AutoCAD® 2005 Tutorial

First Level: 2D Fundamentals

Text by

Randy H. Shih
Oregon Institute of Technology

MultiMedia CD by

Jack Zecher
Indiana University Purdue University Indianapolis

ISBN: 1-58503-199-2

Mission, Kansas

Schroff Development Corporation
P.O. Box 1334
Mission KS 66222
(913) 262-2664
WWW.SDCACAD.COM

Trademarks
The following are registered trademarks of Autodesk, Inc.: 3D Studio, ADI, Advanced Modeling Extension, AME, AutoCAD, AutoCAD Mechanical Desktop, AutoCAD Development System, AutoCAD LT, Autodesk, Autodesk Animator, AutoLISP, AutoShade, AutoVision, and Heidi.
The following are trademarks of Autodesk, Inc.: ACAD, Autodesk Device Interface, AutoCAD DesignCenter, AutoTrack, Heads-up Design, ObjectARX and Visual LISP.
Microsoft, Windows are either registered trademarks or trademarks of Microsoft Corporation.
All other trademarks are trademarks of their respective holders.

Shih, Randy H.
AutoCAD® 2005 Tutorial / First Level: 2D Fundamentals

Randy H. Shih

ISBN 1-58503-199-2 (Text Only)
ISBN 1-58503-201-8 (Text bundled with AutoCAD 2005)

Printed and bound in the United States of America.

Preface

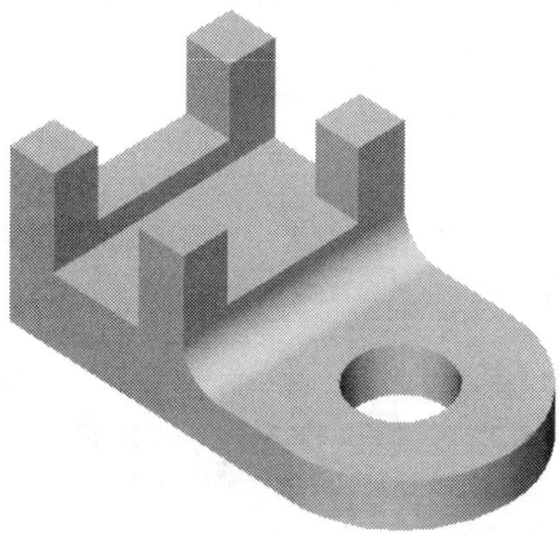

The primary goal of ***AutoCAD® 2005 Tutorial: 2D Fundamentals*** is to introduce the aspects of **Computer Aided Design and Drafting (CADD)**. This text is intended to be used as a training guide for students and professionals. This text covers *AutoCAD® 2005* and the lessons proceed in a pedagogical fashion to guide you from constructing basic shapes to making multiview drawings. This text takes a hands-on, exercise-intensive approach to all the important CAD techniques and concepts. This textbook contains a series of ten tutorial style lessons designed to introduce beginning CAD users to **AutoCAD® 2005**. This text is also helpful to AutoCAD users upgrading from a previous release of the software. The new improvements and key enhancements of the software are incorporated into the lessons. You will learn to use the new AutoCAD Heads-up Design™ interface, which enables you to focus on the design, not on the keyboard. Other features, such as the AutoCAD® 2005 AutoTrack™ feature, the WYSIWYG (What You See Is What You Get) plotting feature, the Named Plot Style feature, and Layout plotting are also introduced in the lessons. The CAD techniques and concepts discussed in this text are also designed to serve as the foundation to the more advanced parametric feature-based CAD packages such as AutoCAD® Mechanical Desktop and AutoCAD® Inventor. The basic premise of this book is that the more designs you create using AutoCAD® 2005, the better you learn the software. With this in mind, each lesson introduces a new set of commands and concepts, building on previous lessons. This book does not attempt to cover all of AutoCAD® 2005's features, only to provide an introduction to the software. It is intended to help you establish a good basis for exploring and growing in the exciting field of Computer Aided Engineering.

Acknowledgments

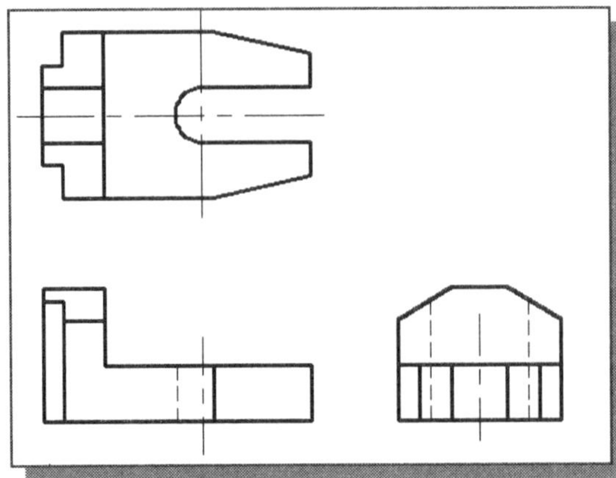

This book would not have been possible without a great deal of support. First, special thanks to two great teachers, Prof. George R. Schade of University of Nebraska-Lincoln and Mr. Denwu Lee, who taught me the fundamentals, the intrigue, and the sheer fun of Computer Aided Engineering.

My deep appreciation goes to Prof. Jack Zecher, Indiana University Purdue University Indianapolis, for the production of the multimedia CD, the audio-visual format of this text.

The effort and support of the editorial and production staff of Schroff Development Corporation is gratefully acknowledged. I would especially like to thank Stephen Schroff and Mary Schmidt for their support and helpful suggestions during this project.

I am grateful that the Mechanical Engineering Technology Department of Oregon Institute of Technology has provided me with an excellent environment in which to pursue my interests in teaching and research. I would especially like to thank Professor Brian Moravec and Emeritus Professor Charles Hermach for helpful comments and encouragement.

Finally, truly unbounded thanks are due to my wife Hsiu-Ling and our daughter Casandra for their understanding and encouragement throughout this project.

Randy H. Shih
Klamath Falls, Oregon
Summer, 2004

Table of Contents

Basic Object Construction Tools

Chapter 3
Geometric Construction and Editing Tools

Chapter 4
Object Properties and Organization

Chapter 5
Orthographic Views in Multiview Drawings

Chapter 6
Basic Dimensioning and Notes

Chapter 7
Templates and Plotting

Chapter 8

Auxiliary Views and Editing with GRIPS

Chapter 9
Section Views

Chapter 10
Assembly Drawings and Blocks

Index

Introduction
Getting Started

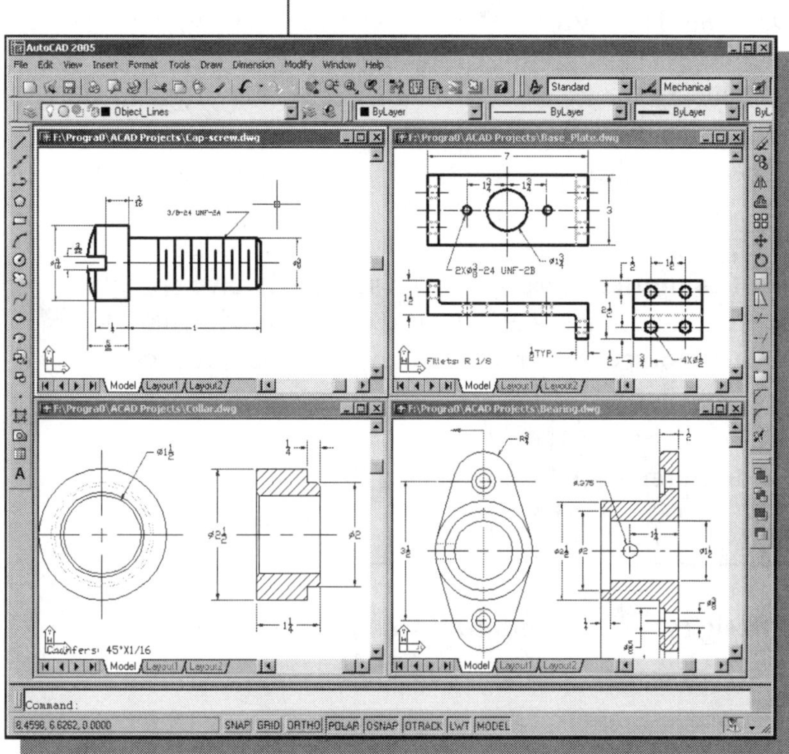

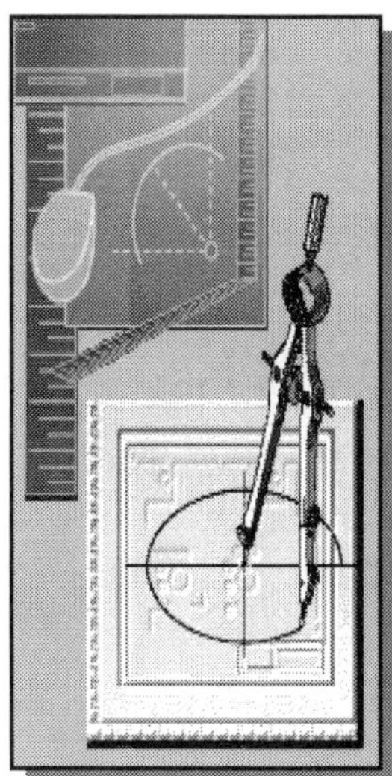

Learning Objectives

- ♦ **Development of Computer Aided Design**
- ♦ **Why use AutoCAD 2005?**
- ♦ **Getting started with AutoCAD 2005**
- ♦ **The AutoCAD Startup dialog box and Units setup**
- ♦ **AutoCAD 2005 screen layout**
- ♦ **Mouse buttons**

Introduction

Computer Aided Design (CAD) is the process of doing designs with the aid of computers. This includes the generation of computer models, analysis of design data, and the creation of the necessary drawings. **AutoCAD® 2005** is a computer aided design software developed by *Autodesk Inc*. The **AutoCAD® 2005** software is a tool that can be used for design and drafting activities. The two-dimensional and three-dimensional models created in **AutoCAD® 2005** can be transferred to other computer programs for further analysis and testing. The computer models can also be used in manufacturing equipment such as machining centers, lathes, mills, or rapid prototyping machines to manufacture the product.

The rapid changes in the field of **computer aided engineering** (CAE) have brought exciting advances in industry. Recent advances have made the long-sought goal of reducing design time, producing prototypes faster, and achieving higher product quality closer to a reality.

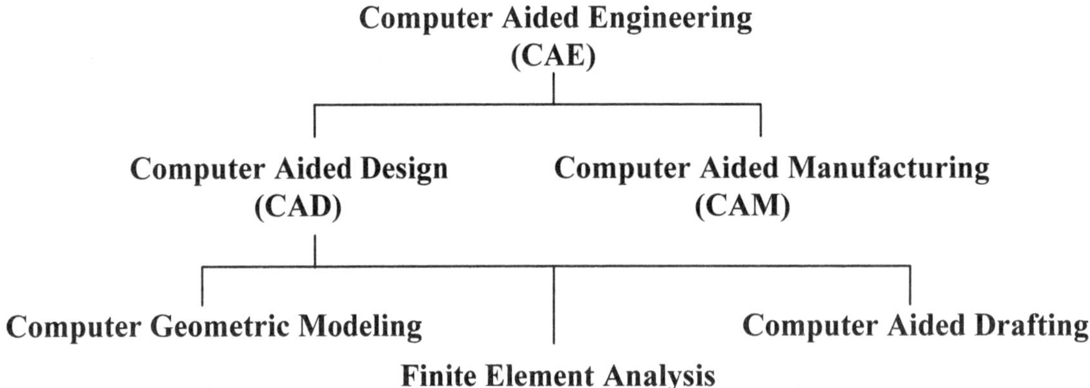

Development of Computer Geometric Modeling

Computer Aided Design is a relatively new technology and its rapid expansion in the last fifty years is truly amazing. Computer modeling technology advanced along with the development of computer hardware. The first generation CAD programs, developed in the 1950s, were mostly non-interactive; CAD users were required to create program codes to generate the desired two-dimensional (2D) geometric shapes. Initially, the development of CAD technology occurred mostly in academic research facilities. The Massachusetts Institute of Technology, Carnegie-Mellon University, and Cambridge University were the lead pioneers at that time. The interest in CAD technology spread quickly and several major industry companies, such as General Motors, Lockheed, McDonnell, IBM, and Ford Motor Co., participated in the development of interactive CAD programs in the 1960s. Usage of CAD systems was primarily in the automotive industry, aerospace industry, and government agencies that developed their own programs for their specific needs. The 1960s also marked the beginning of the development of finite element analysis methods for computer stress analysis and computer aided manufacturing for generating machine toolpaths.

The 1970s are generally viewed as the years of the most significant progress in the development of computer hardware, namely the invention and development of **microprocessors**. With the improvement in computing power, new types of 3D CAD programs that were user-friendly and interactive became reality. CAD technology quickly expanded from very simple **computer aided drafting** to very complex **computer aided design**. The use of 2D and 3D wireframe modelers was accepted as the leading edge technology that could increase productivity in industry. The developments of surface modeling and solid modeling technology were taking shape by the late 1970s; but the high cost of computer hardware and programming slowed the development of such technology. During this time period, the available CAD systems all required extremely expensive room-sized mainframe computers.

In the 1980s, improvements in computer hardware brought the power of mainframes to the desktop at less cost and with more accessibility to the general public. By the mid-1980s, CAD technology had become the main focus of a variety of manufacturing industries and was very competitive with traditional design/drafting methods. It was during this period of time that 3D solid modeling technology had major advancements, which boosted the usage of CAE technology in industry.

In the 1990s, CAD programs evolved into powerful design/manufacturing/management tools. CAD technology has come a long way, and during these years of development, modeling schemes progressed from two-dimensional (2D) wireframe to three-dimensional (3D) wireframe, to surface modeling, to solid modeling and, finally, to feature-based parametric solid modeling.

The first generation CAD packages were simply 2D **Computer Aided Drafting** programs, basically the electronic equivalents of the drafting board. For typical models, the use of this type of program would require that several to many views of the objects be created individually as they would be on the drafting board. The 3D designs remained in the designer's mind, not in the computer database. The mental translation of 3D objects to 2D views is required throughout the use of the packages. Although such systems have some advantages over traditional board drafting, they are still tedious and labor intensive. The need for the development of 3D modelers came quite naturally, given the limitations of the 2D drafting packages.

The development of the 3D wireframe modeler was a major leap in the area of computer modeling. The computer database in the 3D wireframe modeler contains the locations of all the points in space coordinates and it is sufficient to create just one model rather than multiple models. This single 3D model can then be viewed from any direction as needed. The 3D wireframe modelers require the least computer power and achieve reasonably good representation of 3D models. But because surface definition is not part of a wireframe model, all wireframe images have the inherent problem of ambiguity.

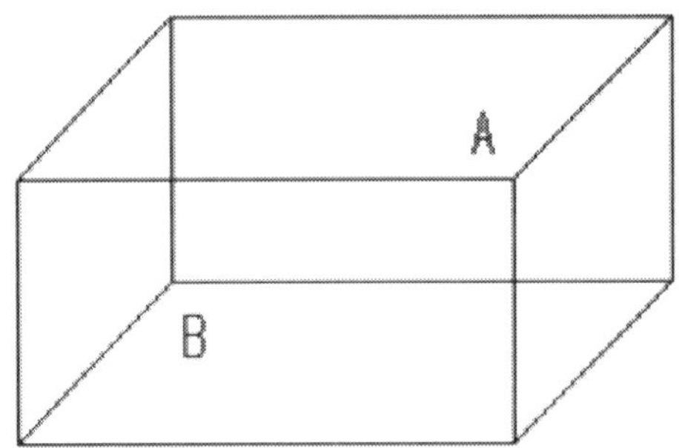

Wireframe Ambiguity: Which corner is in front, A or B?

A non-realizable object: Wireframe models contain no surface definitions.

Surface modeling is the logical development in computer geometry modeling to follow the 3D wireframe modeling scheme by organizing and grouping edges that define polygonal surfaces. Surface modeling describes the part's surfaces but not its interiors. Designers are still required to interactively examine surface models to insure that the various surfaces on a model are contiguous throughout. Many of the concepts used in 3D wireframe and surface modelers are incorporated in the solid modeling scheme, but it is solid modeling that offers the most advantages as a design tool.

In the solid modeling presentation scheme, the solid definitions include nodes, edges, and surfaces, and it is a complete and unambiguous mathematical representation of a precisely enclosed and filled volume. Unlike the surface modeling method, solid modelers start with a solid or use topology rules to guarantee that all of the surfaces are stitched together properly. Two predominant methods for representing solid models are **constructive solid geometry** (CSG) representation and **boundary representation** (B-rep).

The CSG representation method can be defined as the combination of 3D solid primitives. What constitutes a "primitive" varies somewhat with the software but typically includes a rectangular prism, a cylinder, a cone, a wedge, and a sphere. Most solid modelers allow the user to define additional primitives, which can be very complex.

In the B-rep representation method, objects are represented in terms of their spatial boundaries. This method defines the points, edges, and surfaces of a volume, and/or issues commands that sweep or rotate a defined face into a third dimension to form a solid. The object is then made up of the unions of these surfaces that completely and precisely enclose a volume.

By the 1990s, a new paradigm called *concurrent engineering* had emerged. With concurrent engineering, designers, design engineers, analysts, manufacturing engineers, and management engineers all work closely right from the initial stages of the design. In this way, all aspects of the design can be evaluated and any potential problems can be identified right from the start and throughout the design process. Using the principles of concurrent engineering, a new type of computer modeling technique appeared. The technique is known as the *feature-based parametric modeling technique*. The key advantage of the *feature-based parametric modeling technique* is its capability to produce very flexible designs. Changes can be made easily and design alternatives can be evaluated with minimum effort. Various software packages offer different approaches to feature-based parametric modeling, yet the end result is a flexible design defined by its design variables and parametric features.

In this text, we will follow a logical order, parallel to the development of computer geometric modeling, in learning the fundamental concepts and commands of **AutoCAD® 2005**. We will begin with creating 2½D models by modifying the entities properties of 2D designs and then move toward creating 3D wireframe and surface models. We will also discuss and demonstrate several procedures for creating three-dimensional solid models. The techniques presented in this text will also serve as the foundation for entering the world of advanced three-dimensional solid modeling using packages such as **AutoCAD Mechanical Desktop, AutoCAD Architectural Desktop** and **Autodesk Inventor**.

Why use AutoCAD® 2005?

AutoCAD® was first introduced to the public in late 1982, and was one of the first CAD software products that were available for personal computers. Since 1984, **AutoCAD®** has established a reputation for being the most widely used PC-based CAD software around the world. By 2003, it is estimated that there are over 3.5 million **AutoCAD®** users in more than 150 countries worldwide. **AutoCAD® 2005** is the ninteenth release, with many added features and enhancements, of the original **AutoCAD®** software produced by *Autodesk Inc*.

CAD provides us with a wide range of benefits; in most cases, the result of using CAD is increased accuracy and productivity. First of all, the computer offers much higher accuracy than the traditional methods of drafting and design. Traditionally, drafting and detailing are the most expensive cost element in a project and the biggest bottleneck. With CAD systems, such as **AutoCAD® 2005,** the tedious drafting and detailing tasks are simplified through the use of many of the CAD geometric construction tools, such as *grids*, *snap*, *trim,* and *auto-dimensioning*. Dimensions and notes are always legible in

CAD drawings, and in most cases, CAD systems can produce higher quality prints compared to traditional hand drawings.

CAD also offers much-needed flexibility in design and drafting. A CAD model generated on a computer consists of numeric data that describe the geometry of the object. This allows the designers and clients to see something tangible and to interpret the ramifications of the design. In many cases, it is also possible to simulate operating conditions on the computer and observe the results. Any kind of geometric shape stored in the database can be easily duplicated. For large and complex designs and drawings, particularly those involving similar shapes and repetitive operations, CAD approaches are very efficient and effective. Because computer designs and models can be altered easily, a multitude of design options can be examined and presented to a client before any construction or manufacturing actually takes place. Making changes to a CAD model is generally much faster than making changes to a traditional hand drawing. Only the affected components of the design need to be modified and the drawings can be plotted again. In addition, the greatest benefit is that, once the CAD model is created, it can be used over and over again. The CAD models can also be transferred into manufacturing equipment such as machining centers, lathes, mills, or rapid prototyping machines to manufacture the product directly.

CAD, however, does not replace every design activity. CAD may help, but it does not replace the designer's experience with geometry and graphical conventions and standards for the specific field. CAD is a powerful tool, but the use of this tool does not guarantee correct results; the designer is still responsible for using good design practice and applying good judgment. CAD will supplement these skills to ensure that the best design is obtained.

CAD designs and drawings are stored in binary form, usually as CAD files, to magnetic devices such as diskettes and hard disks. The information stored in CAD files usually requires much less physical space in comparison to traditional hand drawings. However, the information stored inside the computer is not indestructible. On the contrary, the electronic format of information is very fragile and sensitive to the environment. Heat or cold can damage the information stored on magnetic storage devices. A power failure while you are creating a design could wipe out the many hours you spent working in front of the computer monitor. It is a good habit to save your work periodically, just in case something might go wrong while you are working on your design. In general, one should save one's work onto the disk at an interval of every 15 to 20 minutes. You should also save your work before you make any major modifications to the design. It is also a good habit to periodically make backup copies of your work and put them in a safe place.

Getting started with AutoCAD® 2005

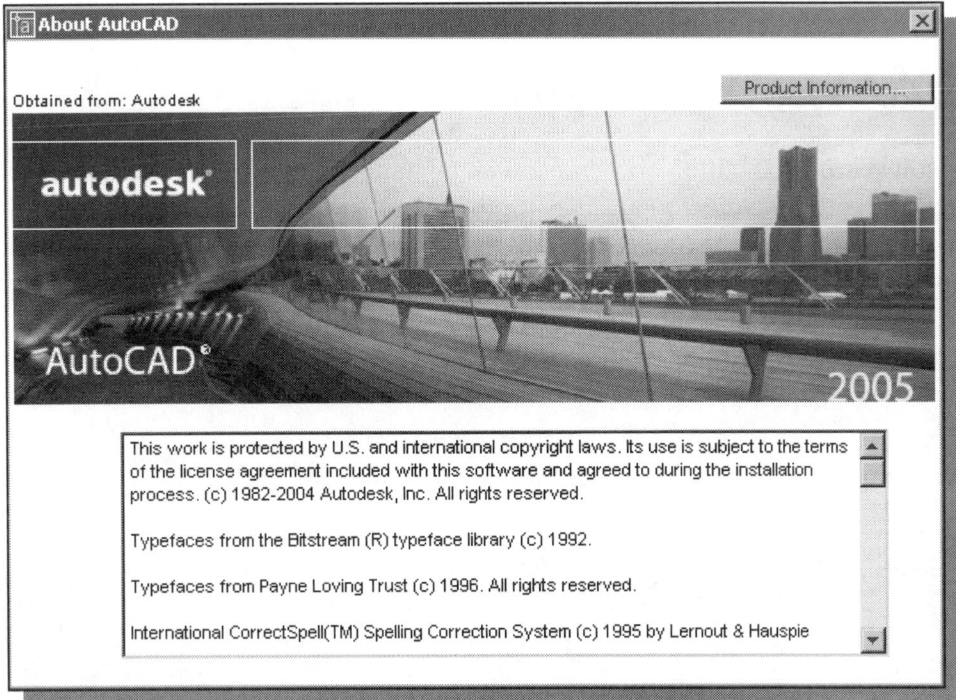

How to start **AutoCAD® 2005** depends on the type of workstation and the particular software configuration you are using. With most *Windows* systems, you may select the **AutoCAD 2005** option on the *Start* menu or select the **AutoCAD 2005** icon on the *Desktop*. Consult with your instructor or technical support personnel if you have difficulty starting the software.

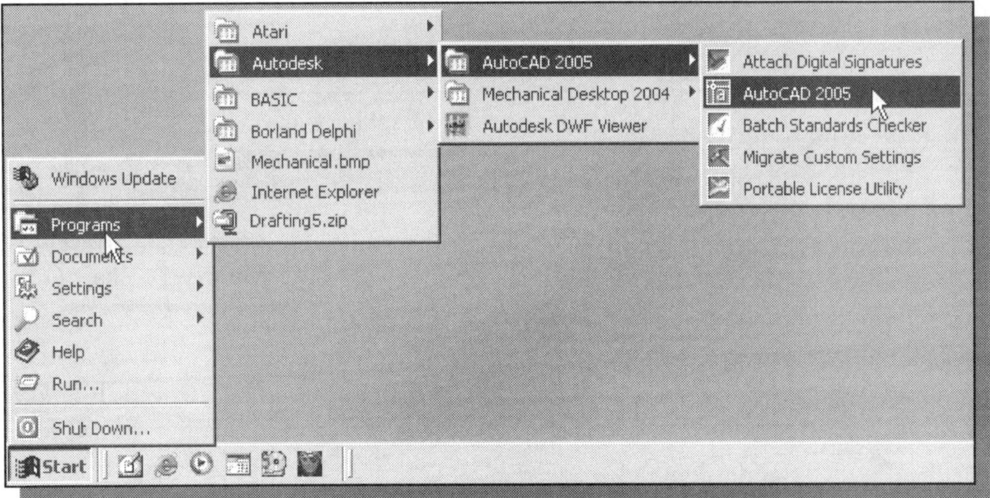

The program takes a while to load, so be patient. Eventually the **AutoCAD® 2005** main *drawing screen* will appear on the screen. The tutorials in this text are based on the assumption that you are using **AutoCAD® 2005**'s default settings. If your system has been customized for other uses, some of the settings may not work with the step-by-step instructions in the tutorials. Contact your instructor and/or technical support personnel to restore the default software configuration.

AutoCAD® 2005 Screen Layout

The default **AutoCAD® 2005** *drawing screen* contains the *pull-down* menus, the *Standard* toolbar, the *Object Properties* toolbar, the *Draw* toolbar, the *Modify* toolbar, the *command prompt area*, the *Status Bar* and the *Tool Palettes window.* A line of quick help text appears at the bottom of the window as you move the *mouse cursor* over different icons. You may resize the **AutoCAD® 2005** drawing window by click and drag at the edges of the window, or relocate the window by click and drag at the window title area.

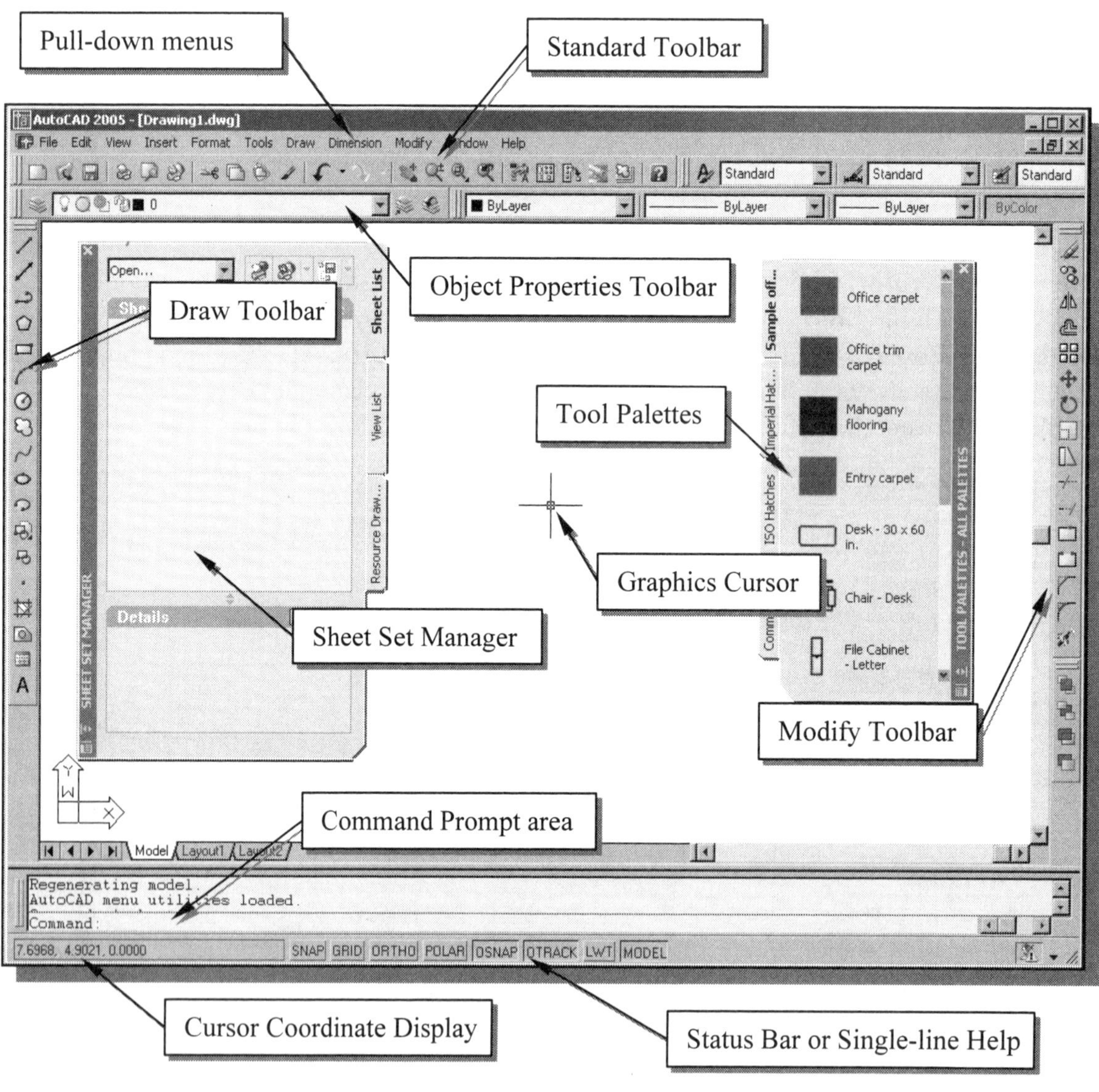

- **Pull-down Menus**
  The *pull-down* menus at the top of the main window contain operations that you can use for all modes of the system.

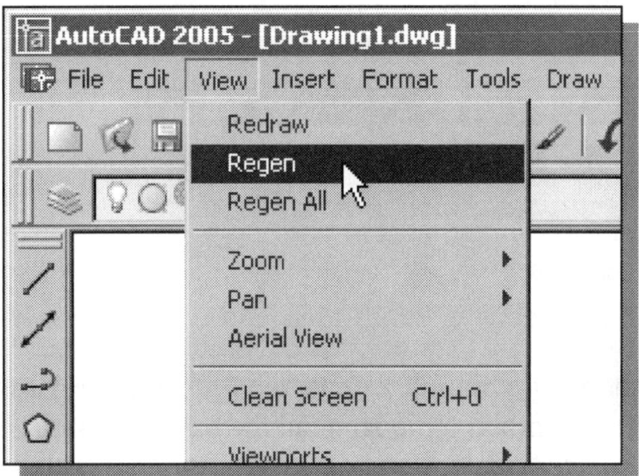

- **Standard Toolbar**
  The *Standard* toolbar at the top of the *AutoCAD* window allows us quick access to frequently used commands. We can customize the toolbar by adding and removing sets of options or individual commands.

- **Object Properties Toolbar**
  The *Object Properties* toolbar contains tools to help manipulate the graphical object properties, such as color, line type, and layer.

- **Graphics Window**
  The *graphics window* is the area where models and drawings are displayed.

- **Graphics Cursor or Crosshairs**
  The *graphics cursor*, or *crosshairs*, shows the location of the pointing device in the graphics window. The coordinates of the cursor are displayed at the bottom of the screen layout. The cursor's appearance depends on the selected command or option.

- **Command Prompt Area**
  The bottom section of the screen layout provides status information for an operation and it is also the area for data input.

Command:
Command:
Command:

- **Draw Toolbar and Modify Toolbar**
  Additional toolbars are available in **AutoCAD® 2005**, and contain groups of buttons that allow us to pick commands quickly, without searching through a menu structure. The *Draw* toolbar and *Modify* toolbar contain icons for basic draw and modify commands.

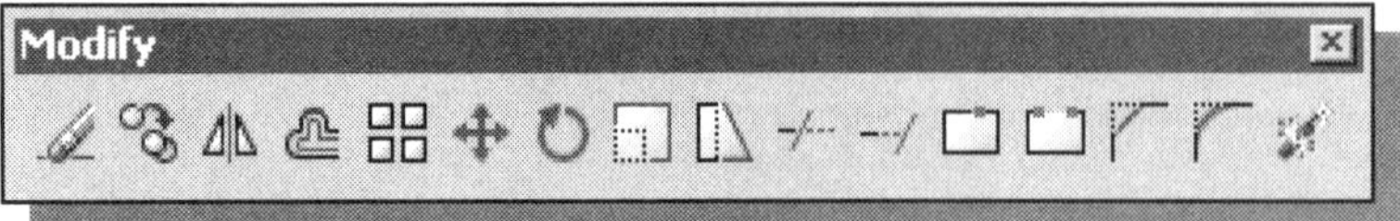

Mouse Buttons

AutoCAD® 2005 utilizes the mouse buttons extensively. In learning **AutoCAD® 2005**'s interactive environment, it is important to understand the basic functions of the mouse buttons. It is highly recommended that you use a mouse or a tablet with **AutoCAD® 2005** since the package uses the buttons for various functions.

- **Left mouse button**
  The **left-mouse-button** is used for most operations, such as selecting menus and icons, or picking graphic entities. One click of the button is used to select icons, menus and form entries, and to pick graphic items.

- **Right mouse button**
  The **right-mouse-button** is used to bring up additional available options. The software also utilizes the **right-mouse-button** as the same as the **ENTER** key, and is often used to accept the default setting to a prompt or to end a process.

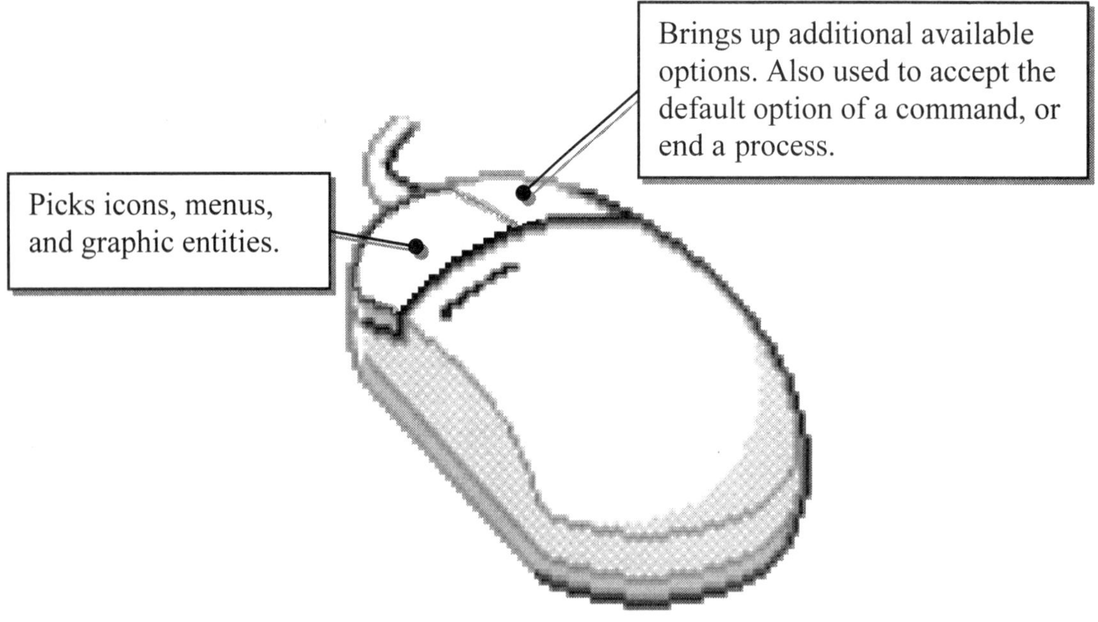

[Esc] - Canceling commands

The [**Esc**] key is used to cancel a command in **AutoCAD® 2005**. The [**Esc**] key is located near the top-left corner of the keyboard. Sometimes, it may be necessary to press the [**Esc**] key twice to cancel a command; it depends on where we are in the command sequence. For some commands, the [**Esc**] key is used to exit the command.

On-Line Help

❖ Several types of on-line help are available at any time during an **AutoCAD® 2005** session. The **AutoCAD® 2005** software provides many on-line help options:

- **Info Palette**:

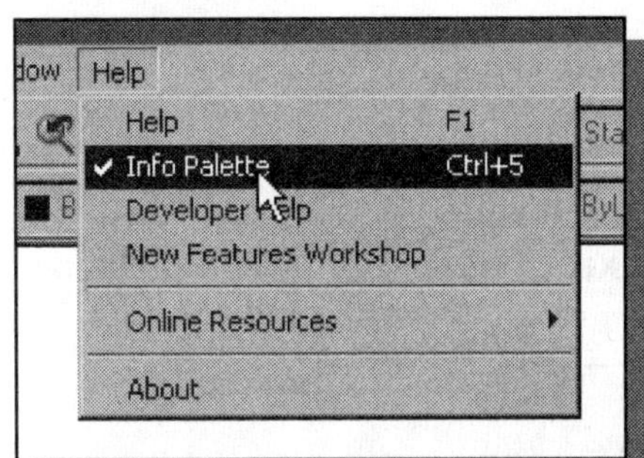

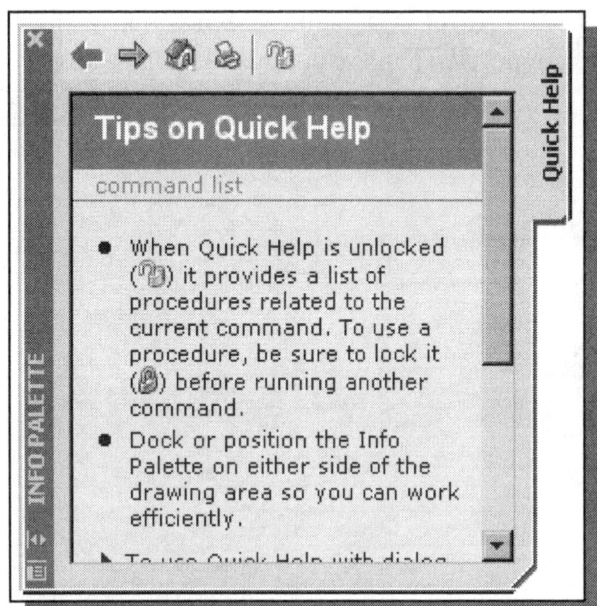

The **Info Palette** option provides an instant help that dynamically displays information on the activated command. The guidance from the **Info Palette** system enables users to quickly get started on performing desired tasks. In the **Info Palette** window, links to additional information are also available. Clicking a blue-text-link expands the current **Info Palette** topic.

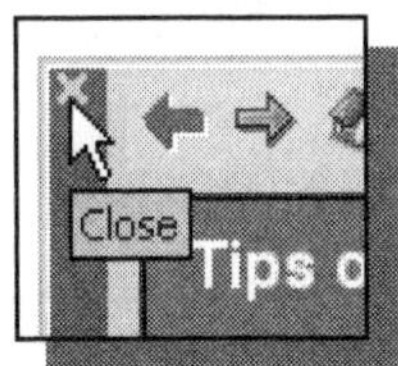

- To *close* the **Info Palette**, left-click the [**X**] icon located in the upper left corner of the ***Info Palette*** window as shown.

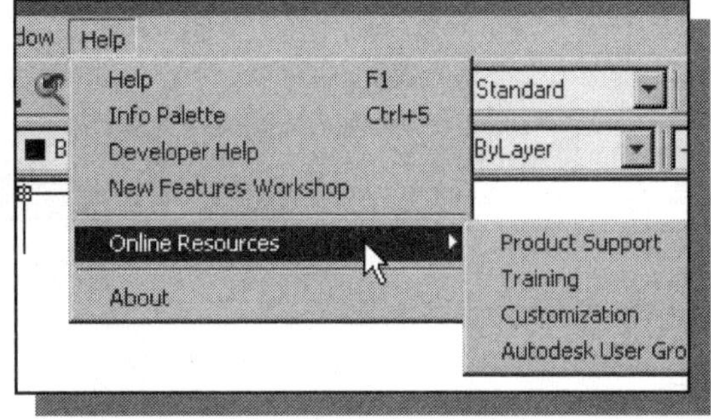

- **Online Resources**: Click on the **HELP** option in the pull-down menu to access the **AutoCAD® 2005 Help menu system**. Notice the different online resources available in the pull-down list.

- **Standard toolbar**: Click on the **[?]** icon in the *Standard* toolbar to access Autodesk On-line Help: User Documentation.

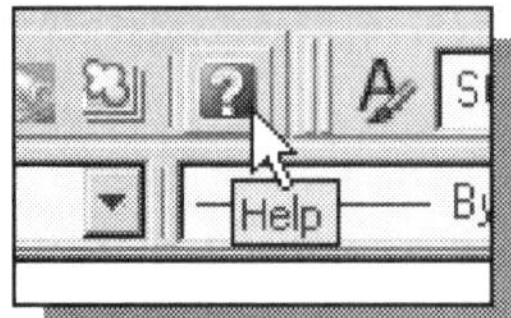

- **Command line and function key [F1]**: Press the [**F1**] key or enter a question mark [**?**] at the command prompt to access the **AutoCAD On-line Help system**.

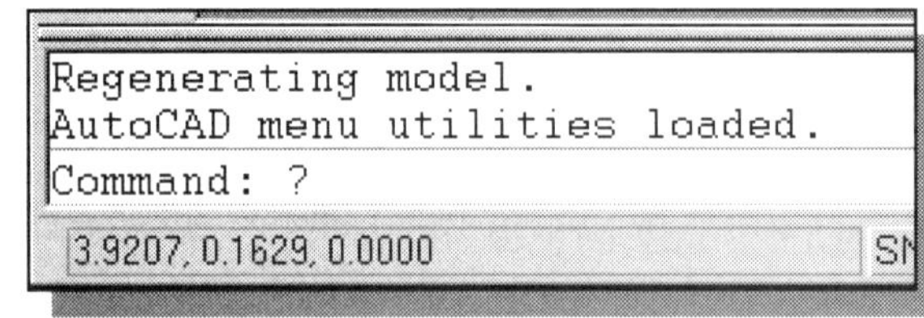

Leaving AutoCAD® 2005

➤ To leave **AutoCAD® 2005**, use the left-mouse-button and click on **File** at the top of the **AutoCAD® 2005** screen window, then choose **Exit** from the pull-down menu or type ***QUIT*** in the command prompt area.

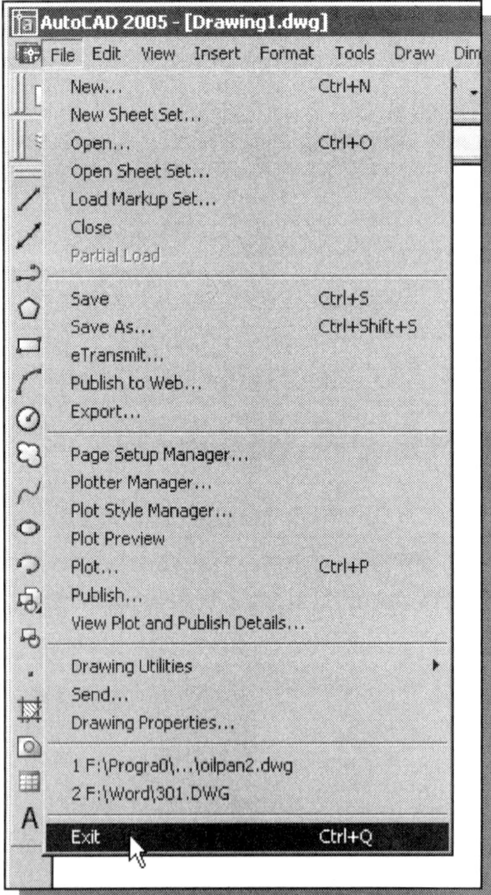

Creating a CAD file folder

❖ It is a good practice to create a separate folder to store your CAD files. You should not save your CAD files in the same folder where the **AutoCAD® 2005** application is located. It is much easier to organize and backup your project files if they are in a separate folder. Making folders within this folder for different types of projects will help you organize your CAD files even further. When creating CAD files in **AutoCAD® 2005**, it is strongly recommended that you *save* your CAD files on the hard drive. However, if you do want to save your files on a floppy drive, be sure to exit the **AutoCAD® 2005** program before removing the diskette from the drive. The better alternative is to save the files on the hard drive and then copy the files onto a floppy diskette under the operating system.

➢ To create a new folder in the Windows environment:

1. In *My Computer*, or start the ***Windows Explorer*** under the *Start* menu, open the folder in which you want to create a new folder.

2. On the **File** menu, point to **New**, and then click **Folder**. The new folder appears with a temporary name.

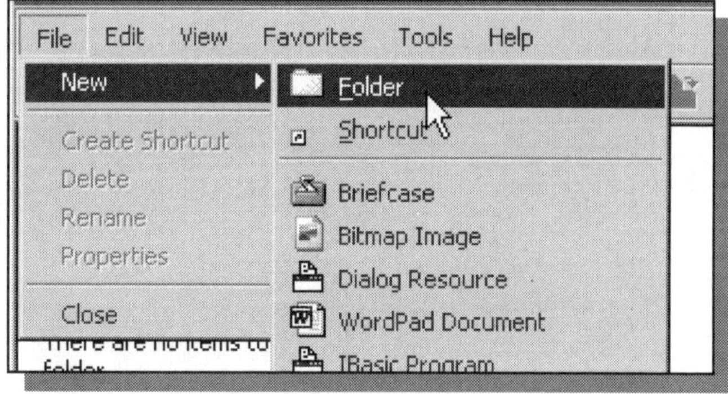

3. Type a name for the new folder, and then press **ENTER**.

NOTES:

Chapter 1
AutoCAD Fundamentals

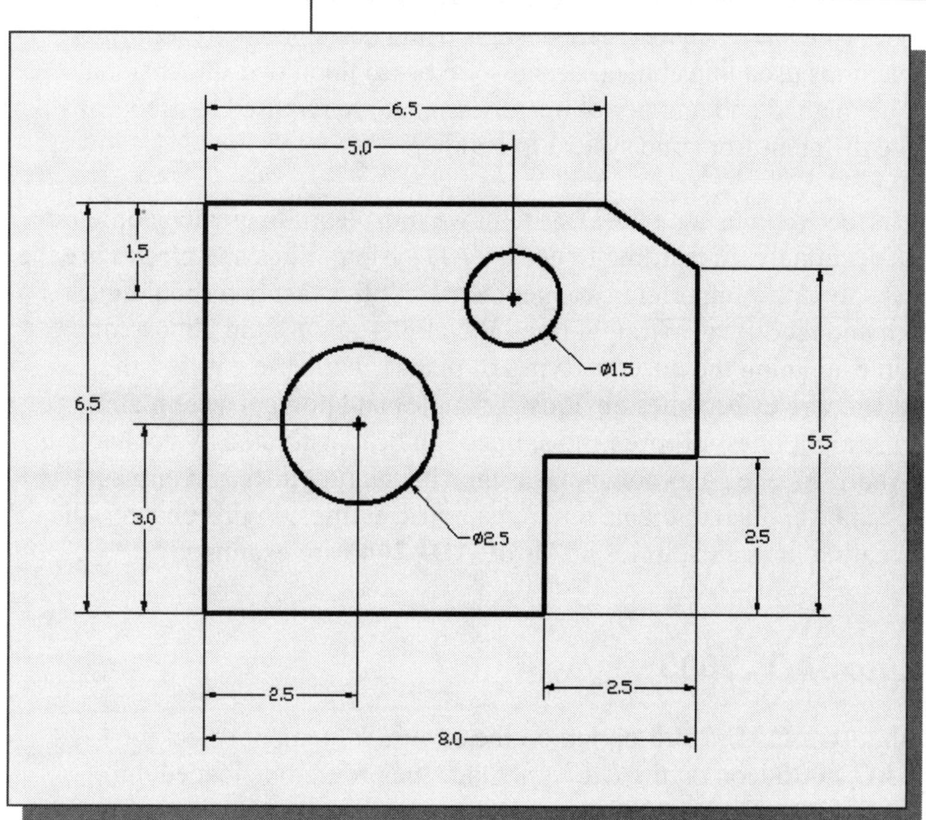

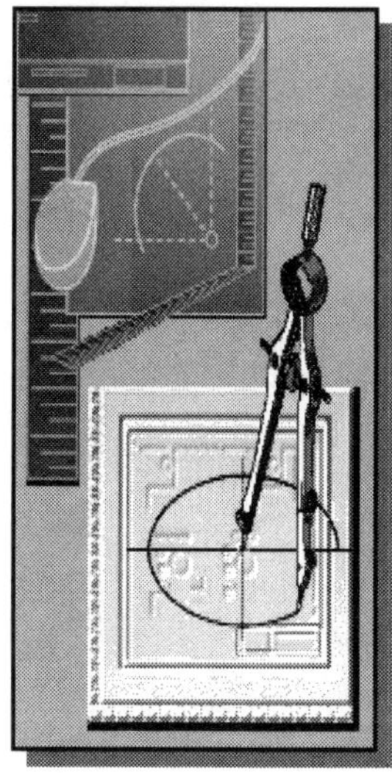

Learning Objectives

- **Create and Save AutoCAD drawing files.**
- **Use the AutoCAD visual reference commands.**
- **Draw, using the LINE and CIRCLE commands.**
- **Use the ERASE command.**
- **Define Positions using the Basic Entry methods.**
- **Use the AutoCAD Pan Realtime option.**

Introduction

Learning to use a CAD system is similar to learning a new language. It is necessary to begin with the basic alphabet and learn how to use it correctly and effectively through practice. This will require learning some new concepts and skills as well as learning a different vocabulary. All CAD systems create designs using basic geometric entities. Many of the constructions used in technical designs are based upon two-dimensional planar geometry. The method and number of operations that are required to accomplish the constructions are different from one system to another.

In order to become effective in using a CAD system, we must learn to create geometric entities quickly and accurately. In learning to use a CAD system, **lines** and **circles** are the first two, and perhaps the most important two, geometric entities that one should master the skills of creating and modifying. Straight lines and circles are used in almost all technical designs. In examining the different types of planar geometric entities, the importance of lines and circles becomes obvious. Triangles and polygons are planar figures bounded by straight lines. Ellipses and splines can be constructed by connecting arcs with different radii. As one gains some experience in creating lines and circles, similar procedures can be applied to create other geometric entities. In this chapter, the different ways of creating lines and circles in **AutoCAD® 2005** are examined.

Starting Up AutoCAD® 2005

1. Select the **AutoCAD 2005** option on the *Program* menu or select the **AutoCAD 2005** icon on the *Desktop*. Once the program is loaded into memory, the **AutoCAD® 2005** drawing screen will appear on the screen.

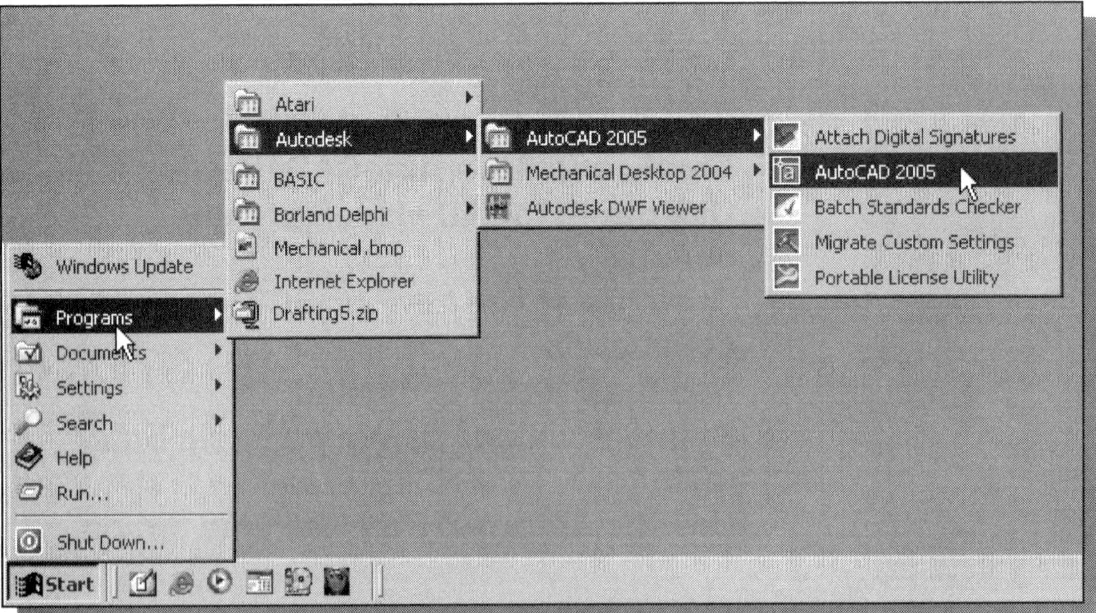

➢ Note that AutoCAD automatically assigns generic name, *Drawing X*, as new drawings are created. In our example, AutoCAD opened the graphics window using the default system units and assigned the drawing name *Drawing1*.

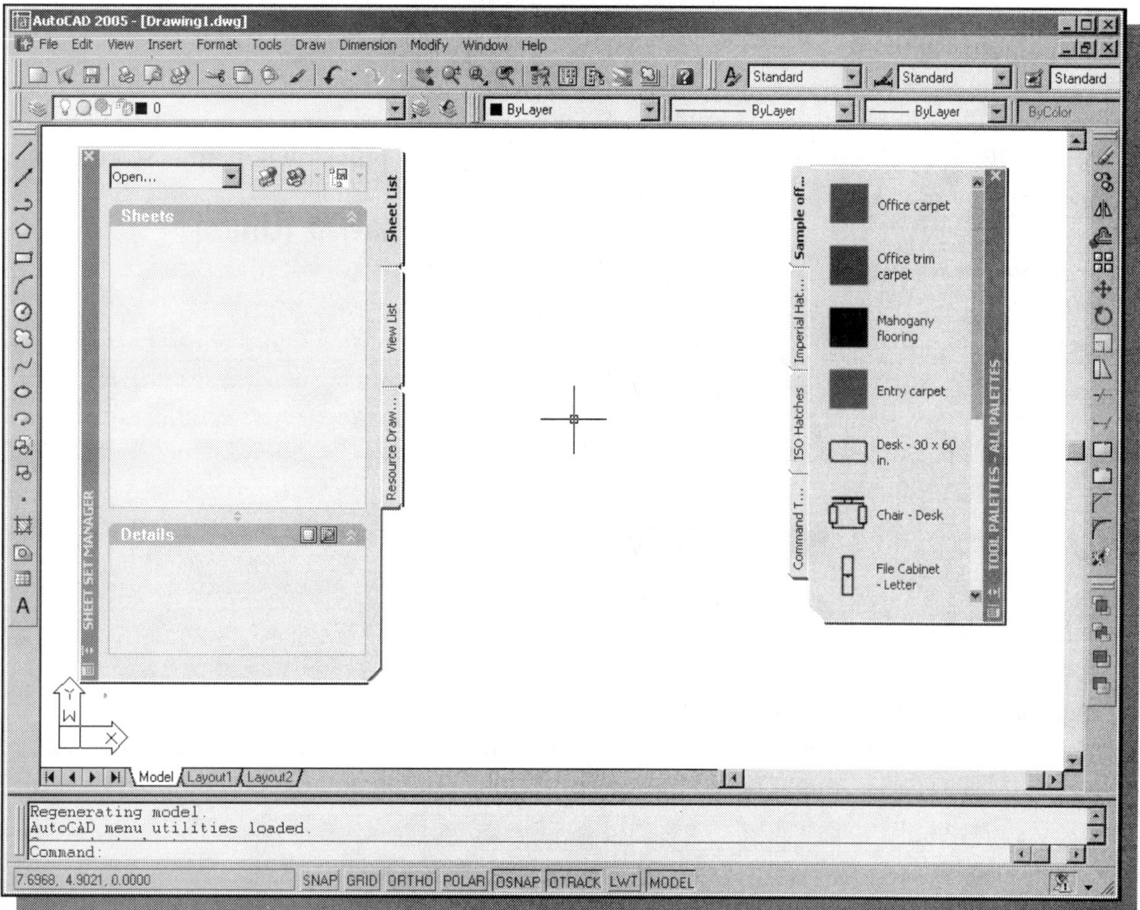

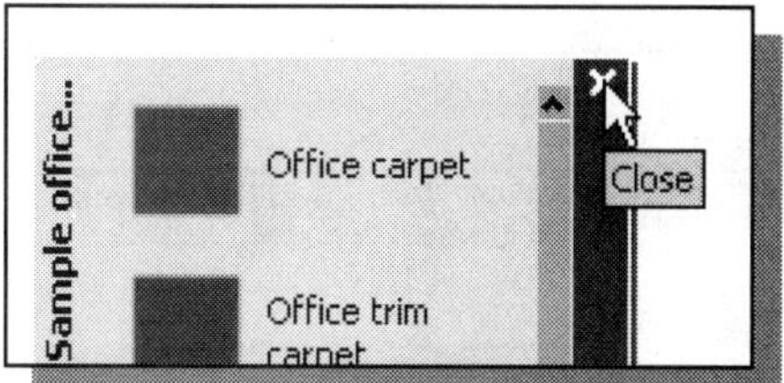

2. Close the *Tool Palettes* by clicking once on **Close** button located at the upper right corner of the window as shown.

3. Close the *Sheet Set Manager* by clicking once on the **Close** button located at the upper right corner of the window as shown.

Drawing Units Setup

➢ Every object we construct in a CAD system is measured in **units**. We should determine the value of the units within the CAD system before creating the first geometric entities.

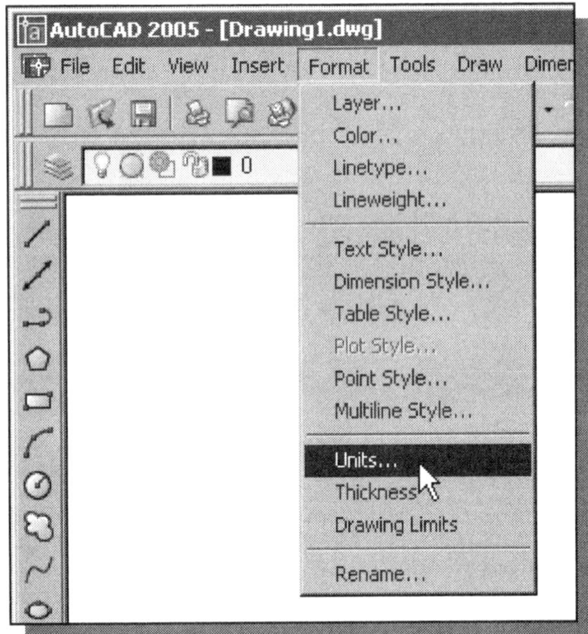

1. In the pull-down menus, select:

   [Format] → [Units]

2. In the *Drawing Units* dialog box, set the *Length Type* to **Decimal**. This will set the measurement to the default *English* units, inches.

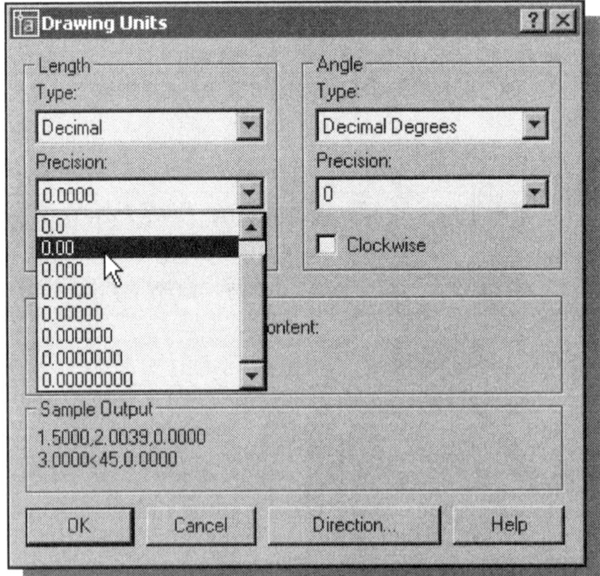

3. Set the *Precision* to **two digits** after the decimal point as shown in the above figure.

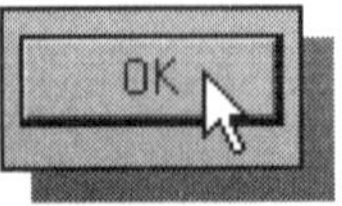

4. Pick **OK** to exit the *Drawing Units* dialog box.

Drawing Area Setup

❖ Next, we will set up the **Drawing Limits**; setting the Drawing Limits controls the extents of the display of the *grid*. It also serves as a visual reference that marks the working area. It can also be used to prevent construction outside the grid limits and as a plot option that defines an area to be plotted/printed. Note that this setting does not limit the region for geometry construction.

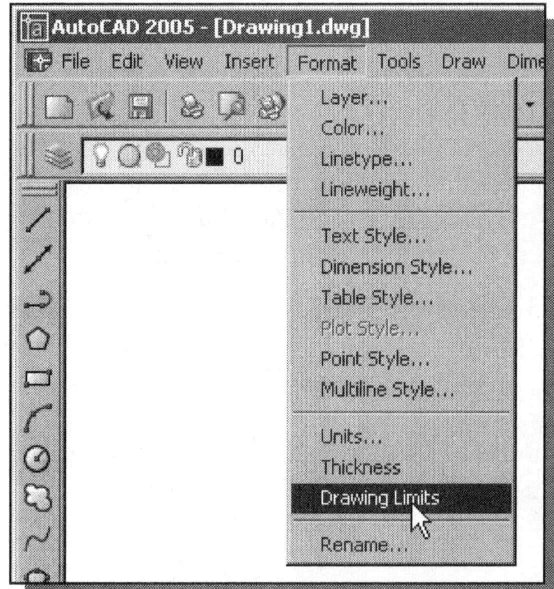

1. In the pull-down menus, select:

   [Format] → [Drawing Limits]

2. In the command prompt area, near the bottom of the AutoCAD drawing screen, the message "*Reset Model Space Limits: Specify lower left corner or [On/Off] <0.00,0.00>:*" is displayed. Press the **ENTER** key once to accept the default coordinates <**0.00,0.00**>.

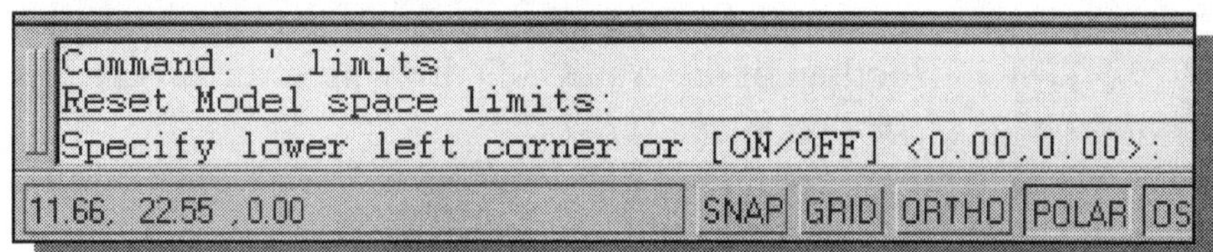

3. In the command prompt area, the message "*Specify upper right corner <0.00,0.00>:*" is displayed. Press the **ENTER** key once to accept the default coordinates <**12.00,9.00**>.

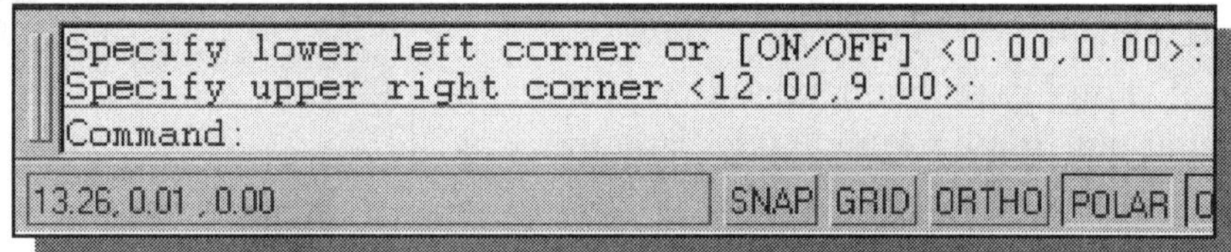

4. On your own, move the graphic cursor near the upper-right comer inside the drawing area and note that the drawing area is unchanged. (The Drawing Limits command is used to set the drawing area; but the display will not be adjusted until a display command is used.)

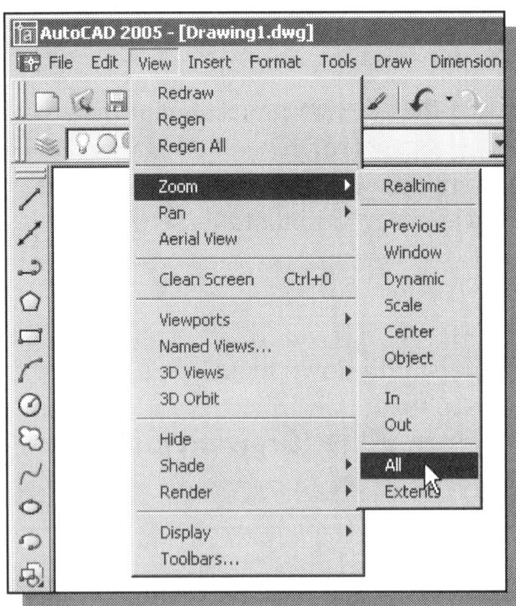

5. In the pull-down menus, select:

   [View] → [Zoom] → [All]

❖ The **Zoom All** command will adjust the display so that all objects in the drawing are displayed to be as large as possible. If no objects are constructed, the Drawing Limits are used to adjust the current viewport.

6. Move the graphic cursor near the upper-right comer inside the drawing area and note that the display area is updated.

Using the *Line* command

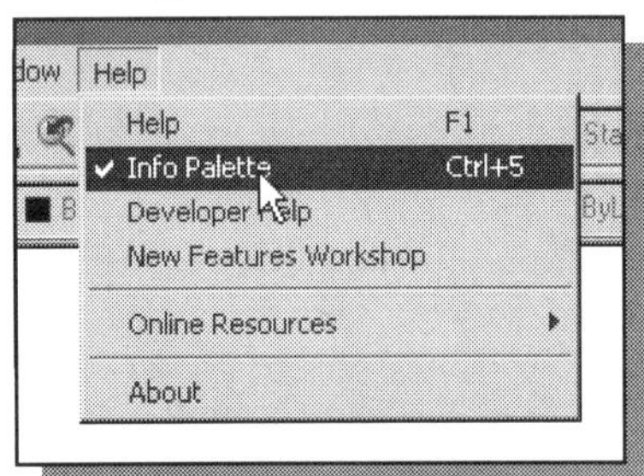

1. Click on the **Info Palette** option in the **Help** pull-down menu to activate the **Quick Help** option.

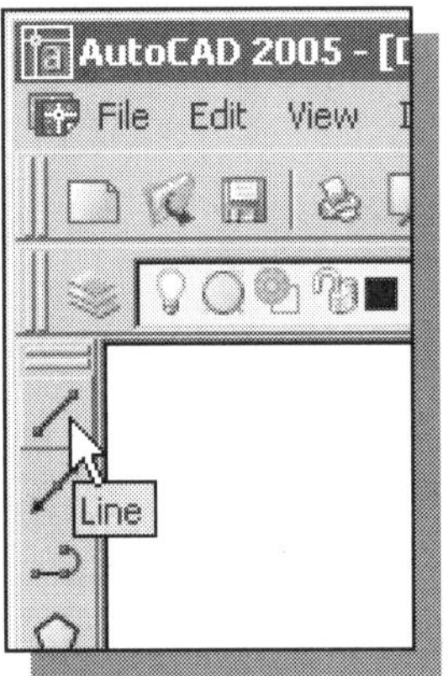

2. Move the graphics cursor to the first icon in the *Draw* toolbar. This icon is the **Line** icon. A *help-tip* box appears next to the cursor and a brief description of the icon is displayed at the bottom of the AutoCAD drawing screen: "*Creates Straight line segments: LINE.*"

3. Select the icon by clicking once with the **left-mouse-button**, which will activate the Line command.

➢ Notice a brief explanation of the selected command is displayed in the *Info Palette* window. It is highly recommended that you read the explanations to gain some insights on the general procedure of using AutoCAD.

4. In the *Info Palette* window, click **To draw lines** to open the *AutoCAD Help* window and get a more detailed explanation on the procedure.

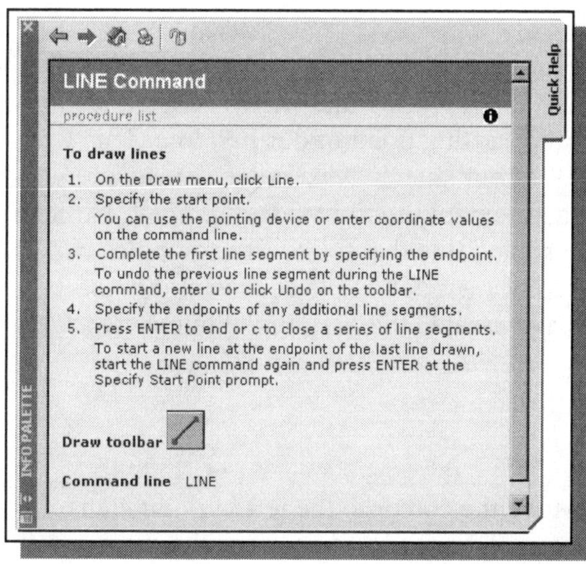

❖ The general procedure to create a line in AutoCAD is displayed in the *Info Palette* window.

5. Click on **Close** button located at the upper left corner of the ***Info Palette*** window as shown.

6. In the command prompt area, near the bottom of the AutoCAD drawing screen, the message "*_line Specify first point:*" is displayed. AutoCAD expects us to identify the starting location of a straight line. Move the graphics cursor inside the graphics window and watch the display of the coordinates of the graphics cursor at the bottom of the AutoCAD drawing screen. The three numbers represent the location of the cursor in the X, Y, and Z directions. We can treat the graphics window as if it was a piece of paper and we are using the graphics cursor as if it were a pencil with which to draw.

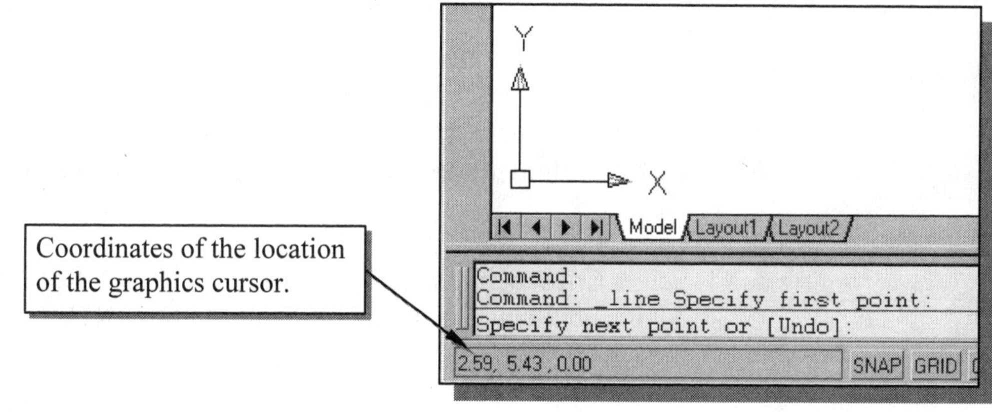

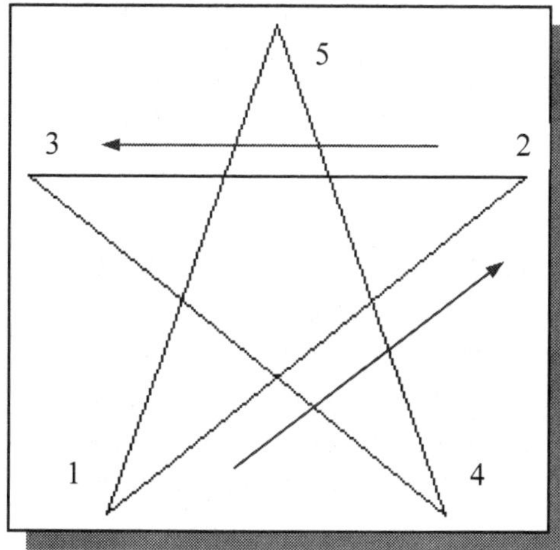

❖ We will create a freehand sketch of a five-point star using the Line command. Do not be overly concerned with the actual size or the accuracy of your freehand sketch. This exercise is to give you a feel for the **AutoCAD® 2005** user interface.

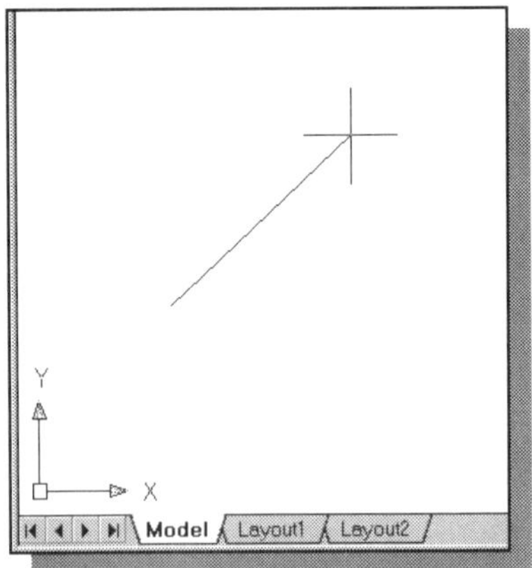

7. We will start at a location about one-third from the bottom of the graphics window. Left-click once to position the starting point of our first line. This will be *point 1* of our sketch. Next move the cursor upward and toward the right side of *point 1*. Notice the rubber-band line that follows the graphics cursor in the graphics window. Left-click again (*point 2*) and we have created the first line of our sketch.

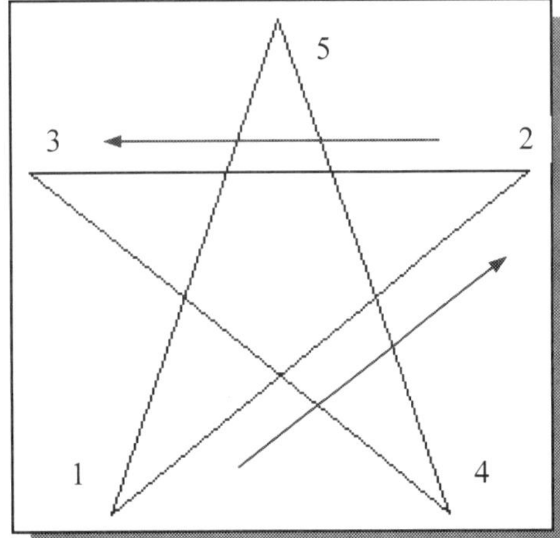

8. Move the cursor to the left of *point 2* and create a horizontal line about the same length as the first line on the screen.

9. Repeat the above steps and complete the freehand sketch by adding three more lines (from *point 3* to *point 4*, *point 4* to *point 5*, and then connect to *point 5* back to *point 1*).

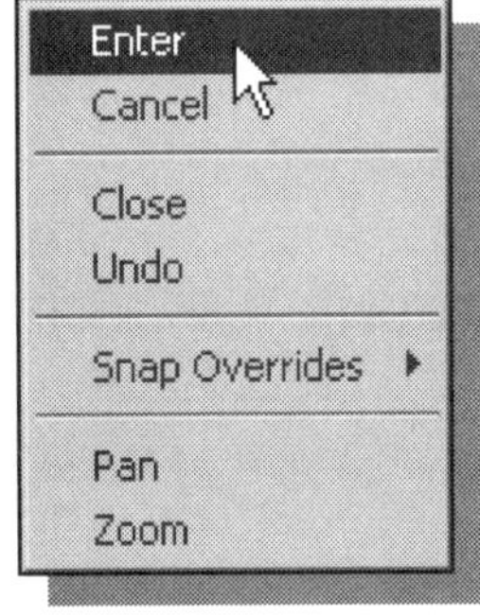

10. Notice that the Line command remains activated even after we connected the last segment of the line to the starting point *(point 1)* of our sketch. Inside the graphics window, **click once with the right-mouse-button** and a popup menu appears on the screen.

11. Select **Enter** with the left-mouse-button to end the Line command. (This is equivalent to hitting the [**ENTER**] key on the keyboard.)

12. On your own, move the cursor near *point 2* and *point 3*, and estimate the length of the horizontal line by watching the displayed coordinates for each point at the bottom of the screen.

Visual reference

The method we just used to create the freehand sketch is known as the **interactive method**, where we use the cursor to specify locations on the screen. This method is perhaps the fastest way to specify locations on the screen. However, it is rather difficult to try to create a line of a specific length by watching the displayed coordinates. It would be helpful to know what one inch or one meter looks like on the screen while we are creating entities. **AutoCAD® 2005** provides us with many tools to aid the construction of our designs. We will use the ***GRID*** and ***SNAP*** options to get a visual reference as to the size of objects and learn to restrict the movement of the cursor to a set increment on the screen.

The *Status Bar* area is located at the bottom of the AutoCAD drawing screen. The words *SNAP*, *GRID*, *ORTHO*, *POLAR*, *OSNAP*, *OSNAP*, *OTRACK*, *LWT* and *MODEL* appearing to the right of the coordinates are buttons that we can left-click to turn these special options *ON* and *OFF*. When the corresponding button is *highlighted*, the specific option is turned *ON*. These buttons act as toggle switches; each click of the button will toggle the option *ON* or *OFF*. Using the buttons is a quick and easy way to make changes to these *drawing aid* options. We can toggle the options on and off in the middle of another command.

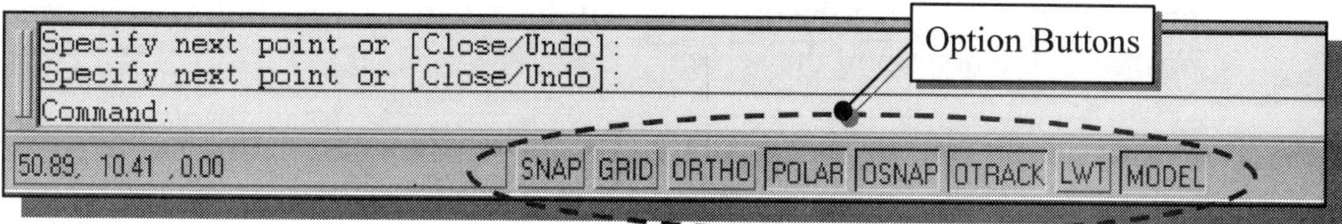

GRID ON

1. Left-click the ***GRID*** button in the *Status Bar* to turn ***ON*** the *GRID* option. (Notice in the command prompt area, the message *"<Grid on>"* is also displayed.)

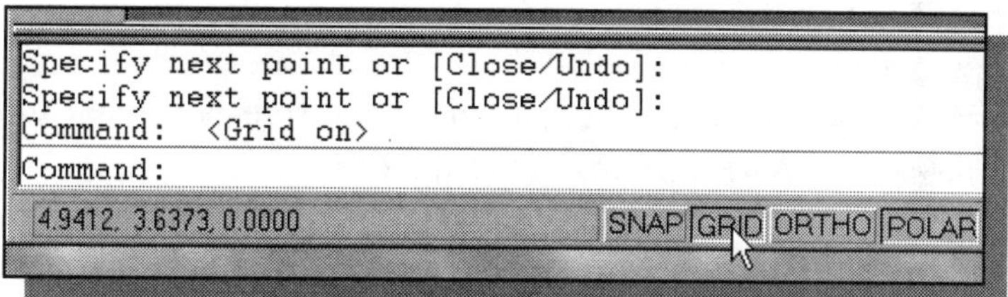

2. Move the cursor inside the graphics window, and estimate the distance in between the grid points by watching the coordinates display at the bottom of the screen.

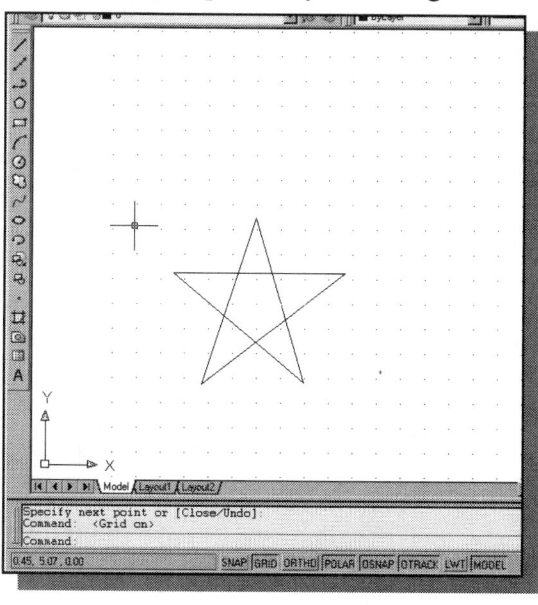

- The *GRID* option creates a pattern of dots that extends over an area on the screen. Using the grid is similar to placing a sheet of grid paper under a drawing. The grid helps you align objects and visualize the distance between them. The grid is not displayed in the plotted drawing. The default grid spacing, which means the distance in between two dots on the screen, is 0.5 inches. We can see that the sketched horizontal line in the above sketch is about 3.5 inches long.

SNAP ON

1. Left-click the ***SNAP*** button in the *Status Bar* to turn ***ON*** the *SNAP* option.

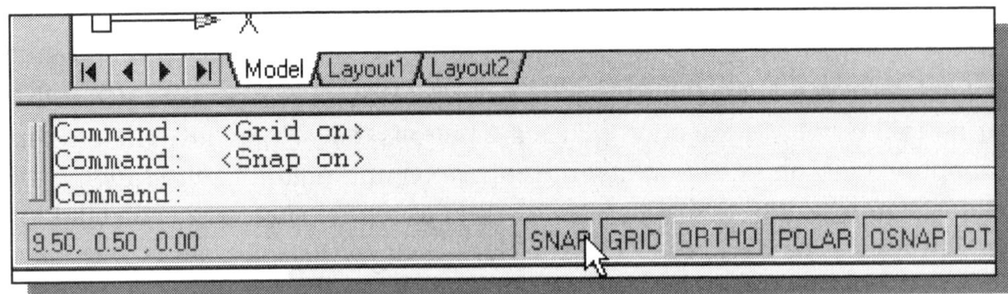

2. Move the cursor inside the graphics window, and move the cursor diagonally on the screen. Observe the movement of the cursor and watch the *coordinates display* at the bottom of the screen.

➢ The *SNAP* option controls an invisible rectangular grid that restricts cursor movement to specified intervals. When *SNAP* mode is on, the screen cursor and all input coordinates are snapped to the nearest point on the grid. The default snap interval is 0.5 inches, and aligned to the grid points on the screen.

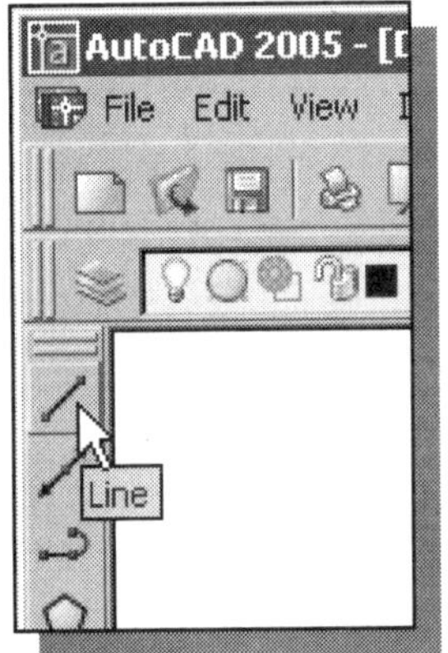

3. Click on the **Line** icon in the *Draw* toolbar. In the command prompt area, the message "*_line Specify first point:*" is displayed.

4. Create another sketch of the five-point star with the *GRID* and *SNAP* options switched *ON*.

5. Use the **right-mouse-button** and select **Enter** in the popup menu to end the Line command if you have not done so.

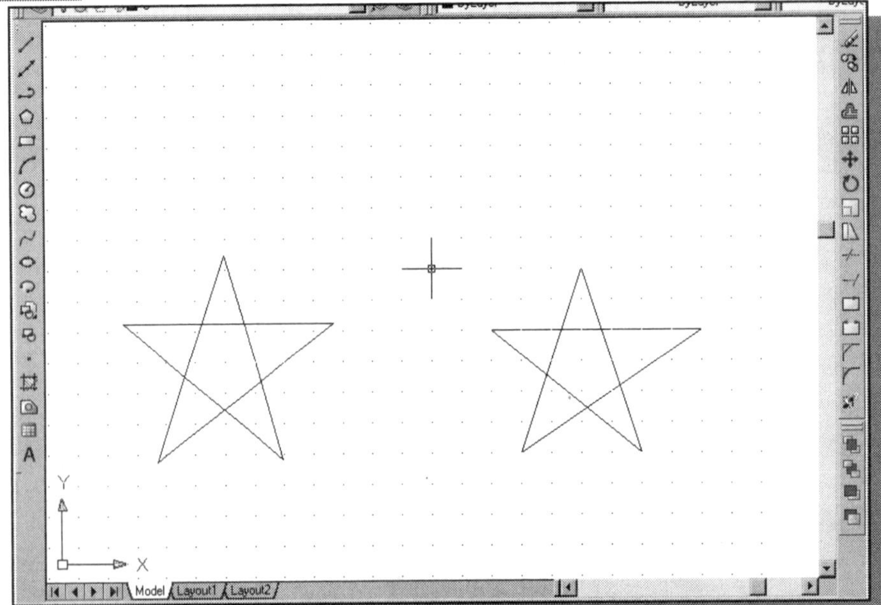

Using the *ERASER*

❖ One of the advantages of using a CAD system is the ability to remove entities without leaving any marks. We will erase two of the lines using the **Erase** command.

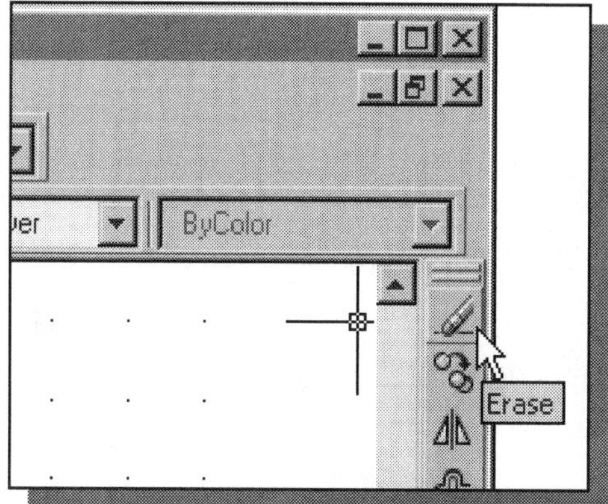

1. Pick **Erase** in the *Modify* toolbar. (The icon is the first icon in the *Modify* toolbar. The icon is a picture of an eraser at the end of a pencil.) The message "*Select objects*" is displayed in the command prompt area and AutoCAD awaits us to select the objects to erase.

2. Left-click the ***SNAP*** button on the *Status Bar* to turn off the *SNAP* option so that we can more easily move the cursor on top of objects. We can toggle the *Status Bar* options ***ON*** or ***OFF*** in the middle of another command.

3. Select any two lines on the screen, and right-mouse-click once to accept the selections. The selected two lines are erased.

Repeat the last command

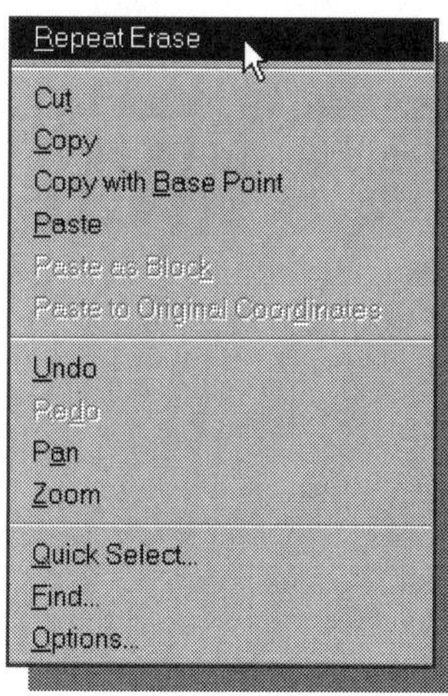

1. Inside the graphics window, click once with the right-mouse-button to bring up the popup option menu.

2. Pick **Repeat Erase**, with the left-mouse-button, in the popup menu to repeat the last command. Notice the other options available in the popup menu.

➢ **AutoCAD® 2005** offers many options to accomplish the same task. Throughout this text, we will emphasize the use of the **AutoCAD Heads-up Design™** interface, which means we focus on the screen, not on the keyboard.

3. Move the cursor to a location that is above and toward the left side of the entities on the screen. Left-mouse-click once to start a corner of a rubber-band window.

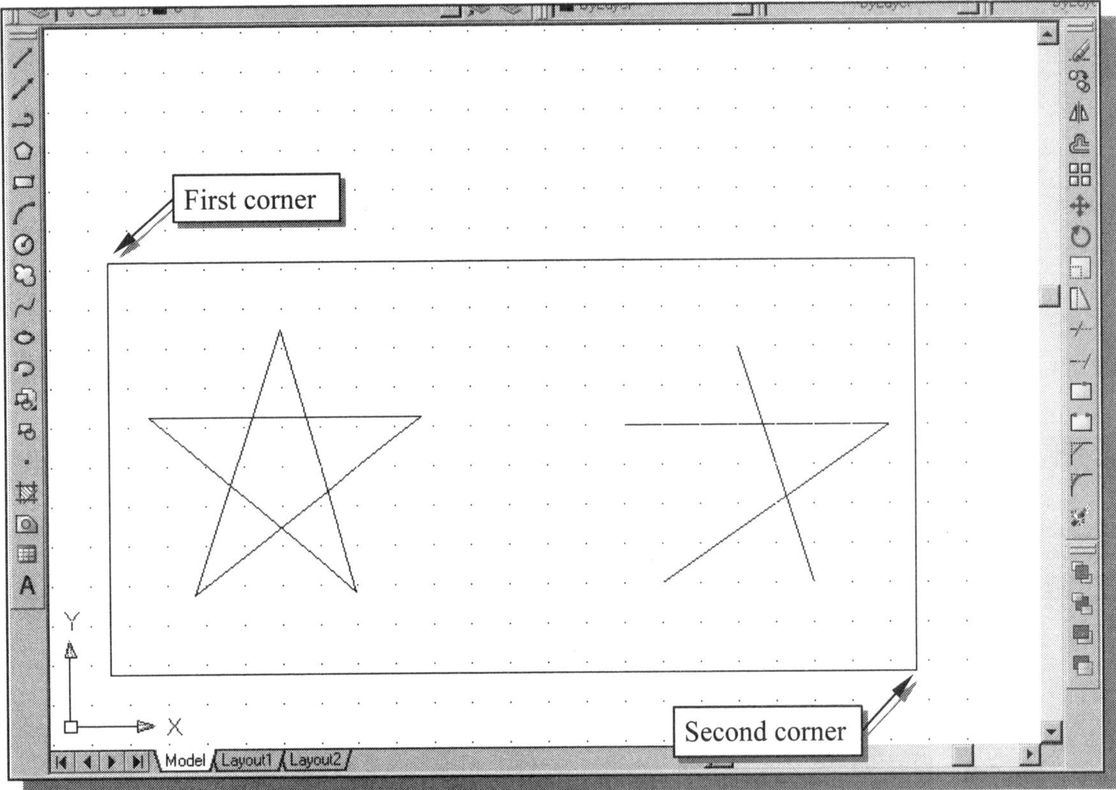

4. Move the cursor toward the right and below the entities, and then left-mouse-click to enclose all the entities inside the **selection window**. Notice all entities that are inside the window are selected.

5. Inside the graphics window, right-mouse-click to proceed with erasing the selected entities.

➢ On your own, create a sketch of your choice using the **Line** command. Experiment with using the different commands we have discussed so far, such as switching the *GRID* and *SNAP* options *ON* and *OFF* in the middle of a command.

❖ Do not be in a hurry to rush through the tutorials. Build up your CAD skills by familiarizing yourself with the commands and options demonstrated, along with the concepts discussed in the chapters. Feel free to repeat, at any time, any portions of the chapters.

The CAD Database and the User Coordinate System

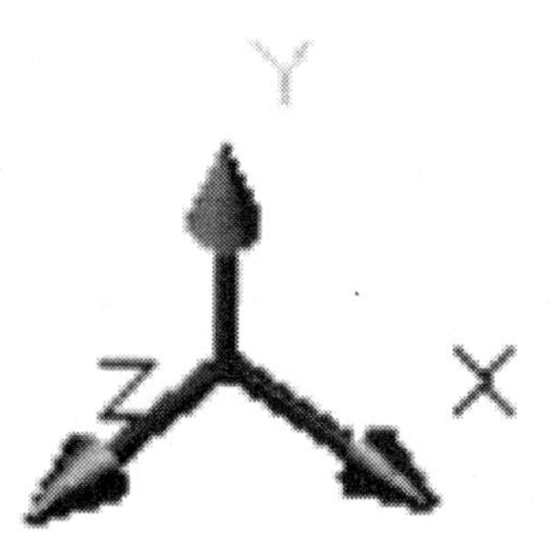

❖ Designs and drawings created in a CAD system are usually defined and stored using sets of points in what is called **world space**. In most CAD systems, the world space is defined using a three-dimensional *Cartesian coordinate system*. Three mutually perpendicular axes, usually referred to as the X-, Y-, and Z-axes, define this system. The intersection of the three coordinate axes forms a point called the **origin**. Any point in world space can then be defined as the distance from the origin in the X-, Y- and Z-directions. In most CAD systems, the directions of the arrows shown on the axes identify the positive sides of the coordinates.

A CAD file, which is the electronic version of the design, contains data that describe the entities created in the CAD system. Information such as the coordinate values in world space for all endpoints, center points, etc., along with the descriptions of the types of entities are all stored in the file. Knowing that AutoCAD stores designs by keeping coordinate data helps us understand the inputs required to create entities.

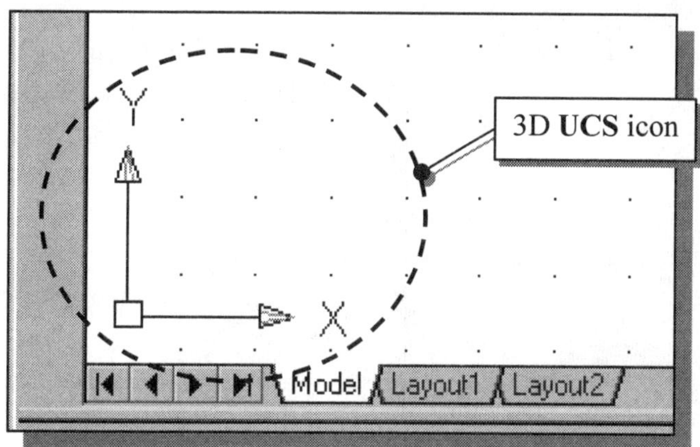

The icon near the bottom left corner of the default AutoCAD graphics window shows the positive X-direction and positive Y-direction of the coordinate system that is active. In AutoCAD, the coordinate system that is used to create entities is called the **user coordinate system** (UCS). By default, the **user coordinate system** is aligned to the **world coordinate system (WCS)**. The **world coordinate system** is a coordinate system used by AutoCAD as the basis for defining all objects and other coordinate systems defined by the users. We can think of the **origin** of the **world coordinate system** as a fixed point being used as a reference for all measurements. The default orientation of the Z-axis can be considered as positive values in front of the monitor and negative values inside the monitor.

Changing to the 2D UCS icon Display

❖ In **AutoCAD® 2005**, the **UCS** icon is displayed in various ways to help us visualize the orientation of the drawing plane.

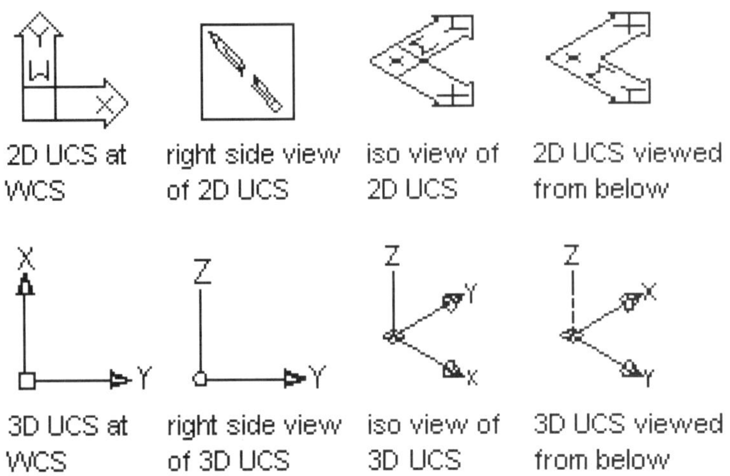

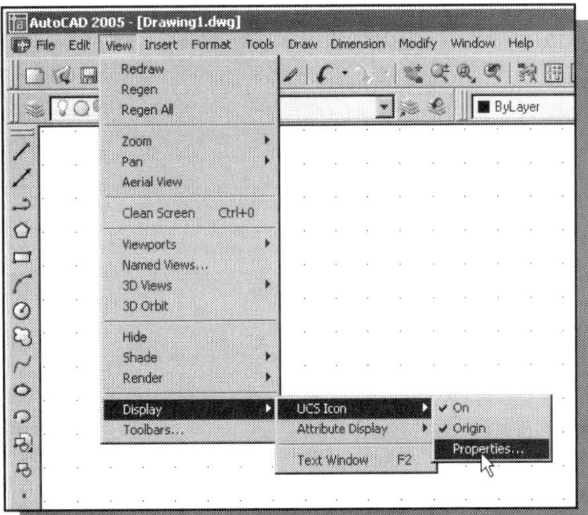

1. In the pull-down menus, select:

   [View] → [Display] → [UCS Icon] → [Properties]

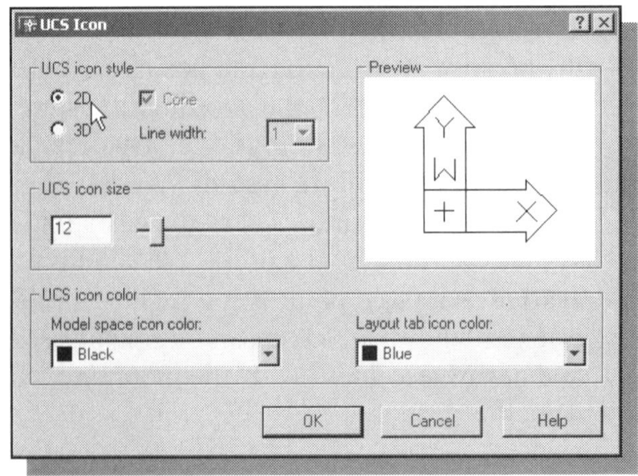

2. In the **UCS icon style** section, switch to the **2D** option as shown.

3. Click **OK** to accept the settings.

❖ Note the W symbol in the **UCS** icon indicates the UCS is aligned to the world coordinate system.

Cartesian and Polar Coordinate Systems

In a two-dimensional space, a point can be represented using different coordinate systems. The point can be located, using a *Cartesian coordinate system*, as X and Y units away from the origin. The same point can also be located using the *polar coordinate system*, as r and θ units away from the origin.

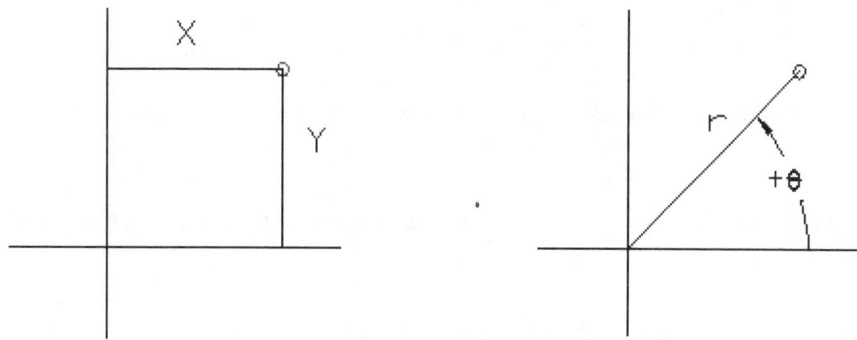

For planar geometry, the polar coordinate system is very useful for certain applications. In the polar coordinate system, points are defined in terms of a radial distance, r, from the origin and an angle θ between the direction of r and the positive X axis. The default system for measuring angles in **AutoCAD® 2005** defines positive angular values as counter-clockwise from the positive X-axis.

Absolute and Relative Coordinates

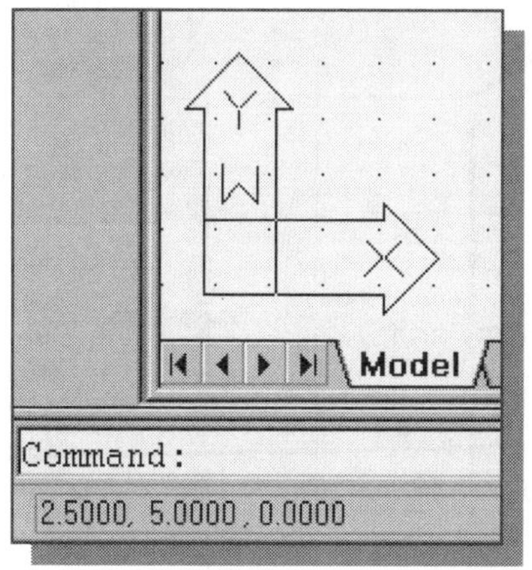

- **AutoCAD® 2005** also allows us to use *absolute* and *relative coordinates* to quickly construct objects. **Absolute coordinate values** are measured from the current coordinate system's origin point. **Relative coordinate values** are specified in relation to previous coordinates.

➢ Note that the *coordinate display area* can also be used as a toggle switch; each left-mouse-click will toggle the coordinate display *on* or *off*.

In **AutoCAD® 2005**, the *absolute* coordinates and the *relative* coordinates can be used in conjunction with the *Cartesian* and *polar* coordinate systems. By default, AutoCAD expects us to enter values in *absolute Cartesian coordinates*, distances measured from the current coordinate system's origin point. We can switch to using the *relative coordinates* by using the @ symbol. The @ symbol is used as the *relative coordinates specifier*, which means that we can specify the position of a point in relation to the previous point.

Defining Positions

In AutoCAD, there are five methods for specifying the locations of points when we create planar geometric entities.

- **Interactive method:** Use the cursor to select on the screen.
- **Absolute coordinates (Format: X,Y):** Type the X and Y coordinates to locate the point on the current coordinate system relative to the origin.
- **Relative rectangular coordinates (Format: @X,Y):** Type the X and Y coordinates relative to the last point.
- **Relative polar coordinates (Format: @Distance<angle):** Type a distance and angle relative to the last point.
- **Direct Distance entry technique**: Specify a second point by first moving the cursor to indicate direction and then entering a distance.

The *GuidePlate*

We will next create a mechanical design using the different coordinate entry methods.

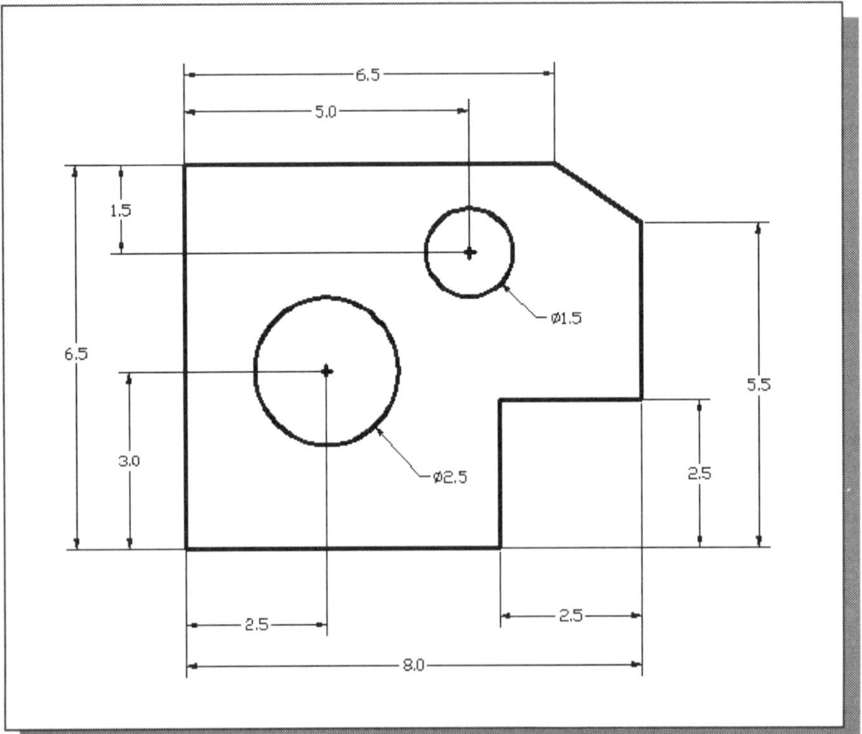

- Use the Erase command and erase all entities on the screen before proceeding to the next section.

❖ The rule for creating CAD designs and drawings is that they should be created at **full size** using real-world units. The CAD database contains all the definitions of the geometric entities and the design is considered as a virtual, full-sized object. Only when a printer or plotter transfers the CAD design to paper is the design scaled to fit on a sheet. The tedious task of determining a scale factor so that the design will fit on a sheet of paper is taken care of by the CAD system. This allows the designers and CAD operators to concentrate their attention on the more important issues – the design.

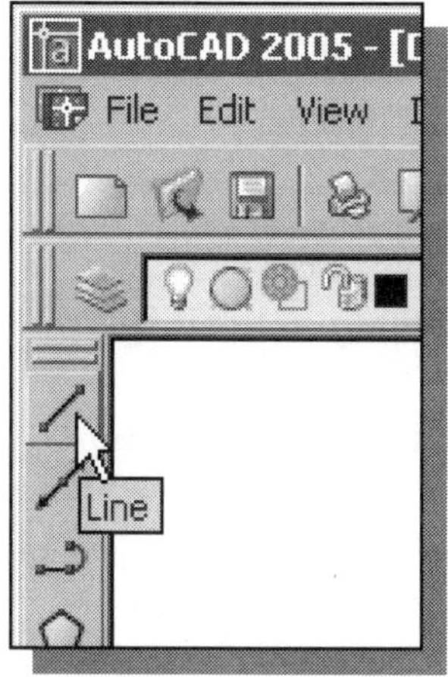

1. Select the **Line** command icon in the *Draw* toolbar. In the command prompt area, near the bottom of the AutoCAD graphics window, the message "*_line Specify first point:*" is displayed. AutoCAD expects us to identify the starting location of a straight line.

2. In the command prompt area, we will locate the starting point of our design at the origin of the *world coordinate system*.

   Command: _line Specify first point: **0,0 [ENTER]**
   (Type ***0,0*** in the command prompt area and press the [**ENTER**] key once.)

3. We will create a horizontal line by entering the absolute coordinates of the second point.

   Specify next point or [Undo]: **5.5,0 [ENTER]**

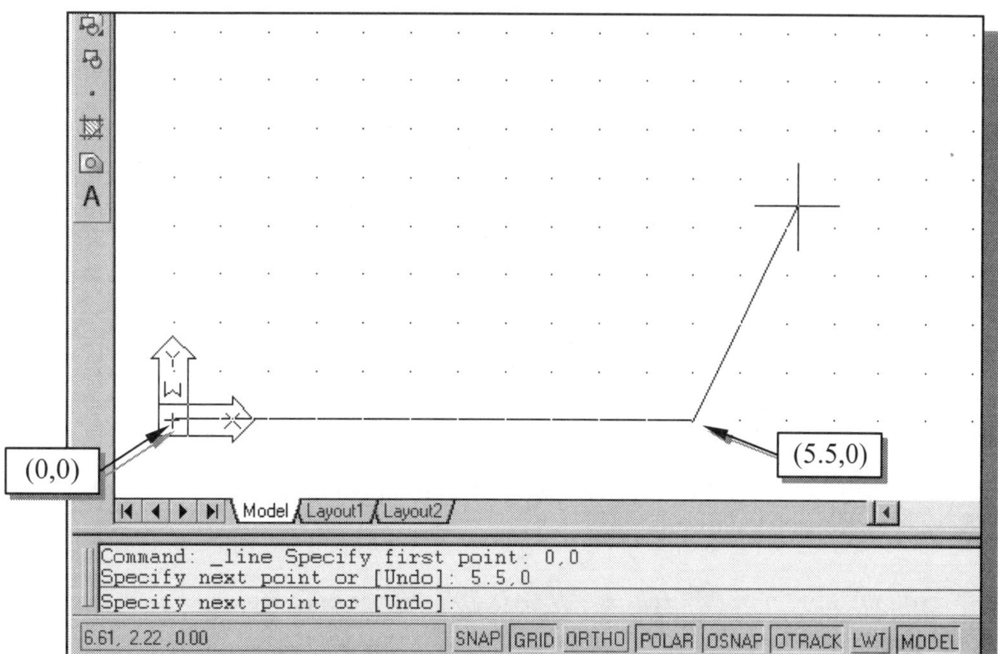

- The line we created is aligned to the bottom edge of the drawing window. Let us adjust the view of the line by using the Pan Realtime command.

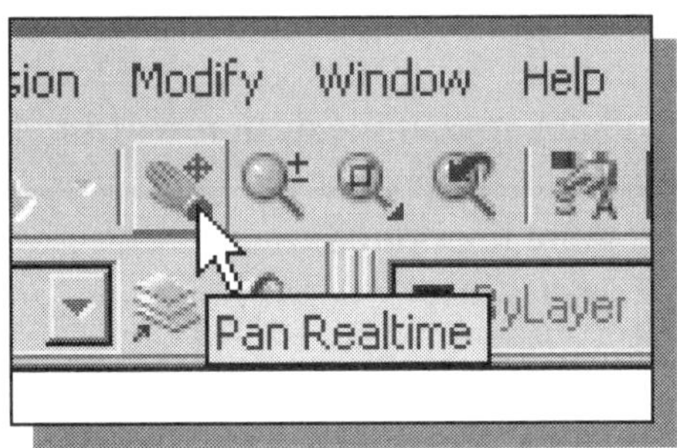

4. Click on the **Pan Realtime** icon in the *Standard* toolbar area. The icon is the picture of a hand with four arrows.

❖ The Pan command enables us to move the view to a different position. This function acts as if you are using a video camera.

5. Move the cursor, which appears as a hand inside the graphics window, near the center of the drawing window, then push down the left-mouse-button and drag the display toward the right and top side until we can see the sketched line. (Notice the scroll bars can also be used to adjust viewing of the display.)

6. Press the **[Esc]** key to exit the Pan command. Notice that AutoCAD goes back to the Line command.

7. We will create a vertical line by using the *relative rectangular coordinates entry method*, relative to the last point we specified:

   Specify next point or [Close/Undo]: **@0,2.5** **[ENTER]**

8. We can mix any of the entry methods in positioning the locations of the endpoints. Move the cursor to the *Status Bar* area, and turn *ON* the *GRID* and *SNAP* options.

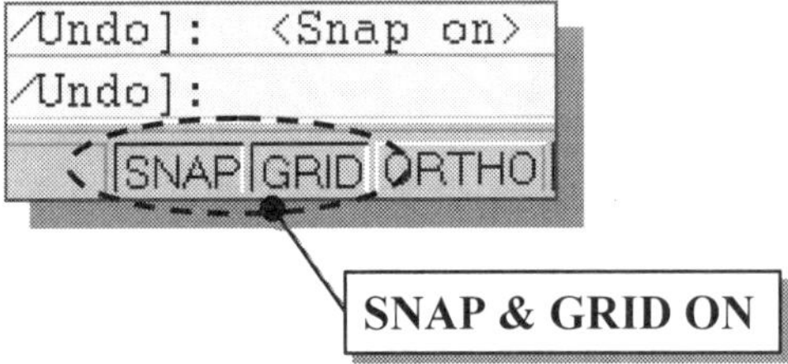

9. Create the next line by picking the location, world coordinates **(8,2.5)**, on the screen.

10. We will next use the *relative polar coordinates entry method*, relative to the last point we specified:

    Specify next point or [Close/Undo]: **@3<90** **[ENTER]**
    (Distance is **3** inches with an angle of **90** degrees.)

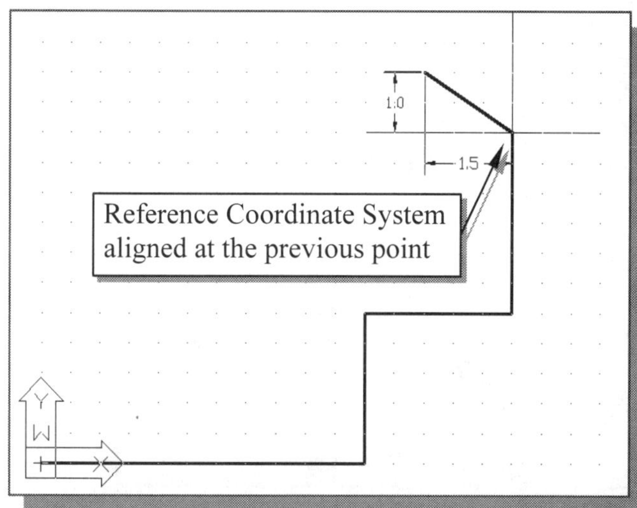

11. Using the *relative rectangular coordinates entry method* to create the next line, we can imagine a *reference coordinate system* aligned at the previous point. Coordinates are measured along the two reference axes.

Specify next point or [Close/Undo]: **@-1.5,1** **[ENTER]**

(**-1.5** and **1** inches are measured relative to the reference point.)

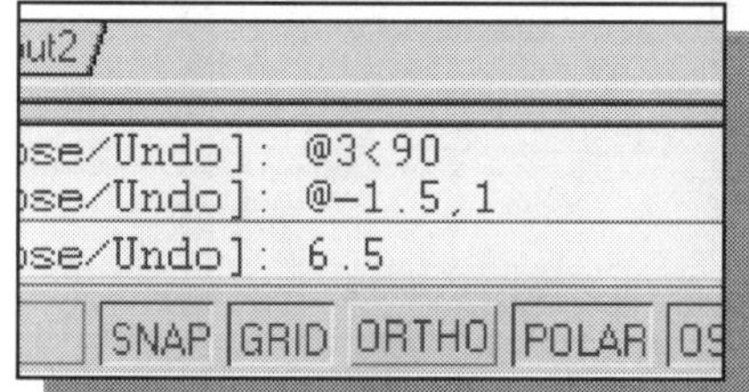

12. Move the cursor directly to the left of the last point and use the *direct distance entry technique* by entering ***6.5*** **[ENTER]**.

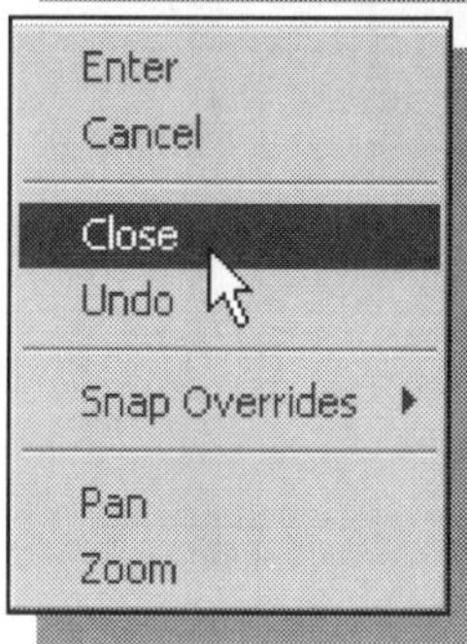

13. For the last segment of the sketch, we can use the **Close** option to connect back to the starting point. Inside the graphics window, right-mouse-click and a popup menu appears on the screen.

14. Select **Close** with the left-mouse-button to connect back to the starting point and end the Line command.

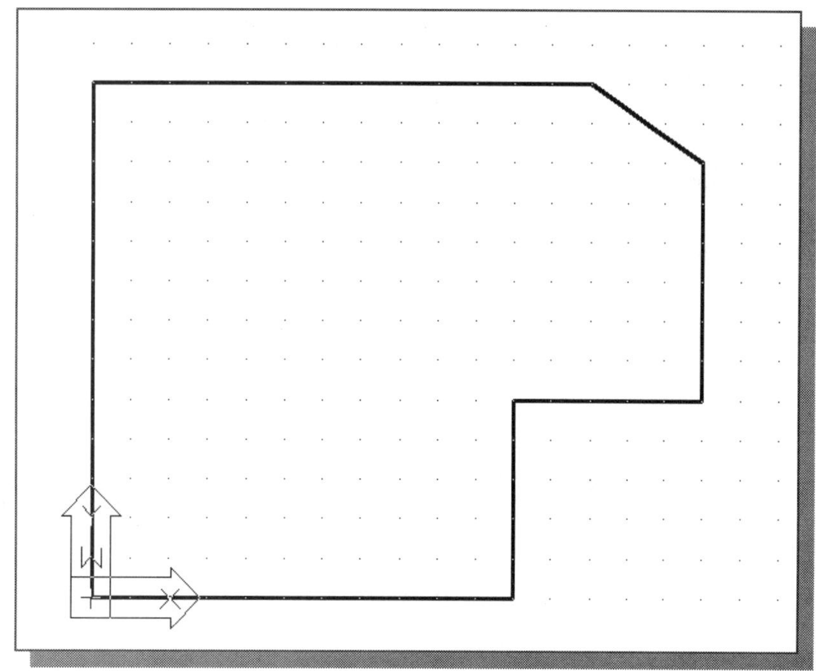

Creating *Circles*

The menus and toolbars in **AutoCAD® 2005** are designed to allow the CAD operators to quickly activate the desired commands. Besides using the *Draw* toolbar, we can also select the different *Draw* commands through the pull-down menus.

1. In the pull-down menus, select:
   [Draw] → [Circle] → [Center, Diameter]

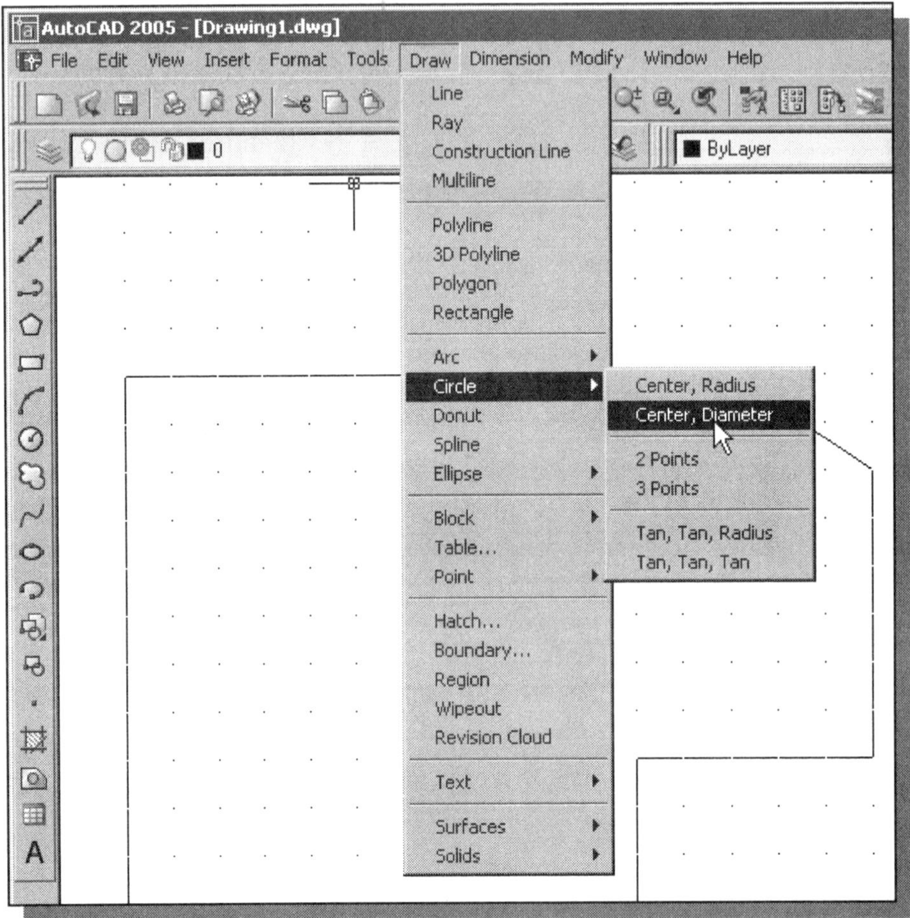

Notice the different options available under the circle submenu:

- **Center Point**: Draws a circle based on a center point and a diameter or a radius.
- **3 Points**: Draws a circle based on three points on the circumference.
- **2 Points**: Draws a circle based on two endpoints of the diameter.
- **TTR–Tangent, Tangent, Radius**: Draws a circle with a specified radius tangent to two objects.
- **TTT–Tangent, Tangent, Tangent**: Draws a circle tangent to three objects.

2. In the command prompt area, the message "*Specify center point for circle or [3P/2P/Ttr (tan tan radius)]:*" is displayed. AutoCAD expects us to identify the location of a point or enter an option. We can use any of the four coordinate entry methods to identify the desired location. We will enter the **world coordinates (2.5,3)** as the center point for the first circle.

   Specify center point for circle or [3P/2P/Ttr (tan tan radius)]: **2.5,3 [ENTER]**

3. In the command prompt area, the message "*Specify diameter of circle:*" is displayed.

   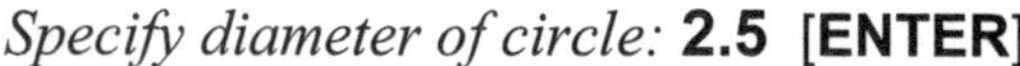
   Specify diameter of circle: **2.5 [ENTER]**

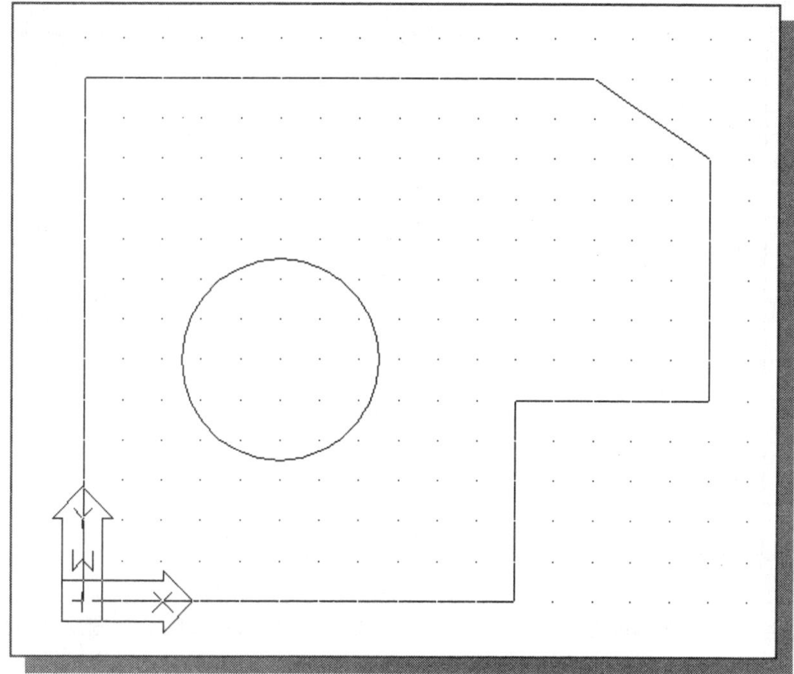

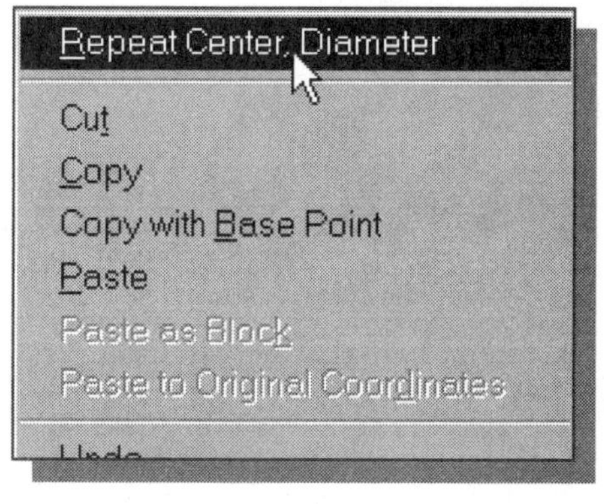

4. Inside the graphics window, right-mouse-click to bring up the popup option menu.

5. Pick **Repeat Center, Diameter** with the left-mouse-button in the popup menu to repeat the last command.

6. Using the *relative rectangular coordinates entry method*, relative to the center-point coordinates of the first circle, we specify the location as **(2.5,2)**.

Specify center point for circle or [3P/2P/Ttr (tan tan radius)]: **@2.5,2 [ENTER]**

7. In the command prompt area, the message "*Specify Diameter of circle: <2.50>*" is displayed. The default option for the Circle command in AutoCAD is to specify the *radius* and the last radius used is also displayed in brackets.

   Specify Diameter of circle<2.50>: **1.5** [**ENTER**]

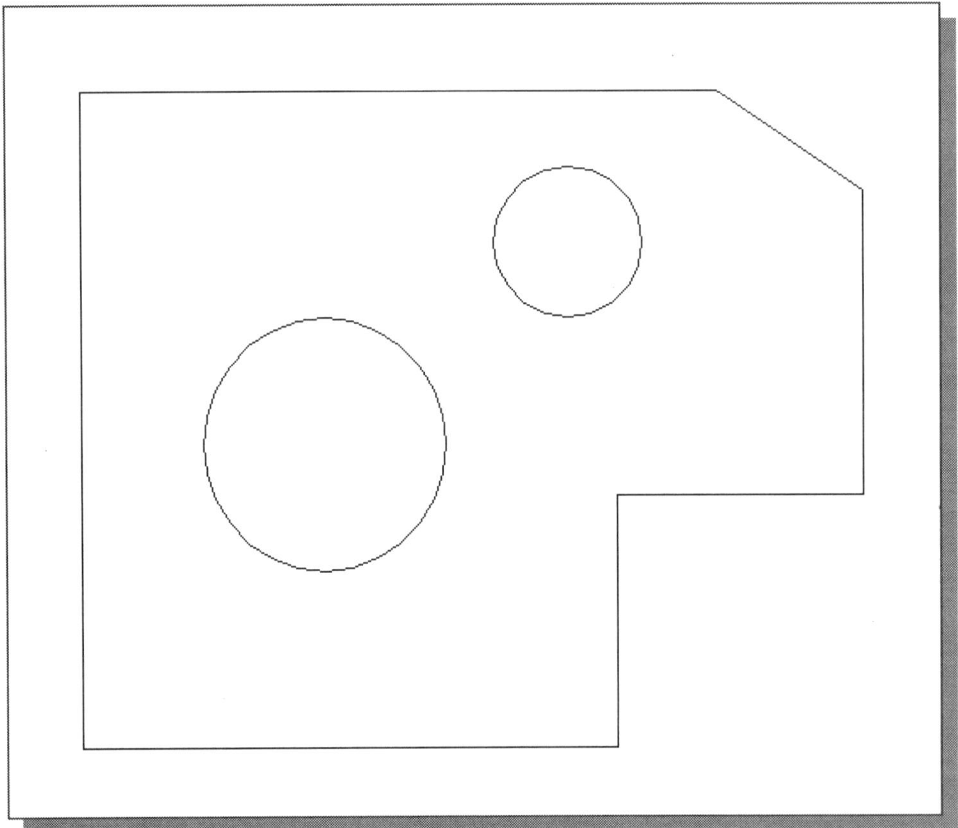

Saving the CAD Design

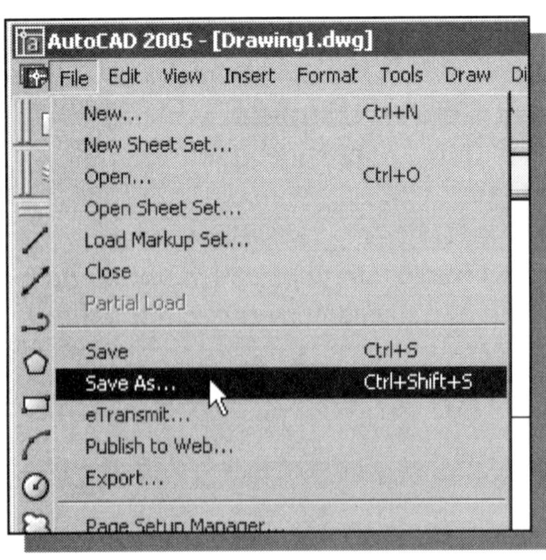

1. In the pull-down menus, select:

   [File] → [Save As]

❖ Note the command can also be activated with quick-key combination of **[Ctrl]**+**[Shift]**+**[S]**.

2. In the *Save Drawing As* dialog box, select the folder in which you want to store the CAD file and enter ***GuidePlate*** in the *File name* box.

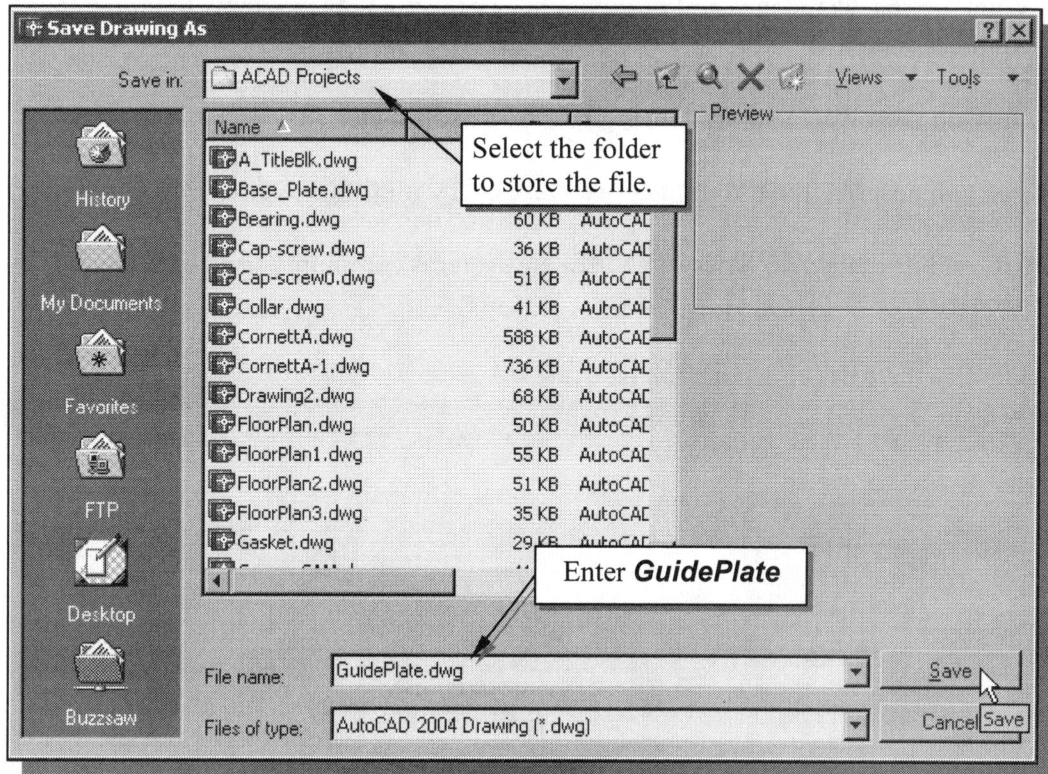

3. Pick **Save** in the *Save Drawing As* dialog box to accept the selections and save the file.

Exit AutoCAD 2005

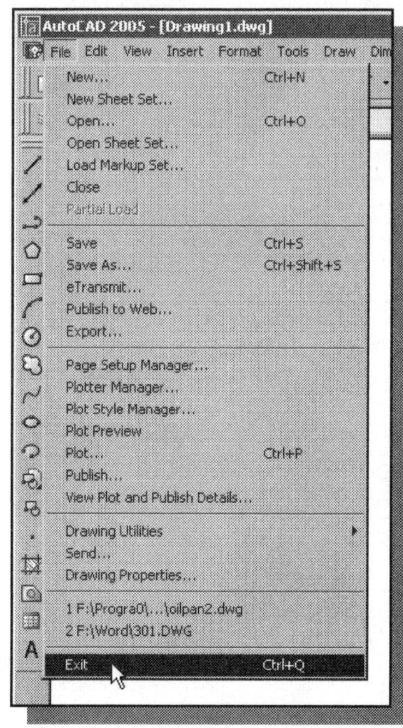

❖ To exit **AutoCAD® 2005**, select **File** then choose **Exit** from the pull-down menu or type ***QUIT*** at the command prompt. Note the command can also be activated with quick-key combination of **[Ctrl]+[Q]**.

Questions:

1. What are the advantages and disadvantages of using CAD systems to create engineering drawings?

2. How do the ***GRID*** and ***SNAP*** options assist us in sketching?

3. List and describe the different **coordinate entry methods** available in AutoCAD?

4. List and describe two types of coordinate systems commonly used for planar geometry.

5. Identify the following commands:

(a)

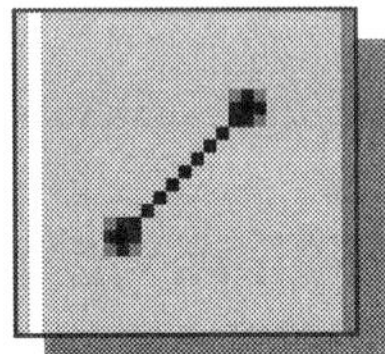

(b)

(c)

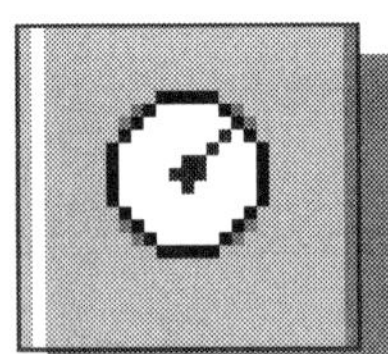

(d)

Tan, Tan, Radius

Exercises: (All dimensions are in inches.)

1.

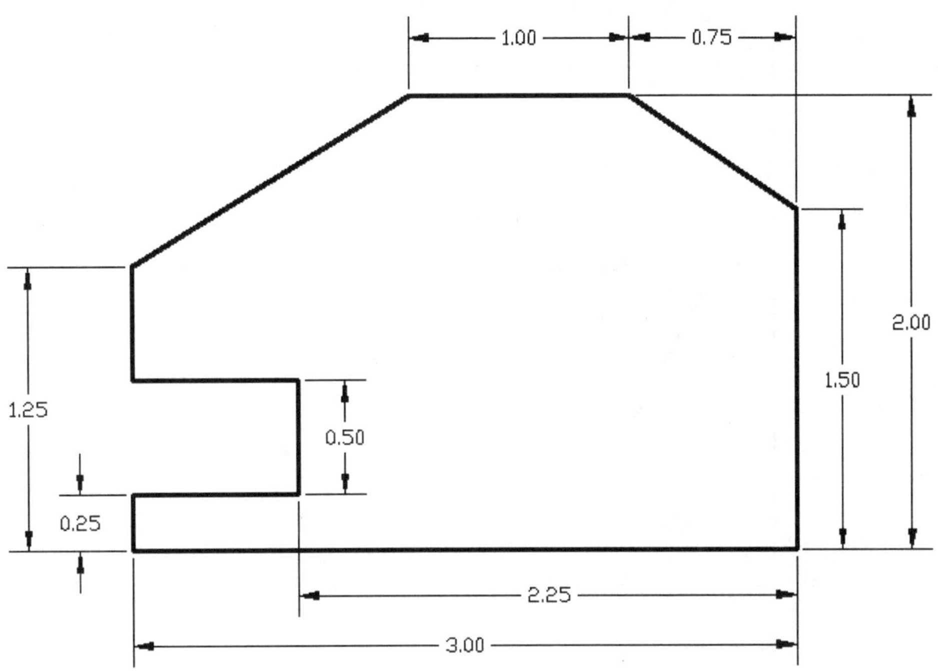

2.

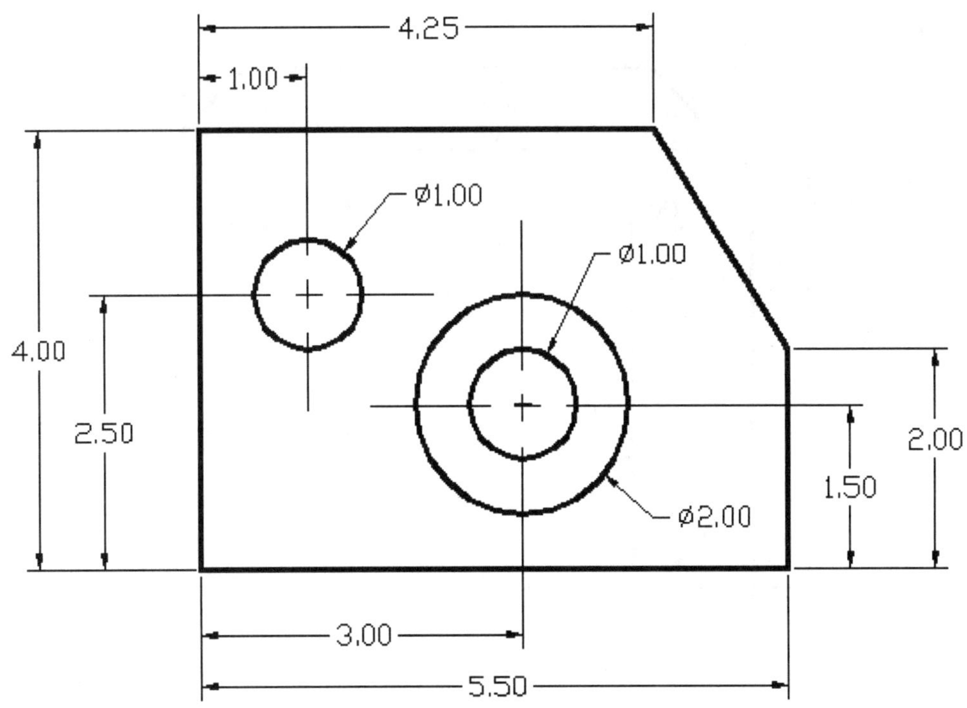

3.

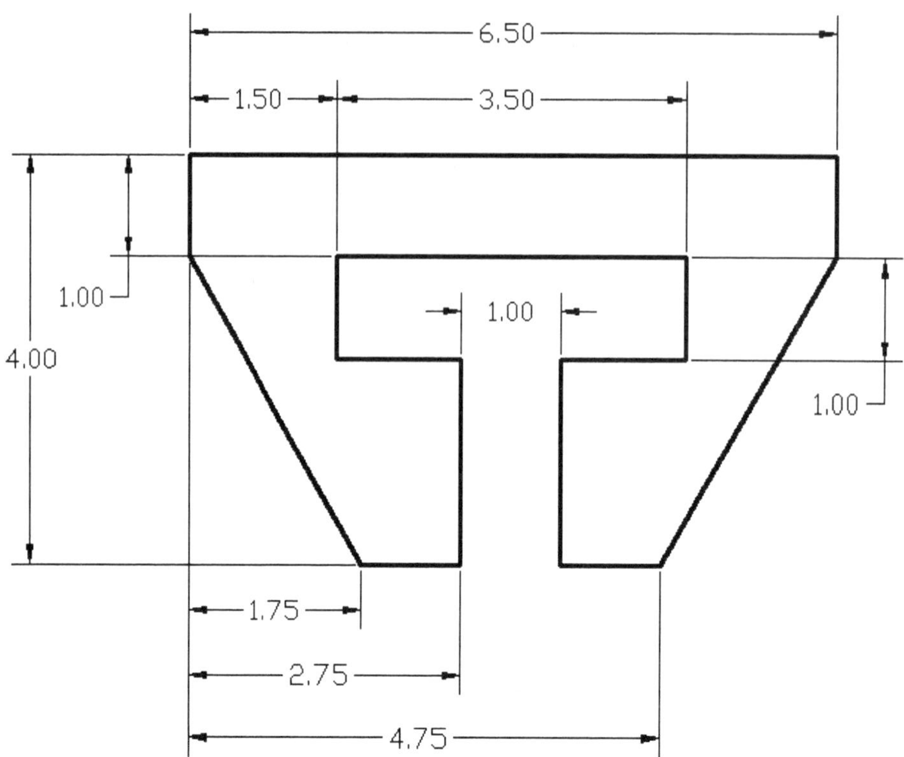

6.50
1.50
3.50
1.00
4.00
1.00
1.00
1.75
2.75
4.75

1.25
0.25
45°
0.20
45°
0.125
1.25
0.75
0.30
0.50
0.50
0.125
0.375
0.25
45°
0.20
45°
0.25
1.25
1.50

4.

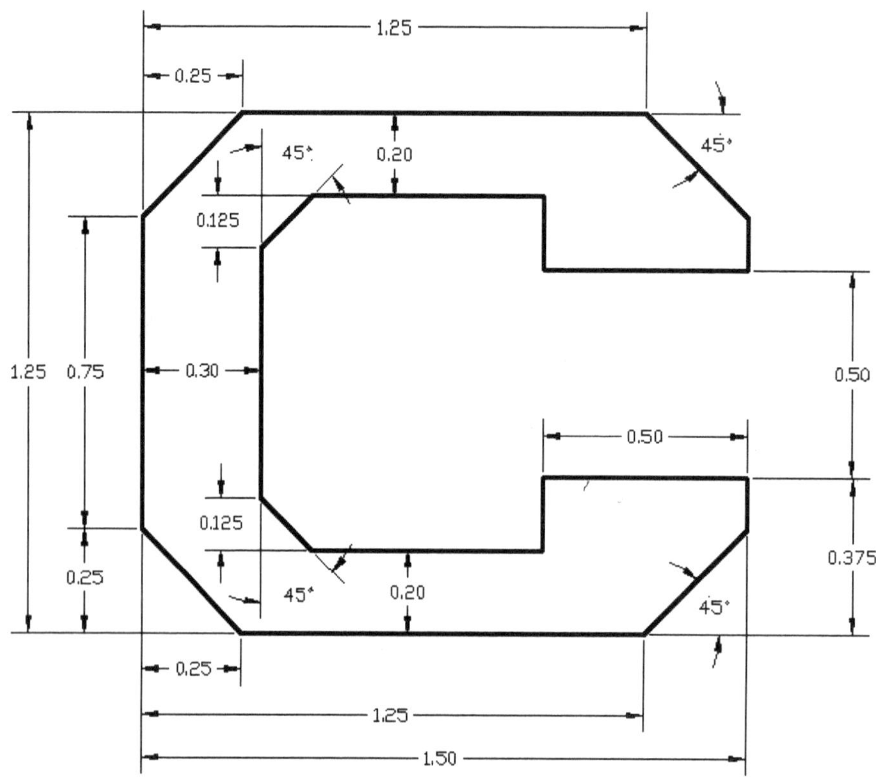

Chapter 2
Basic Object Construction Tools

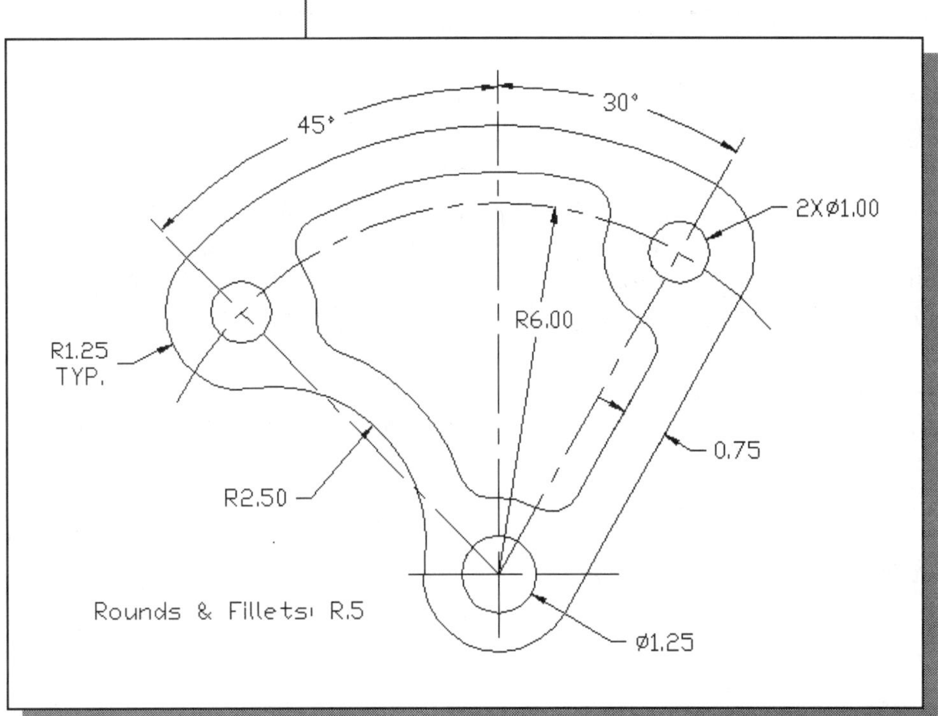

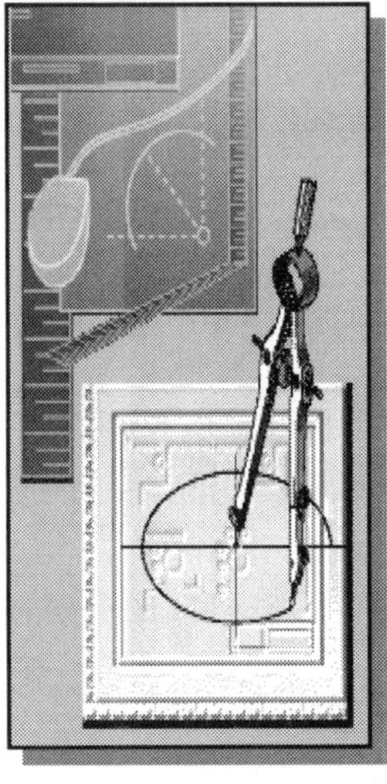

Learning Objectives

- **Referencing the WCS.**
- **Use the Startup dialog box.**
- **Set up GRID & SNAP intervals.**
- **Display AutoCAD's toolbars.**
- **Set up and use OBJECT SNAPS.**
- **Edit, using the TRIM command.**
- **Use the Polygon command.**
- **Create TTR circles.**
- **Create Tangent lines.**

Introduction

The main characteristic of any CAD system is its ability to create and modify 2D/3D geometric entities quickly and accurately. Most CAD systems provide a variety of object construction and editing tools to relieve the designer of the tedious drudgery of this task, so that the designer can concentrate more on design content. It is important to note that CAD systems can be used to replace traditional drafting with pencil and paper, but the CAD user must have a good understanding of the basic geometric construction techniques to fully utilize the capability of the CAD systems.

The use of the **User Coordinate System (UCS)** and the **World Coordinate System (WCS)** is further discussed in this chapter. In working CAD, one simple approach to creating designs in CAD systems is to create geometry by referencing the **World Coordinate System**. The general procedure of this approach is illustrated in this chapter.

In this chapter, we will examine the basic geometric construction and editing tools provided by **AutoCAD® 2005**. We will first look at tools such as *UNITS*, *GRID*, *SNAP* intervals setup and the *OSNAP* option, followed by construction tools such as circles and polygons; we will also look at the basic Trim command.

The *RockerArm* design:

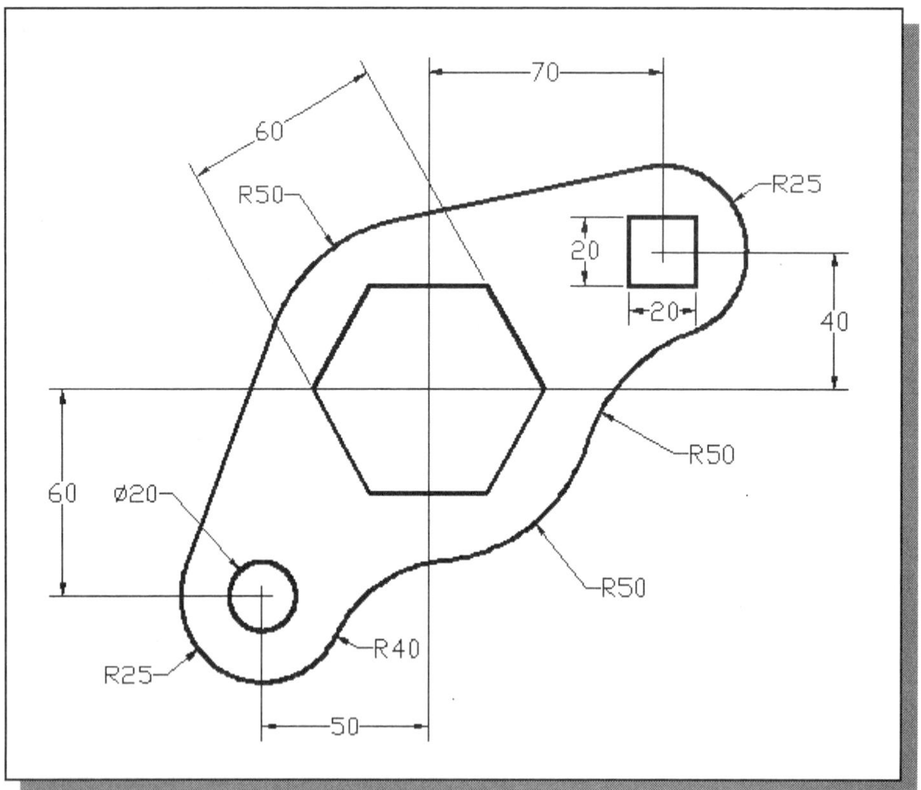

- ❖ Before continuing to the next page, on your own make a rough sketch showing the steps that can be used to create the design. Be aware that there are many different approaches to accomplishing the same task.

Starting Up AutoCAD® 2005

1. Select the **AutoCAD 2005** option on the *Program* menu or select the **AutoCAD 2005** icon on the *Desktop*. Once the program is loaded into the memory, the **AutoCAD® 2005** drawing screen will appear on the screen.

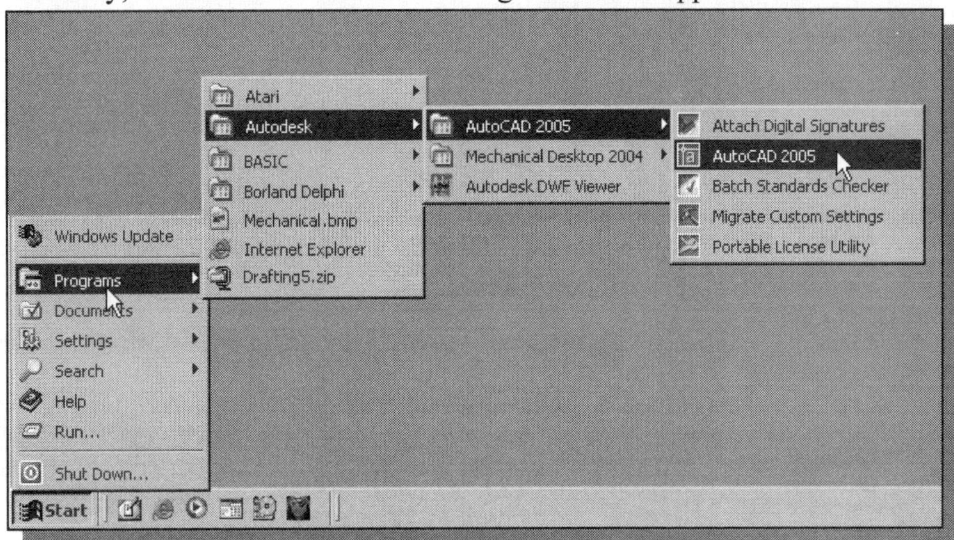

Activate the Startup option

❖ In **AutoCAD® 2005**, we can use the *Startup* dialog box to establish different types of the drawing settings. This option can be activated through the **Options** command.

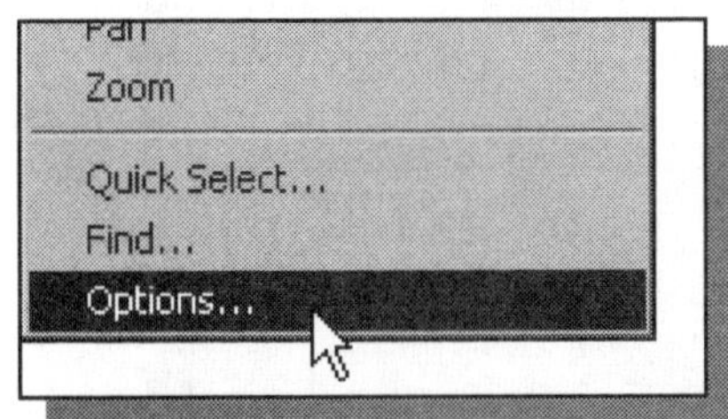

1. Inside the graphics area, right-mouse-click once to display the option list.

2. Select **Options**, with the left-mouse-button, to display the *Options* dialog box.

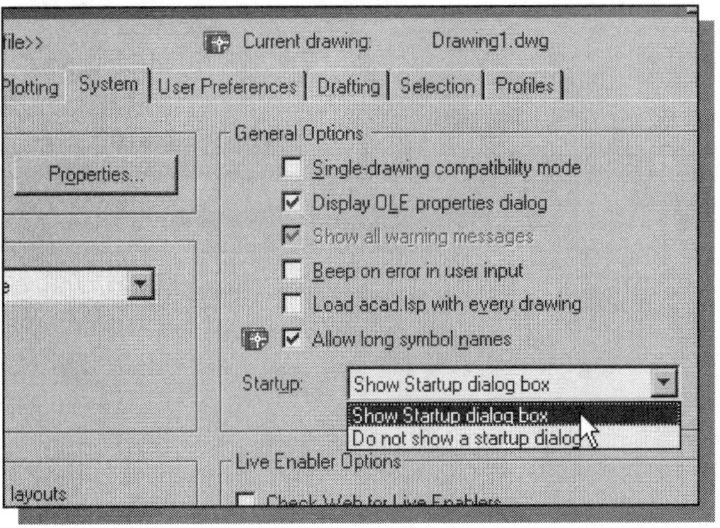

3. Switch to the **System** tab as shown.

4. In the *General Options* list, set the ***Startup*** option to **Show Startup dialog box** as shown.

5. Pick **OK** to exit the *Options* dialog box.

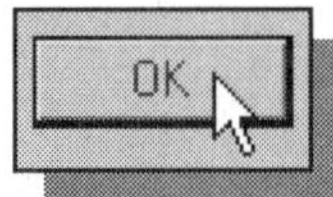

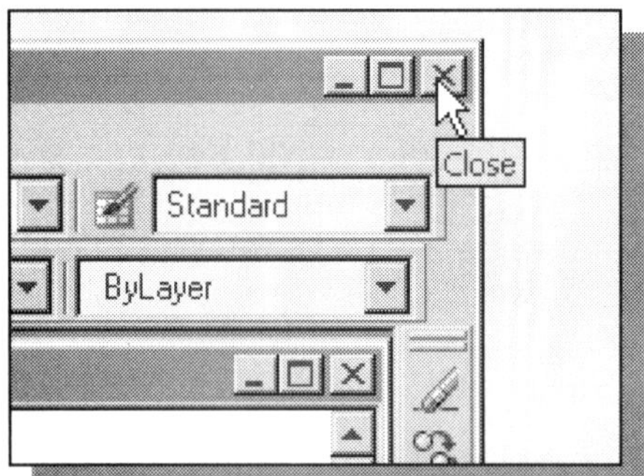

6. To show the effect of the *Startup* option, **exit** AutoCAD by clicking on the **Close** icon as shown.

7. Restart AutoCAD by selecting the **AutoCAD 2005** option on the *Program* menu.

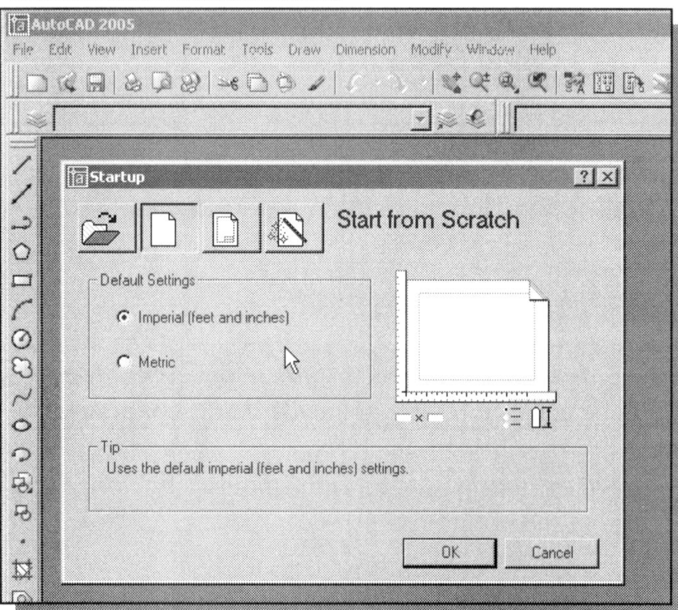

8. The *Startup* dialog box appears on the screen with different options to assist the creation of drawings. Move the cursor on top of the four icons and notice the four options available:
(1) **Open a drawing**,
(2) **Start from Scratch,**
(3) **Use a Template** and
(4) **Use a Setup Wizard**.

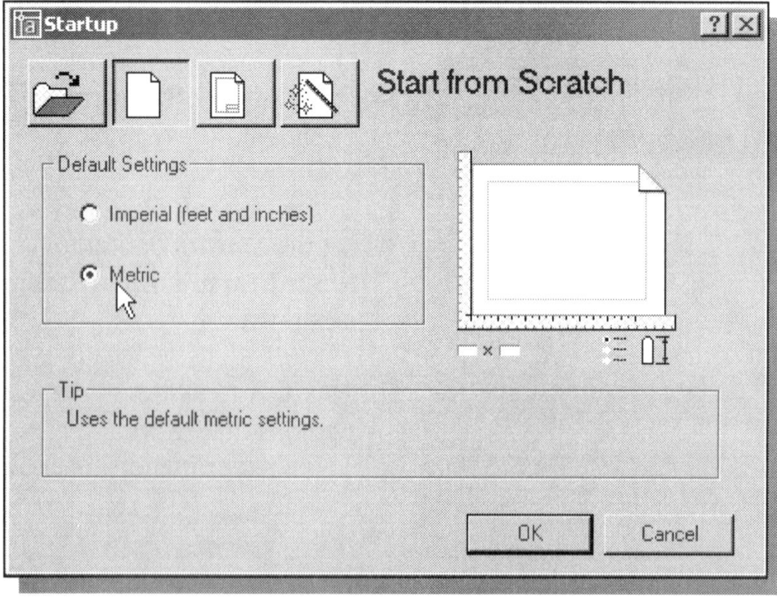

9. In the *Create New Drawing* dialog box, select the **Start from Scratch** option as shown in the figure.

10. Choose **Metric** to use the metric settings.

11. Click **OK** to accept the setting.

Drawing Units Display Setup

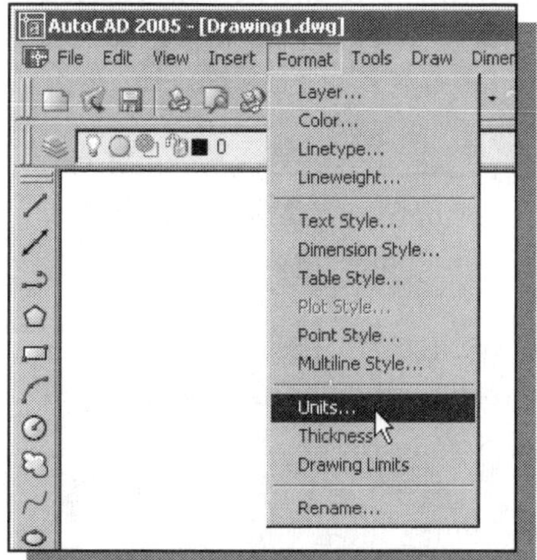

1. In the pull-down menus, select:

   [Format] → [Units]

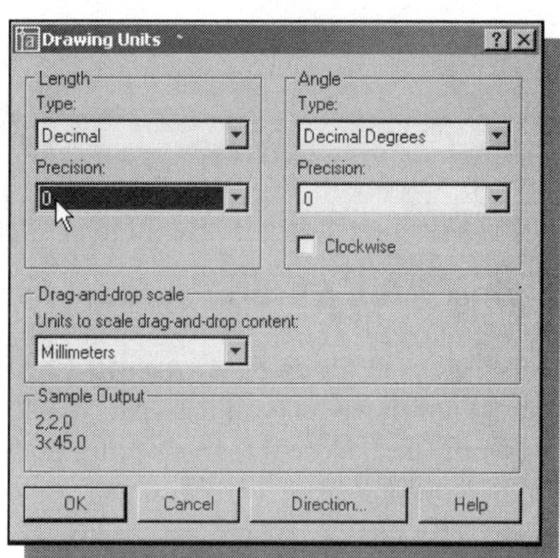

2. Set the *Precision* to **no digits** after the decimal point.

3. Click **OK** to exit the *Drawing Units* dialog box.

GRID and *SNAP* Intervals Setup

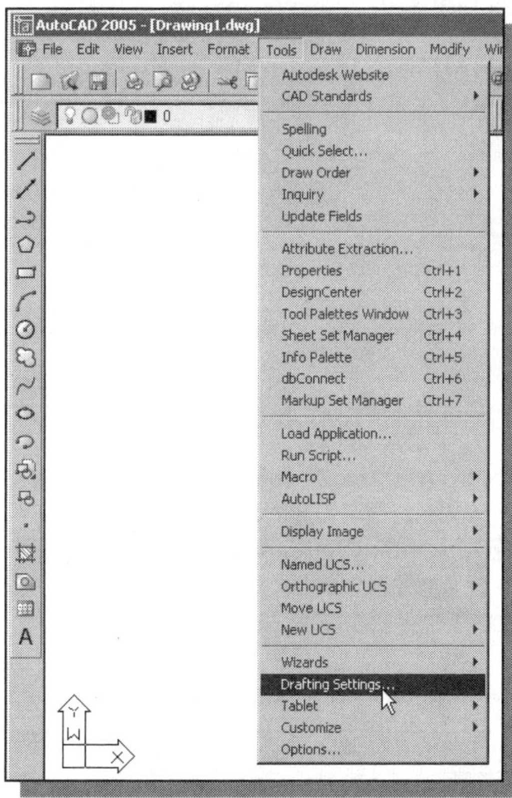

1. In the pull-down menus, select:

   [Tools] → [Drafting Settings]

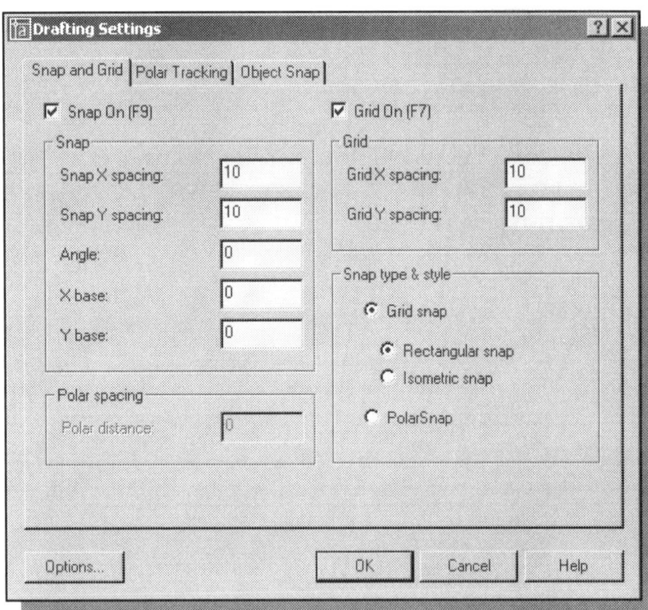

2. In the *Drafting Settings* dialog box, select the **Snap and Grid** tab if it is not the page on top.

3. Change *Grid Spacing* and *Snap Spacing* to ***10.00*** for both X and Y directions.

4. Switch ***ON*** the *Grid On* and *Snap On* options as shown.

5. Pick **OK** to exit the *Drawing Units* dialog box.

Drawing Area Setup

❖ Next, we will set up the **Drawing Limits**; setting the Drawing Limits controls the extents of the display of the *grid*. It also serves as a visual reference that marks the working area. Note that this setting does not limit the region for geometry construction.

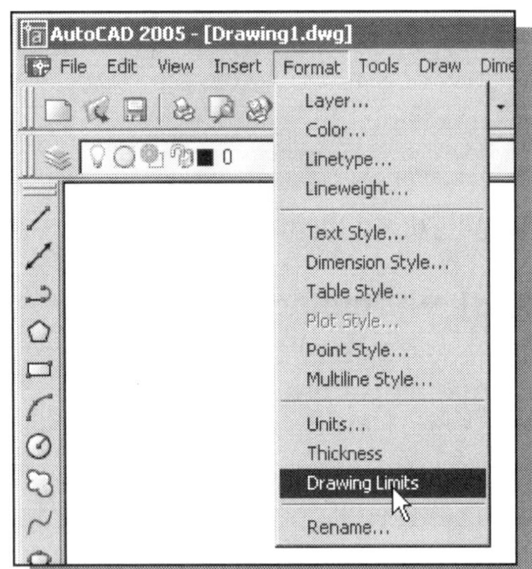

1. In the pull-down menus, select:

   [Format] → [Drawing Limits]

2. In the command prompt area, near the bottom of the AutoCAD drawing screen, the message "*Reset Model Space Limits: Specify lower left corner or [On/Off] <0,0>:*" is displayed. Enter ***-200,-150*** as the new lower left coordinates.

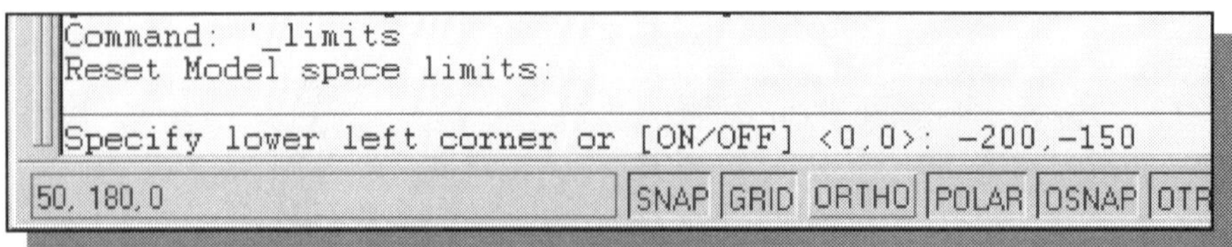

3. In the command prompt area, the message "*Specify upper right corner <420,297>:*" is displayed. Enter ***200,150*** as the new upper right coordinates.

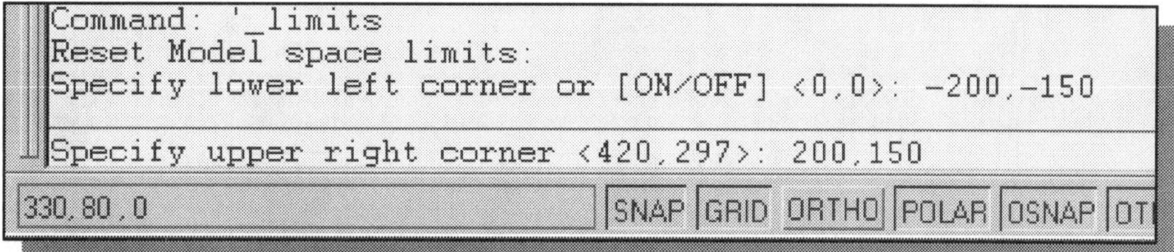

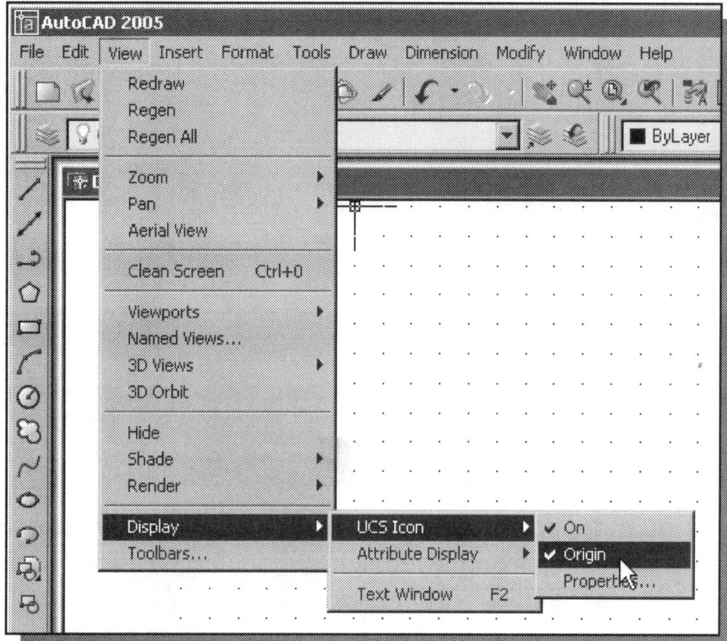

4. Confirm the **[UCS Icon]** → **[Origin]** option is switched *ON* as shown.

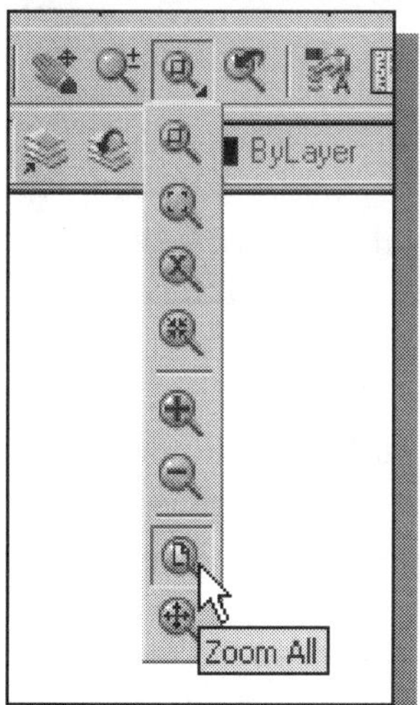

5. In the *Standard* toolbar, select **Zoom All** with the left-mouse-button on the **Zoom** icon stack.

❖ Notice the *UCS Icon*, which is aligned to the origin, is displayed at the center of the graphics window.

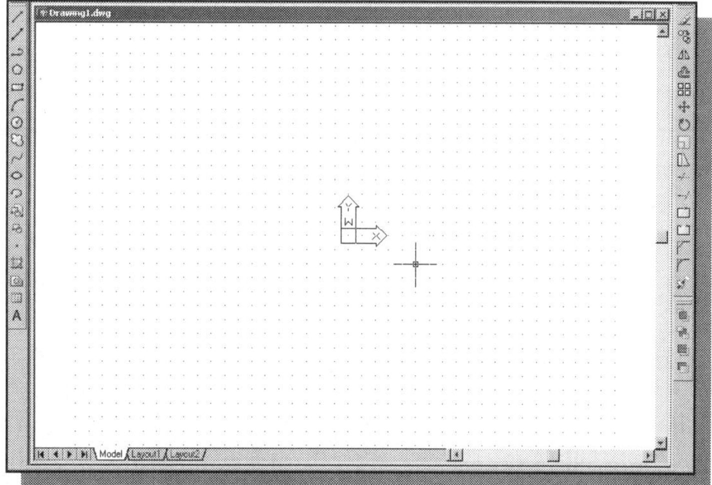

Referencing the World Coordinate System

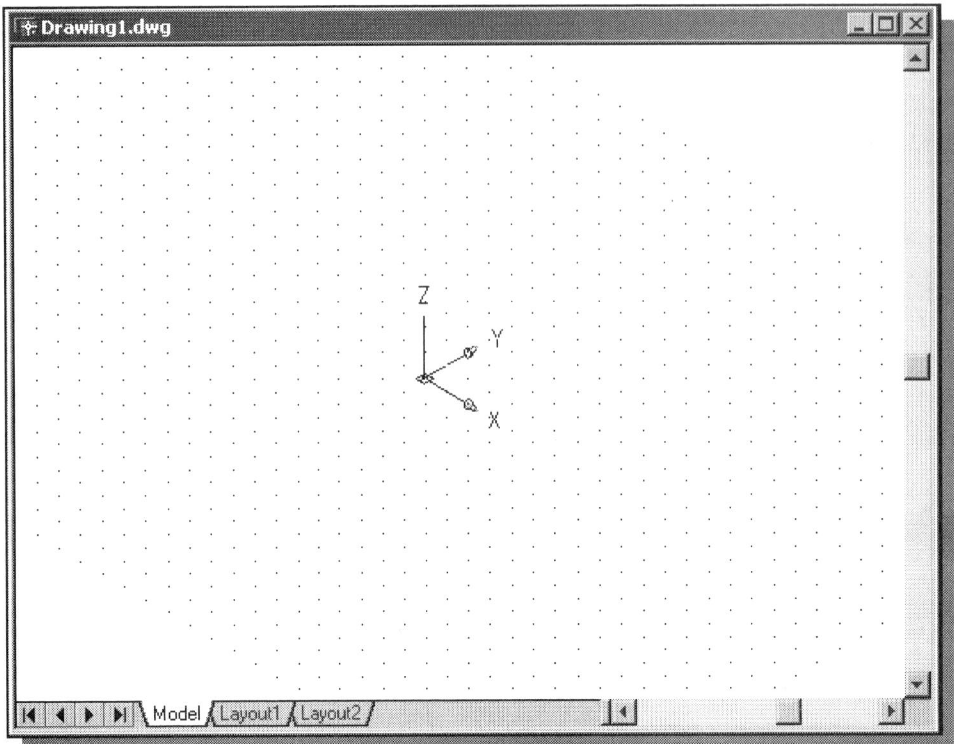

Design modeling software is becoming more powerful and user friendly, yet the system still does only what the user tells it to do. When using a geometric modeler, we therefore need to have a good understanding of what the inherent limitations are. We should also have a good understanding of what we want to do and what to expect, as the results are based on what is available.

In most geometric modelers, objects are located and defined in what is usually called **world space** or **global space**. Although a number of different coordinate systems can be used to create and manipulate objects in a 3D modeling system, the objects are typically defined and stored using the world space. The world space is usually a **3D Cartesian coordinate system** that the user cannot change or manipulate.

In most engineering designs, models can be very complex, and it would be tedious and confusing if only one coordinate system were available in CAD systems. Practical CAD systems provide the user with definable **Local Coordinate Systems (LCS)** or **User Coordinate Systems** (**UCS**), which are measured relative to the world coordinate system. Once a local coordinate system is defined, we can then create geometry in terms of this more convenient system. For most CAD systems, the default construction coordinate system is initially aligned to the world coordinate system.

In AutoCAD, the default **User Coordinate System (UCS)** is initially aligned to the XY plane of the **World Coordinate System (WCS)**. One simple approach to creating designs in CAD systems is to create geometry by referencing the **World Coordinate System**. The general procedure of this approach is illustrated in the following sections.

Creating *Circles*

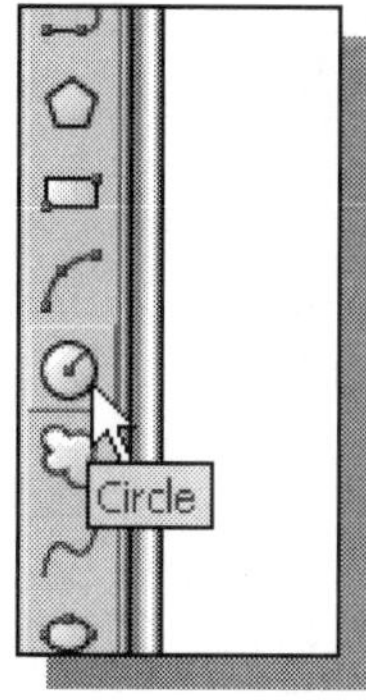

1. Select the **Circle** command icon in the *Draw* toolbar. In the command prompt area, the message "*_circle Specify center point for the circle or [3P/2P/Ttr (tan tan radius)]:*" is displayed. AutoCAD expects us to identify the center location first.

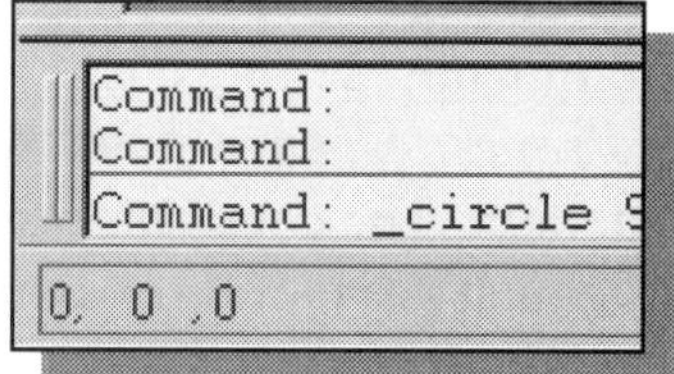

2. Select the **origin** of the world coordinate system as the center point location.

3. In the command prompt area, the message "*Specify radius of circle or [Diameter]:*" is displayed. AutoCAD expects us to identify the radius of the circle. Enter ***50*** as the value of the radius.

4. Hit the **[SPACE BAR]** once to repeat the circle command. In the command prompt area, the message "*_circle Specify center point for the circle or [3P/2P/Ttr (tan tan radius)]:*" is displayed. AutoCAD expects us to identify the center location of the new circle.

5. In the command prompt area, enter ***70,40*** as the absolute coordinate values of the center point coordinates of the second circle.

6. In the command prompt area, enter ***25*** as the value of the radius.

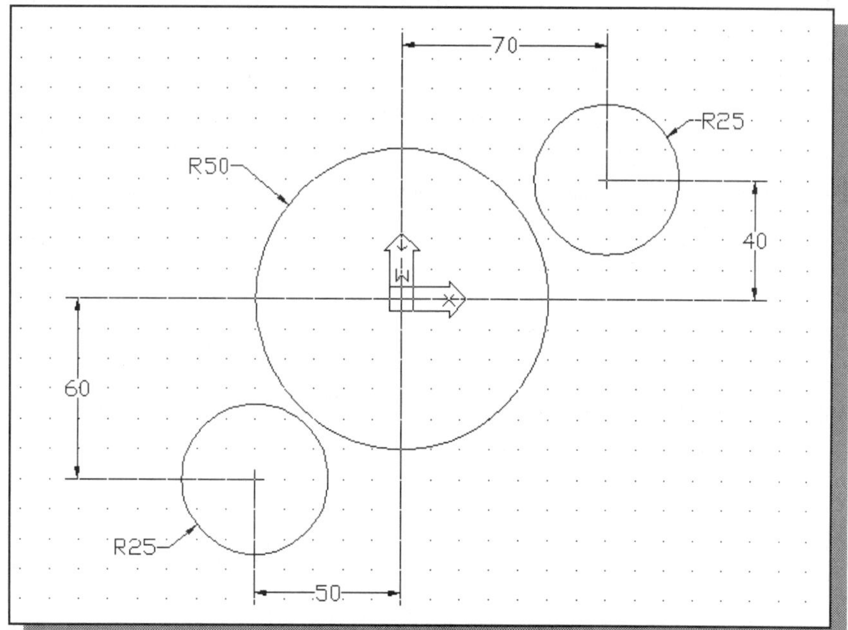

7. On your own, repeat the above procedure and create another circle (radius **25**) at coordinates **-50,-60** that is measured relative to the origin of the world coordinate system as shown in the above figure.

Object Snap Toolbar

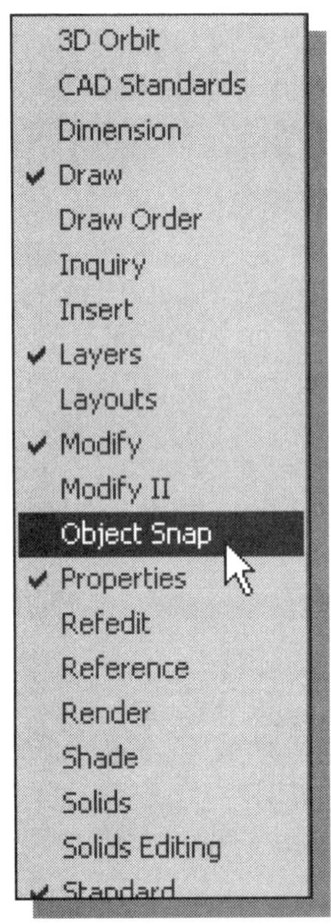

1. Move the cursor to the *Standard* toolbar area and **right-mouse-click** once on any icon in the toolbar area to display a list of toolbar menu groups.

   ❖ AutoCAD provides 29 predefined toolbars for access to frequently used commands, settings, and modes. The *Standard*, *Object Properties*, *Draw*, and *Modify* toolbars are displayed by default. The *check marks* in the list identify the toolbars that are currently displayed on the screen.

2. Select **Object Snap**, with the left-mouse-button, to display the *Object Snap* toolbar on the screen.

❖ **Object Snap** is an extremely powerful construction tool available on most CAD systems. During an entity's creation operations, we can snap the cursor to points on objects such as endpoints, midpoints, centers, and intersections. For example, we can turn on **Object Snap** and quickly draw a line to the center of a circle, the midpoint of a line segment, or the intersection of two lines.

3. Move the cursor over the icons in the *Object Snap* toolbar and read the description of each icon in the *Status Bar* area.

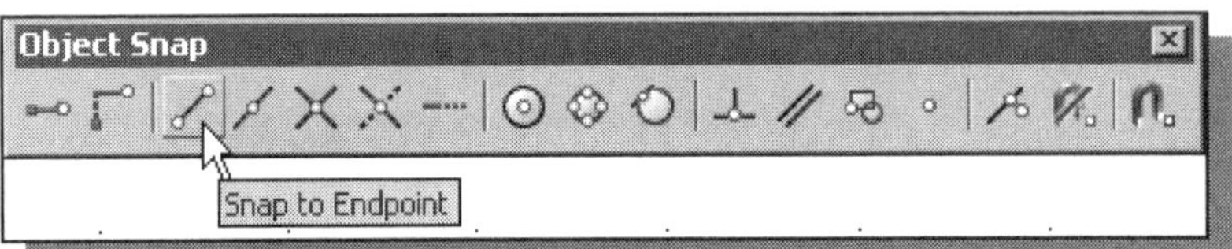

4. We will next turn off the *Grid Snap* option by toggling off the ***Snap*** button in the *Status Bar* area.

5. On your own, move the cursor inside the graphics window and confirm the grid snapping option is switched off.

6. On your own, in the *Status Bar* area, reset the option buttons so that only the *GRID*, and *MODEL* options are switched ***ON***.

Using the *LINE* command

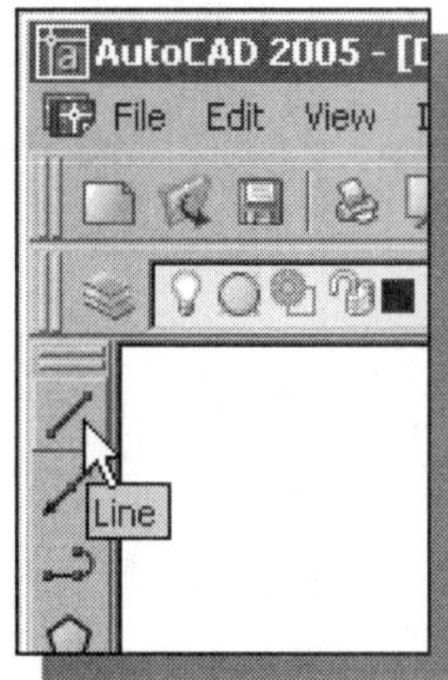

1. Select the **Line** command icon in the *Draw* toolbar. In the command prompt area, near the bottom of the AutoCAD drawing screen, the message "*_line Specify first point:*" is displayed. AutoCAD expects us to identify the starting location of a straight line.

2. Pick **Snap to Tangent** in the *Object Snap* toolbar. In the command prompt area, the message "*_tan to*" is displayed. AutoCAD now expects us to select a circle or an arc on the screen.

❖ The **Snap to Tangent** option allows us to snap to the point on a circle or arc that, when connected to the last point, forms a line tangent to that object.

3. Pick a location that is near the top left side of the smaller circle on the right; note the tangent symbol is displayed as shown.

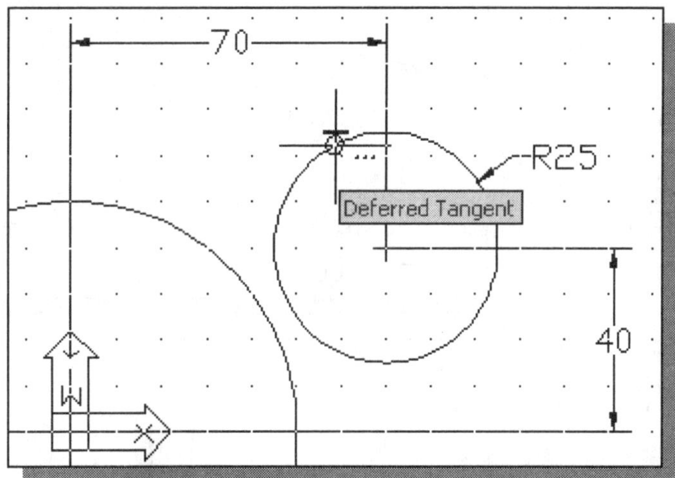

❖ Note that the note "Deferred Tangent" indicates that AutoCAD will calculate the tangent location when the other endpoint of the line is defined.

4. Pick **Snap to Tangent** in the *Object Snap* toolbar. In the command prompt area, the message "*_tan to*" is displayed. AutoCAD now expects us to select a circle or an arc on the screen.

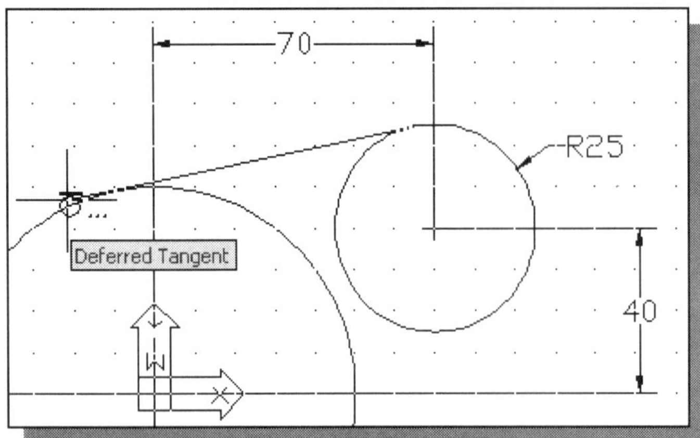

5. Pick a location that is near the top left side of the center circle; note the tangent symbol is displayed as shown.

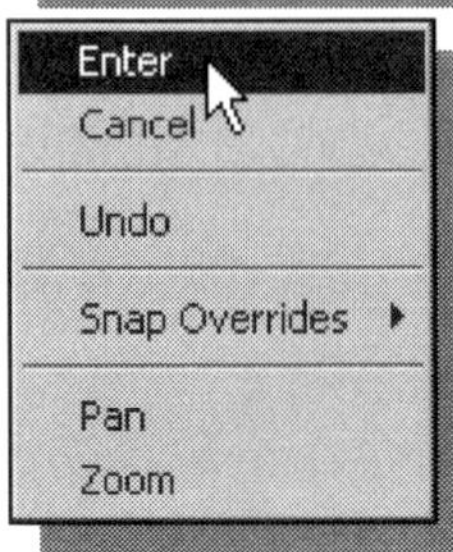

6. Inside the graphics window, **right-mouse-click** to activate the option menu and select **Enter** with the left-mouse-button to end the Line command.

❖ A line tangent to both circles is constructed as shown in the figure.

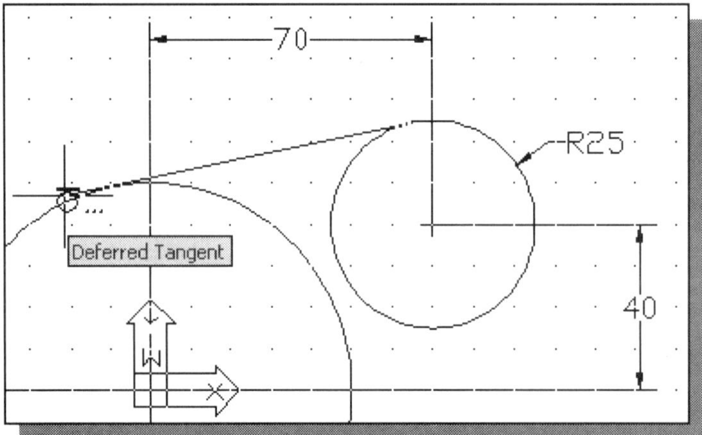

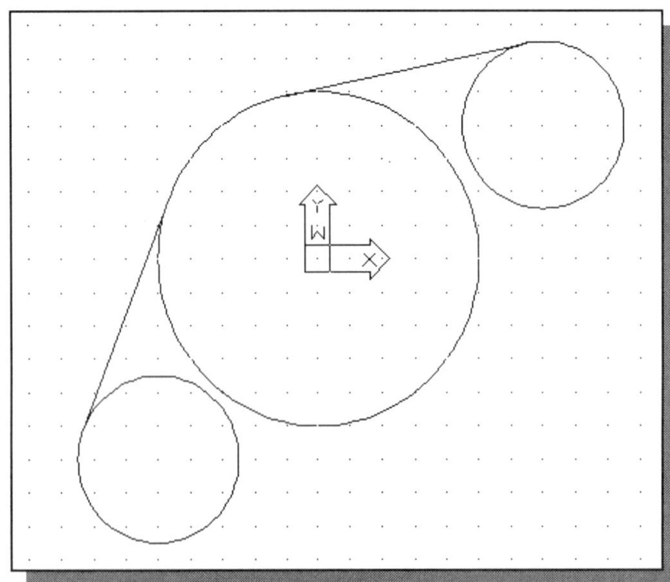

7. On your own, repeat the above steps and create the other tangent line between the center circle and the circle on the left. Your drawing should appear as the figure.

Creating *TTR Circles*

1. Select the **Circle** command icon in the *Draw* toolbar. In the command prompt area, the message "*Specify center point for circle or [3P/2P/Ttr (tan tan radius)]:*" is displayed.

2. Inside the graphics window, right-mouse-click to activate the option menu and select the **Ttr (tan tan radius)** option. This option allows us to create a circle that is tangent to two objects.

3. Pick a location near the **bottom of the smaller circle** on the right. We will create a circle that is tangent to this circle and the center circle.

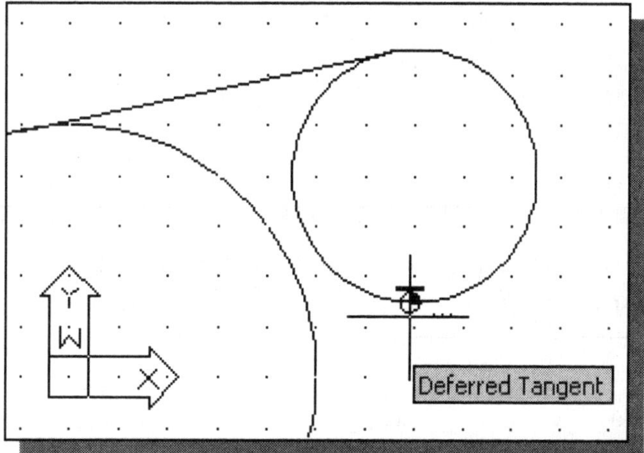

4. Pick the **center circle** by selecting a location that is near the right side of the circle. AutoCAD interprets the locations we selected as being near the tangency.

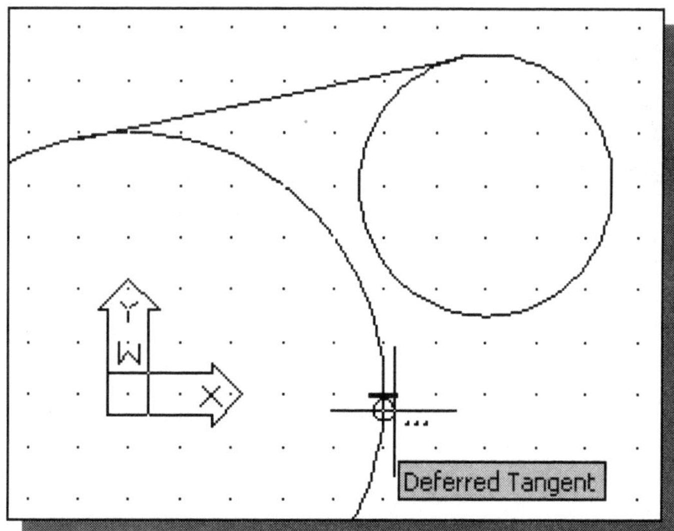

5. In the command prompt area, the message "*Specify radius of circle* " is displayed. Enter ***50*** as the radius of the circle.

   Specify radius of circle : **50 [ENTER]**

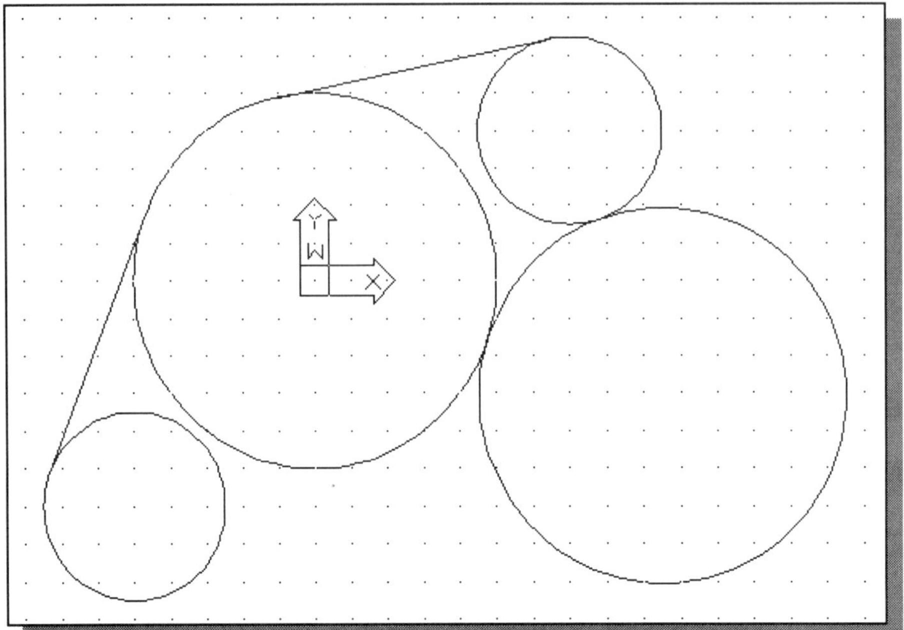

6. On your own, repeat the above steps and create the other TTR circle (radius **40**). Your drawing should appear as the figure below.

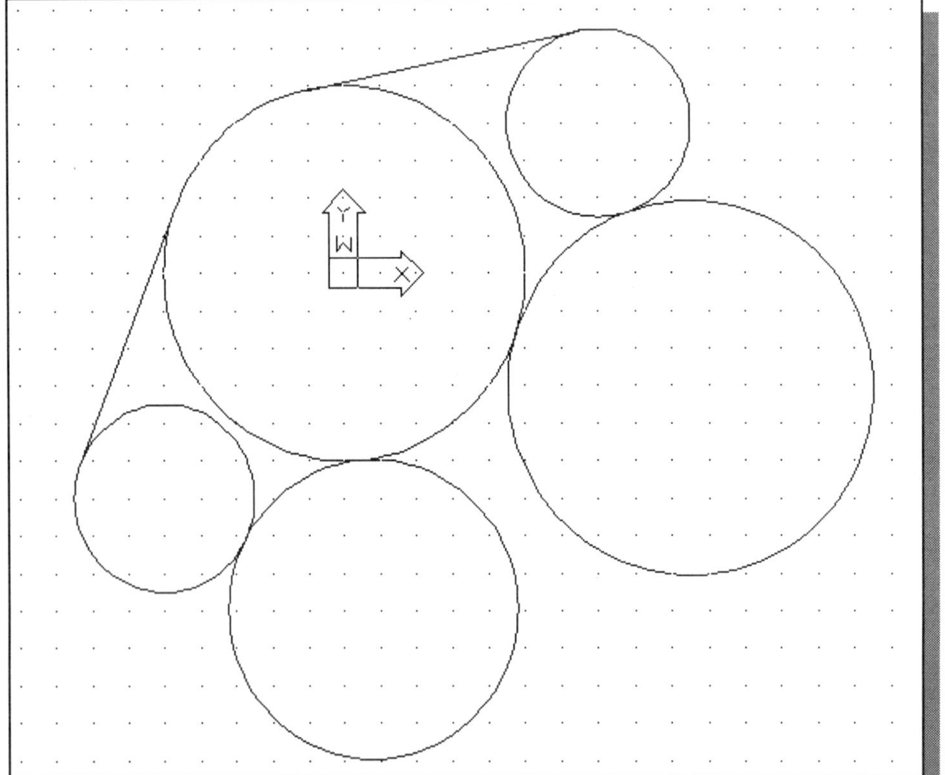

Using the *Trim* Command

- The **Trim** command shortens an object so that it ends precisely at a selected boundary.

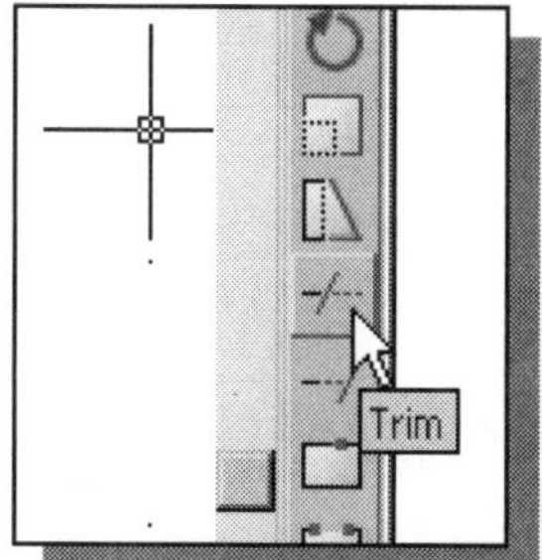

1. Select the **Trim** command icon in the *Modify* toolbar. In the command prompt area, the message "*Select boundary edges... Select objects:*" is displayed.

- First, we will select the objects that define the boundary edges to which we want to trim the object.

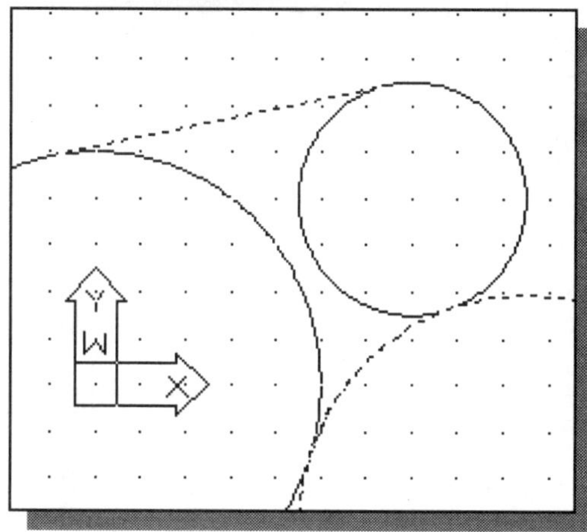

2. Pick the tangent line connecting the center circle and the top right circle.

3. Pick the lower right circle. The two selected entities are highlighted as shown in the figure.

4. Inside the graphics window, **right-mouse-click** to proceed with the Trim command.

5. The message "*Select object to trim or shift-select object to extend or [Project/Edge/Undo]:*" is displayed in the command prompt area. Pick the **left** section of the upper right circle and note the selected portion is trimmed as shown.

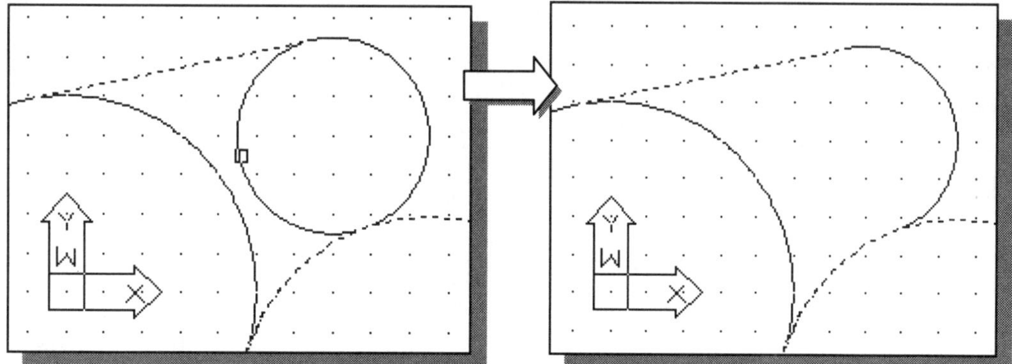

❖ In AutoCAD, the Trim command requires first selection of objects that define the cutting edges at which an object is to stop. Valid cutting edge objects include most 2D geometry such as lines, arcs, circles, ellipses, polylines, splines, and text. For 3D objects, a 2D projection method is used, where the cutting edges and the objects to be trimmed are projected onto the XY plane of the current user coordinate system (UCS).

6. Select the upper right side of the center circle to remove the selected portion.

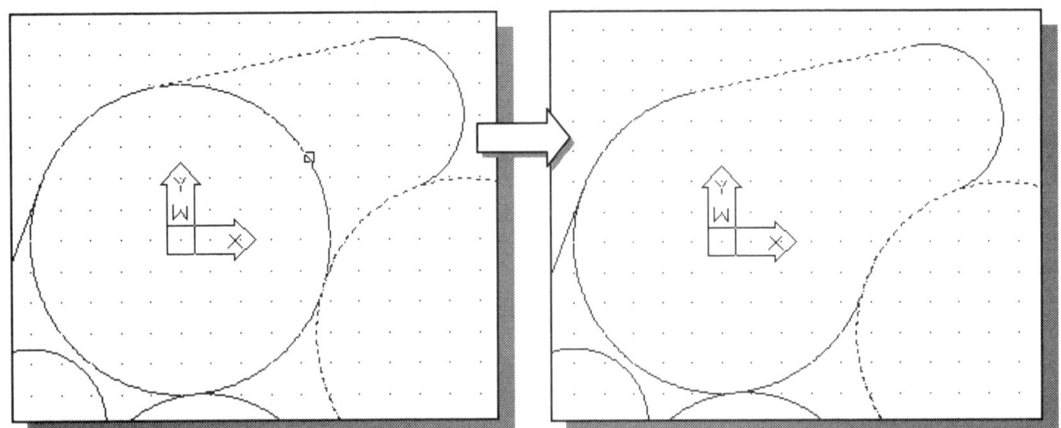

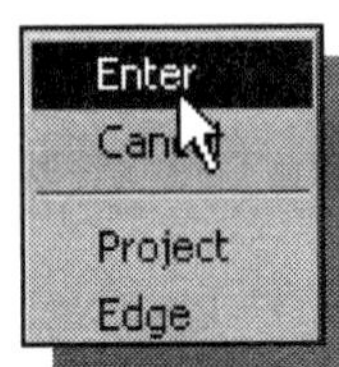

7. Inside the graphics window, **right-mouse-click** to activate the option menu and select **Enter** to end the Trim command.

8. Hit the [**SPACE BAR**] once to repeat the **Trim** command.

9. Select the two arcs that were trimmed as the two cutting edges and trim the lower section of the TTR circle as shown.

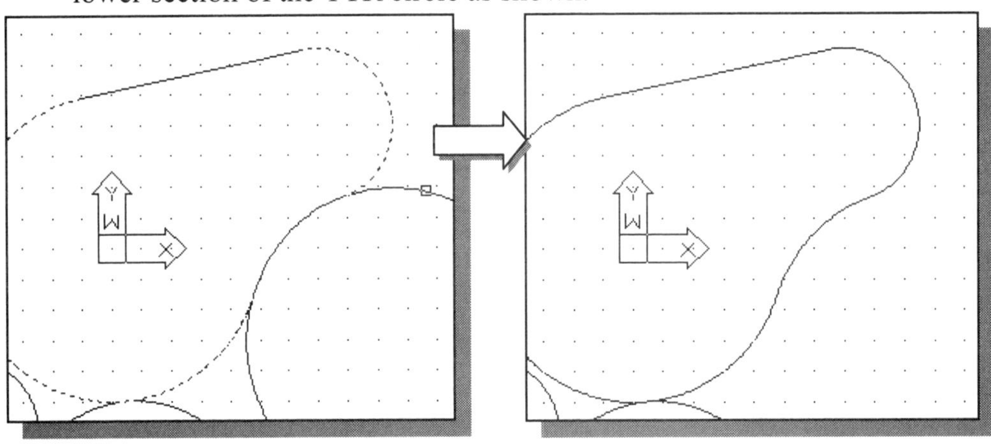

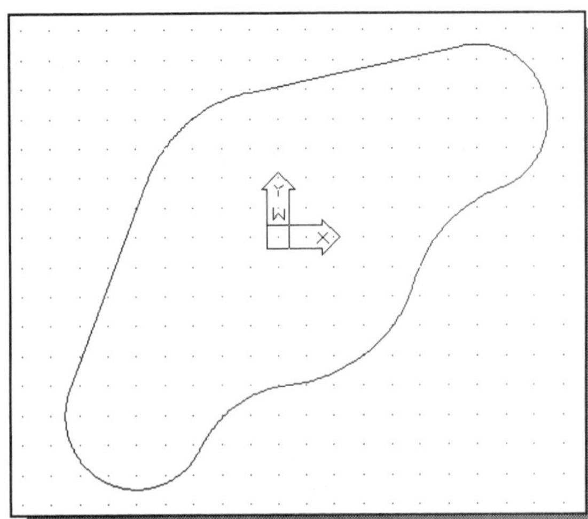

10. On your own, trim the other geometry so that the drawing appears as shown.

11. Inside the graphics window, **right-mouse-click** to activate the option menu and select **Enter** with the left-mouse-button to end the Trim command.

Using the *Polygon* command

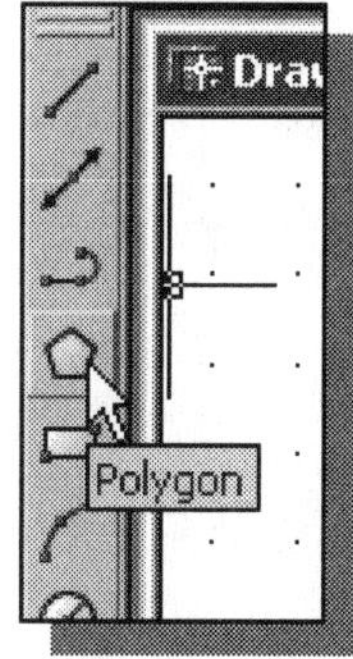

1. Select the **Polygon** command icon in the *Draw* toolbar. In the command prompt area, the message "*_polygon Enter number of sides <4>:*" is displayed. AutoCAD expects us to identify the number of sides.

2. Enter ***6*** to create a six sided hexagon.
   _polygon Enter number of sides <4>: **6 [ENTER]**

3. In the command prompt area, the message "*Specify center of polygon or [Edge]:*" is displayed. Since the center of the large circle is aligned to the origin of the WCS, the center of the polygon can be positioned using several methods. Let's use the "absolute coordinates input method."
   Specify center of polygon or [Edge]: **0,0 [ENTER]**

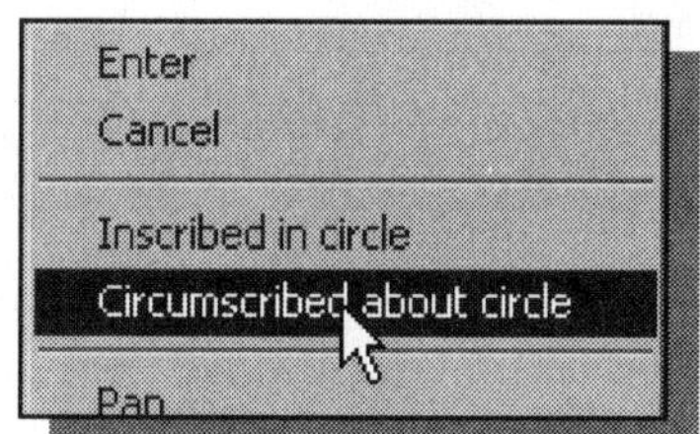

4. In the command prompt area, the message "*Enter an option [Inscribed in circle/Circumscribed about circle] <I>:*" is displayed. Inside the graphics window, **right-mouse-click** to activate the option menu and select **Circumscribed about circle**.

5. In the command prompt area, the message *Specify radius of circle :*" is displayed. Enter ***30*** as the radius.
   Specify radius of circle : **30 [ENTER]**

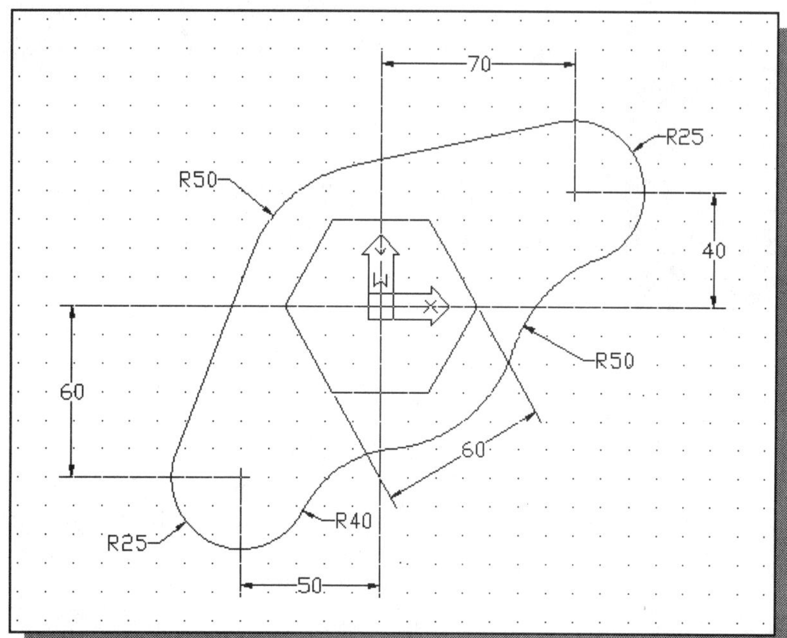

❖ Note that the polygon option [Inscribed in circle/Circumscribed about circle] allows us to create either **flat to flat** or **corner to corner** distance.

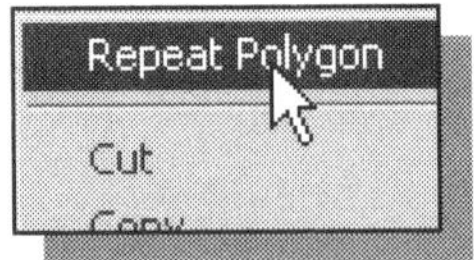

6. Inside the graphics window, **right-mouse-click** to activate the option menu and select **Repeat Polygon**. In the command prompt area, the message "*_polygon Enter number of sides <6>:*" is displayed. AutoCAD expects us to identify the number of sides.

7. Enter **4** to create a six sided hexagon.
   _polygon Enter number of sides <6>: **4 [ENTER]**

8. In the command prompt area, the message "*Specify center of polygon or [Edge]:*" is displayed. Let's use the *OBJECT SNAP* option to locate its center location. Pick **Snap to Center** in the *Object Snap* toolbar as shown.

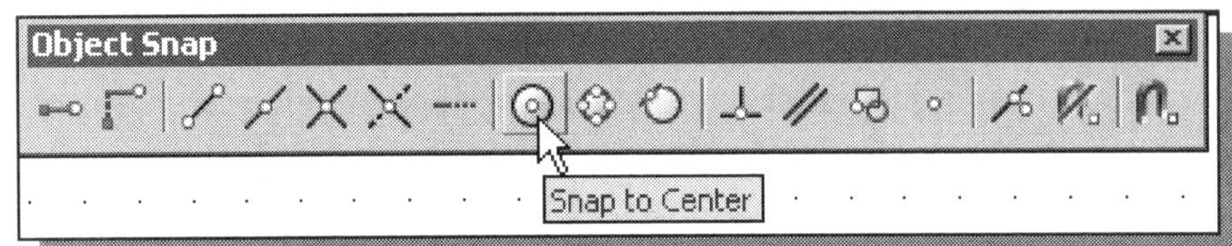

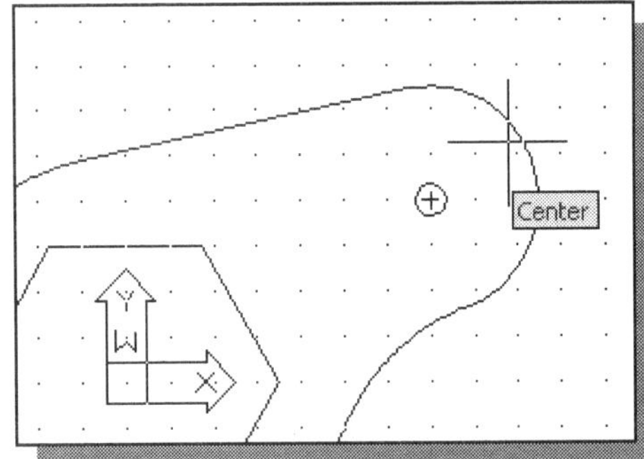

9. Move the cursor on top of the arc on the right and notice the center point is automatically highlighted. Select the arc to accept the highlighted location.

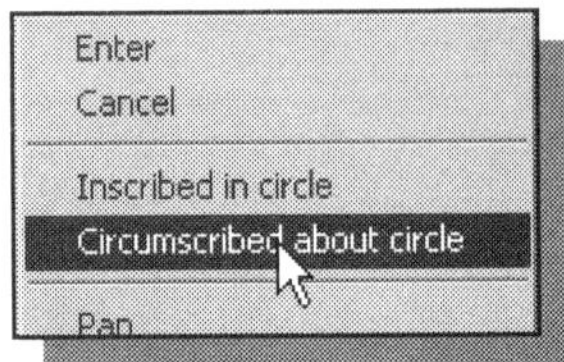

10. Inside the graphics window, **right-mouse-click** to activate the option menu and select **Circumscribed about circle**.

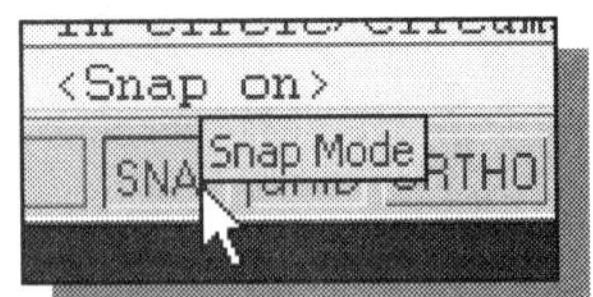

11. Switch ***ON*** the ***GRID SNAP*** option in the *Status Bar* as shown.

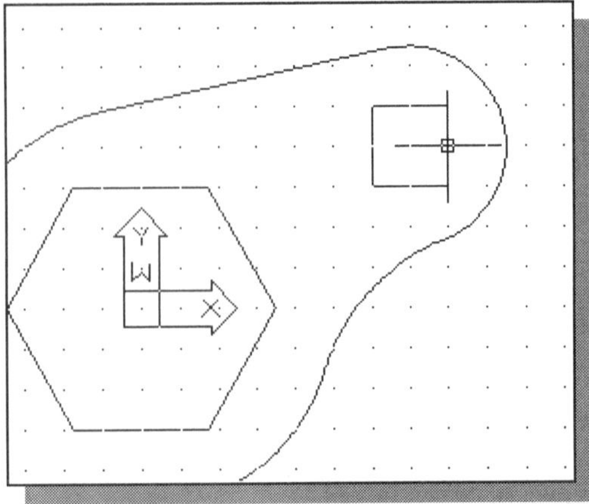

12. Create a square by selecting one of the adjacent grid points next to the center point as shown. Note that the orientation of the polygon can also be adjusted as the cursor is moved to other locations.

Creating a Concentric *Circle*

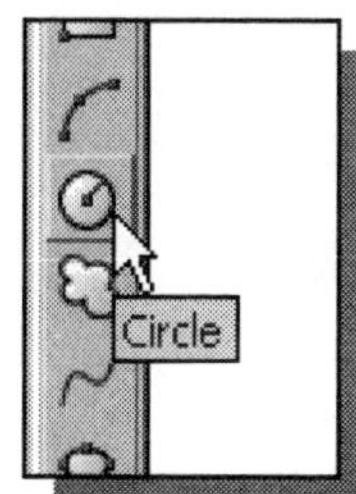

1. Select the **Circle** command icon in the *Draw* toolbar. In the command prompt area, the message "*Specify center point for circle or [3P/2P/Ttr (tan tan radius)]:*" is displayed.

2. Let's use the *OBJECT SNAP* option to assure the center location is aligned properly. Pick **Snap to Center** in the *Object Snap* toolbar as shown.

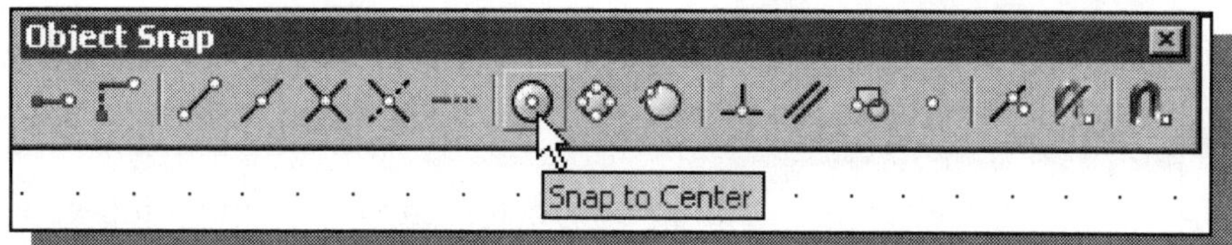

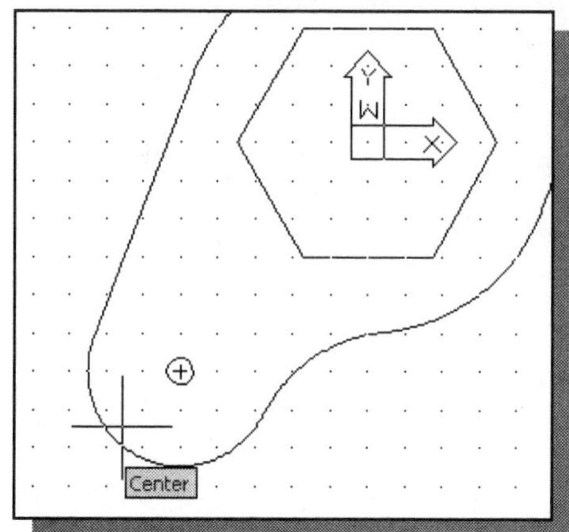

3. Move the cursor on top of the lower arc on the left and notice the center point is automatically highlighted. Select the arc to accept the highlighted location.

4. In the command prompt area, the message "*Specify radius of circle <25>*" is displayed. Enter ***10*** to complete the Circle command.
   Specify radius of circle <25>: **10 [ENTER]**

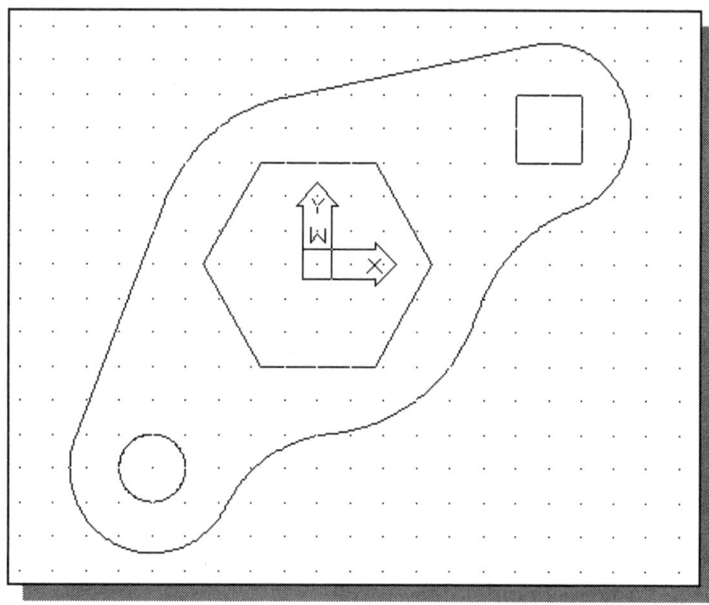

Saving the CAD file

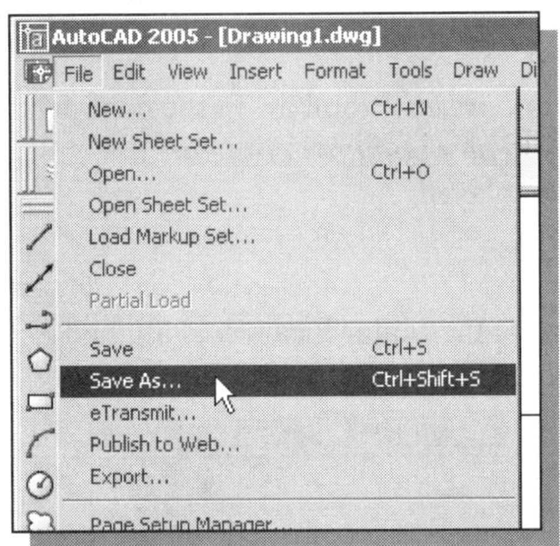

1. In the pull-down menus, select:

   [File] → [Save As]

2. In the *Save Drawing As* dialog box, select the folder in which you want to store the CAD file and enter ***RockerArm*** in the *File name* box.

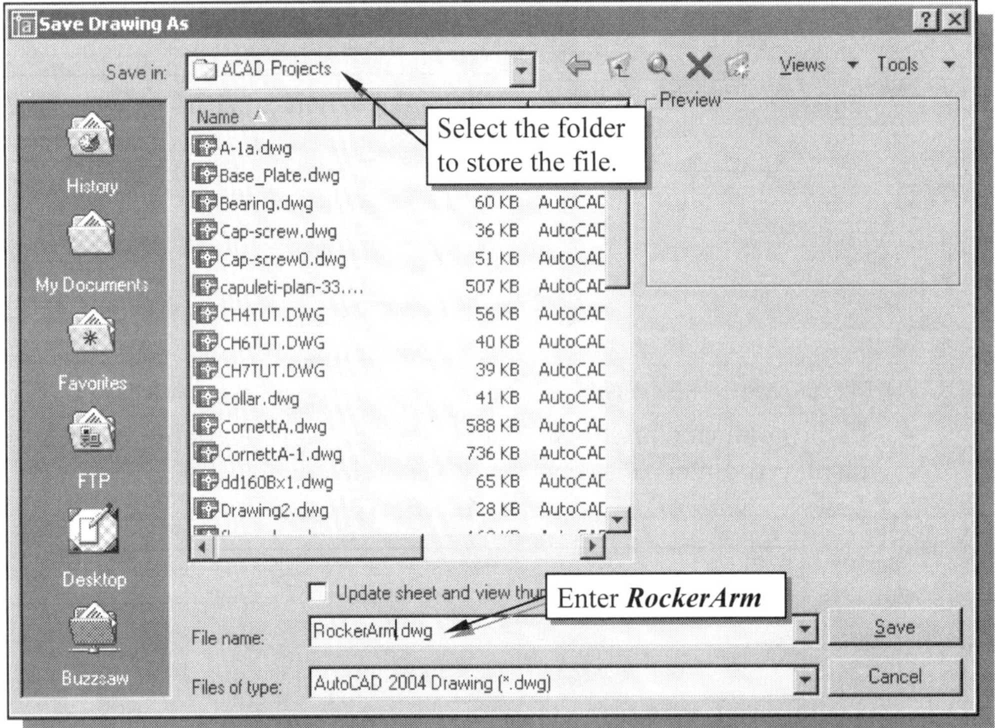

3. Pick **Save** in the *Save Drawing As* dialog box to accept the selections and save the file.

Exit AutoCAD

- To exit **AutoCAD® 2005**, select **File** then choose **Exit** from the pull-down menu or type ***QUIT*** at the command prompt.

Questions:

1. Describe the procedure to activate the AutoCAD **Startup** option.

2. List and describe three options in the AutoCAD **OBJECT SNAP** toolbar.

3. Which AutoCAD command can we use to remove a portion of an existing entity?

4. Describe the AutoCAD **Polygon** command.

5. Identify the following commands:

(a)

(b)

(c)

(d)

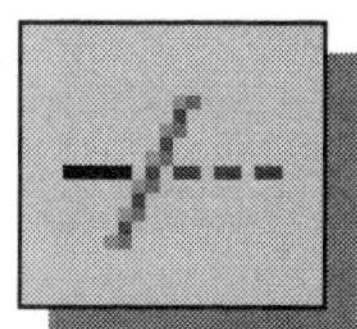

Exercises: Unless otherwise specified, dimensions are in inches.

1.

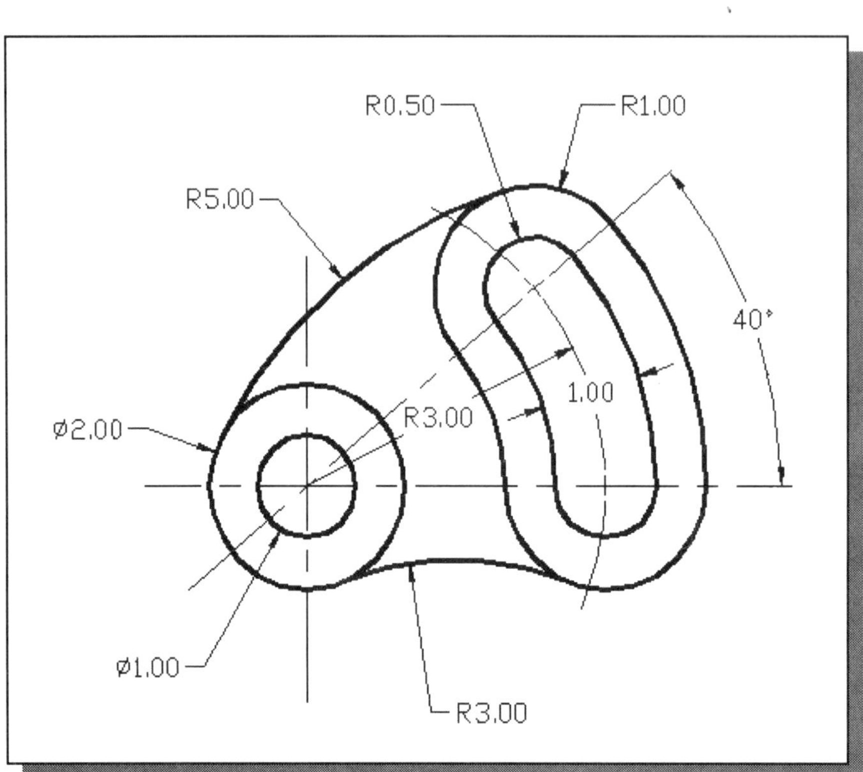

2. (Note: This design has two sets of parallel lines with implied tangency.)

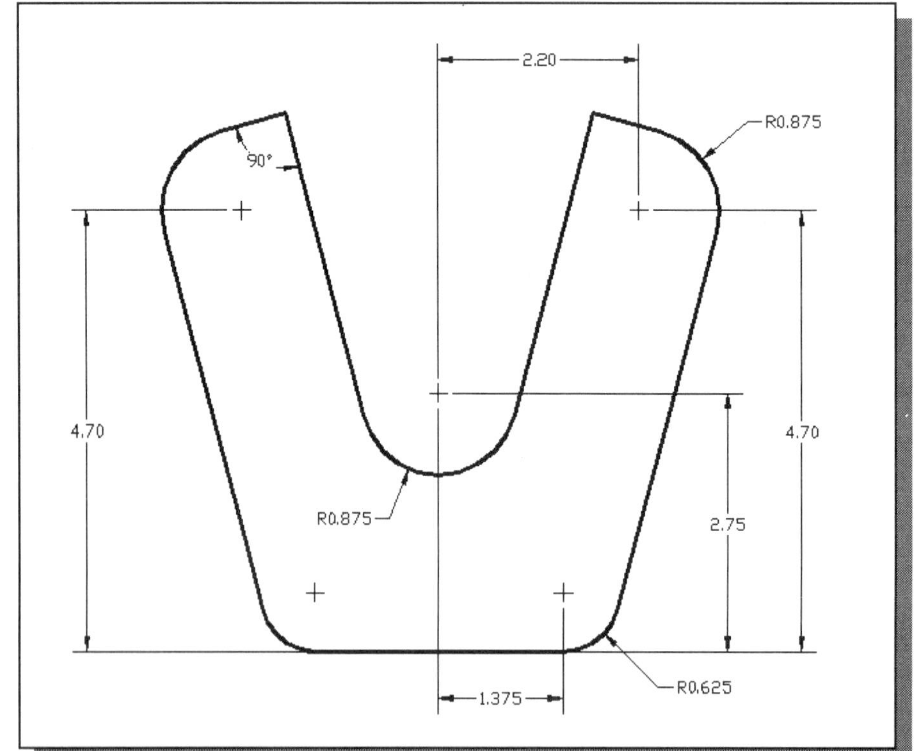

3. Dimensions are in Millimeters.

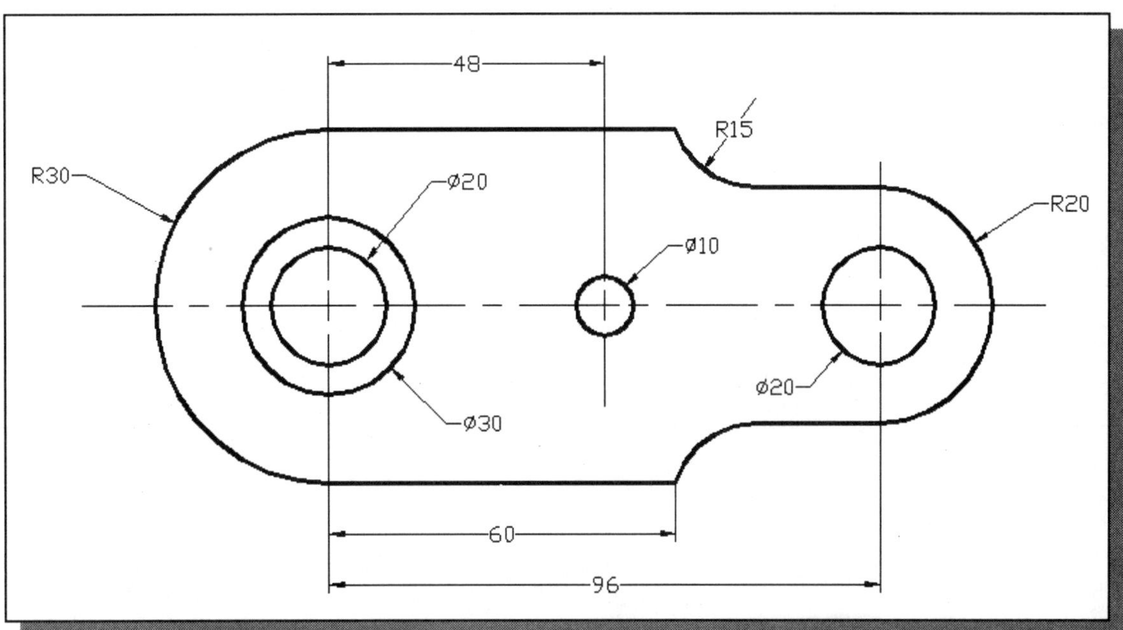

4.

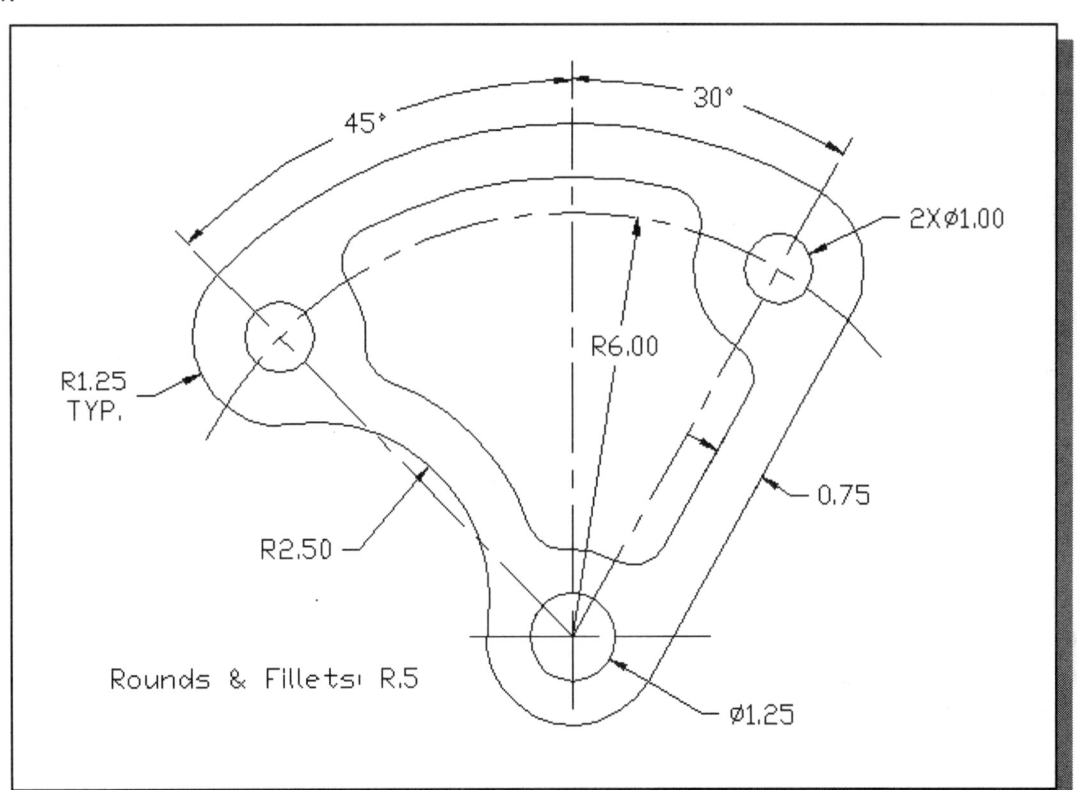

NOTES:

Chapter 3
Geometric Construction and Editing Tools

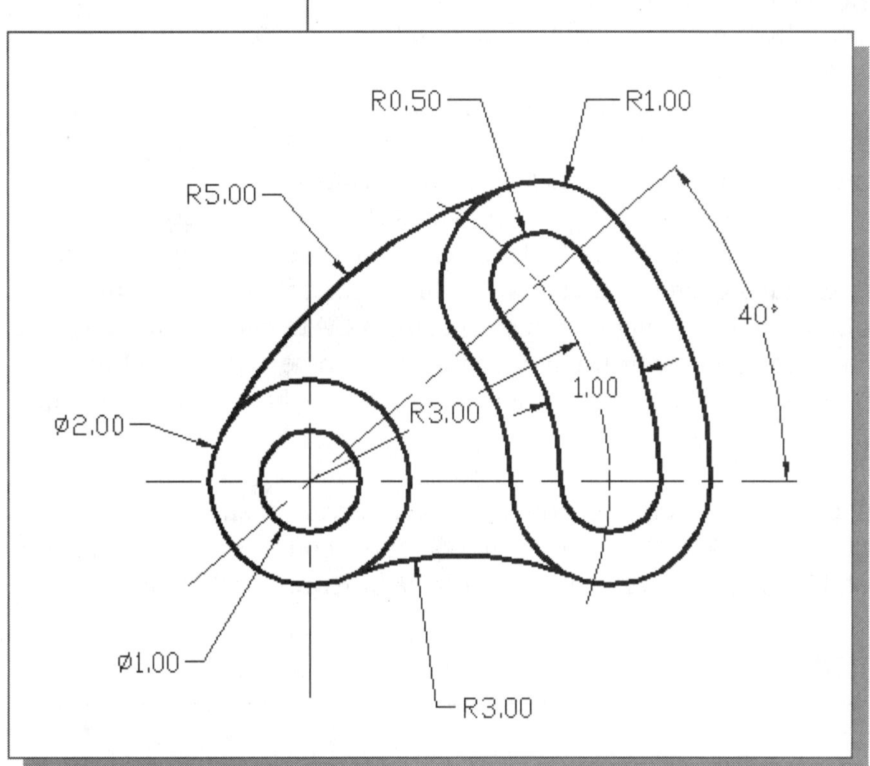

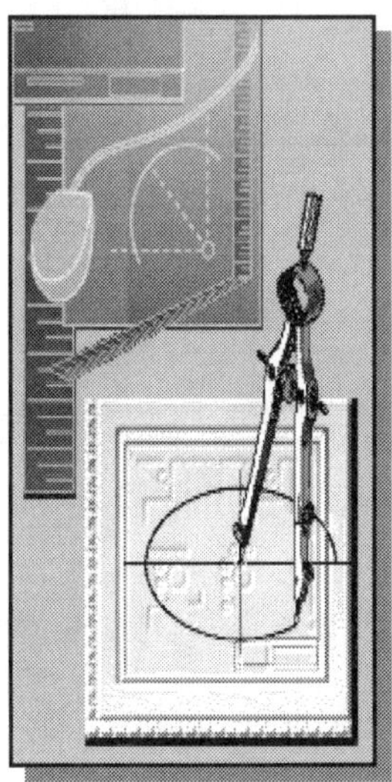

Learning Objectives

- **Set up the display of Drawing Units.**
- **Display AutoCAD's toolbars.**
- **Set up and use OBJECT SNAPS.**
- **Edit, using EXTEND and TRIM.**
- **Use the FILLET command.**
- **Create parallel geometric entities.**
- **Using the PEDIT command.**
- **Use the EXPLODE command.**

Introduction

Exploring the possibilities of a CAD system can be very exciting. For persons who have board drafting experiences, the transition from the drafting board to the computer does require some adjusting. But, the essential skills required to work in front of a computer are not that much different from those needed for board drafting. In fact, many of the basic skills acquired in board drafting can also be applied to a computer system. For example, the geometric construction techniques that are typically used in board drafting can be used in AutoCAD. The main difference between using a CAD system over the traditional board drafting is the ability to create and modify geometric entities very quickly and accurately. As it was illustrated in the previous chapters, a variety of object construction and editing tools, which are available in AutoCAD, are fairly easy to use. It is important to emphasize that a good understanding of the geometric construction fundamentals remains to be the most important part of using a CAD system. A good understanding of the basic geometric construction commands can be very helpful in expanding one's understanding of the more complex commands/techniques involved in using CAD systems.

In this chapter, we will continue to examine more of the geometric construction and editing tools provided by **AutoCAD® 2005**. We will look at the construction tools such as Trim, Extend, Fillet, Pedit and Offset that are available in **AutoCAD® 2005.**

The *Gasket* design:

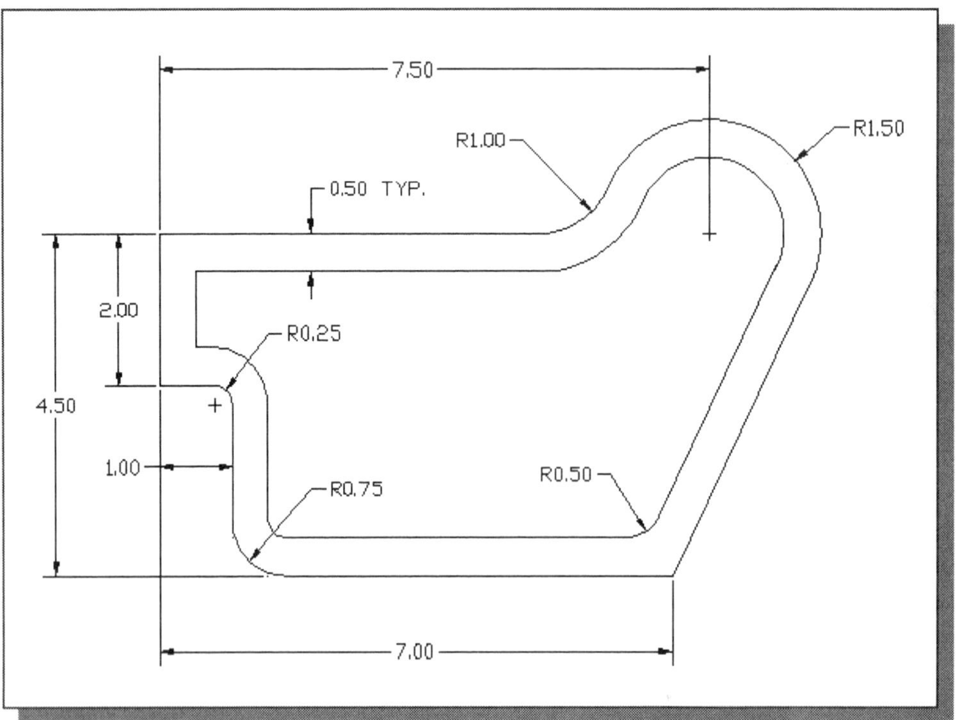

❖ Before continuing to the next page, on your own make a rough sketch showing the steps that can be used to create the design. Be aware that there are many different approaches to accomplishing the same task.

Starting Up AutoCAD® 2005

1. Select the AutoCAD 2005 option on the *Program* menu or select the AutoCAD 2005 icon on the *Desktop*. Once the program is loaded into the memory, the **AutoCAD® 2005** drawing screen will appear on the screen.

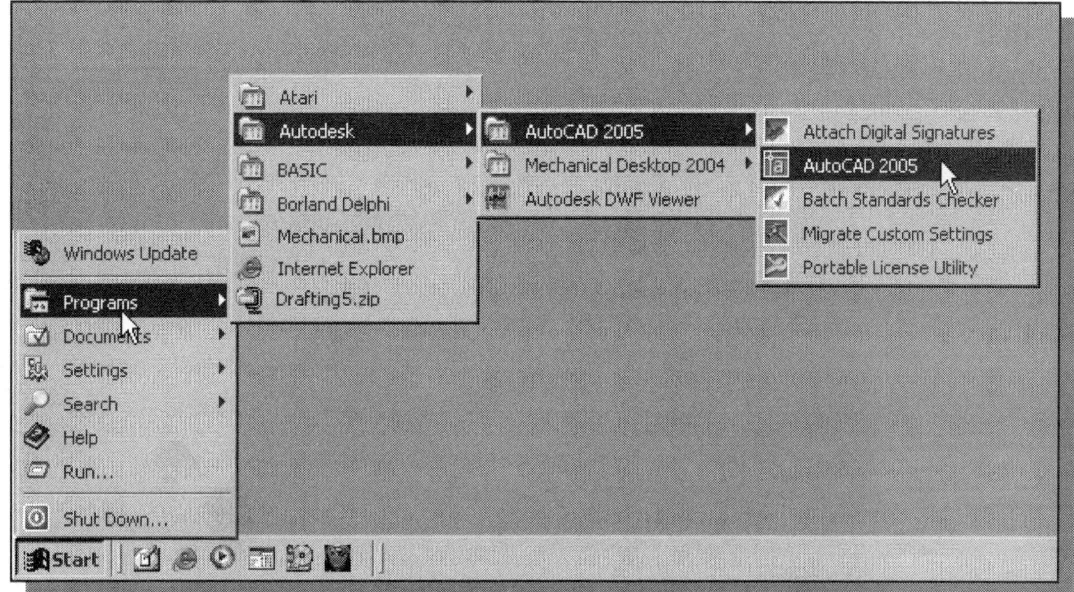

2. In the *Startup* window, select **Start from Scratch**, as shown in the figure below.

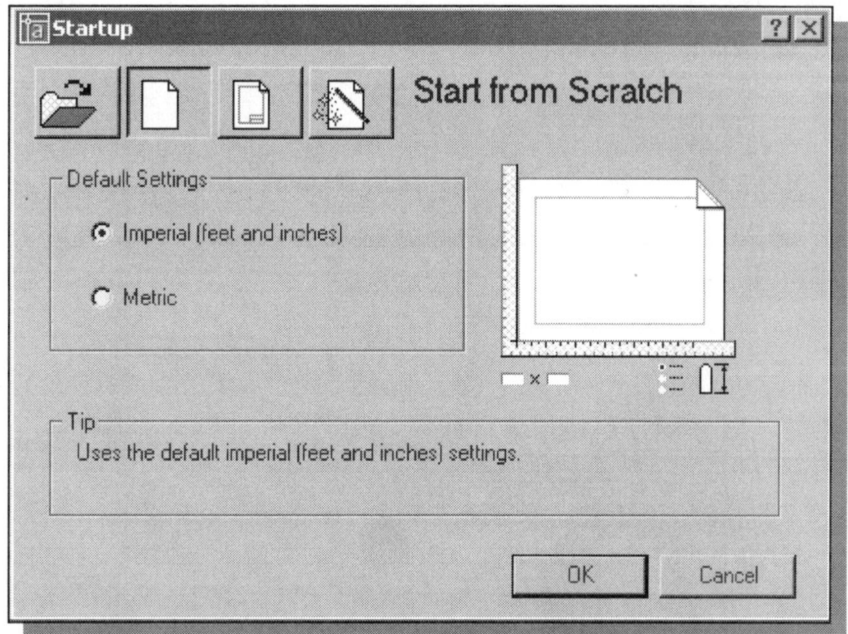

3. In the *Default Settings* section, pick **Imperial (feet and inches)** as the drawing units.

4. Pick **OK** in the *Startup* dialog box to accept the selected settings.

Drawing Units Display Setup

Before creating the first geometric entity, the value of the units within the CAD system should be determined. For example, in one drawing, a unit might equal one millimeter of the real-world object. In another drawing, a unit might equal an inch. The unit type and number of decimal places for object lengths and angles can be set through the **UNITS** command. These *drawing units settings* control how AutoCAD interprets the coordinate and angle entries and how it displays coordinates and units in the *Status Bar* and in the dialog boxes.

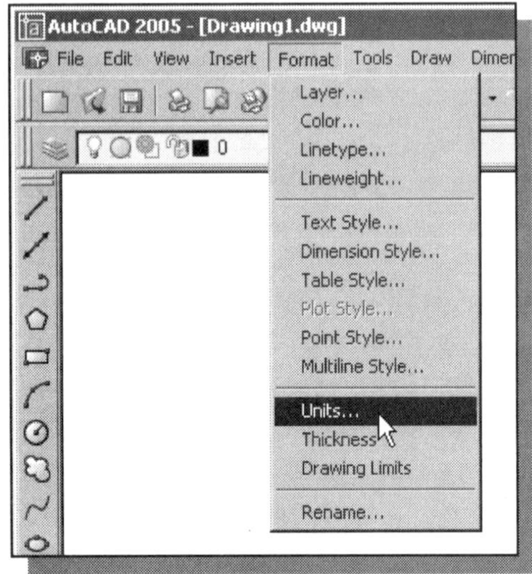

1. In the pull-down menus, select:

   [Format] → [Units]

2. In the *Drawing Units* dialog box, confirm the *Length Type* to **Decimal**. This is the default measurement to the default English units, inches.

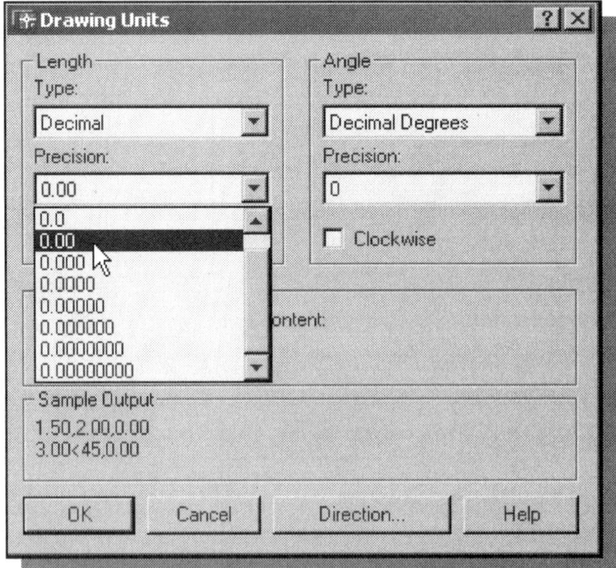

3. Set the *Precision* to **two digits** after the decimal point.

4. Pick **OK** to exit the *Drawing Units* dialog box.

GRID **and** ***SNAP*** **Intervals Setup**

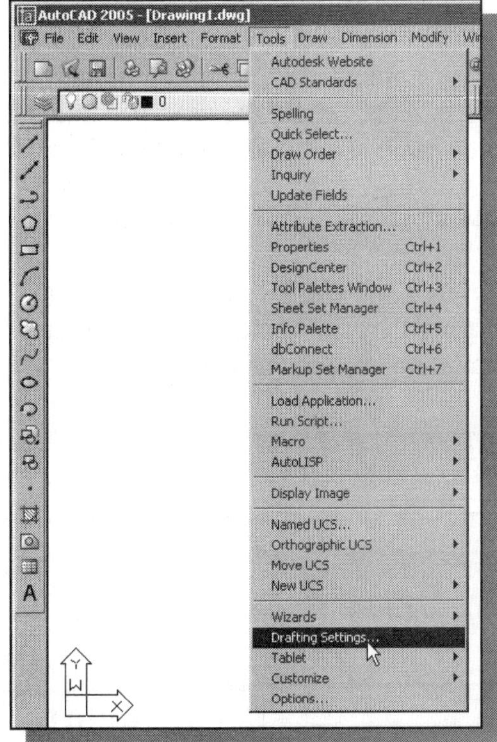

1. In the pull-down menus, select:

   [Tools] → [Drafting Settings]

2. In the *Drafting Settings* dialog box, select the **Snap and Grid** tab if it is not the page on top.

3. Change *Grid Spacing* to ***1.00*** for both X and Y directions.

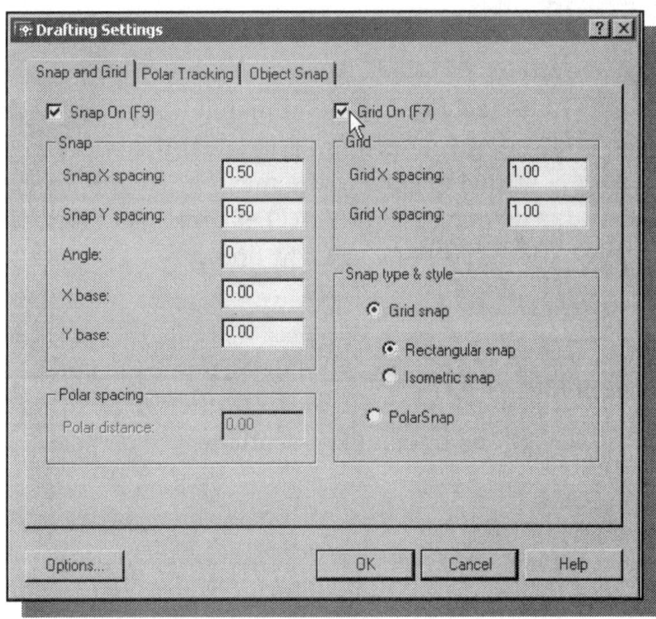

4. Switch *ON* the *Grid On* and *Snap On* options as shown.

5. Pick **OK** to exit the *Drawing Units* dialog box.

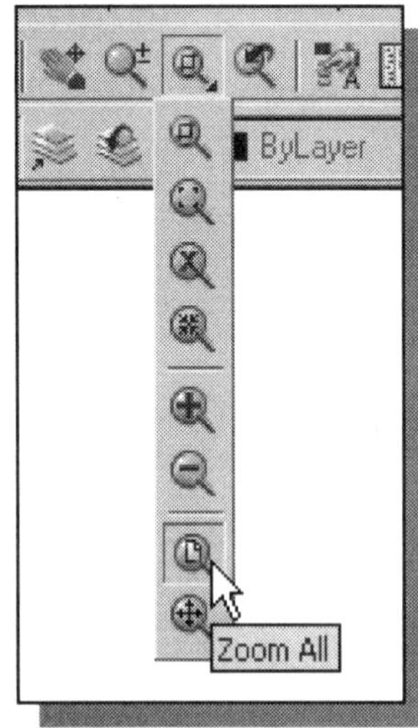

6. In the *Standard* toolbar, select **Zoom All** with the left-mouse-button on the Zoom icon stack.

❖ Notice in the *Status Bar* area, the *GRID* and *SNAP* options are pressed down indicating they are switched *ON*. The grid spacing is set to 1 inch and the snap interval is set to 0.5 inch.

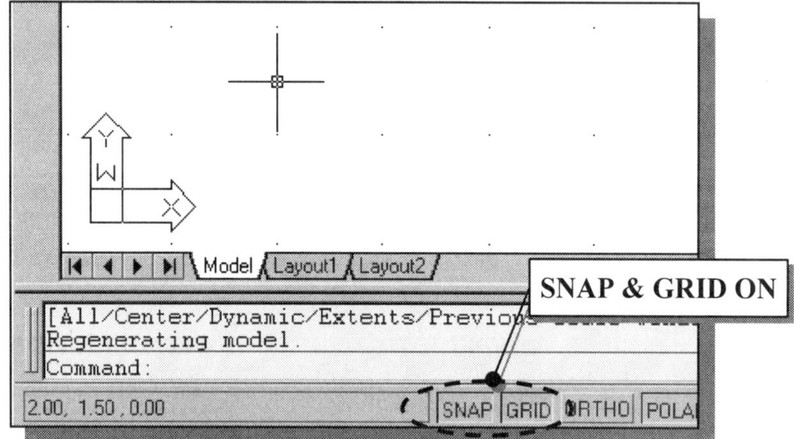

Using the *LINE* command

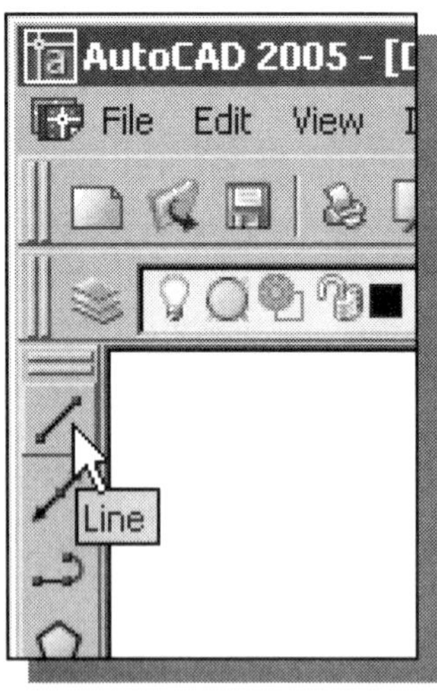

1. Select the **Line** command icon in the *Draw* toolbar. In the command prompt area, near the bottom of the AutoCAD drawing screen, the message "*_line Specify first point:*" is displayed. AutoCAD expects us to identify the starting location of a straight line.

2. In the graphics window, move the cursor to **world coordinates (2,6). Left-click** to position the starting point of the line at that location.

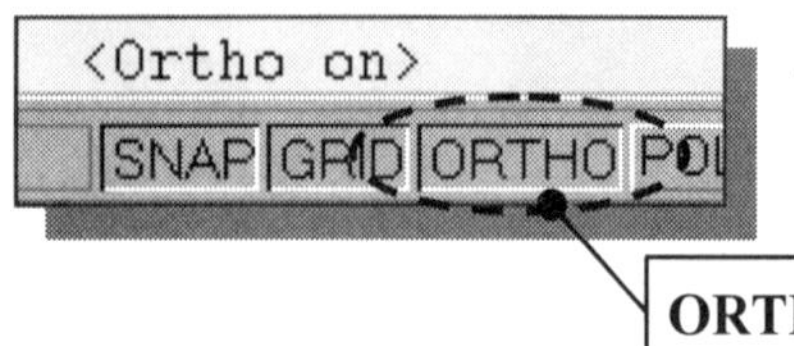

3. We will next turn *ON* the *ORTHO* option by toggling on the ***ORTHO*** button in the *Status Bar* area.

❖ The *ORTHO* option constrains cursor movement to the horizontal or vertical directions, relative to the current coordinate system. With the **Line** command, we are now restricted to creating only horizontal or vertical lines with the *ORTHO* option.

4. Move the graphics cursor below the last point we selected on the screen and create a vertical line that is two units long (*Y coordinate: 4.00*).

5. Move the graphics cursor to the right of the last point and create a horizontal line that is one unit long (*X coordinate: 3.00*).

6. Move the graphics cursor below the last point and create a vertical line that is 2.5 units long (*Y coordinate: 1.50*).

7. **Turn *OFF*** the *SNAP* option in the *Status Bar* area.

8. Move the graphics cursor to the right of the last point and create a horizontal line that is about seven units long (near *X coordinate: 10.00*). As is quite common during the initial design stage, we do not always know all of the dimensions at the beginning.

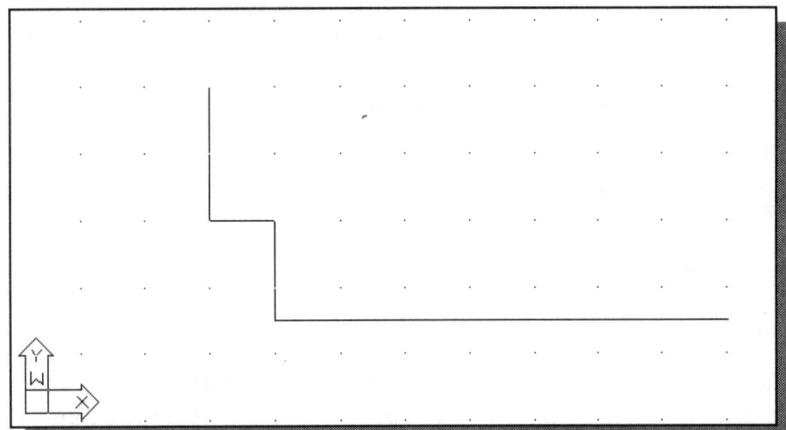

9. Inside the graphics window, **right-mouse-click** to activate the option menu and select **Enter** with the left-mouse-button to end the **Line** command.

10. In the *Status Bar* area, reset the option buttons so that only the *GRID*, *ORTHO*, and *MODEL* options are switched ***ON***.

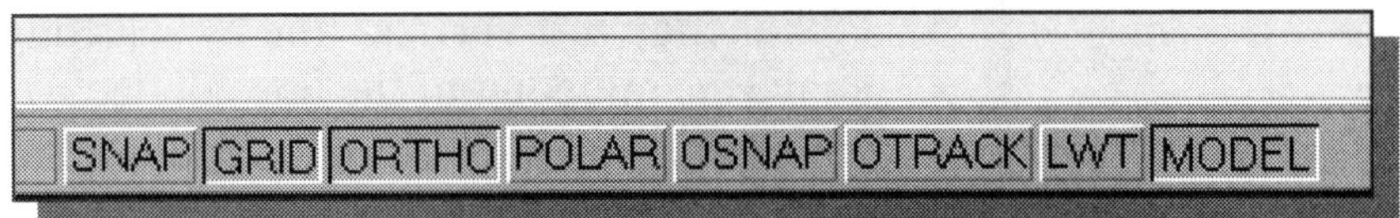

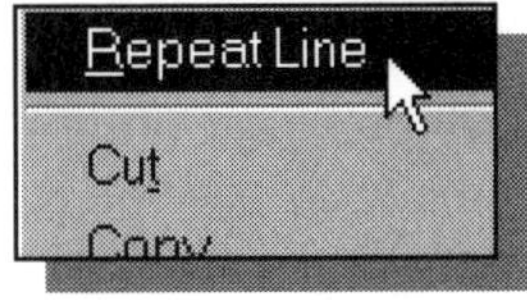

11. Activate the **Line** command by picking the icon in the *Draw* toolbar or **right-mouse-click** to activate the option menu and select **Repeat Line**.

Object Snap Toolbar

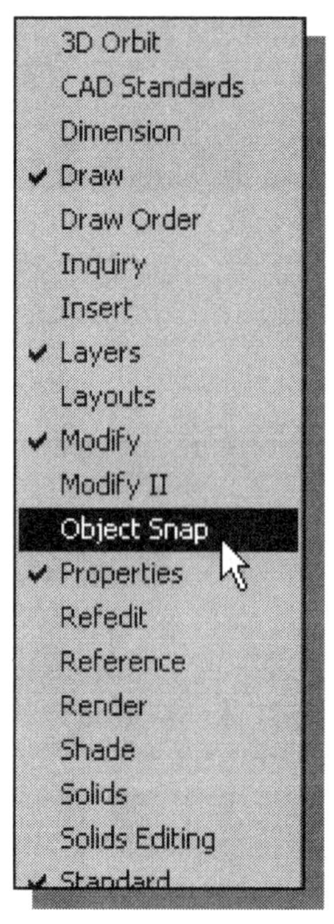

1. Move the cursor to the *Standard* toolbar area and **right-mouse-click** once on any icon in the toolbar area to display a list of toolbar menu groups.

❖ AutoCAD provides 24 toolbars for access to frequently used commands, settings, and modes. The *Standard, Object Properties*, *Draw*, and *Modify* toolbars are displayed by default. The *check marks* in the list identify the toolbars that are currently displayed on the screen.

2. Select **Object Snap**, with the left-mouse-button, to display the *Object Snap* toolbar on the screen.

❖ **Object Snap** is an extremely powerful construction tool available on most CAD systems. During an entity's creation operations, we can snap the cursor to points on objects such as endpoints, midpoints, centers, and intersections. For example, we can quickly draw a line to the center of a circle, the midpoint of a line segment, or the intersection of two lines.

3. Move the cursor over the icons in the *Object Snap* toolbar and read the description of each icon in the *Status Bar* area.

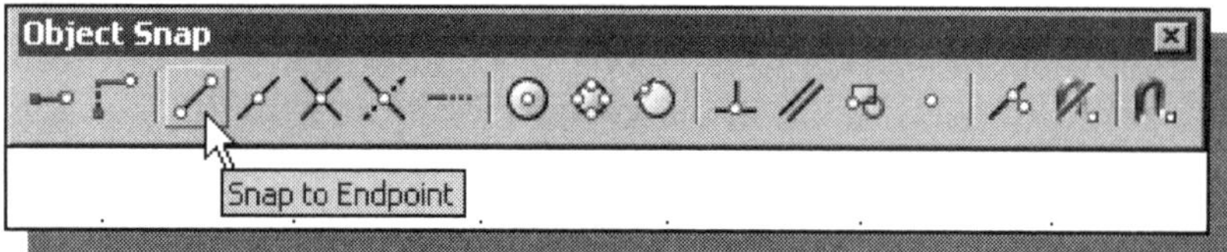

4. In the *Object Snap* toolbar, pick **Snap to Endpoint**. In the command prompt area, the message "*_endp of*" is displayed. AutoCAD now expects us to select a geometric entity on the screen.

❖ The Snap to Endpoint option allows us to snap to the closest endpoint of objects such as lines or arcs. AutoCAD uses the midpoint of the entity to determine which end to snap to.

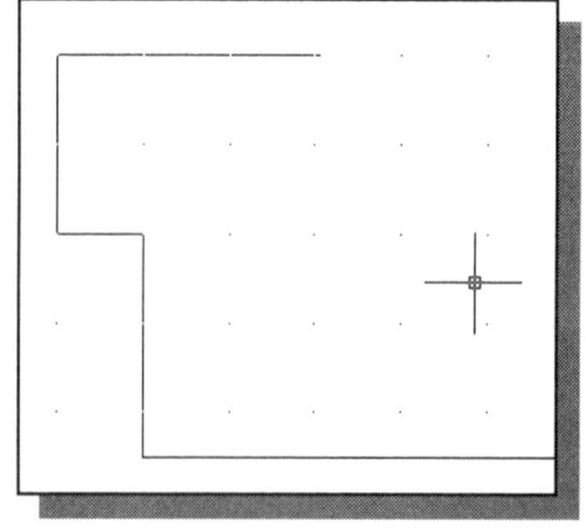

5. Pick the **top left vertical line** by selecting a location above the midpoint of the line. Notice AutoCAD automatically snaps to the top endpoint of the line.

6. Move the graphics cursor to the right of the last point and create a horizontal line that is about three units long (near *X coordinate: 5.00*).

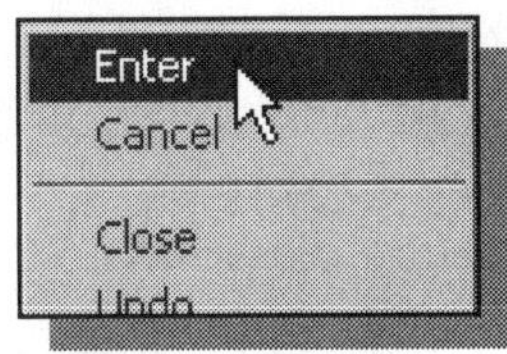

7. Inside the graphics window, **right-mouse-click** to activate the option menu and select **Enter** with the left-mouse-button to end the Line command.

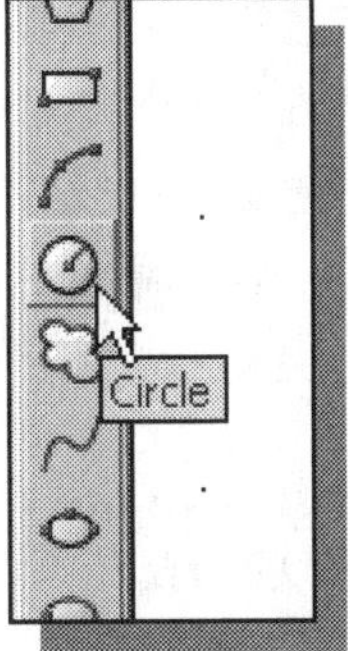

8. Select the **Circle** command icon in the *Draw* toolbar. In the command prompt area, the message "*Specify center point for circle or [3P/2P/Ttr (tan tan radius)]:*" is displayed.

9. In the *Status Bar* area, switch ***ON*** the *SNAP* option.

10. In the graphics window, move the cursor to world coordinates **(9.5,6)**. **Left-click** to position the center point of the circle at this location.

11. Move the graphics cursor to world coordinates **(11,6)**. **Left-click** at this location to create a circle (radius **1.5** inches).

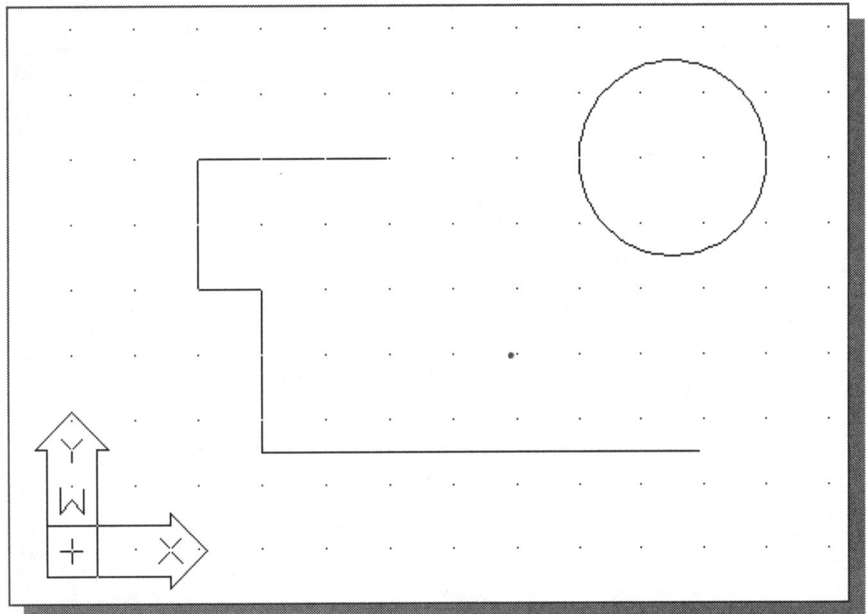

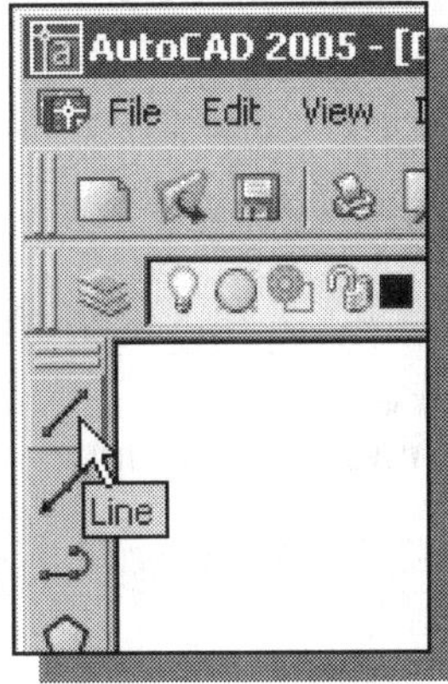

12. Select the **Line** command icon in the *Draw* toolbar. In the command prompt area, the message "*_line Specify first point:*" is displayed.

13. In the graphics window, move the cursor to world coordinates **(9,1.5)**. **Left-click** to position the first point of a line at this location.

14. Pick **Snap to Tangent** in the *Object Snap* toolbar. In the command prompt area, the message "*_tan to*" is displayed. AutoCAD now expects us to select a circle or an arc on the screen.

❖ The **Snap to Tangent** option allows us to snap to the point on a circle or arc that, when connected to the last point, forms a line tangent to that object.

15. Pick a location on the right side of the circle and create the line tangent to the circle. Note that the *Object Snap* options take precedence over the *ORTHO* option.

16. Inside the graphics window, **right-mouse-click** to activate the option menu and select **Enter** with the left-mouse-button to end the Line command.

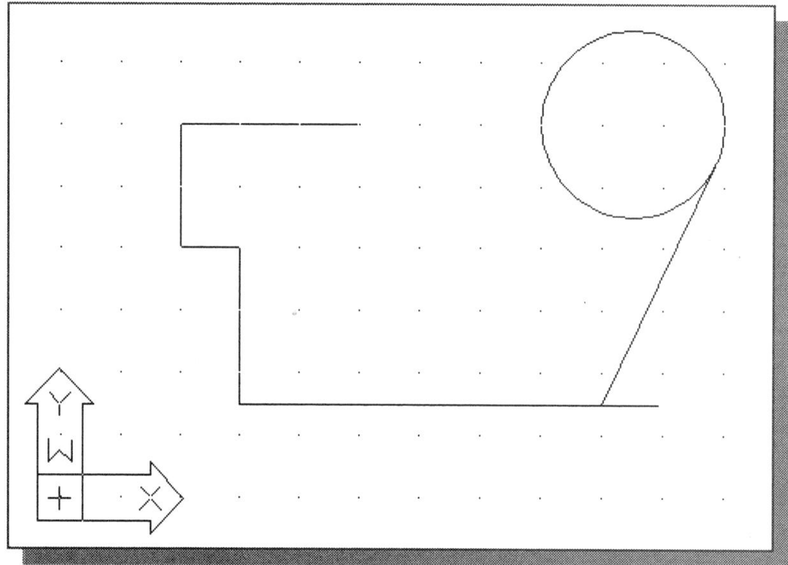

17. In the *Status Bar* area, reset the option buttons so that only the *MODEL* button is switched ***ON***.

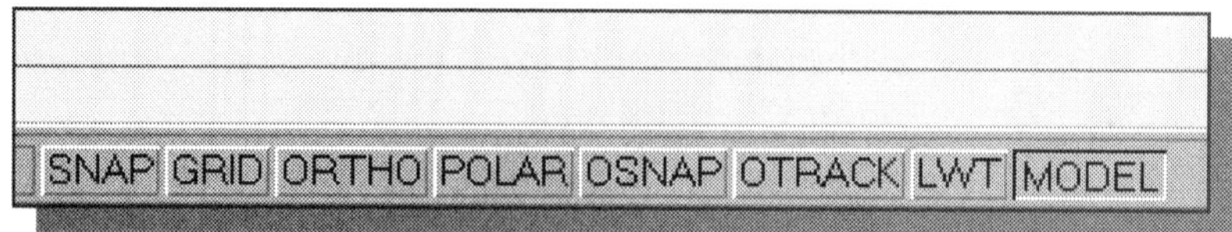

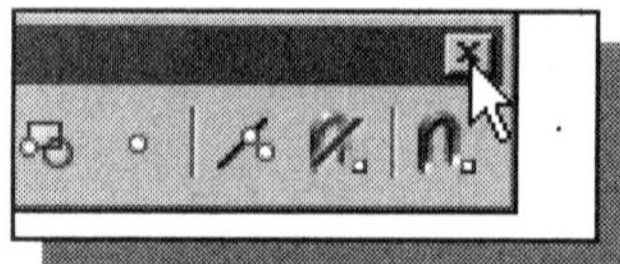

18. Close the *Object Snap* toolbar by **left-clicking** the upper right corner **X** icon.

Using the *Extend* command

- The **Extend** command lengthens an object so that it ends precisely at a selected boundary.

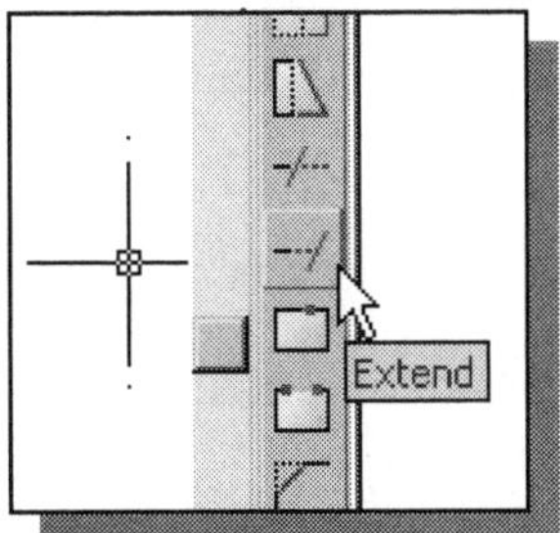

1. Select the **Extend** command icon in the *Modify* toolbar. In the command prompt area, the message "*Select boundary edges... Select objects:*" is displayed.

   ❖ First, we will select the objects that define the boundary edges to which we want to extend the object.

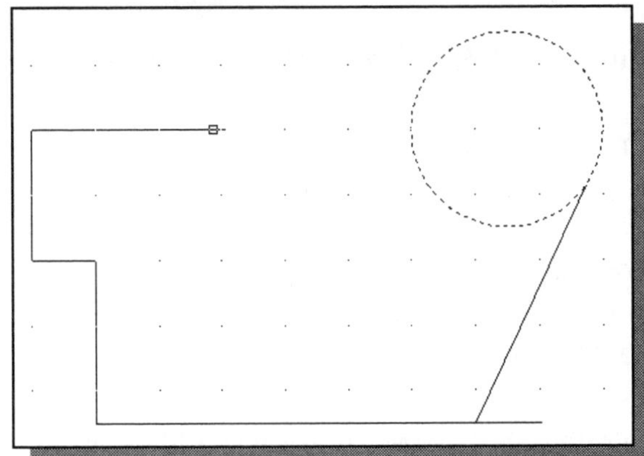

2. Pick the **circle** as the *boundary edge*.

3. Inside the graphics window, **right-mouse-click** to proceed with the **Extend** command.

4. The message "*Select object to extend or shift-select object to trim or [Project/Edge/Undo]:*" is displayed in the command prompt area. Extend the **horizontal line** that is to the left side of the circle by clicking near the right endpoint of the line.

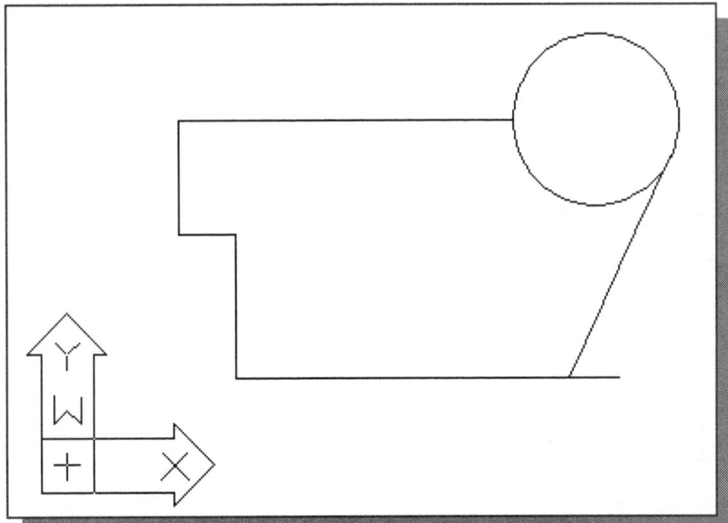

5. Inside the graphics window, **right-mouse-click** to activate the option menu and select **Enter** with the left-mouse-button to end the **Extend** command.

Using the *Trim* Command

- The Trim command shortens an object so that it ends precisely at a selected boundary.

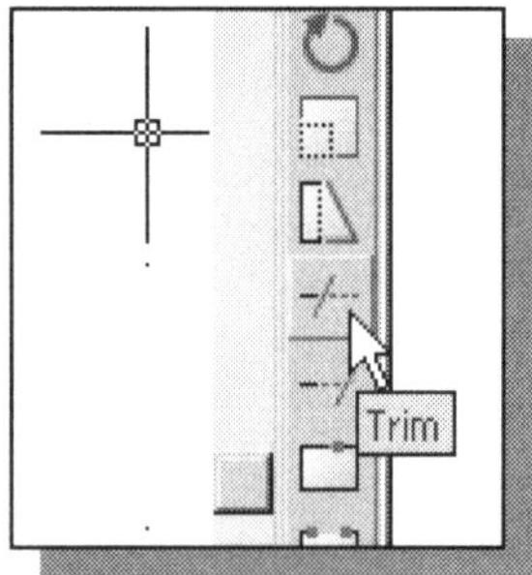

1. Select the **Trim** command icon in the *Modify* toolbar. In the command prompt area, the message "*Select boundary edges... Select objects:*" is displayed.

- First, we will select the objects that define the boundary edges to which we want to trim the object.

2. Pick the **inclined line** and the **top horizontal line** as the *boundary edges*.

3. Inside the graphics window, **right-mouse-click** to proceed with the Trim command.

4. The message "*Select object to trim or shift-select object to extend or [Project/Edge/Undo]:*" is displayed in the command prompt area. Pick the **right endpoint** of the bottom horizontal line.

5. Pick the **bottom of the circle** by clicking on the lower portion of the circle.

6. Inside the graphics window, **right-mouse-click** to activate the option menu and select **Enter** with the left-mouse-button to end the Trim command.

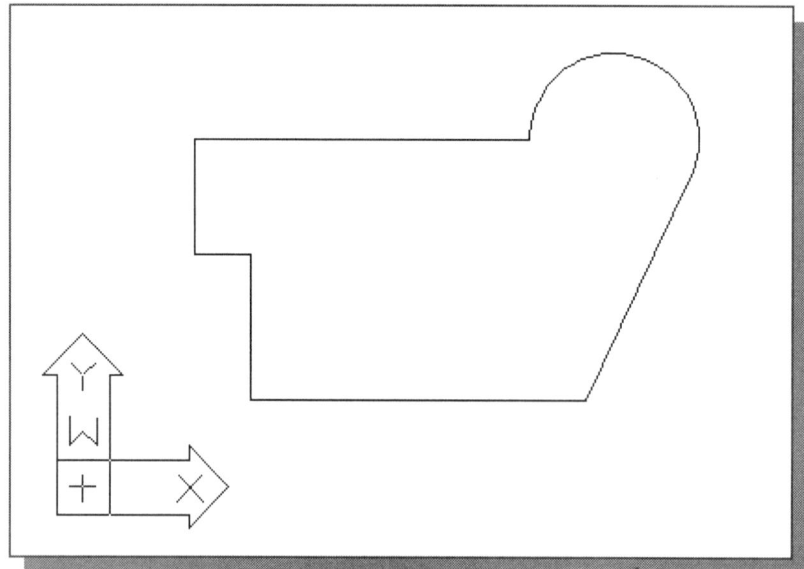

- Note that in **AutoCAD® 2005**, we can perform either trimming or extending an object using the Extend command or the Trim command. For example, when using the **Extend** command, we can select an object to *extend* or hold down **SHIFT** and select an object to *trim*.

Creating a *TTR Circle*

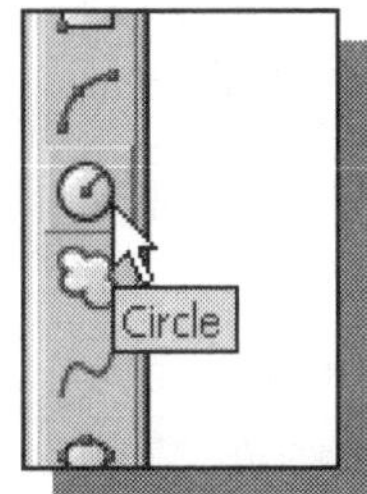

1. Select the **Circle** command icon in the *Draw* toolbar. In the command prompt area, the message "*Specify center point for circle or [3P/2P/Ttr (tan tan radius)]:*" is displayed.

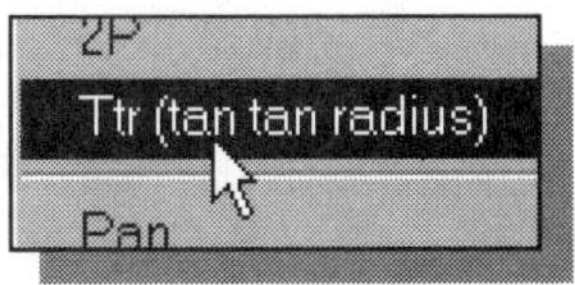

2. Inside the graphics window, right-mouse-click to activate the option menu and select the **Ttr (tan tan radius)** option. This option allows us to create a circle that is tangent to two objects.

3. Pick the **top horizontal line** that is to the left side of the arc. We will create a circle that is tangent to this line and the circle.

4. Pick the **circle** by selecting a location that is above the right endpoint of the horizontal line. AutoCAD interprets the location we selected as being near the tangency.

5. In the command prompt area, the message "*Specify radius of circle <1.50>*" is displayed.

   Specify radius of circle <1.50>: **1.0 [ENTER]**

➢ On your own, use the **Trim** command and trim the circle, the horizontal line, and the arc as shown.

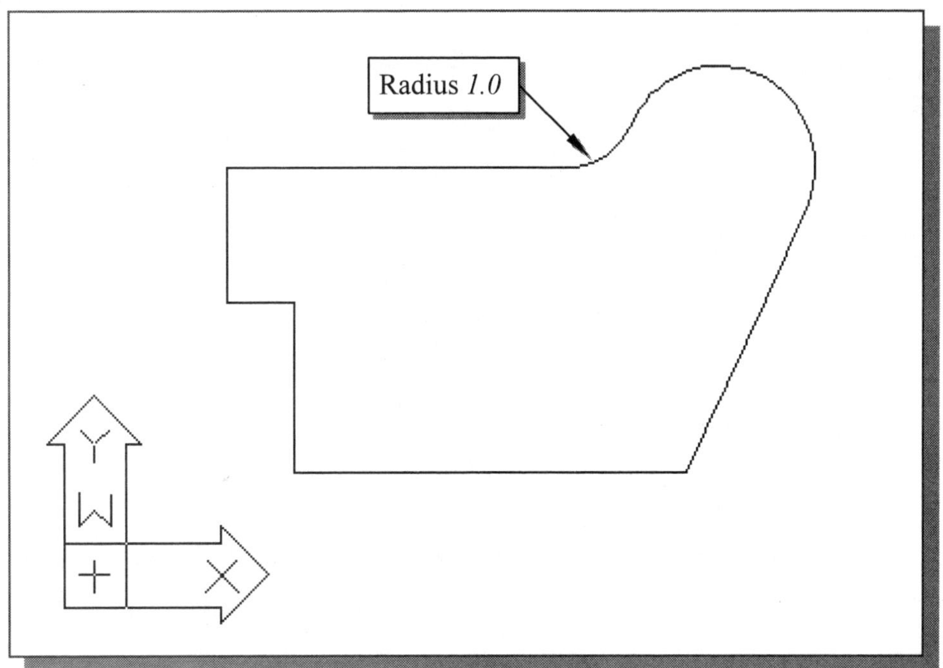

Using the *FILLET* command

- **Fillet** rounds or fillets the edges of two arcs, circles, elliptical arcs, or lines with an arc of a specified radius.

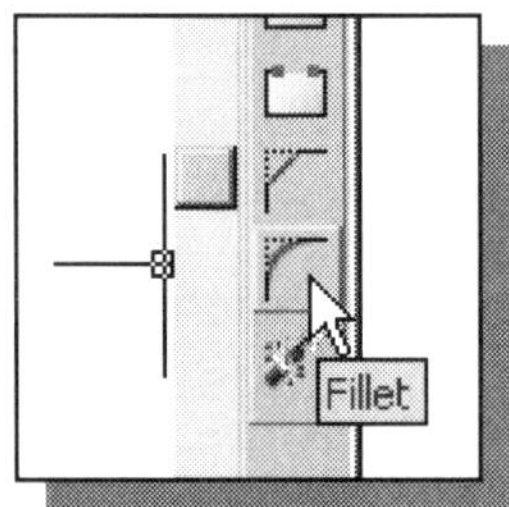

1. Select the **Fillet** command icon in the *Modify* toolbar. In the command prompt area, the message "*Select first object or [Polyline/Radius/Trim]:*" is displayed.

2. Inside the graphics window, right-mouse-click to activate the option menu and select the **Radius** option with the left-mouse-button to specify the radius of the fillet.

3. In the command prompt area, the message "*Specify fillet radius:*" is displayed.

   Specify fillet radius: **0.75** **[ENTER]**

4. Pick the **bottom horizontal line** and the **adjacent vertical line** to create a rounded corner as shown.

➢ On your own, use the **Fillet** command and create a 0.25 fillet at the corner as shown.

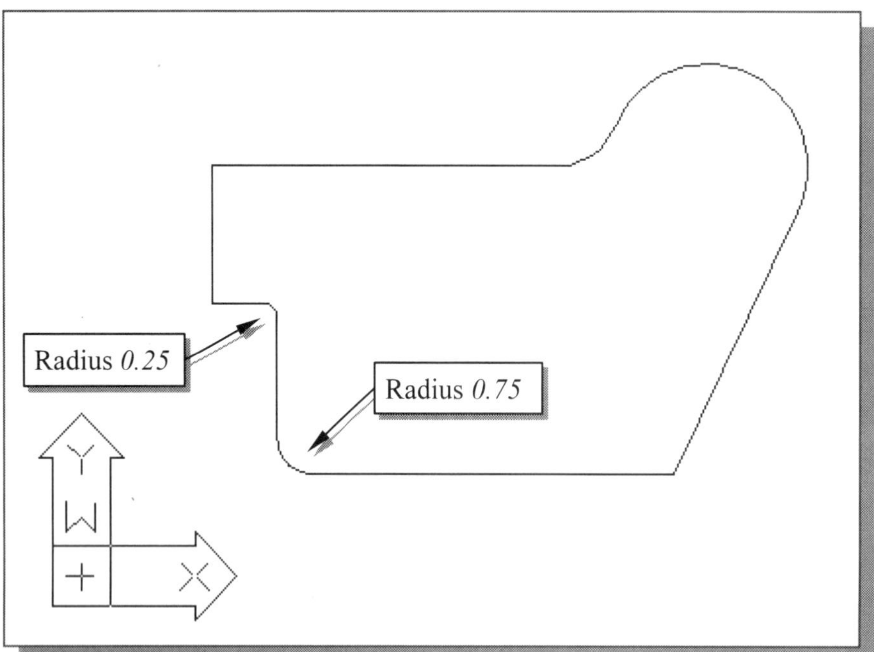

Converting objects into a *Polyline*

- The next task in our project is to use the **Offset** command and create a scaled copy of the constructed geometry. Prior to using the **Offset** command, we will simplify the procedure by converting all objects into a **compound object – a *polyline***.

❖ A *polyline* in AutoCAD is a 2D line of adjustable width composed of line and arc segments. A polyline is treated as a single object with definable options.

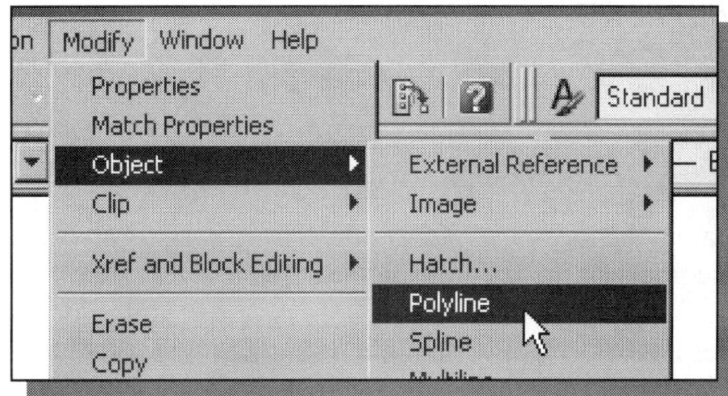

1. In the pull-down menus, select:
   [Modify] → [Object] → [Polyline]

2. The message "*Select polyline:*" is displayed in the command prompt area. Select any of the objects on the screen.

3. The message "*Object selected is not a polyline, Do you want to turn it into one? <Y>*" is displayed in the command prompt area. **Right-mouse-click** to accept the *Yes* default.

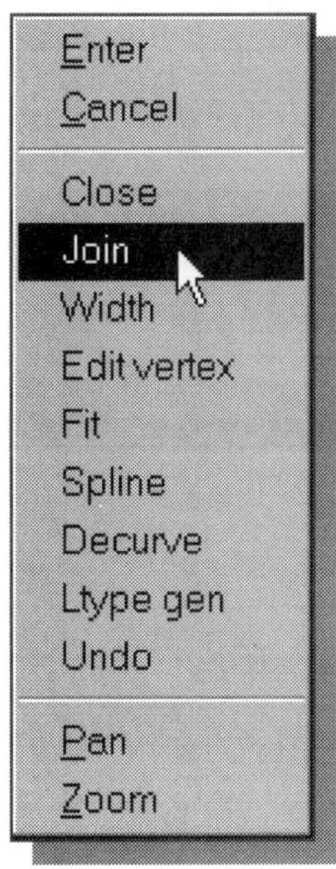

4. Inside the graphics window, right-mouse-click to activate the option menu and select the **Join** option with the left-mouse-button to add objects to the polyline.

5. **Pick all objects** by enclosing them inside a *selection window*.

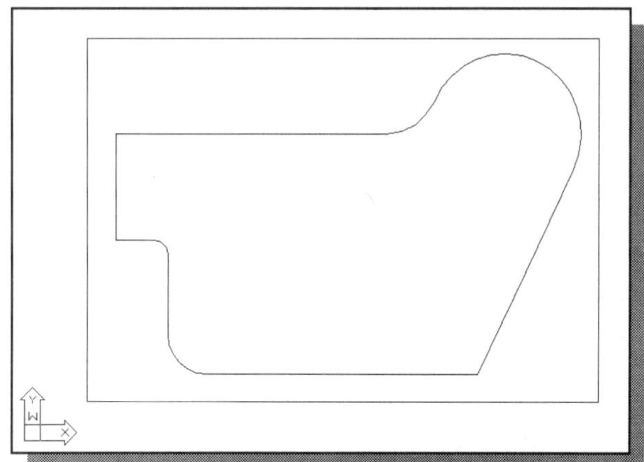

6. Inside the graphics window, **right-mouse-click** to accept the selected objects.

7. Inside the graphics window, right-mouse-click to activate the option menu and select **Enter** to end the **Pedit** command.

Using the *OFFSET* command

- The Offset command creates a new object at a specified distance from an existing object or through a specified point.

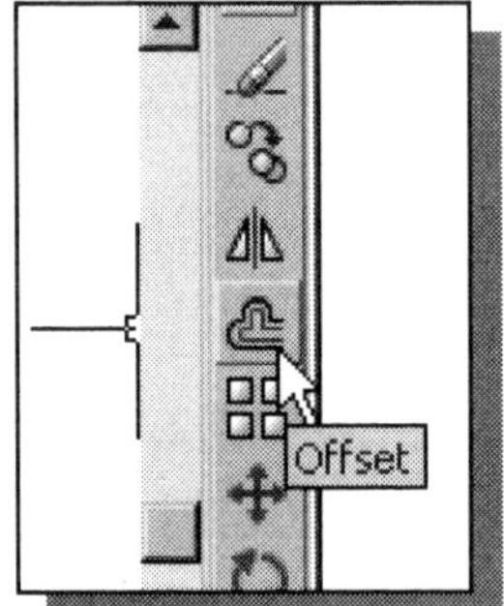

1. Select the **Offset** command icon in the *Modify* toolbar. In the command prompt area, the message "*Specify offset distance or [Through]:*" is displayed.

   Specify offset distance or [Through]: **0.5 [ENTER]**

2. In the command prompt area, the message "*Select object to offset or <exit>:*" is displayed. Select any segment of the polyline on the screen.

3. Since all the lines and arcs have been converted into a single object, all segments are selected.

4. AutoCAD next asks us to identify the direction of the offset. Pick a location that is *inside* the polyline.

5. Inside the graphics window, right-mouse-click to end the Offset command.

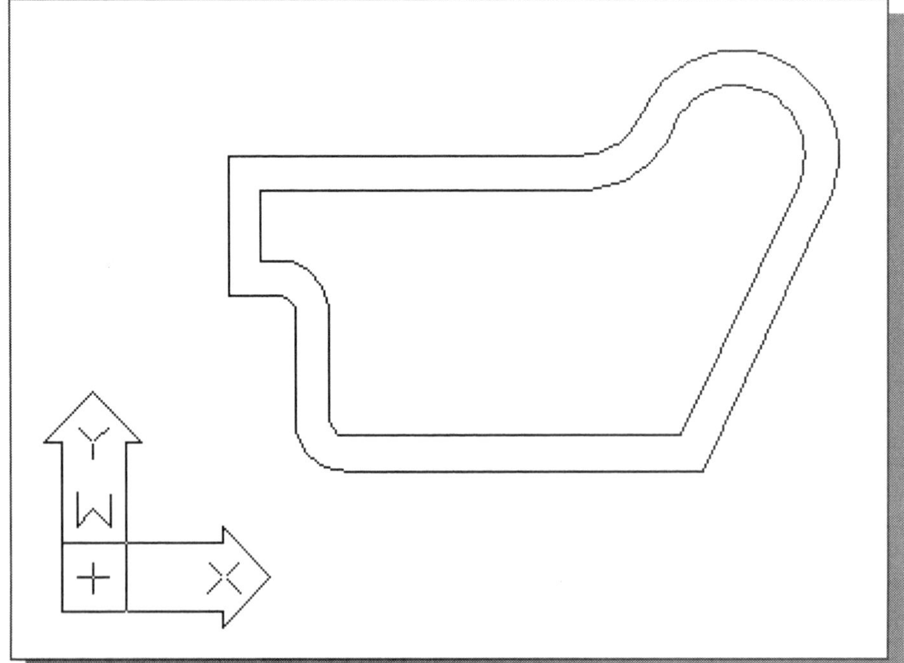

Using the *Explode* command

- The Explode command breaks a compound object into its component objects.

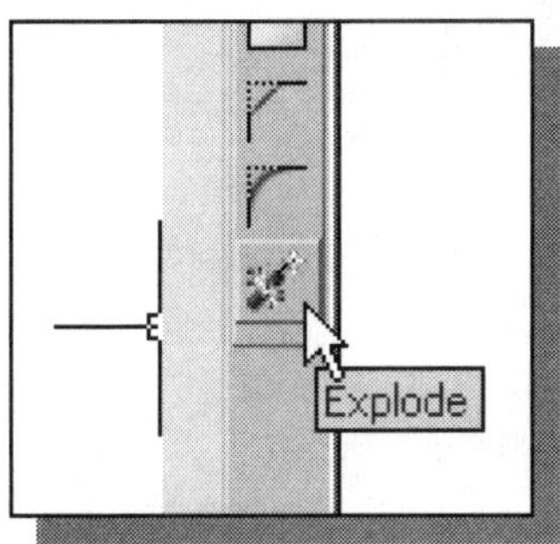

1. Select the **Explode** command icon in the *Modify* toolbar. In the command prompt area, the message "*Select objects:*" is displayed.

2. Pick the **polyline** that we created using the Offset command.

3. Inside the graphics window, right-mouse-click to end the Explode command.

Create another *Fillet*

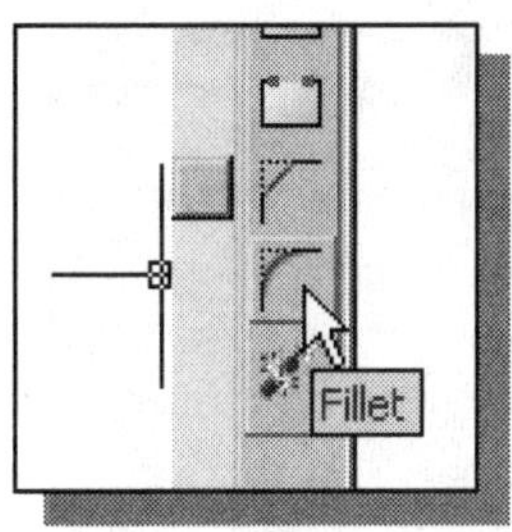

1. Select the **Fillet** command icon in the *Modify* toolbar. In the command prompt area, the message "*Select first object or [Polyline/Radius/Trim]:*" is displayed.

2. Inside the graphics window, right-mouse-click to activate the option menu and select the **Radius** option with the left-mouse-button to specify the radius of the fillet.

3. In the command prompt area, the message "*Specify fillet radius:*" is displayed.

   Specify fillet radius: **0.5 [ENTER]**

4. Pick the **horizontal line** and the **adjacent inclined line** to create a rounded corner as shown.

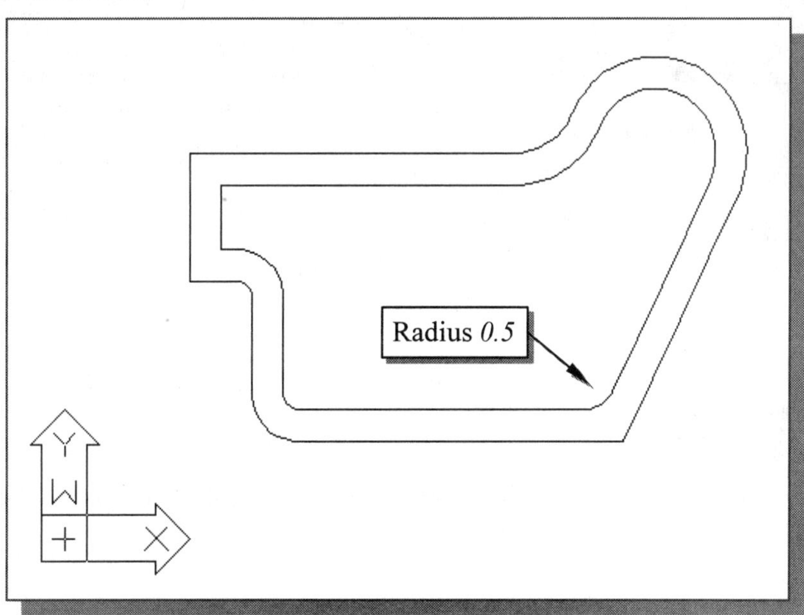

Saving the CAD file

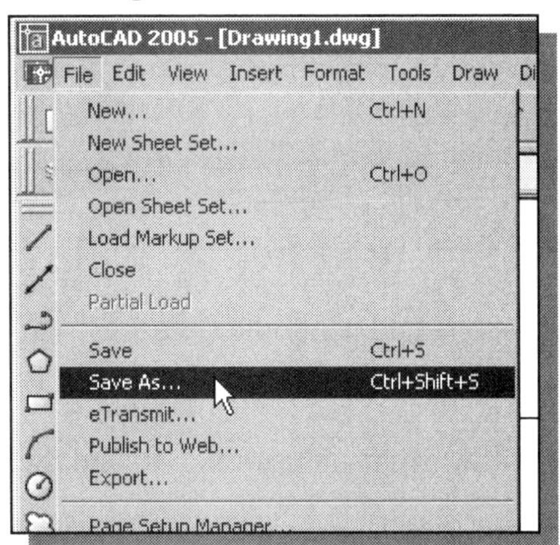

1. In the pull-down menus, select:

   [File] → [Save As]

2. In the *Save Drawing As* dialog box, select the folder in which you want to store the CAD file and enter ***Gasket*** in the *File name* box.

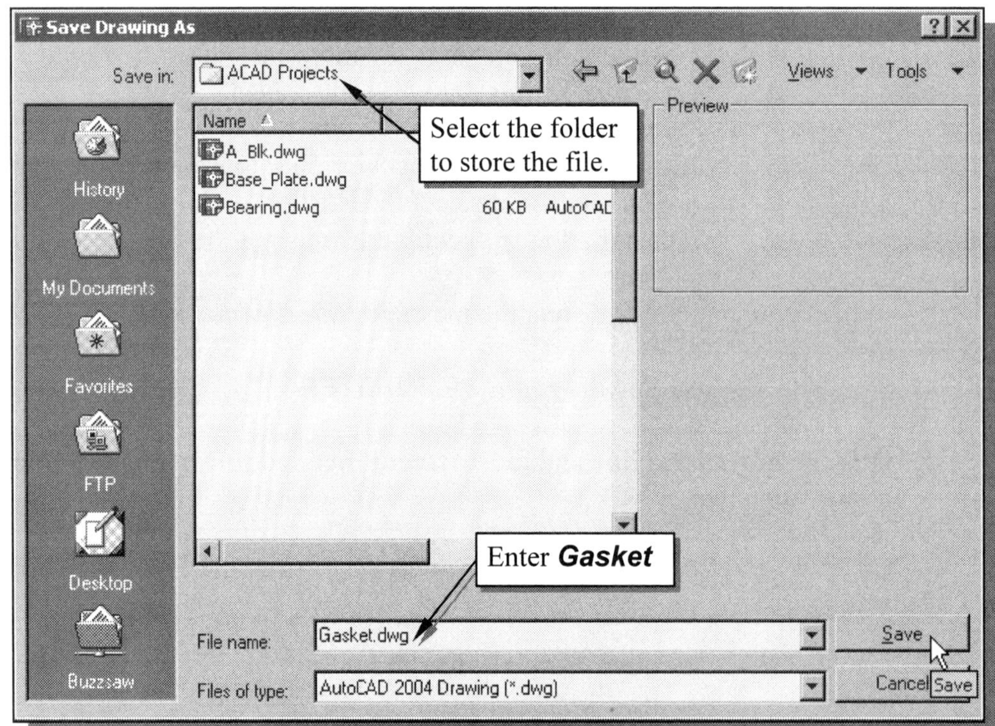

3. Pick **Save** in the *Save Drawing As* dialog box to accept the selections and save the file.

Exit AutoCAD

- To exit **AutoCAD® 2005**, select **File** then choose **Exit** from the pull-down menu or type ***QUIT*** at the command prompt.

Questions:

1. Describe the AutoCAD ***ORTHO*** option.

2. Describe the advantages of using **Polyline** in AutoCAD.

3. Which AutoCAD command can we use to create rounded corners?

4. Describe the AutoCAD **Offset** command.

5. Identify the following commands:

   (a)

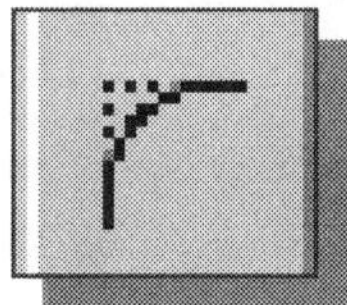

   (b)

   (c)

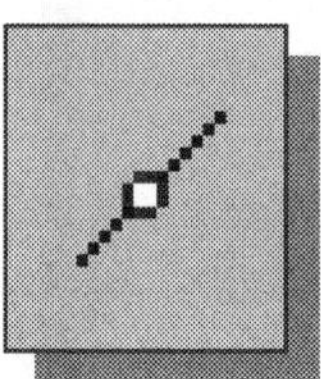

   (d)

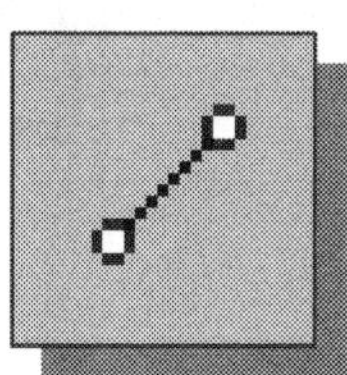

Exercises: Unless otherwise specified, dimensions are in inches.

1.

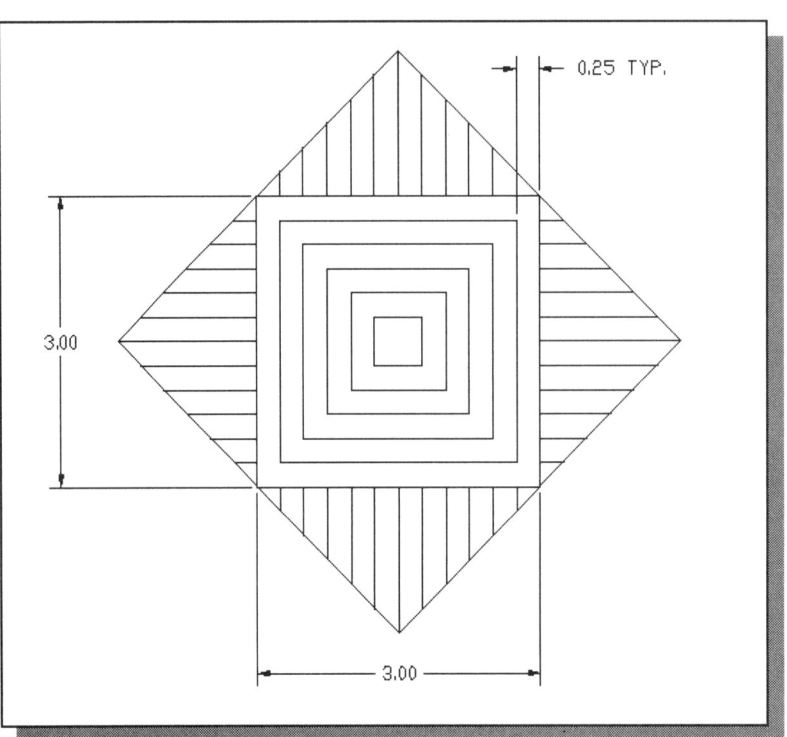

2.

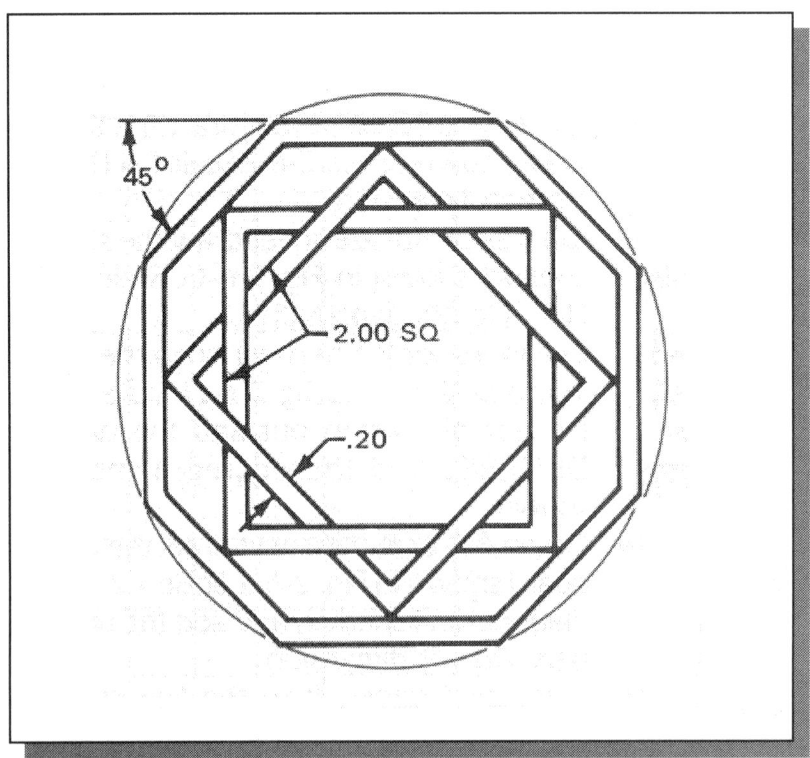

3.

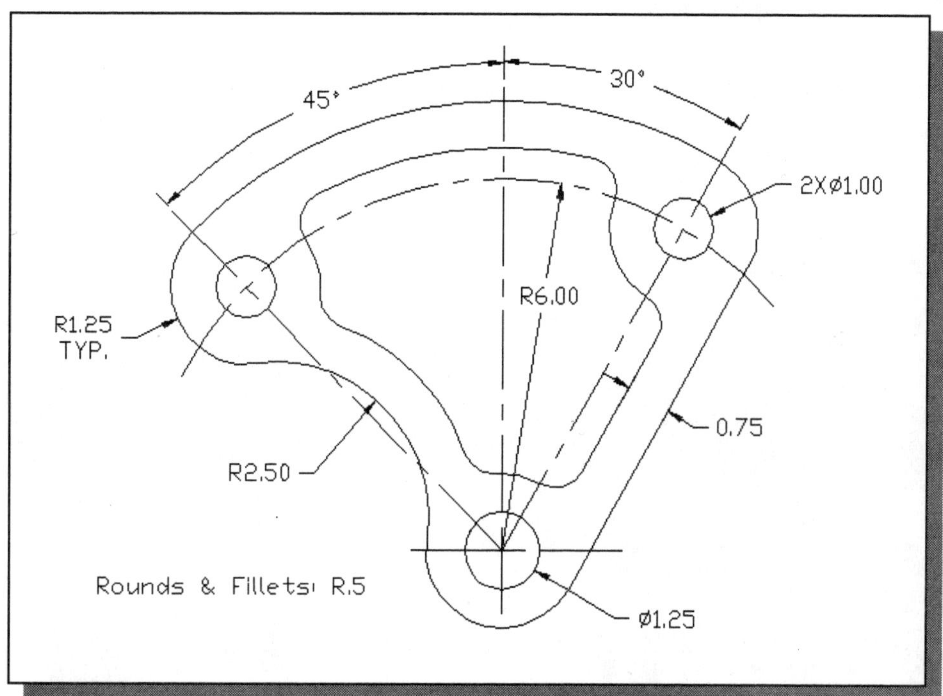

45°
30°
2X⌀1.00
R6.00
R1.25
TYP.
0.75
R2.50
Rounds & Fillets: R.5
⌀1.25

R2.00
R4.00
R6.00
30°
R1.00
R3.25
1.50
⌀1.50
60°
R3.00

4.

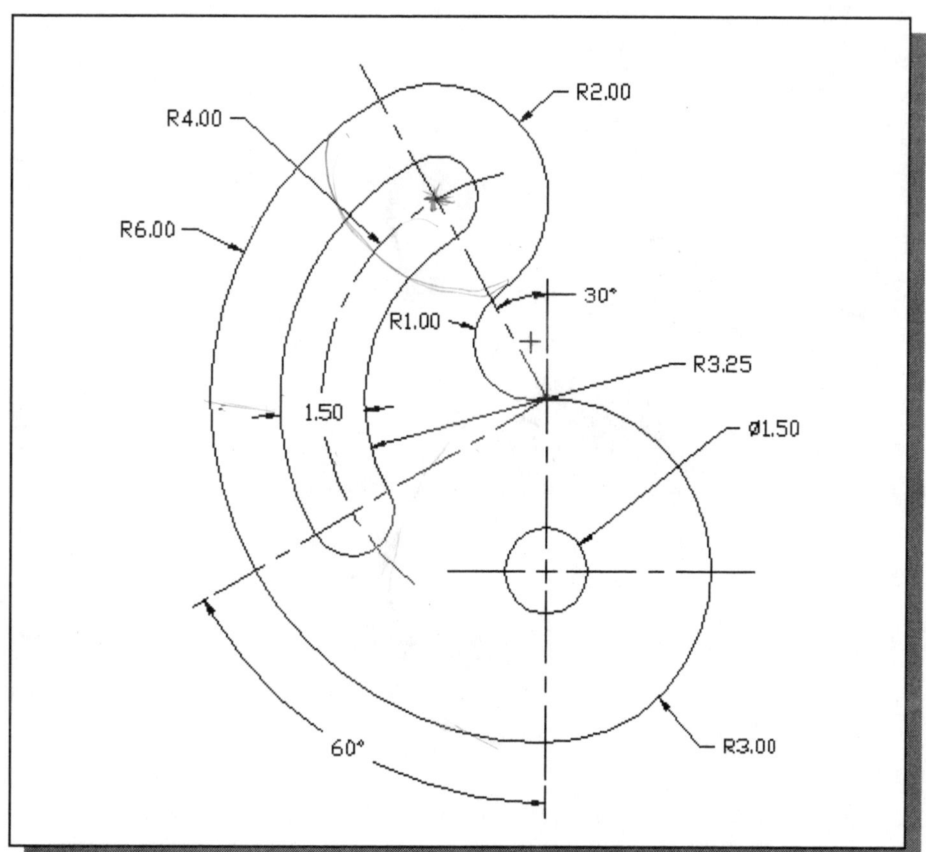

NOTES:

Chapter 4
Object Properties and Organization

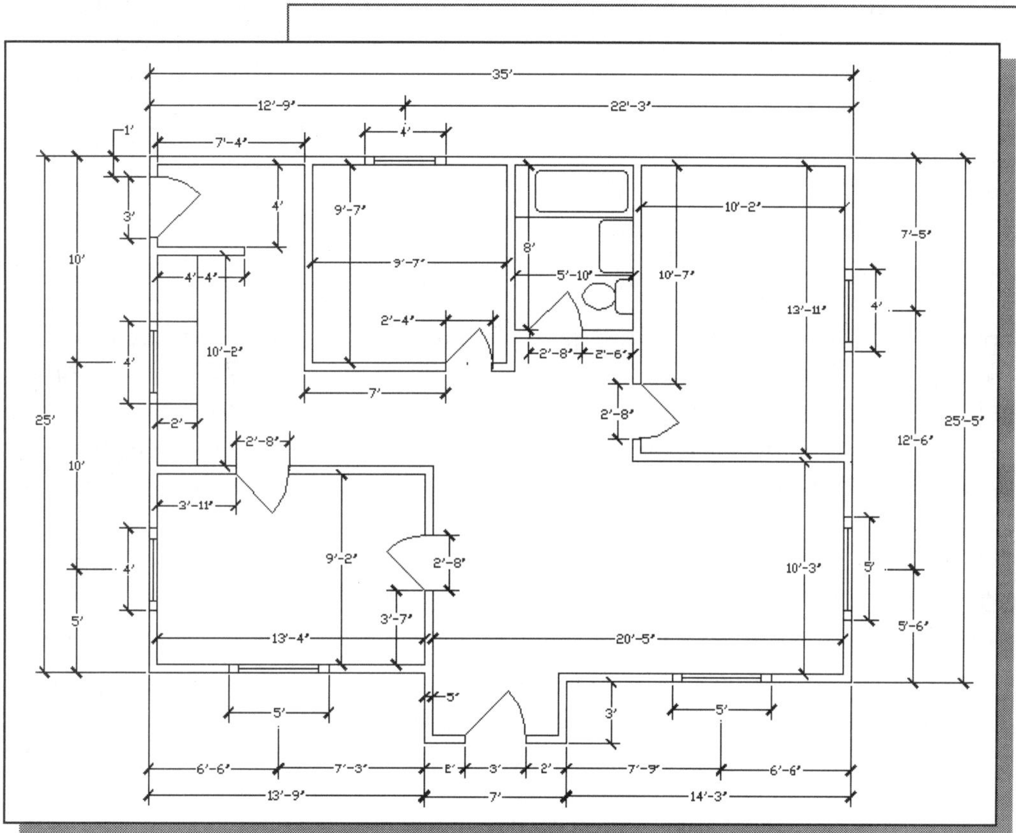

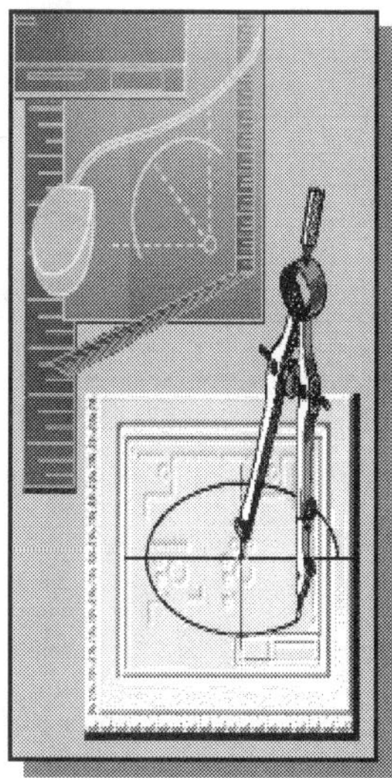

Learning Objectives

- Using the AutoCAD Quick Setup wizard.
- Create new Multiline Styles.
- Draw, using the MULTILINE command.
- Use the ZOOM ALL command.
- Create new layers.
- Pre-selection of objects.
- Controlling Layer Visibility.
- Moving objects to a different layer.

Introduction

The CAD database of a design may contain information regarding the hundreds of CAD entities that are used to create the CAD model. One of the advantages of using a CAD system is its ability to organize and manage the database so that the designer can access the information quickly and easily. Typically, CAD entities that are created to describe one feature, function, or process of a design are perceived as related information and therefore are organized into the same group. In AutoCAD, the **Layer** command is used extensively for this purpose. For example, an architectural drawing typically will show walls, doors, windows, and dimensions. Using layers, we can choose to display or hide sub-systems for clarity; we can also change object properties, such as colors and linetypes, quickly and easily.

In this chapter, we will continue to explore the different construction and editing tools that are available in **AutoCAD® 2005**. We will demonstrate the use of the Limits, Mline, Medit, and Layer commands. As you become proficient with the CAD tools and understand the underlying CAD modeling concepts, you are encouraged to experiment with new ideas in using the CAD tools and develop your own style of using the system.

The *Floor Plan* Design

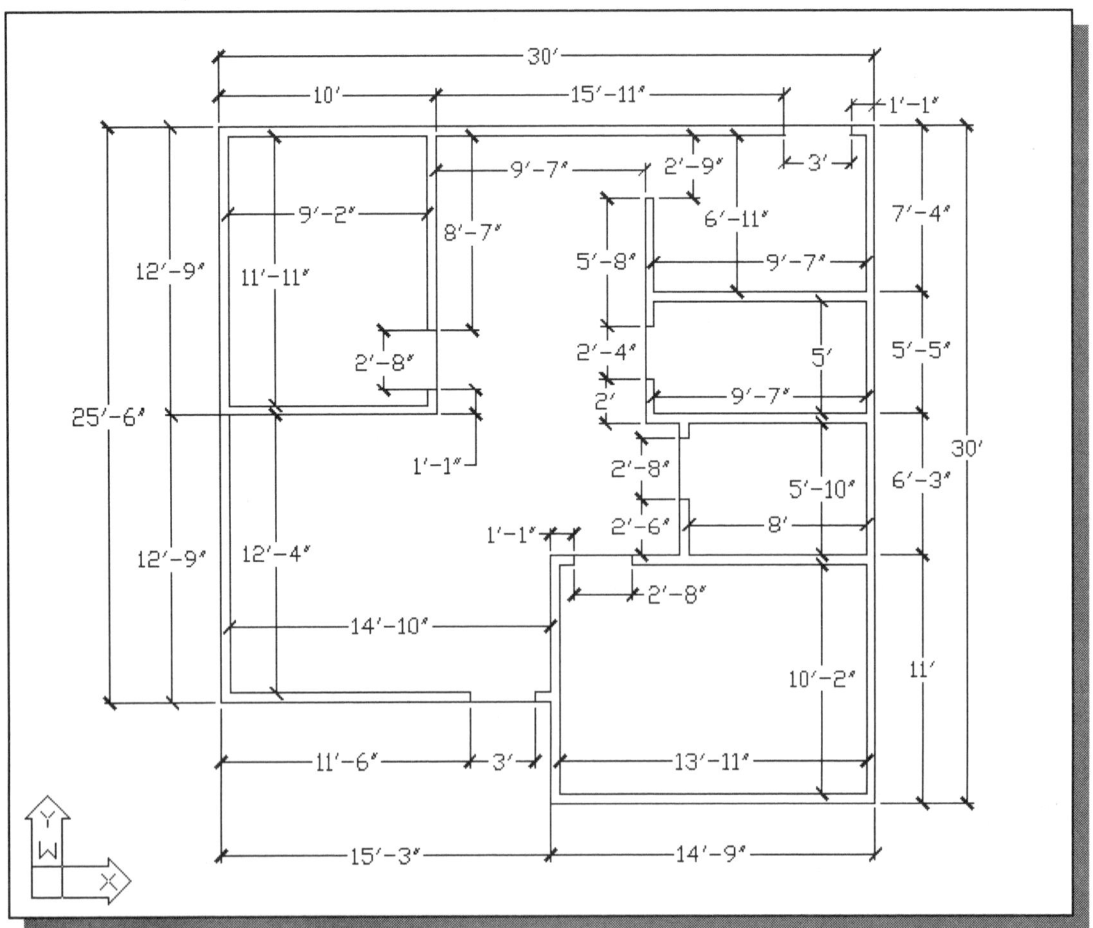

Starting Up AutoCAD® 2005

1. Select the **AutoCAD 2005** option on the *Program* menu or select the **AutoCAD 2005** icon on the *Desktop*. Once the program is loaded into the memory, the **AutoCAD® 2005** drawing screen will appear on the screen.

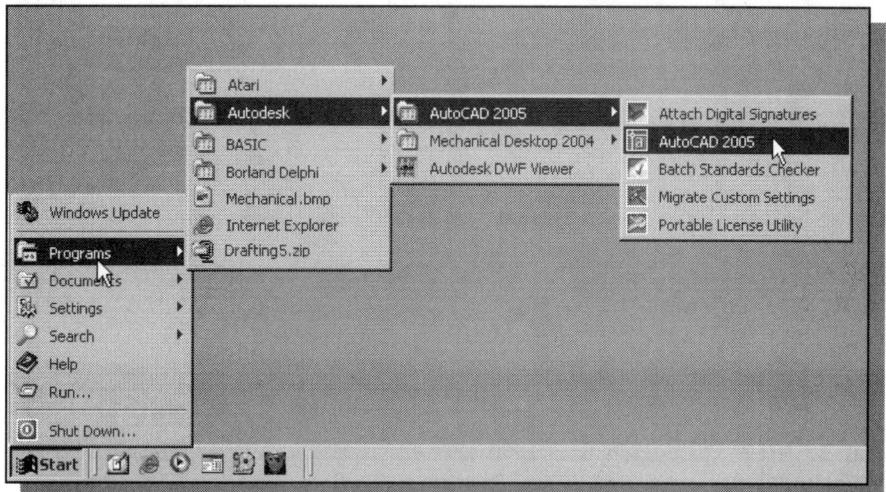

Using the Setup wizard

1. In the *Startup* dialog box, select the **Use a Wizard** option as shown in the figure below.

2. In the *Select a Wizard* section, pick **Quick Setup**.

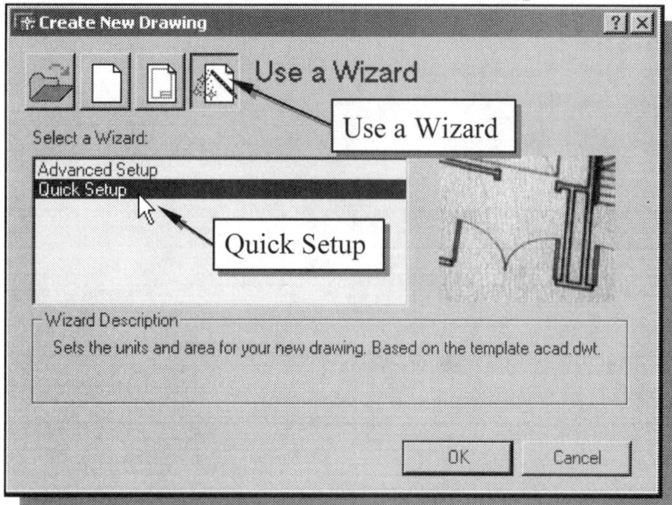

- AutoCAD setup wizards allow us to customize several of the AutoCAD settings depending on the wizard we choose. The *Quick Setup* wizard sets the units and grid display area. Choices for units include *Decimal, Engineering, Architectural, Fractional,* and *Scientific*. We can also specify the width and length of a two-dimensional area to establish the extents of the *grid* displayed, also known as the *limits* of the working area.

Drawing Units Setup

1. In the *Quick Setup Units* option, select **Architectural**.

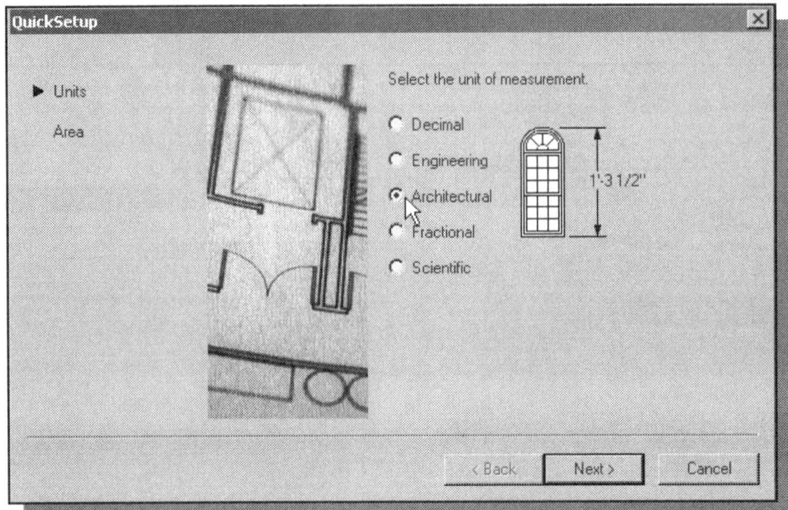

2. Pick **Next** to continue with the *Quick Setup* settings.

Reference Area Setup

1. In the *Quick Setup Area* option, enter **60′** and **40′** for the width and length.

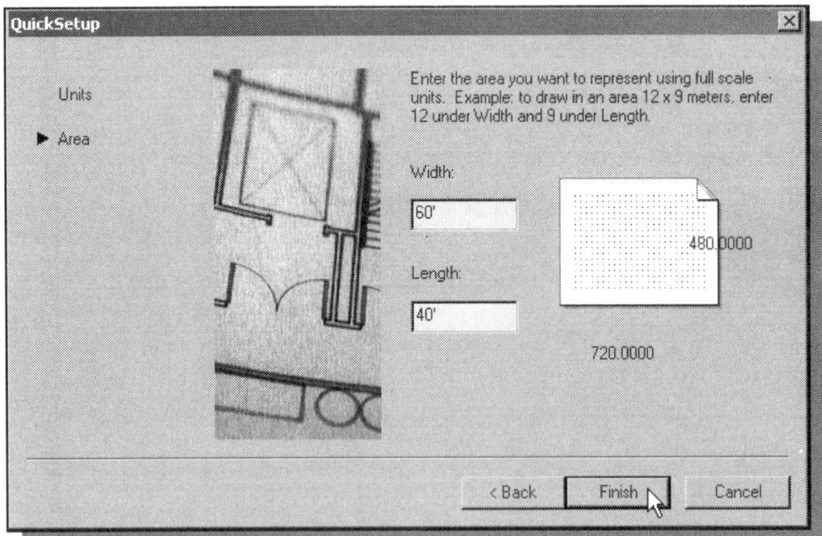

- The two-dimensional area we set up in the *Quick Setup* is the *drawing limits* in AutoCAD.

2. Pick **Finish** to accept the settings and end the *Quick Setup* wizard.

GRID and *SNAP* Intervals Setup

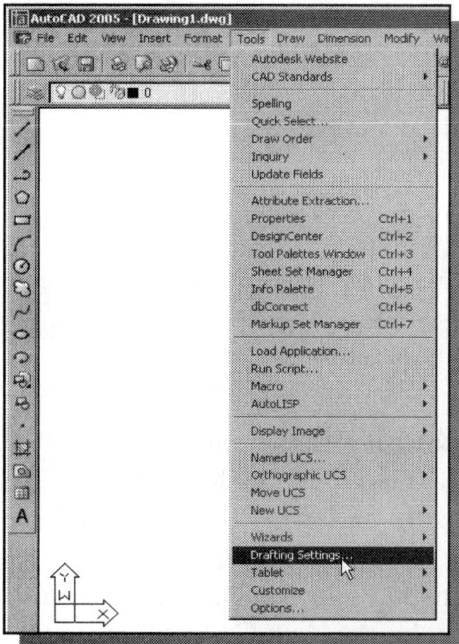

1. In the pull-down menus, select:

   [Tools] → [Drafting Settings]

2. In the *Drafting Settings* dialog box, select the **SNAP and GRID** tab if it is not the page on top.

3. Change *Grid Spacing* to ***6″*** for both X and Y directions.

4. Also adjust the *Snap Spacing* to ***6″*** for both X and Y directions.

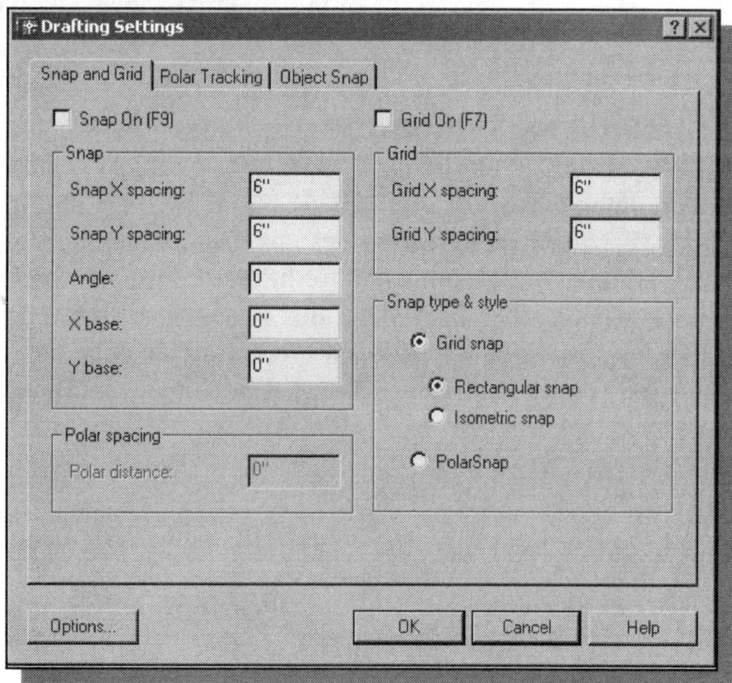

5. Pick **OK** to exit the *Drafting Settings* dialog box.

6. In the *Status Bar* area, reset the option buttons so that only *SNAP, GRID*, and *MODEL* are switched ***ON***.

Using the *Zoom All* command

1. Move the cursor inside the graphics window and notice that, although we have set the *limits* to 40′ by 60′, the default display is still 9″ by 12″. In the graphics window, only a few grid points are displayed.

2. In the *Standard* toolbar area, click and hold down the **Zoom** options button, and the list of available Zoom options appears. Move the cursor over the different icons and read the brief description of each icon to get a feel for what each option does.

3. Move the cursor over the **Zoom All** icon, the second icon from the bottom of the list, and release the left-mouse-button to select the command.

   The Zoom All command displays all objects in the current design. In a two-dimensional view, AutoCAD zooms to the drawing limits or the area that shows all objects, whichever is greater.

The AutoCAD *Multiline* command

- The **Multiline** command in **AutoCAD® 2005** is used to create multiple parallel lines. This command is very useful for creating designs that contain multiple parallel lines, such as walls for architectural designs and for highway designs in civil engineering. The Multiline command creates a set of parallel lines and all line segments are grouped together to form a single *multiline object*, which can be modified using Multiline Edit and Explode commands. We will first create a new ***multiline style*** for our floor plan design.

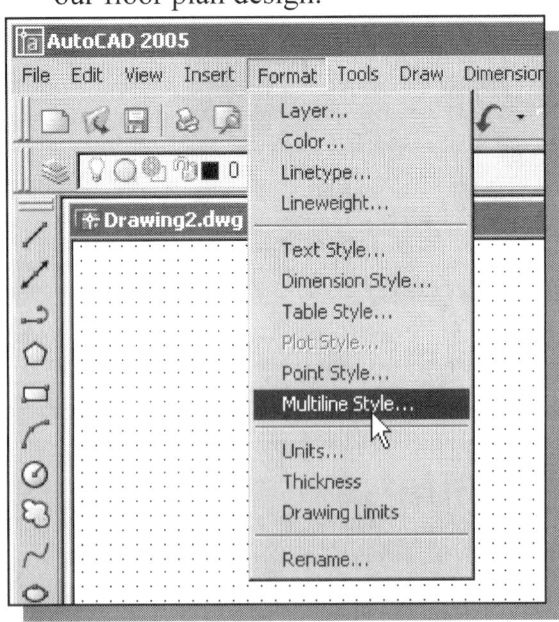

1. In the pull-down menus, select:

   [Format] → [Multiline Style]

❖ The default AutoCAD multiline style is called *STANDARD*, and it consists of two elements (two parallel lines) with an offset distance of 1.0 inch.

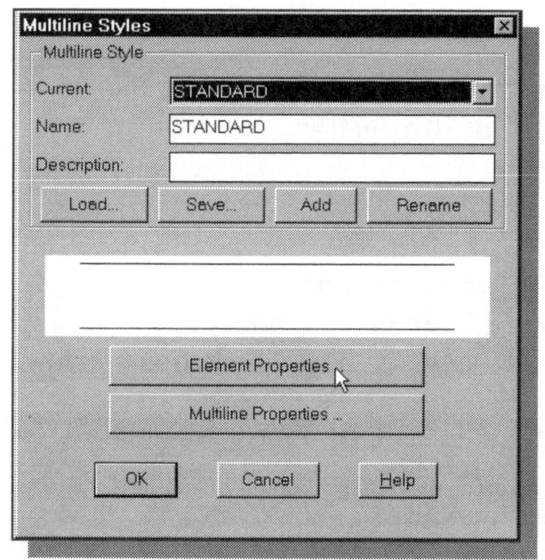

2. In the *Multiline Styles* dialog box choose **Element Properties**.

❖ In the *Element Properties* dialog box, all the line elements in the current multiline style are displayed. Each line element in the style is defined by its offset from a reference line, the *multiline origin.*

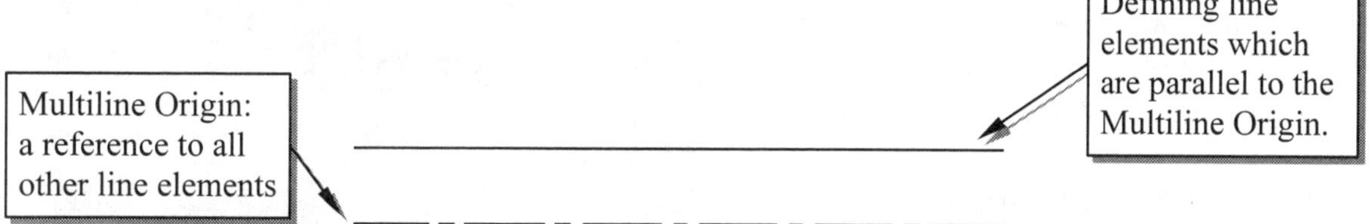

❖ Note that, in the *Element Properties* dialog box, all the line elements are listed in descending order with respect to their offsets. We will create two line elements representing a six-inch wall (offsetting on both sides of the reference location).

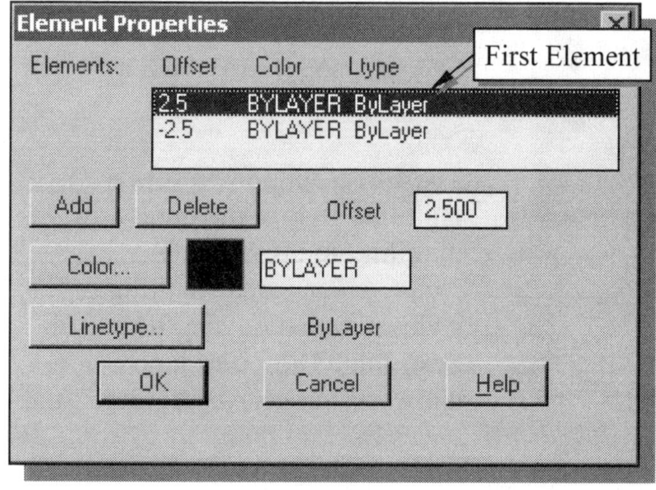

3. In the *Element Properties* dialog box, highlight the first element in the list, and change the *Offset* to ***2.5***.

4. Pick the *second element* in the *Element Properties* dialog box and change the *Offset* to ***-2.5***.

5. Choose **OK** to exit the *Element Properties* dialog box.

❖ Notice the Add and Delete options are also available in the dialog box, which allow us to create or remove as many as 16 elements in a multiline style.

6. In the *Multiline Styles* dialog box choose **Multiline Properties**.

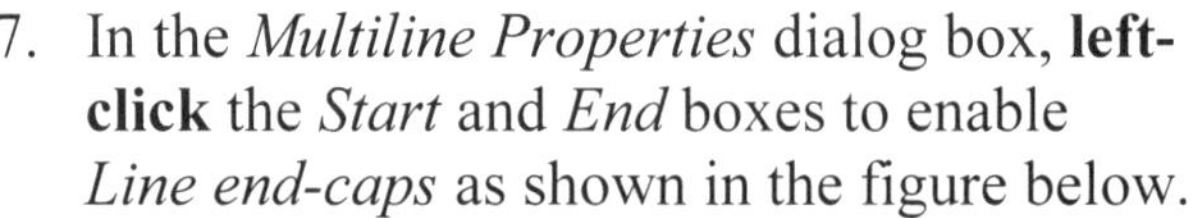

7. In the *Multiline Properties* dialog box, **left-click** the *Start* and *End* boxes to enable *Line end-caps* as shown in the figure below.

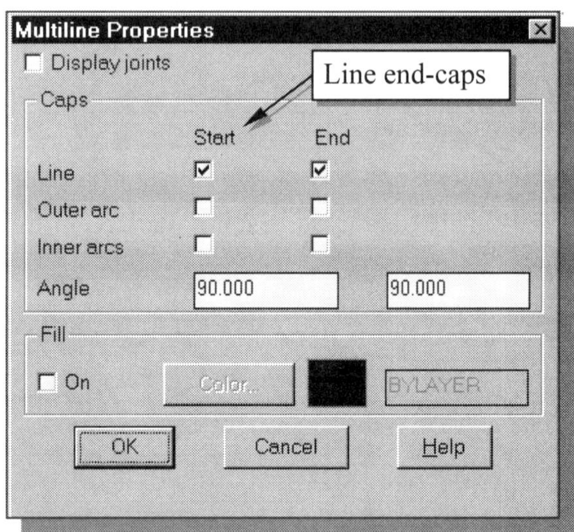

8. Choose **OK** to exit the *Multiline Properties* dialog box.

9. In the *Multiline Styles* dialog box: in the ***Name*** box, enter ***WALL*** as the new *Multiline Style Name*.

10. Enter ***5″ wall with line endcaps*** in the *Description* box.

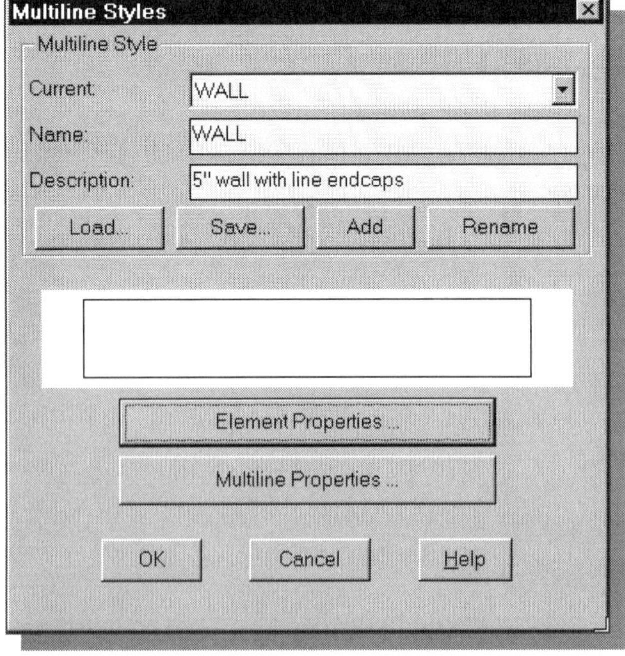

11. Click the **Add** button to add the new multiline style to the database of the current CAD design. (The *Current Multiline Style* is also set to **WALL** as shown.)

    The **Save** button will save a multiline style to the library of multiline styles. By default, AutoCAD saves the multiline styles information to a file called **acad.mln**. The **Load** button allows us to retrieve multiline styles from a library.

12. Choose **OK** to exit the *Multiline Styles* dialog box.

Drawing Multilines

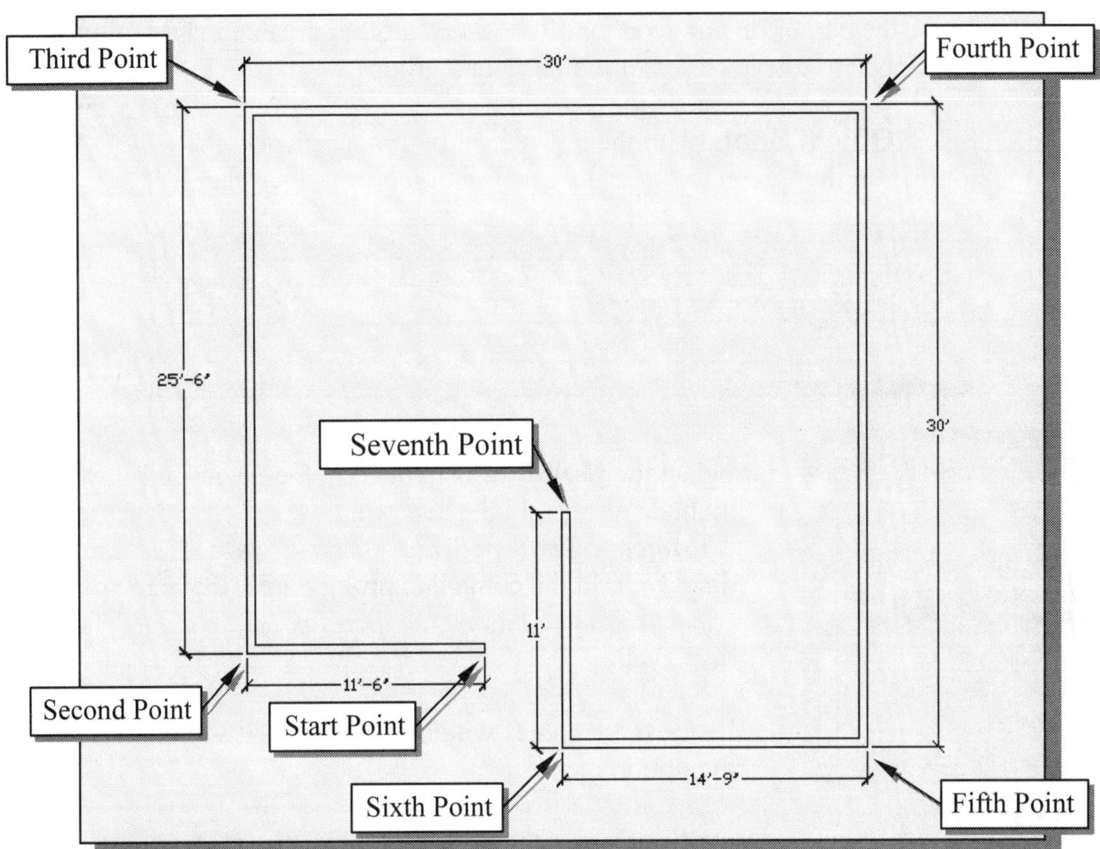

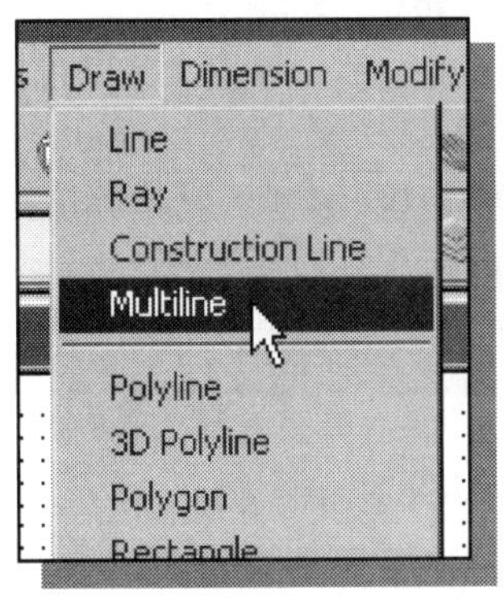

1. Select the **Multiline** command icon in the *Draw* pull-down menu as shown. In the text window, the current settings "*Justification = **Top**, Scale = 1.00, Style = **Wall***" are displayed.

2. In the command prompt area, the message "*Specify start point or [Justification/Scale/Style]:*" is displayed. Select a location near the bottom of the graphics window as the **start point** of the multiline by left-clicking the mouse.

3. In the command prompt area, create a vertical line by using the *relative rectangular coordinates entry method*, relative to the last point we specified

   Specify next point: **@-11'6",0** **[ENTER]**

4. On your own, complete the multiline by specifying the points, *point three* through *point seven*, as shown in the above figure.

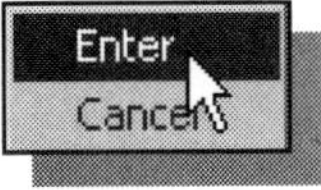

5. Inside the graphics window, right-mouse-click and select **Enter** to end the Multiline command.

Creating interior walls

1. Move the cursor on any icon in the *Standard* toolbar area and **right-mouse-click** once to display a list of toolbar menu groups.

2. Select **Object Snap**, with the left-mouse-button, to display the *Object Snap* toolbar on the screen to assist the construction of the floor plan.

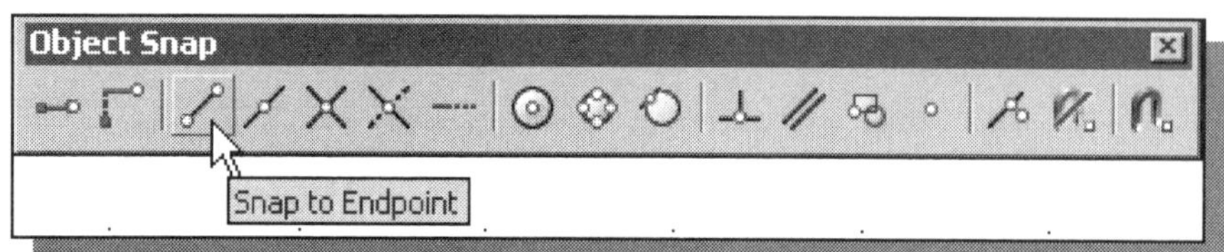

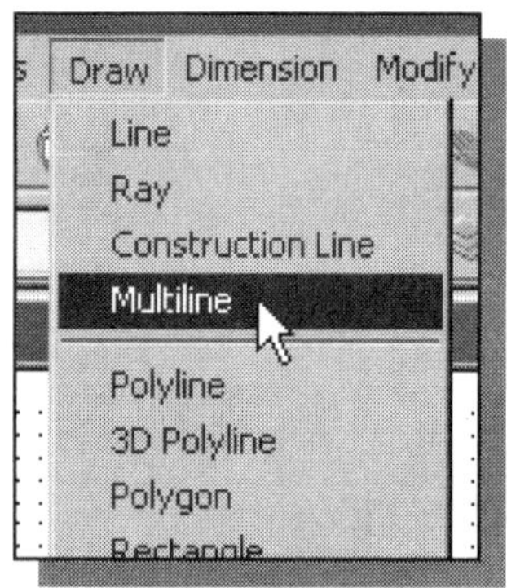

3. Select the **Multiline** command in the *Draw* pull-down menu as shown. In the text window, the current settings "*Justification = Top, Scale = 1.00, Style = Wall*" are displayed. In the command prompt area, the message "*Specify start point or [Justification/Scale/Style]:*" is displayed.

4. Inside the graphics window, **right-mouse-click** to display the option menu.

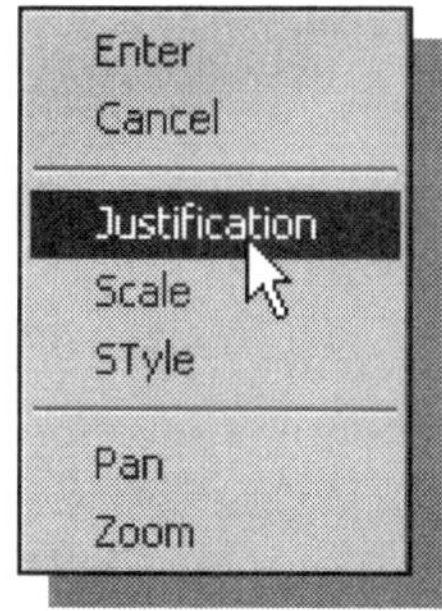

5. Pick **Justification** in the option menu. In the command prompt area, the message "*Enter justification type [Top/Zero/Bottom] <Top>:*" is displayed.

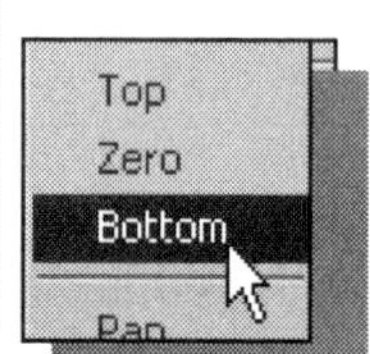

6. Inside the graphics window, right-mouse-click to display the option menu and select **Bottom** so that the points we select will be set as alignments for the bottom element.

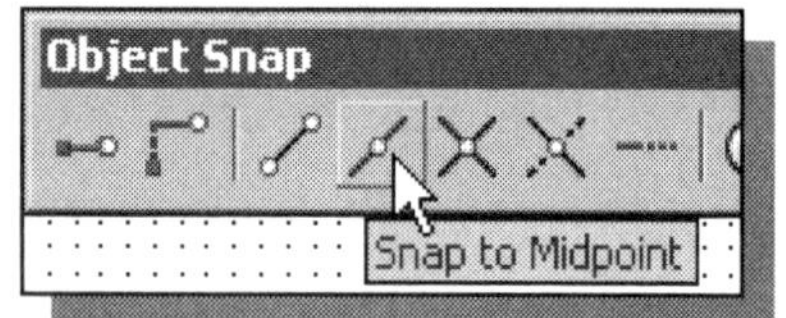

7. In the *Object Snap* toolbar, pick **Snap to Midpoint**. In the command prompt area, the message "*_mid of*" is displayed. AutoCAD now expects us to select a geometric entity on the screen.

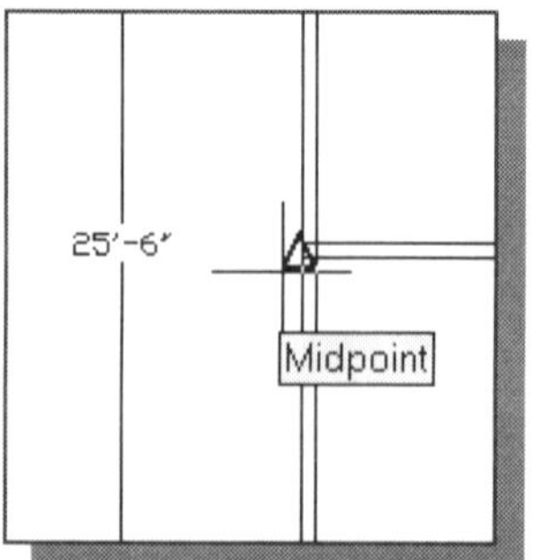

8. Select the vertical line on the left as shown.

9. At the command prompt, enter ***@10',0*** **[ENTER]**.

10. Now enter ***@0,1'1"***, to define the vertical stub wall.

11. Inside the graphics window, right-mouse-click and select **Enter** to end the Multiline command.

- Next, we will create a line representing the location of a 2′-8″ door.

12. Select the **Line** command icon in the *Draw* toolbar. In the command prompt area, the message "*_line Specify first point:*" is displayed.

13. In the *Object Snap* toolbar, pick **Snap to Endpoint**. In the command prompt area, the message "*_endp of*" is displayed. AutoCAD now expects us to select a geometric entity on the screen.

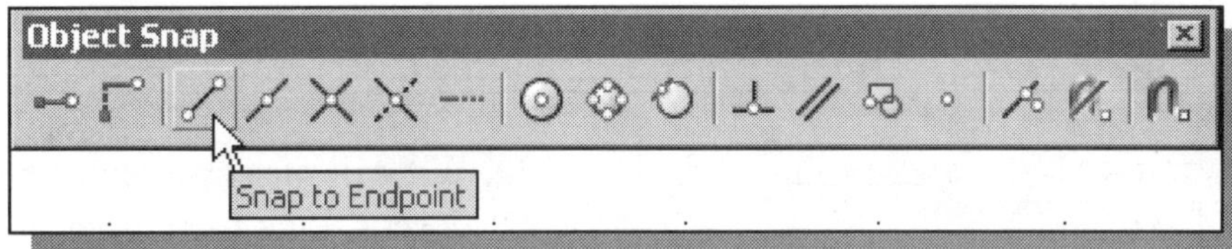

14. Pick the **top right corner** of the multiline we just created.

15. At the command prompt, enter ***@0,2'8"*** **[ENTER]**.

16. Inside the graphics window, right-mouse-click and select **Enter** to end the Line command.

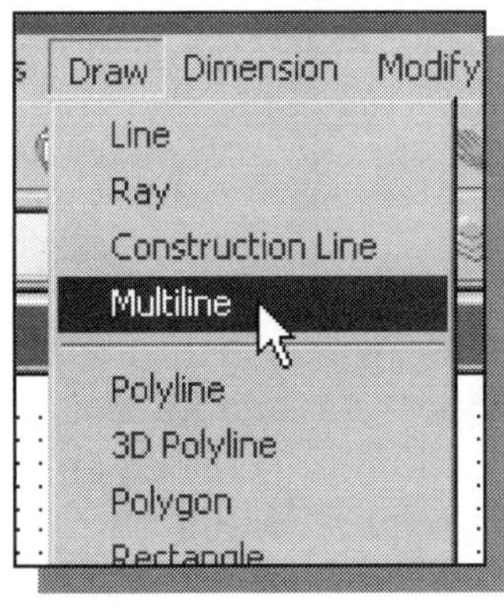

17. Select the **Multiline** command in the *Draw* pull-down menu. In the text window, the current settings "*Justification = Bottom, Scale = 1.00, Style = Wall*" are displayed. In the command prompt area, the message "*Specify start point or [Justification/Scale/Style]:*" is displayed.

18. Inside the graphics window, right-mouse-click to display the option menu.

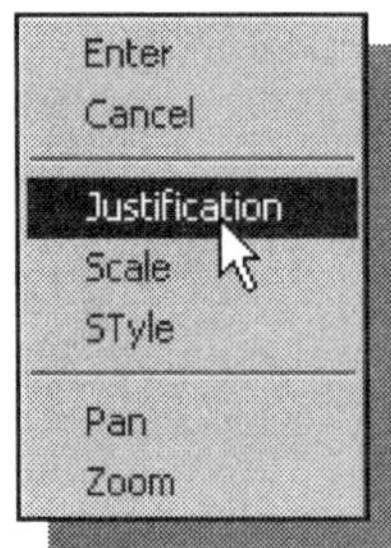

19. Pick **Justification** in the option menu. In the command prompt area, the message "*Enter justification type [Top/Zero/Bottom] <Bottom>:*" is displayed.

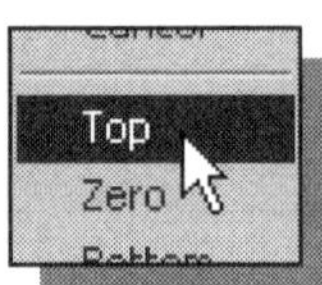

20. Inside the graphics window, right-mouse-click to display the option menu and select **Top** so that the points we select will align to the top element.

21. In the *Object Snap* toolbar, pick **Snap From**. In the command prompt area, the message "*_from Base point*" is displayed. AutoCAD now expects us to select a geometric entity on the screen.

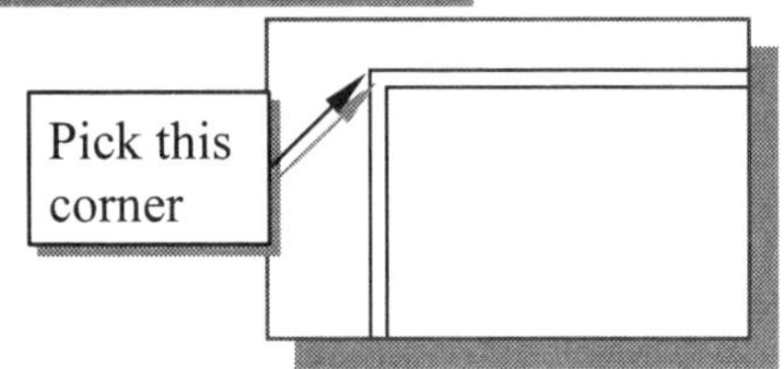

22. We will measure relative to the top left corner. Pick the corner as shown.

23. At the command prompt, enter **@10',0** [ENTER].

24. In the *Object Snap* toolbar, pick **Snap to Endpoint**. In the command prompt area, the message "*_endp of*" is displayed.

25. Pick the top endpoint of the reference line.

26. Inside the graphics window, right-mouse-click once and select **Enter** to end the Multiline command. The drawing should appear as shown in the figure below.

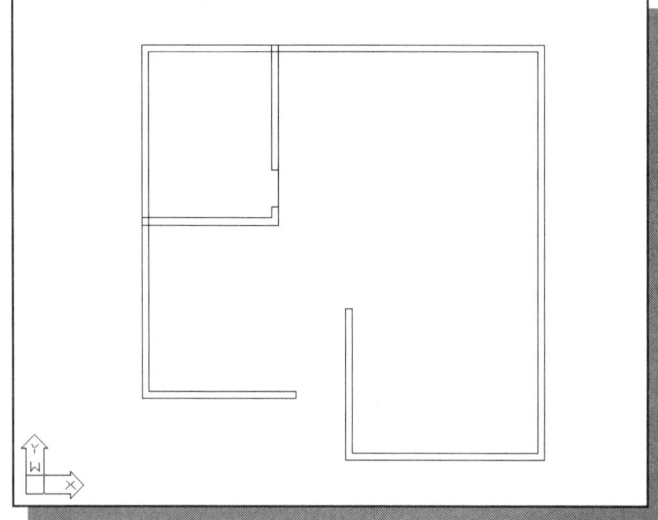

❖ One of the main advantages of using a CAD system to create drawings is the ability to create and remove geometric entities quickly, using many of the available tools. Unlike traditional board drafting, where only the necessary entities are created on paper, CAD provides a much more flexible environment that requires a slightly different way of thinking, as well as taking a different view of the tasks at hand.

Joining the walls using *Multiline Edit*

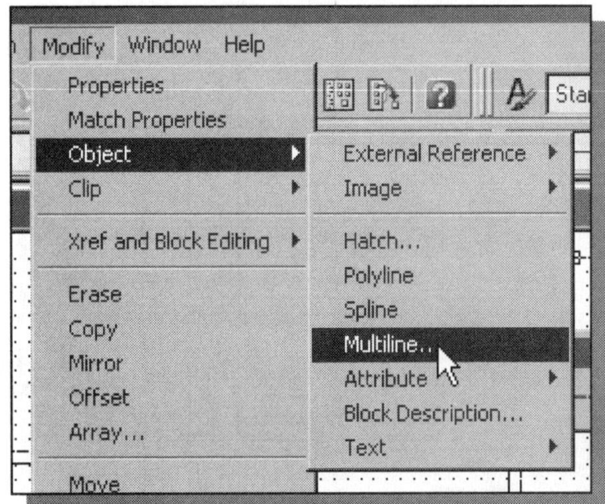

1. In the pull-down menus, select:

   [Modify] → [Object] → [Multiline]

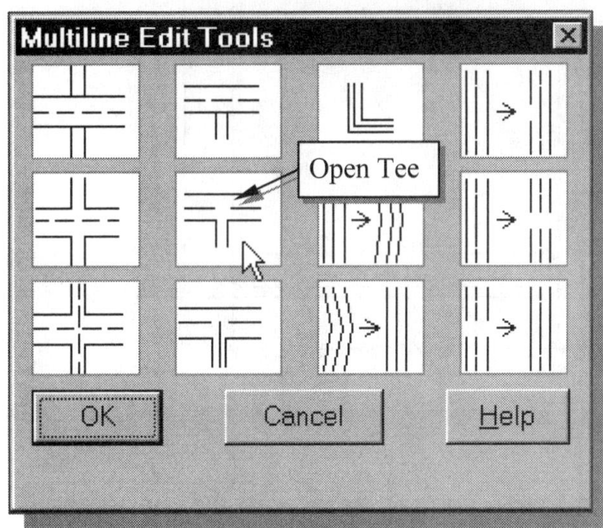

The *Multiline Edit Tools* dialog box appears. Select the **Help** button to see the description of the available *Multiline Edit Tools*.

2. Pick the **Open Tee** option in the dialog box.

3. Click **OK** to accept the selection of the Open Tee option.

➢ We will need to select two multilines for this option: first, select the multiline to trim or extend and, second, select the intersecting multiline.

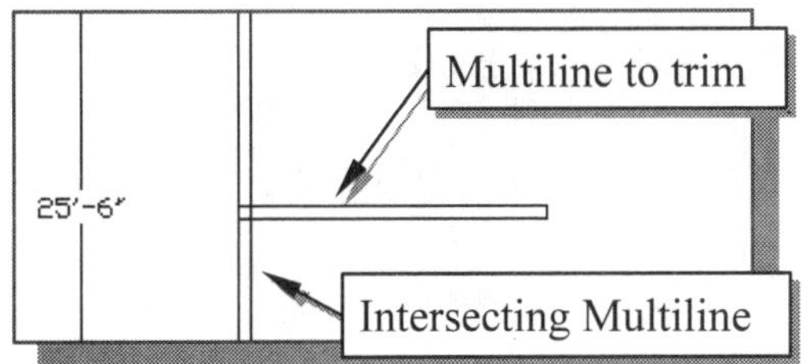

4. Pick the **horizontal multiline** as the *multiline to trim* as shown.

5. Pick the **vertical multiline** as the *intersecting multiline.*

6. Repeat the above steps and modify the connection of the other inside wall.

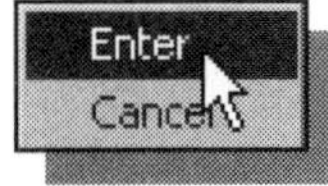

7. Inside the graphics window, right-mouse-click once and select **Enter** to end the Mledit command.

8. Using the *Multiline* options, create the additional walls and doorways as shown.

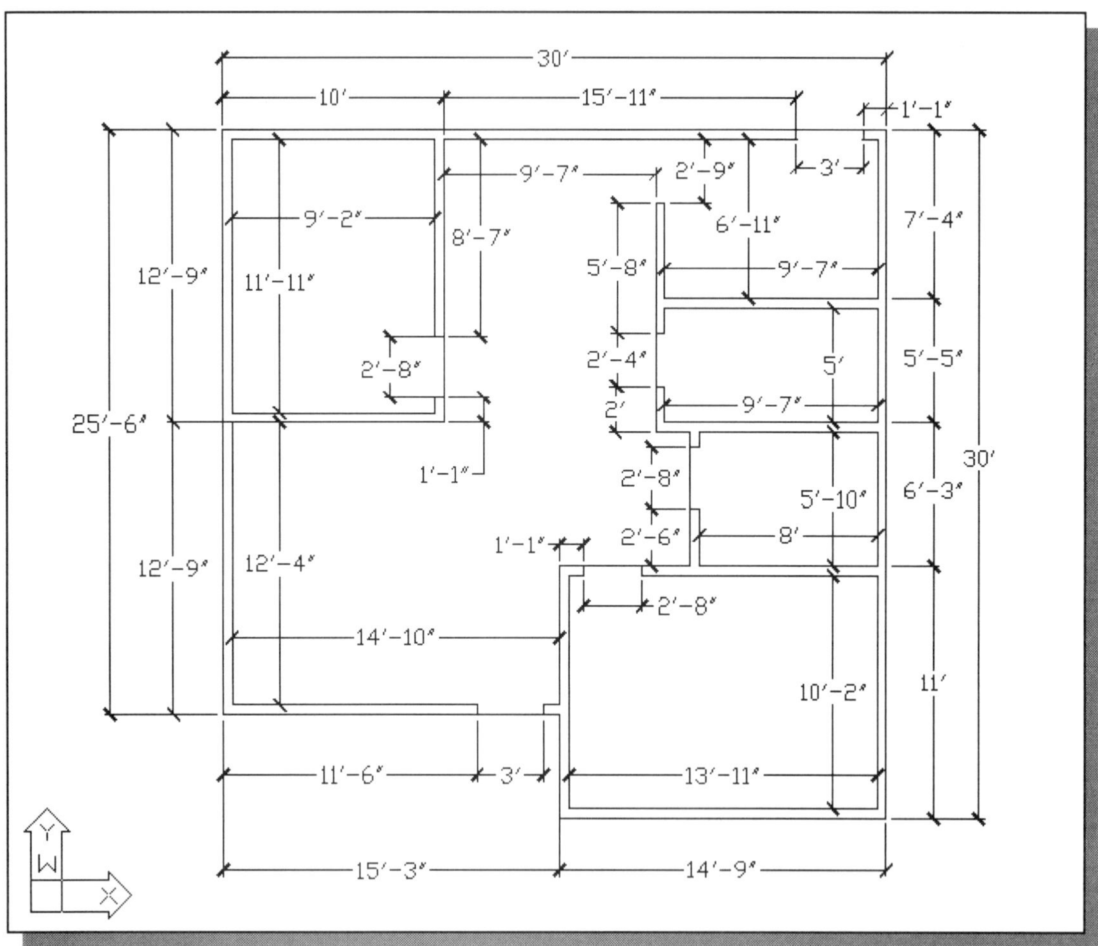

➢ Hint: Use the **Trim/Extend**, **Undo**, and **Erase** commands to assist the construction of the floor plan.

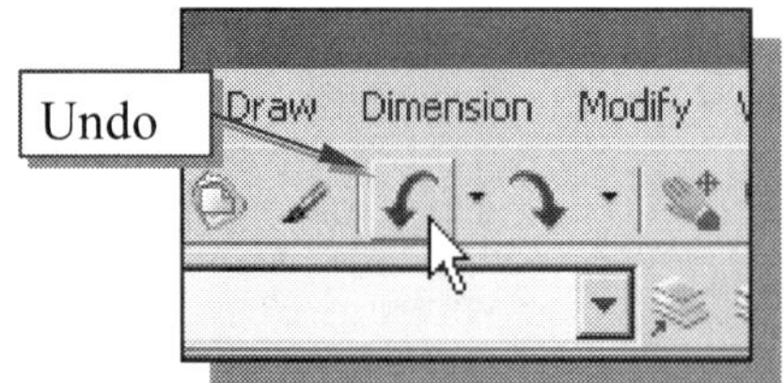

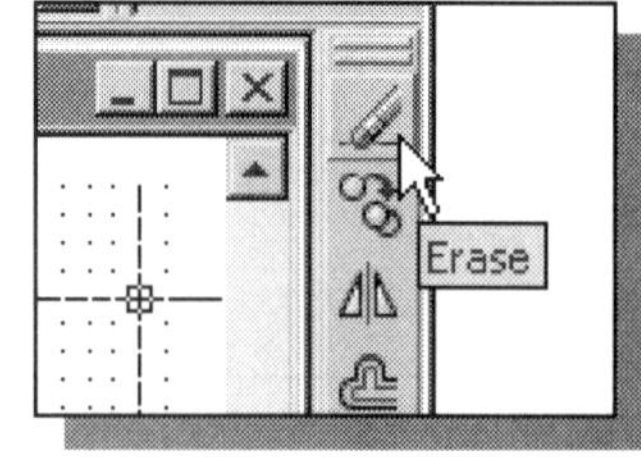

❖ Now is a good time to save the design. Select **[File] → [Save As]** in the pull-down menu and use ***FloorPlan*** as the *File name.*

Using *Layers* and Object Properties

In **AutoCAD® 2005**, ***layers*** can be thought of as transparent overlays on which we organize different kinds of design information. Typically, CAD entities that are created to describe one feature or function of a design are considered as related information and therefore can be organized into the same group. The objects we organized into the same group will usually have common properties such as colors, linetypes, and lineweights. Color helps us visually distinguish similar elements in our designs. Linetype helps us identify easily the different drafting elements, such as centerlines or hidden lines. Lineweight increases the legibility of an object through width. Consider the floor plan we are currently working on. The floor plan can be placed on one layer, electrical layout on another, and plumbing on a third layer. Organizing layers and the objects on layers makes it easier to manage the information in our designs. Layers can be used as a method to control the visibility of objects. We can temporarily switch *ON* or *OFF* any layer to help construction and editing of our designs.

AutoCAD allows us to create an infinite number of layers. In general, twenty to thirty layers are sufficient for most designs. Most companies also require designers and CAD operators to follow the company standards in organizing objects in layers.

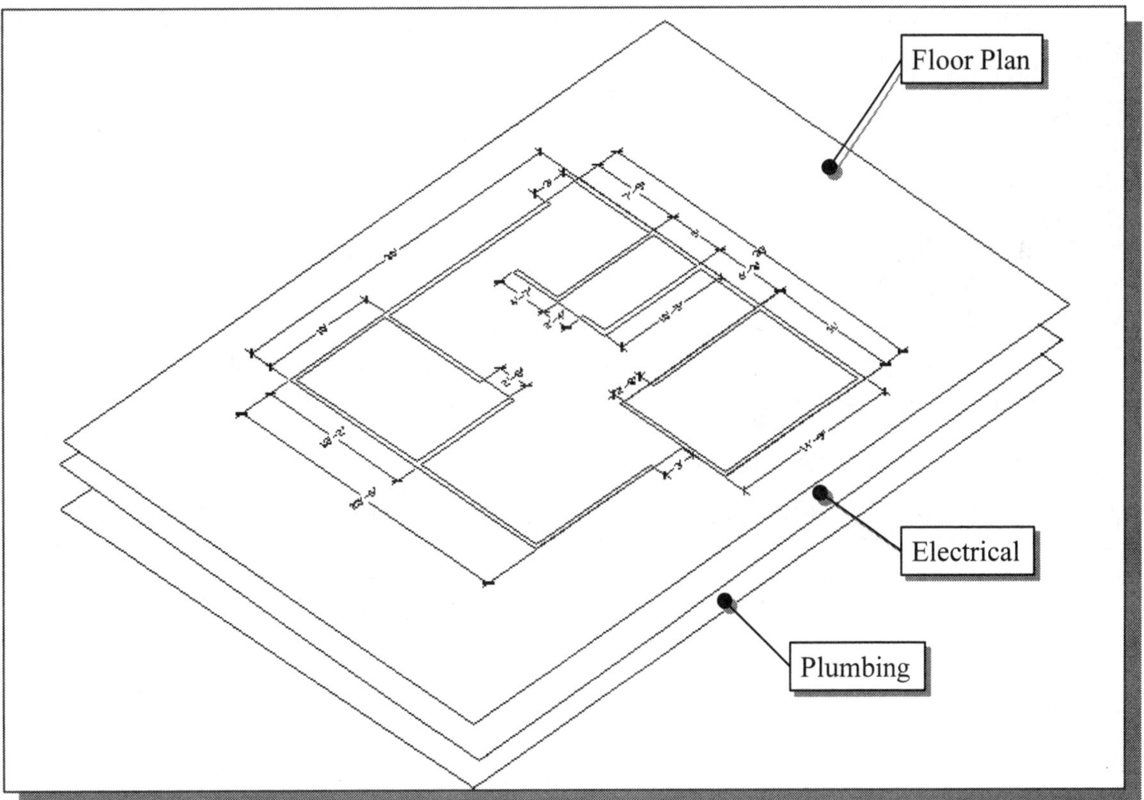

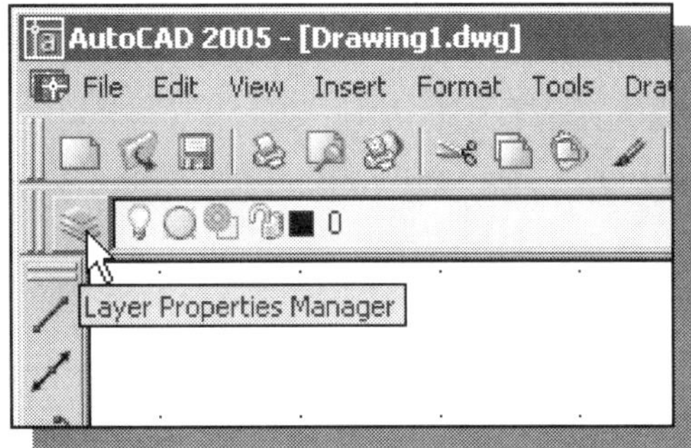

1. Pick **Layers Properties Manager** in the *Object Properties* toolbar.

❖ The *Layer Properties Manager* dialog box appears. AutoCAD creates a default layer, *layer 0*, which we cannot rename or delete. *Layer 0* has special properties used by the system.

❖ In AutoCAD, we always construct entities on a layer. It may be the default layer or a layer that we create. Each layer has associated properties such as the visibility setting, color, linetype, lineweight, and plot style.

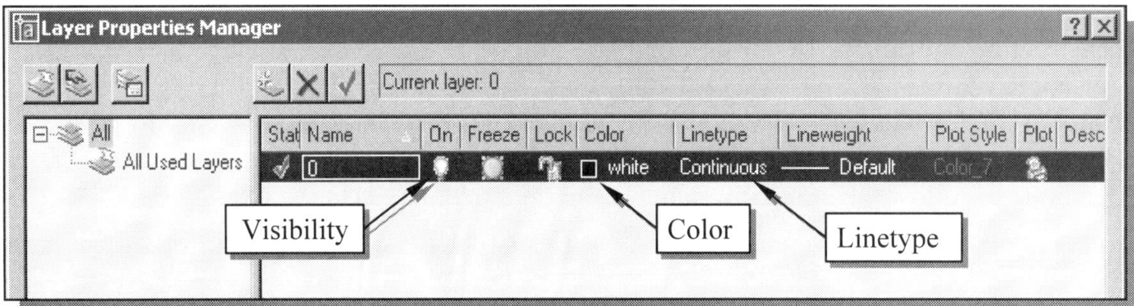

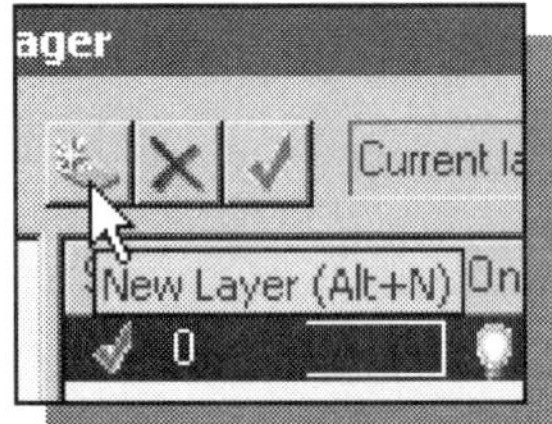

2. Click on the **New** button. Notice a layer is automatically added to the list of layers.

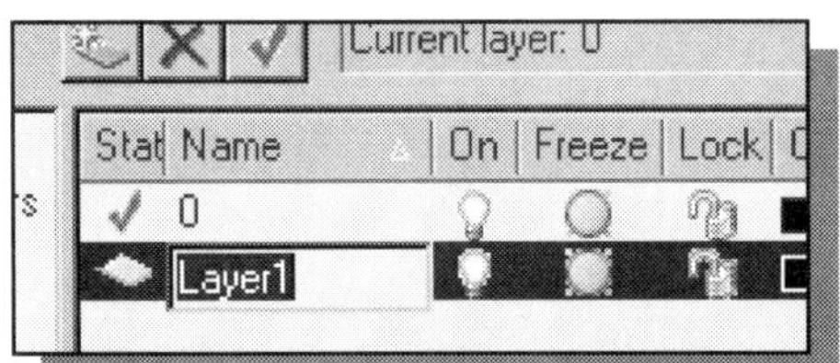

3. AutoCAD will assign a generic name to the new layer (*Layer1*). Enter ***BathRoom*** as the name of the new layer as shown in the figure below.

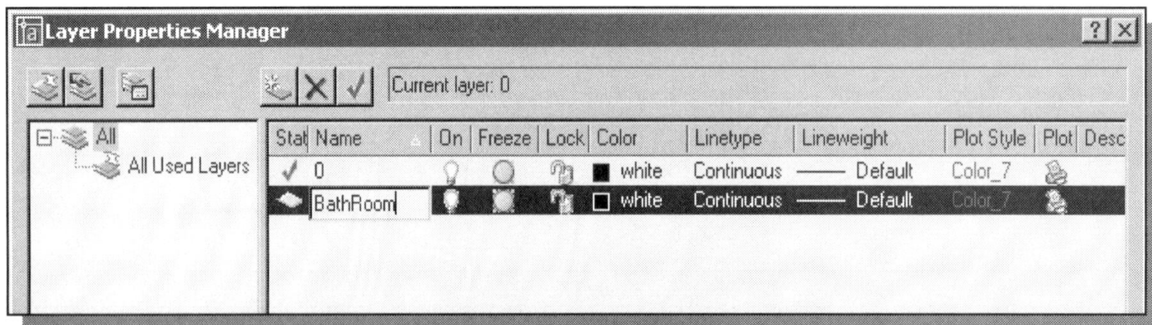

❖ Layer properties can be adjusted by clicking on the icon or name of a property. For example, clicking on the *light-bulb* icon will toggle the visibility of the layer *ON* or *OFF*.

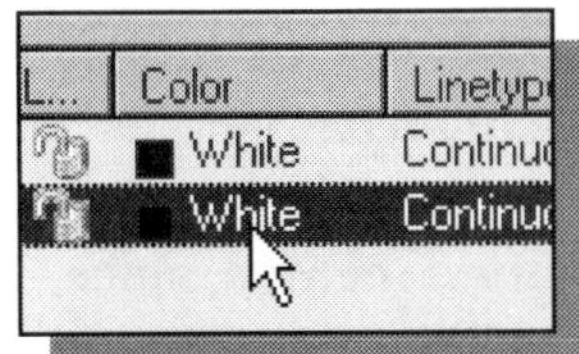

4. Pick the color swatch or the color name (**White**) of the *BathRoom* layer. The *Select Color* dialog box appears.

5. Pick **Cyan** (*Index color: 4*)in the *Standard Colors* section. Notice the current color setting is displayed at the bottom of the dialog box.

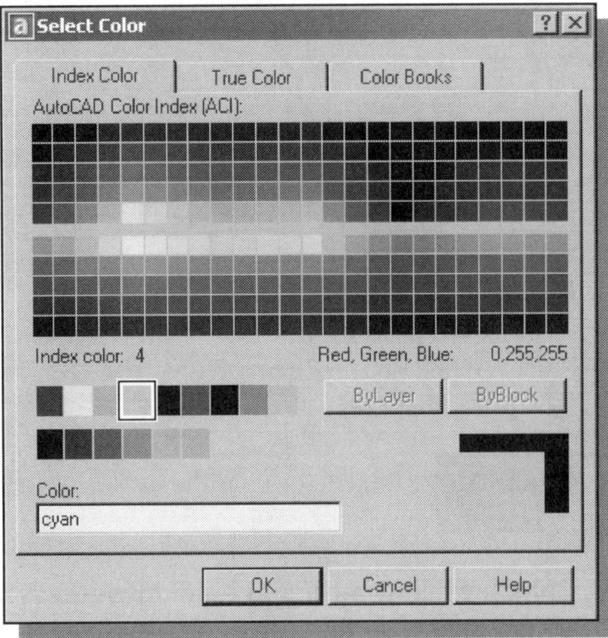

6. Click on the **OK** button to accept the color assignment.

7. Click on the **Set Current** button to make *BathRoom* the *Current Layer*. There can only be one *Current Layer*, and new entities are automatically placed on the layer that is set to be the *Current Layer*.

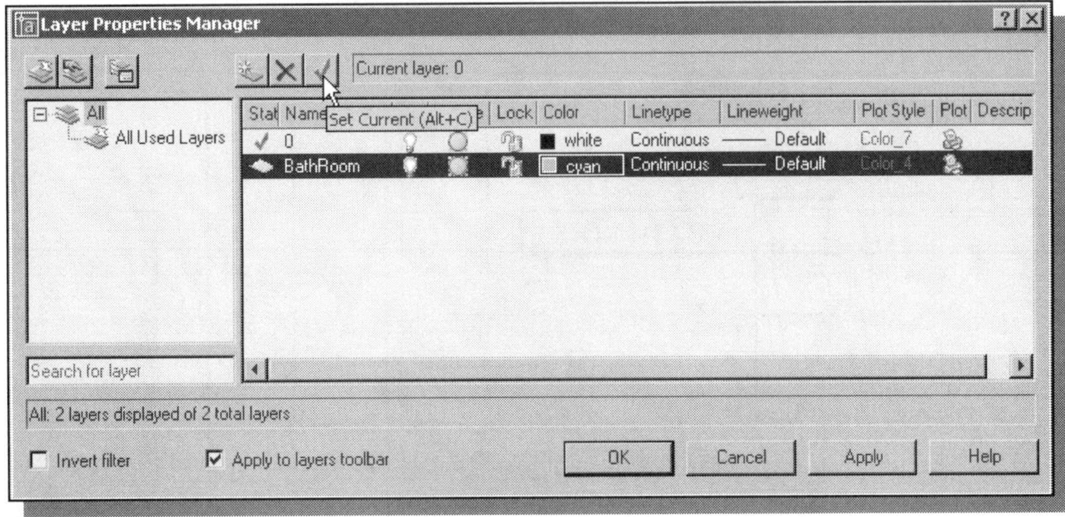

8. Click on the **OK** button to accept the settings and exit the *Layer Properties Manager* dialog box.

❖ The *Object Properties* toolbar near the top of the AutoCAD screen shows the status of object properties. There are two strategies for assigning *colors, linetypes*, and *lineweights* in AutoCAD. The two methods are (a) assign to individual objects, or (b) assign ***ByLayer*** properties. Using the *ByLayer* method is the preferred method, since it allows us to modify all related objects quickly and easily.

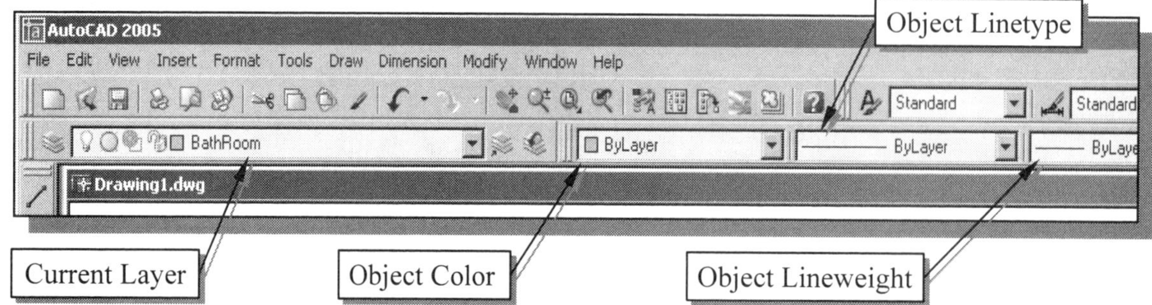

Using *Zoom Realtime*

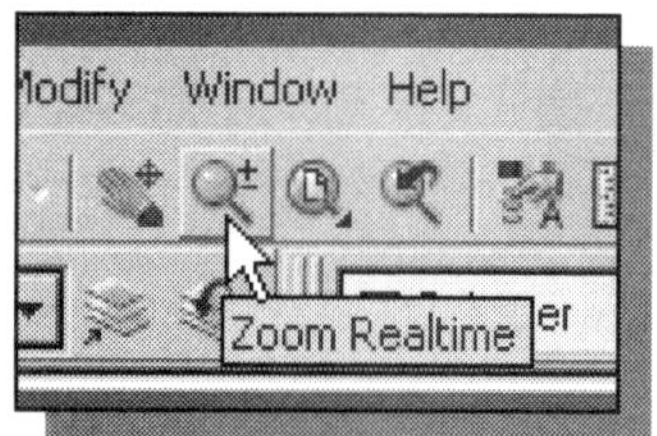

1. Click on the **Zoom Realtime** icon in the *Standard* toolbar area.

2. Move the cursor near the center of the graphics window.

3. Inside the graphics window, **push and hold down the left-mouse-button**, then move upward to enlarge the current display scale factor. (Press the **[Esc]** key to exit the Zoom command.)

4. Use the **Pan Realtime** option to reposition the display so that we can work on the bathroom of the floor plan.

Modeling the bathroom

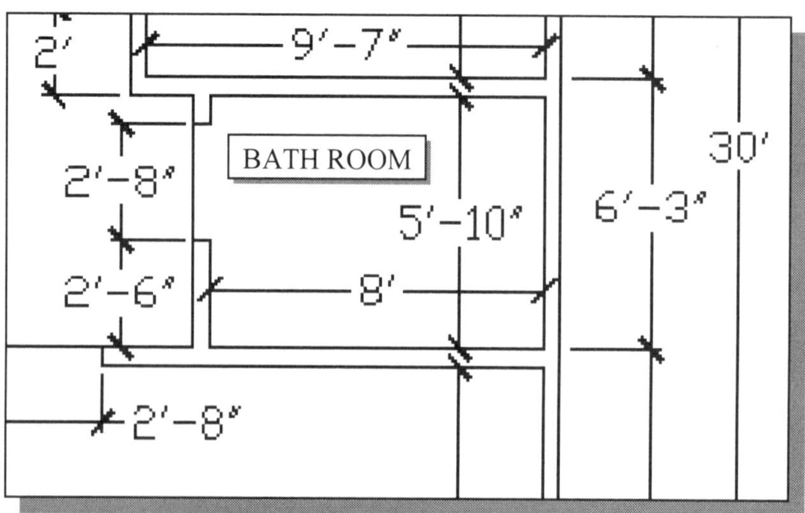

1. In the *Status Bar* area, reset the option buttons so that only the *MODEL* button is switched ***ON***.

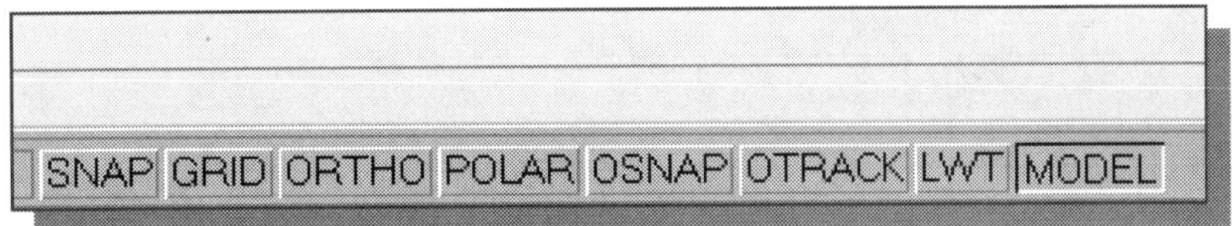

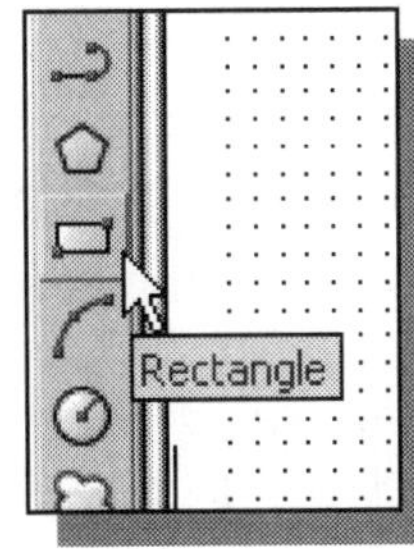

2. Click on the **Rectangle** command icon in the *Draw* toolbar. In the command prompt area, the message "*Specify first corner point:*" is displayed.

3. In the *Object Snap* toolbar, pick **Snap to Endpoint**. In the command prompt area, the message "*_endp of*" is displayed. AutoCAD now expects us to select a geometric entity on the screen.

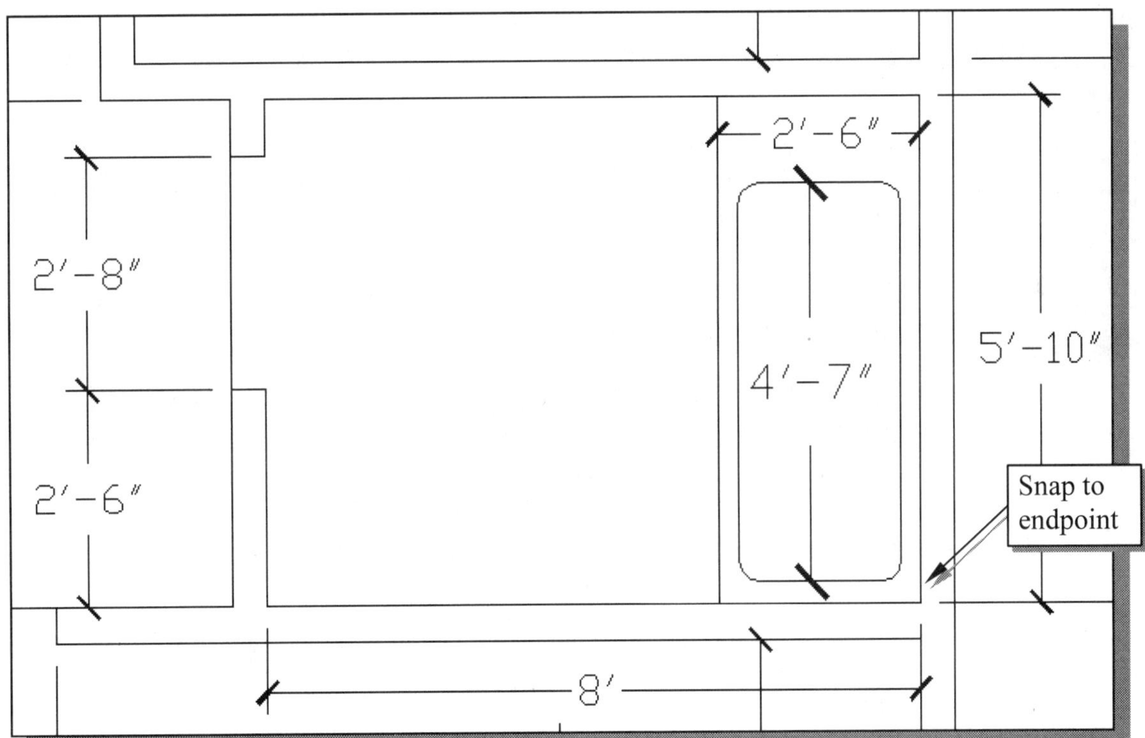

4. Use the *relative coordinate entry method* and create the outer rectangle of the tub (2′-6″ × 5′-10″.)

5. Complete the inner shape by creating a rectangle with a distance of 3″ from the outer rectangle and rounded corners of 3″ radius.

6. Create two rectangles (*10″ × 20″* and *20″ × 30″*) with rounded corners (radius **3**″) and position them as shown.

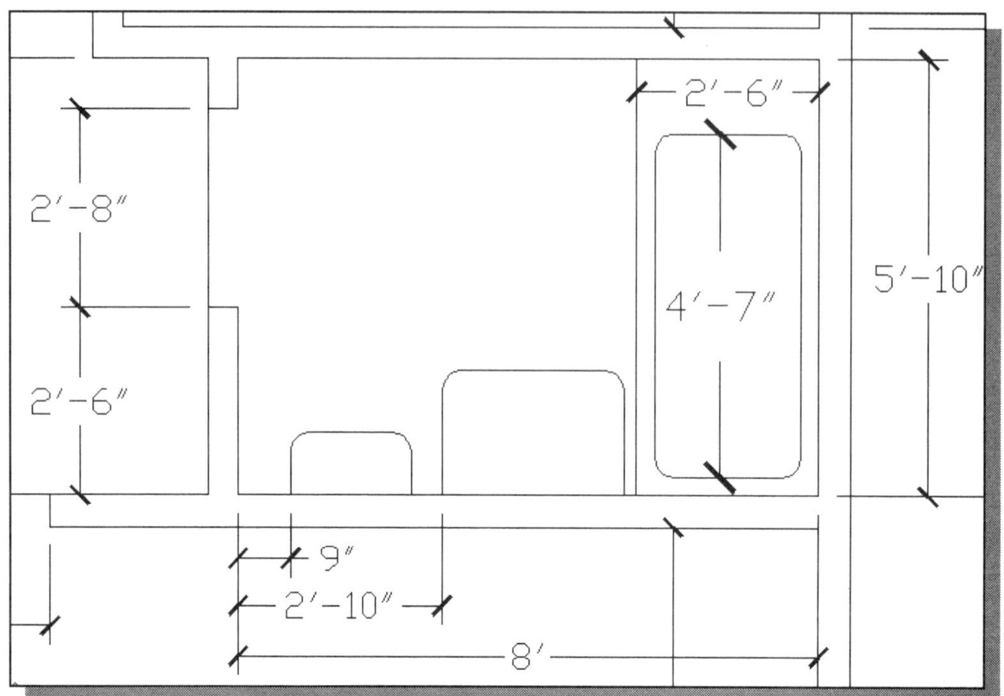

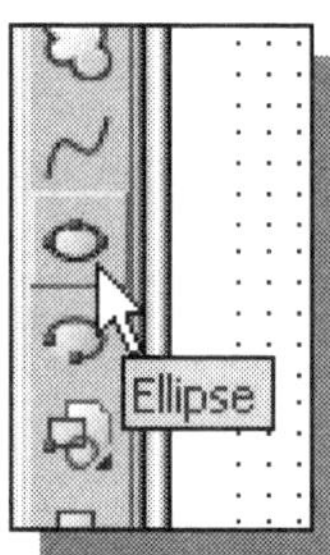

7. Select the **Ellipse** command icon in the *Draw* toolbar. In the command prompt area, the message "*Specify axis endpoint of ellipse or [Arc/Center]:*" is displayed.

8. In the *Object Snap* toolbar, pick **Snap to Midpoint**. In the command prompt area, the message "*_mid of*" is displayed.

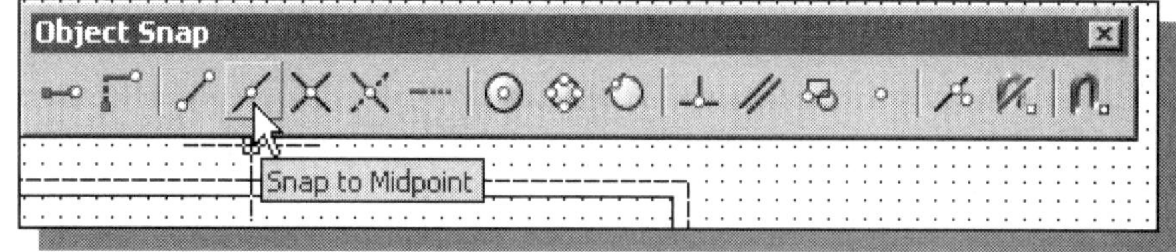

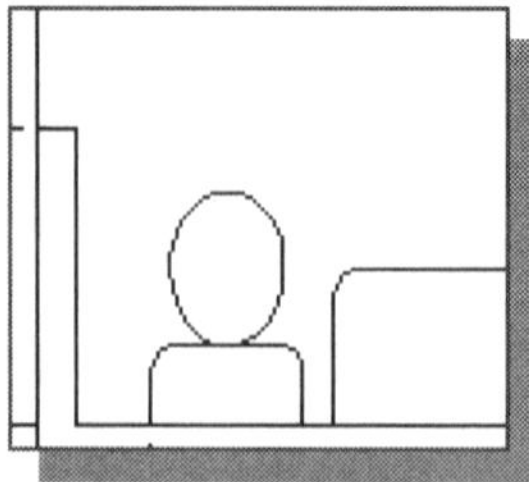

9. Pick the top horizontal line of the small rectangle we just created.

10. For the second point location, enter ***@0,20″*** **[ENTER]**.

11. For the third point, enter ***@7.5″,0*** **[ENTER]**.

❖ An ellipse has a major axis, the longest distance between two points on the ellipse, and a minor axis, the shorter distance across the ellipse. The three points we specified identify the two axes.

Controlling *Layer Visibility*

AutoCAD does not display or plot the objects that are on invisible layers. To make layers invisible, we can ***freeze*** or ***turn off*** those layers. Turning off layers only temporarily removes the objects from the screen; the objects remain active in the CAD database. Freezing layers will make the objects invisible and also disable the objects in the CAD database. Freezing layers will improve object selection performance and reduce regeneration time for complex designs. When we ***thaw*** a frozen layer, AutoCAD updates the CAD database with the screen coordinates for all objects in the design.

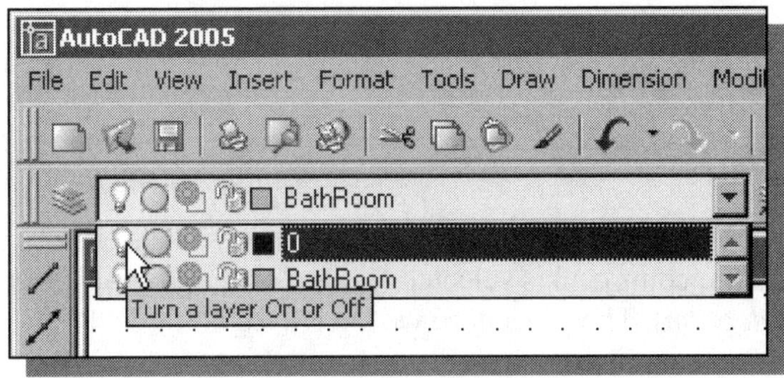

1. On the *Object Properties* toolbar, choose the ***Layer Control*** box with the left-mouse-button.

2. Move the cursor over the **light-bulb** icon for *layer 0.* The tool tip "*Turn a layer On or Off*" appears.

3. **Left-mouse-click once** and notice the icon color is changed to a dark color, representing the layer (*layer 0*) is turned *OFF.*

4. Move the cursor into the graphics window and **left-mouse-click once** to accept the layer control settings.

➢ On your own, practice turning on *layer 0* and freezing/thawing *layer 0.* What would happen if we turn off all layers?

Adding a New Layer

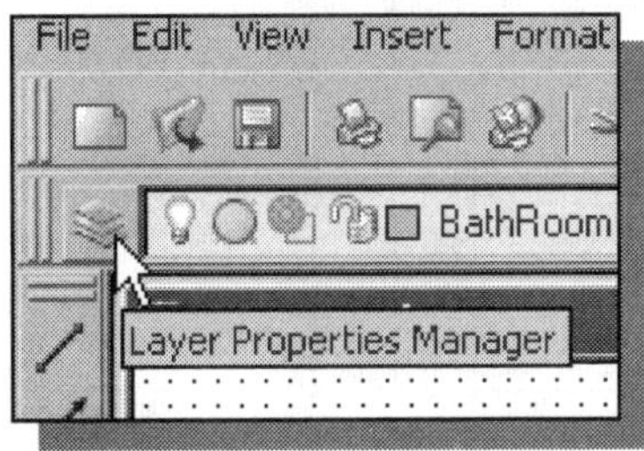

1. Pick **Layer Properties Manager** in the *Object Properties* toolbar. The *Layer Properties Manager* dialog box appears.

2. Create a new layer (layer name: ***Walls***) and change the layer color to **Green**.

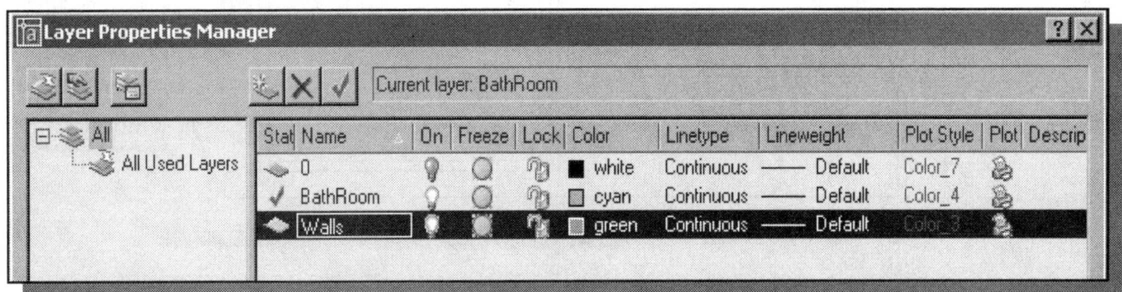

3. Turn ***ON*** the *0* layer, turn ***OFF*** the *BathRoom* layer and set the ***Walls*** layer as the *Current Layer*.

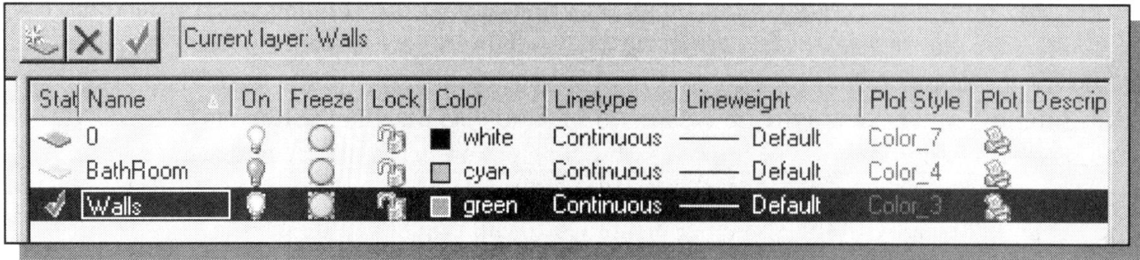

4. Click on the **OK** button to accept the settings.

Moving objects to a different layer

❖ **AutoCAD® 2005** provides a flexible graphical user interface that allows users to select graphical entities BEFORE the command is selected (*pre-selection*), or AFTER the command is selected (*post-selection*). The procedure we have used so far is the *post-selection* option. We can pre-select one or more objects by clicking on the objects at the command prompt (**Command:**). To deselect the selected items, press the **[Esc]** key twice.

1. Inside the graphics window, pre-select all objects by enclosing all objects inside a **selection window** as shown.

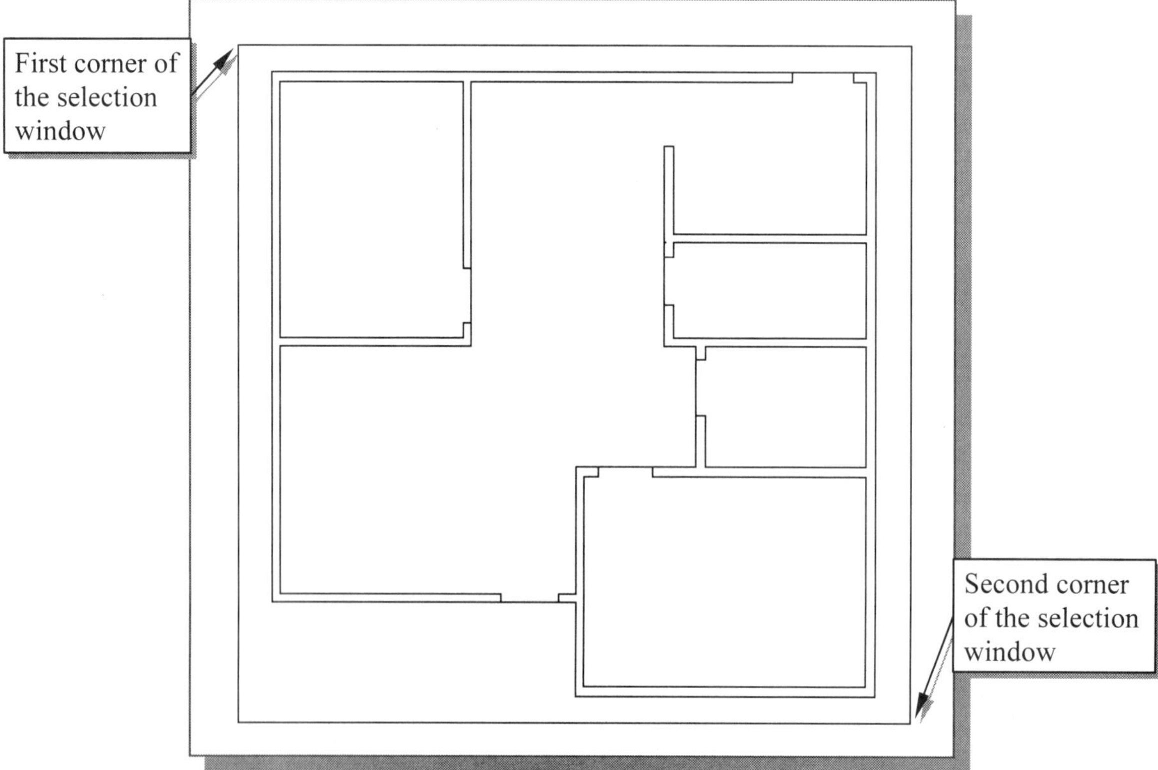

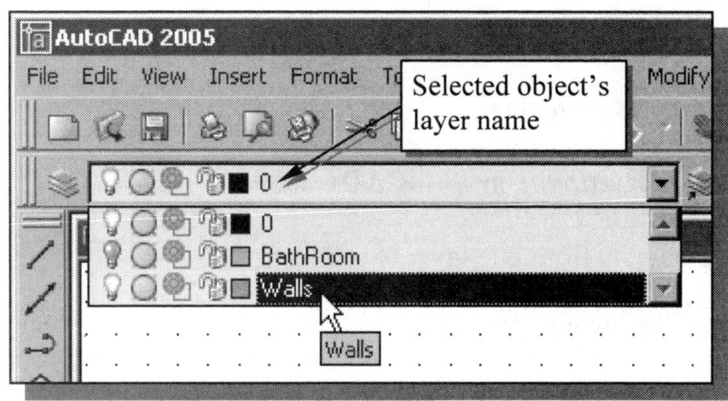

2. On the *Object Properties* toolbar, choose the ***Layer Control*** box with the left-mouse-button.

❖ Notice the layer name displayed in the *Layer Control* box is the selected object's assigned layer and layer properties.

3. In the *Layer Control* box, click on the ***Walls*** layer name.

4. Make *Walls* invisible by turning the layer ***OFF***.

➢ On your own, complete the floor plan by creating the 4′ and 5′ windows in a new layer *Windows*. The dimensions are as shown in the figure below.

Questions:

1. Describe some of the advantages of using *layers*.

2. List two methods to control the *layer visibility* in **AutoCAD® 2005**.

3. Describe the procedure to move objects from one layer to another.

4. When and why would you use the Multiline command?

5. Identify the following commands:

(a)

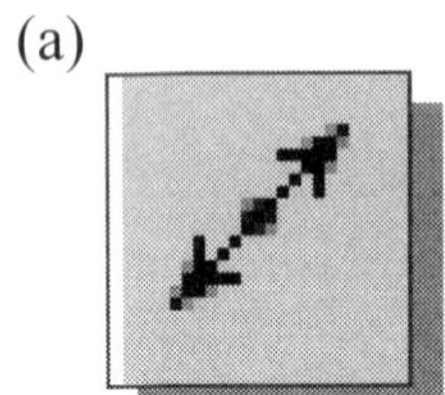

(b)

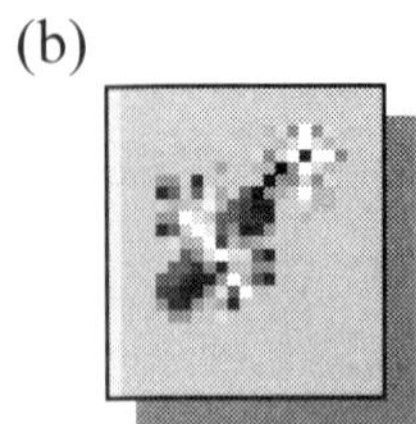

(c)

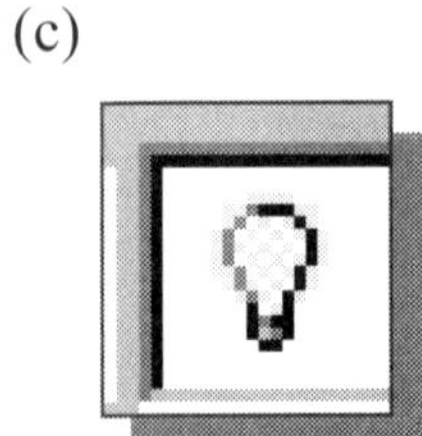

(d)

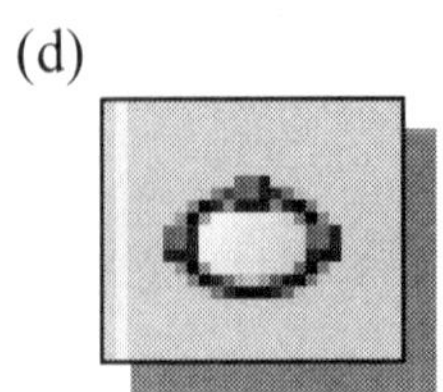

Exercises:

1. Wall thickness: 5 inch

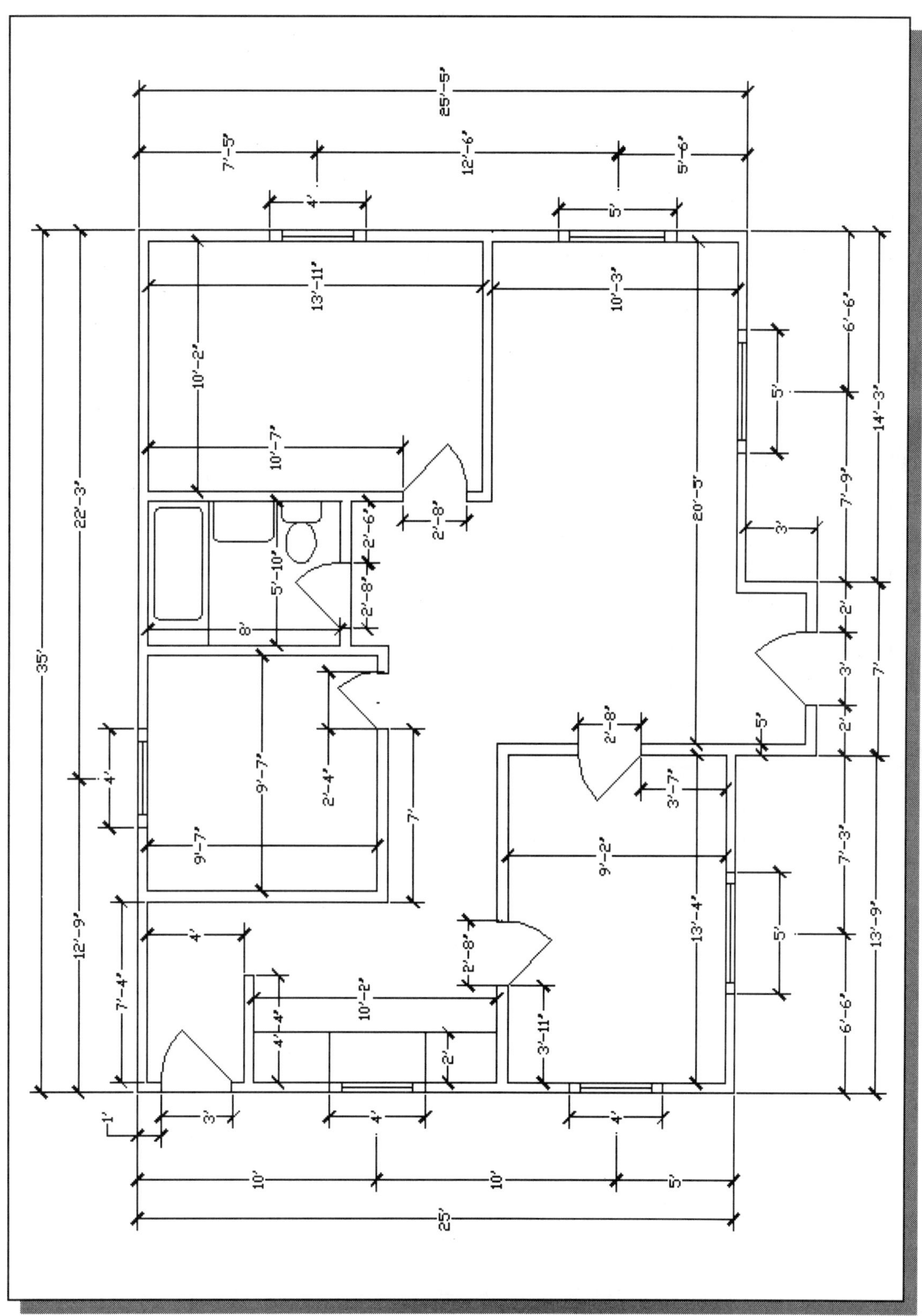

2. Wall thickness: 5 inch

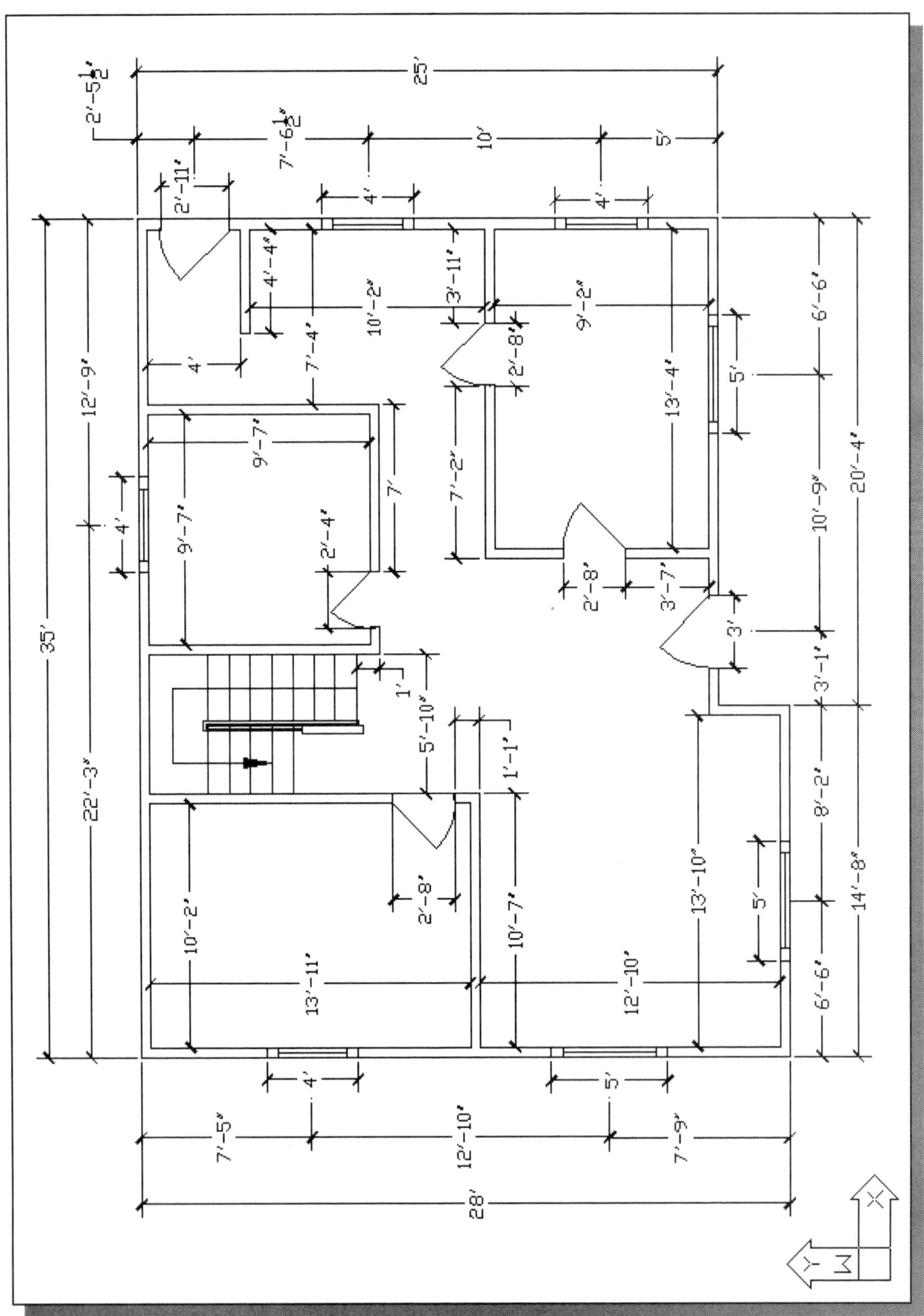

Chapter 5
Orthographic Views in Multiview Drawings

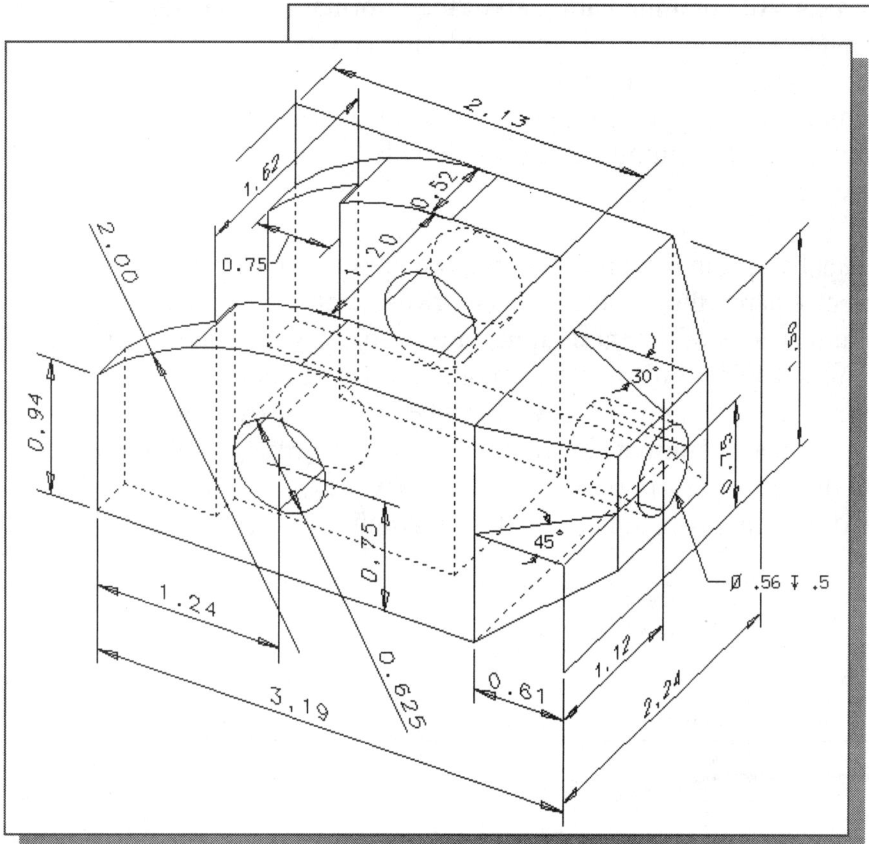

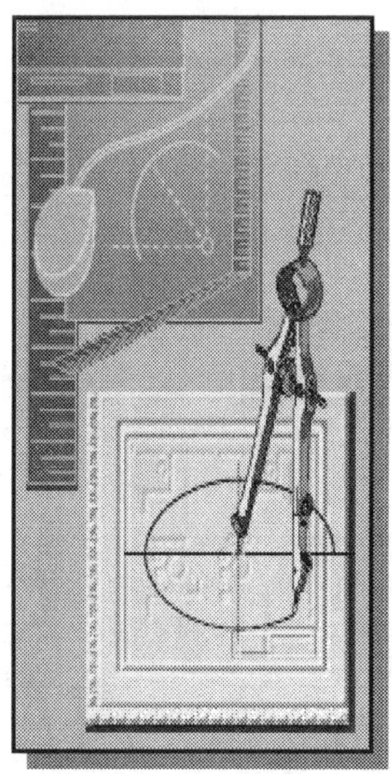

Learning Objectives

- Create 2D orthographic views using AutoCAD.
- Using the CONSTRUCTION LINE command to draw.
- Using Running Object Snaps.
- Use AutoCAD's *AutoSnap* and *AutoTrack* features.
- Create a Miter line to transfer dimensions.
- Using Projection lines between orthographic views.
- Use the POLAR Tracking option.

Introduction

Most drawings produced and used in industry are ***multiview drawings***. Multiview drawings are used to provide accurate three-dimensional object information on two-dimensional media, a means of communicating all of the information necessary to transform an idea or concept into reality. The standards and conventions of multiview drawings have been developed over many years, which equip us with a universally understood method of communication. The age of computers has greatly altered the design process, and several CAD methods are now available to help generate multiview drawings using CAD systems.

Multiview drawings usually require several orthographic views to define the shape of a three-dimensional object. Each orthographic view is a two-dimensional drawing showing only two of the three dimensions of the three-dimensional object. Consequently, no individual view contains sufficient information to completely define the shape of the three-dimensional object. All orthographic views must be looked at together to comprehend the shape of the three-dimensional object. The arrangement and relationship between the views are therefore very important in multiview drawings. In this chapter, the common methods of creating two-dimensional orthographic views with AutoCAD are examined.

The *Locator* Design

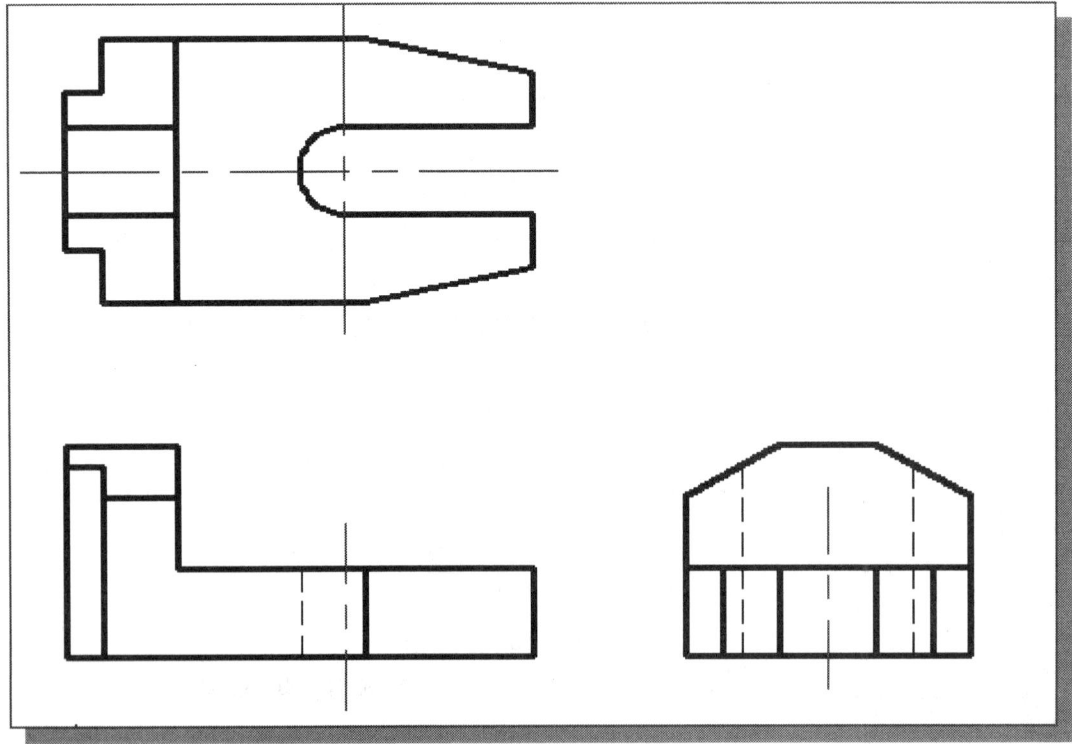

The *Locator* part

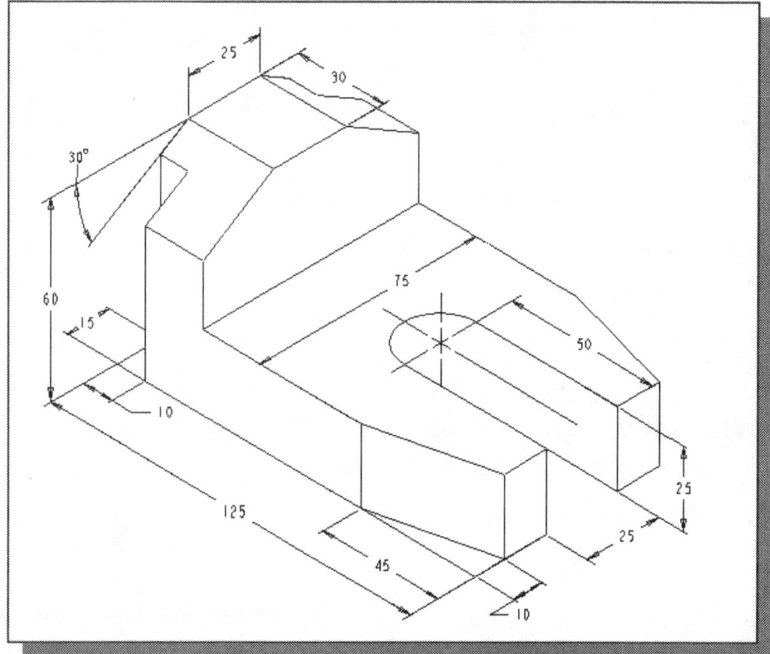

➢ Before going through the tutorial, make a rough sketch of a multiview drawing of the part. How many 2D views will be necessary to fully describe the part? Based on your knowledge of **AutoCAD® 2005** so far, how would you arrange and construct these 2D views? Take a few minutes to consider these questions and do preliminary planning by sketching on a piece of paper. You are also encouraged to construct the orthographic views on your own prior to following through the tutorial.

Starting Up AutoCAD® 2005

1. Select the **AutoCAD 2005** option on the *Program* menu or select the **AutoCAD 2005** icon on the *Desktop*.

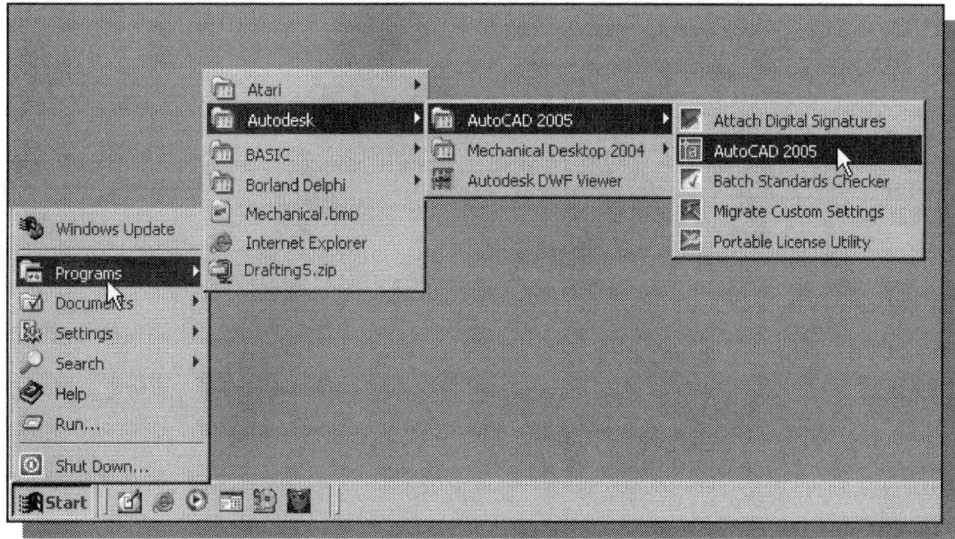

2. In the *Startup* dialog box, select the ***Start from Scratch*** option with a single click of the left-mouse-button.

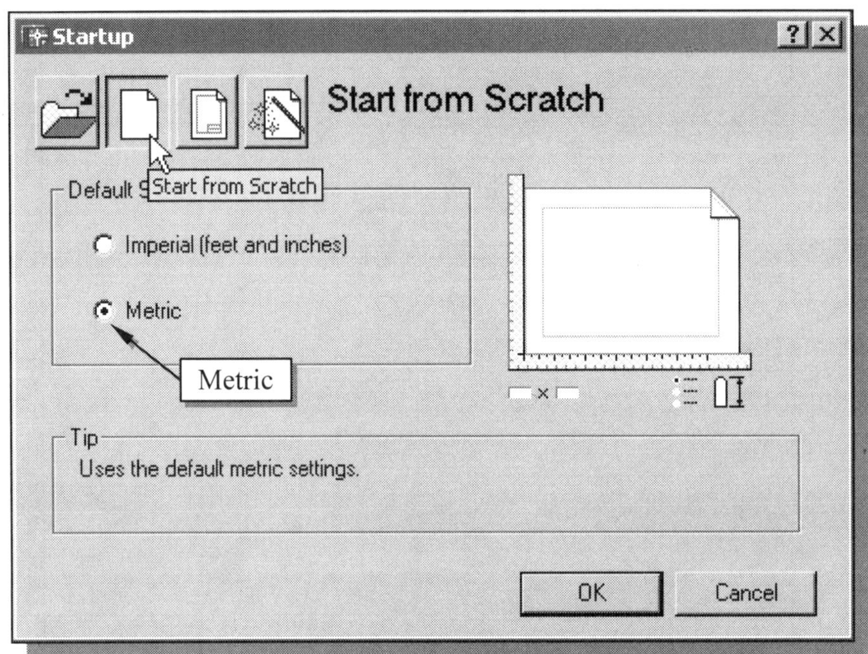

3. In the *Default Settings* section, pick **Metric** as the drawing units.

4. Click **OK** to accept the settings and exit the *Startup* window.

GRID and *SNAP* Intervals Setup

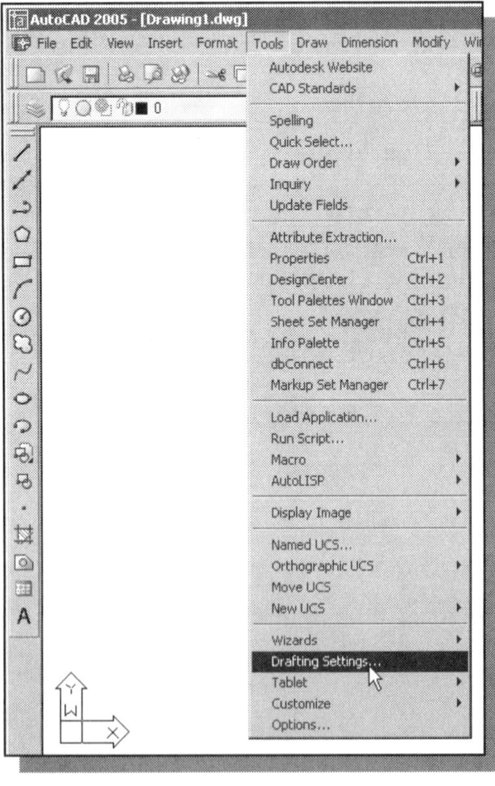

1. In the pull-down menus, select:

   [Tools] → [Drafting Settings]

2. In the *Drafting Settings* dialog box, select the **SNAP and GRID** tab if it is not the page on top.

3. Change *Grid Spacing* to ***10*** for both X and Y directions.

4. Also adjust the *Snap Spacing* to ***10*** for both X and Y directions.

5. Pick **OK** to exit the *Drafting Settings* dialog box.

Layers setup

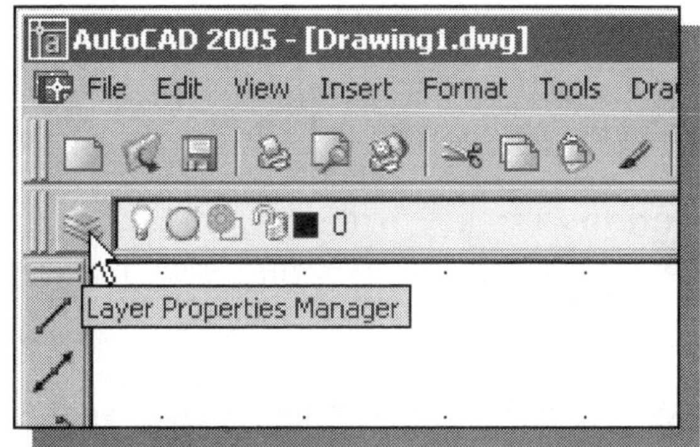

1. Pick **Layer Properties Manager** in the *Object Properties* toolbar.

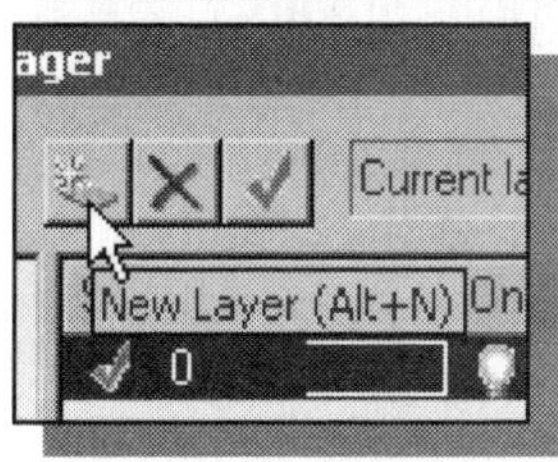

2. Click on the **New** icon to create new layers.

3. Create two **new** layers with the following settings:

Layer	***Color***	***LineType***
Construction	**White**	**Continuous**
Object	**Yellow**	**Continuous**

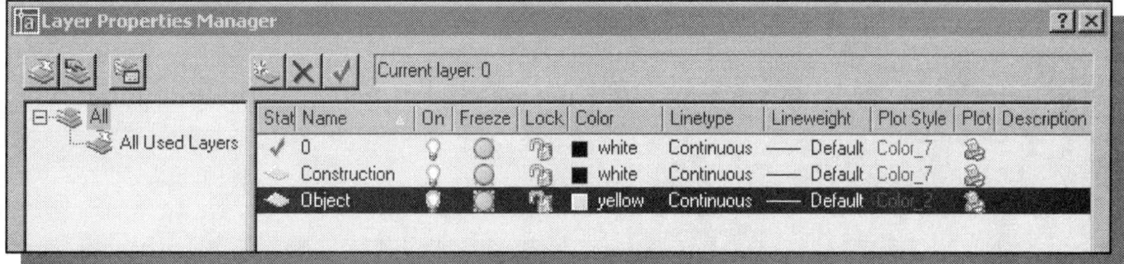

4. Highlight the layer ***Construction*** in the list of layers.

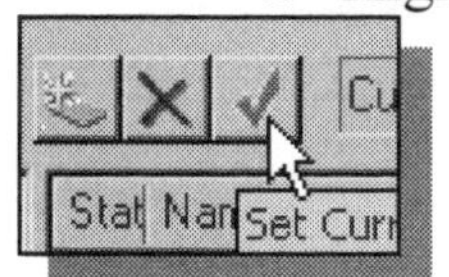

5. Click on the **Current** button to set layer ***Construction*** as the *Current Layer*.

6. Click on the **OK** button to accept the settings and exit the *Layer Properties Manager* dialog box.

7. In the *Status Bar* area, reset the option buttons so that only *SNAP, GRID*, and *MODEL* are switched ***ON***.

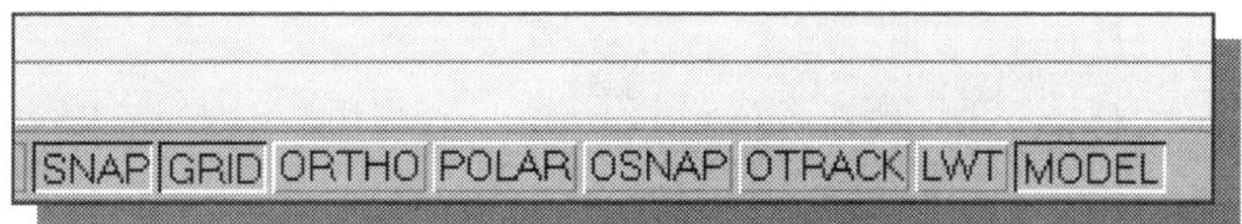

Drawing *Construction Lines*

❖ Construction lines are lines that extend to infinity. Construction lines are usually used as references for creating other objects. We will also place the construction lines on the *Construction* layer so that the layer can later be frozen or turned off.

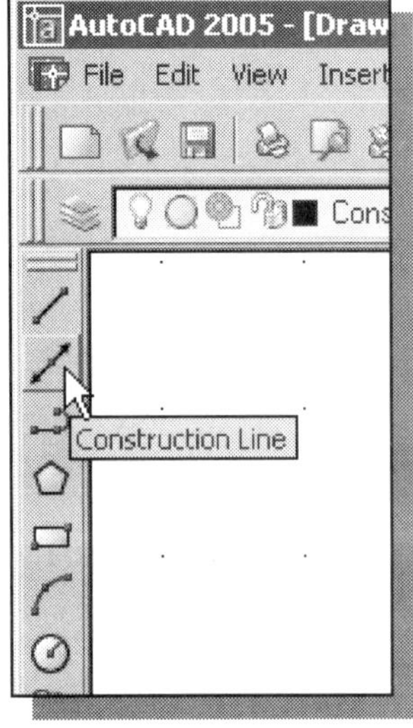

1. Select the **Construction Line** icon in the *Draw* toolbar. In the command prompt area, the message "*_xline Specify a point or [Hor/Ver/Ang/Bisect/Offset]:*" is displayed.

   - To orient construction lines, we generally specify two points. Note that other orientation options are also available.

2. Select a location near the lower left corner of the graphics window. It is not necessary to align objects to the world coordinate origin. CAD systems provide us with many powerful tools to manipulate geometry. Our main goal is to use the CAD system as a flexible and powerful tool, and to be very efficient and effective with the systems.

3. Pick a location above the last point to create a **vertical line**.

4. Move the cursor toward the right of the first point and pick a location to create a **horizontal line**.

5. Inside the graphics window, **right-mouse-click** to end the Construction Line command.

6. In the *Status Bar* area, turn ***OFF*** the *SNAP* option.

Using the *Offset* command

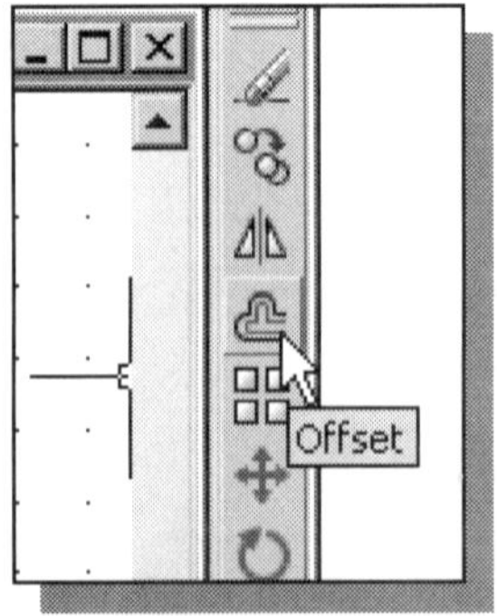

1. Select the **Offset** icon in the *Modify* toolbar. In the command prompt area, the message "*Specify offset distance or [Through]:*" is displayed.

2. In the command prompt area, enter: ***125*** **[ENTER]**.

3. In the command prompt area, the message "*Select object to offset or <exit>:*" is displayed. Pick the **vertical line** on the screen.

4. AutoCAD next asks us to identify the direction of the offset. Pick a location that is to the **right** of the vertical line.

5. Inside the graphics window, **right-mouse-click** to end the Offset command.

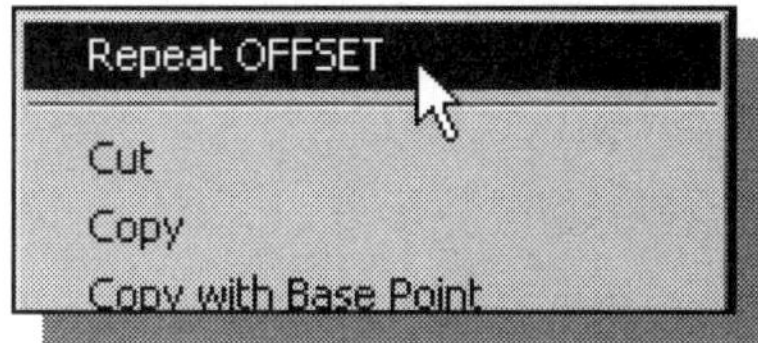

6. Hit the [**SPACE BAR**], or right-mouse-click inside the graphics window and select **Repeat Offset** in the popup list, to repeat the Offset command.

7. In the command prompt area, enter: ***60*** [**ENTER**].

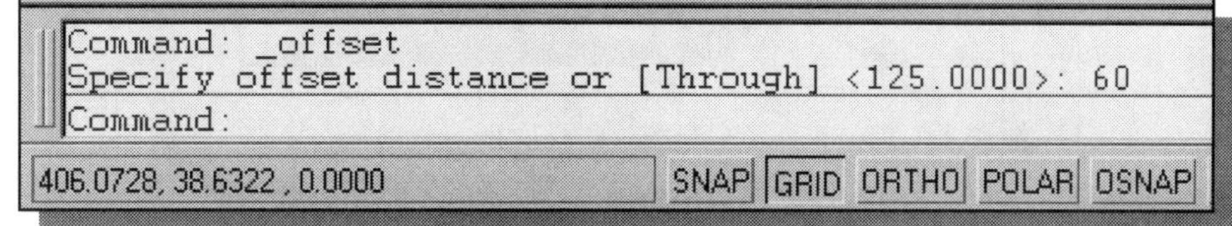

8. In the command prompt area, the message "*Select object to offset or <exit>:*" is displayed. Pick the **horizontal line** on the screen.

9. AutoCAD next asks us to identify the direction of the offset. Pick a location that is **above** the horizontal line.

10. Inside the graphics window, **right-mouse-click** to end the Offset command.

11. Repeat the **Offset** command and create the offset lines as shown.

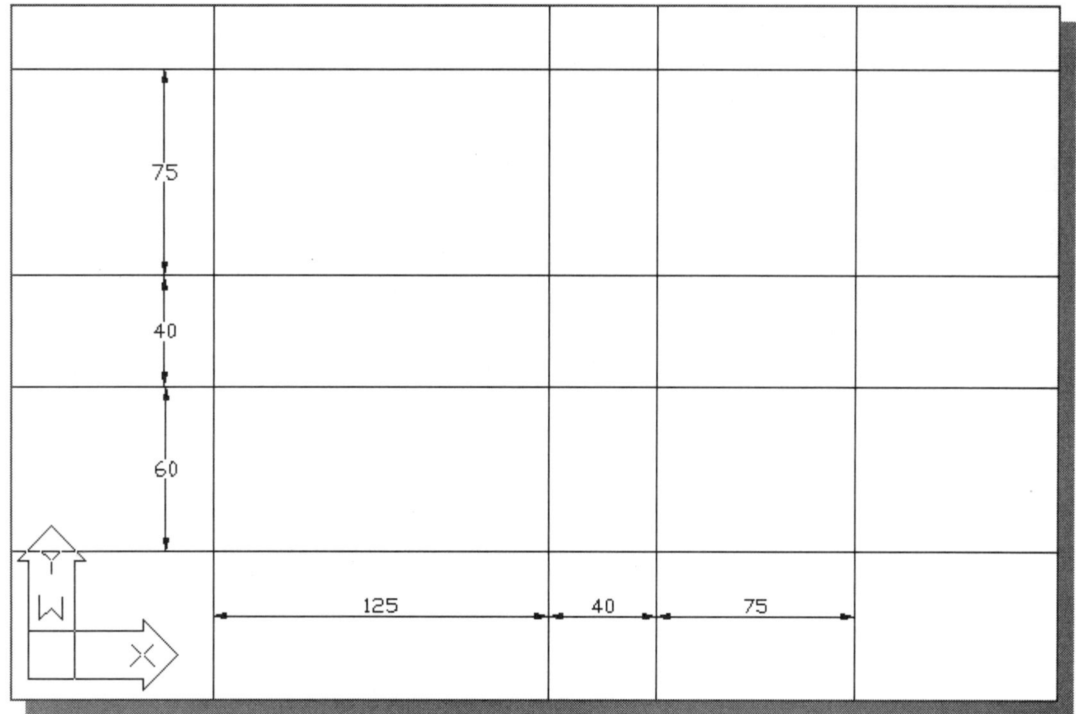

Set layer *Object* as the current layer

1. On the *Object Properties* toolbar, choose the ***Layer Control*** box with the left-mouse-button.

2. Move the cursor over the name of the layer ***Object***. The tool tip "*Object*" appears.

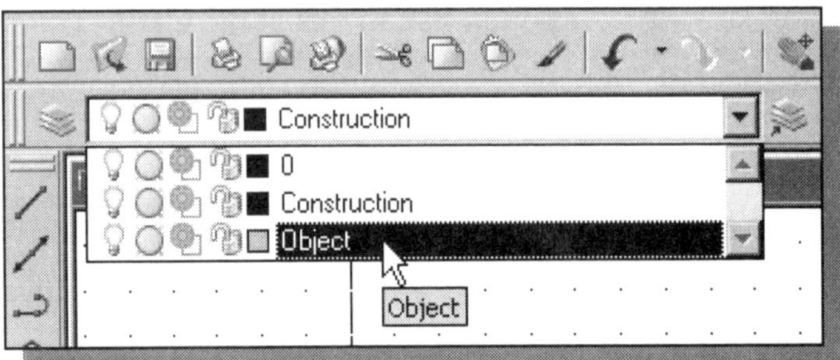

3. **Left-mouse-click once** and the layer *Object* is set as the *Current Layer*.

Using the *Running Object Snaps*

In **AutoCAD® 2005**, while using geometry construction commands, the cursor can be placed to points on objects such as endpoints, midpoints, centers, and intersections. In AutoCAD, this tool is called the ***Object Snap***.

Object snaps can be turned on in one of two ways:

- **Single Point (or override) Object Snaps**: Sets an object snap for one use.
- **Running Object Snaps**: Sets object snaps *active* until we turn them off.

The procedure we have used so far is the *Single Point Object Snaps* option, where we select the specific object snap from the *Object Snap* toolbar for one use only. The use of the *Running Object Snaps* option to assist the construction is illustrated next.

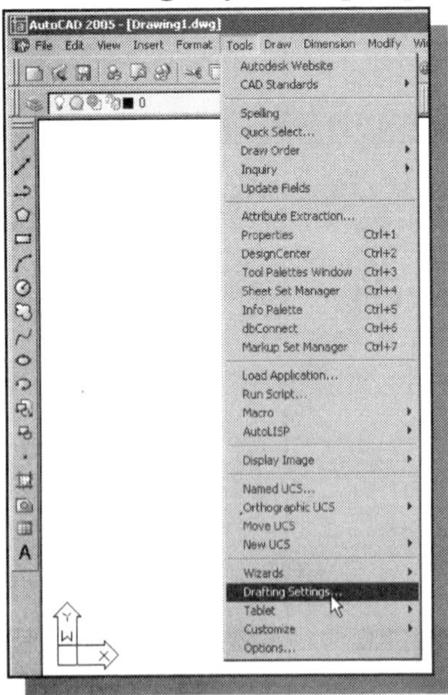

1. In the pull-down menus, select:

   [Tools] → [Drafting Settings]

2. In the *Drafting Settings* dialog box select the **Object Snap** tab.

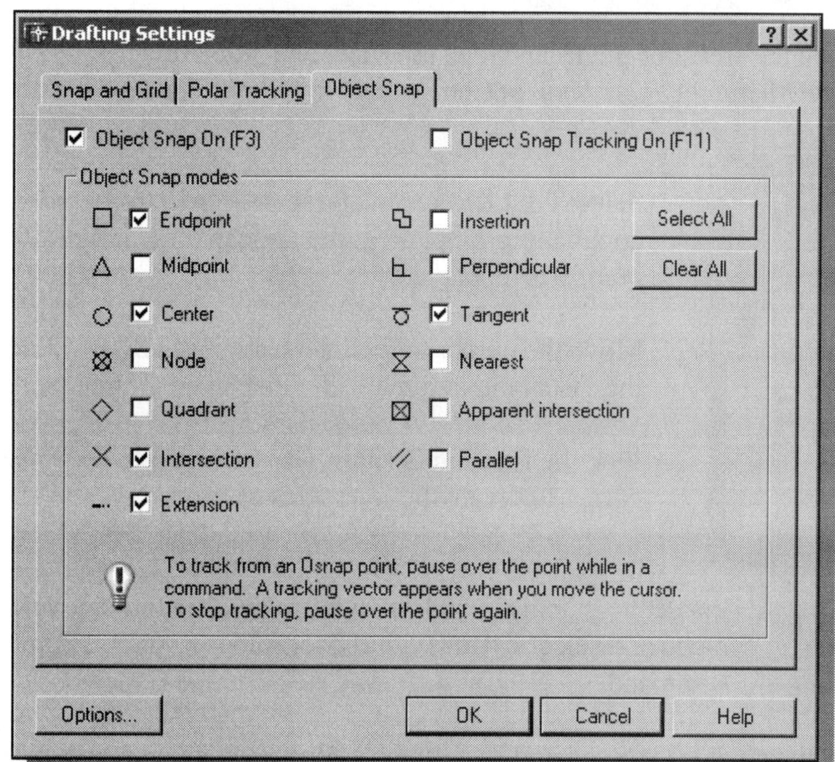

The *Running Object Snap* options can be turned on or off by clicking the different options listed. Notice the different symbols for the different *Object Snap* options.

3. Turn ***ON*** the *Running Object Snap* by clicking the **Object Snap On** box, or hit the **[F3]** key once.

4. Confirm the ***Intersection, Endpoint*** and ***Extension*** options are switched ***ON*** and click on the **OK** button to accept the settings and exit from the *Drafting Settings* dialog box.

❖ Notice in the *Status Bar* area the ***OSNAP*** button is switched ***ON***. We can toggle the *Running Object Snap* option on or off by clicking the *OSNAP* button.

5. Press the **[F3]** key once and notice the *OSNAP* button is switched ***OFF*** in the *Status Bar* area.

6. Press the **[F3]** key again and notice the *OSNAP* button is now switched ***ON*** in the *Status Bar* area.

➢ **AutoCAD® 2005** provides many input methods and shortcuts; you are encouraged to examine the different options and choose the option that best fits your own style.

Creating *Object Lines*

We will define the areas for the front-view, top-view and side-view by adding object lines using the *Running Object Snap* option.

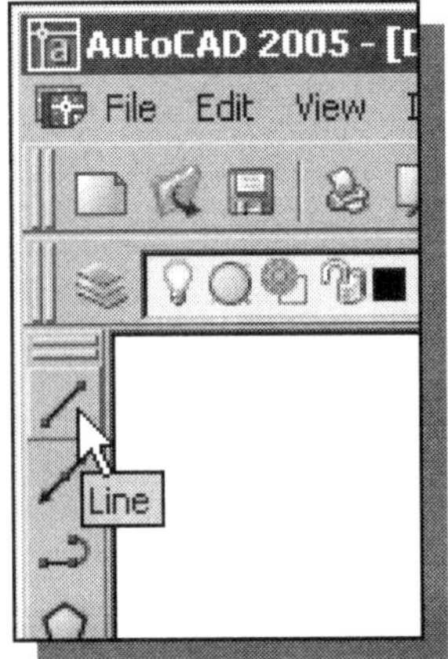

1. Select the **Line** command icon in the *Draw* toolbar. In the command prompt area, the message "*_line Specify first point:*" is displayed.

2. Move the cursor to the intersection of any two lines and notice the visual aid automatically displayed at the intersection.

3. Pick the four intersection points closest to the lower left corner to create the four sides of the area of the front view.

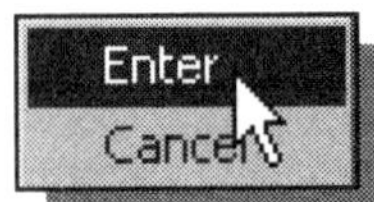

4. Inside the graphics window, right-mouse-click to activate the option menu and select **Enter** with the left-mouse-button to end the Line command.

5. Repeat the Line command to define the top view and side view as shown.

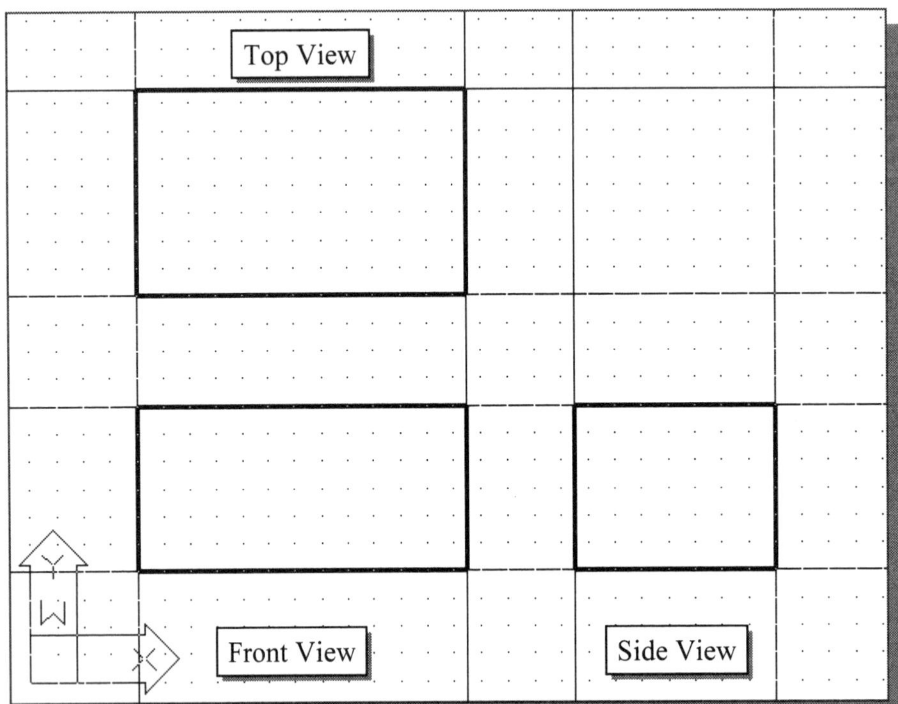

Turn *OFF* the Construction Lines layer

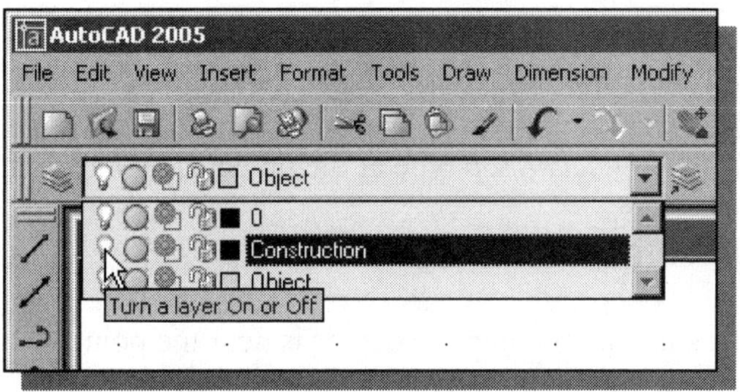

1. On the *Object Properties* toolbar, choose the ***Layer Control*** box with the left-mouse-button.

2. Move the cursor over the light-bulb icon for layer ***Construction***. The tool tip "*Turn a layer On or Off*" appears.

3. **Left-mouse-click once** and notice the icon color is changed to gray, representing the layer (layer *Construction*) is turned *OFF*.

Adding more objects in the Front View

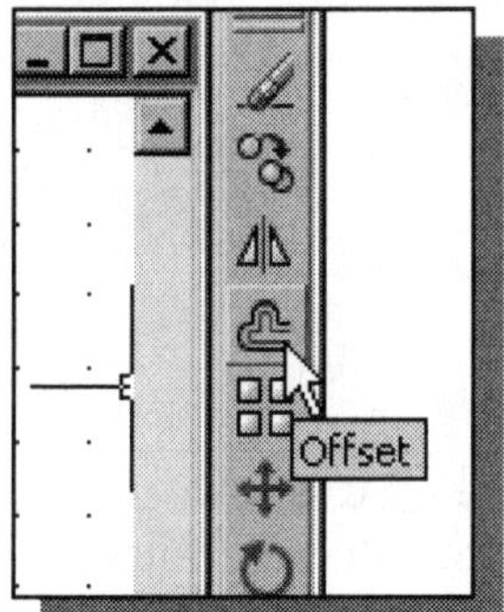

1. Use the **Offset** command and create the two parallel lines in the front view as shown.

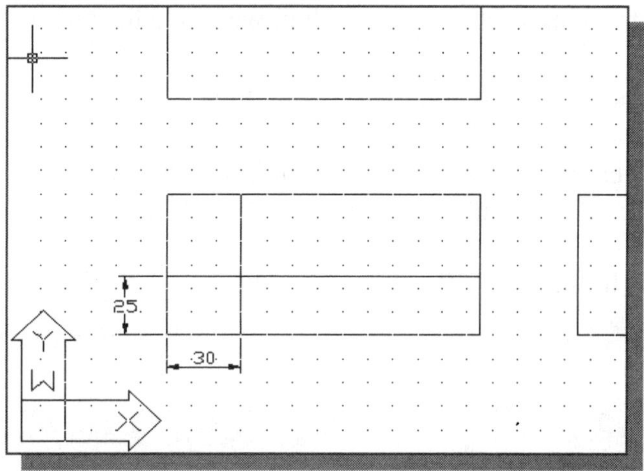

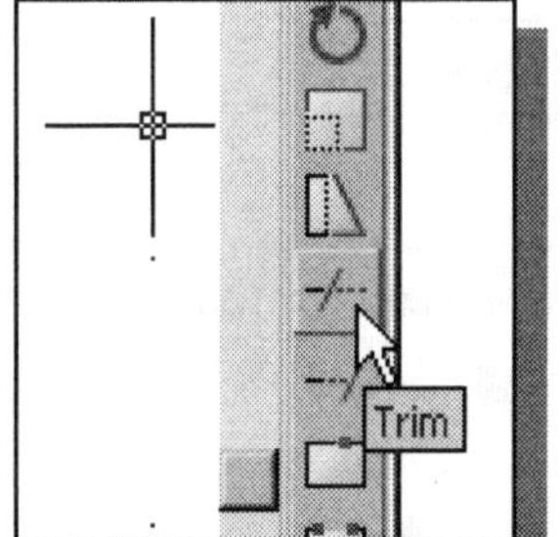

2. Use the **Trim** command and modify the front view as shown.

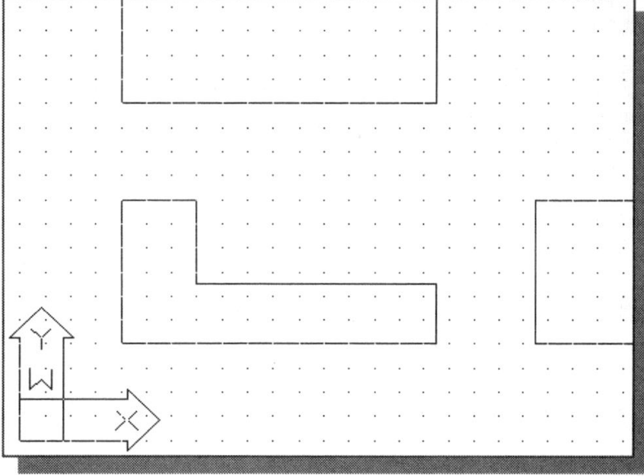

AutoCAD's *AutoSnap*™ and *AutoTrack*™ features

AutoCAD's *AutoSnap* and *AutoTrack* provide visual aids when the *Object Snap* options are switched *on*. The main advantages of *AutoSnap* and *AutoTrack* are as follows:

- **Symbols**: Automatically displays the *Object Snap* type at the object snap location.
- **Tooltips**: Automatically displays the *Object Snap* type below the cursor.
- **Magnet**: Locks the cursor onto a snap point when the cursor is near the point.

With ***Object Snap Tracking***, the cursor can track along alignment paths based on other object snap points when specifying points in a command. To use *Object Snap Tracking*, one or more object snaps must be switched on. The basic rules of using the ***Object Snap Tracking*** option are as follows:

- To track from a *Running Object Snap* point, pause over the point while in a command.
- A tracking vector appears when we move the cursor.
- To stop tracking, pause over the point again.
- When multiple *Running Object Snaps* are on, press the **[TAB]** key to cycle through available snap points when the object snap aperture box is on an object.

1. In the *Status Bar* area, turn *ON* the *OTRACK* option.

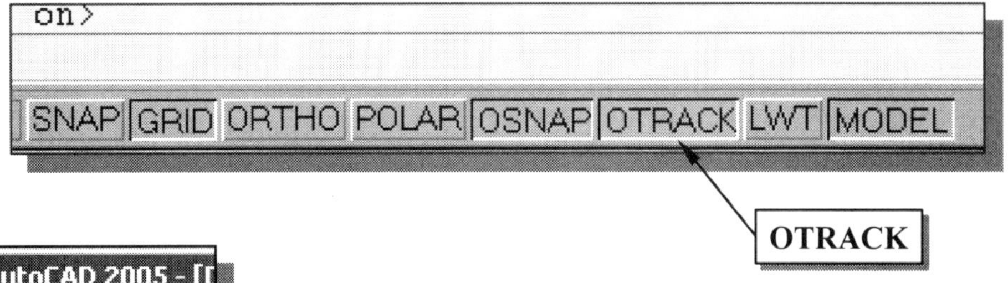

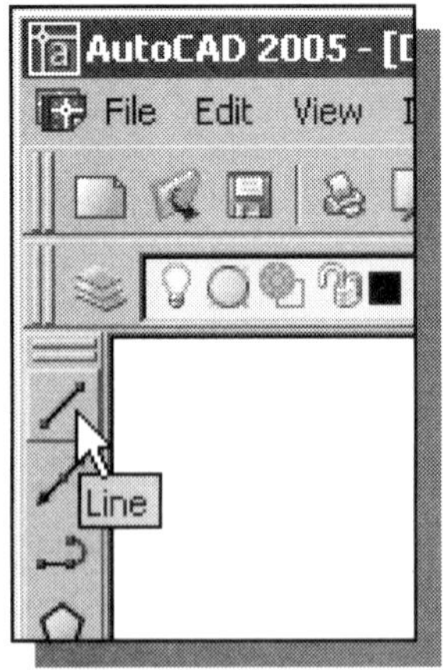

2. Select the **Line** command icon in the *Draw* toolbar. In the command prompt area, the message "*_line Specify first point:*" is displayed.

3. Move the cursor near the top right corner of the vertical protrusion in the front view. Notice that *AutoSnap* automatically locks the cursor to the corner and displays the ***Endpoint*** symbol.

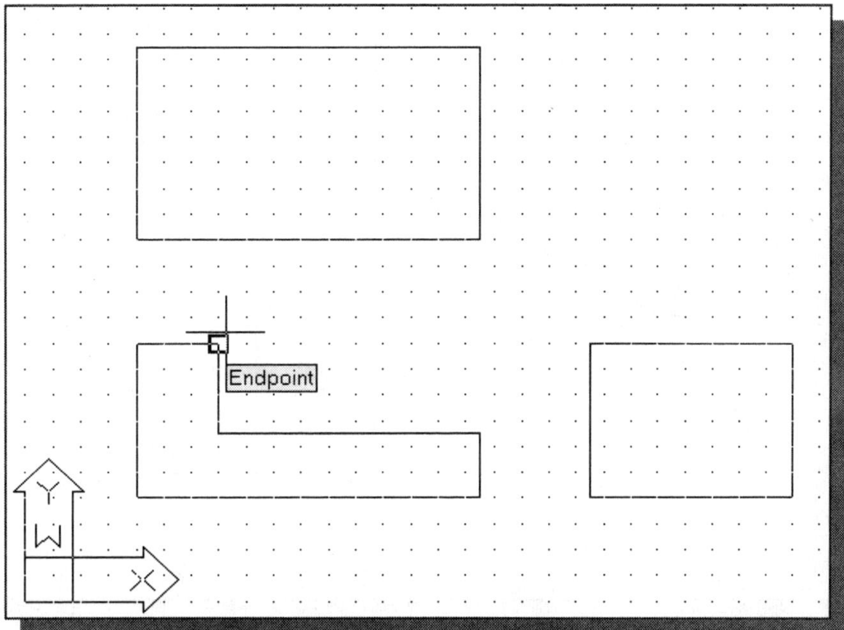

4. Move the cursor upward and notice that *Object Tracking* displays a dashed line, showing the alignment to the top right corner of the vertical protrusion in the front view. Move the cursor near the top horizontal line of the top view and notice that *AutoSnap* displays the intersection point.

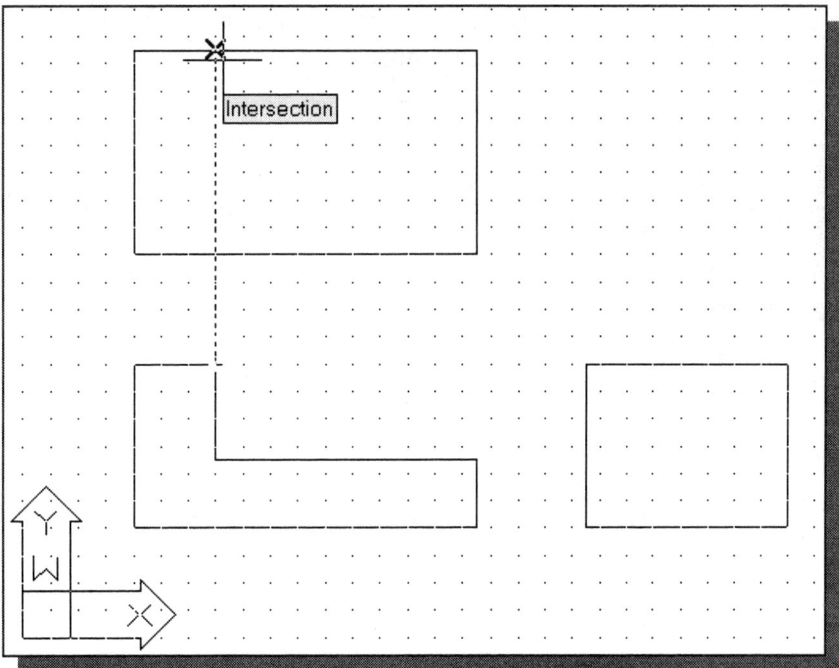

5. Left-mouse-click to place the starting point of a line at the intersection.

6. Move the cursor to the top left corner of the front view to activate the tracking feature.

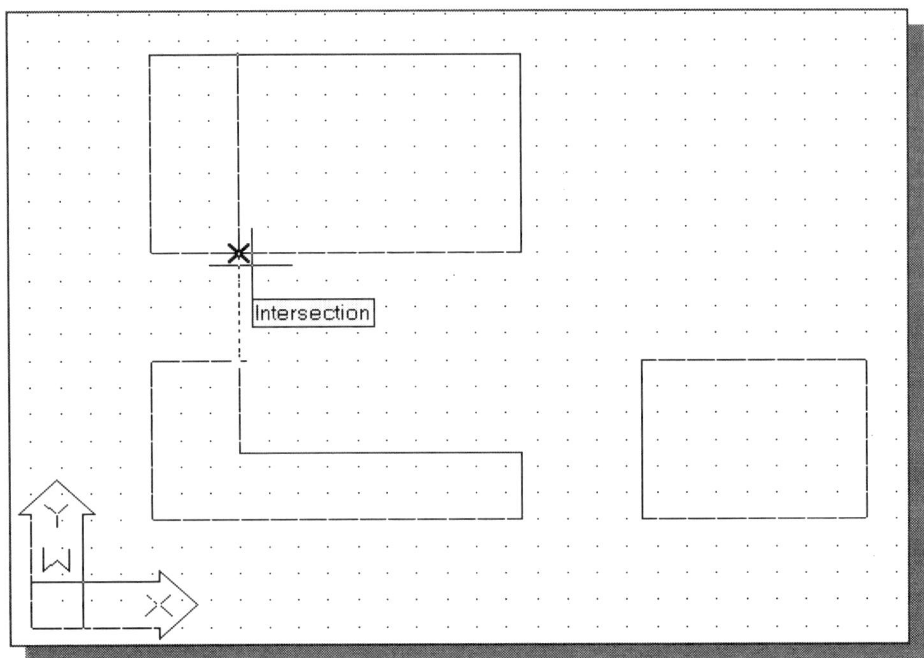

7. Create the line as shown in the above figure.

Adding more objects in the Top View

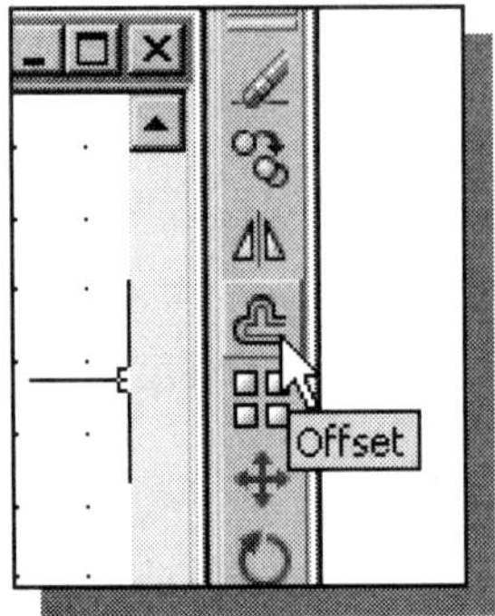

1. Use the **Offset** command and create the two parallel lines in the top view as shown.

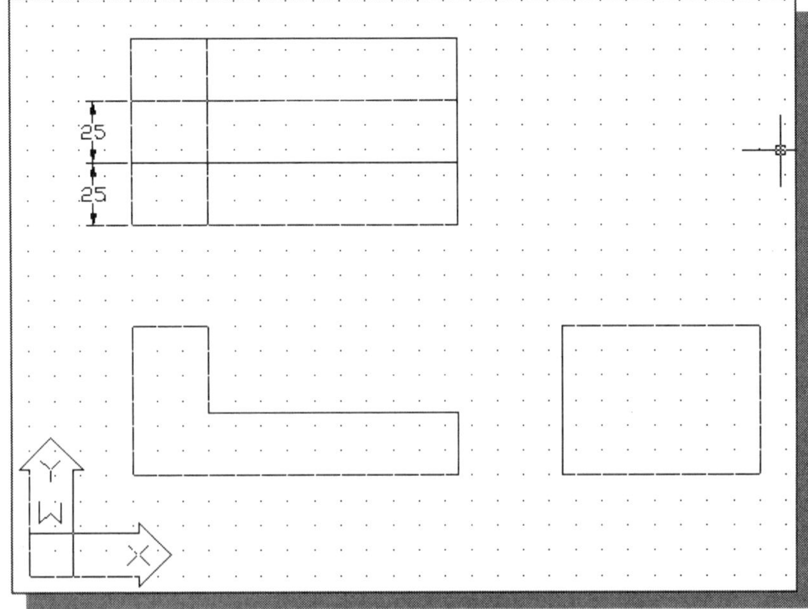

2. Move the cursor to the *Standard* toolbar area and **right-mouse-click** on any icon to display a list of toolbar menu groups.

3. Select **Object Snap**, with the left-mouse-button, to display the *Object Snap* toolbar on the screen.

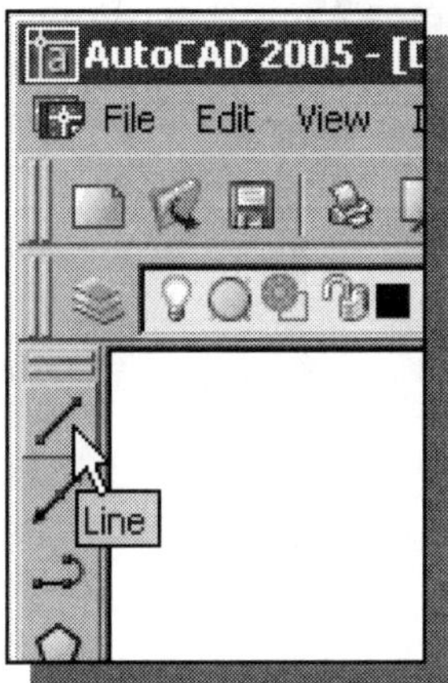

4. Select the **Line** command icon in the *Draw* toolbar. In the command prompt area, the message "*_line Specify first point:*" is displayed.

5. In the *Object Snap* toolbar, pick **Snap From**. In the command prompt area, the message "*_from Base point*" is displayed. AutoCAD now expects us to select a geometric entity on the screen.

➢ The ***Single Point Object Snap*** overrides the ***Running Object Snap*** option.

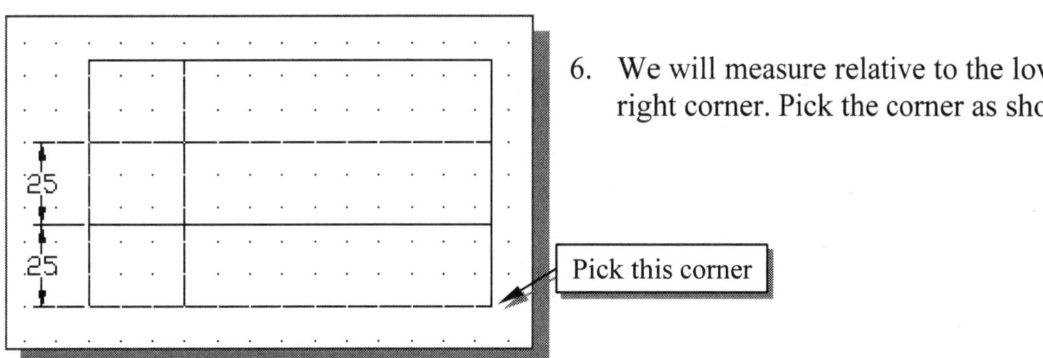

6. We will measure relative to the lower right corner. Pick the corner as shown.

7. In the *command prompt* area, enter ***@0,10*** **[ENTER]**.

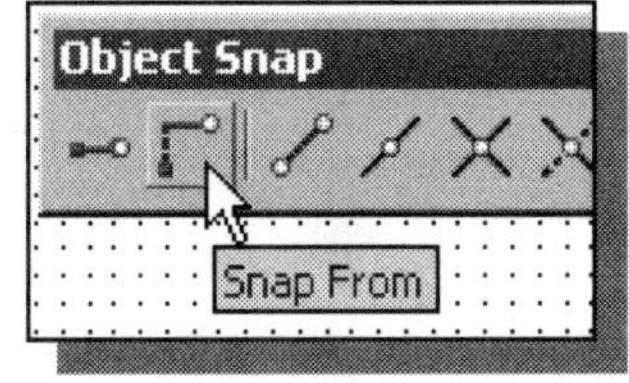

8. In the *Object Snap* toolbar, pick **Snap From**. Pick the lower right corner of the top view again.

9. In the command prompt area, enter ***@-45,0*** **[ENTER]**.

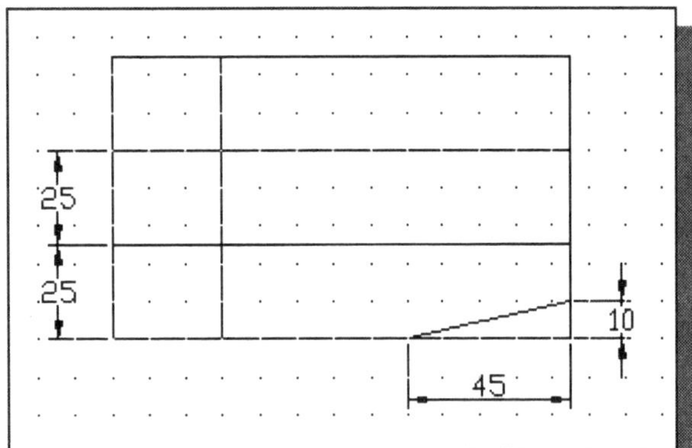

10. Inside the graphics window, right-mouse-click to activate the option menu and select **Enter** with the left-mouse-button to end the **Line** command.

11. Repeat the procedure and create the line and circle (diameter **25**mm) as shown in the figure below.

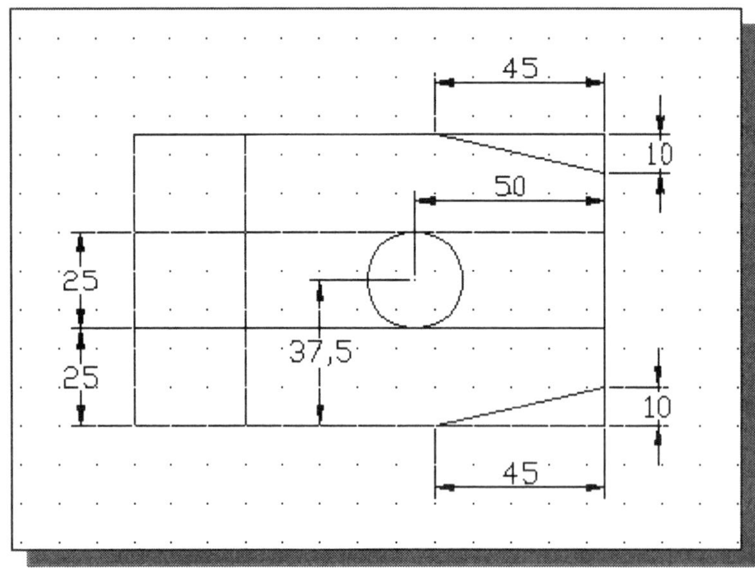

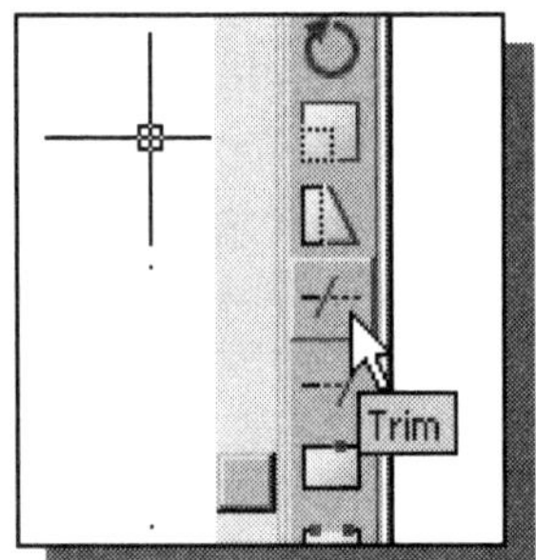

12. Select the **Trim** icon in the *Modify* toolbar. In the command prompt area, the message "*Select boundary edges... Select objects:*" is displayed.

13. Pick the following objects as boundary edges: the circle, and the lines that are near the circle.

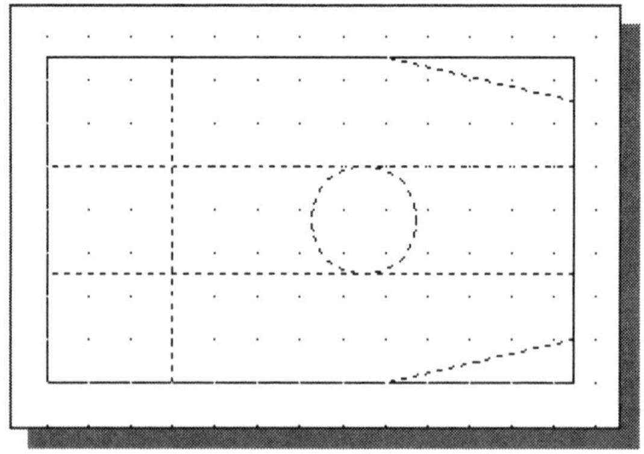

14. Inside the graphics window, **right-mouse-click** to accept the selected objects.

15. Select the unwanted portions and modify the objects as shown.

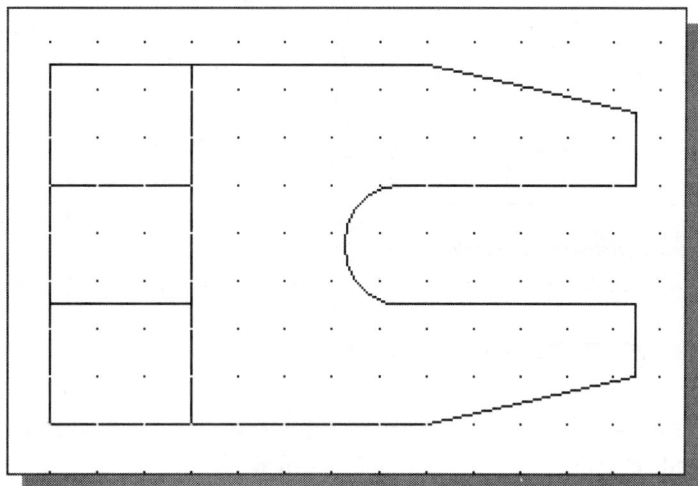

16. On your own, use the **Offset** and **Trim** commands and modify the top view as shown.

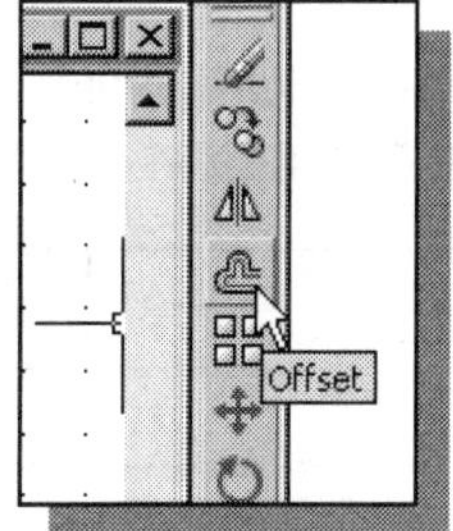

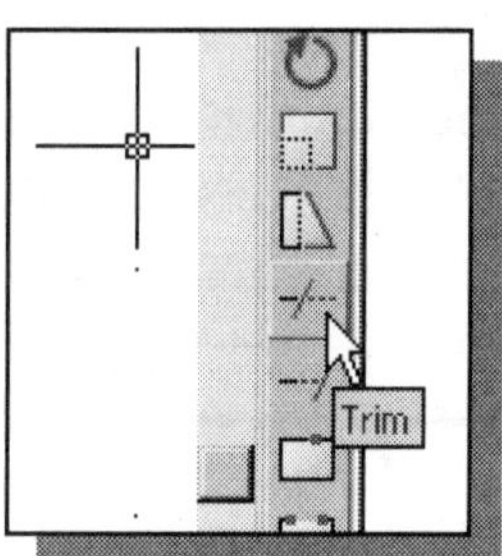

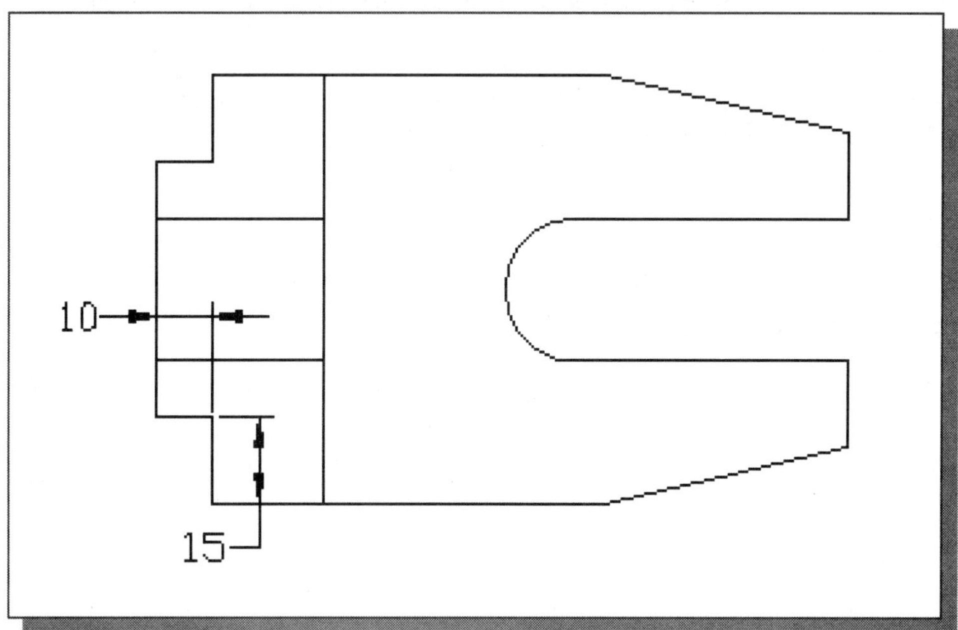

Drawing using the *Miter Line* method

❖ The *45 ° miter line* method is a simple and straightforward procedure to transfer measurements in between the top view and the side view.

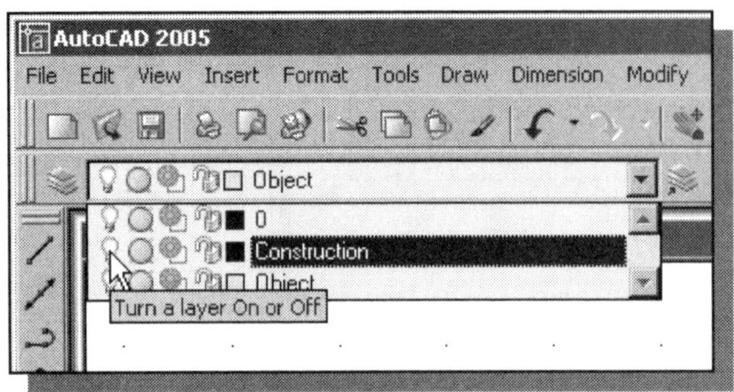

1. On the *Object Properties* toolbar, choose the ***Layer Control*** box with the left-mouse-button.

2. Move the cursor over the **light-bulb** icon for layer ***Construction***. The tool tip "*Turn a layer On or Off*" appears.

3. **Left-mouse-click once** and notice the icon color is changed to a light color, representing the layer (layer *Construction*) is turned *ON*.

4. **Left-mouse-click once** over the name of the layer ***Construction*** to set it as the *Current Layer*.

5. Use the **Line** command and create the *miter line* by connecting the two intersections of the construction lines as shown.

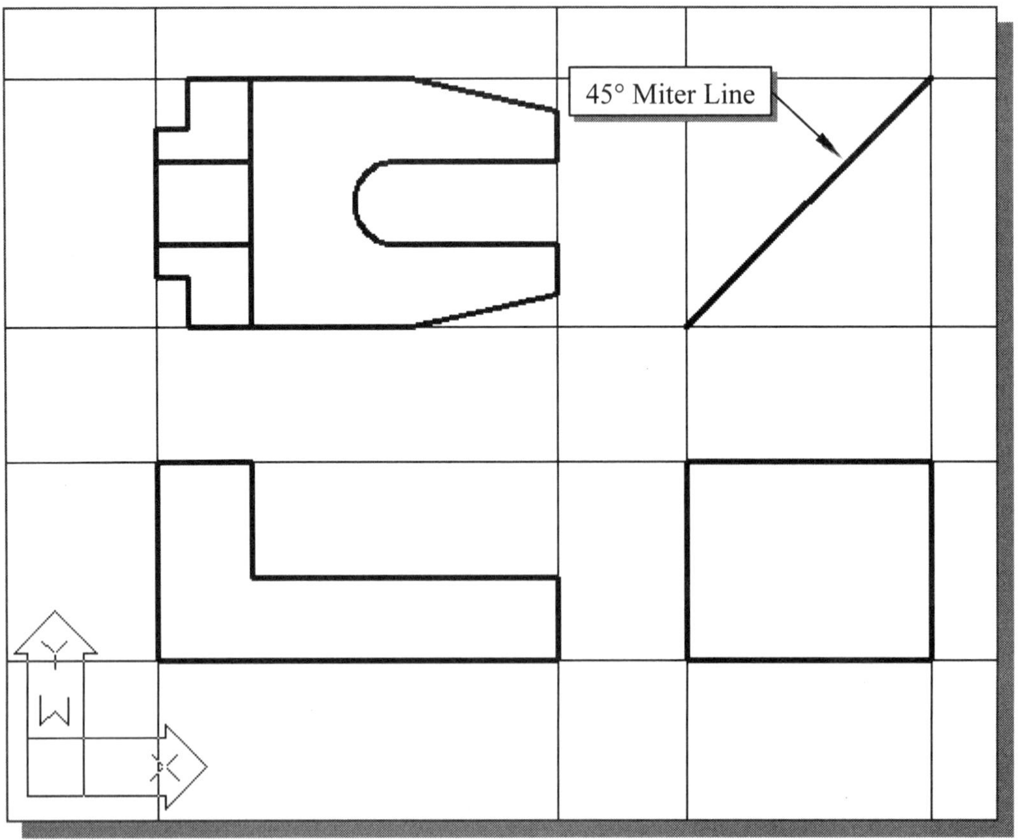

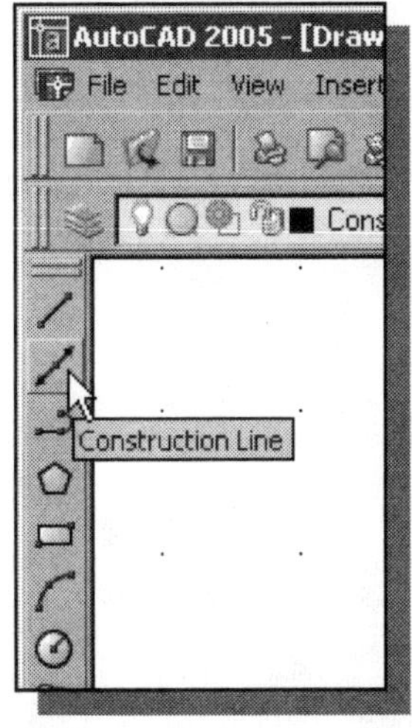

6. Select the **Construction Line** command in the *Draw* toolbar as shown.

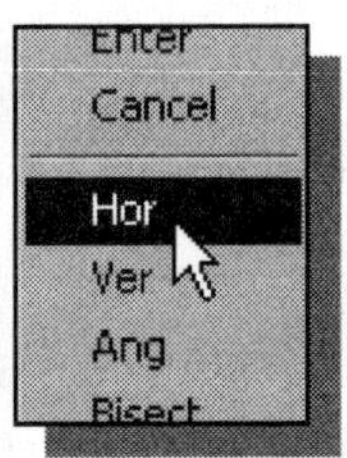

7. Inside the graphics area, right-mouse-click once and select the **Horizontal** option as shown.

8. On your own, create horizontal projection lines through all the corners in the top view as shown.

9. Use the **Trim** command and trim the projection lines as shown in the figure below.

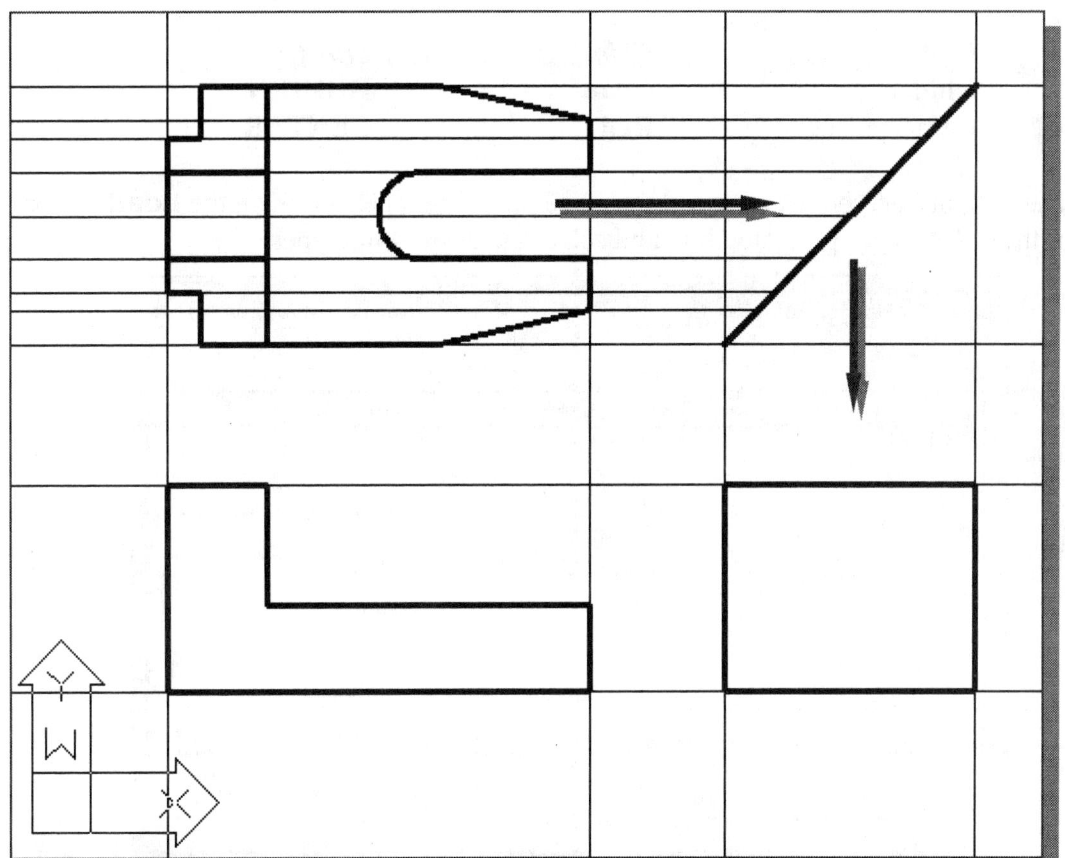

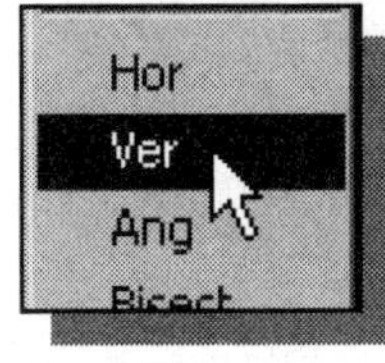

10. Add **Construction Lines** (vertical option) through all the intersection points that are on the *miter line*.

More Layers setup

1. Pick ***Layers*** in the *Object Properties* toolbar.

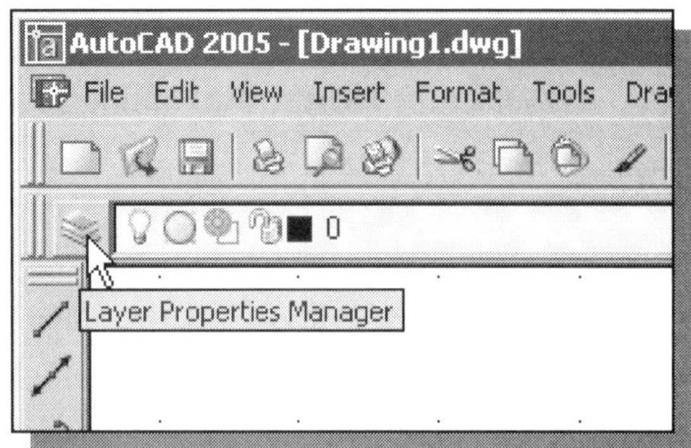

2. Click on the **New** icon to create new layers.

3. Create two **new layers** with the following settings:

Layer	***Color***	***LineType***
Hidden	**Cyan**	**HIDDEN**
Center	**Red**	**CENTER**

- The default linetype is *Continuous.* To use other linetypes, click on the **Load** button in the *Select Linetype* dialog box and select the desired linetypes.

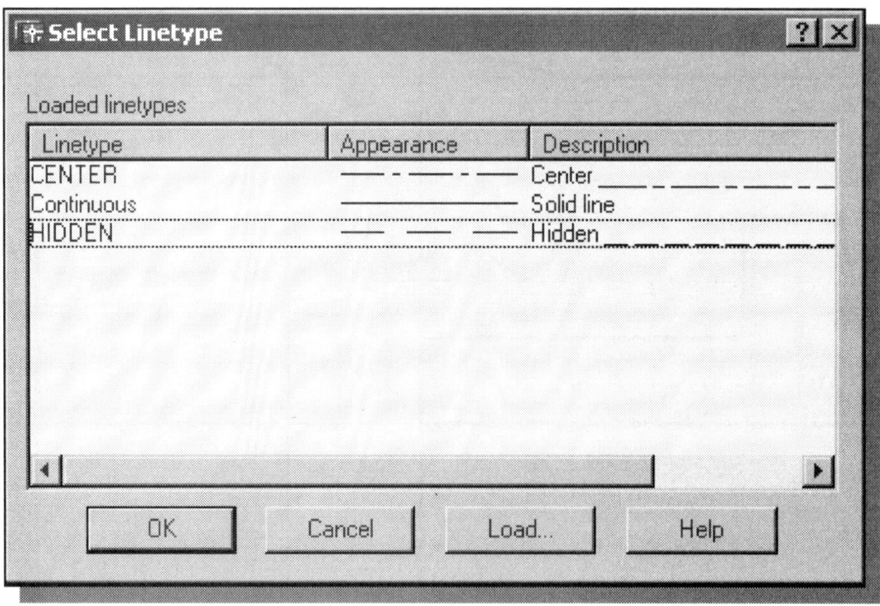

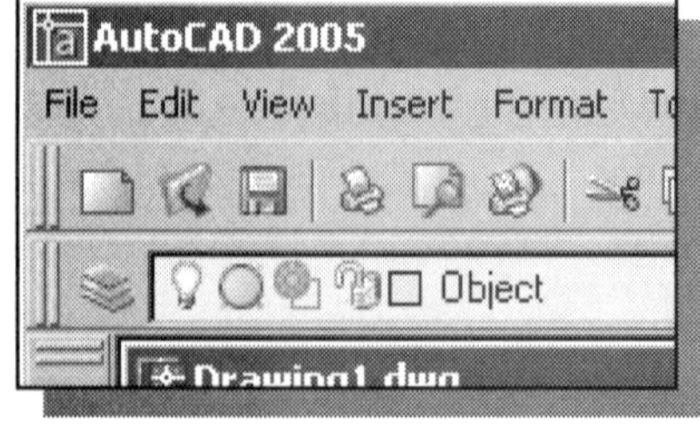

4. On your own, set the layer ***Object*** as the *Current Layer.*

Top View to Side View Projection

1. Using the *Running Object Snaps*, create the necessary **object-lines** in the side view.

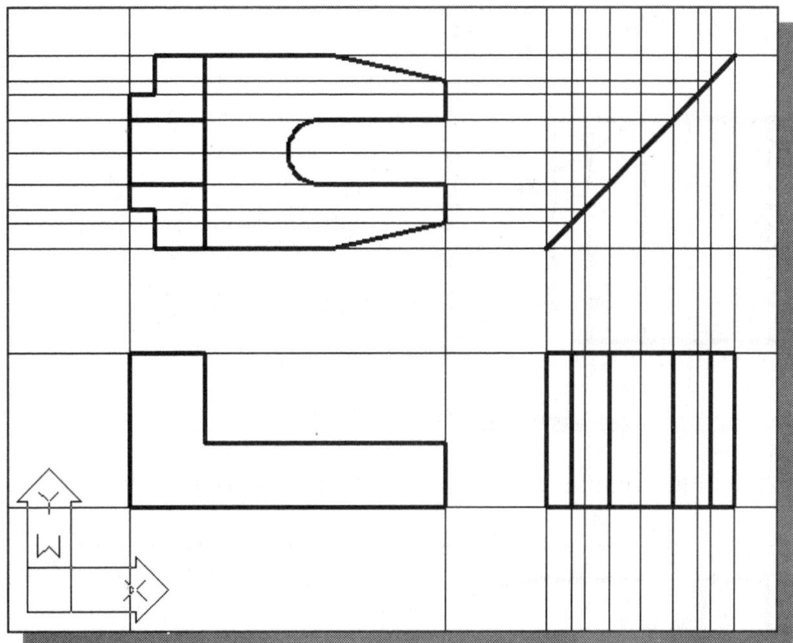

2. Set layer ***Hidden*** as the *Current Layer* and create the two necessary hidden lines in the side view.

3. Set layer ***Center*** as the *Current Layer* and create the necessary centerlines in the side view.

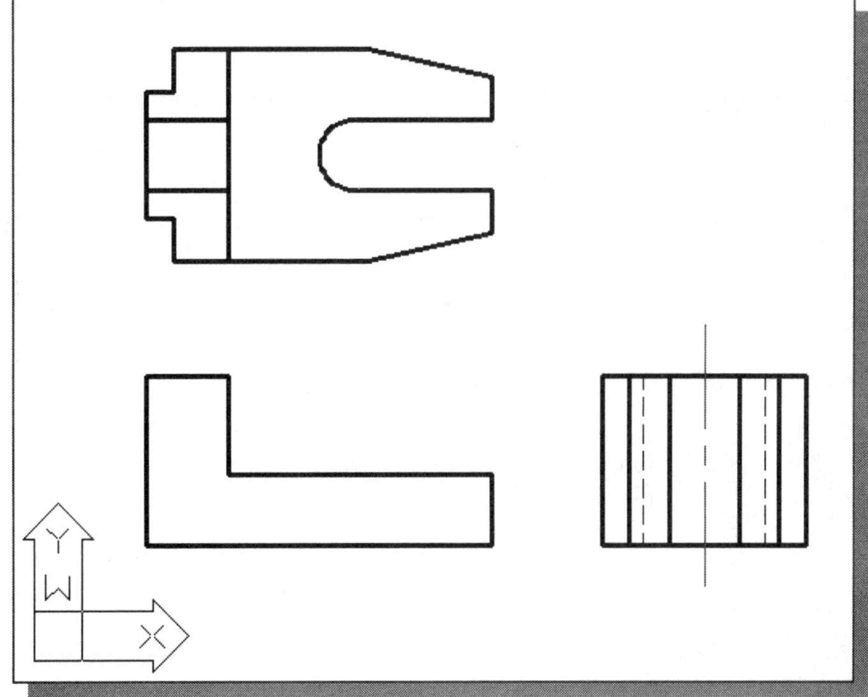

4. In the *Layer Control* box, turn ***OFF*** the construction lines.

5. Set layer ***Object*** as the *Current Layer*.

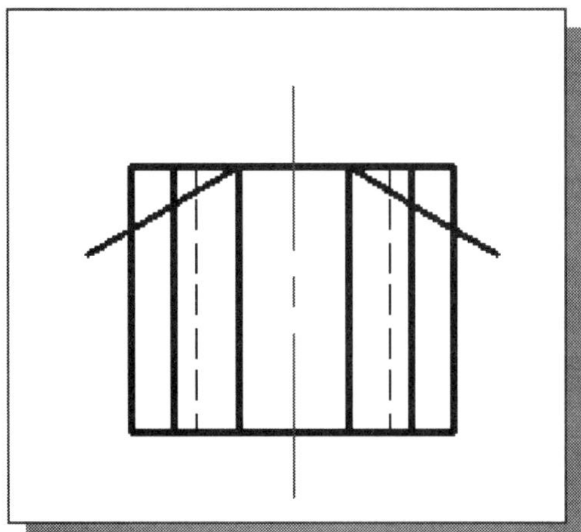

6. Use the **Line** command and create the two 30° inclined lines as shown.

   (Hint: Relative coordinate entries of @40<-30 and @40<210)

7. Use the Line command and create a horizontal line in the side view as shown.

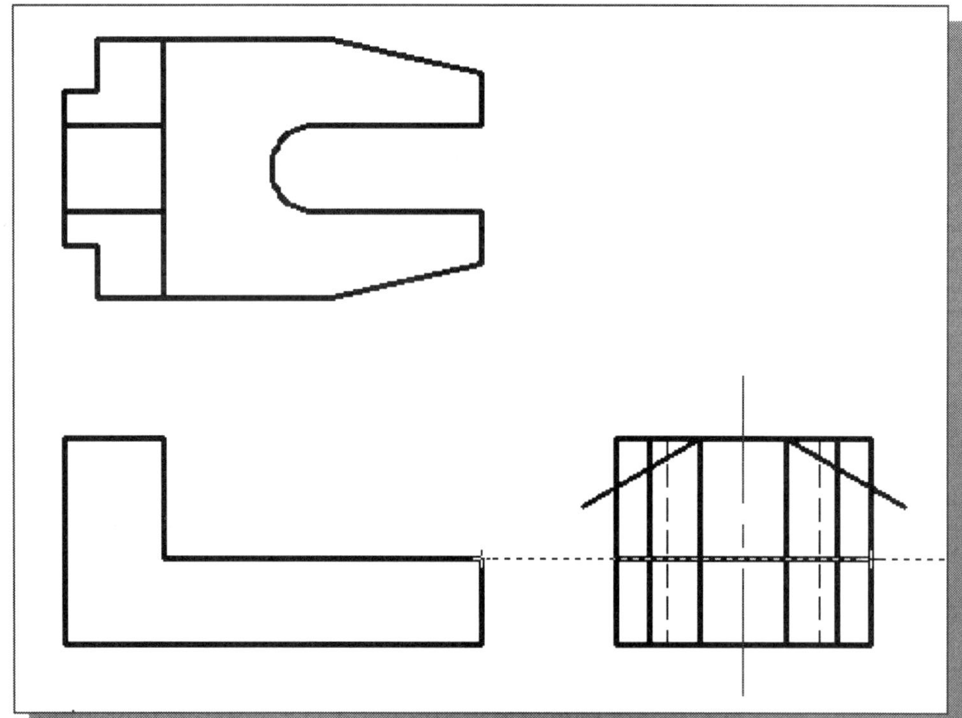

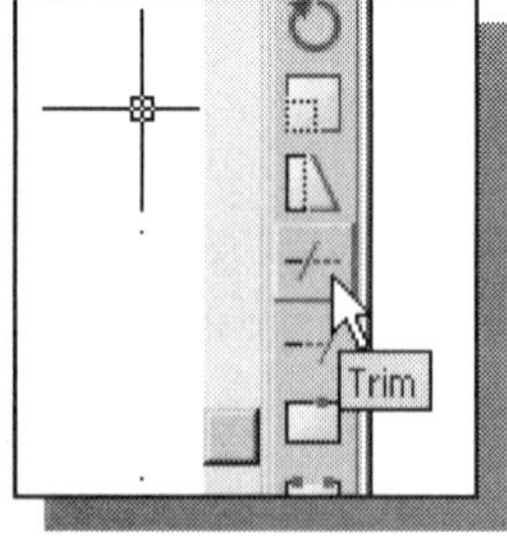

8. On your own, use the **Trim** command and remove the unwanted portions in the side view.

Completing the Front View

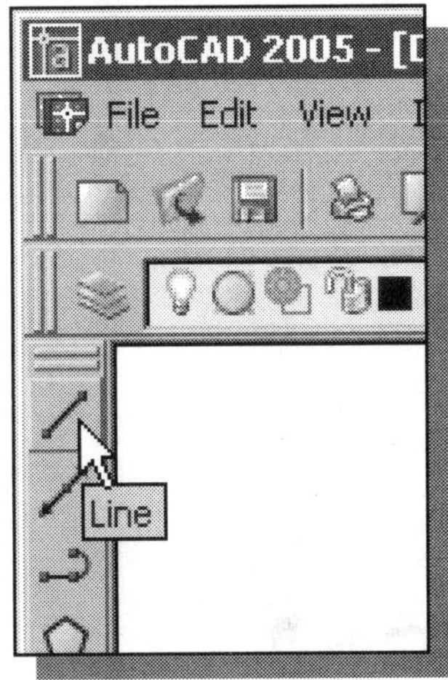

1. Select the **Line** command icon in the *Draw* toolbar. In the command prompt area, the message "*_line Specify first point:*" is displayed.

2. Move the cursor to the top left corner in the side view and the bottom left corner in the top view to activate the *Object Tracking* option to both corners.

3. Left-mouse-click once when the cursor is aligned to both corners as shown.

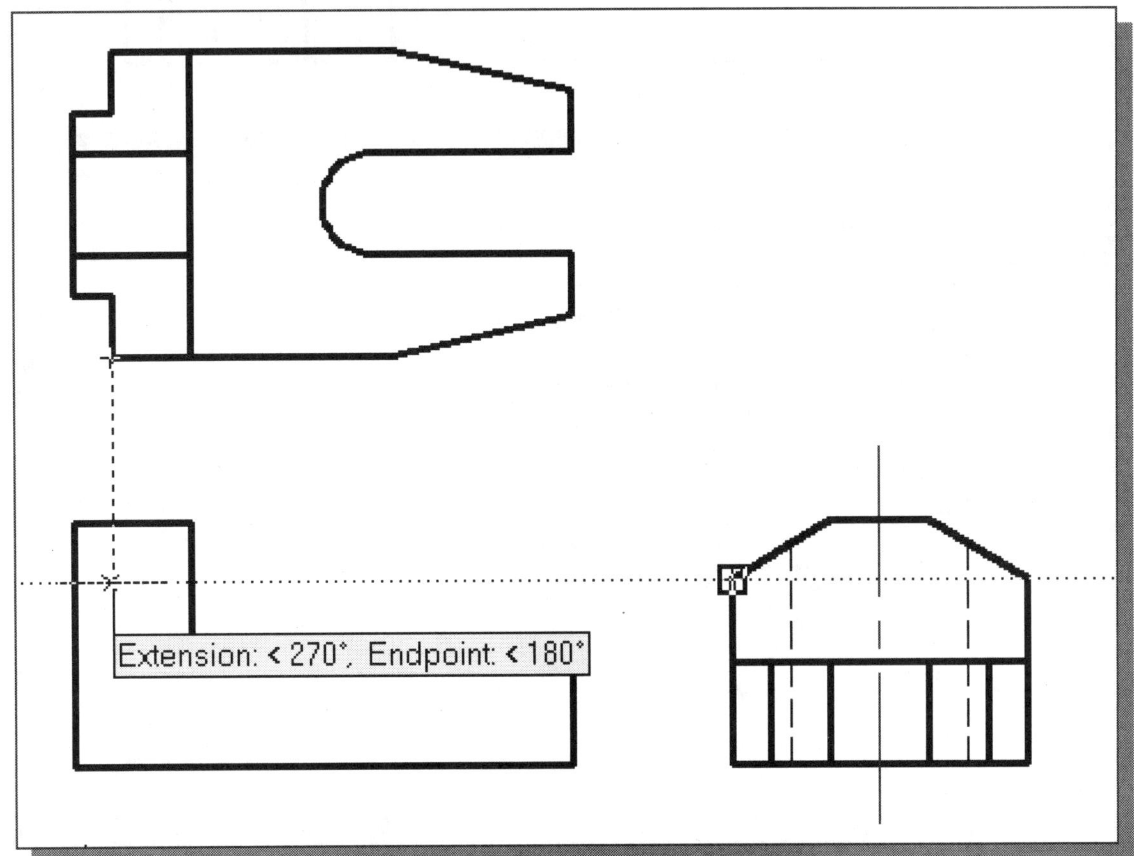

4. Create the **horizontal line** as shown.

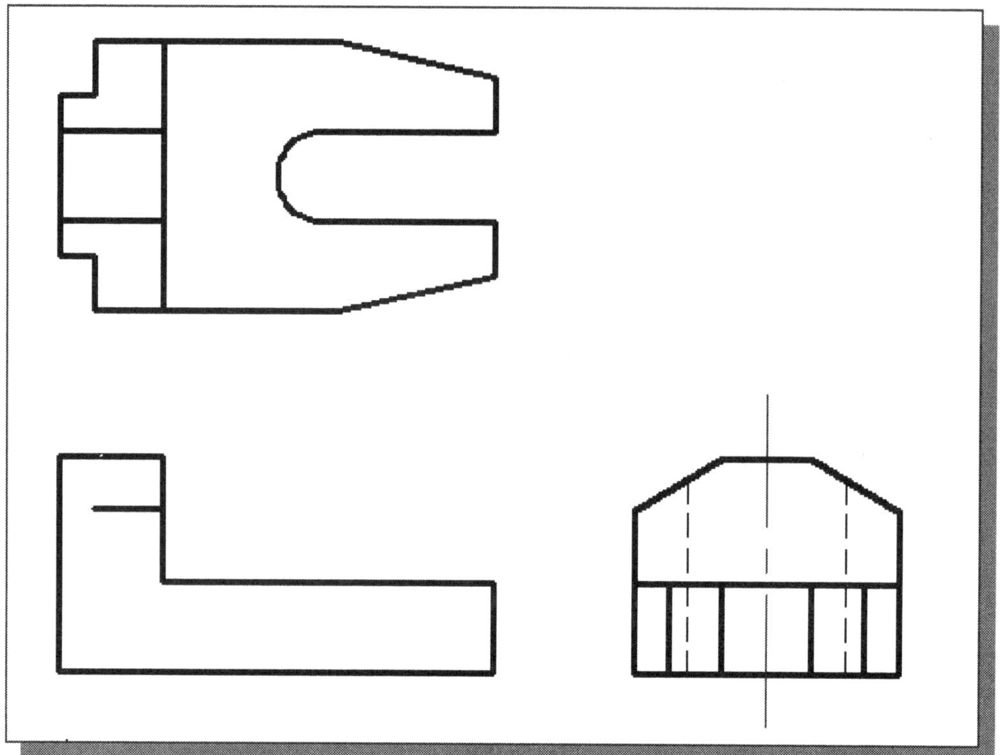

5. Repeat the procedure and create the lines in the front view as shown.

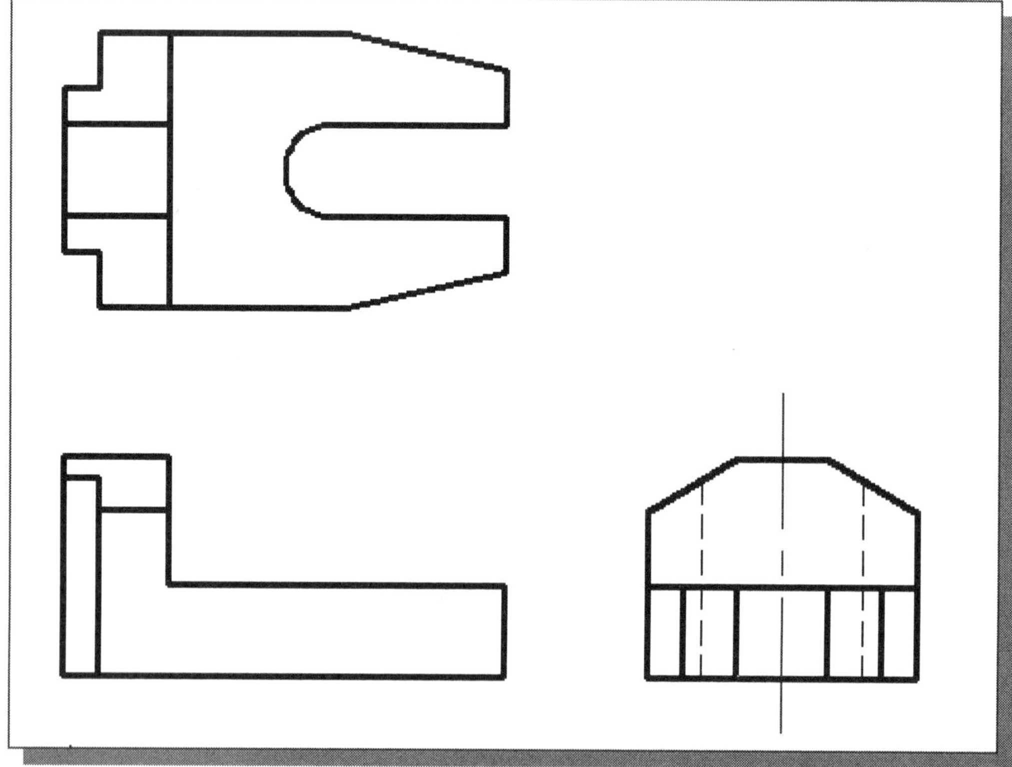

6. Add in any additional object lines that are necessary.

7. Set layer ***Hidden*** as the *Current Layer* and create the necessary hidden lines in the front view.

8. Set layer ***Center*** as the *Current Layer* and create the necessary centerlines in the top view and front view.

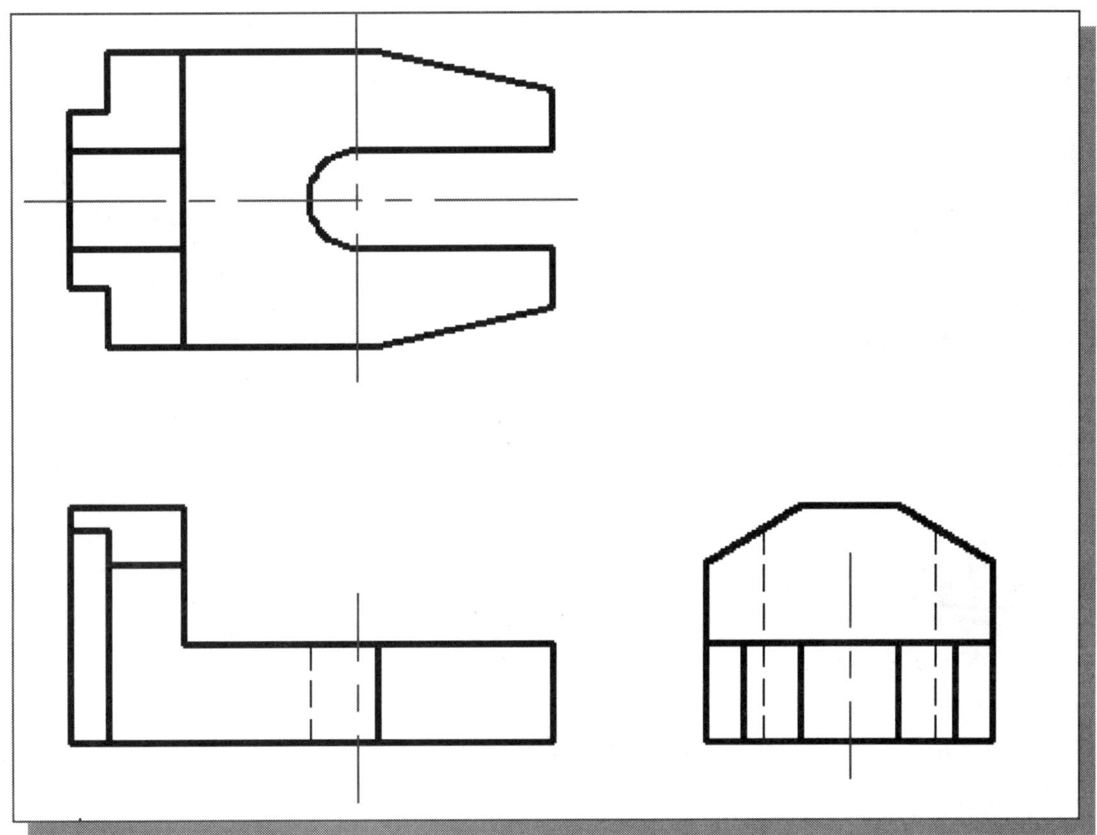

Saving the CAD file

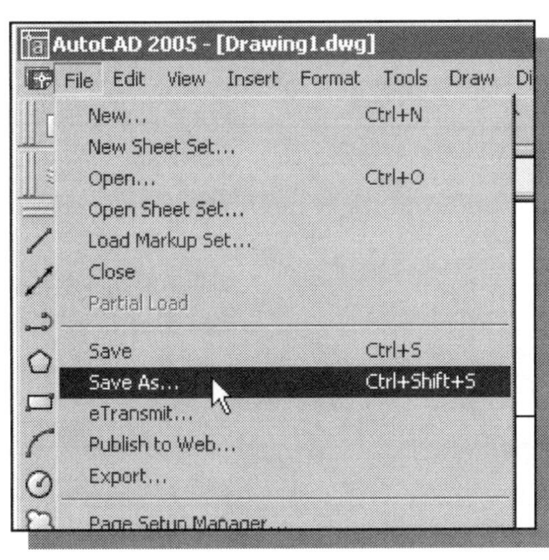

1. In the pull-down menus, select:

   [File] → [Save As]

2. In the *Save Drawing As* dialog box, select the folder you want to store the CAD file and enter ***Locator*** in the *File name* box.

3. Pick **Save** in the *Save Drawing As* dialog box to accept the selections and save the file.

Questions:

1. Explain what an orthographic view is and why it is important to engineering graphics.

2. What does the *Running Object Snaps* option allow us to do?

3. Explain how a *miter line* can assist us in creating orthographic views.

4. Describe the AutoCAD *AutoSnap* and *AutoTrack* options.

5. Identify the following commands:

(a)

(b)

(c)

(d)

Exercises: (Unless otherwise specified, dimensions are in inches.)

1.

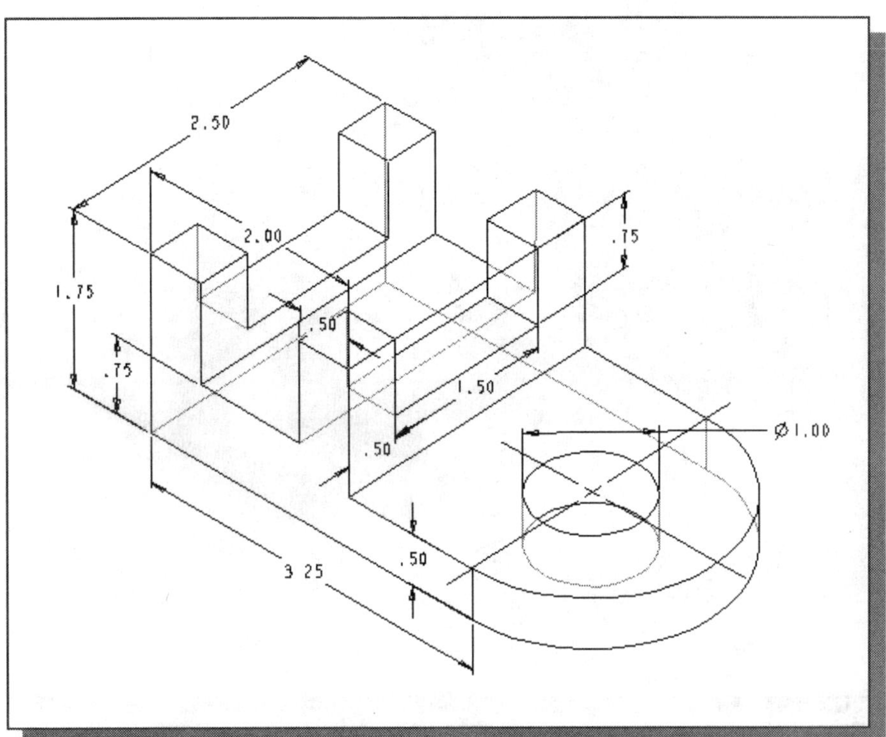

2.

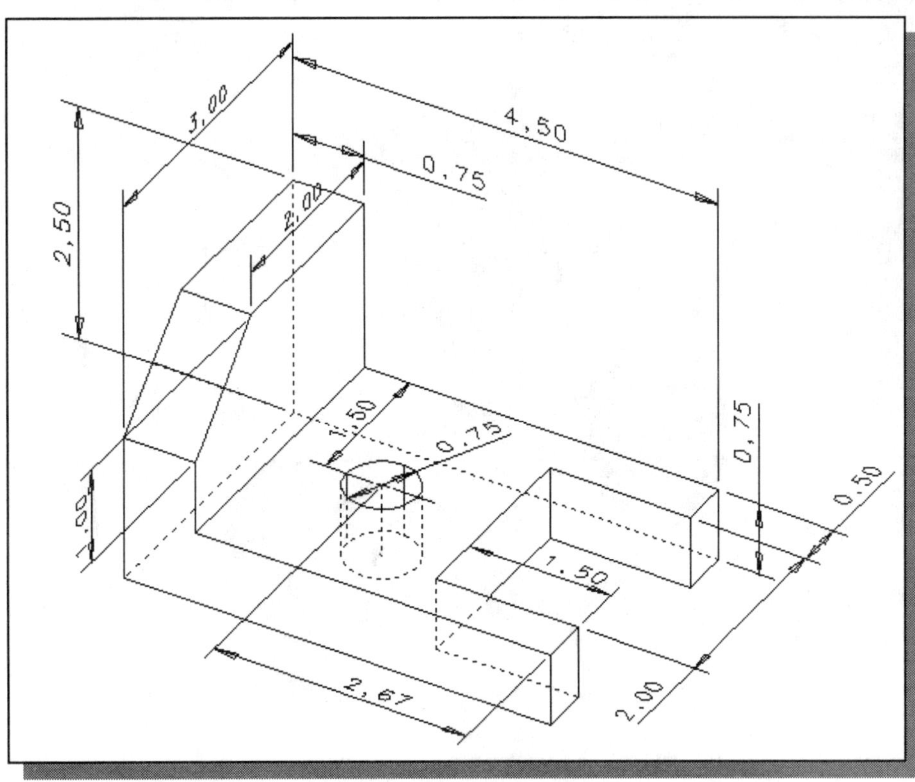

3.

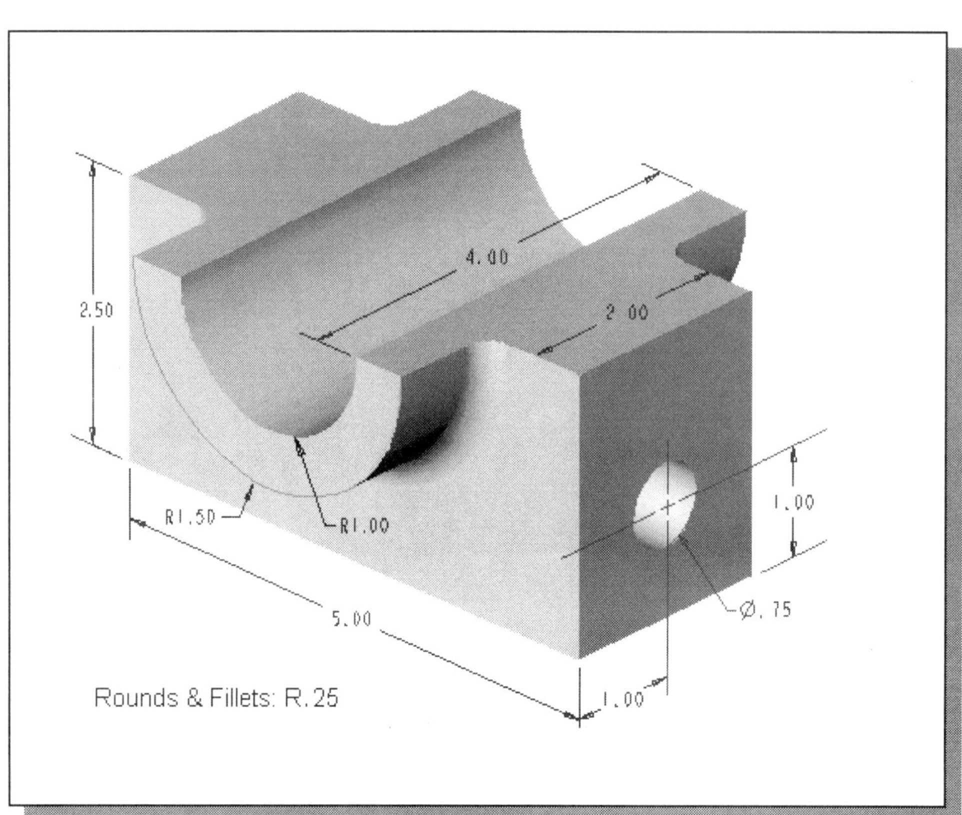

4. Dimensions are in Millimeters.

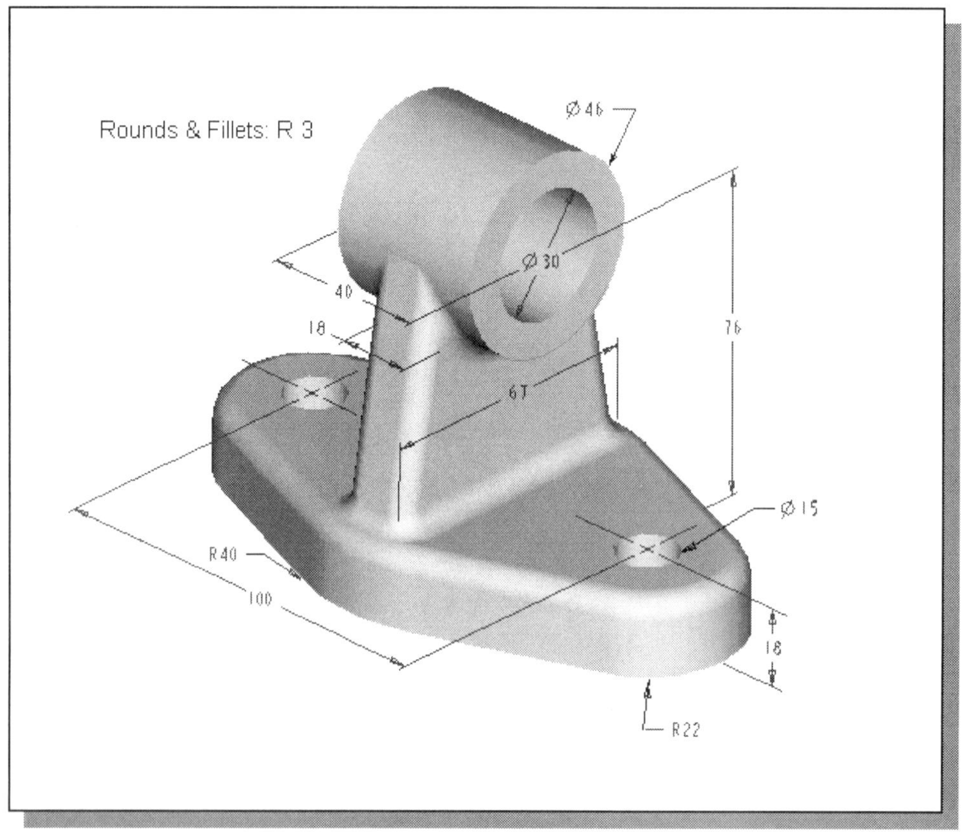

5.

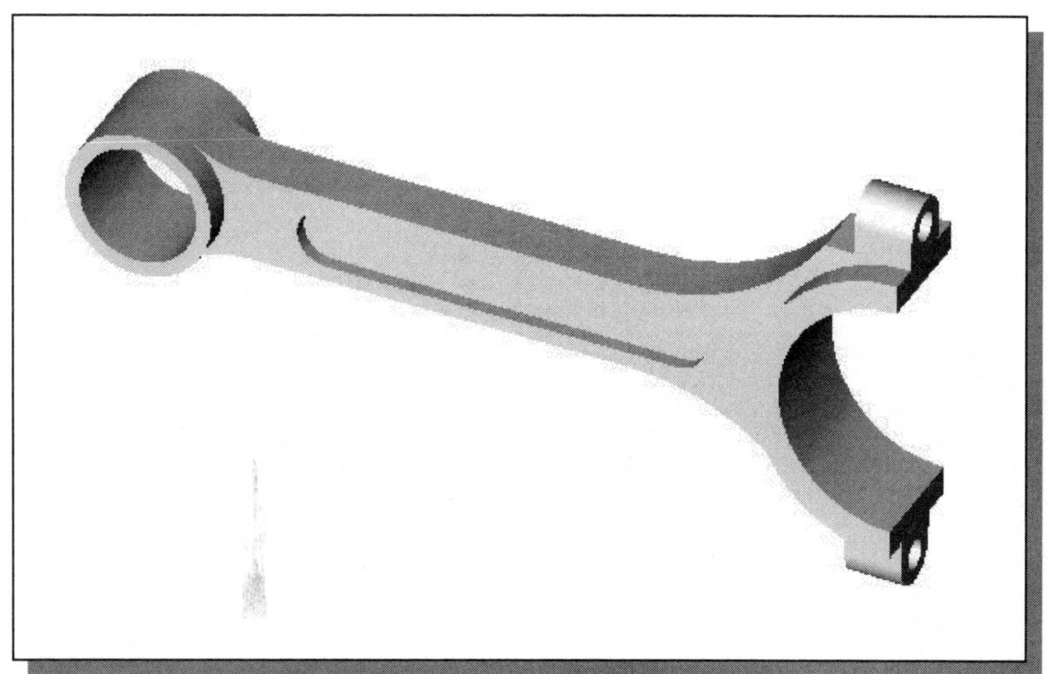

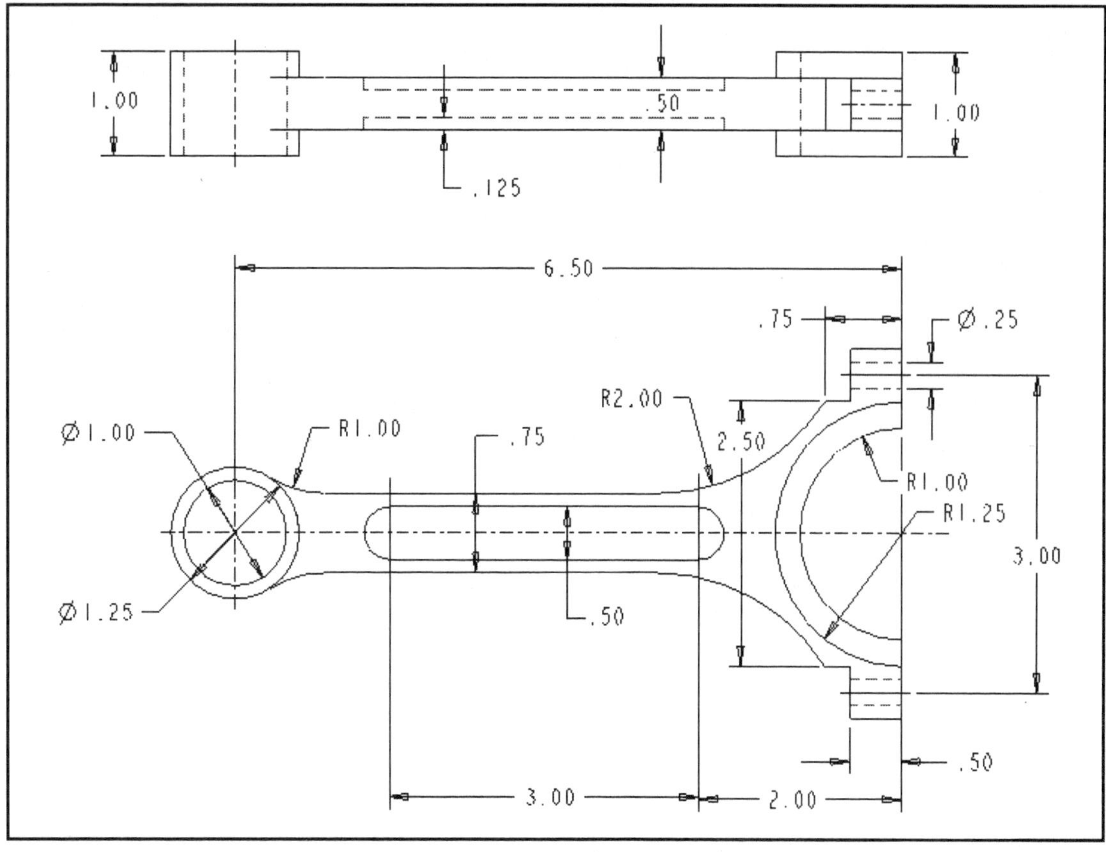

1.00
.50
1.00
.125
6.50
.75
Ø.25
R2.00
Ø1.00
R1.00
.75
2.50
R1.00
R1.25
3.00
Ø1.25
.50
.50
3.00
2.00

NOTES:

Chapter 6
Basic Dimensioning and Notes

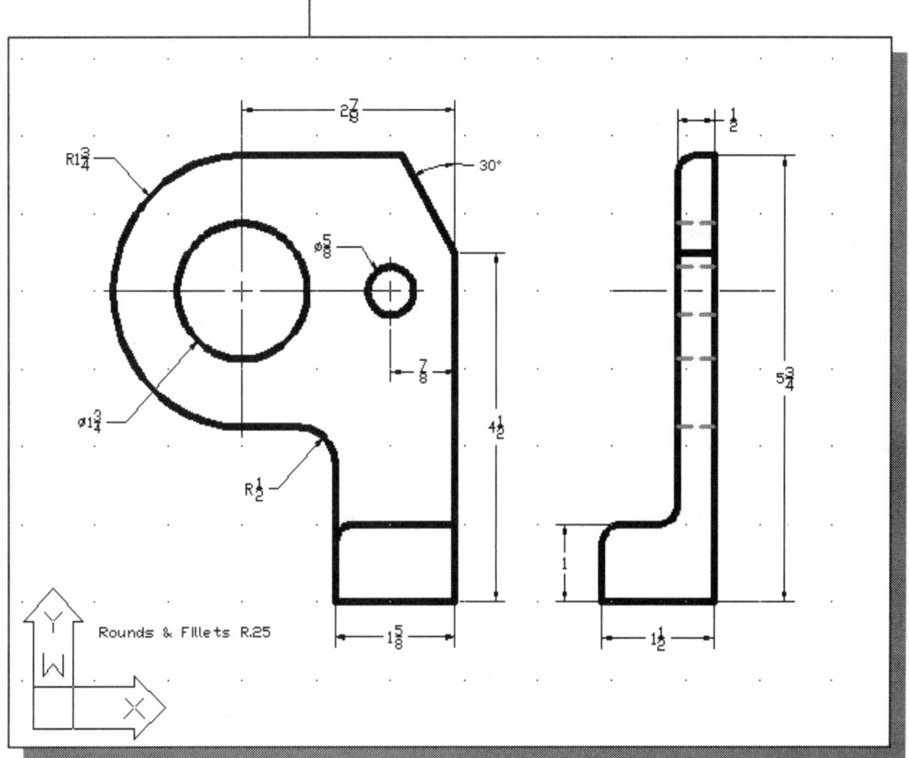

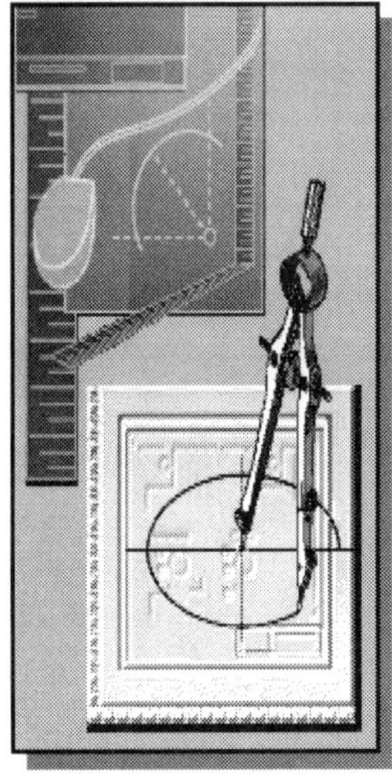

Learning Objectives

- Understand dimensioning nomenclature and basics.
- Display and use the Dimension toolbar.
- Use the AutoCAD Dimension Style Manager.
- Create Center Marks.
- Add Linear and Angular Dimensions.
- Use the SINGLE LINE TEXT command.
- Create SPECIAL CHARACTERS in Notes.

Introduction

In order to manufacture a finalized design, the complete ***shape*** and ***size*** description must be shown on the drawings of the design. Thus far, the use of **AutoCAD® 2005** to define the ***shape*** of designs have been illustrated. In this chapter, the procedures to convey the ***size*** definitions of designs using **AutoCAD® 2005** is discussed. The *tools of size description* are known as *dimensions* and *notes*.

Considerable experience and judgment is required for accurate size description. Detail drawings should contain only those dimensions that are necessary to make the design. Dimensions for the same feature of the design should be given only once in the same drawing. Nothing should be left to chance or guesswork on a drawing. Drawings should be dimensioned to avoid any possibility of questions. Dimensions should be carefully positioned; preferably near the profile of the feature being dimensioned. The designer and the CAD operator should be as familiar as possible with materials, methods of manufacturing, and shop processes.

Traditionally, detailing a drawing is the biggest bottleneck of the design process; and when doing board drafting, dimensioning is one of the most time consuming and tedious tasks. Today, most CAD systems provide what is known as an **auto-dimensioning feature**, where the CAD system automatically creates the extension lines, dimensional lines, arrowheads, and dimension values. Most CAD systems also provide an **associative dimensioning feature** so that the system automatically updates the dimensions when the drawing is modified.

The *Bracket* Design

Starting Up AutoCAD 2005

1. Select the **AutoCAD 2005** option on the *Program* menu or select the **AutoCAD 2005** icon on the *Desktop*.

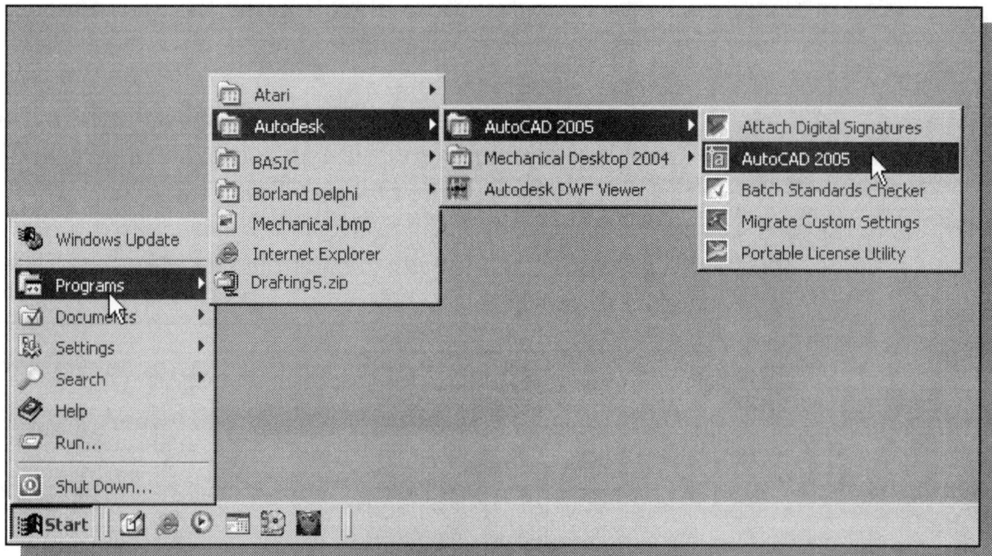

2. In the *Startup* window, select ***Start from Scratch***, as shown in the figure below.

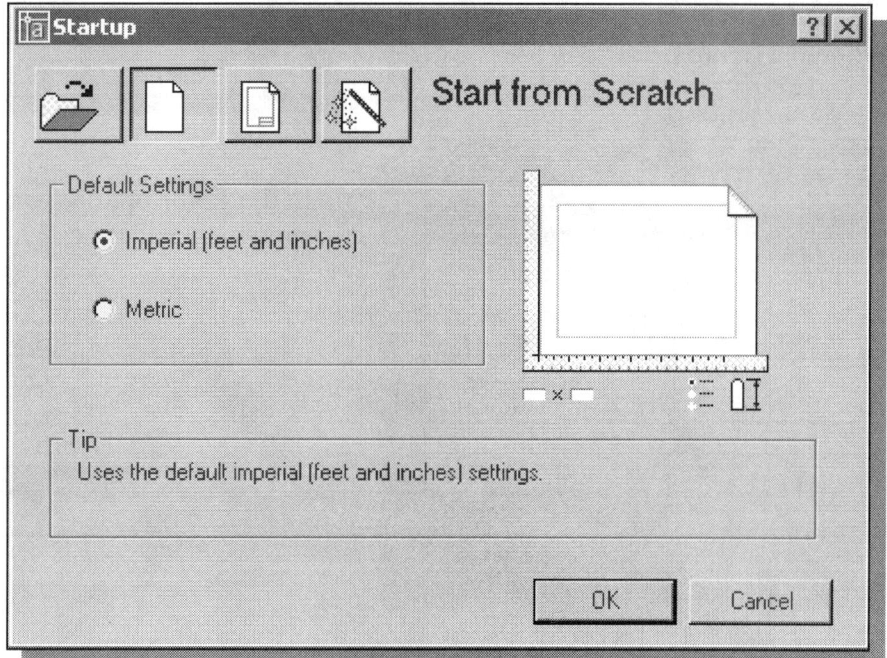

3. In the *Default Settings* section, pick **Imperial (feet and inches)** as the drawing units.

4. Pick **OK** in the *Startup* dialog box to accept the selected settings.

Change the Background Color of the Graphics window

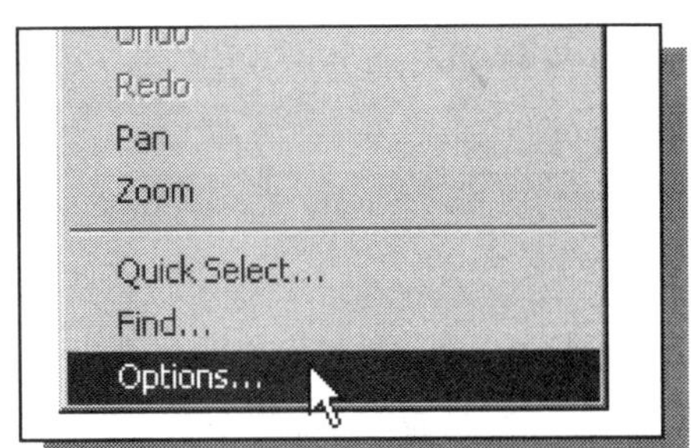

1. Move the cursor inside the graphics window, right-mouse-click to bring the option menu and select **Options** with the left-mouse-button.

❖ Note that many of the AutoCAD interface and drawing environment settings can be changed through the *Options* dialog box.

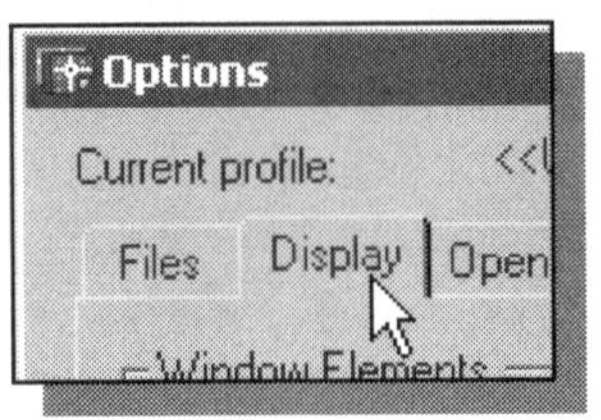

2. In the *Options* dialog box, select the **Display** tab if it is not the page on top.

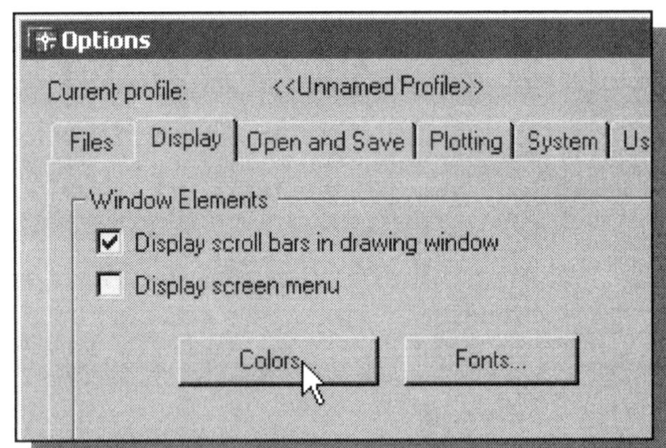

3. In the *Window Elements* section, click the **Colors** button as shown in the figure.

4. In the *Color Options* dialog box, select ***Model tab background*** as shown in the figure below.

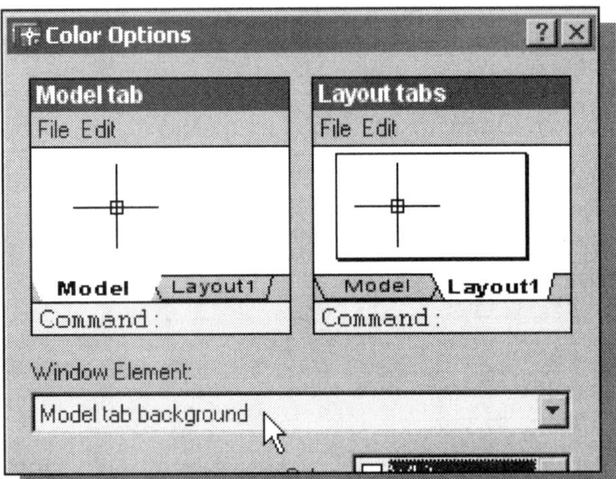

5. In the *Color* option, select ***White*** as shown.

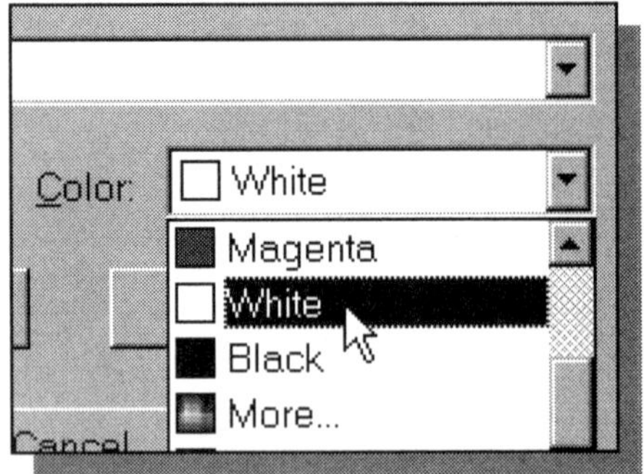

6. Click the **Apply & Close** button to accept the settings. Note the color of the background in the graphics window is adjusted.

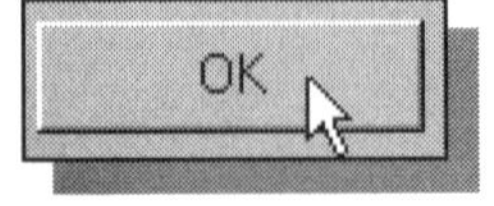

7. Click the **OK** button to exit the *Options* dialog box.

GRID and ***SNAP*** Intervals Setup

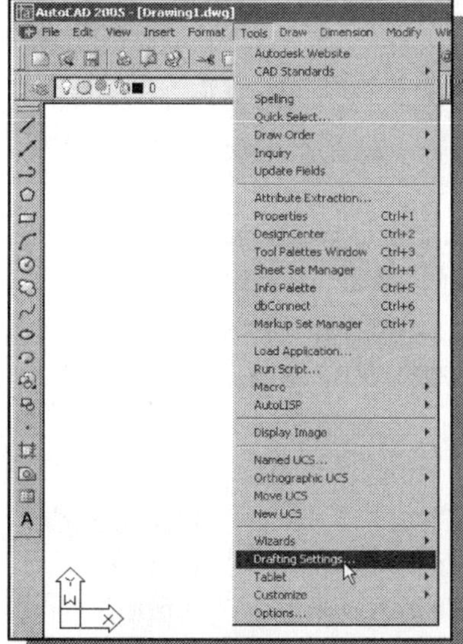

1. In the pull-down menus, select:

   [Tools] → [Drafting Settings]

2. In the *Drafting Settings* dialog box, select the **SNAP and GRID** tab if it is not the page on top.

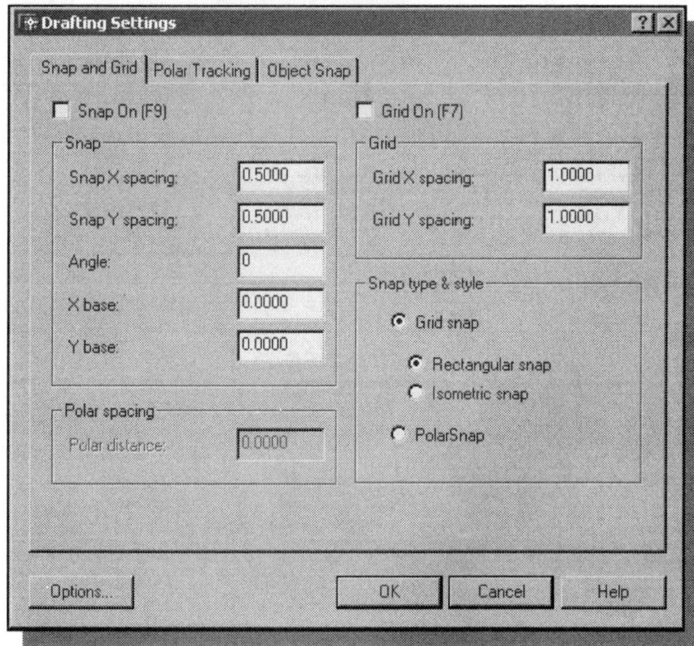

3. Change *Grid Spacing* to ***1.0*** for both X and Y directions.

4. Also adjust the *Snap Spacing* to ***0.5*** for both X and Y directions.

5. Pick **OK** to exit the *Drafting Settings* dialog box.

Layers setup

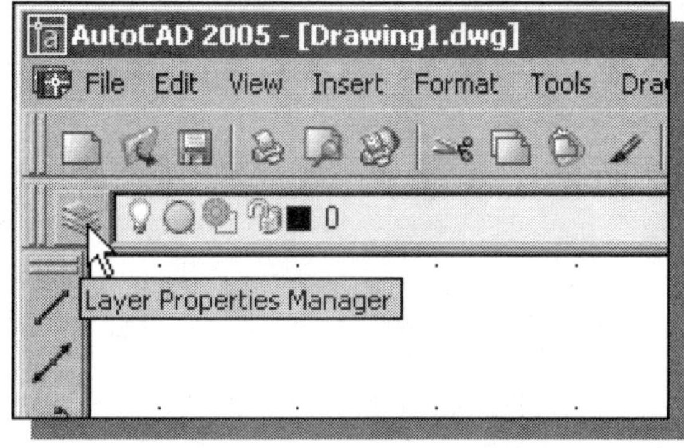

1. Pick ***Layer Properties Manager*** in the *Object Properties* toolbar.

2. In the *Layer Properties Manager* dialog box, click on the **New** button (or the key combination [**Alt+N**]) to create a new layer.

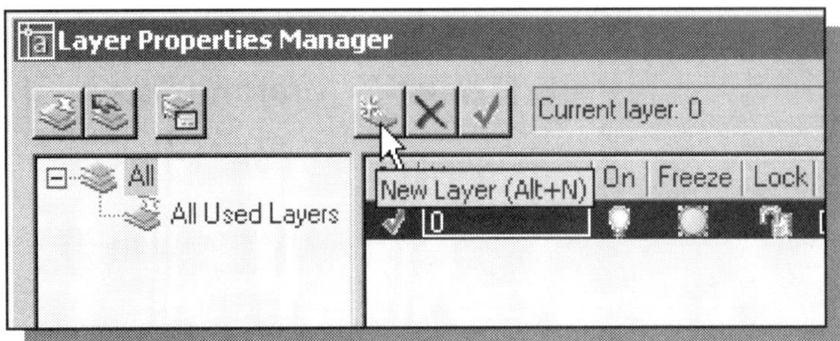

3. Create **layers** with the following settings:

Layer	*Color*	*LineType*	*Lineweight*
Construction	**Gray(9)**	**Continuous**	**Default**
Object_Lines	**Blue**	**Continuous**	**0.6mm**
Hidden_Lines	**Cyan**	**Hidden**	**0.3mm**
Center_Lines	**Red**	**Center**	**Default**
Dimensions	**Magenta**	**Continuous**	**Default**
Section_Lines	**White**	**Continuous**	**Default**
CuttingPlane_Lines	**Dark Gray**	**Phantom**	**0.6mm**
Title_Block	**Green**	**Continuous**	**1.2mm**
Viewport	**White**	**Continuous**	**Default**

4. Highlight the layer ***Construction*** in the list of layers.

5. Click on the **Current** button to set layer ***Construction*** as the *Current Layer*.

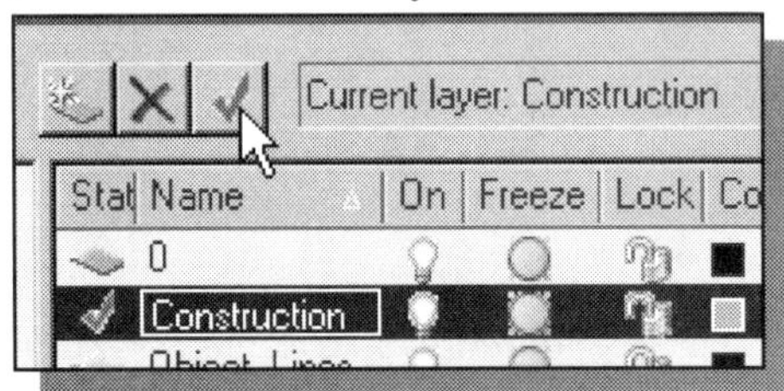

6. Click on the **OK** button to accept the settings and exit the *Layer Properties Manager* dialog box.

7. In the *Status Bar* area, reset the option buttons so that only *SNAP, GRID* and *MODEL* are switched ***ON***.

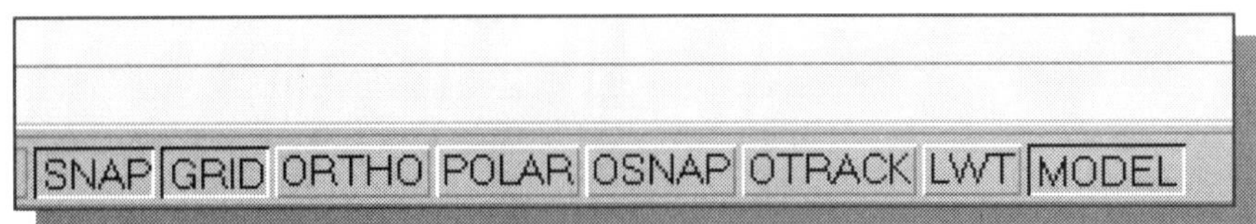

The *Bracket* Design

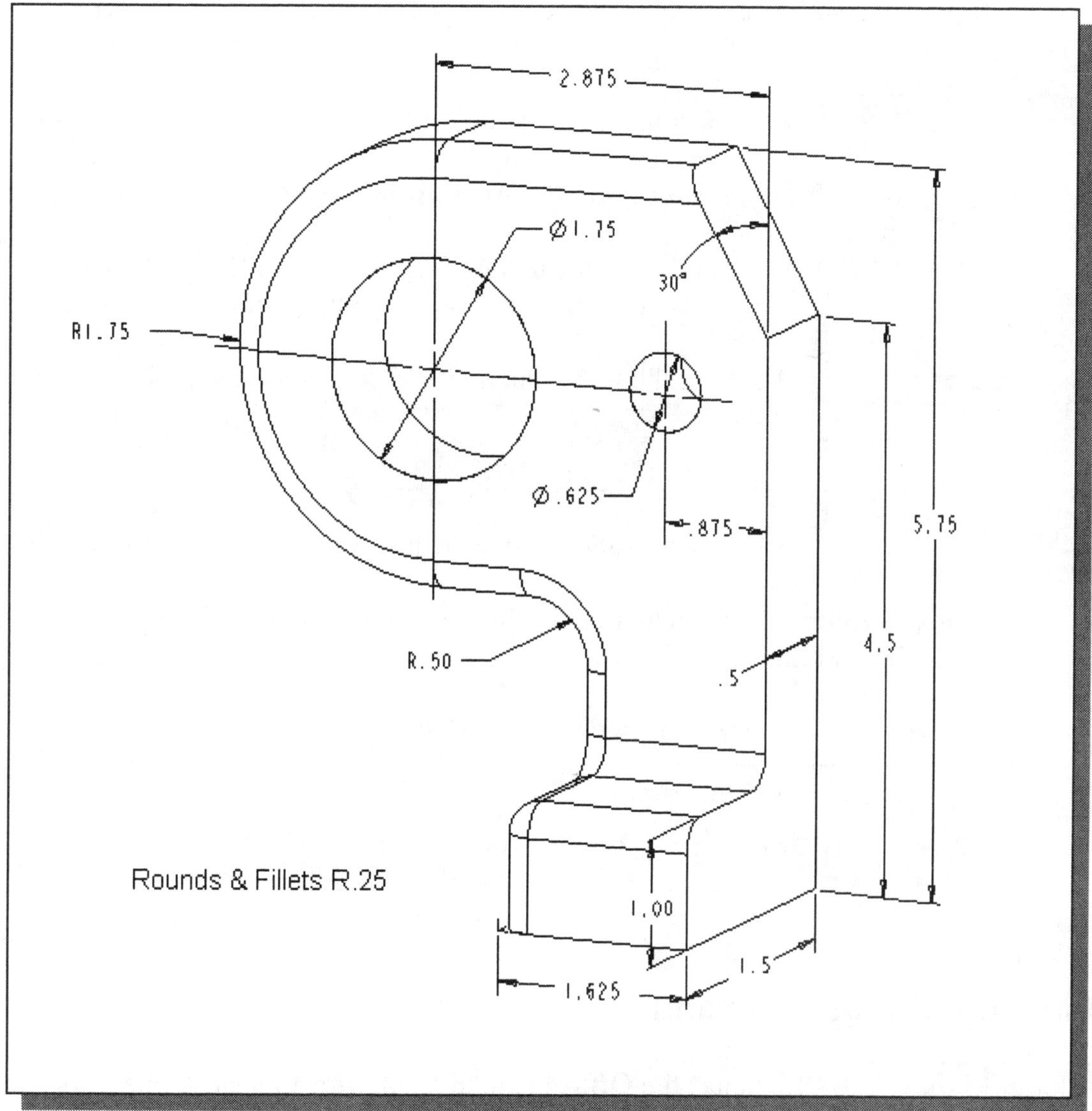

➢ Before going through the tutorial, make a rough sketch of a multiview drawing of the part. How many 2D views will be necessary to fully describe the part? Based on your knowledge of **AutoCAD® 2005** so far, how would you arrange and construct these 2D views? Take a few minutes to consider these questions and do preliminary planning by sketching on a piece of paper. You are also encouraged to construct the orthographic views on your own prior to going through the tutorial.

Drawing Construction Lines

❖ We will place the construction lines on the *Construction* layer so that the layer can later be frozen or turned off.

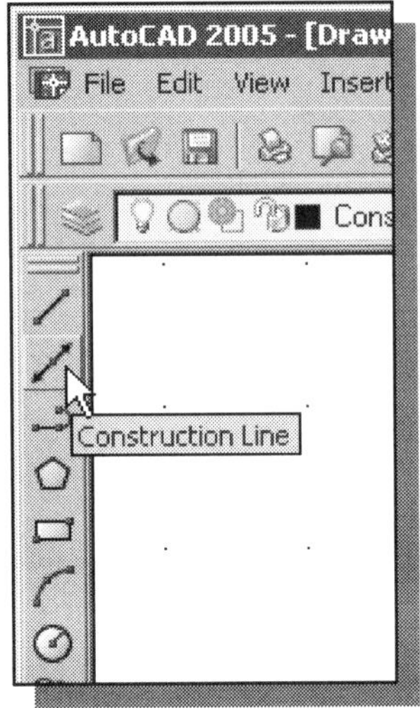

1. Select the **Construction Line** icon in the *Draw* toolbar. In the command prompt area, the message "*_xline Specify a point or [Hor/Ver/Ang/Bisect/Offset]:*" is displayed.

   To orient construction lines, we generally specify two points, although other orientation options are also available.

2. Place the first point at world coordinate (**3,2**) on the screen.

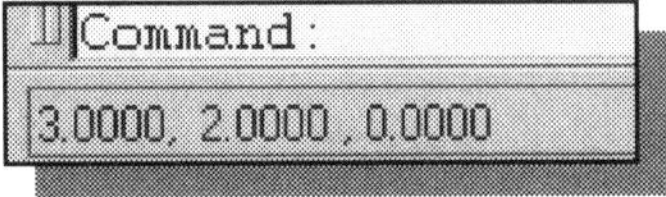

3. Pick a location above the last point to create a **vertical line**.

4. Move the cursor toward the right of the first point and pick a location to create a **horizontal line**.

5. In the *Status Bar* area, turn ***OFF*** the *SNAP* option.

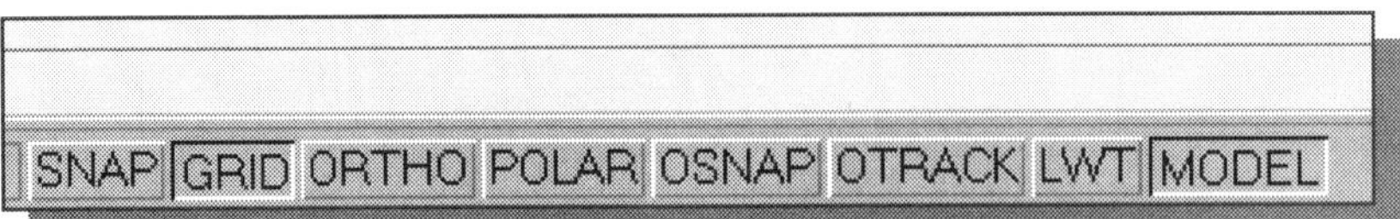

Using the *Offset* command

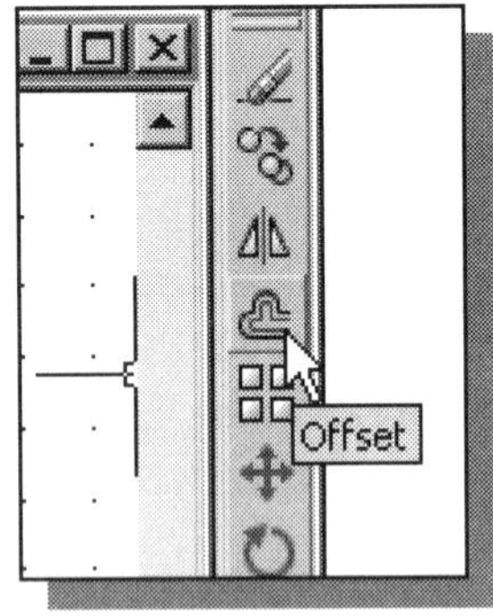

1. Select the **Offset** icon in the *Modify* toolbar. In the command prompt area, the message "*Specify offset distance or [Through]:*" is displayed.

2. In the command prompt area, enter: ***2.875*** **[ENTER]**.

3. In the command prompt area, the message "*Select object to offset or <exit>:*" is displayed. Pick the **vertical line** on the screen.

4. AutoCAD next asks us to identify the direction of the offset. Pick a location that is to the **right** of the vertical line.

5. Inside the graphics window, right-mouse-click twice to **end** the Offset command.

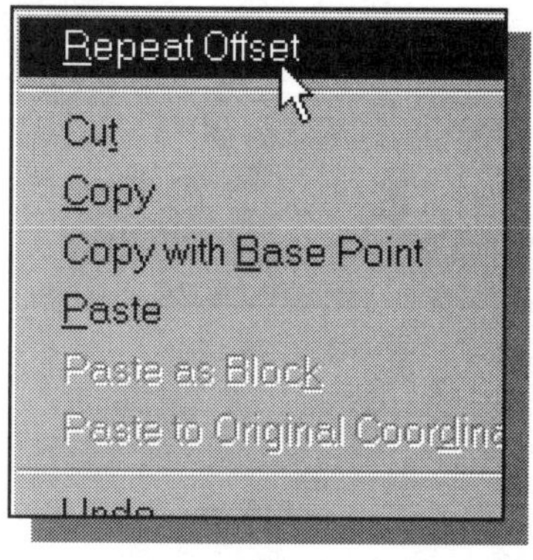

6. Hit the **[SPACE BAR]**, or **right-mouse-click** inside the graphics window and select **Repeat Offset** in the popup list, to repeat the Offset command.

7. In the command prompt area, enter: ***5.75*** **[ENTER]**.

8. In the command prompt area, the message "*Select object to offset or <exit>:*" is displayed. Pick the **horizontal line** on the screen.

9. AutoCAD next asks us to identify the direction of the offset. Pick a location that is **above** the horizontal line.

10. Inside the graphics window, right-mouse-click once to **end** the Offset command.

11. Repeat the **Offset** command and create the lines as shown.

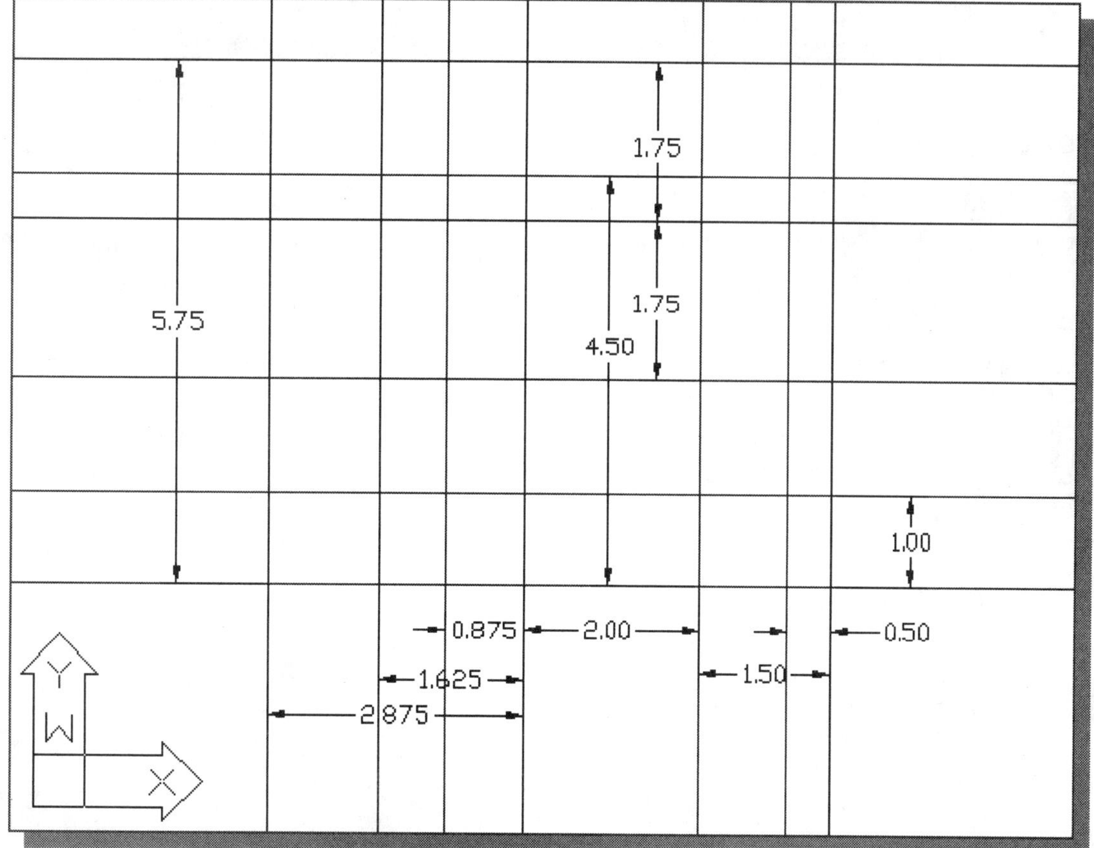

Set layer *Object_Lines* as the *Current Layer*

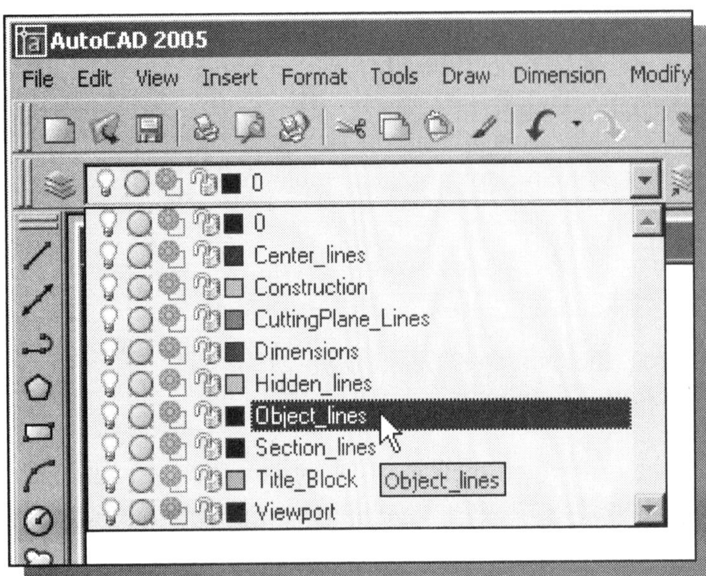

1. On the *Object Properties* toolbar, choose the ***Layer Control*** box with the left-mouse-button.

2. Move the cursor over the name of layer ***Object_Lines*** and the tool tip "*Object_Lines*" appears.

3. **Left-mouse-click once** and layer *Object_Lines* is set as the *Current Layer*.

4. In the *Status Bar* area, turn ***ON*** the *OSNAP, OTRACK*, and *LWT* options.

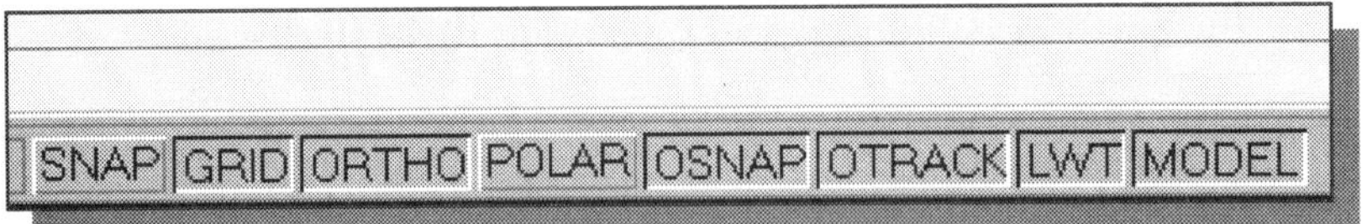

Creating object lines

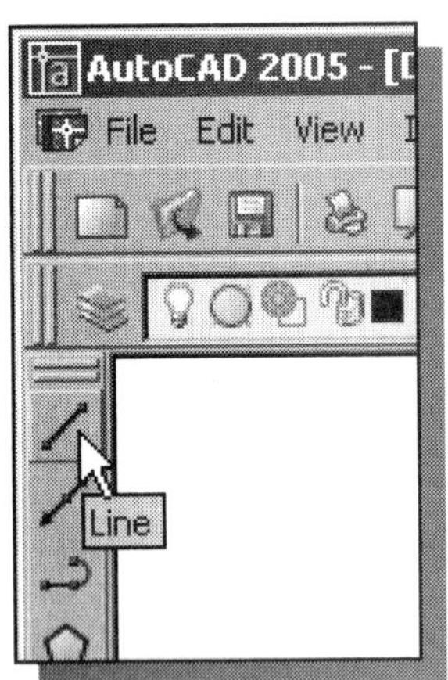

1. Select the **Line** command icon in the *Draw* toolbar. In the command prompt area, the message "*_line Specify first point:*" is displayed.

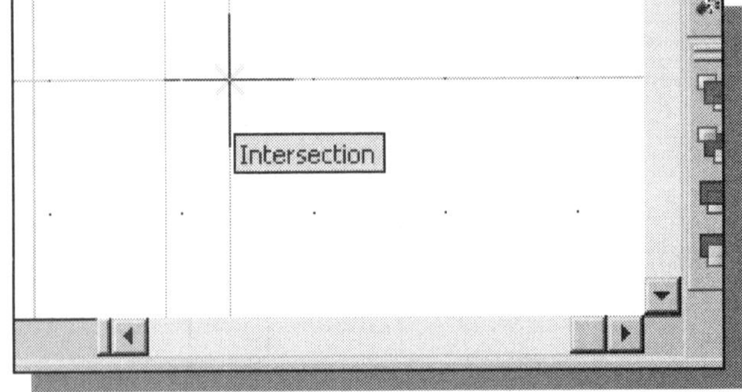

2. Move the cursor to the intersection of the construction lines at the lower right corner and notice the visual aid automatically displayed at the intersection.

3. Create the object lines as shown below. (Use the *relative coordinate entry method* and the Trim command to construct the 30° line.)

4. Use the Arc and Circle commands to complete the object lines as shown.

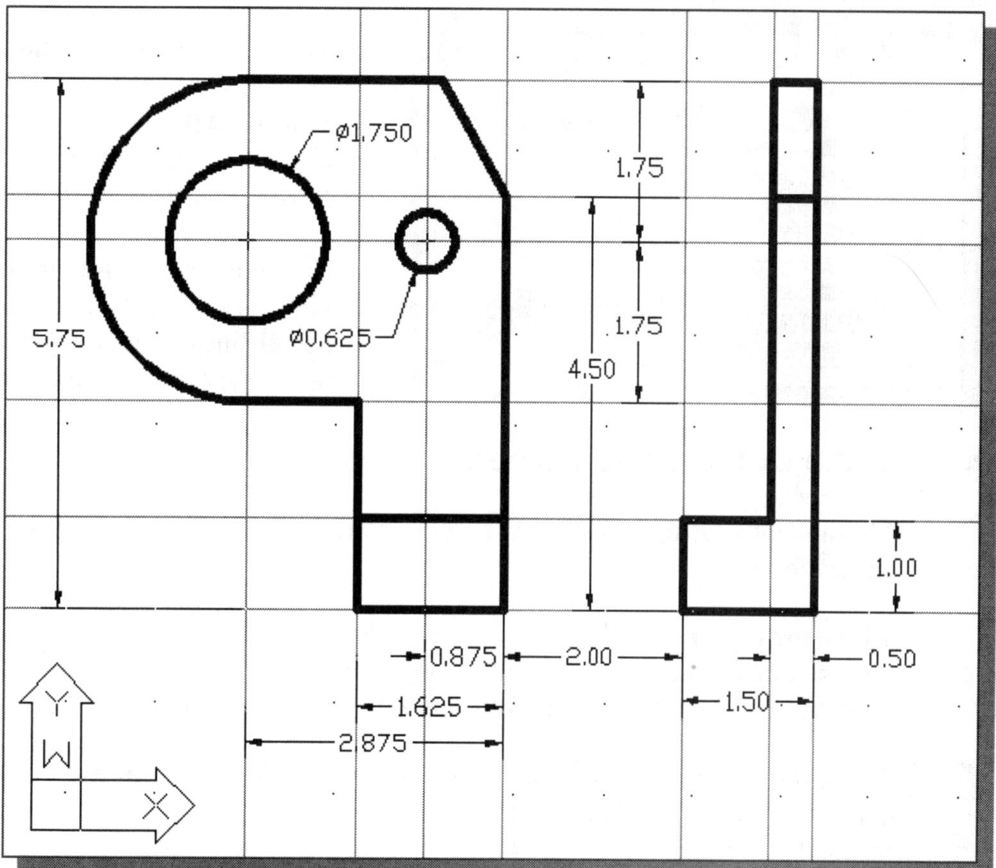

Creating hidden lines

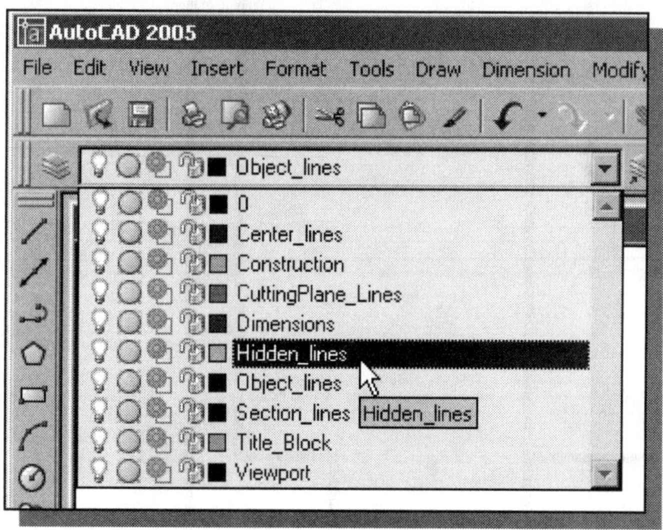

1. On the *Object Properties* toolbar, choose the *Layer Control* box with the left-mouse-button.

2. Move the cursor over the name of layer ***Hidden_Lines***, **left-mouse-click once**, and set layer *Hidden_lines* as the *Current Layer.*

3. Create the five hidden lines in the side view as shown on the next page.

Creating Center lines

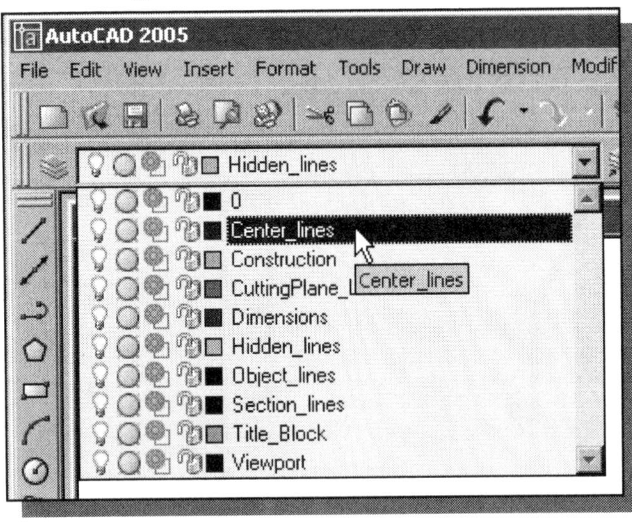

1. On the *Object Properties* toolbar, choose the *Layer Control* box with the left-mouse-button.

2. Move the cursor over the name of layer ***Center_Lines***, **left-mouse-click once**, and set layer *Center_Lines* as the *Current Layer*.

3. Create the center line in the side view as shown. (We will add the center lines in the front-view using the *Center Mark* option.)

Turn *OFF* the Construction Lines

1. On the *Object Properties* toolbar, choose the *Layer Control* box with the left-mouse-button.

2. Move the cursor over the light-bulb icon for layer *Construction_Lines*, **left-mouse-click once**, and notice the icon color is changed to a gray tone color, representing the layer (layer *Construction_Lines*) is turned *OFF*.

3. Move the cursor over the name of layer ***Object_Lines***, **left-mouse-click once**, and set layer *Object_Lines* as the *Current Layer*.

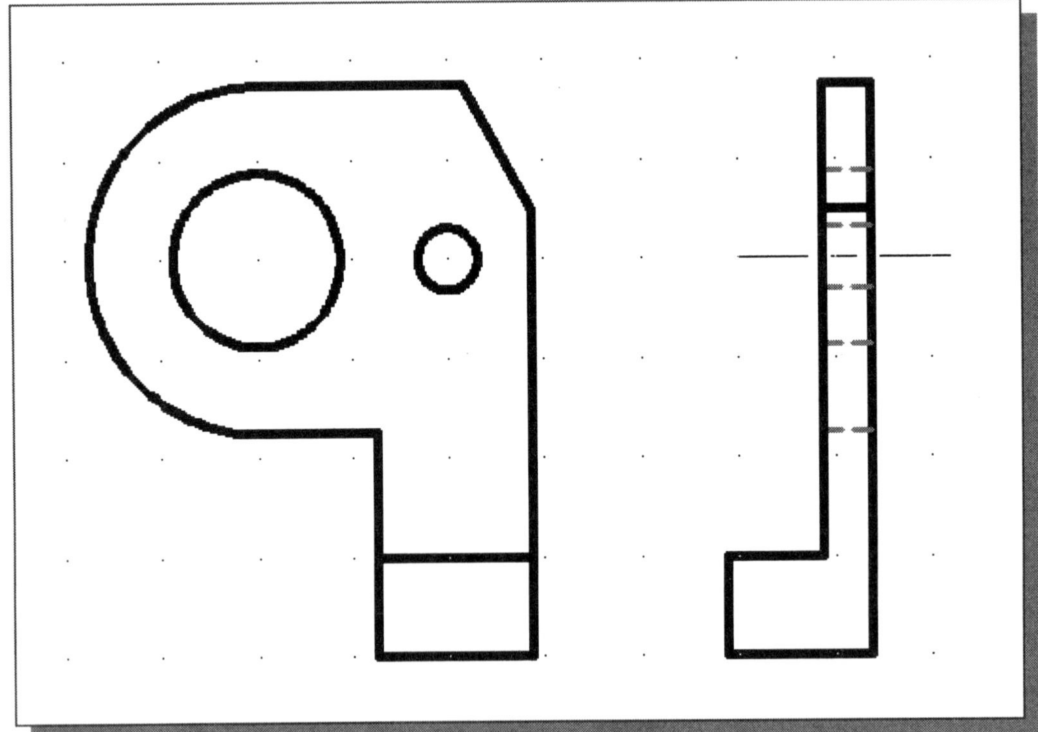

Using the *Fillet* command

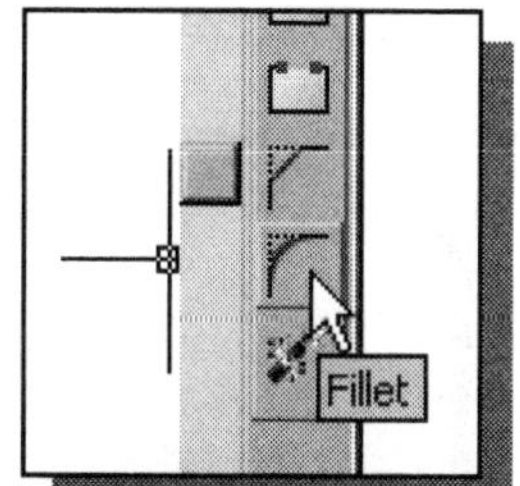

1. Select the **Fillet** command icon in the *Modify* toolbar. In the command prompt area, the message "*Select first object or [Polyline/Radius/Trim]:*" is displayed.

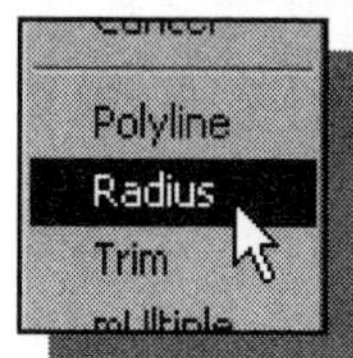

2. Inside the graphics window, right-mouse-click to activate the option menu and select the **Radius** option with the left-mouse-button to specify the radius of the fillet.

3. In the command prompt area, the message "*Specify fillet radius:*" is displayed.

   Specify fillet radius: **0.5** **[ENTER]**.

4. Pick the **bottom horizontal line** as the first object to fillet.

5. Pick the **adjacent vertical line** connected to the arc to create a rounded corner as shown.

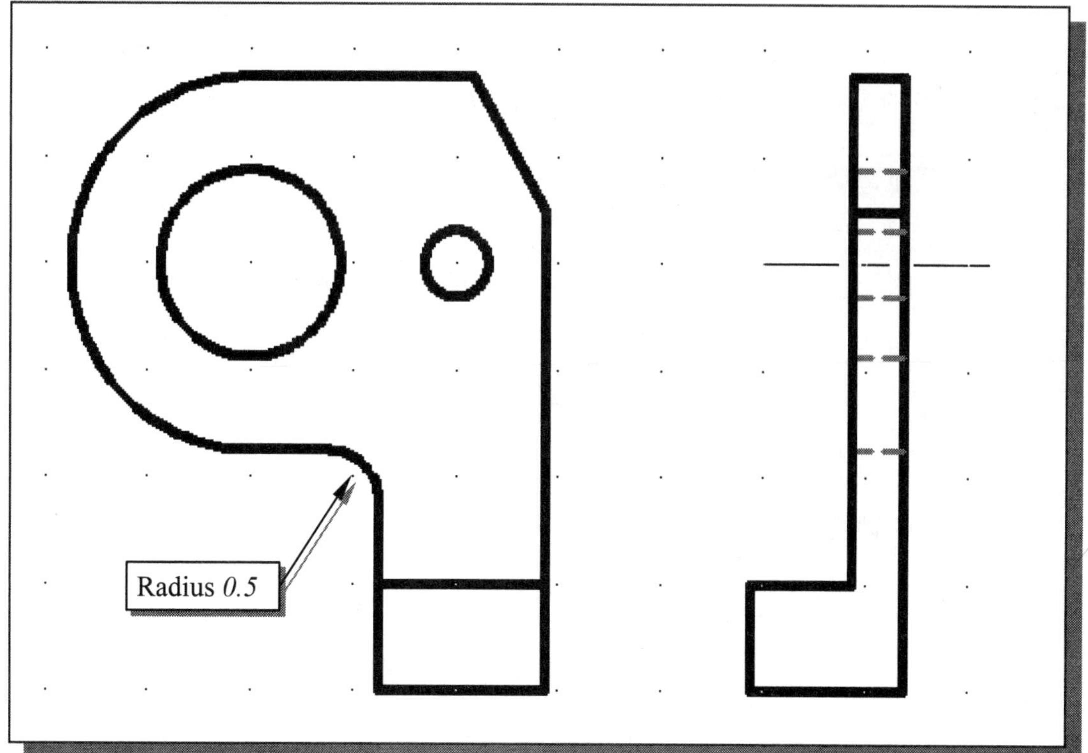

6. Repeat the **Fillet** command and create the four rounded corners (radius **0.25**) as shown.

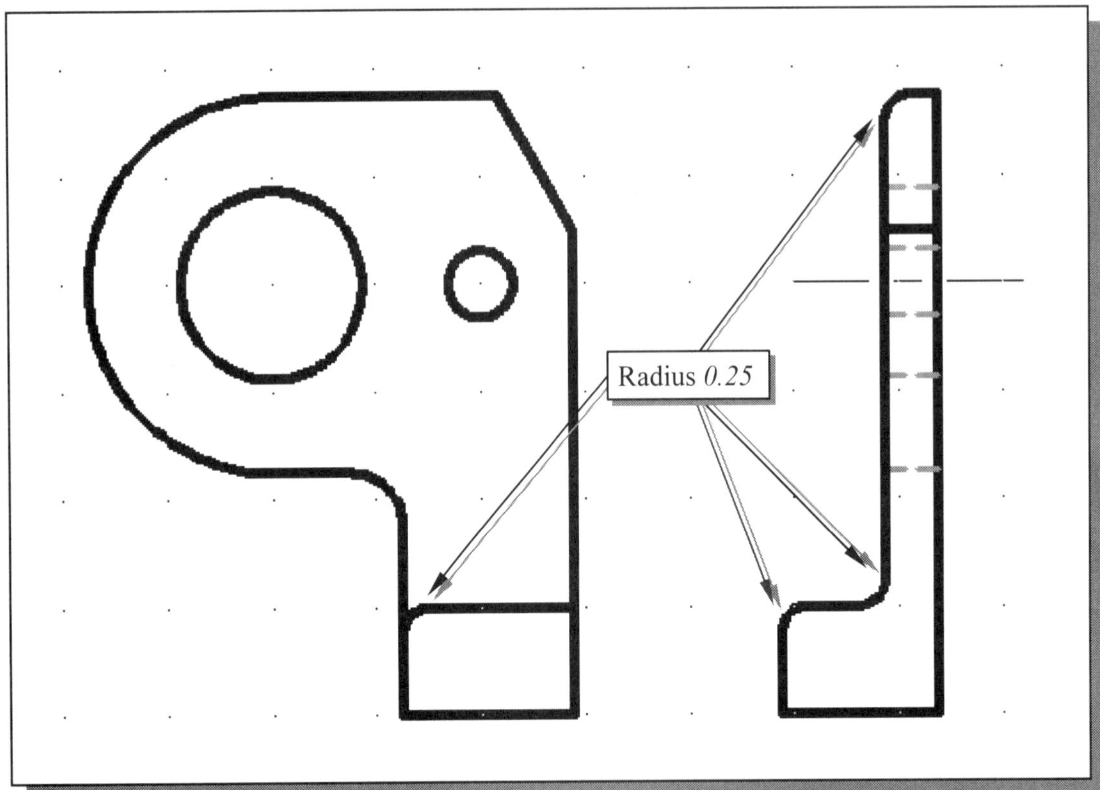

Saving the Completed CAD Design

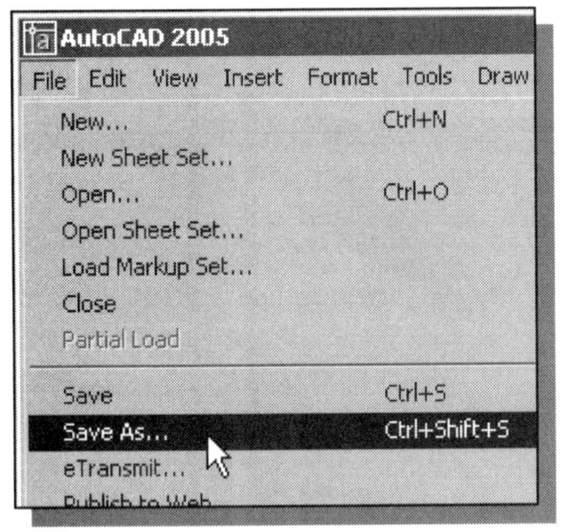

1. In the pull-down menus, select:

   [File] → [Save As]

2. In the *Save Drawing As* dialog box, select the folder in which you want to store the CAD file and enter ***Bracket*** in the *File name* box.

3. Click **Save** in the *Save Drawing As* dialog box to accept the selections and save the file.

The *Dimension* toolbar

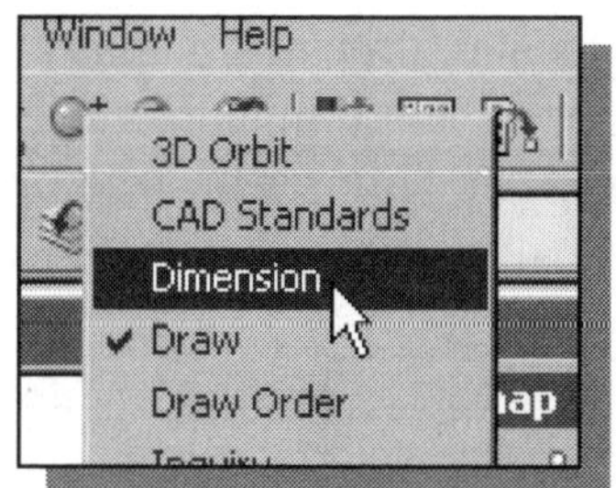

1. Move the cursor to the *Standard* toolbar area and **right-mouse-click** on any icon in the *Standard* toolbar to display a list of toolbar menu groups.

2. Select **Dimension**, with the left-mouse-button, to display the *Dimension* toolbar on the screen.

3. Move the cursor over the icons in the *Dimension* toolbar and read the description of each icon in the *Status Bar* area.

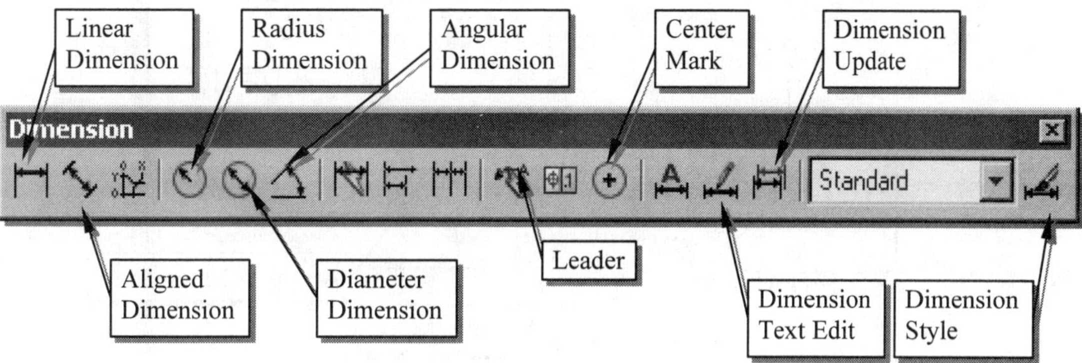

Using *Dimension Style Manager*

❖ The appearance of the dimensions are controlled by *dimension variables*, which we can set using the *Dimension Style Manager* dialog box.

1. In the *Dimension* toolbar, pick **Dimension Style**. The *Dimension Style Manager* dialog box appears on the screen.

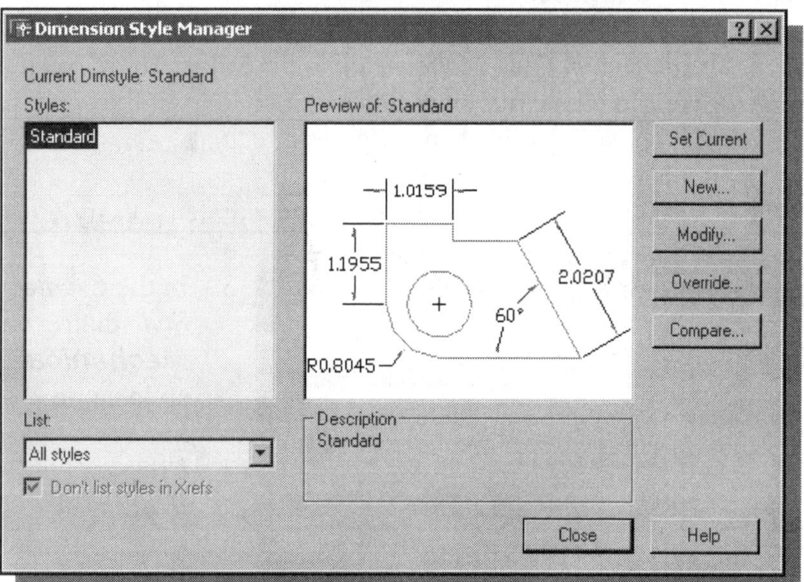

Dimensions nomenclature and basics

As it was stated in *Chapter 2*, the rule for creating CAD designs and drawings is that they should be created **full size** using real-world units. The importance of this practice is evident when we begin applying dimensions to the geometry. The features that we specify for dimensioning are measured and displayed automatically.

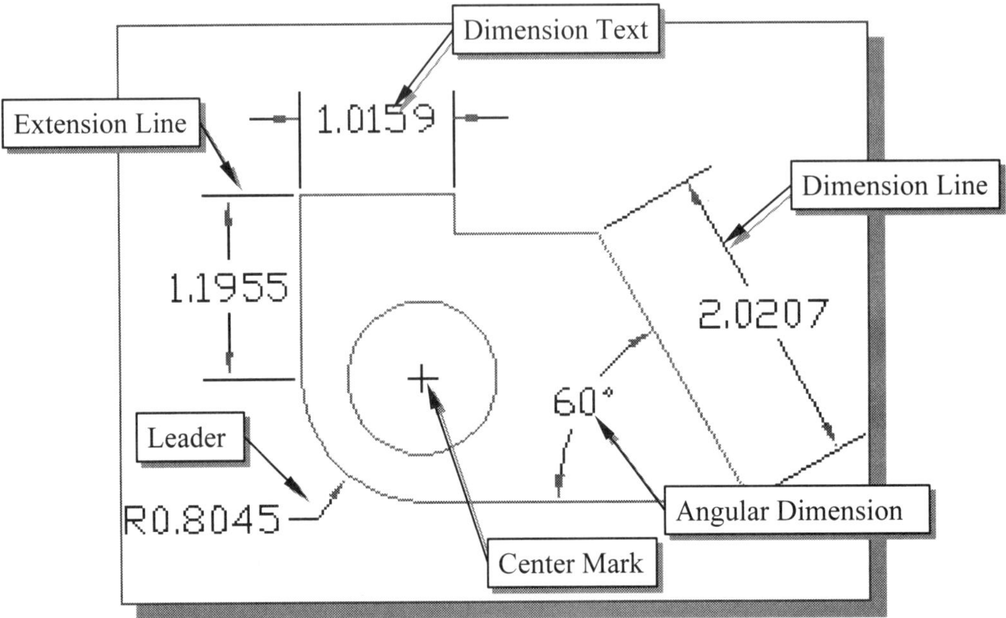

When selecting and placing dimensions, think about (1) the function of the part and (2) the manufacturing operations. Detail drawings should contain only those dimensions that are necessary to make the design. Dimensions for the same feature of the design should be given only once in the same drawing. Nothing should be left to chance or guesswork on a drawing. Drawings should be dimensioned to avoid any possibility of questions. Dimensions should be carefully positioned; preferably near the profile of the feature being dimensioned.

Notice in the *Dimension Style Manager* dialog box, the AutoCAD default style name is *Standard.* We can create our own dimension style to fit the specific type of design we are working on, such as mechanical or architectual.

2. Click on the **New** button to create a new dimension style.

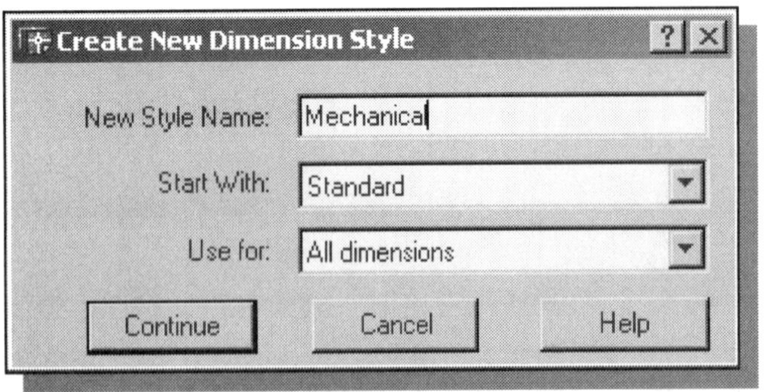

3. In the *Create New Dimension Style* dialog box, enter ***Mechanical*** as the dimension style name.

4. Click on the **Continue** button to proceed.

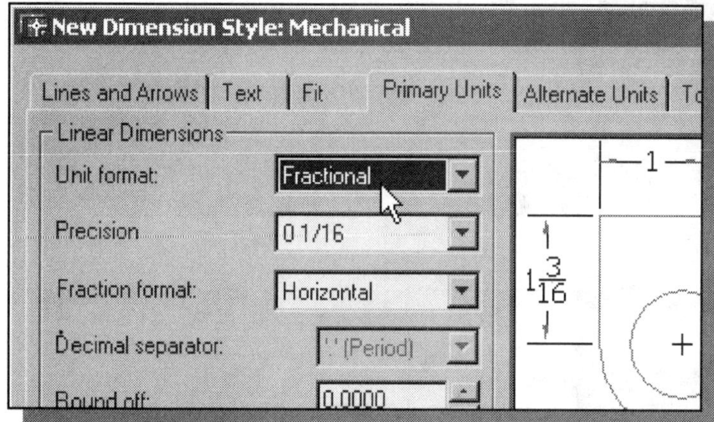

5. Click on the **Primary Units** tab.

6. Select ***Fractional*** as the *Unit format* under the Primary Units tab.

❖ On your own, examine the different options available; most of the settings are self-explanatory.

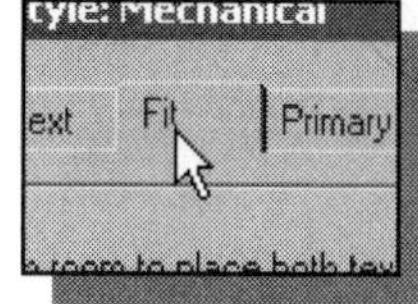

7. Select the **Fit** tab and notice the two options under *Scale for Dimension Features*.

❖ We can manually adjust the dimension scale factor or let AutoCAD automatically adjust the scale factor. For example, our current drawing will fit on A-size paper, and therefore we will use the scale factor of 1. If we decide to plot the same drawing on B-size paper, then we will need to set the dimension scale factor to 2.0. It is possible to let AutoCAD determine the scale factor based on the *layout* settings; we will discuss more about the *layout* in the next chapter.

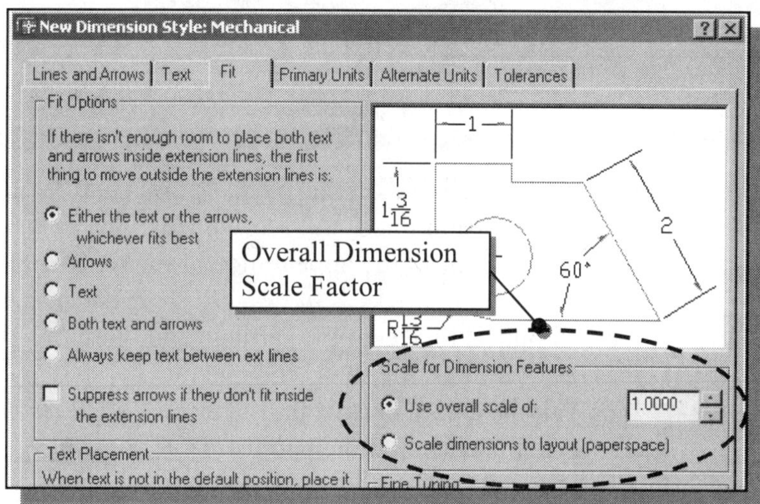

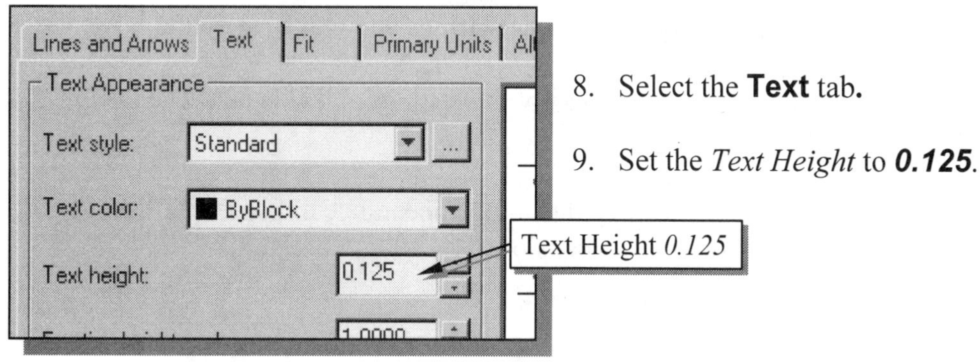

8. Select the **Text** tab.

9. Set the *Text Height* to ***0.125***.

10. Select the **Lines and Arrows** tab and set *Arrow size* and *Extend beyond dim lines* to ***0.125***. Also set the *Center Mark Type* to ***Line***.

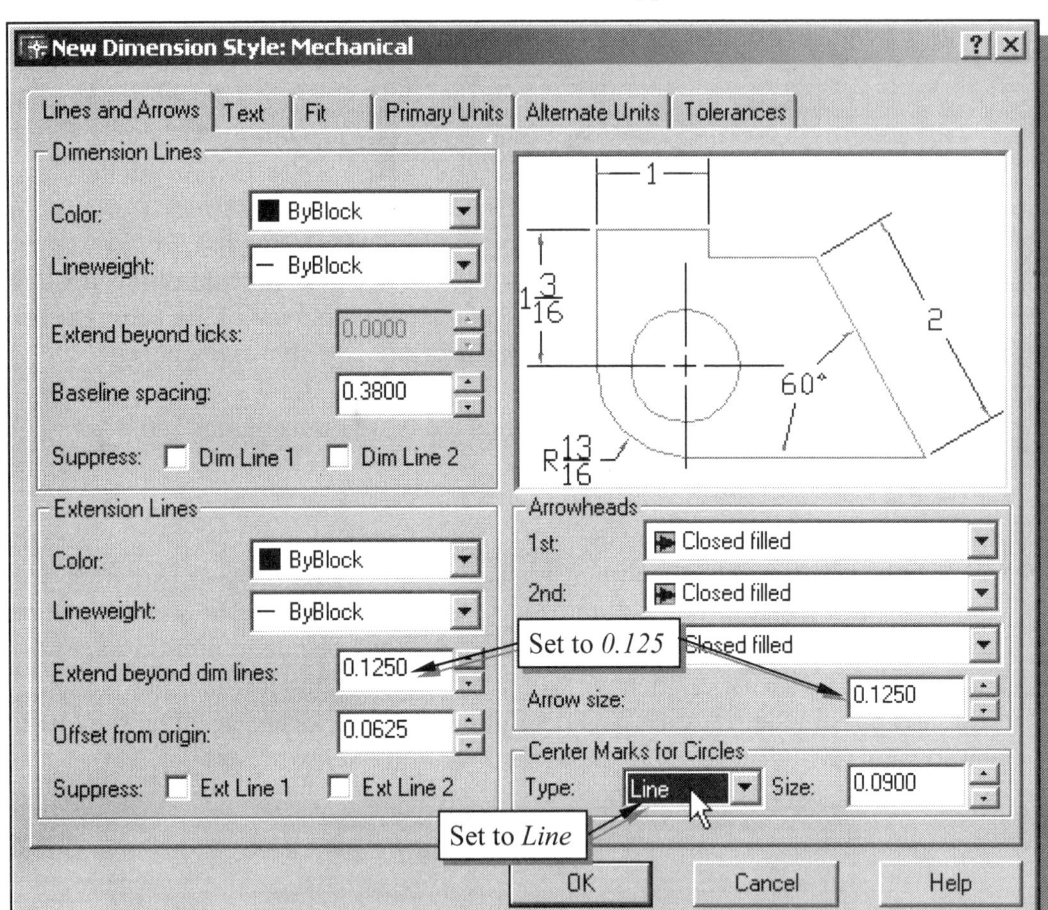

❖ Notice the different options available on this page, options that let us turn off one or both of extension lines, dimension lines, and arrowheads. The *Dimension Style Manager* allows us to easily control the appearance of the dimensions in the drawing.

11. Click on the **OK** button to accept the settings and close the dialog box.

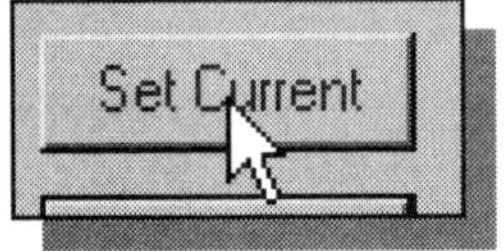

12. Pick the **Set Current** button to make the *Mechanical* dimension style the current dimension style.

13. Click on the **OK** button to accept the settings and close the dialog box.

14. Click on the **Close** button to accept the settings and close the *Dimension Style Manager* dialog box.

❖ The **Center Mark** option is used to control the appearance of center marks and centerlines for diameter and radial dimensions.

Using the *Center Mark* command

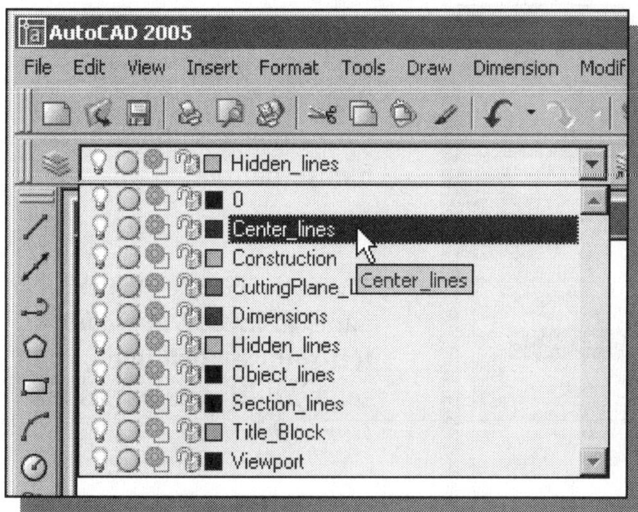

1. On the *Object Properties* toolbar, choose the ***Layer Control*** box with the left-mouse-button.

2. Move the cursor over the name of layer ***Center_Lines***, **left-mouse-click once**, and set layer *Center_lines* as the *Current Layer.*

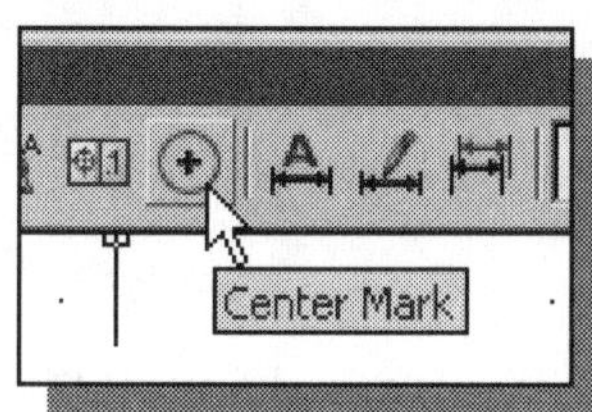

3. In the *Dimension* toolbar, click on the **Center Mark** icon.

4. Pick the **radius 1.75 arc** in the front view and notice AutoCAD automatically places two centerlines through the center of the arc.

5. Repeat the **Center Mark** command and pick the **small circle** to place the centerlines as shown.

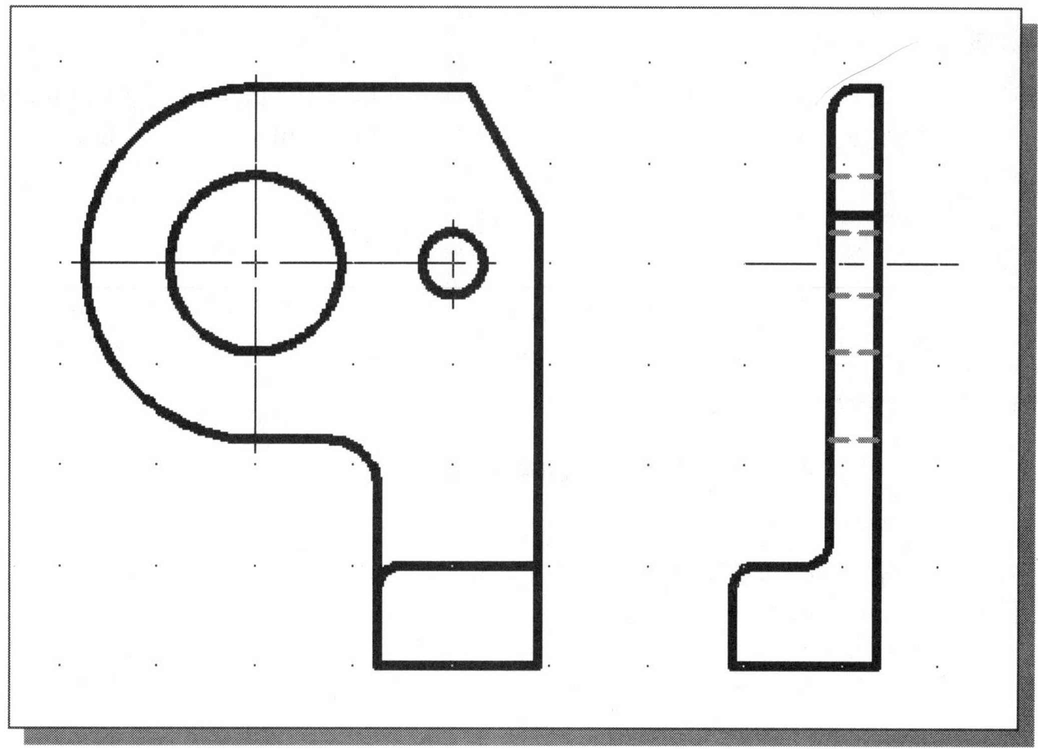

Adding *Linear* dimensions

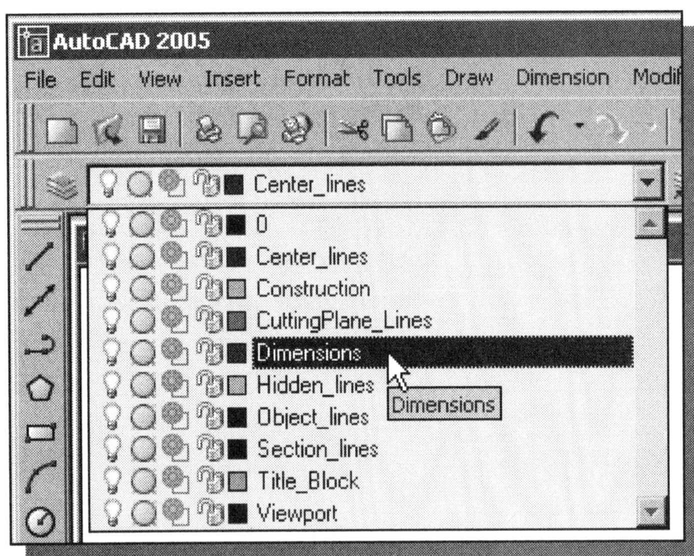

1. On the *Object Properties* toolbar, choose the ***Layer Control*** box with the left-mouse-button.

2. Move the cursor over the name of layer ***Dimensions***, **left-mouse-click once**, and set layer *Dimensions* as the *Current Layer.*

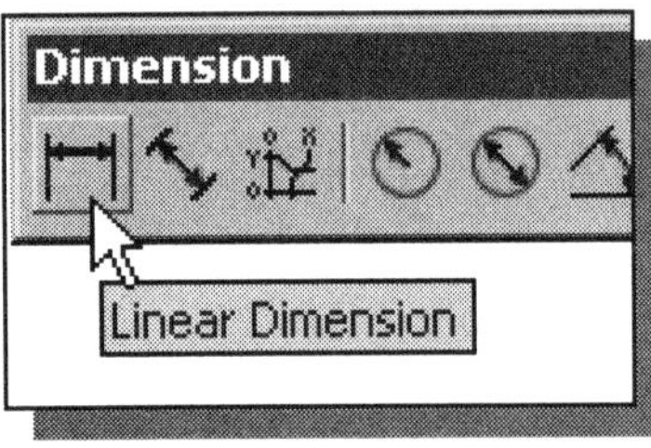

3. In the *Dimension* toolbar, click on the **Linear Dimension** icon.

The Linear Dimension command measures and annotates a feature with a horizontal or vertical dimension.

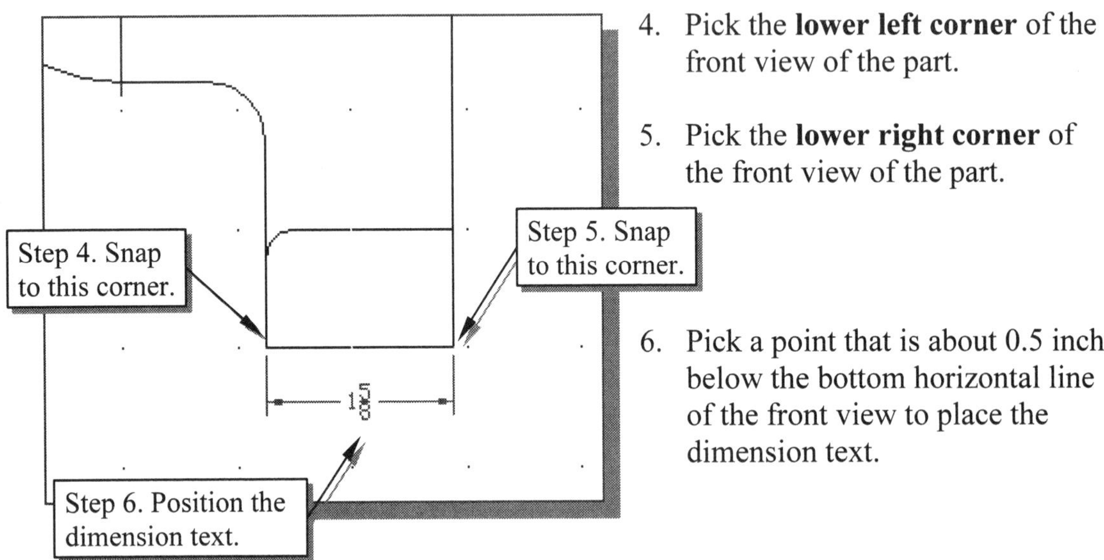

4. Pick the **lower left corner** of the front view of the part.

5. Pick the **lower right corner** of the front view of the part.

6. Pick a point that is about 0.5 inch below the bottom horizontal line of the front view to place the dimension text.

❖ Adding dimensions is this easy with AutoCAD's auto-dimensioning and associative-dimensioning features.

7. Repeat the **Linear Dimension** command and add the necessary linear dimensions as shown.

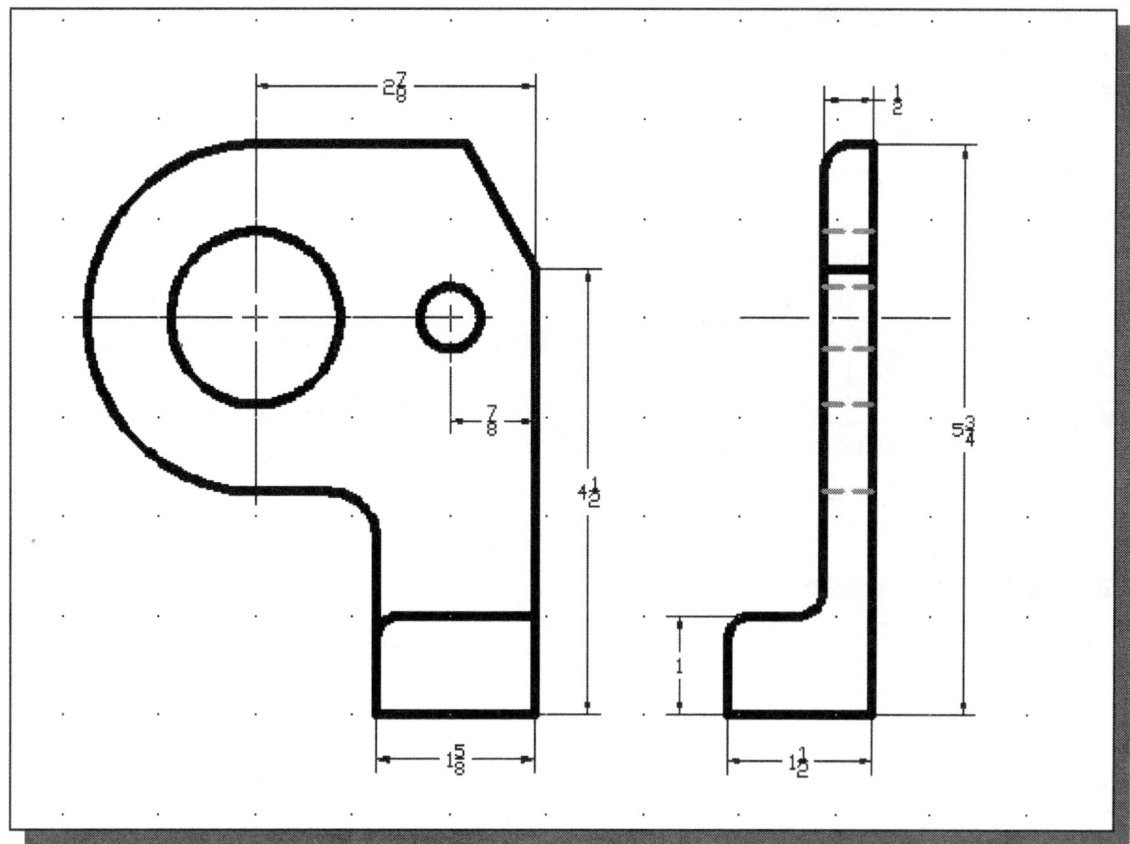

Adding an *Angular* Dimension

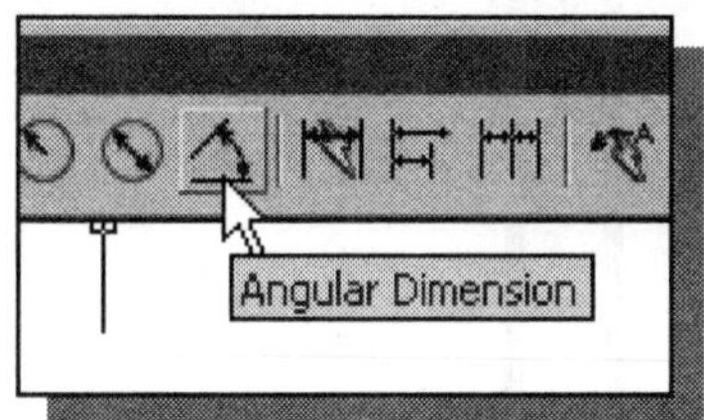

1. In the *Dimension* toolbar, click on the **Angular Dimension** icon.

- The Angular Dimension command measures and annotates a feature with an angle dimension.

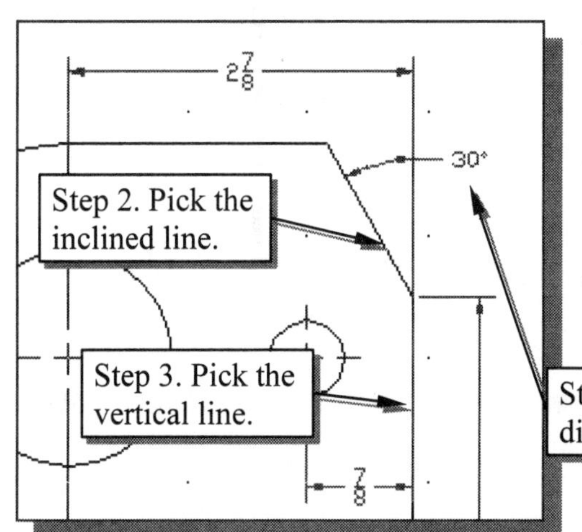

2. Pick the **inclined line** of the part in the front view.
3. Pick the **right vertical line** of the part in the front view.
4. Pick a point toward the right of the front view to place the dimension text.

Adding *Radius* and *Diameter* dimensions

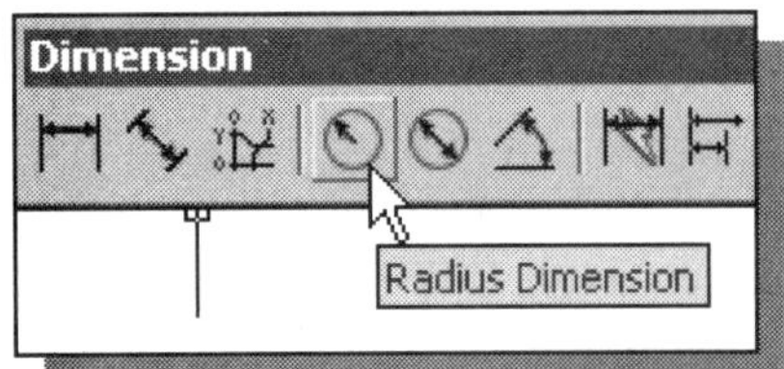

1. In the *Dimension* toolbar, click on the **Radius Dimension** icon.

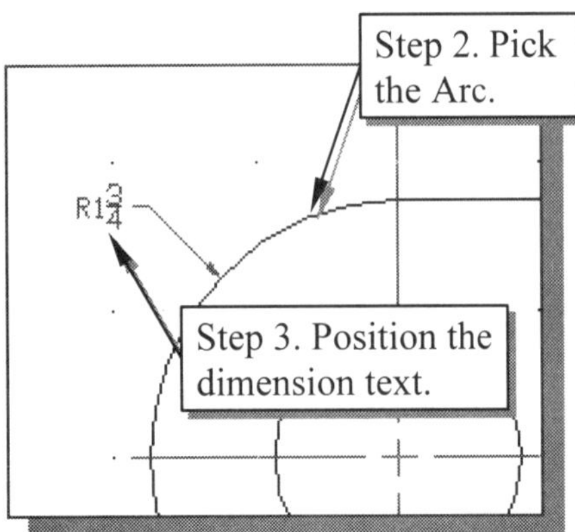

2. Pick the **large arc** in the front view.

3. Pick a point toward the left of the arc to place the dimension text.

4. Use the Radius Dimension and Diameter Dimension commands to add the necessary dimensions as shown.

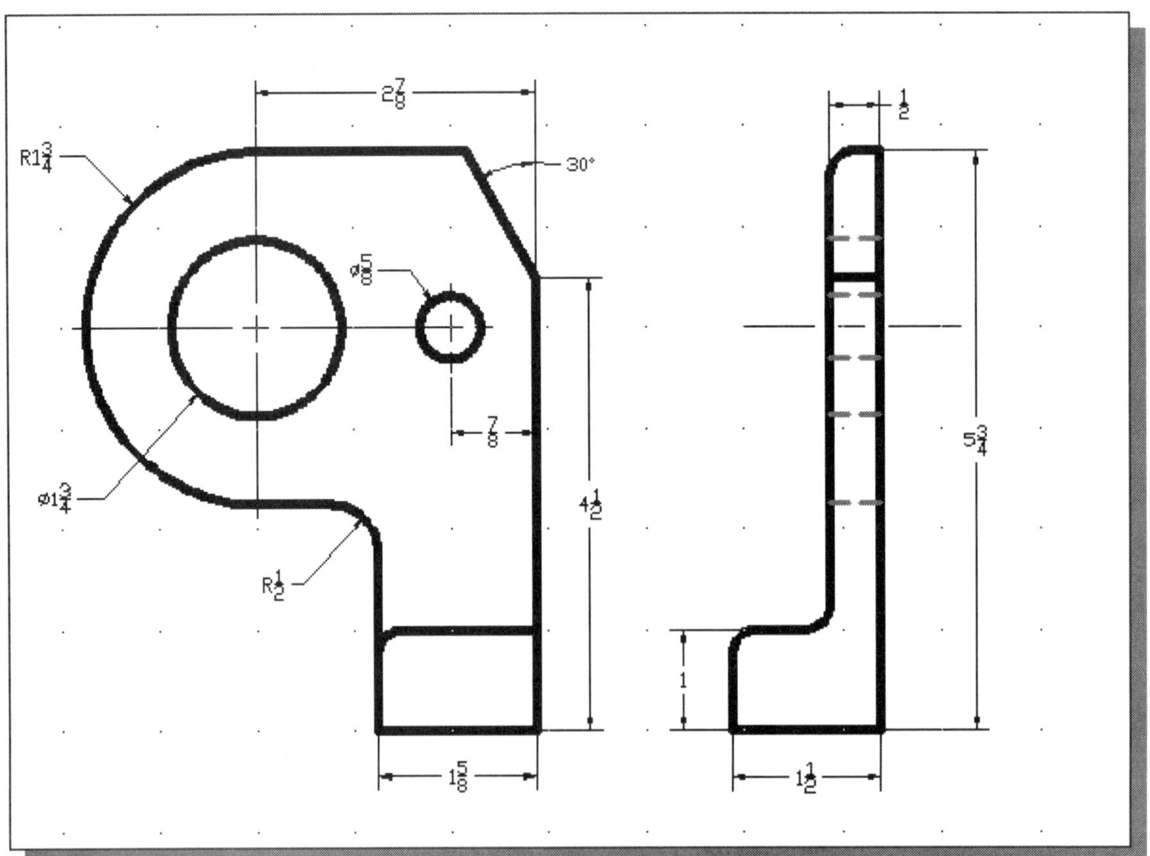

Using the *SINGLE LINE TEXT* command

❖ AutoCAD provides two options to create notes. For simple entries, we can use the **Single Line Text** command. For longer entries with internal formatting, we can use the **Multiline Text** command. The **Single Line Text** command, also known as the **Text** command, can be used to enter several lines of text that can be rotated and resized. The text we are typing is displayed on the screen. Each line of text is treated as a separate object in AutoCAD. To end a line and begin another, press the **[ENTER]** key after entering characters. To end the Text command, press the **[ENTER]** key without entering any characters.

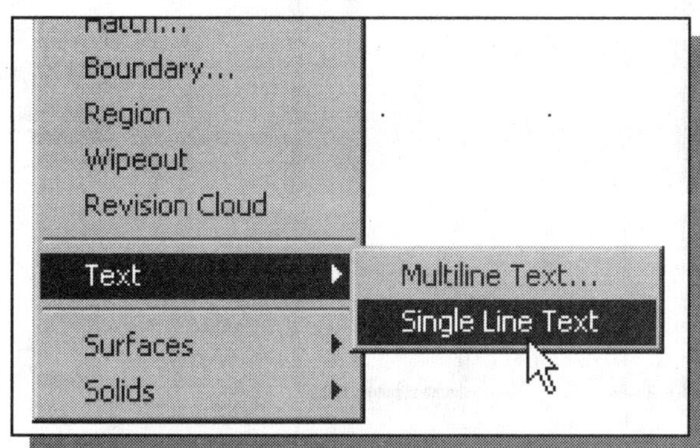

1. In the pull-down menus, select:
   [Draw] → [Text] → [Single Line Text]

2. In the command prompt area, the message "*Specify start point of text or [Justify/Style]:*" is displayed. Pick a location near the world coordinate **(1,1.5)**.

3. In the command prompt area, the message "*Specify Height:*" is displayed. Enter ***0.125*** as the text height.

4. In the command prompt area, the message "*Specify rotation angle of text <0>:*" is displayed. Enter ***0*** at the command prompt.

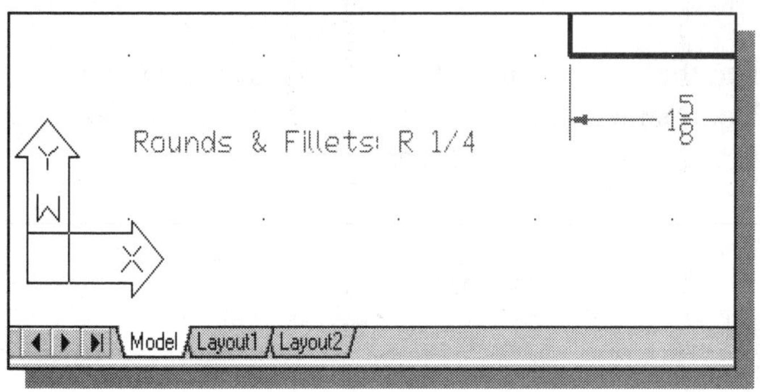

5. In the command prompt area, the message "*Enter Text:*" is displayed.

   Enter: ***Rounds & Fillets R 1/4*** **[ENTER]**.

6. In the command prompt area, the message "*Enter Text:*" is displayed. Press the **[ENTER]** key once to end the command.

7. In the *Status Bar* area, reset the options as shown.

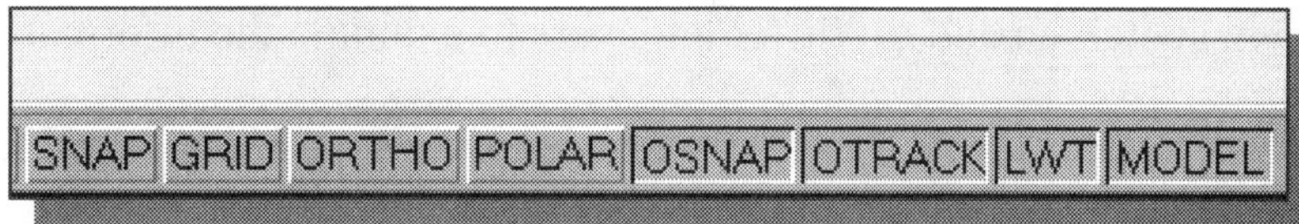

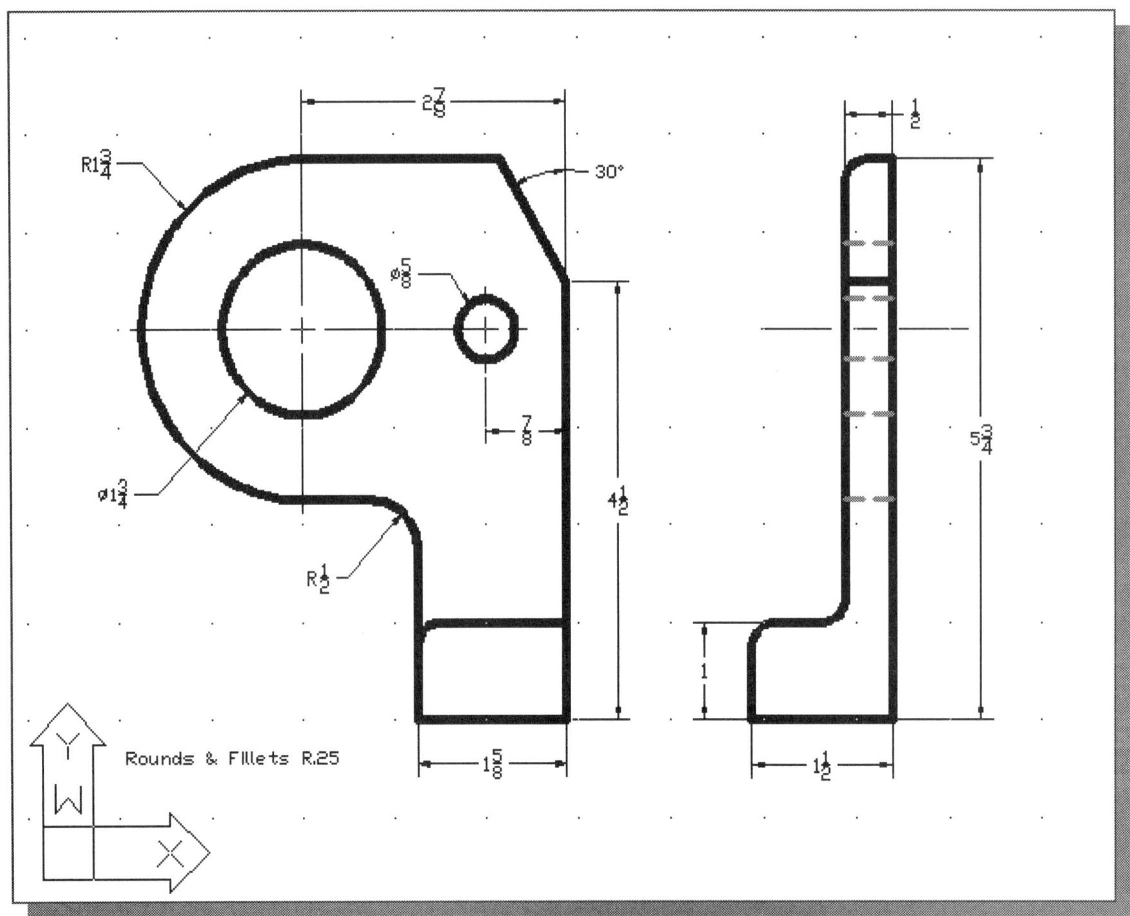

Adding special characters

- We can add special text characters to the dimensioning text and notes. We can type in special characters during any text command and when entering the dimension text. The most common special characters have been given letters to make them easy to remember.

Code	*Character*	*Symbol*
%%C	Diameter symbol	∅
%%D	Degree symbol	°
%%P	Plus/Minus sign	±

➢ On your own, create notes containing some of the special characters listed.

➢ On your own, switch on and off different layers to examine the information stored on each layer.

Saving the Design

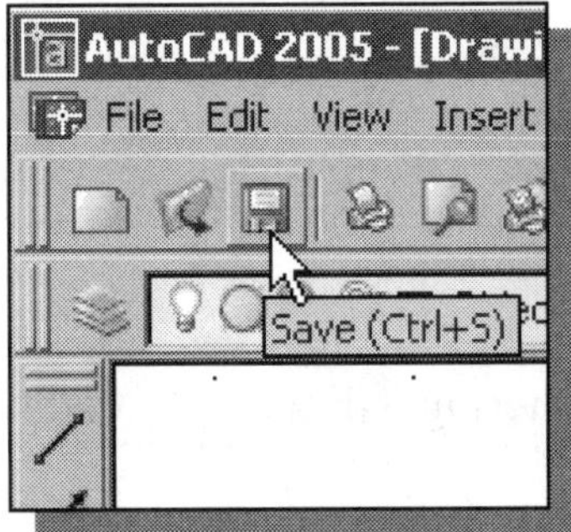

➢ In the *Standard Toolbar* area, select the **Save** icon.

A Special Note on Layers containing Dimensions

AutoCAD creates several hidden **BLOCKS** when we create associative dimensions and we will take a more in depth look at *blocks* in *Chapter 9*. AutoCAD treats **blocks** as a special type of object called a *named object*. Each kind of *named object* has a *symbol table* or a *dictionary*, and each table or dictionary can store multiple *named objects*. For example, if we create five dimension styles, our drawing's dimension style *symbol table* will have five dimension style records. In general, we do not work with *symbol tables* or *dictionaries* directly.

When we create dimensions in AutoCAD, most of the hidden blocks are placed in the same layer where the dimension was first defined. Some of the definitions are placed in the *DEFPOINTS* layer. When moving dimensions from one layer to another, AutoCAD does not move these definitions. When deleting layers, we cannot delete the current layer, *layer 0*, xref-dependent layers, or a layer that contains visible and/or invisible objects. Layers referenced by block definitions, along with the *DEFPOINTS* layer, cannot be deleted even if they do not contain visible objects.

To delete layers with hidden blocks, first use the **Purge** command **[File → Drawing Utilities → Purge → Block]** to remove the invisible blocks. (We will have to remove all visible objects prior to using this command.) The empty layer can now be *deleted* or *purged*.

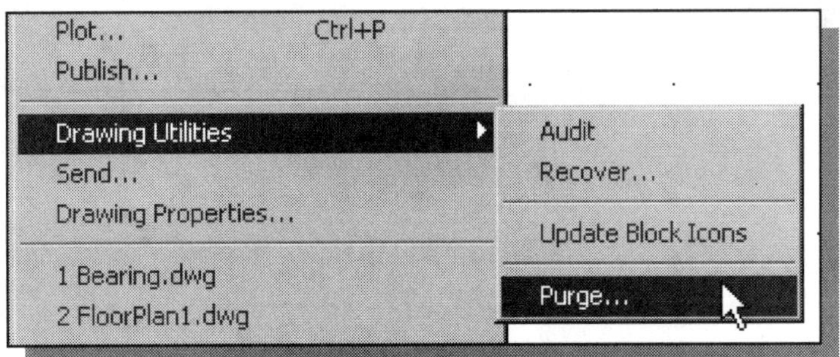

Questions:

1. Why are dimensions and notes important to a technical drawing?

2. List and describe some of the general-dimensioning practices.

3. Describe the procedure in setting up a new *Dimension Style.*

4. What is the special way to create a diameter symbol when entering a dimension text?

5. Identify the following commands:

(a)

(b)

(c)

(d)

Exercises:

1. Dimensions are in inches.

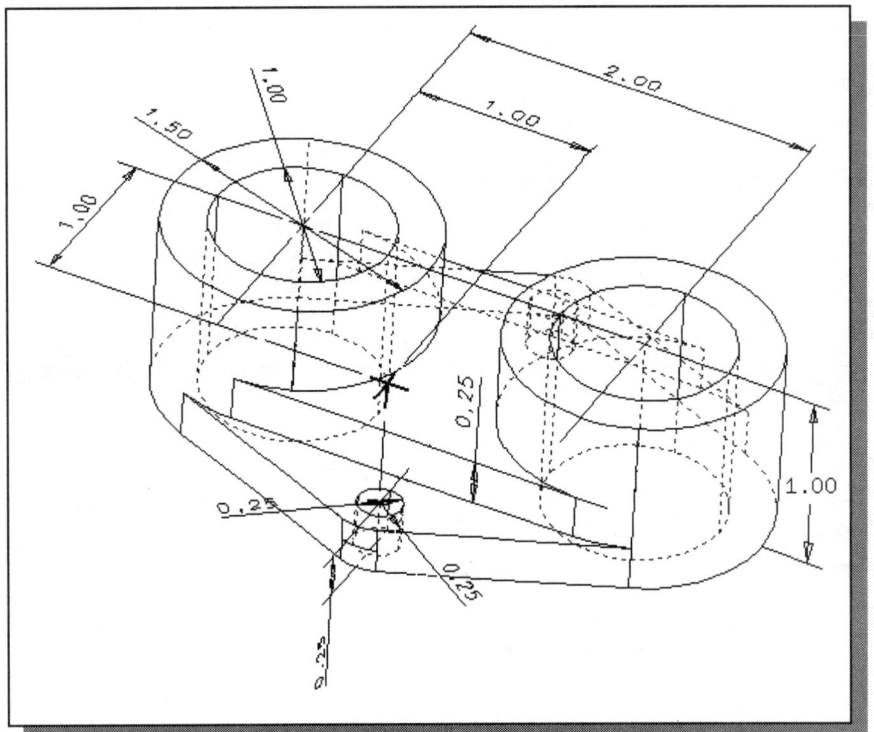

2. Dimensions are in inches.

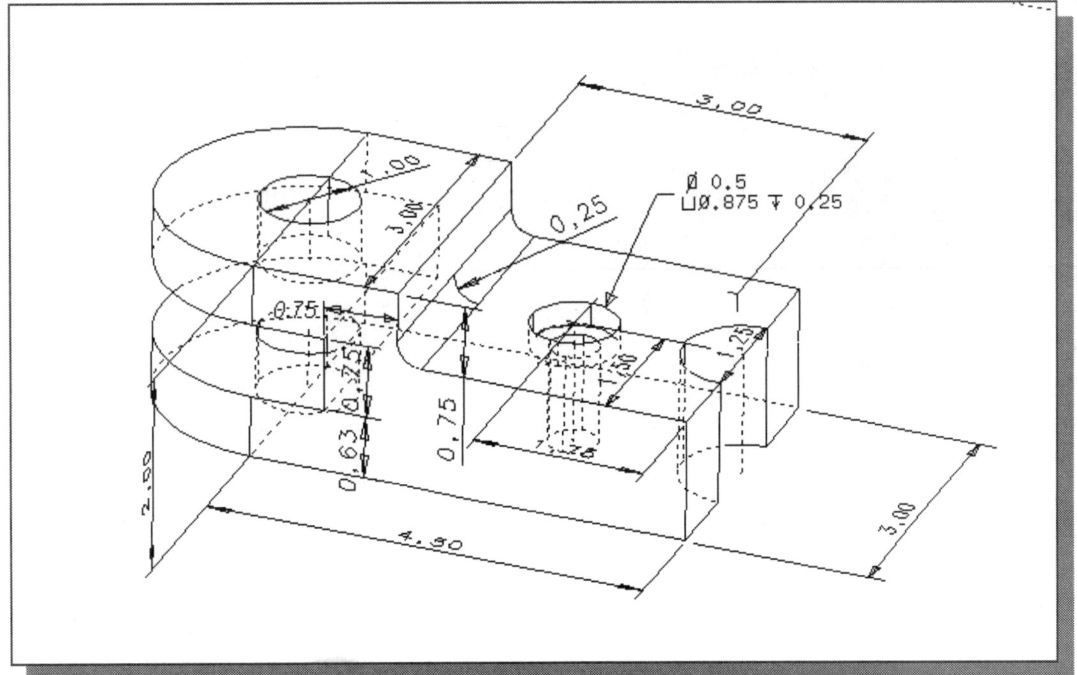

3. Dimensions are in millimeters.

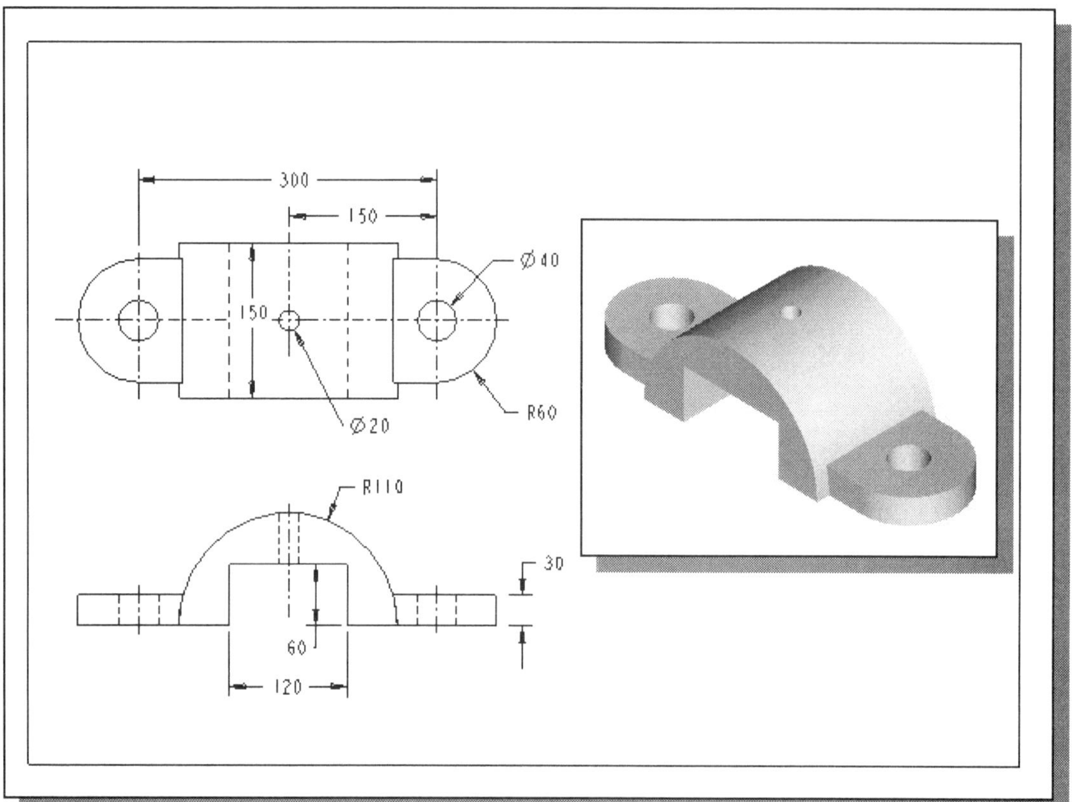

4. Dimensions are in inches.

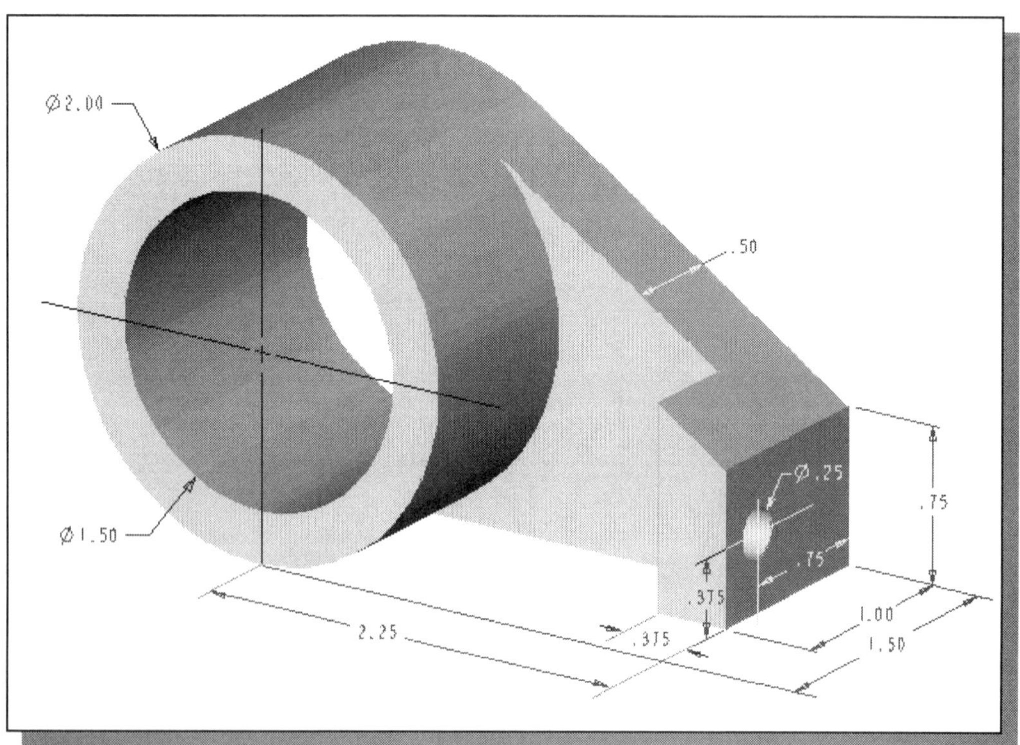

Chapter 7
Templates and Plotting

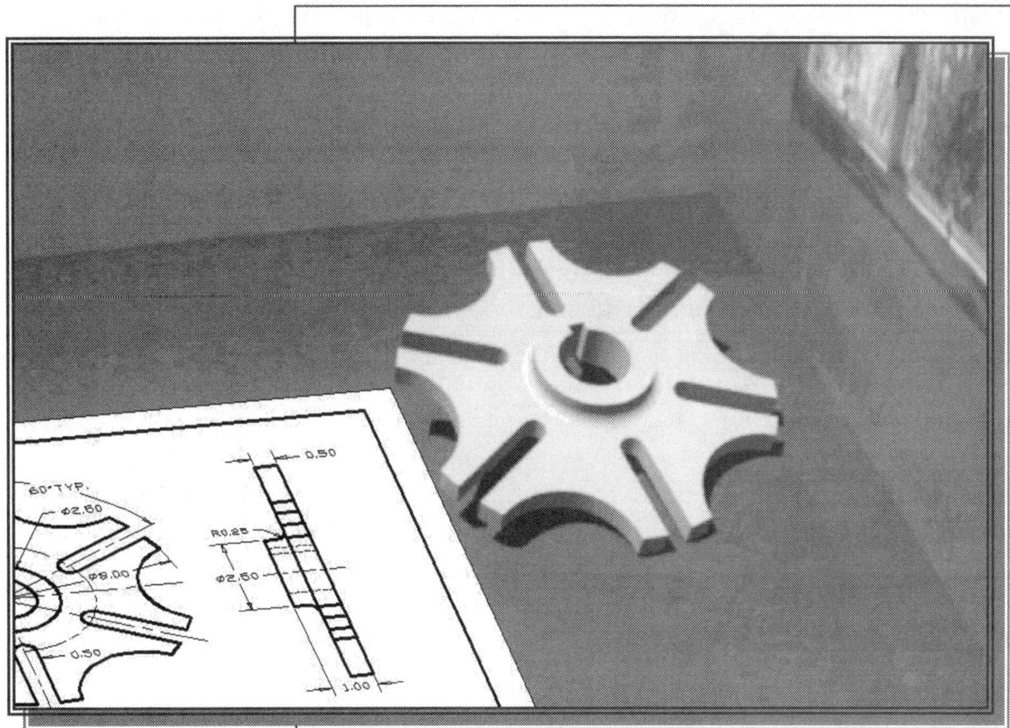

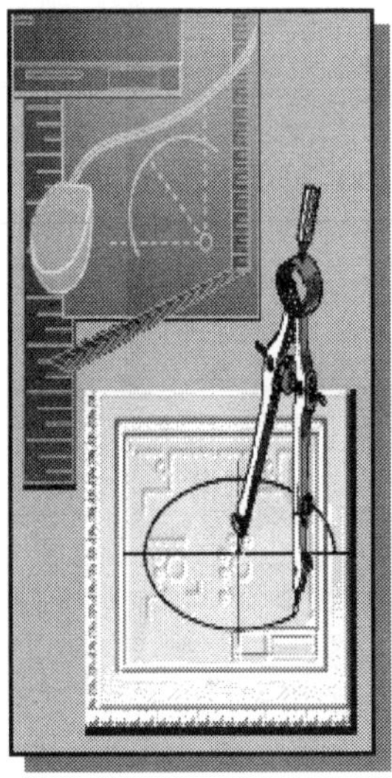

Learning Objectives

- Set up the AutoCAD Plot Style option.
- Create a Template file.
- Use the MIRROR command.
- Create Multiple Copies of objects.
- Set up Layouts in Paper Space.
- Create Viewports in Paper Space.
- Use the PROPERTIES command.
- Adjust the Text Scale for Plotting.

Introduction

One of the main advantages of using CAD systems is that we can easily reuse information that is already in the system. For example, many of the system settings, such as setting up layers, colors, linetypes and grids, are typically performed in all AutoCAD files. In **AutoCAD® 2005**, we can set up **template files** to eliminate these repetitive steps and make our work much more efficient. Using template files also helps us maintain consistent design and drafting standards. In this chapter, we will illustrate the procedure to set up template files that can contain specific plotting settings, system units, environment settings and other drafting standard settings.

We can also reuse any of the geometry information that is already in the system. For example, we can easily create multiple identical copies of geometry with the **Array** command, or create mirror images of objects using the **Mirror** command. In this chapter, we will examine the use of these more advanced construction features and techniques in **AutoCAD® 2005**.

Also in this chapter, we will demonstrate the printing/plotting procedure to create a hardcopy of our design. **AutoCAD® 2005** provides plotting features that are very easy to use. The **AutoCAD® 2005** plotting features include: WYSIWYG (What You See Is What You Get) layouts; onscreen lineweights; plot style tables; device-accurate paper sizes; and creating custom paper sizes.

The *GenevaCam* Design

Starting Up AutoCAD 2005

1. Select the **AutoCAD 2005** option on the *Program* menu or select the **AutoCAD 2005** icon on the *Desktop*.

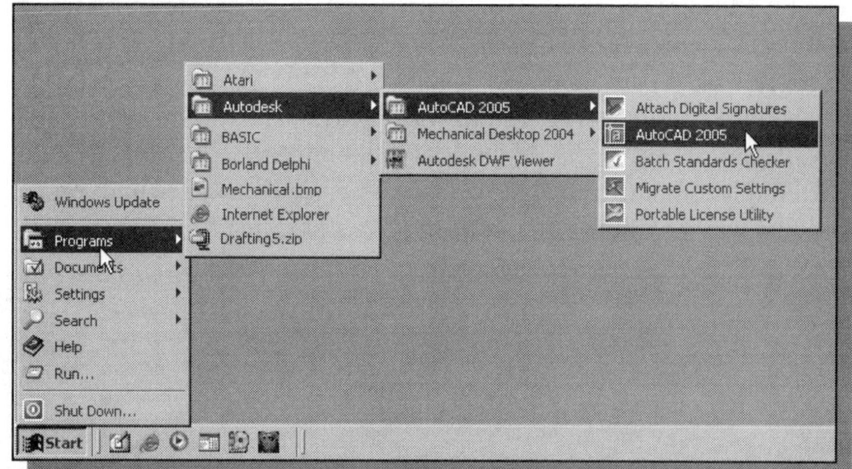

2. In the startup window, select ***Start from Scratch***, as shown in the figure below.

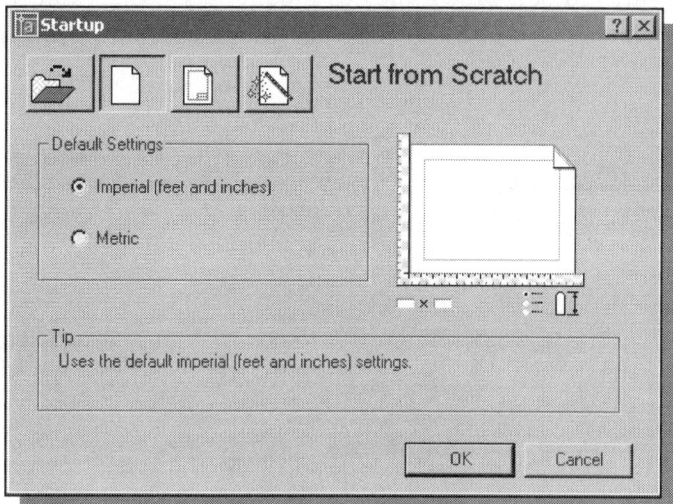

3. In the *Default Settings* section, pick **Imperial (feet and inches)** as the drawing units.

4. Pick **OK** in the startup dialog box to accept the selected settings.

❖ Note the units setting of *Drawing1* is set to the *English units* system. As it was stated in *Chapter 2*, the rule for creating CAD designs and drawings is that they should be created **full size**. The importance of this practice is evident when we are ready to create hardcopies of the design, or transfer the designs electronically to manufacturing equipment, such as a CNC machine. Internally, CAD systems do not distinguish whether the one unit of measurement is one inch or one millimeter. **AutoCAD® 2005** provides several options to control the units settings.

Setting up the *Plot Style Mode*

❖ Using **AutoCAD® 2005** *plot styles* and *plot style tables* allow us to control the way drawings look at plot time. We can reassign object properties, such as color, linetype, and lineweight, and plot the same drawing differently. The default **AutoCAD® 2005** *Plot Style Mode* is set to use the *Color-Dependent plot style*, which controls the plotting of objects based on the object colors and is the *traditional* method of adjusting the plotted hardcopy in AutoCAD. The new method in **AutoCAD® 2005** is to use the *Named plot style table* that works independently of color. In this chapter, we will learn to plot with the new AutoCAD *Named plot style*, which provides a very flexible and fast way to control the plotting of our designs.

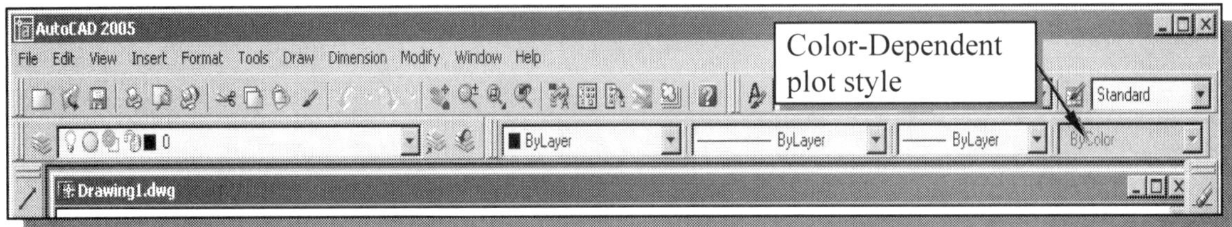

➢ Notice the *Plot Style* box, in the *Object Properties* toolbar, displays the default setting of *ByColor* and is grayed out. This indicates the plot style is set to the *Color-Dependent* plot style, and therefore the object color is used to control plotting.

1. In the pull-down menus, select:

[Tools] → [Options]

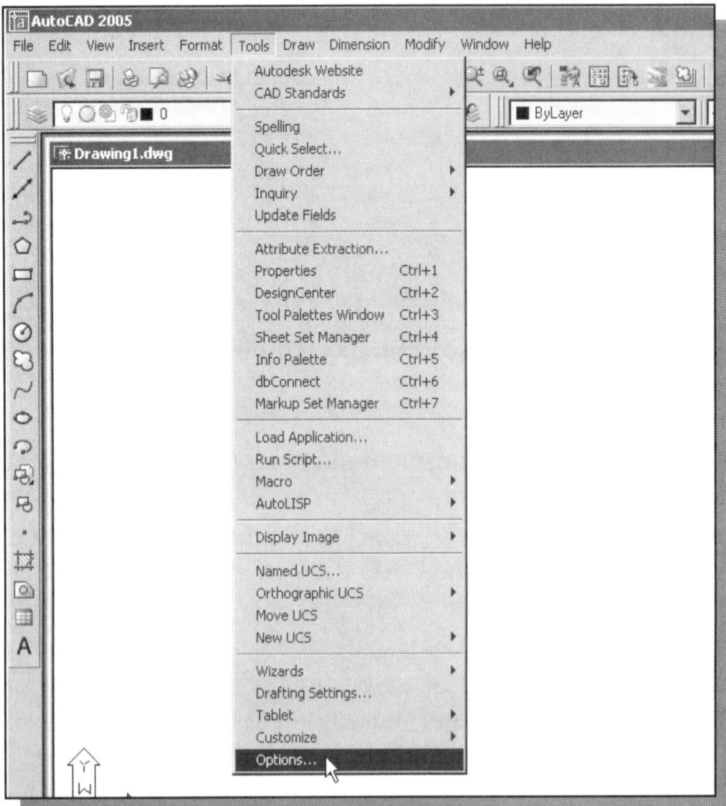

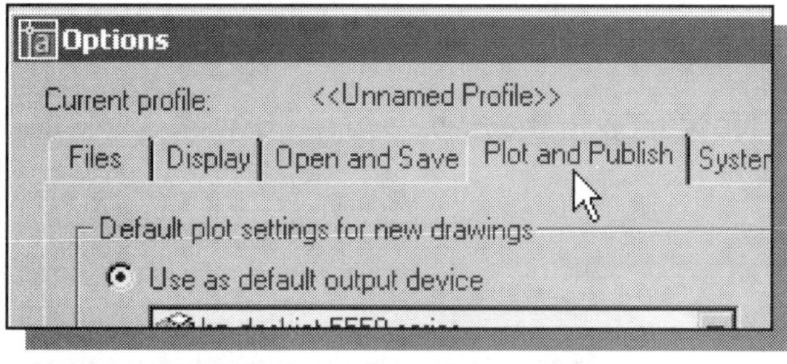

2. In the *Options* dialog box, select the **Plot and Publish** tab if it is not the page on top.

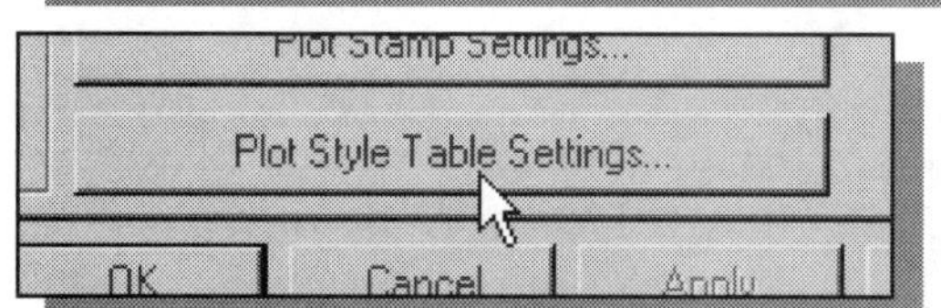

3. Click on the **Plot Style Table Settings** button as shown.

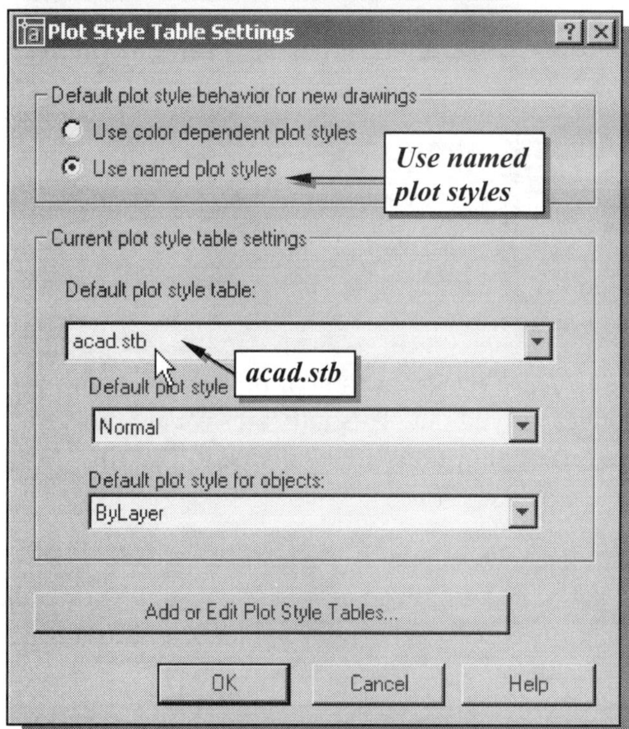

4. Switch *ON* the **Use named plot styles** as shown.

5. In the *Default plot style table*, select ***acad.stb*** from the list of plot style tables.

6. Click on the **OK** button to accept the modified plot style table settings.

7. Pick **OK** to accept the selected settings and close the ***Options*** dialog box.

❖ Notice the *Plot Style* box in the *Object Properties* toolbar still displays the setting of *ByColor* and is still grayed out. This is because the plotting settings are stored in each file. We will close this file and start a new file to have the new settings take effect.

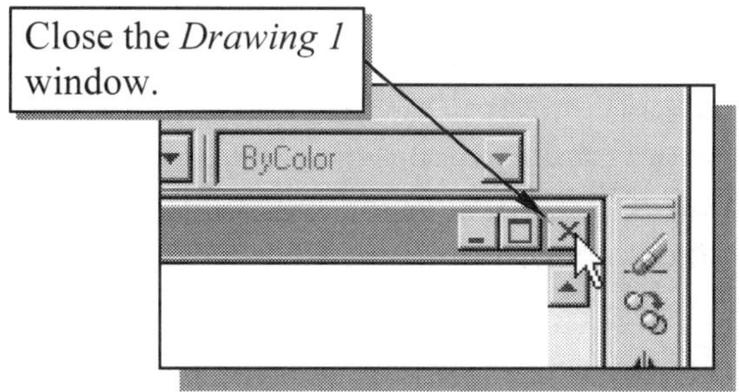

8. Click on the **[X]** button, located near the top right corner of the *Drawing 1* window, to close the file.

9. In the AutoCAD *Warning* dialog box, select **NO** to close the file without saving.

Starting a new file

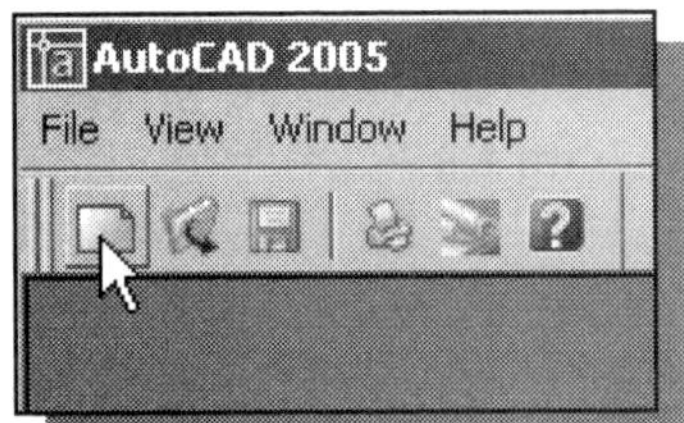

1. Select the **New** icon in the *Standard* toolbar.

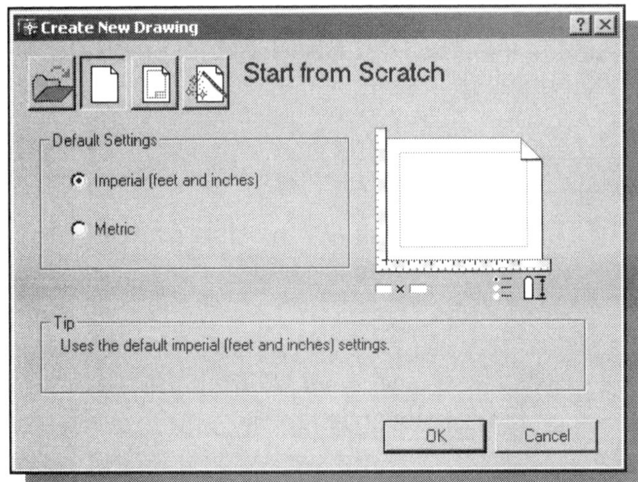

2. In the *AutoCAD* startup dialog box, select the ***Start from Scratch*** option as shown.
3. Pick **Imperial (Feet and Inches)** as the drawing units
4. Pick **OK** in the startup dialog box to accept the selected settings.

❖ Notice the *Plot Style* box in the *Object Properties* toolbar now displays the setting of ***ByLayer*** and is no longer grayed out. This indicates we are now using the *Named plot style*, and different options are available to control plotting of the design.

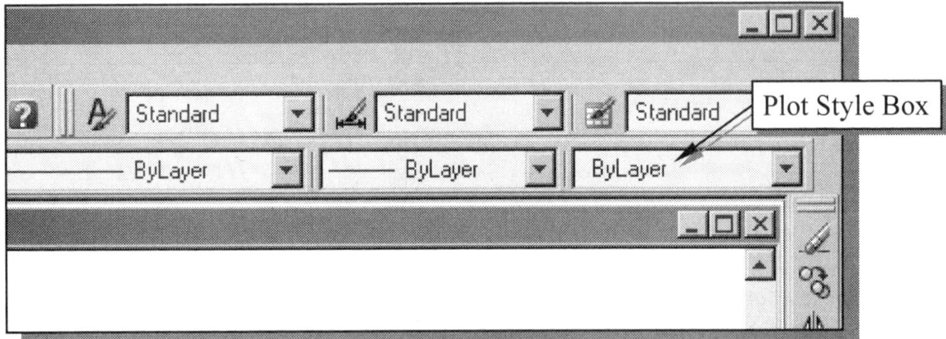

➢ We will demonstrate the use of the ***Named plot style*** to create a hardcopy of the *Geneva Cam* design. The steps described in the above sections are required to set up the settings for the named plot style to be used in new drawings, and it should be done prior to creating the design. We can also convert an existing drawing to use named plot styles; it will require installing the ***AutoCAD Migration*** application and use the **Convertpstyles** command to perform the conversion. Note that after the conversion, any color-dependent plot style tables attached to layouts in the drawing are removed.

GRID and *SNAP* Intervals Setup

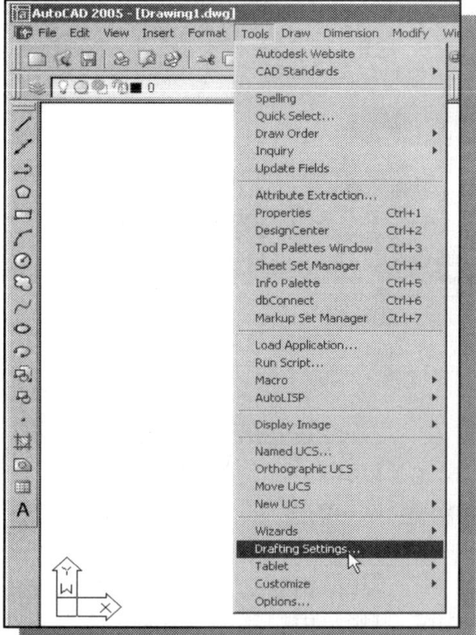

1. In the pull-down menus, select:

   [Tools] → [Drafting Settings]

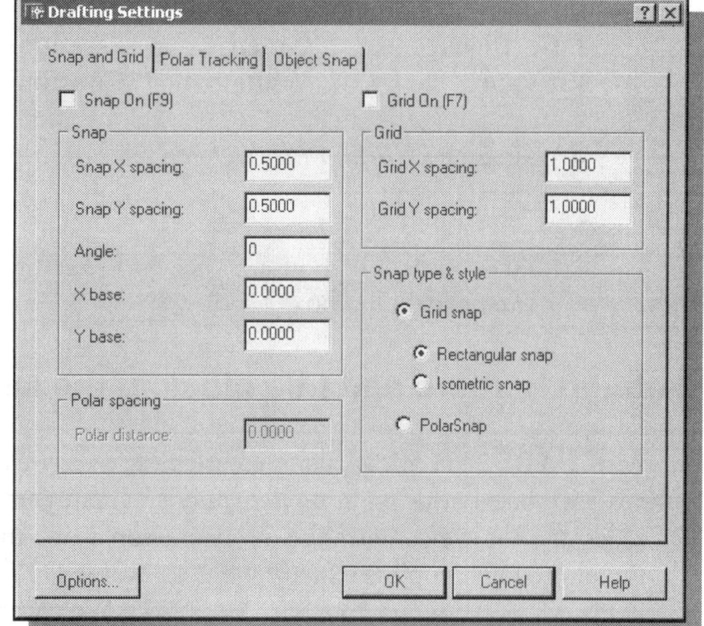

2. In the *Drafting Settings* dialog box, select the **SNAP and GRID** tab if it is not the page on top.

3. Change *Grid Spacing* to ***1.0*** for both X and Y directions.

4. Also adjust the *Snap Spacing* to ***0.5*** for both X and Y directions.

5. Pick **OK** to exit the *Drafting Settings* dialog box.

6. In the *Status Bar* area, reset the option buttons so that only *SNAP, GRID*, and *MODEL* are switched ***ON***.

Layers setup

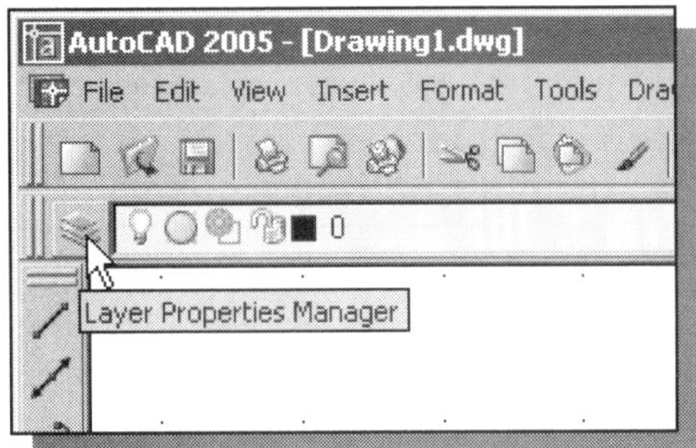

1. Pick **Layer Properties Manager** in the *Object Properties* toolbar.

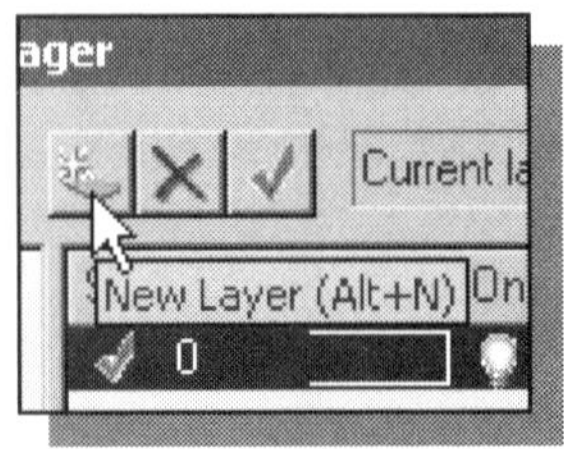

2. Click on the **New** icon to create new layers.

3. Create **layers** with the following settings:

Layer	***Color***	***LineType***	***Lineweight***	***PlotStyle***
Construction	**Gray**	**Continuous**	**Default**	**Normal**
Object_Lines	**Blue**	**Continuous**	**0.6mm**	**Normal**
Hidden_Lines	**Cyan**	**Hidden**	**0.3mm**	**Normal**
Center_Lines	**Red**	**Center**	**Default**	**Normal**
Dimensions	**Magenta**	**Continuous**	**Default**	**Normal**
Section_Lines	**White**	**Continuous**	**Default**	**Normal**
CuttingPlane_Lines	**Dark Gray**	**Phantom**	**0.6mm**	**Normal**
Title_Block	**Green**	**Continuous**	**1.2mm**	**Normal**
Viewport	**White**	**Continuous**	**Default**	**Normal**

➢ Using the ***Normal*** *PlotStyle* enables plotting of ***lineweights*** defined in the specific layer.

4. Click on the **OK** button to accept the settings and exit the *Layer Properties Manager* dialog box.

Adding borders and title block in the layout

AutoCAD® 2005 allows us to create plots to any exact scale on the paper. Until now, we have been working in ***model space*** to create our design in **full size**. When we are ready to plot, we can arrange our design on a two-dimensional sheet of paper so that the plotted hardcopy is exactly what we wanted. This two-dimensional sheet of paper is known as the ***paper space*** in AutoCAD. We can place borders and title blocks on *paper space*, the objects that are less critical to our design.

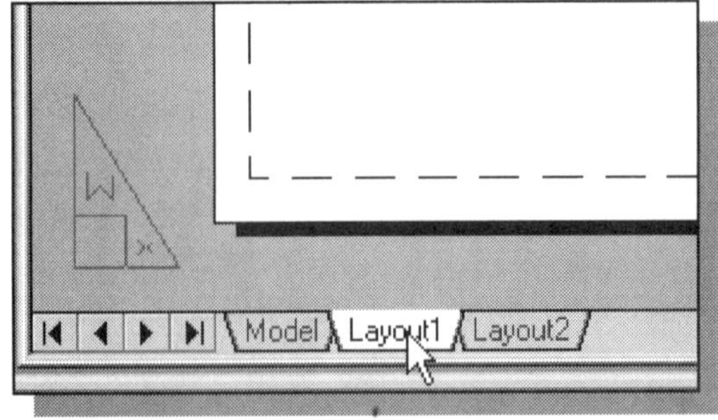

1. Pick the **Layout1** tab to switch to the two-dimensional paper space.

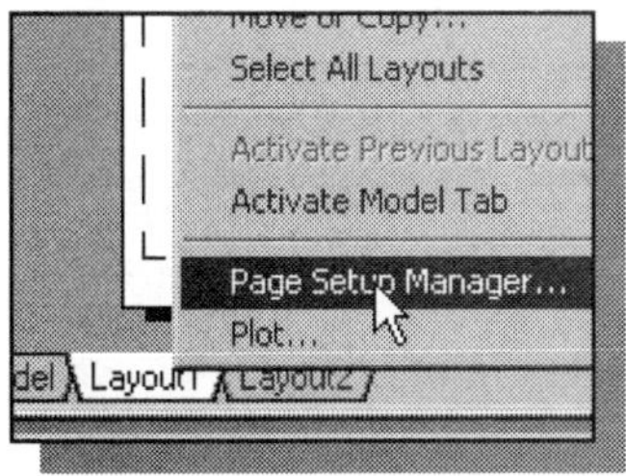

2. To adjust any *Page Setup* options, right-mouse-click once on the tab and slect **Page Setup Manager**.

3. Choose the default layout in the *Page Setup Manager*.

4. In the *Page Setup* dialog box, select a plotter/printer that is available to plot/print your design. Consult with your instructor or technical support personnel if you have difficulty identifying the hardware.

❖ In this chapter, we will demonstrate the plotting procedure for an A-size plot on a LaserJet printer. The procedure described here is also applicable to other types of printers and plotters.

Notice the *Printable area* listed in the *Paper size and paper units* section is typically smaller than the actual paper size, which is due to the limitations of the hardware.

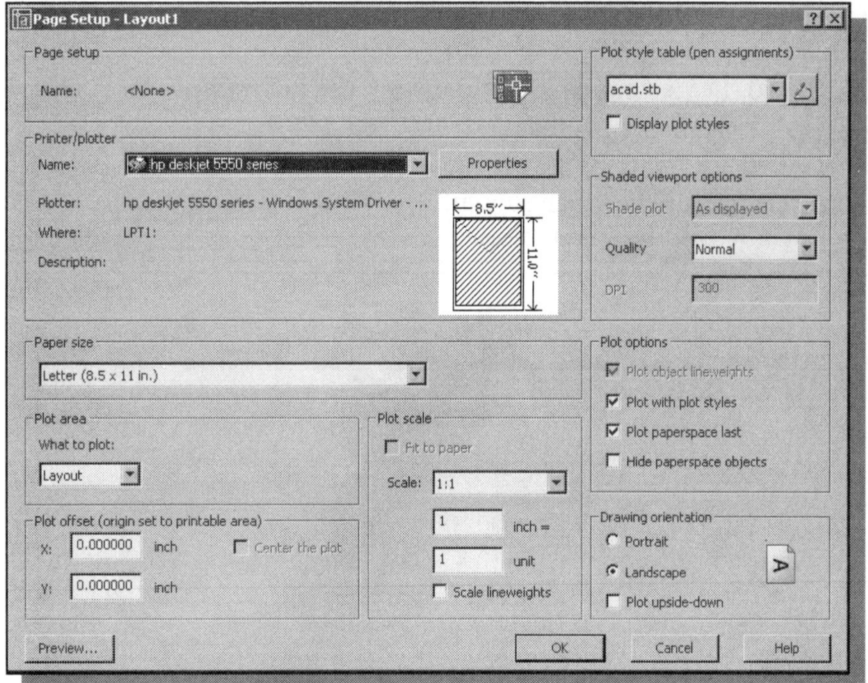

5. Confirm the *Paper size* is set to **Letter** or equivalent (8.5″ by 11″) and the *Drawing orientation* is set to **Landscape**.

6. Click on the **OK** button to accept the settings and exit the *Page Setup* dialog box.

❖ In the graphics window, a rectangular outline on a gray background indicates the paper size. The dashed lines displayed within the paper indicate the *printable area*.

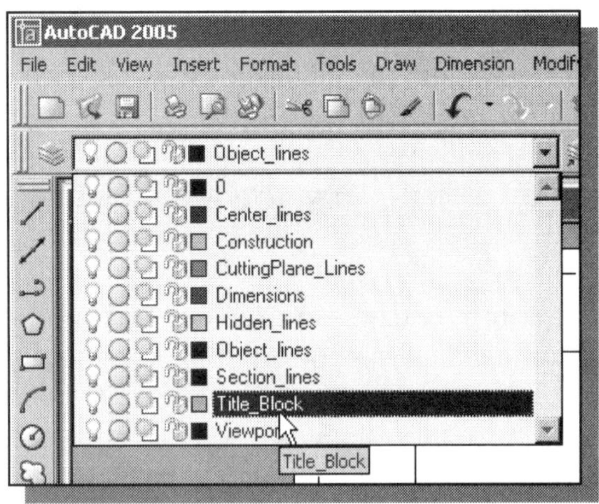

7. In the *Object Properties* toolbar area, select the ***Layer Control*** box and set layer ***Title_Block*** as the *Current Layer*.

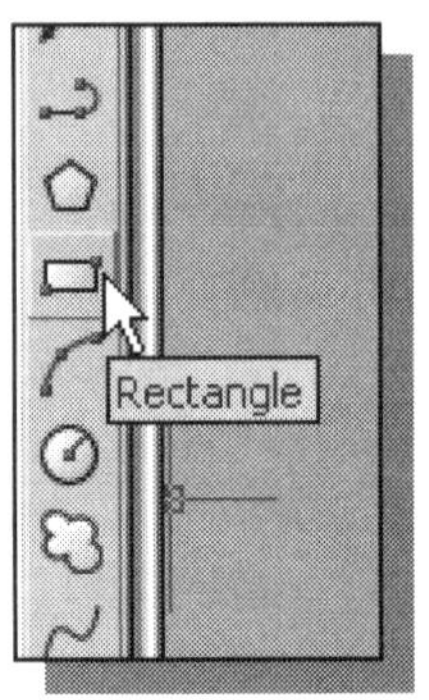

8. Select the **Rectangle** icon in the *Draw* toolbar. In the command prompt area, the message "*Specify first corner point or [Chamfer/Elevation/Fillet/Thickness/Width]:*" is displayed.

9. Pick a location that is on the inside and near the lower left corner of the dashed rectangle.

10. In the command prompt area, use the *relative coordinate entry method* and create a 10.25″ × 7.75″ rectangle.

11. Complete the title block as shown.

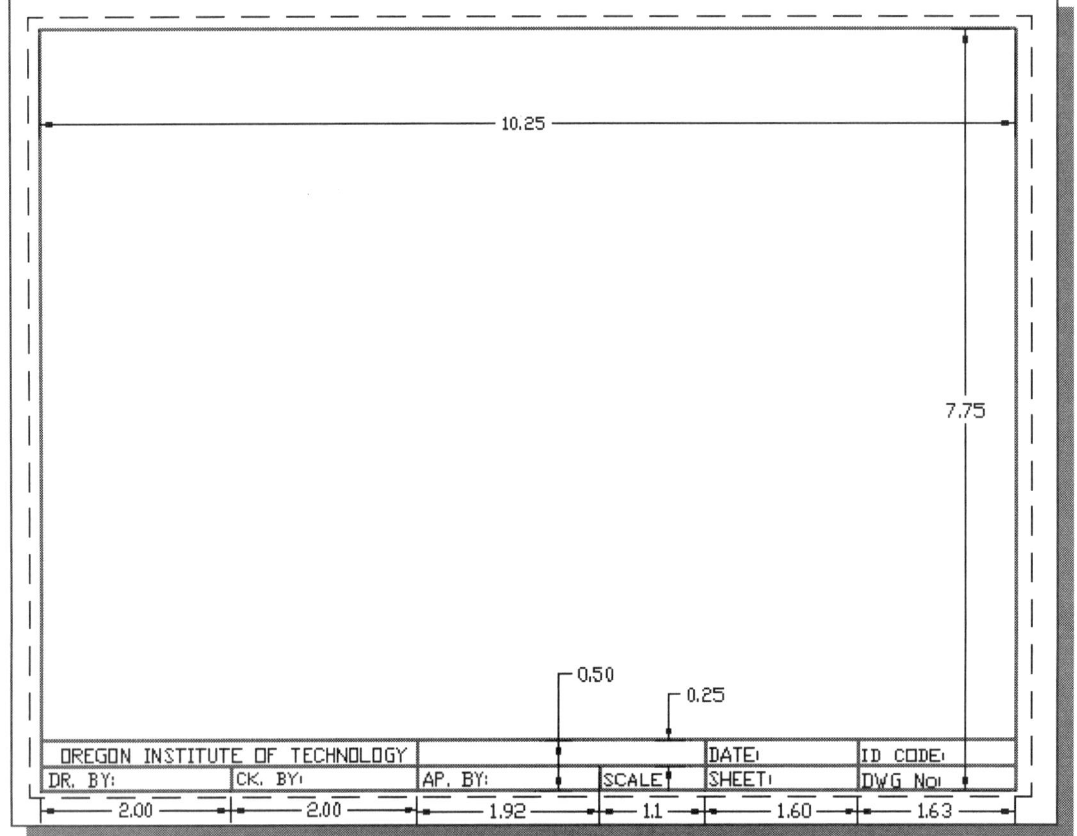

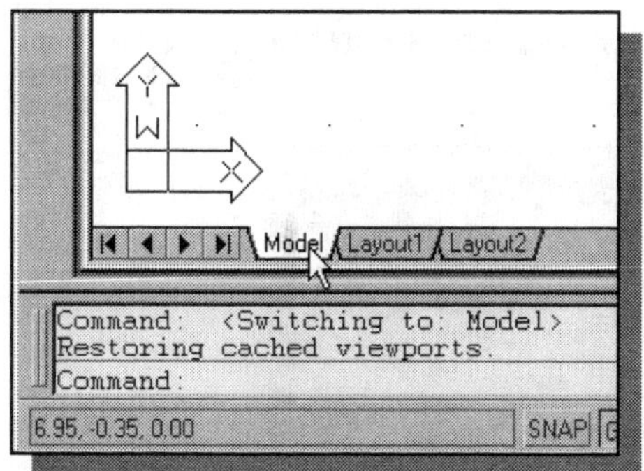

12. Pick the **Model** tab to switch back to *model space*.

➢ Notice the title block we created is shown only in *paper space*.

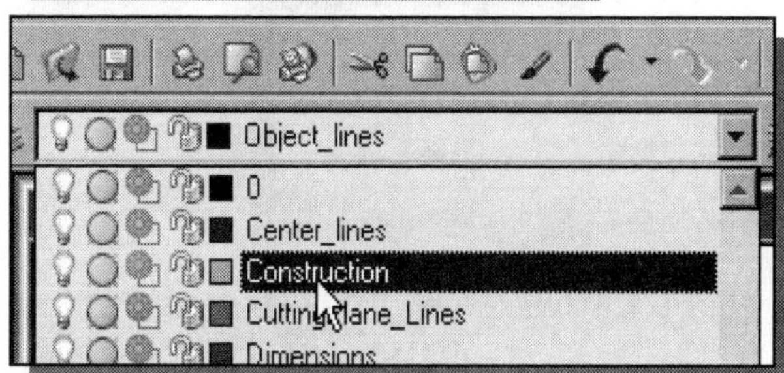

13. In the *Object Properties* toolbar area, select the ***Layer Control*** box and set layer *Construction_Lines* as the *Current Layer*.

Create a Template file

The heart of any CAD system is the ability to reuse information that is already in the system. In the preceding sections, we spent a lot of time setting up system variables, such as layers, colors, linetypes and plotting settings. We will make a **template file** containing all of the settings and the title block we have created so far.

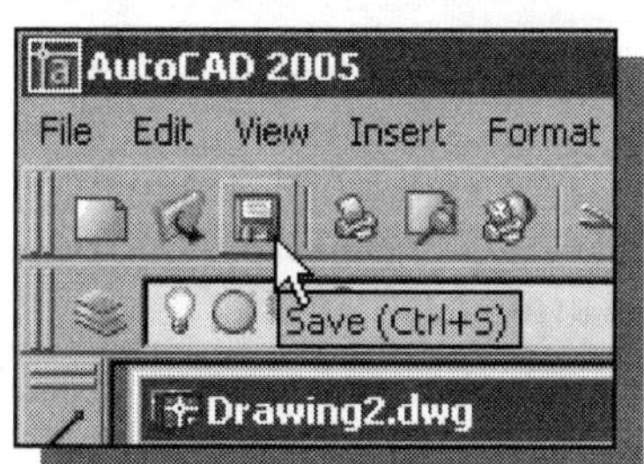

1. In the *Standard* toolbar area, select the **Save** icon.

2. In the *Save Drawing As* dialog box, save to the default template folder (or select the folder in which you want to store the *template file).* Enter ***Acad_A_Title*** in the *File name* box.

3. Pick **Save** in the *Save Drawing As* dialog box to close the dialog box.

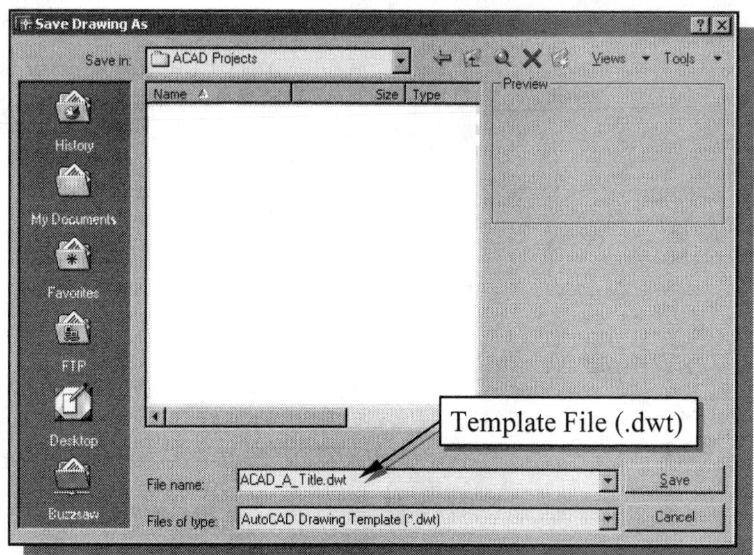

4. In the *Template Description* dialog box, enter ***A-size layout with title block*** in the *Description* box.

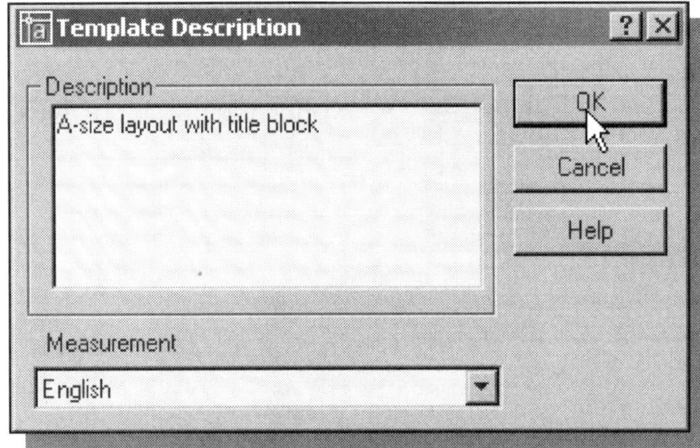

5. Pick **OK** to close the dialog box and save the template file.

➢ The only difference between an AutoCAD template file and a regular AutoCAD drawing file is the filename extension, (.dwt) versus (.dwg). We can convert any AutoCAD drawing into an AutoCAD template file by changing the filename extension to *.dwt*. It is recommended that you keep a second copy of any template files on a separate floppy disk as a backup.

Exit AutoCAD 2005

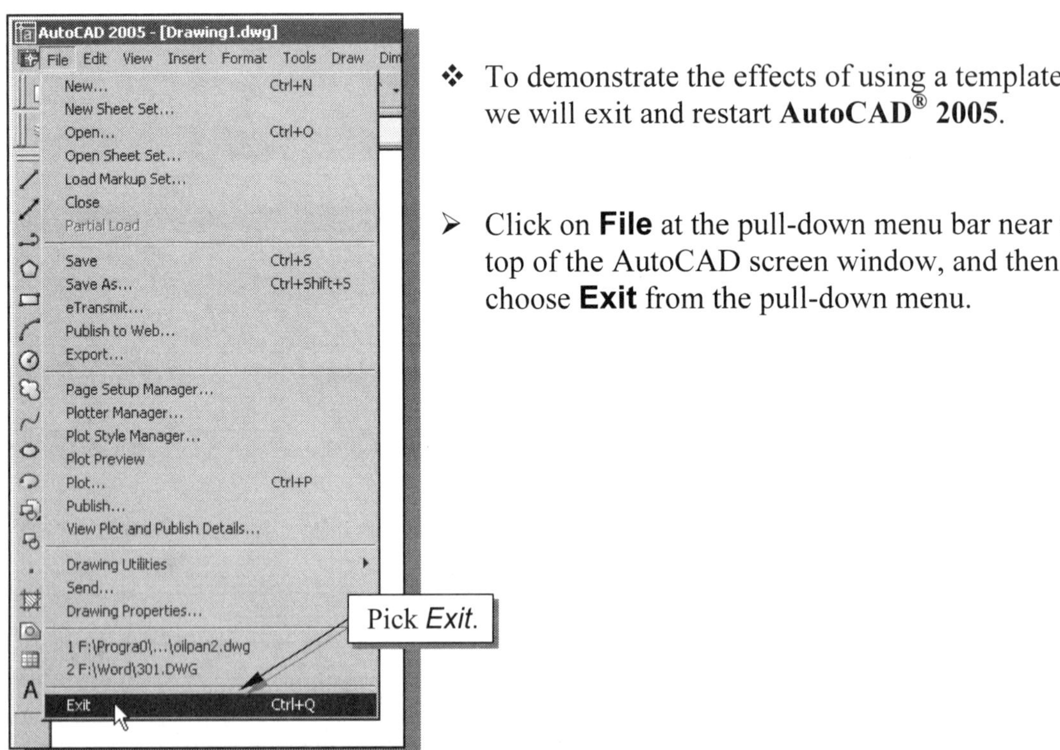

❖ To demonstrate the effects of using a template file, we will exit and restart **AutoCAD® 2005**.

➢ Click on **File** at the pull-down menu bar near the top of the AutoCAD screen window, and then choose **Exit** from the pull-down menu.

Starting Up AutoCAD 2005

1. Select the **AutoCAD 2005** option on the *Program* menu or select the **AutoCAD 2005** icon on the *Desktop*.

2. In the AutoCAD *Startup* dialog box, select the ***Template*** option.

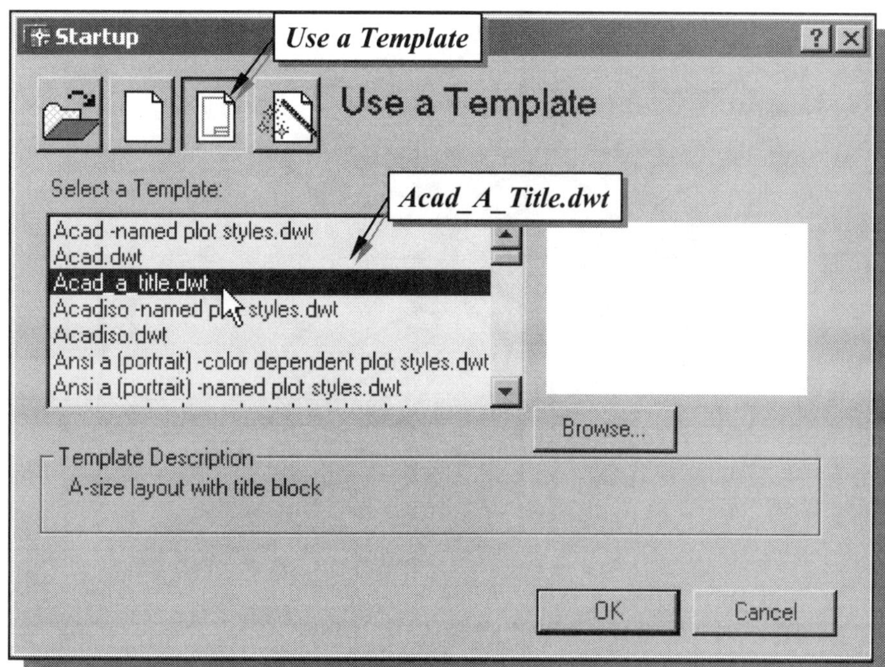

3. Select the ***Acad_A_Title*** template file from the list of template files. If the template file is not listed, click on the **Browse** button to locate it and proceed to open a new drawing file.

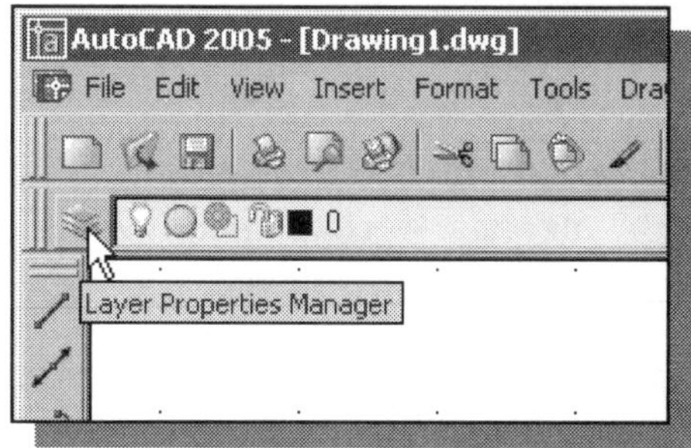

4. Pick **Layer Properties Manager** in the *Object Properties* toolbar.

5. Examine the layer property settings in the *Layer Properties Manager* dialog box.

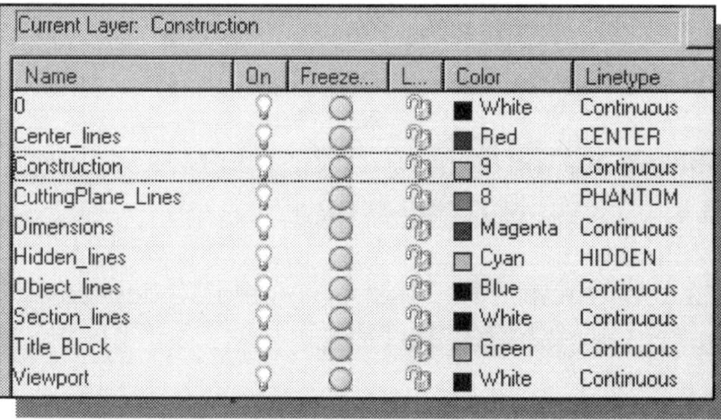

6. On your own, set layer ***Construction*** as the *Current Layer*.

7. Click on the **OK** button to exit the *Layer Properties Manager* dialog box.

The *Geneva Cam* Drawing

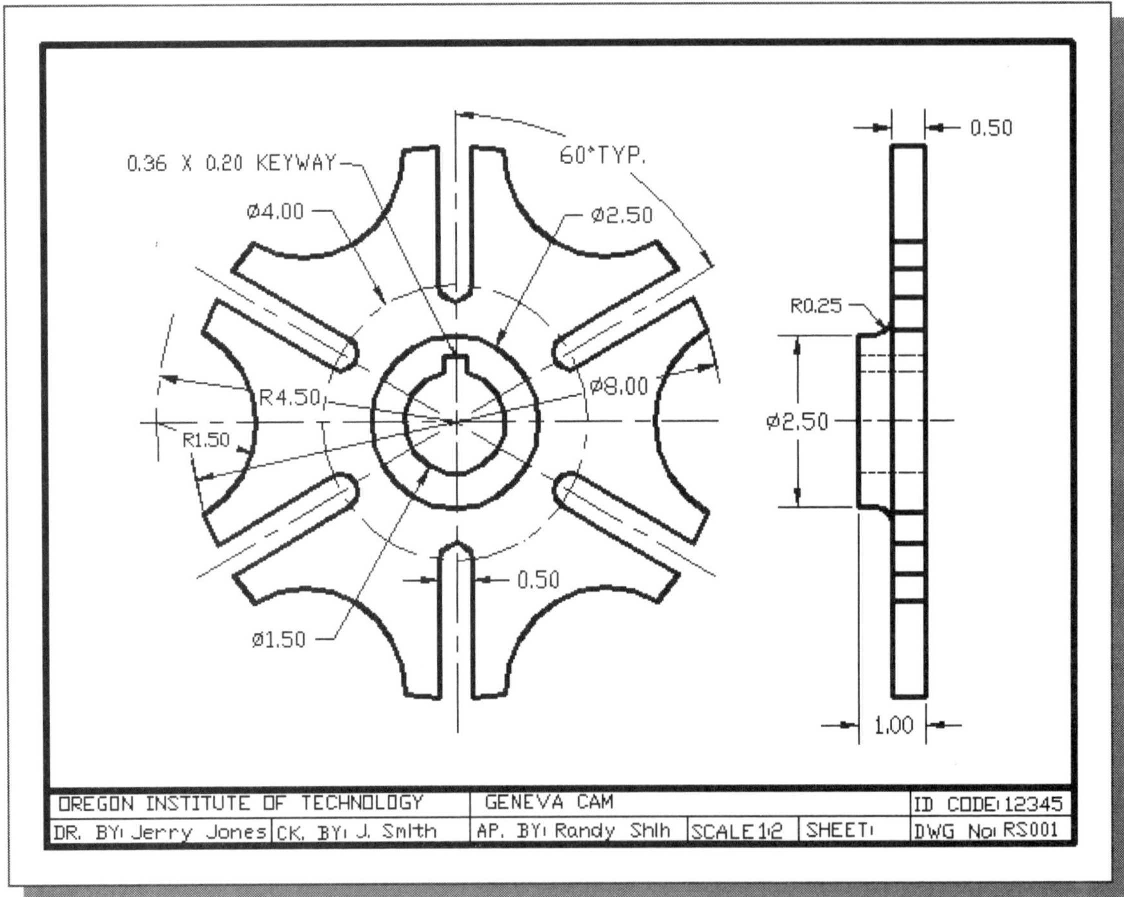

Drawing construction lines

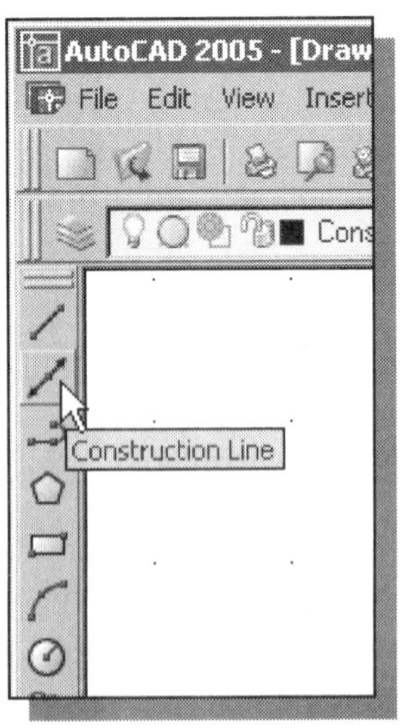

1. Select the **Construction Line** icon in the *Draw* toolbar. In the command prompt area, the message "*_xline Specify a point or [Hor/Ver/Ang/Bisect/Offset]:*" is displayed.

2. Place the first point at world coordinate (**5,4.5**) on the screen.

3. Pick a location above the last point to create a **vertical line**.

4. Move the cursor toward the right of the first point, and then pick a location to create a **horizontal line**.

5. Next to create a construction line that is rotated 30 degrees from horizontal, enter ***@2<30*** **[ENTER]**.

6. Inside the graphics window, **right-mouse-click** to end the Construction Line command.

7. Select the **Circle** icon in the *Draw* toolbar. In the command prompt area, the message "*CIRCLE Specify center point for circle or [3P/2P/Ttr]:*" is displayed.

8. Pick the intersection of the lines as the center point of the circle.

9. In the command prompt area, the message "*Specify radius of circle or [Diameter]:*" is displayed. Enter ***0.75*** **[ENTER]**.

10. Repeat the Circle command and create four additional circles of radii **1.25**, **2.0**, **4.0** and **4.5** as shown.

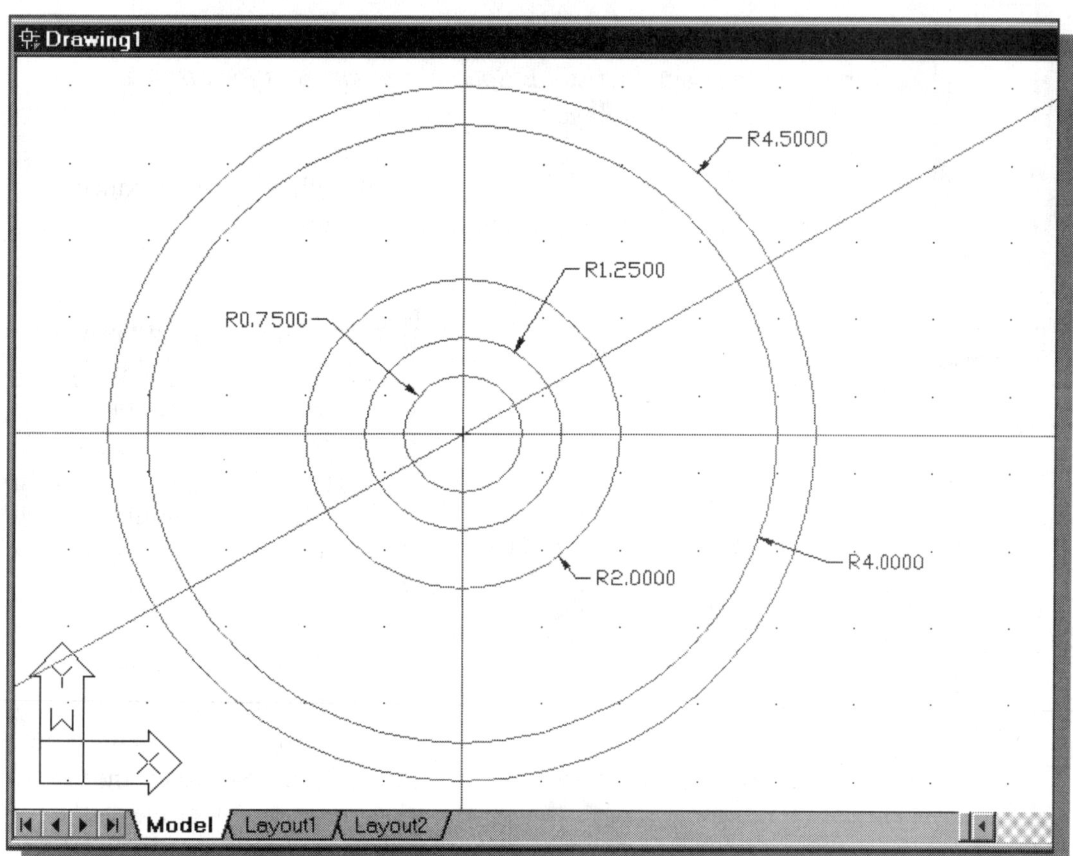

11. In the *Status Bar* area, reset the options and turn ***ON*** the *GRID*, *OSNAP*, *OTRACK*, and *LWT* options.

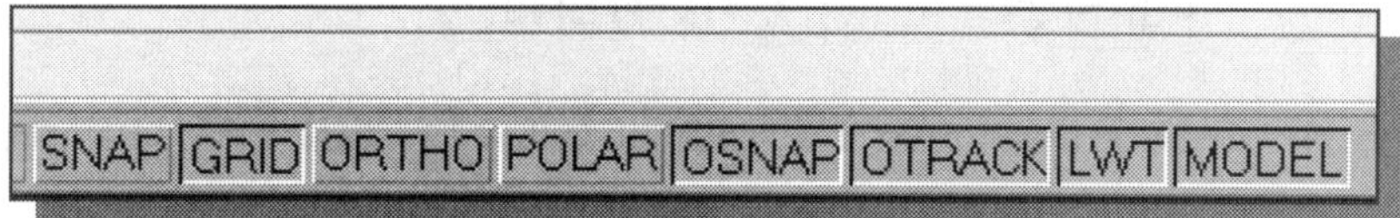

Creating object lines

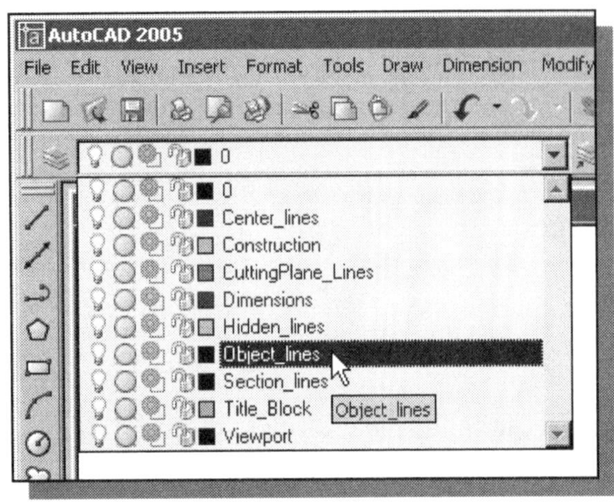

1. On the *Object Properties* toolbar, choose the ***Layer Control*** box with the left-mouse-button.

2. Move the cursor over the name of layer ***Object_Lines***; the tool tip "*Object_Lines*" appears.

3. **Left-mouse-click once** and layer *Object_Lines* is set as the *Current Layer*.

4. Select the **Circle** icon in the *Draw* toolbar. In the command prompt area, the message "*CIRCLE Specify center point for circle or [3P/2P/Ttr]:*" is displayed.

5. Move the cursor to the center of the circles, then left-click once to select the intersection as the center of the new circle.

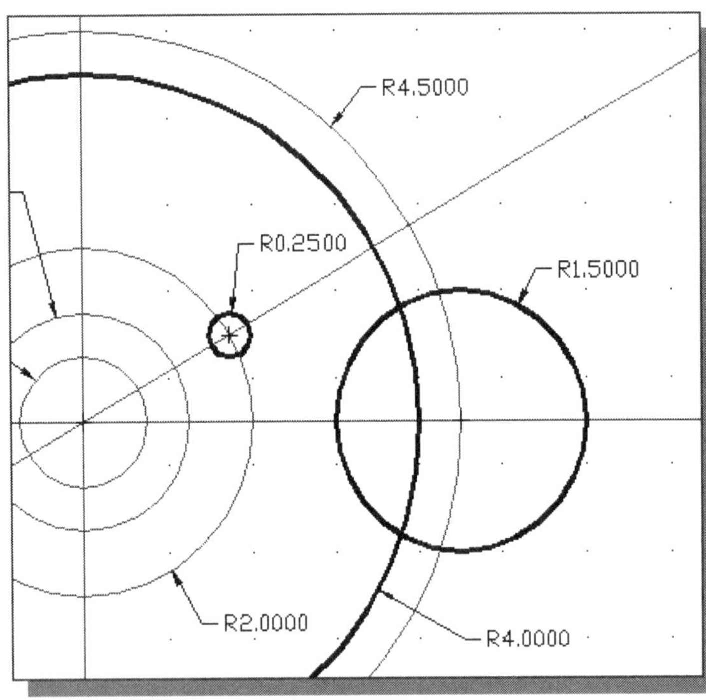

6. In the command prompt area, the message "*Specify radius of circle or [Diameter]:*" is displayed. Pick the **right intersection** of the horizontal line and the radius 4.0 circle.

7. Repeat the Circle command and pick the **right intersection** of the horizontal line and the radius 4.5 circle as the center point of the circle.

8. In the command prompt area, the message "*Specify radius of circle or [Diameter]:*" is displayed. Enter ***1.5*** **[ENTER]**.

9. Repeat the Circle command and create a circle of radius **0.25** centered at the intersection of the inclined line and the radius **2.0** circle as shown.

Using the *Offset* command

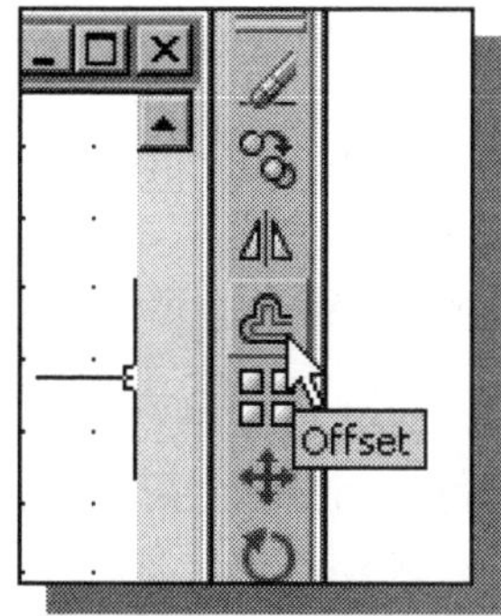

1. Select the **Offset** icon in the *Modify* toolbar. In the command prompt area, the message "*Specify offset distance or [Through]:*" is displayed.

2. In the command prompt area, enter: ***0.25* [ENTER]**.

3. In the command prompt area, the message "*Select object to offset or <exit>:*" is displayed. Pick the **inclined line** on the screen.

4. AutoCAD next asks us to identify the direction of the offset. Pick a location that is **below** the inclined line.

5. Inside the graphics window, **right-mouse-click** to end the Offset command.

❖ Notice that the new line created by the Offset command is placed on the same layer as the line we selected to offset. Which layer is current does not matter; the offset object will always be on the same layer as the original object.

6. Use the **Zoom Window** command and zoom-in on the 30 degrees region as shown.

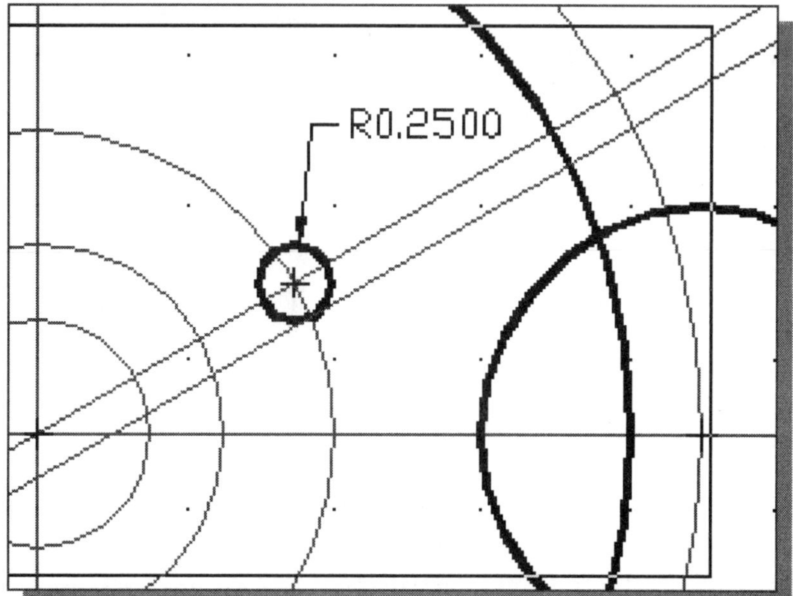

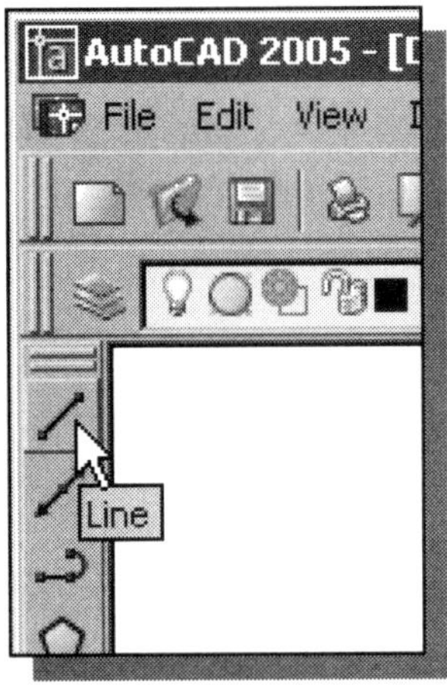

7. Select the **Line** command icon in the *Draw* toolbar. In the command prompt area, the message "*_line Specify first point:*" is displayed.

8. Move the cursor to the intersection of the small circle and the lower inclined line and notice the visual aid that automatically displays at the intersection. Left-click once to select the point.

9. Pick the next intersection point, toward the right side, along the inclined line.

➢ On your own, use the **Trim** and **Erase** commands to remove the unwanted portions of the objects until your drawing contains only the objects shown below.

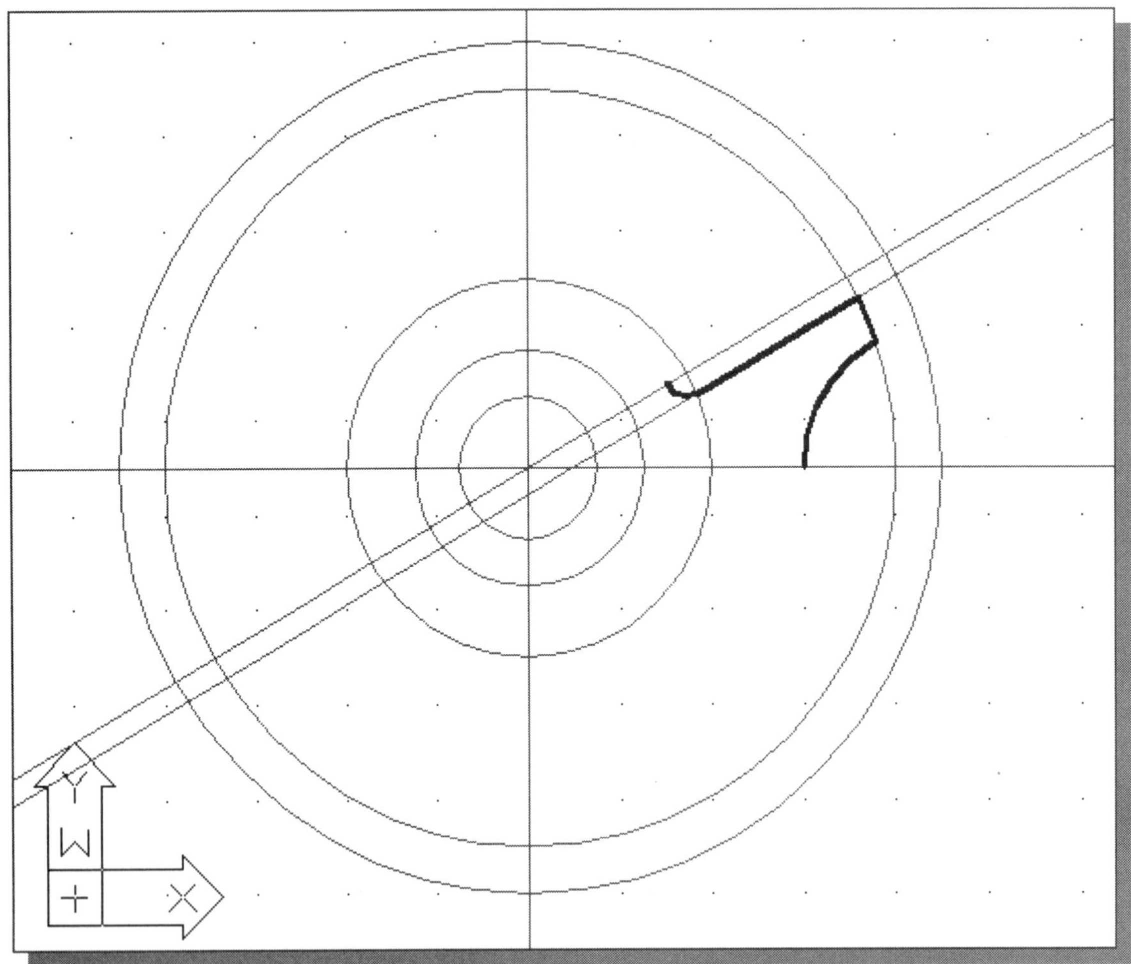

Using the *Mirror* command

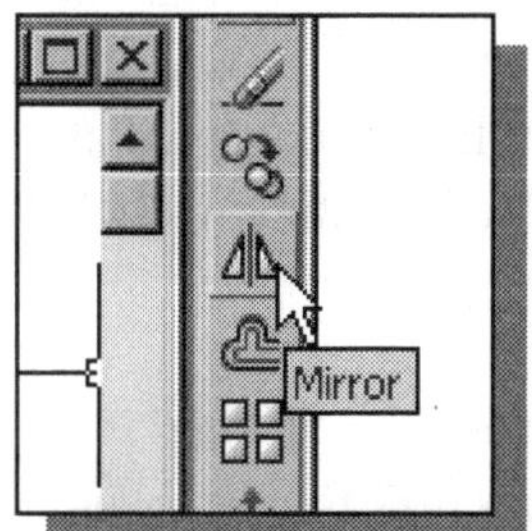

1. Select the **Mirror** command icon in the *Modify* toolbar. In the command prompt area, the message "*Select objects:*" is displayed.

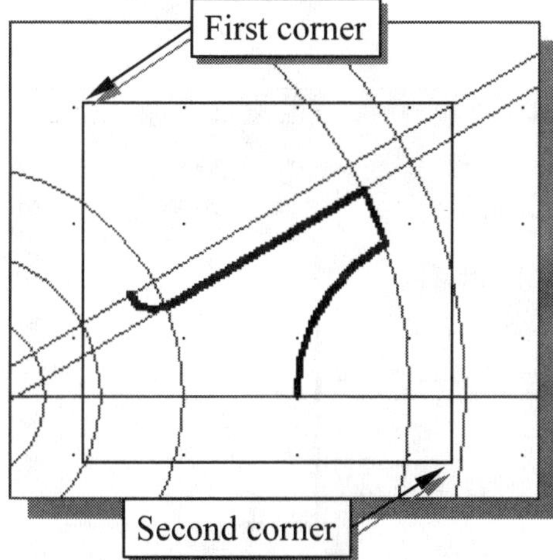

2. Create a *selection window* by selecting the two corners as shown.

Note that in **AutoCAD® 2005**, creating the selection window from left to right will select only objects entirely within the selection area. Going from right to left (crossing selection) selects objects within and objects crossing the selection area. Objects must be at least partially visible to be selected.

3. Inside the graphics window, **right-mouse-click** to accept the selection and continue with the Mirror command.

4. In the command prompt area, the message "*Specify the first point of the mirror line:*" is displayed. Pick any intersection point along the horizontal line on the screen.

5. In the command prompt area, the message "*Specify the second point:*" is displayed. Pick any other intersection point along the horizontal line on the screen.

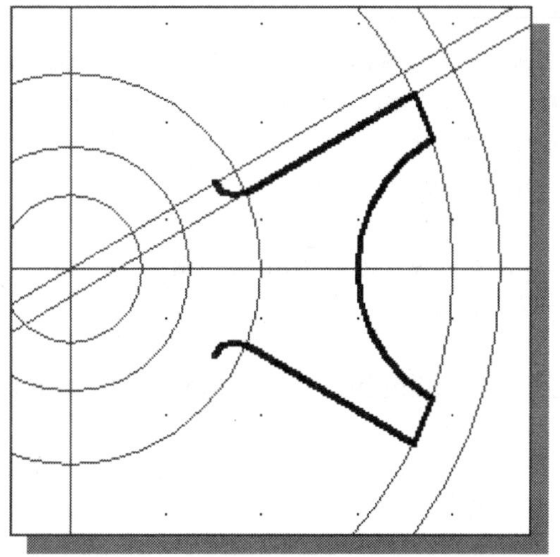

6. In the command prompt area, the message "*Delete source objects? [Yes/No] <N>:*" is displayed. Inside the graphics window, **right-mouse-click** and select **Enter** to retain the original objects.

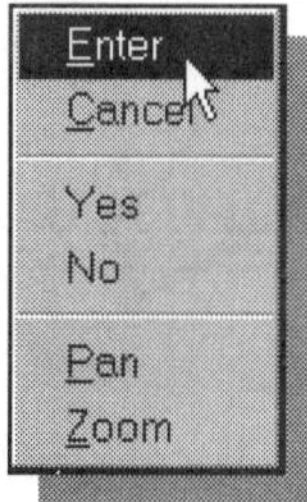

Using the *Array* command

❖ We can make multiple copies of objects in polar or rectangular arrays (patterns). For polar arrays, we control the number of copies of the object and whether the copies are rotated. For rectangular arrays, we control the number of rows and columns and the distance between them.

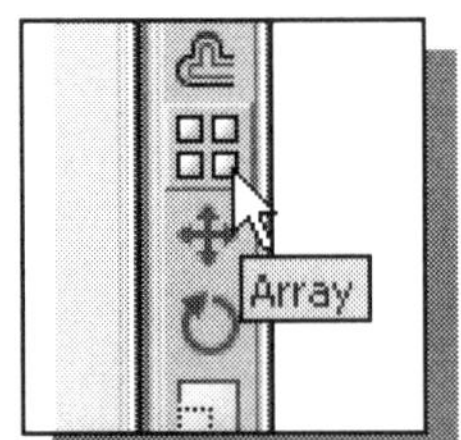

1. Select the **Array** command icon in the *Modify* toolbar. In the command prompt area, the message "*Select objects:*" is displayed.

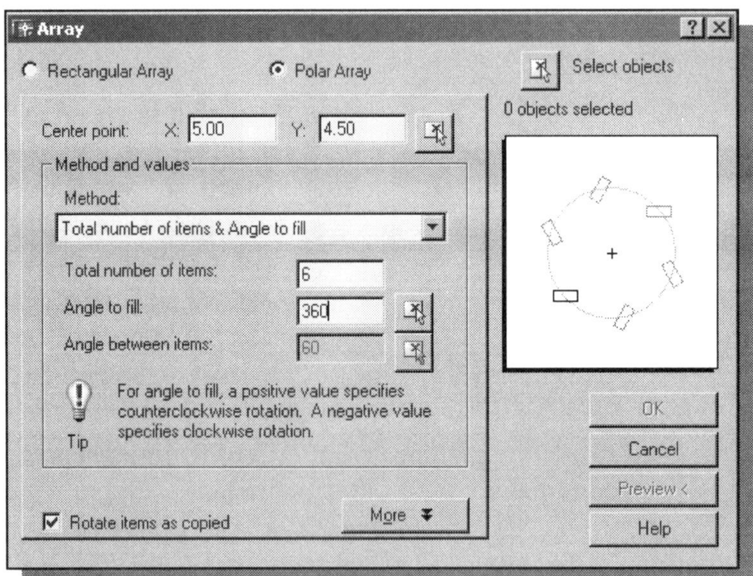

2. In the *Array* dialog box, select the ***Polar Array*** option.

3. Enter ***5.0*** and ***4.5*** as the X and Y coordinates of the *Center point* of the array.

4. Enter ***6*** as the number of items in the array.

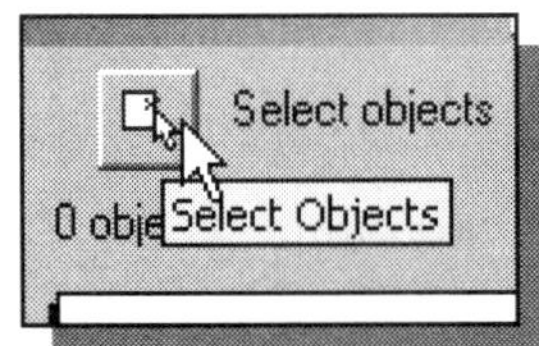

5. Click the **Select Objects** icon, as shown in the figure, to select objects to create the array.

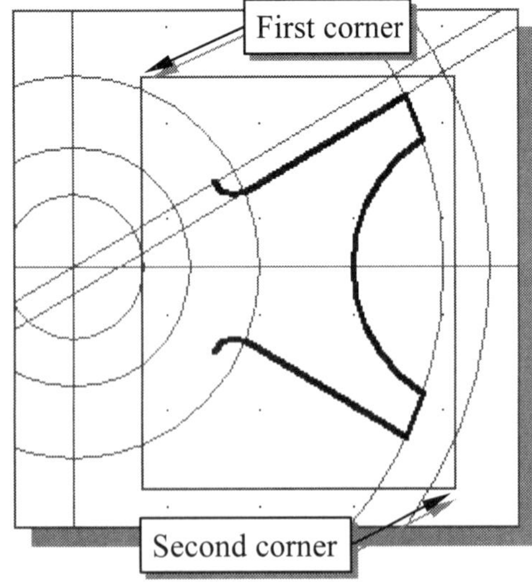

6. Using a *selection* window, enclose the objects we mirrored and the mirrored copies as shown.

7. In the command prompt area, the message "*Select Objects:*" is displayed. Inside the graphics window, **right-mouse-click** to end the selection.

8. In the *Array* dialog box, click the **OK** button to create the array.

9. Next construct the ***0.36 × 0.20*** keyway by first creating parallel lines at 0.95 and 0.18 distance of the horizontal and vertical construction lines.

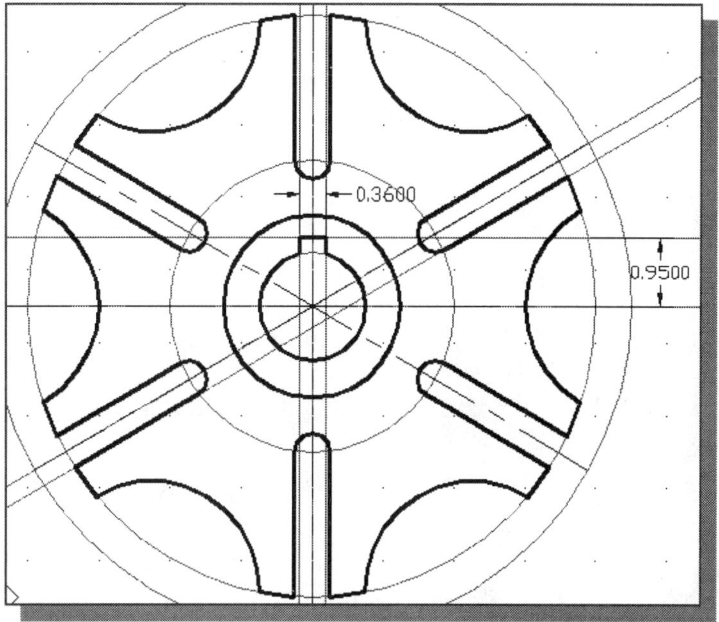

➤ On your own, complete the two views with dimensions. (In the *Dimension Style Manager*, set options under the **Fit** tab to control the appearance of radius and diameter dimensions.)

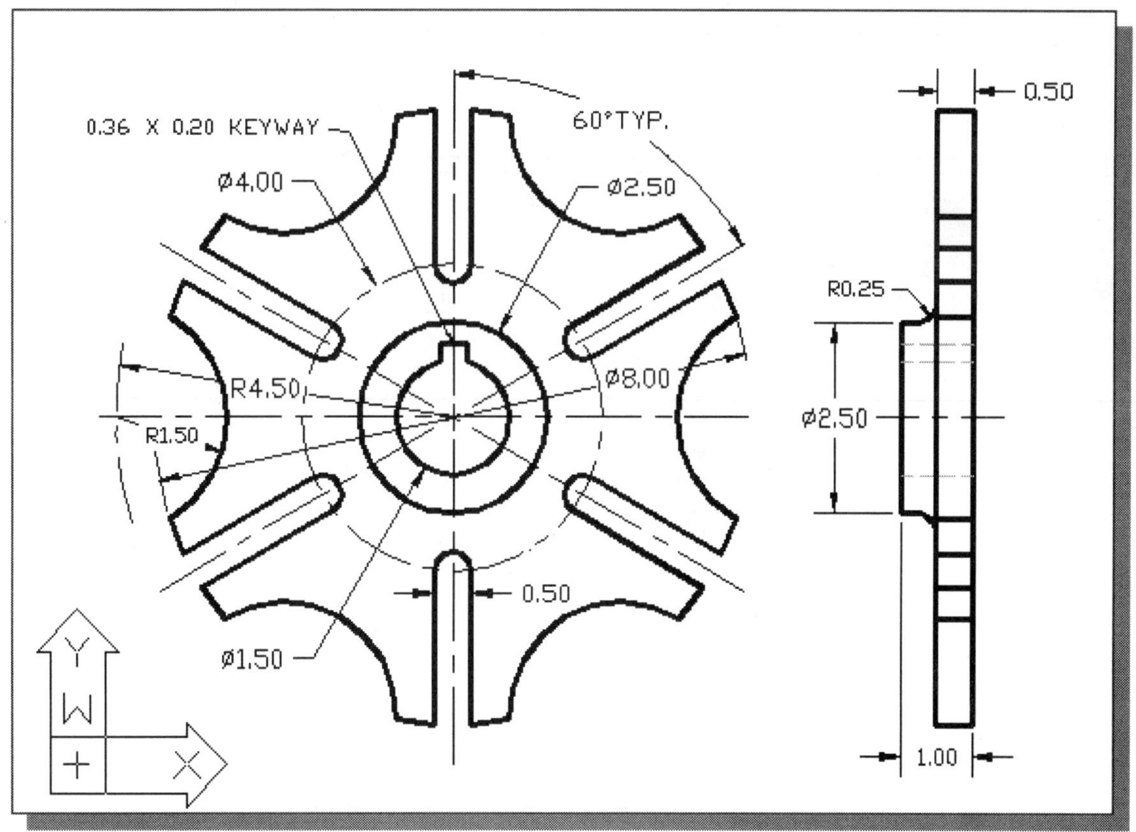

Creating a *Viewport* inside the title block

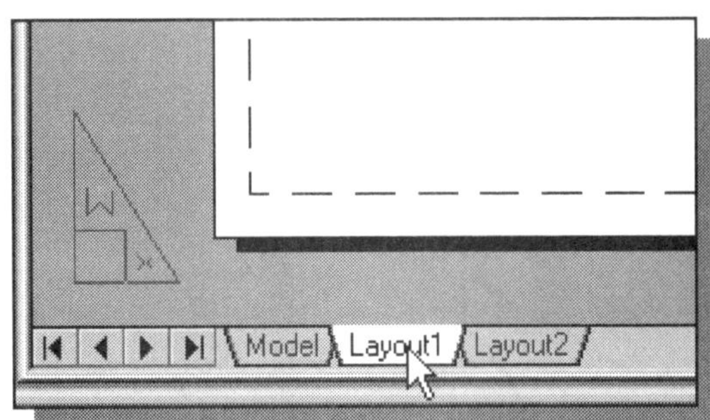

1. Pick the **Layout1** tab to switch to the two-dimensional paper space containing the title block.

2. If a view is displayed inside the title block, use the Erase command and delete the view by selecting any edge of the viewport.

3. Set the ***Viewport*** layer as the *Current Layer*.

4. In the pull-down menus, select:

   [View] → [Viewports] → [1 Viewport]

5. In the *Status Bar* area, turn ***OFF*** the *OSNAP* option.

6. Create a viewport inside the title block area as shown.

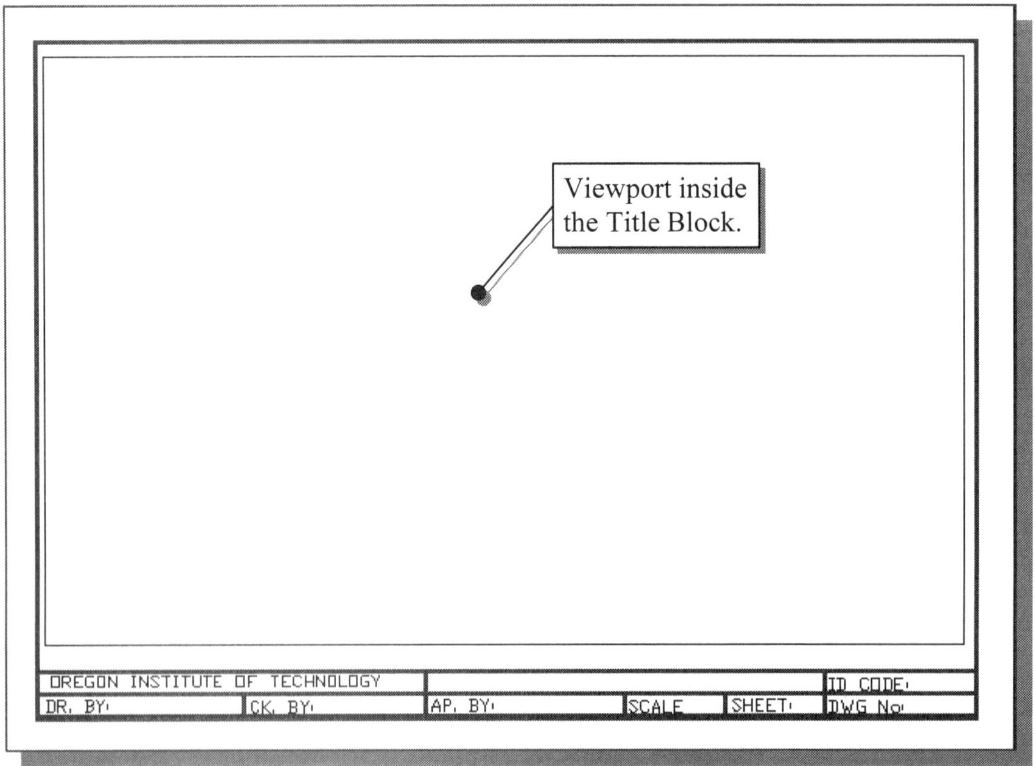

Viewport properties

1. Pre-select the viewport by left-clicking once on any edge of the viewport.

2. In the *Standard* toolbar, select the **Properties** icon.

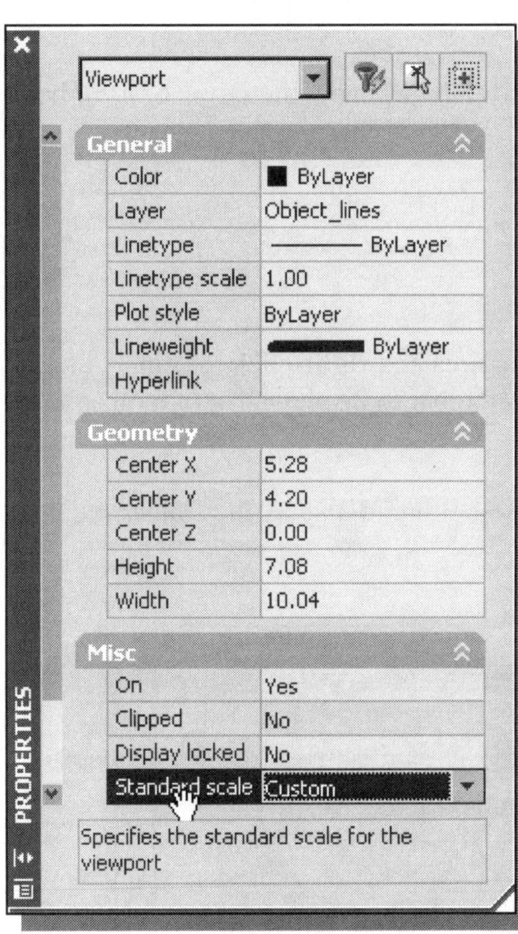

3. In the *Properties* dialog box, scroll down to the bottom of the list. Notice the current scale is set to ***Custom***, ***0.5602***. (The number on your screen might be different.)

4. **Left-click** the *Standard scale* box and notice an arrowhead appears.

5. Click on the arrowhead button and a list of standard scales is displayed. Use the scroll bar to look at the list.

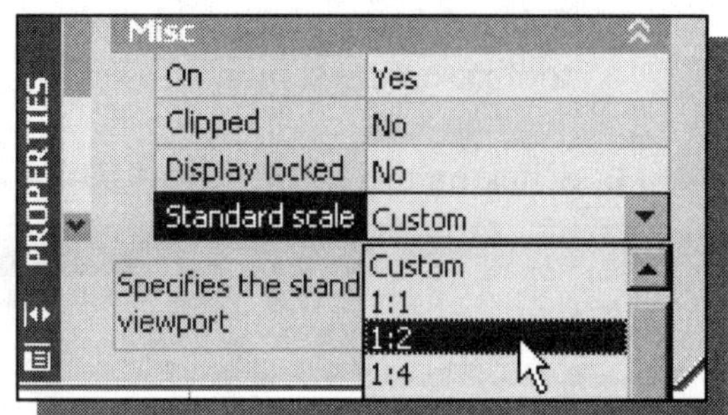

6. Select ***1:2*** in the standard scale list. This will set the plotting scale factor to half scale.

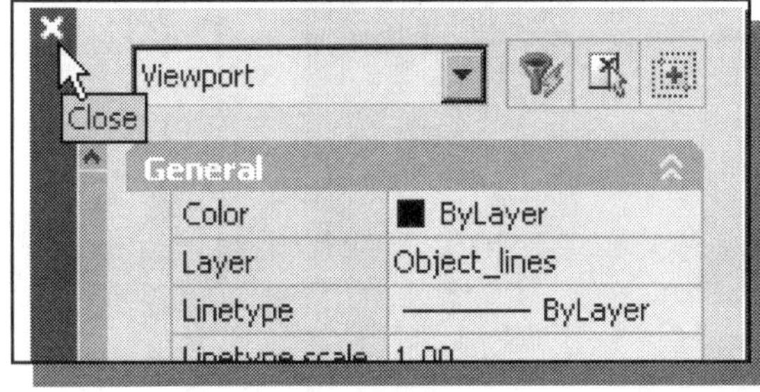

7. Click on the **[X]** button to exit the *Properties* dialog box.

Hide the *Viewport borders*

❖ We will **turn off** the *viewport borders* so that the lines will not be plotted.

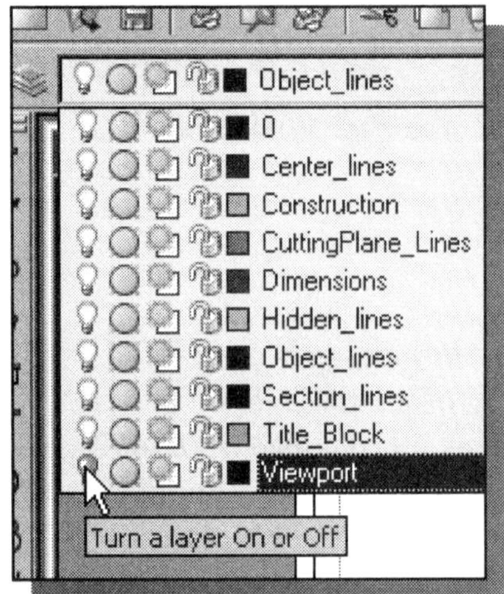

1. With the viewport pre-selected, choose the ***Layer Control*** box with the left-mouse-button.
2. Move the cursor over the name of layer ***Viewport***, **left-mouse-click once**, and move the viewport to layer *Viewport.*
3. Turn ***OFF*** layer *Viewport* in the *Layer Control* box.

Adjusting the dimension scale

1. Move the cursor to the *Standard* toolbar area and **right-click** the empty area (in between two icons) of the *Standard* toolbar to display a list of toolbar menu groups.
2. Select **Dimension**, with the left-mouse-button, to display the *Dimension* toolbar on the screen.
3. Click on the **Dimension Style** icon.

4. In the *Dimension Style Manager* dialog box, select **Modify**.

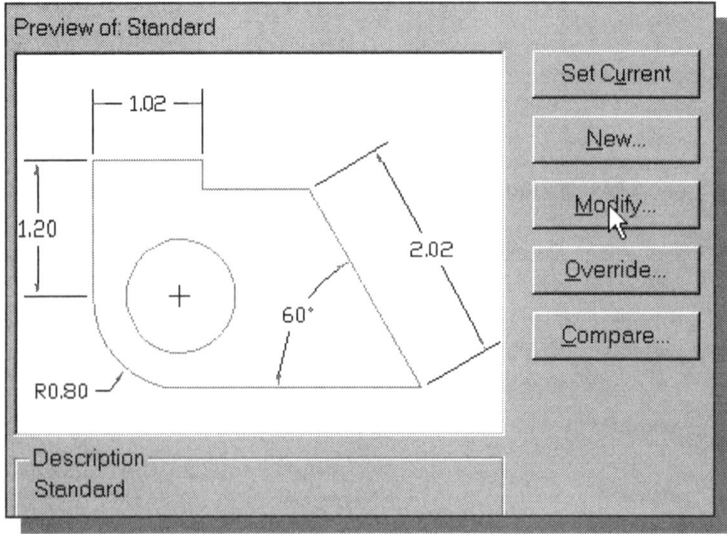

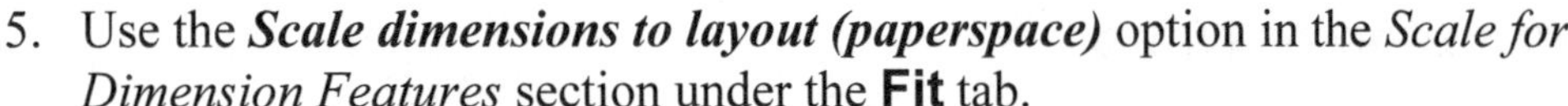

5. Use the ***Scale dimensions to layout (paperspace)*** option in the *Scale for Dimension Features* section under the **Fit** tab.

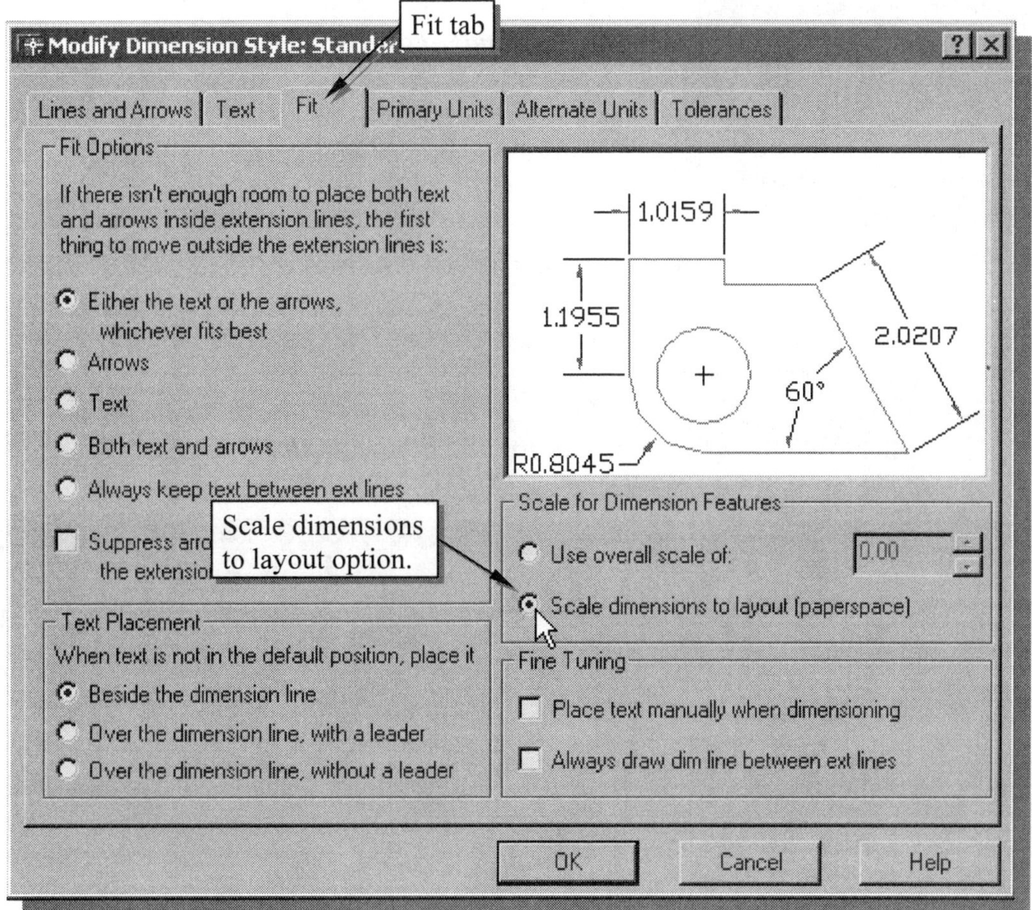

6. Click on the **OK** button to close the *Modify Dimension Style* dialog box.

7. Click on the **Close** button to close the *Dimension Style Manager* dialog box.

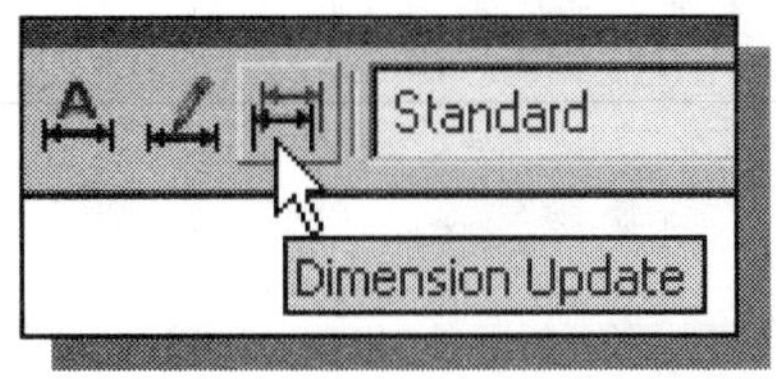

8. Click on the **Dimension Update** icon.

9. Pick one of the radius dimensions.

10. Inside the graphics window, right-mouse-click to update the selected dimension.

11. Repeat the **Dimension Update** command on all the dimensions.

Plot/Print the drawing

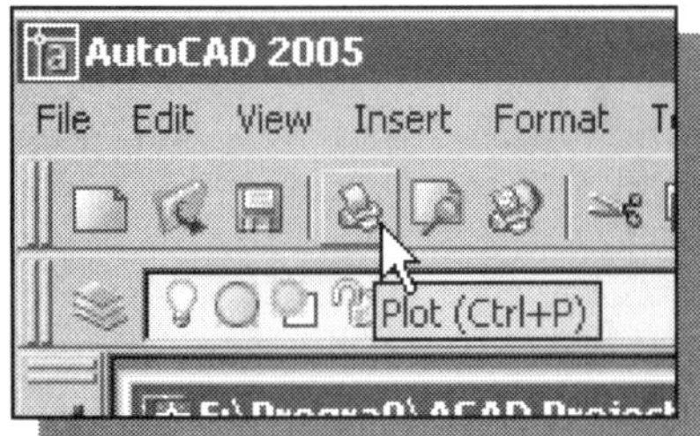

1. In the *Standard* toolbar, select the **Plot** icon.

2. Confirm the proper ***Plot device*** is selected.

3. In the *Plot area* section, confirm it is set to ***Layout***.

4. In the *Plot scale* section, confirm it is set to ***1:1***. Our *paper space* is set to the correct paper size.

5. In the *Plot options* section, confirm the ***Plot with plot styles*** and ***Plot paper space last*** options are selected.

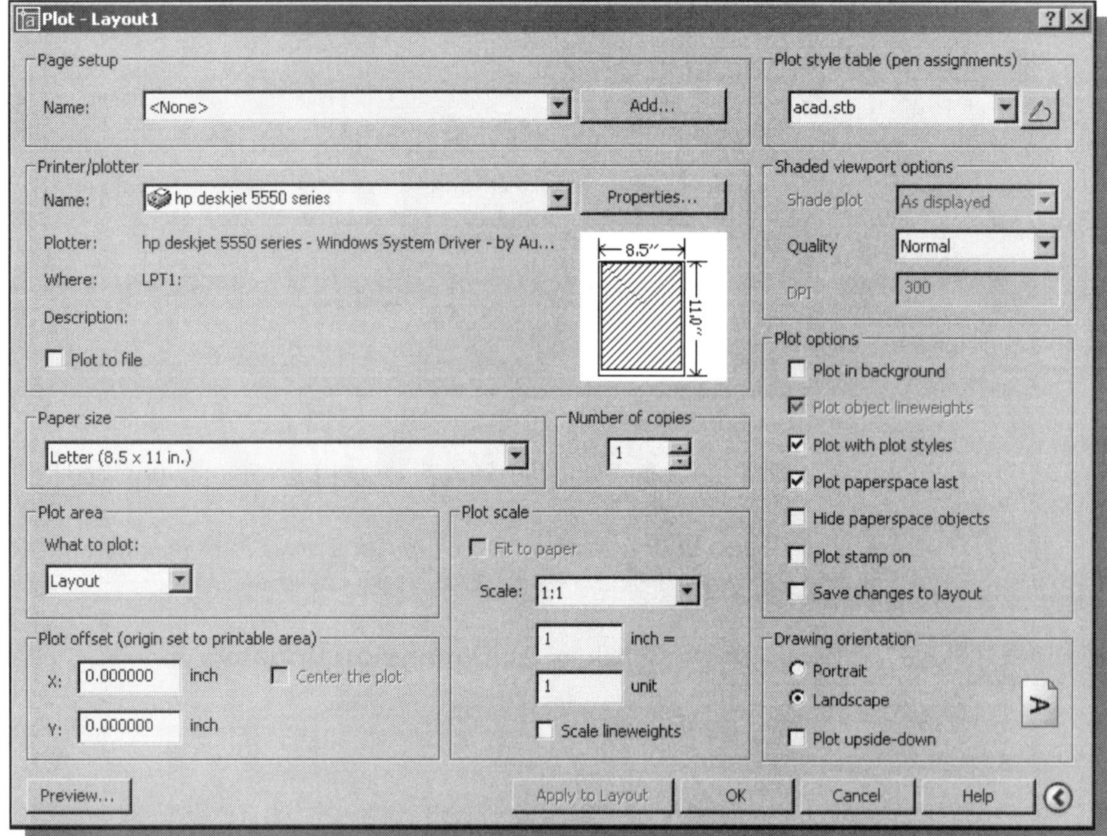

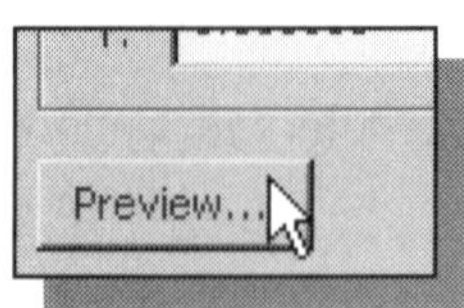

❖ Note the Preview option is also available.

6. Click on the **OK** button to proceed with plotting the drawing.

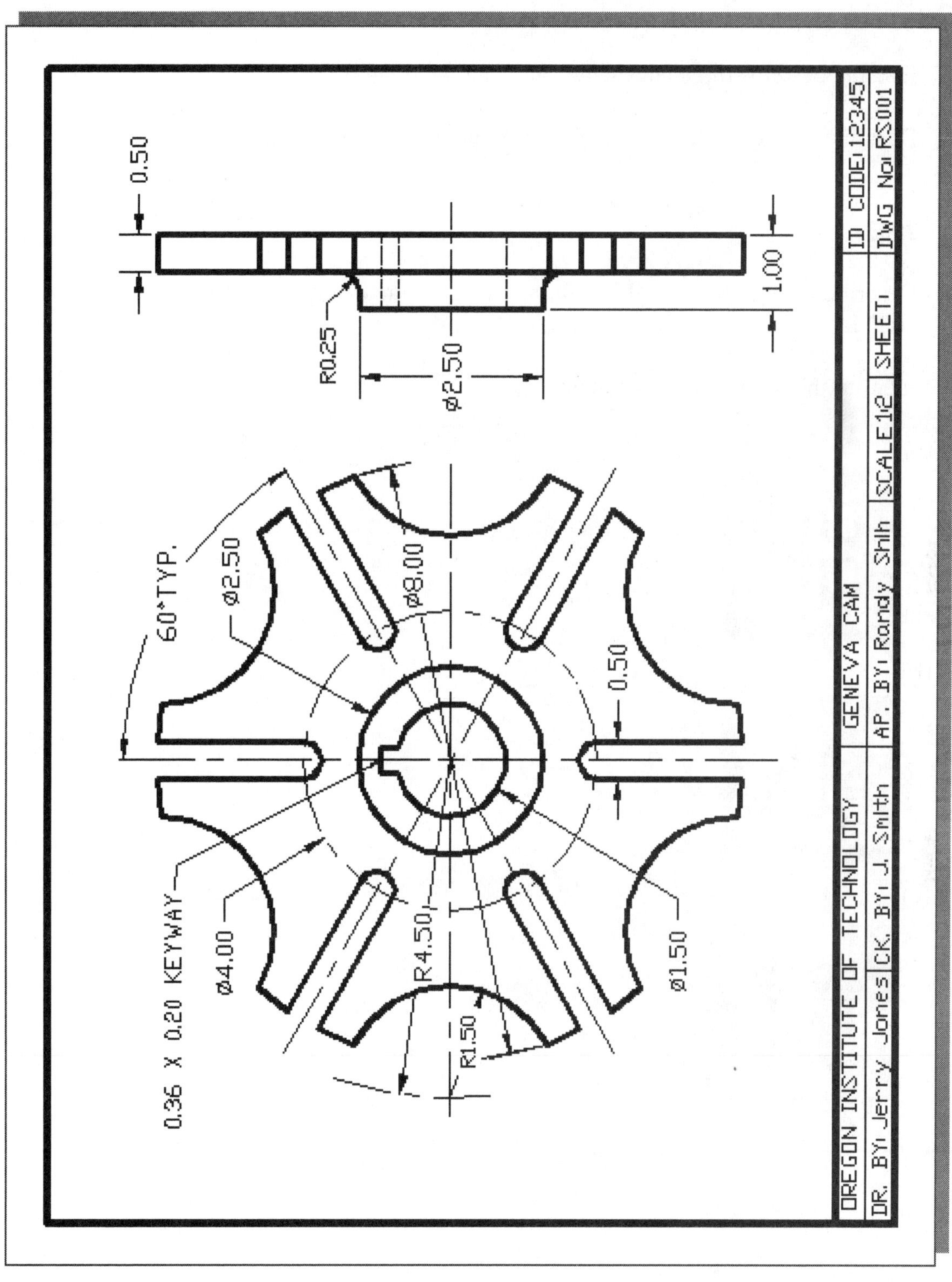
0.50
1.00
R0.25
Ø2.50
60°TYP.
Ø2.50
Ø8.00
0.50
0.36 X 0.20 KEYWAY
Ø4.00
R4.50
R1.50
Ø1.50
OREGON INSTITUTE OF TECHNOLOGY
GENEVA CAM
ID CODE: 12345
DR. BY: Jerry Jones
CK. BY: J. Smith
AP. BY: Randy Shih
SCALE 1:2
SHEET:
DWG No: RS001

Questions:

1. List and describe three advantages of using *template files*.

2. Describe the items that were included in the *Acad_A_Title* template file.

3. List and describe two methods of creating multiple copies of objects in **AutoCAD® 2005**.

4. Describe the procedure in determining the scale factor for plotting an **AutoCAD® 2005** layout.

5. Identify the following commands:

(a)

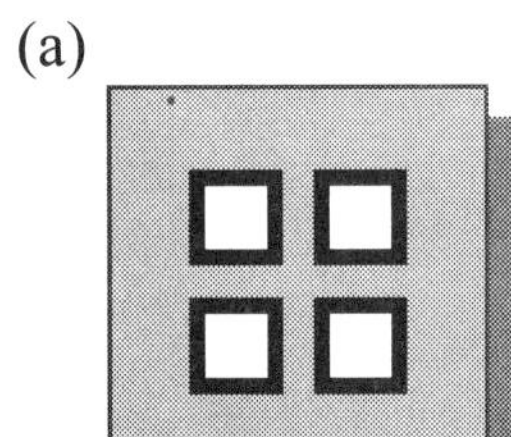

(b)

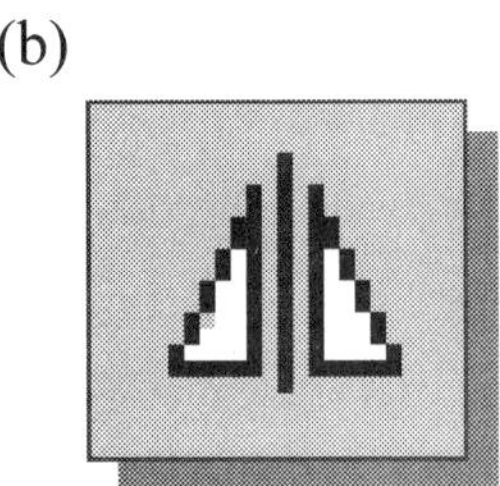

(c)

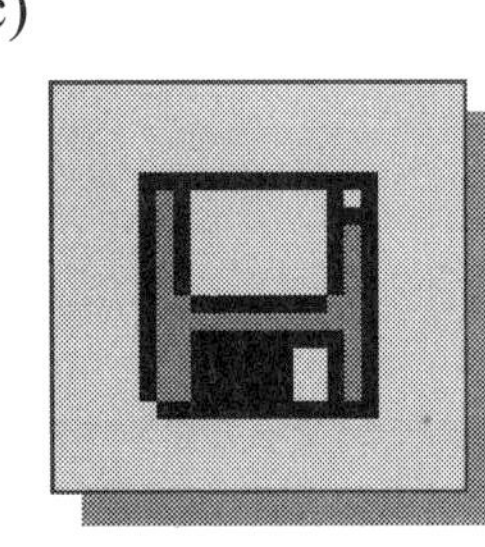

(d)

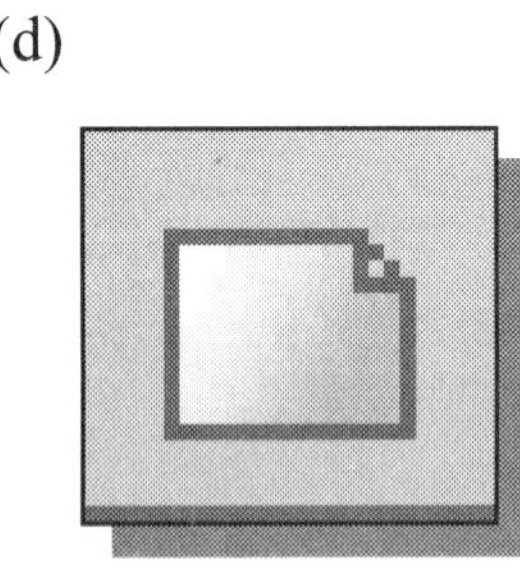

Exercises:

1. Plate thickness: 0.125 inch

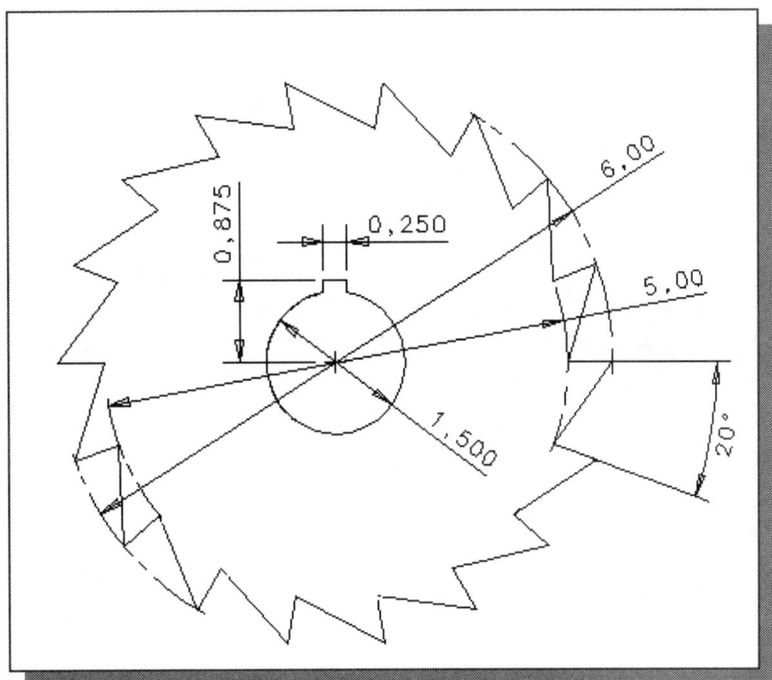

2.

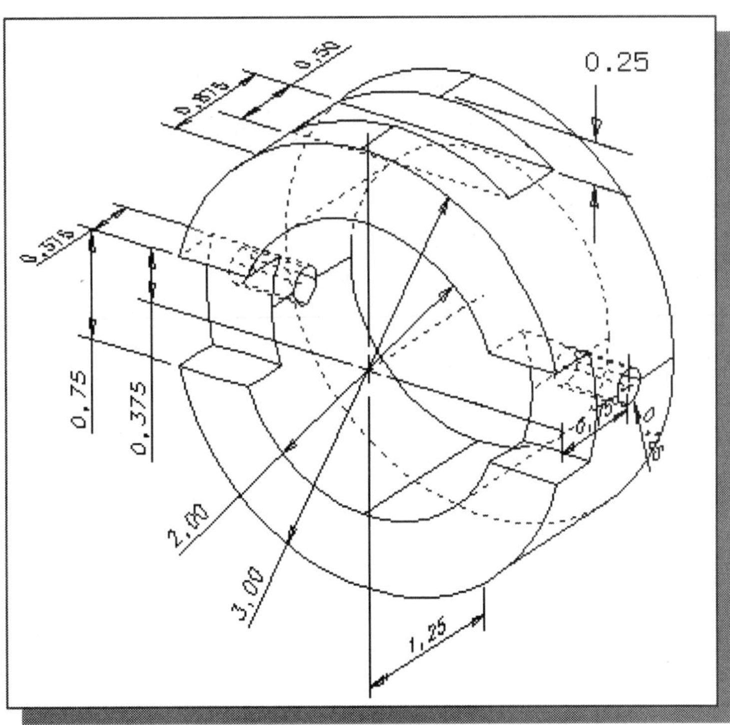

3.

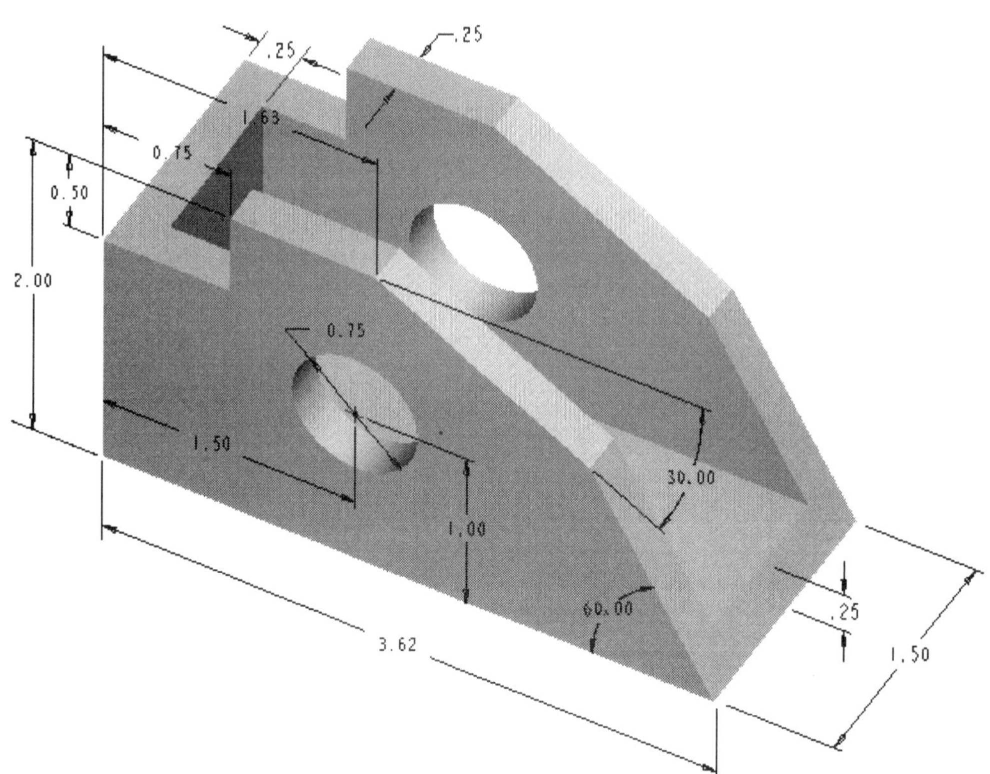

.25
.25
1.63
0.75
0.50
2.00
0.75
1.50
1.00
30.00
60.00
3.62
.25
1.50

3.00
1.25
1.00
.75
.50
1.25
3.00
Ø1.25
Ø2.25
R2.50

4.

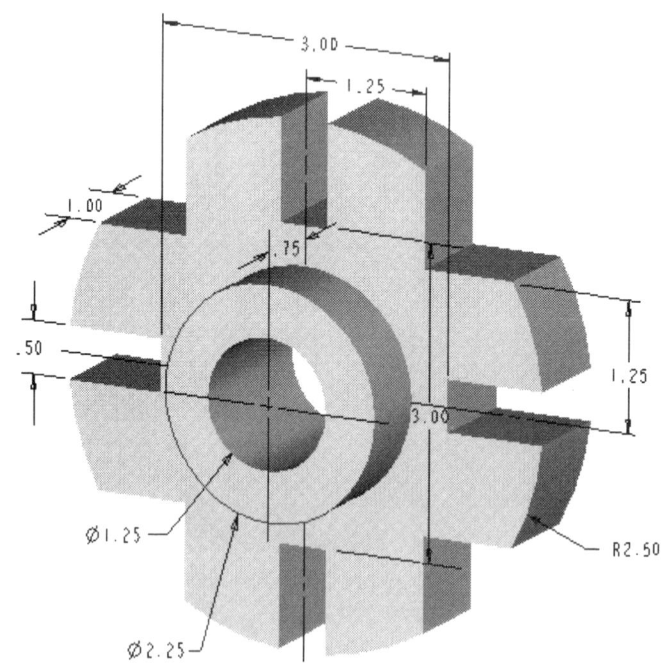

5. Dimensions are in Millimeters. (Thickness: 25 mm.)

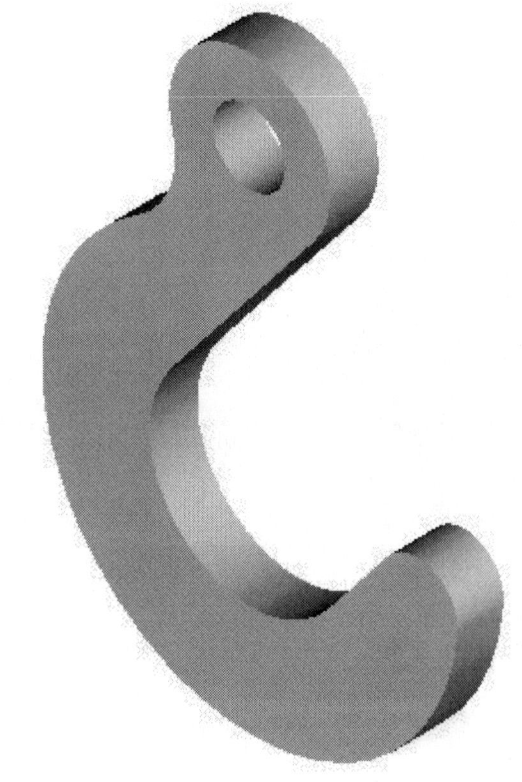

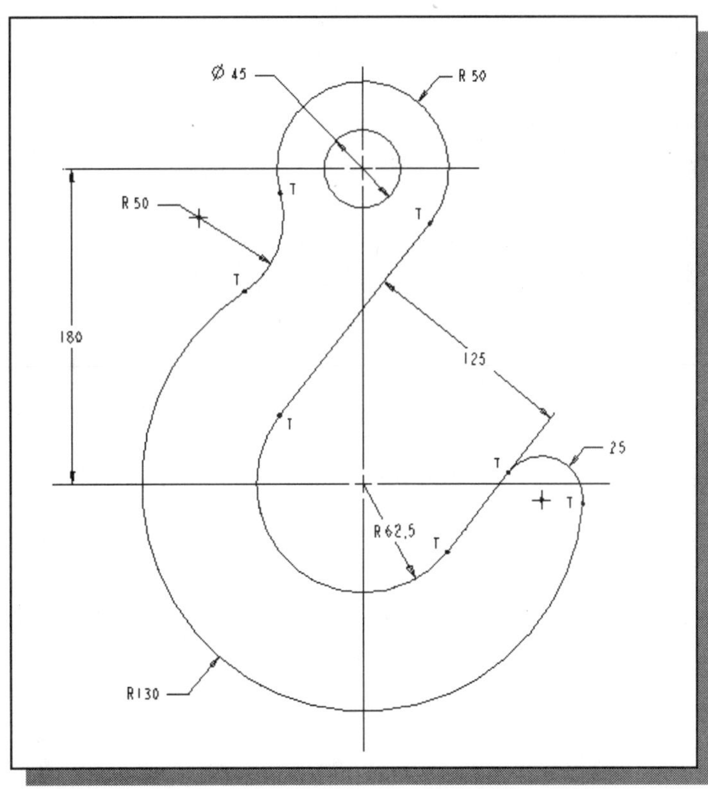

NOTES:

Lesson 8
Auxiliary Views and Editing with GRIPS

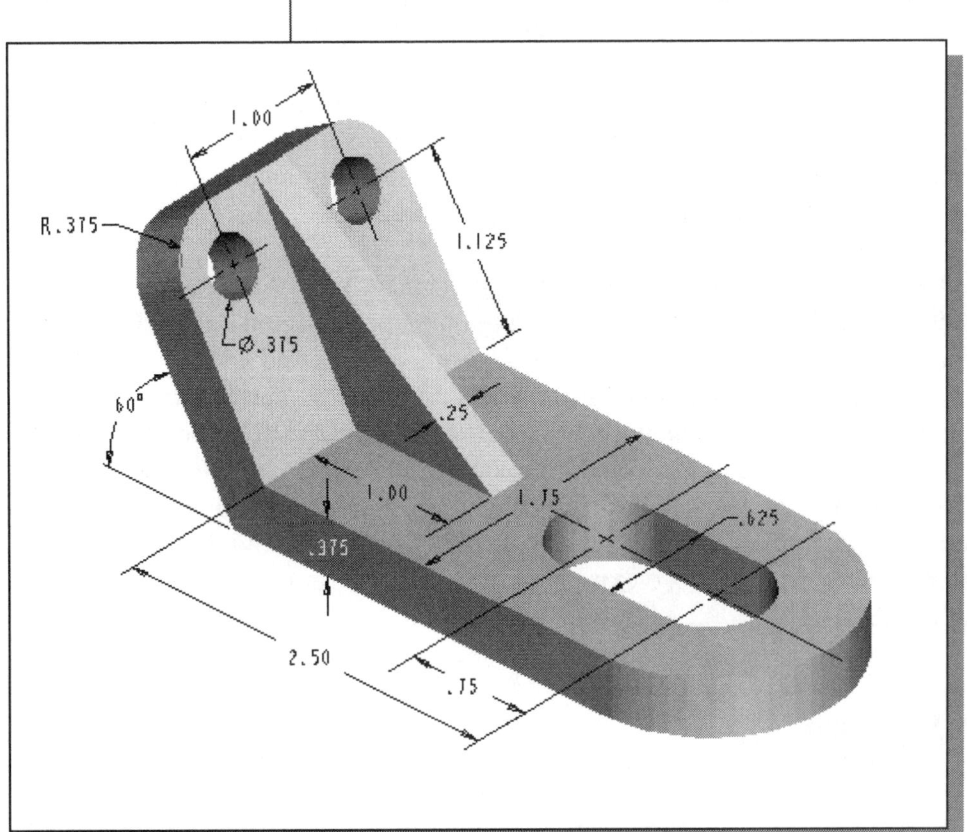

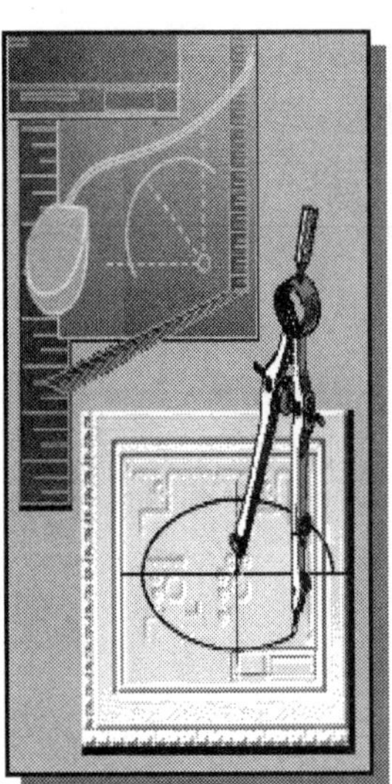

Learning Objectives

- Use 2D Projection method to draw Auxiliary Views.
- Create Rectangles.
- Use the basic GRIPS Editing commands.
- Create and Edit the Plot Style Table.
- Set up and use the Polar Tracking option.
- Create multiple Viewports in Paper Space.

Introduction

An important rule concerning multiview drawings is to draw enough views to accurately describe the design. This usually requires two or three of the regular views, such as a front view, a top view and/or a side view. Many designs have features located on inclined surfaces that are not parallel to the regular planes of projection. To truly describe the feature, the true shape of the feature must be shown using an **auxiliary view**. An *auxiliary view* has a line of sight that is perpendicular to the inclined surface, as viewed looking directly at the inclined surface. An *auxiliary view* is a supplementary view that can be constructed from any of the regular views. This lesson will demonstrate the construction of an auxiliary view using various CAD techniques.

In this lesson, we will examine the use of the very powerful AutoCAD *GRIPS* feature. In **AutoCAD® 2005**, a ***GRIP*** is a small square displayed on a pre-selected object. Grips are key control locations such as the endpoints and midpoints of lines and arcs. Different types of objects display different numbers of grips. Using grips, we can *stretch*, *move*, *mirror*, *scale*, *rotate*, and *copy* objects without entering commands or clicking toolbars. Grips reduce the keystrokes and object selection required in performing common editing commands. To edit with grips, we select the objects before issuing any commands. To remove a specific object from a selection set that displays grips, we hold down the **[SHIFT]** key as we select the object. To exit the *grips mode* and return to the *command prompt*, press the **[ESC]** key.

The *V-Block* Design

Starting Up AutoCAD 2005

1. Select the **AutoCAD 2005** option on the *Program* menu or select the **AutoCAD 2005** icon on the *Desktop*.

2. In the AutoCAD 2005 *Startup* dialog box, select the ***Template*** option.

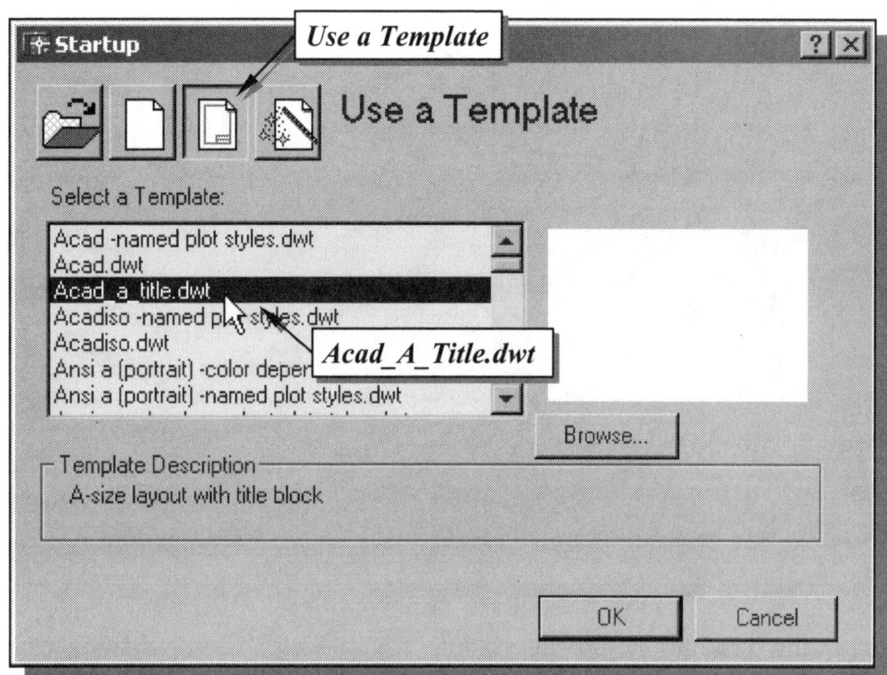

3. Select the ***Acad_A_Title*** template file from the list of template files. If the template file is not listed, click on the **Browse** button to locate and proceed to open a new drawing file.

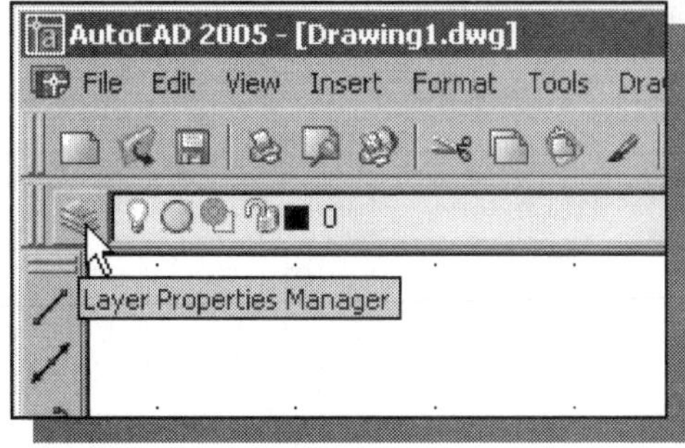

4. Pick ***Layer Properties Manager*** in the *Object Properties* toolbar.

5. Examine the layer property settings in the *Layer Properties Manager* dialog box.

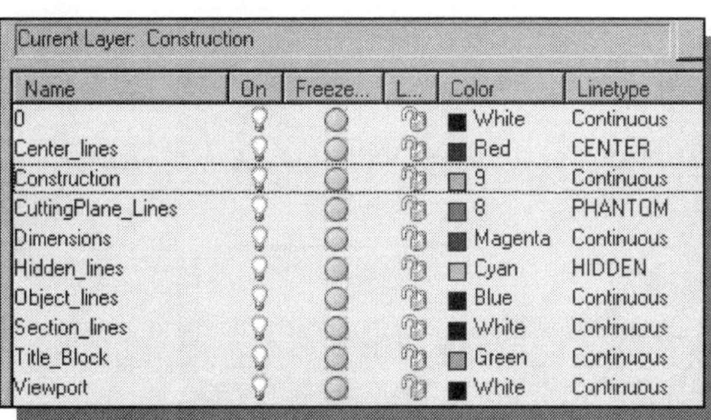

6. Click on the **OK** button to exit the *Layer Properties Manager* dialog box.

The *V-Block* example

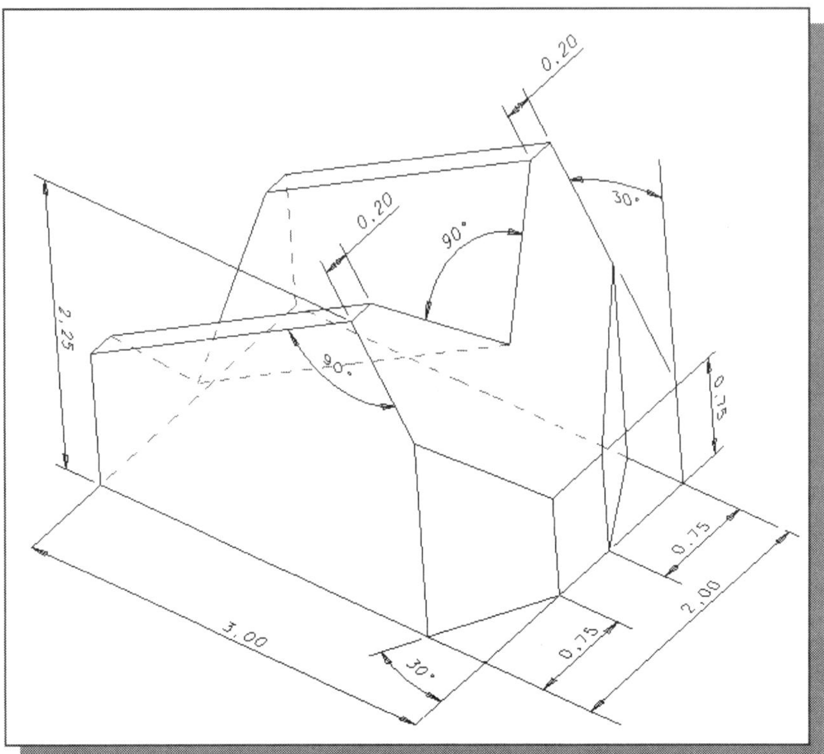

➢ Before going through the tutorial, make a rough sketch of a multiview drawing of the part. How many 2D views will be necessary to fully describe the part? Based on your knowledge of **AutoCAD® 2005** so far, how would you arrange and construct these 2D views? Take a few minutes to consider these questions and do preliminary planning by sketching on a piece of paper. You are also encouraged to construct the orthographic views on your own prior to going through the tutorial.

Setting up the principal views

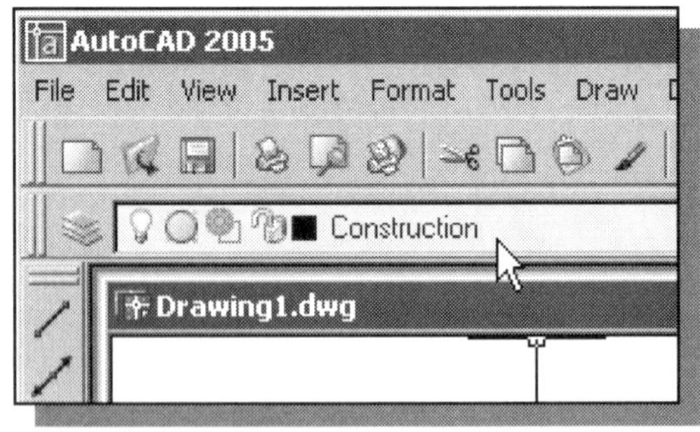

1. In the *Layer Control* box, confirm layer *Construction_Lines* is set as the *Current Layer*.

2. In the *Status Bar* area, reset the options and turn ***ON*** the *OSNAP, OTRACK, LWT*, and *MODEL* options.

- We will first create construction geometry for the front view.

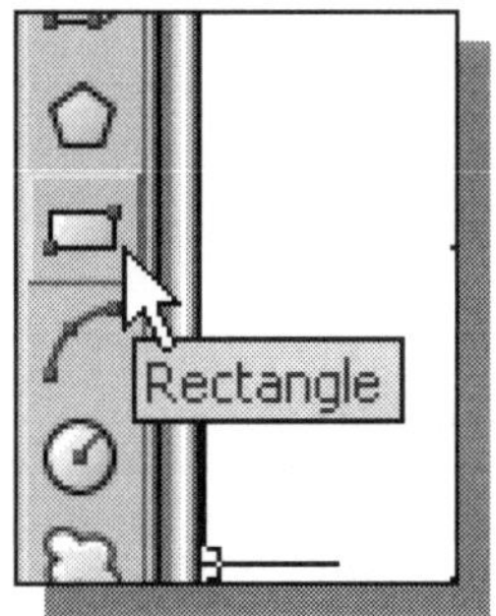

3. Select the **Rectangle** icon in the *Draw* toolbar. In the command prompt area, the message "*Specify first corner point or [Chamfer/Elevation/Fillet/Thickness/Width]:*" is displayed.

4. Place the first corner-point of the rectangle near the lower left corner of the screen. Do not be overly concerned about the actual coordinates of the location; the drawing space is as big as you can imagine.

5. Create a 3″ × 2.25″ rectangle. Enter ***@3,2.25*** **[ENTER]**.

❖ The Rectangle command creates rectangles as *polyline* features, which means all segments of a rectangle are created as a single object.

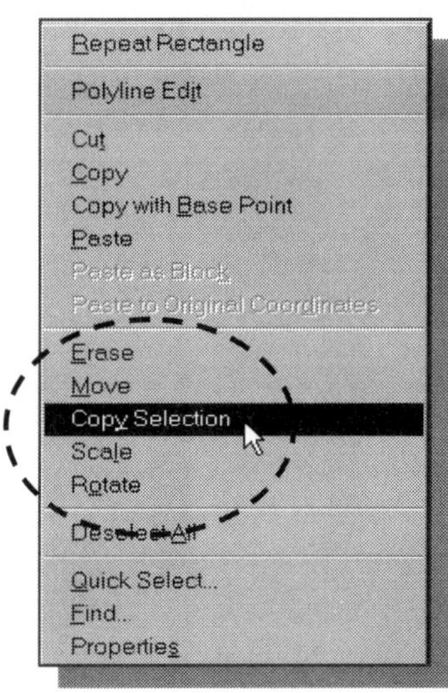

6. Next, use the *GRIPS* editing tools to make a copy of the rectangle. Pick any edge of the rectangle we just created. Notice that small squares appear at different locations on the rectangle.

7. Inside the graphics window, **right-mouse-click** to bring up the popup option menu.

❖ In the center section of the popup menu, the set of GRIPS editing commands includes Erase, Move, Copy Selection, Scale, and Rotate.

8. In the popup menu, select the **Copy Selection** option.

9. In the command prompt area, the message "*Specify base point or displacement, or [Multiple]:*" is displayed. Pick the **lower right corner** as the base point. A copy of the rectangle is attached to the cursor at the base point.

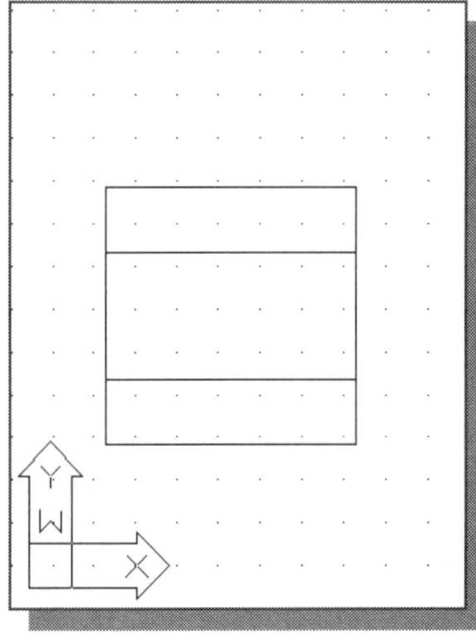

10. In the command prompt area, the message "*Specify second point of displacement, or <use first point as displacement>:*" is displayed. Enter: ***@0,0.75*** **[ENTER]**.

❖ This will position the second rectangle at the location for the 30-degree angle.

11. Pre-select the copy by picking the top horizontal line on the screen. The second rectangle, the copy we just created, is selected.

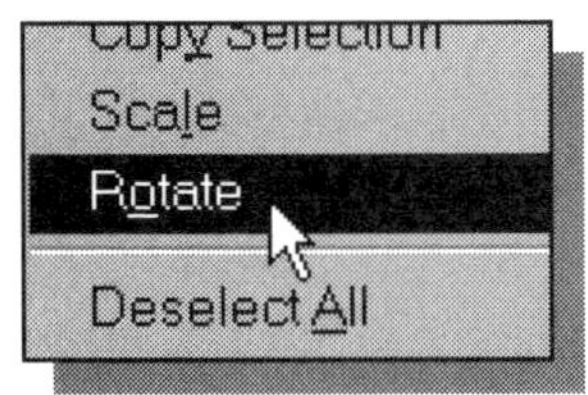

12. Inside the graphics window, **right-mouse-click** to bring up the popup option menu and select the **Rotate** option.

13. In the command prompt area, the message "*Specify base point:*" is displayed. Pick the **lower right corner** of the selected rectangle as the base point.

14. In the command prompt area, the message "*Specify the rotation angle or [Reference]:*" is displayed. Enter: ***30*** **[ENTER]**.

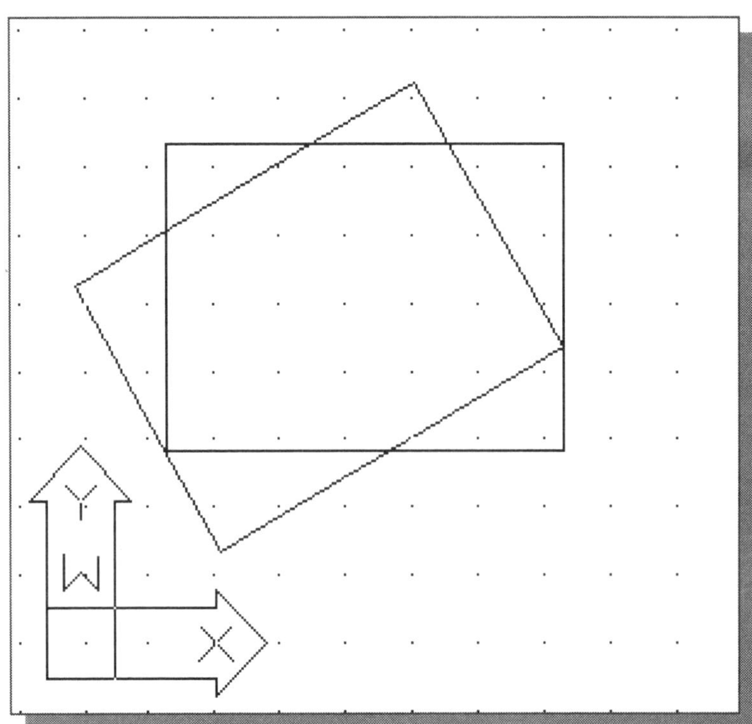

Setting up the Top View

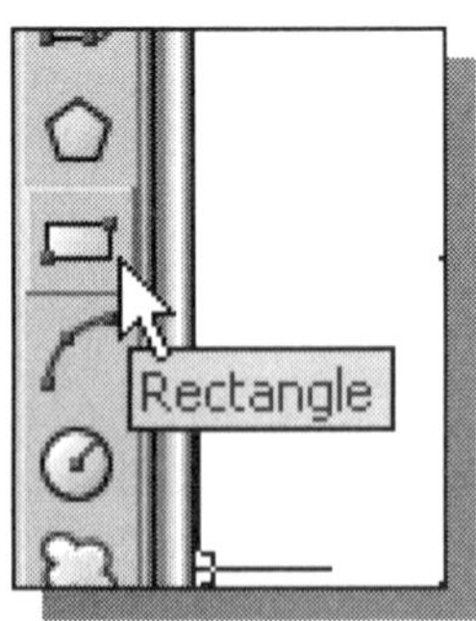

1. Select the **Rectangle** icon in the *Draw* toolbar. In the command prompt area, the message "*Specify first corner point or [Chamfer/Elevation/Fillet/Thickness/Width]:*" is displayed.

2. Move the cursor over the top left corner of the first rectangle we created. This will activate the ***object tracking*** alignment feature to the corner.

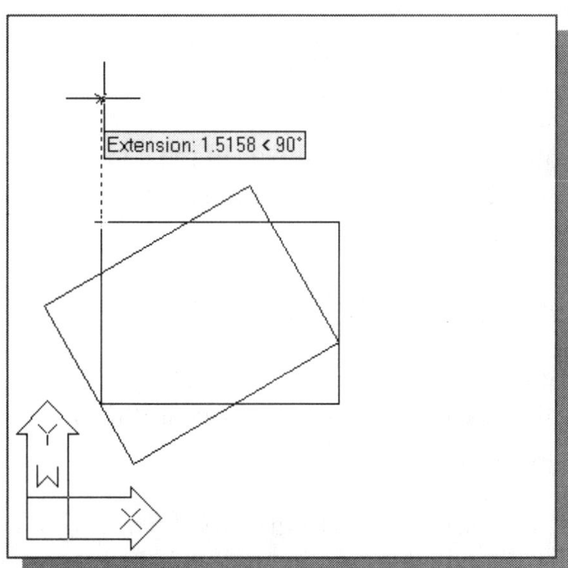

3. Move the cursor upward to a location that is about 1.5″ away from the reference point. (Read the *OTRACK* display on the screen.) Left-click once to place the first corner-point of the rectangle.

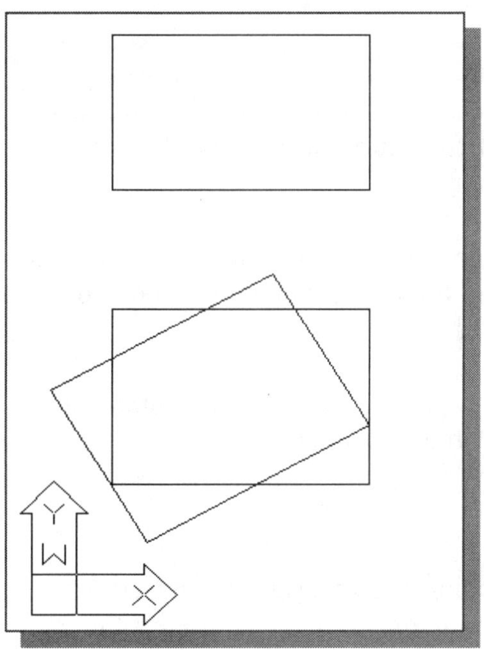

4. We will create a 3″ × 2″ rectangle.
   Enter: ***@3,2*** **[ENTER]**.

- We have created the outline of the top view of the *V-block* design.

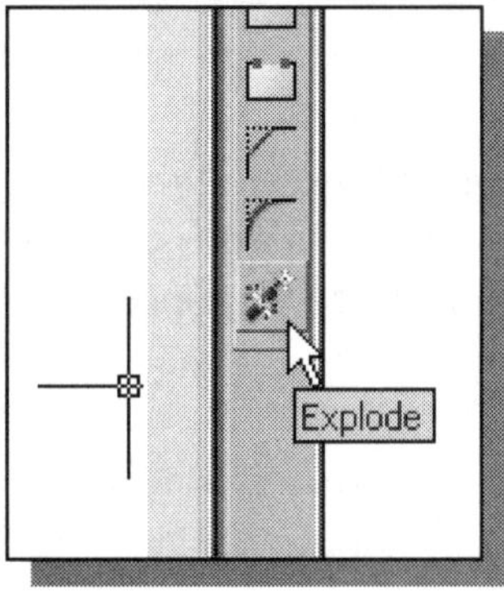

5. Pre-select the rectangle we just created by left-clicking any edge of the rectangle.

6. Select the **Explode** icon in the *Modify* toolbar.

- The top rectangle now consists of four separate line segments.

Using the *Offset* command

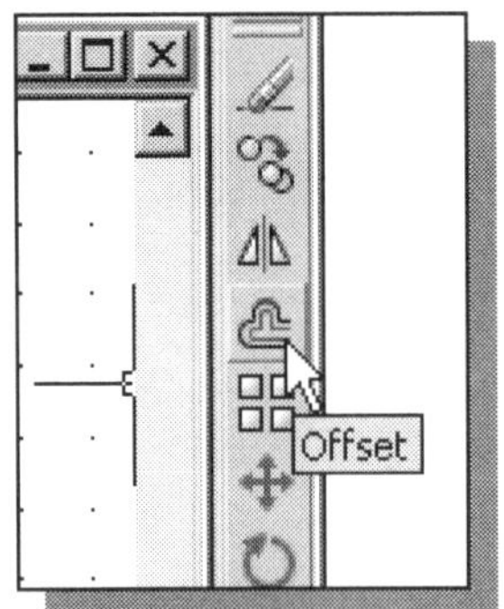

1. Select the **Offset** icon in the *Modify* toolbar. In the command prompt area, the message "*Specify offset distance or [Through]:*" is displayed.

2. In the command prompt area, enter: ***0.2*** **[ENTER]**.

3. In the command prompt area, the message "*Select object to offset or <exit>:*" is displayed. Pick the **top horizontal line** of the top view on the screen.

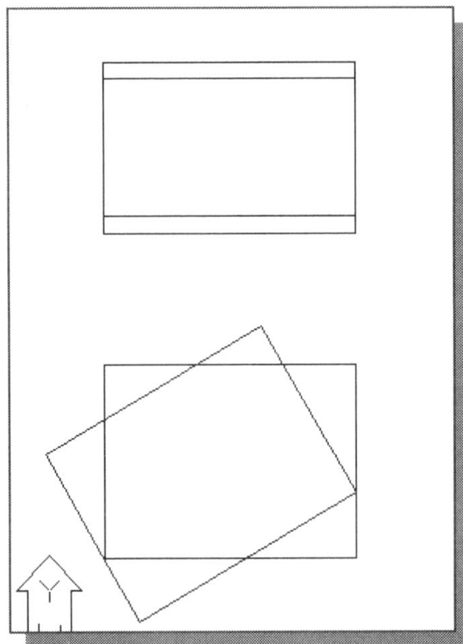

4. AutoCAD next asks us to identify the direction of the offset. Pick a location that is **below** the selected line.

5. In the command prompt area, the message "*Select object to offset or <exit>:*" is displayed. Pick the **bottom horizontal line** of the top view on the screen.

6. AutoCAD next asks us to identify the direction of the offset. Pick a location that is above the selected line.

7. Inside the graphics window, **right-mouse-click** to end the Offset command.

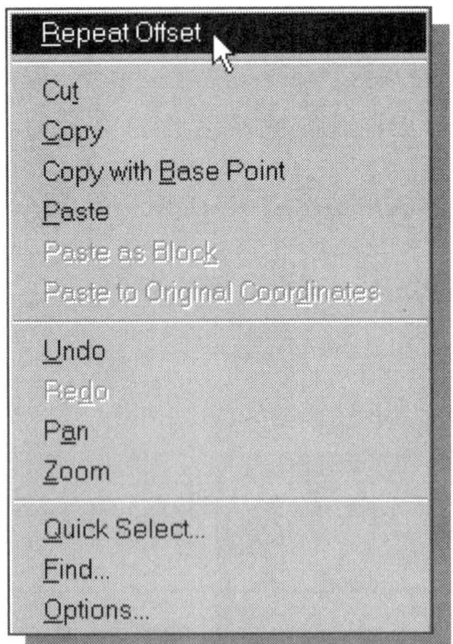

8. Inside the graphics window, right-mouse-click to bring up the popup option menu and select the **Repeat Offset** option.

- Notice in the popup menu, none of the GRIPS editing commands are displayed; the GRIPS editing commands are displayed only if objects are pre-selected.

9. In the command prompt area, the message "*Specify offset distance or [Through]:*" is displayed. Enter: ***0.75*** **[ENTER]**.

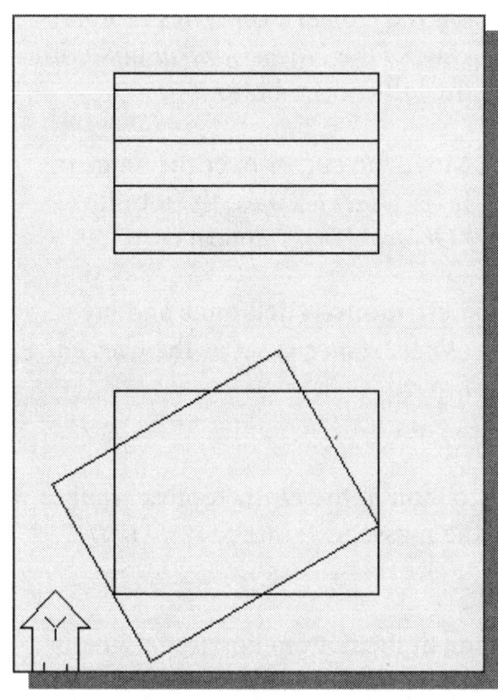

10. In the command prompt area, the message "*Select object to offset or <exit>:*" is displayed. Pick the **top horizontal line** of the top view on the screen.

11. AutoCAD next asks us to identify the direction of the offset. Pick a location that is **below** the selected line.

12. In the command prompt area, the message "*Select object to offset or <exit>:*" is displayed. Pick the **bottom horizontal line** of the top view on the screen.

13. AutoCAD next asks us to identify the direction of the offset. Pick a location that is above the selected line.

14. Inside the graphics window, **right-mouse-click** to end the Offset command.

- The four parallel lines will be used to construct the top v-cut feature and the two 0.75″ × 30° cut features at the base of the *V-block* in the top view.

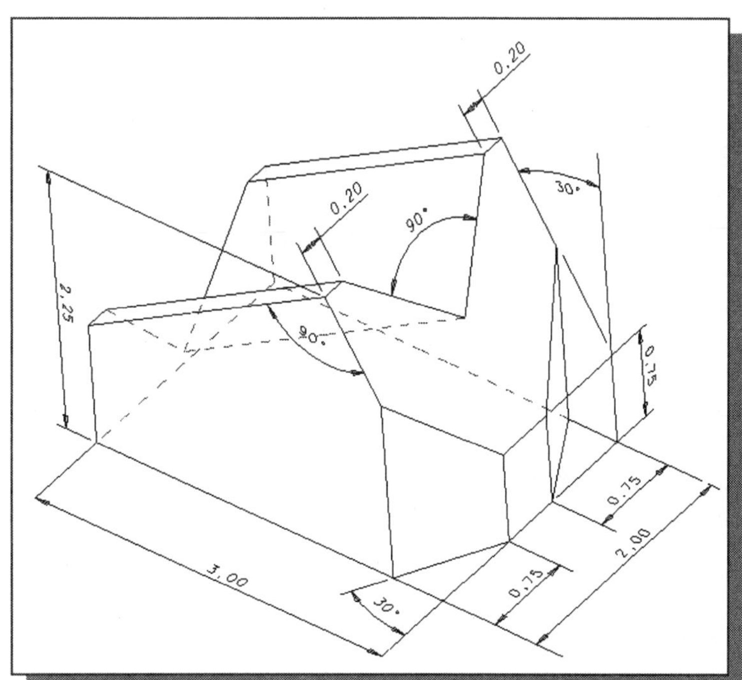

Creating object lines in the front view

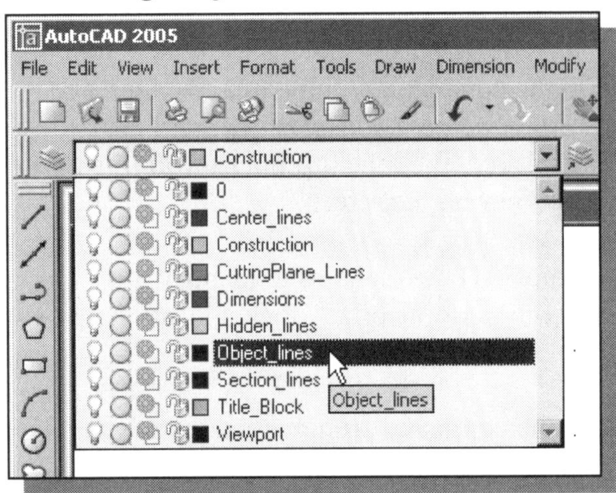

1. On the *Object Properties* toolbar, choose the *Layer Control* box with the left-mouse-button.

2. Move the cursor over the name of layer *Object_Lines*; the tool tip "*Object_Lines*" appears.

3. **Left-mouse-click once** and layer *Object_Lines* is set as the *Current Layer*.

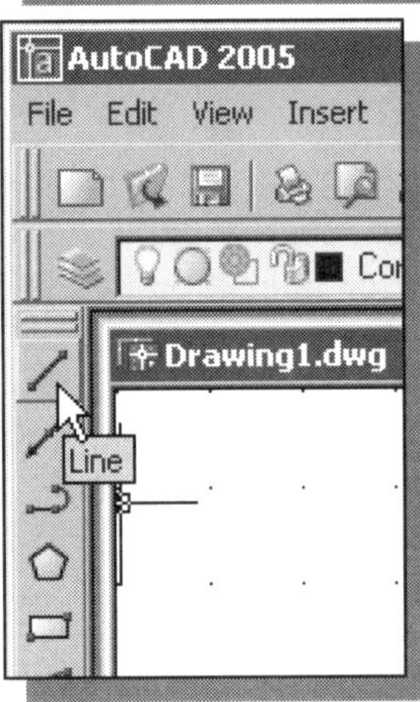

4. Select the **Line** command icon in the *Draw* toolbar. In the command prompt area, the message "*_line Specify first point:*" is displayed.

5. Pick the **lower left corner** of the bottom horizontal line in the front view as the starting point of the line segments.

6. Pick the **lower right corner** of the bottom horizontal line in the front view as the second point.

7. Select the **third** and **fourth** points as shown in the below figure.

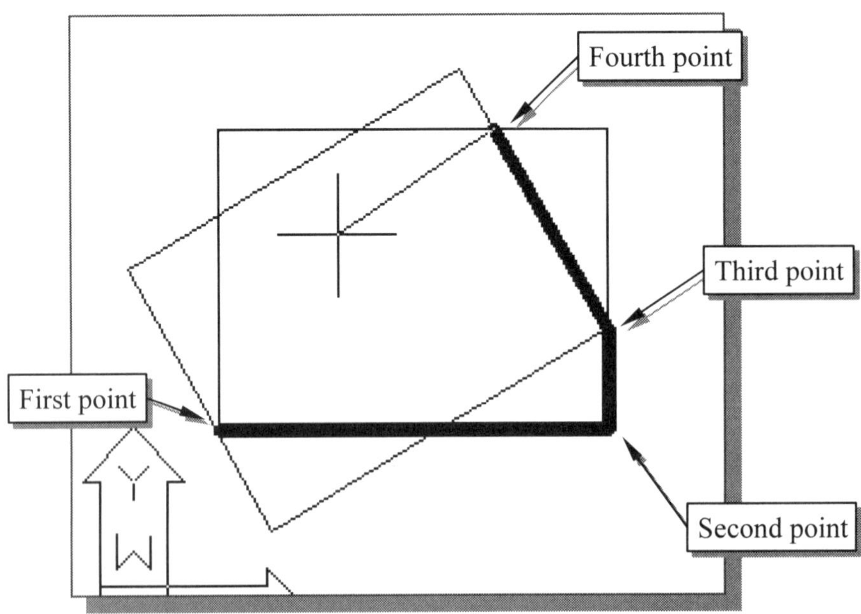

Setting the POLAR TRACKING option

1. In the *Status Bar* area, turn ***ON*** the *POLAR* option.

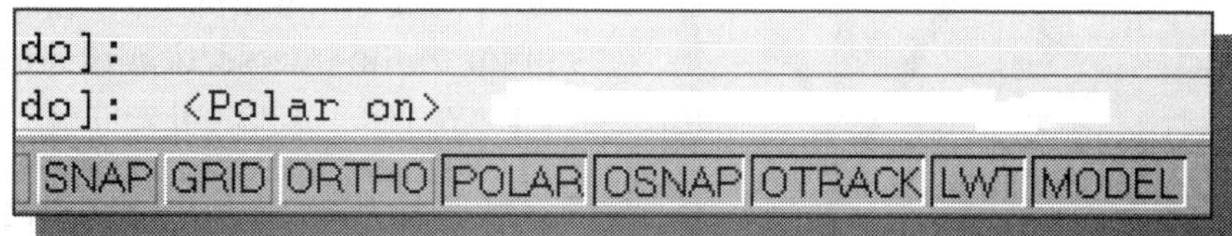

- Note that the *POLAR* option is one of the *AutoCAD AutoTrack*[TM] features. The *AutoTrack* features include two tracking options: polar tracking and object snap tracking. When the *POLAR* option is turned on, alignment markers are displayed to help us create objects at precise positions and angles. A quick way to change the settings of the *AutoTrack* feature is to use the option menu.

2. Move the cursor on top of the *POLAR* option in the *Status Bar* area.

3. Click once with the right-mouse-button to bring up the option menu.

4. Select **Settings** in the option menu as shown in the figure.

5. In the *Drafting Settings* dialog box, set the *Increment angle* to ***30*** as shown in the figure below.

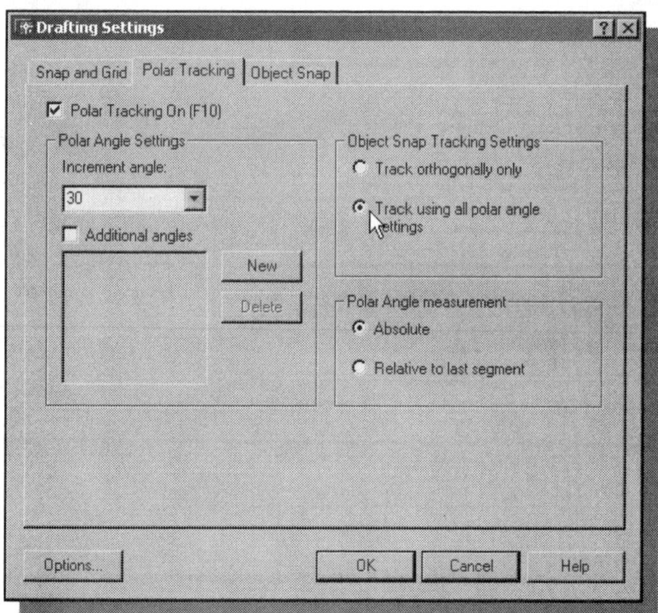

6. Under the *Object Snap Tracking Settings* option, turn ***ON*** the ***Track using all polar angle settings*** as shown in the figure above.

7. Click **OK** to accept the modified settings.

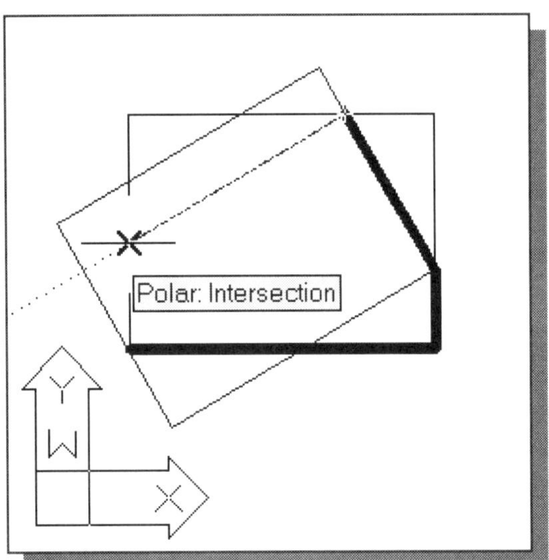

8. Move the cursor near the left vertical line as shown and notice that *AutoCAD AutoTrack* automatically snaps the cursor to the intersection point and displays the alignment marker as shown.

➢ In the following steps, we will illustrate the use of different *POLAR* settings to achieve the same result.

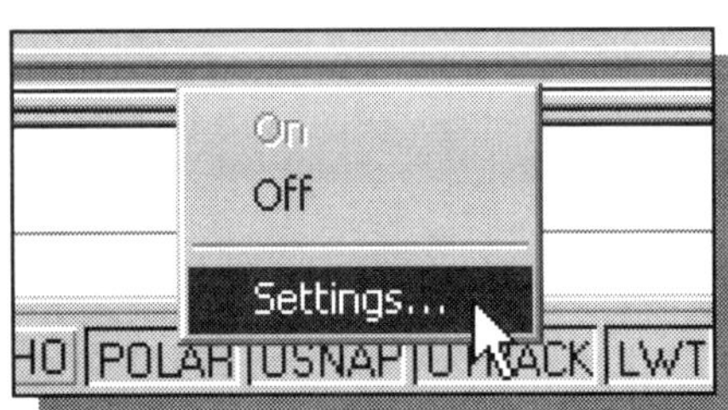

9. Click once with the right-mouse-button on the *POLAR* option in the *Status Bar* area to bring up the option menu.

10. Select **Settings** in the option menu as shown in the figure.

11. In the *Drafting Settings* dialog box, set the *Increment angle* to ***90*** as shown in the figure below.

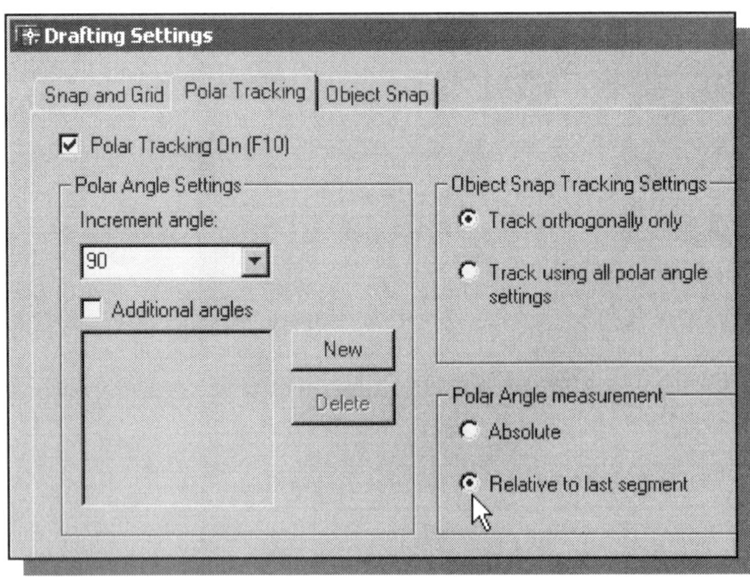

12. Under the *Object Snap Tracking Settings* option, turn ***ON*** the ***Track orthogonally only*** as shown in the figure.

13. Under the *Object Snap Tracking Settings* option, turn ***ON*** the ***Relative to last segment*** option as shown in the figure above.

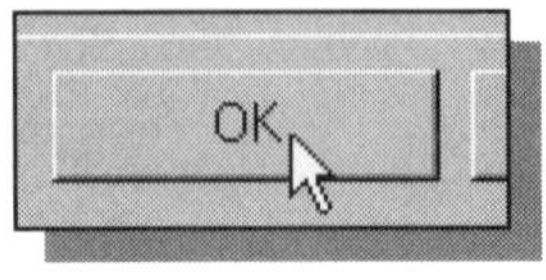

14. Click **OK** to accept the modified settings.

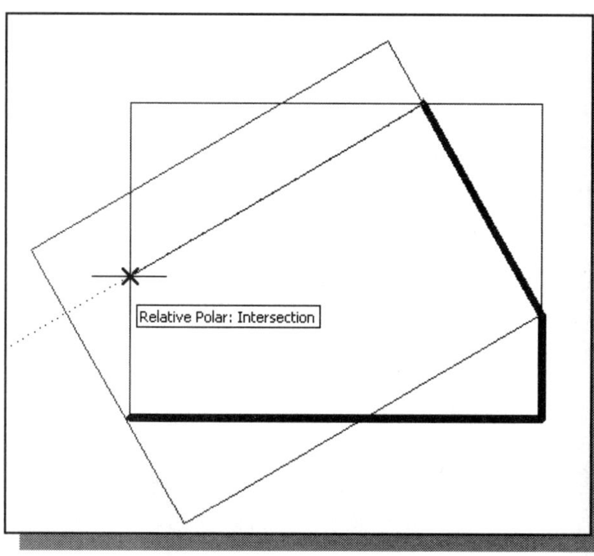

15. Move the cursor near the left vertical line and notice the *AutoTrack* feature automatically snaps the cursor to the intersection point and displays the alignment marker as shown.

➢ On your own, experiment with changing the settings to achieve the same *SNAP/POLAR* results.

16. Left-click at the intersection point as shown.

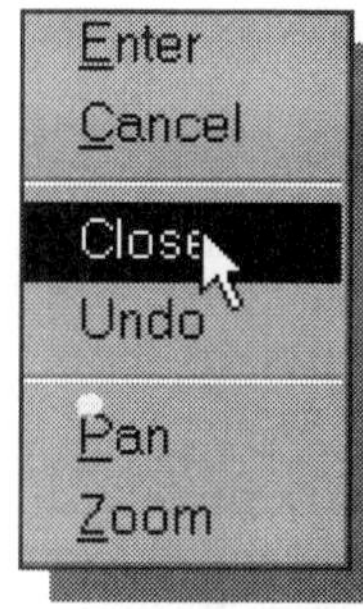

17. Inside the graphics window, right-mouse-click once to bring up the popup menu.

18. Pick the **Close** option in the popup menu. AutoCAD will create a line connecting the last point to the first point of the line sequence.

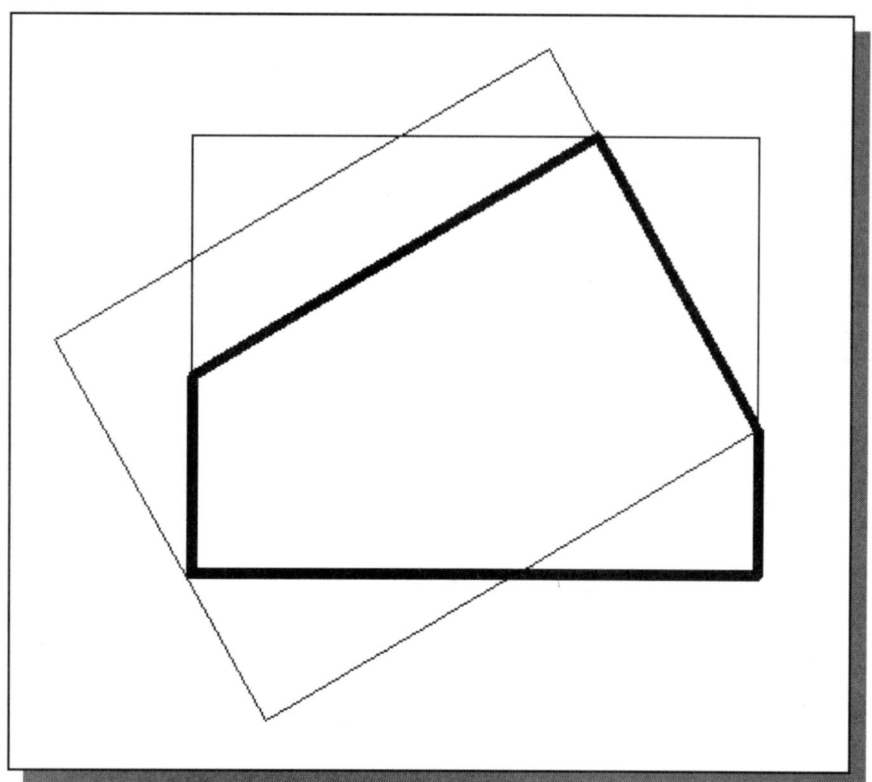

Setting up an auxiliary view

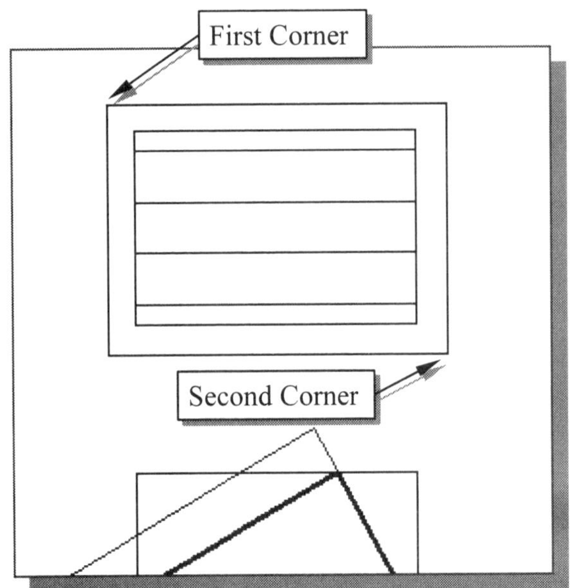

1. **Pre-select** all objects in the top view by enclosing the objects inside a selection window.

2. Inside the graphics window, right-mouse-click to bring up the popup option menu and select the **Copy Selection** option.

3. In the command prompt area, the message "*Specify base point or displacement, or [Multiple]:*" is displayed. Pick the **lower left corner** of the top view as the base point.

4. Using the *AutoTrack* feature, place the copy of the top-view by aligning it to the inclined object line we just created. Left-click once to position the copy about 2″ away from the top corner of the front-view.

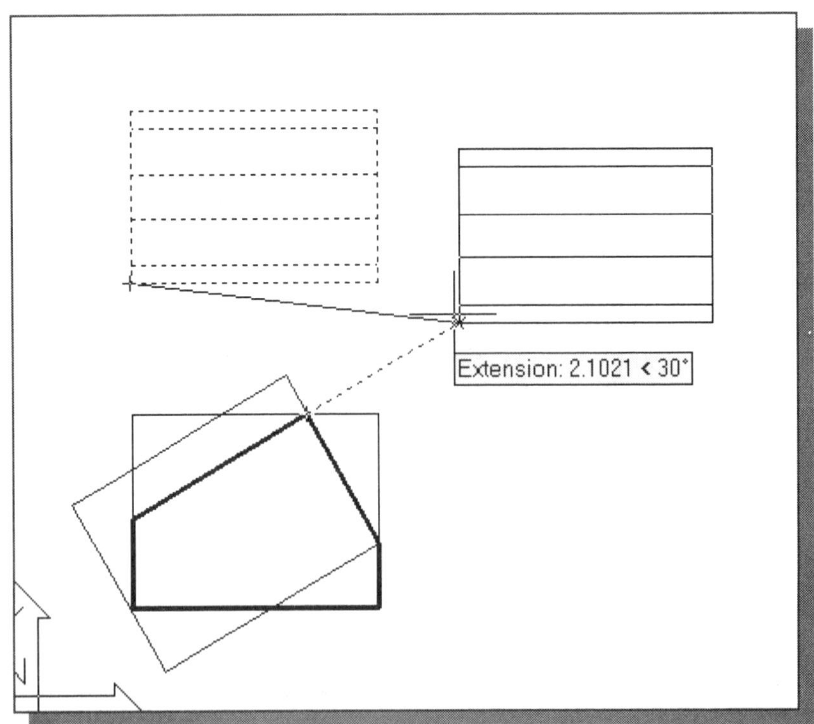

Aligning the auxiliary view to the front view

1. **Pre-select** all objects in the auxiliary view by enclosing the objects inside a selection window.

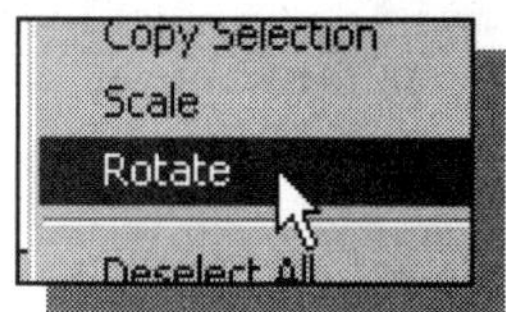

2. Inside the graphics window, right-mouse-click to bring up the popup option menu and select the **Rotate** option.

3. In the command prompt area, the message "*Specify base point:*" is displayed. Pick the **bottom left corner** of the auxiliary view as the base point.

4. In the command prompt area, the message "*Specify the rotation angle or [Reference]:*" is displayed. Enter: ***-60*** **[ENTER]**.

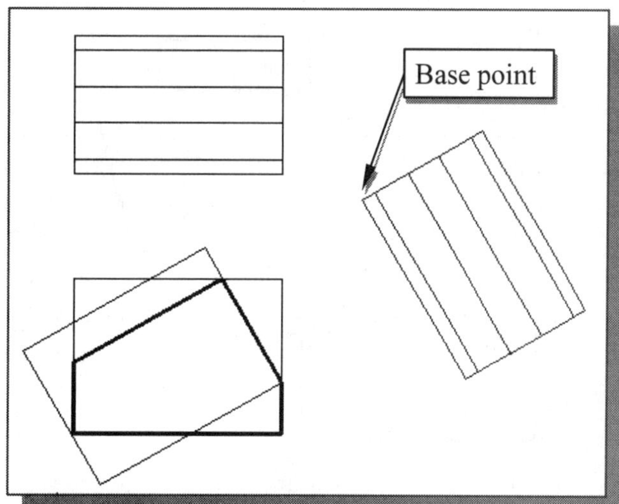

Creating the V-cut in the auxiliary view

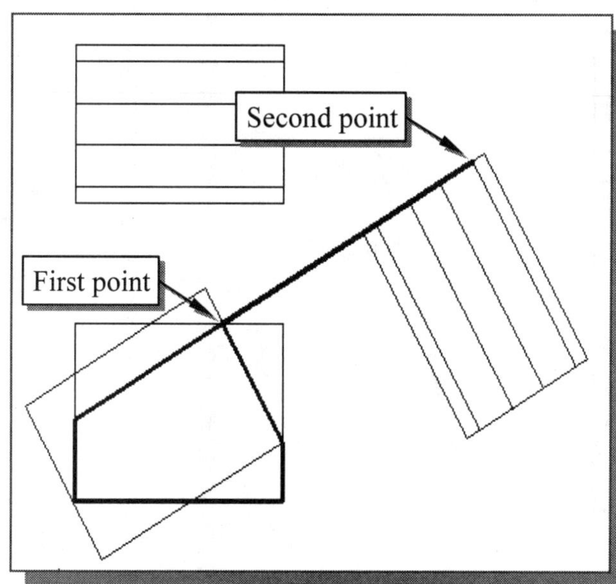

1. Select the **Line** icon in the *Draw* toolbar. In the command prompt area, the message "*_line Specify first point:*" is displayed.

2. Pick the **top corner** of the inclined object line in the front view as the starting point of the line segments.

3. Pick the **second top end point** in the auxiliary view as the second point.

4. Inside the graphics window, right-mouse-click and select **Enter** to end the Line command.

5. Pre-select the line we just created.

6. Inside the graphics window, right-mouse-click to bring up the popup option menu and select the **Rotate** option.

7. In the command prompt area, the message "*Specify base point:*" is displayed. Pick the top right endpoint of the line as the base point.

8. In the command prompt area, the message "*Specify the rotation angle or [Reference]:*" is displayed. Enter: ***45*** **[ENTER]**.

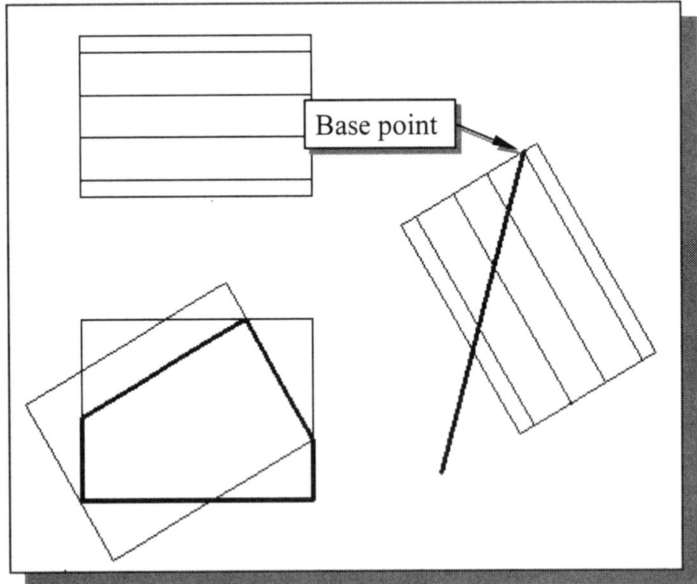

9. On your own, repeat the above steps and create the other line as shown.

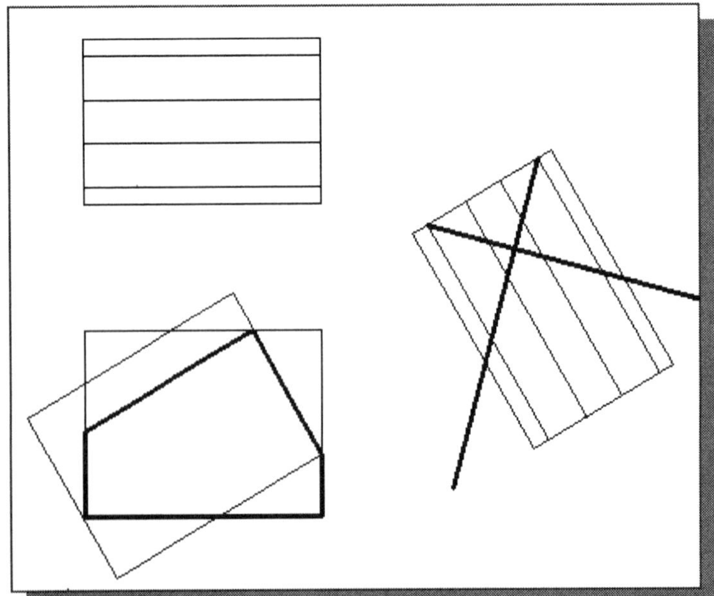

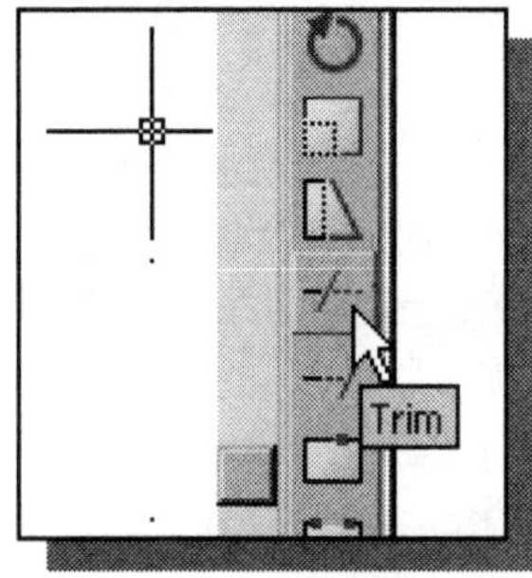

10. Select the **Trim** command icon in the *Modify* toolbar. In the command prompt area, the message "*Select boundary edges... Select objects:*" is displayed.

11. Pick the two inclined lines we just created in the auxiliary view as the *boundary edges*.

12. Inside the graphics window, **right-mouse-click** to proceed with the Trim command. The message "*Select object to trim or [Project/Edge/Undo]:*" is displayed in the command prompt area.

13. Pick the two lower endpoints of the two inclined lines to remove the unwanted portions.

14. Inside the graphics window, right-mouse-click to activate the option menu and select **Enter** with the left-mouse-button to end the Trim command.

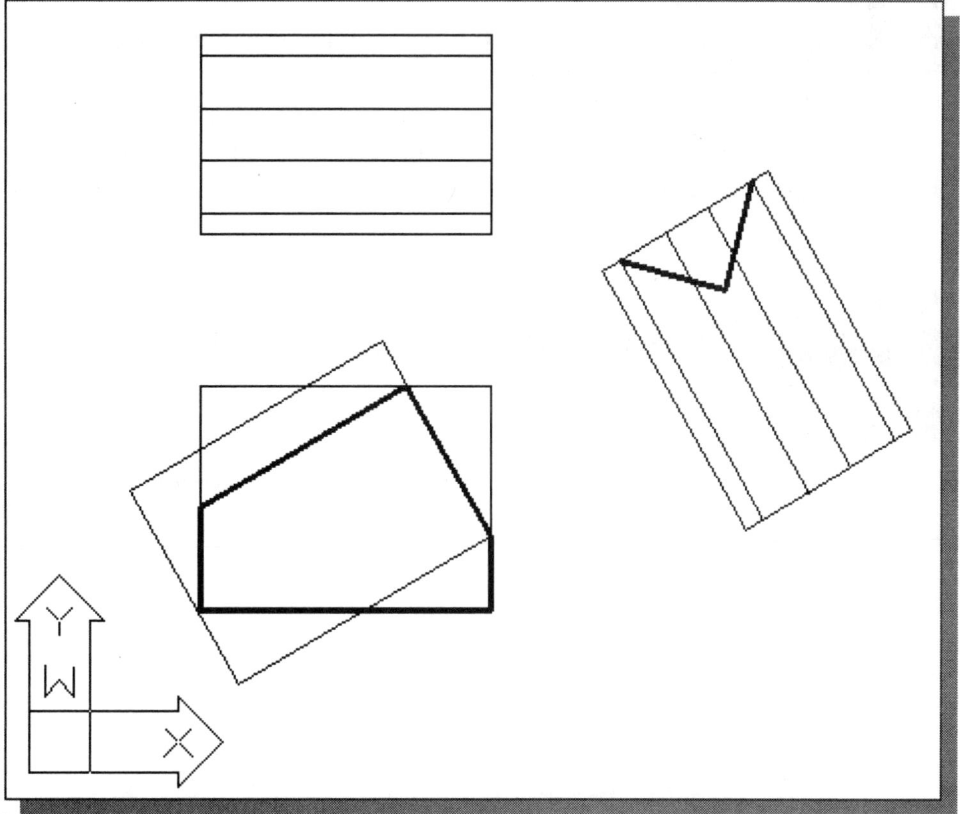

➢ The V-cut is shown at its true size and shape only in the auxiliary view. It is therefore necessary to create the V-cut in the auxiliary view. Now that we have constructed the feature in the auxiliary view, we can use projection lines to transfer the feature to the front view and top view.

Creating the V-cut in the front view and top view

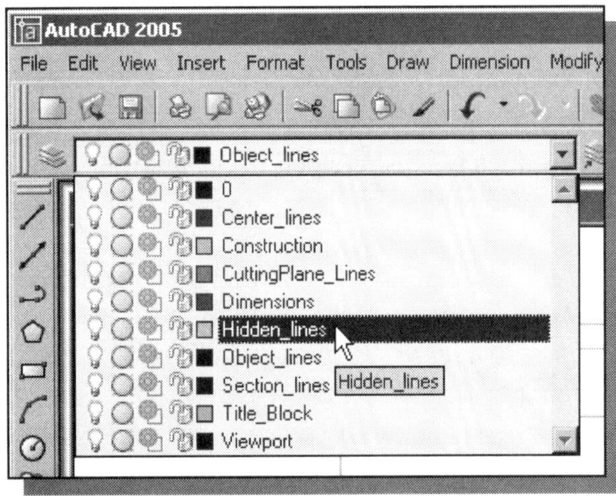

1. On the *Object Properties* toolbar, choose the *Layer Control* box with the left-mouse-button.

2. Move the cursor over the name of layer ***Hidden_Lines***; the tool tip *"Hidden_Lines"* appears.

3. **Left-mouse-click once** and layer *Hidden_Lines* is set as the *Current Layer.*

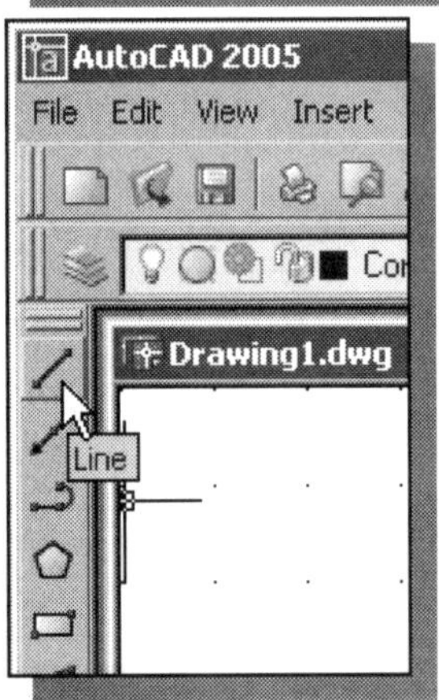

4. Select the **Line** command icon in the *Draw* toolbar. In the command prompt area, the message "*_line Specify first point:*" is displayed.

5. Pick the **vertex** of the V-cut in the *auxiliary view* as the first point of the line.

6. Inside the graphics window, hold down the **[SHIFT]** key and **right-mouse-click** once to bring up the *Object Snap* shortcut menu.

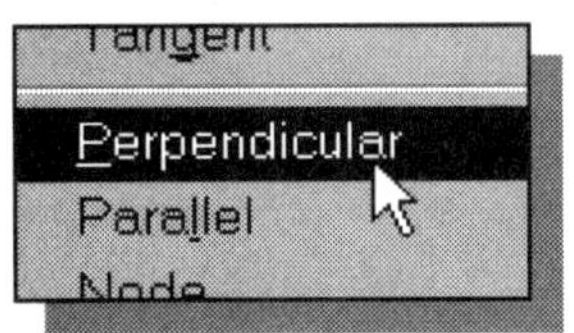

7. Select the **Perpendicular** option in popup window.

8. Move the cursor to the front view and notice the perpendicular symbol appears at different locations. Select the intersection point on the inclined line as shown in the figure below.

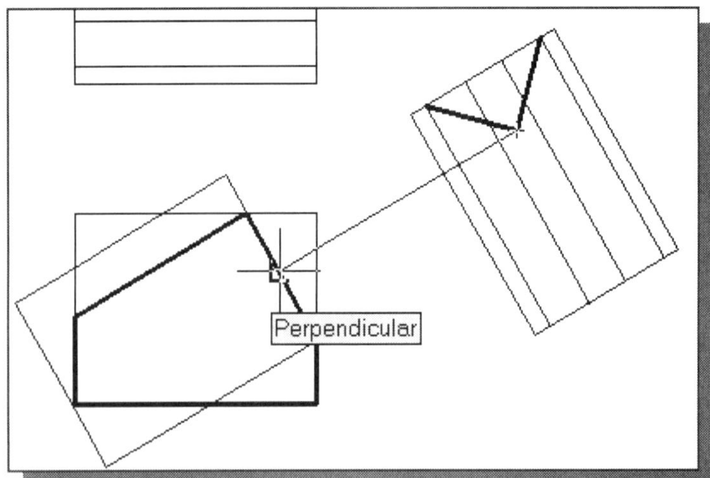

9. Inside the graphics window, right-mouse-click to activate the option menu and select **Enter** with the left-mouse-button to end the **Line** command.

10. On your own, use the **Trim** and **Extend** commands to adjust the hidden lines in the front view.

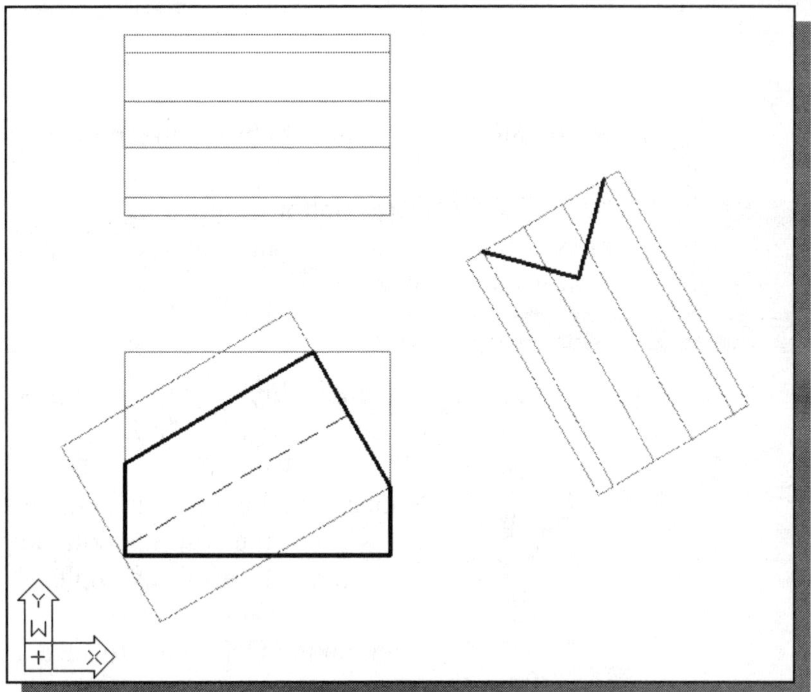

➢ On your own, first create the two construction lines and then construct the V-cut feature in the top-view. Use the **Trim** and **Extend** commands to assist the construction.

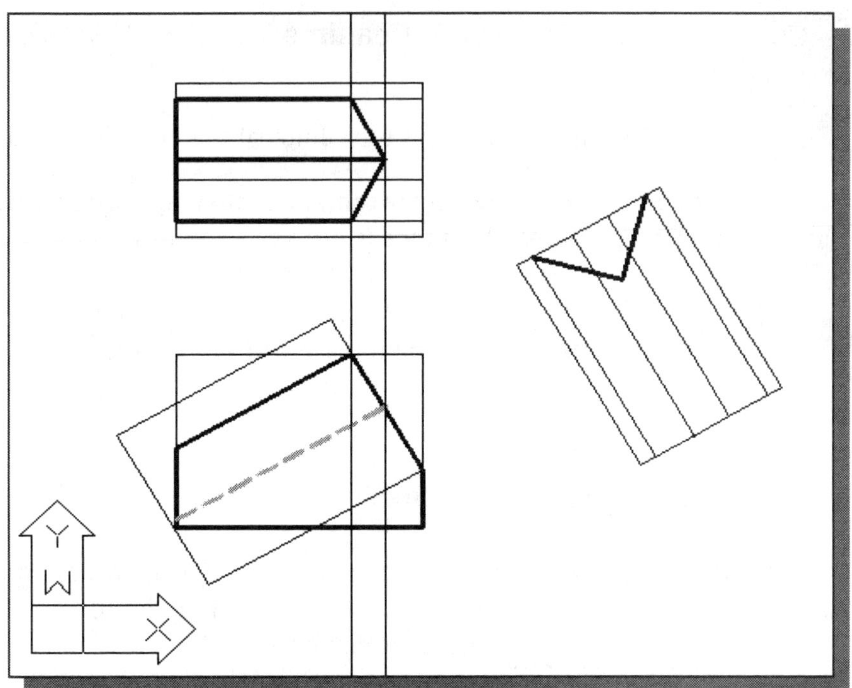

Setting the POLAR TRACKING option

1. Move the cursor to the *Status Bar* area, over the *POLAR* option button.

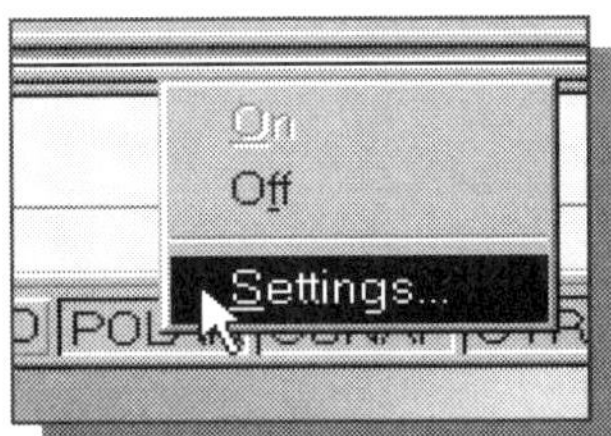

2. **Right-mouse-click once** to bring up a popup option menu.

3. Select the **Settings** option by clicking once with the left-mouse-button. This is the shortcut to bring up the *Drafting Settings* dialog box.

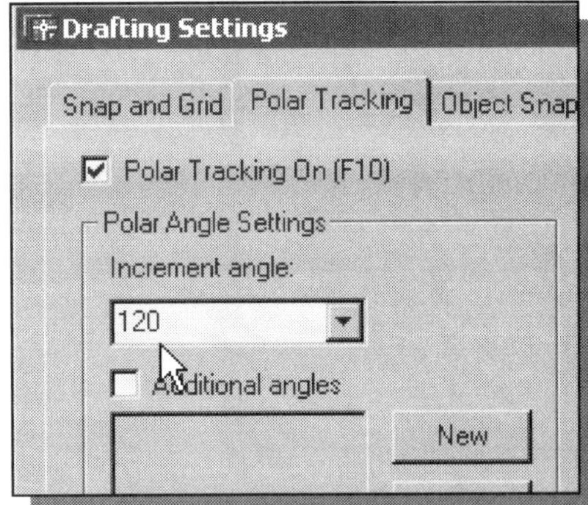

4. In the *Drafting Settings* dialog box, set the *Increment angle* to ***120***.

➢ Notice the other settings that are available. We will use the absolute polar angle measurement for this example.

5. Click on the **OK** button to accept the settings.

Completing the top-view

1. Click on the **Zoom Realtime** icon in the *Standard* toolbar area.

2. Move the cursor near the center of the graphics window.

3. **Push and hold down the left-mouse-button**, then move upward to enlarge the current display scale factor. (Press the **[Esc]** key to exit the command.)

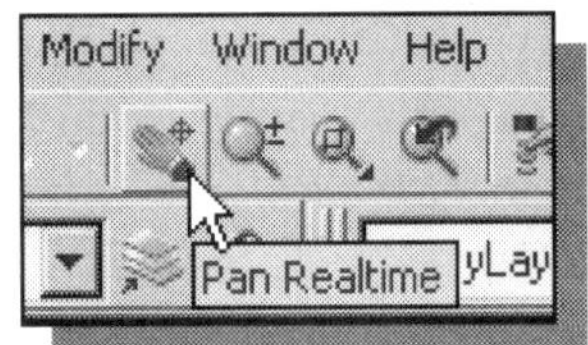

4. Use the **Pan Realtime** option to reposition the display so that we can work on the top view of the *V-block*.

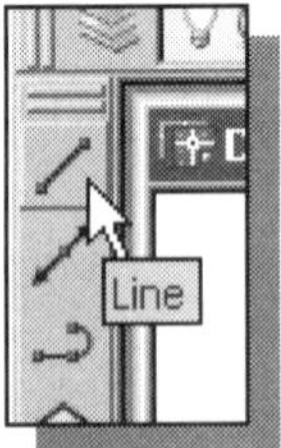

5. Select the **Line** icon in the *Draw* toolbar.

6. In the command prompt area, the message "*_line Specify first point:*" is displayed. Pick the **right endpoint** of the third horizontal line in the top view as the starting point of the line segments.

7. Move the cursor toward the top horizontal line and observe the *AutoTracking* markers over different locations.

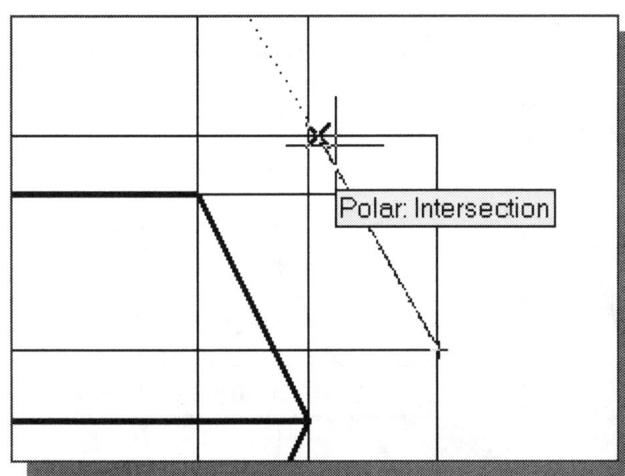

8. **Left-click** at the intersection of the polar tracking and the top horizontal line as shown. Do not select the intersection between the top horizontal line and the vertical line. (Use the **Zoom Realtime** command to zoom-in further, if necessary.)

9. Inside the graphics window, right-mouse-click and select **Enter** to end the **Line** command.

10. Repeat the above steps and create the other inclined line in the top view.

➢ On your own, complete the top view by adding all the necessary object lines in the top view. Use the **Trim** and **Extend** commands to assist the construction.

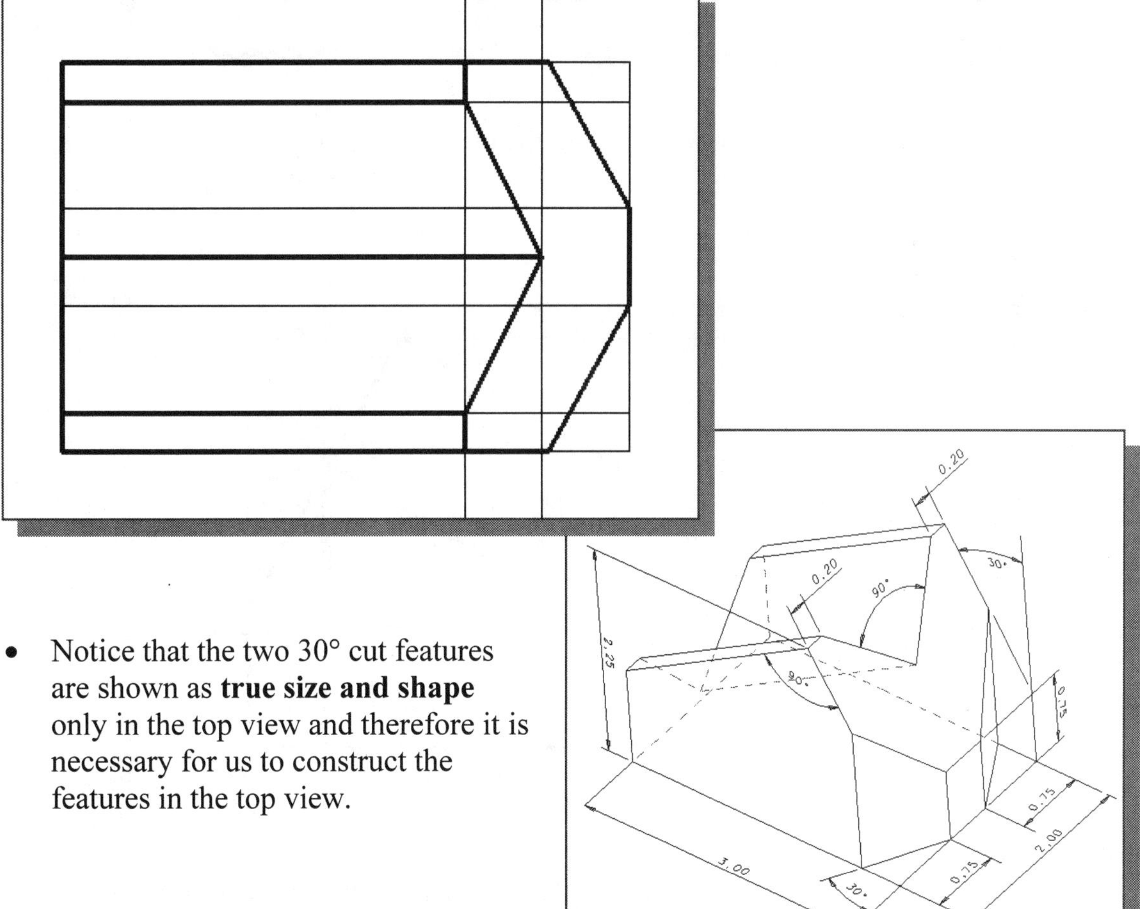

- Notice that the two 30° cut features are shown as **true size and shape** only in the top view and therefore it is necessary for us to construct the features in the top view.

➢ On your own, create the **vertical construction line** through the corner of the 30° cut as shown.

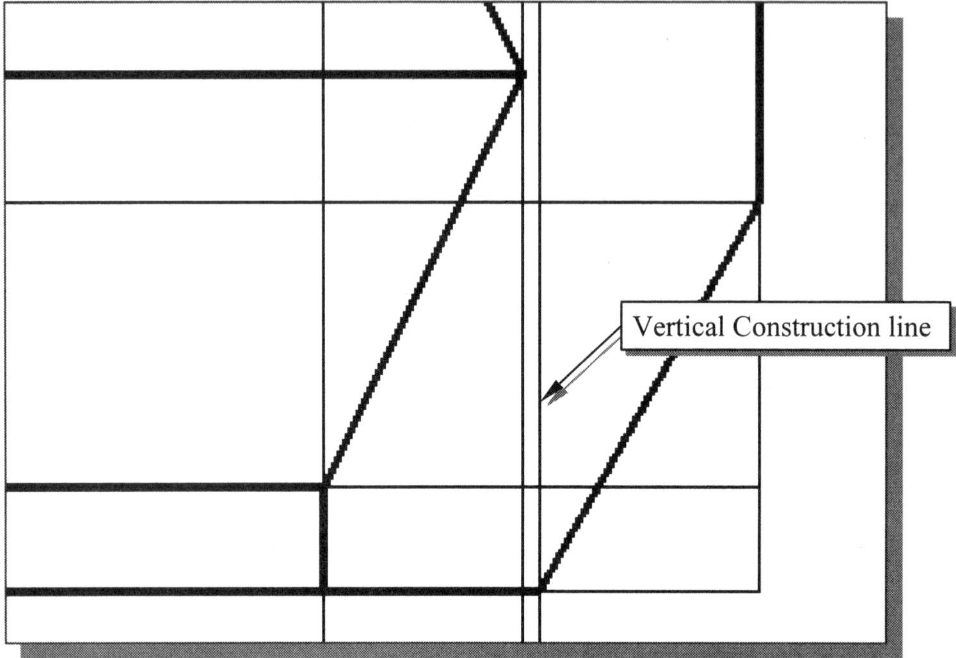

11. Complete the front view by adding the object line along the construction line as shown.

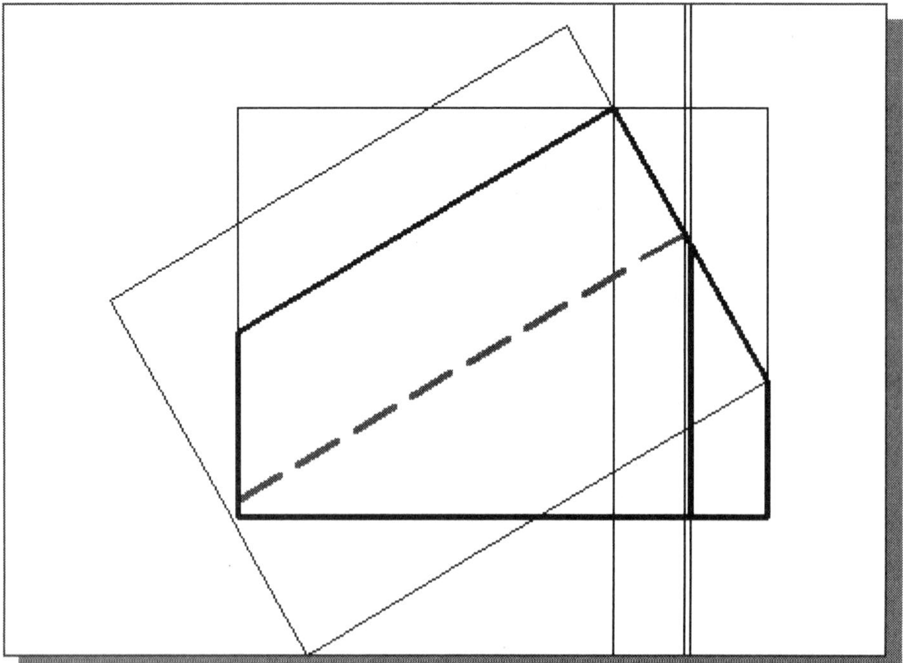

➤ On your own, complete the views by adding all the necessary object lines in the views.

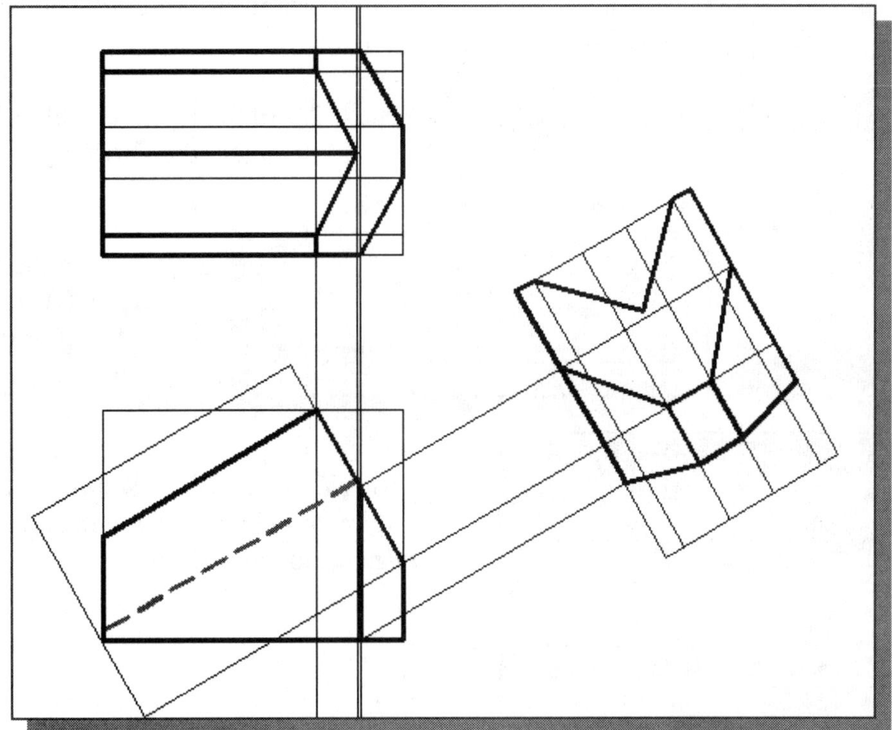

➤ Complete the drawing by adding the proper dimensions.

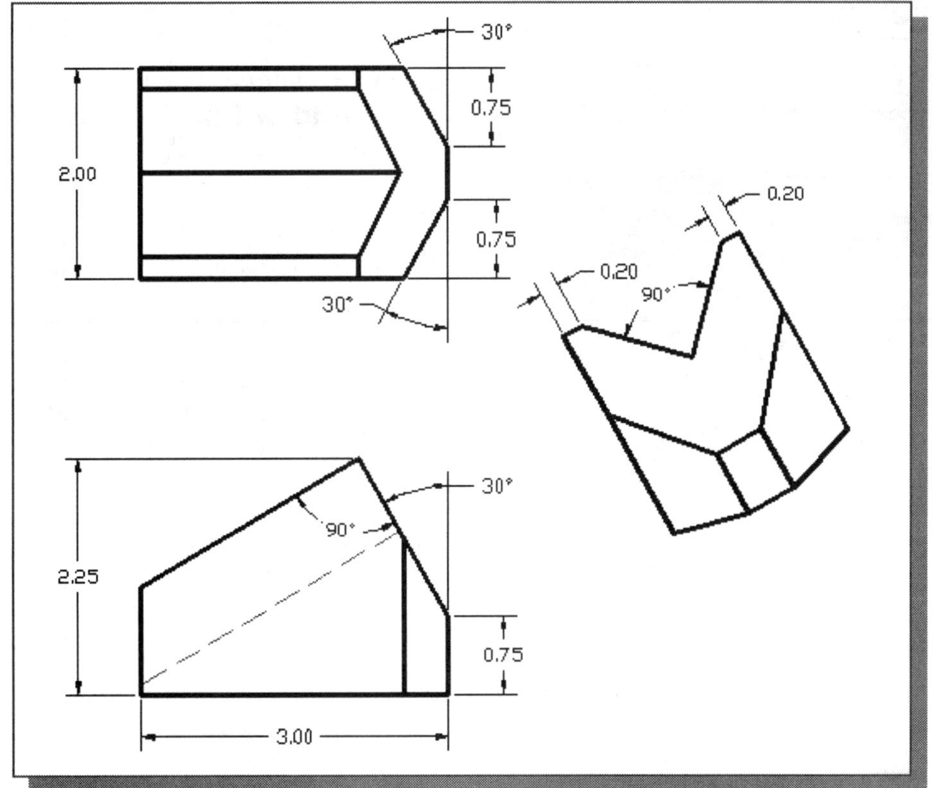

Edit the Plot Style table

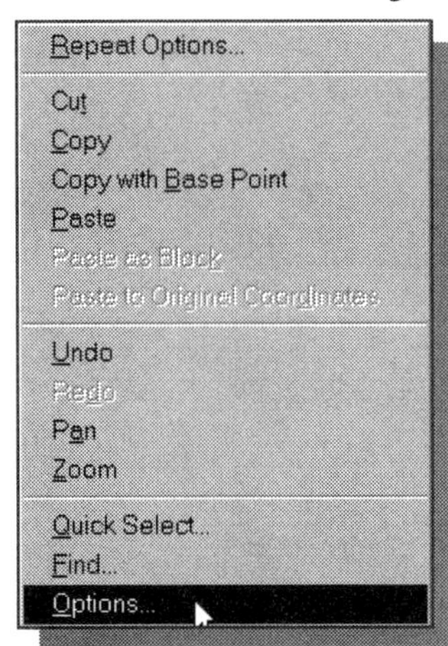

1. Inside the graphics window, right-mouse-click and select **Options** in the popup menu.

2. In the *Options* dialog box, select the **Plotting** tab.

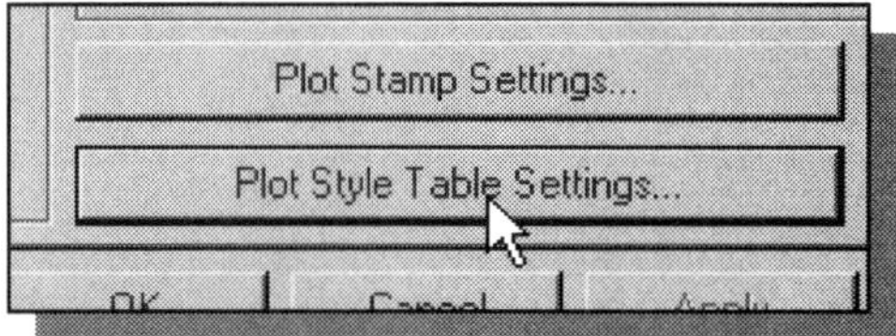

3. Click on the **Plot Style Table Settings** button as shown.

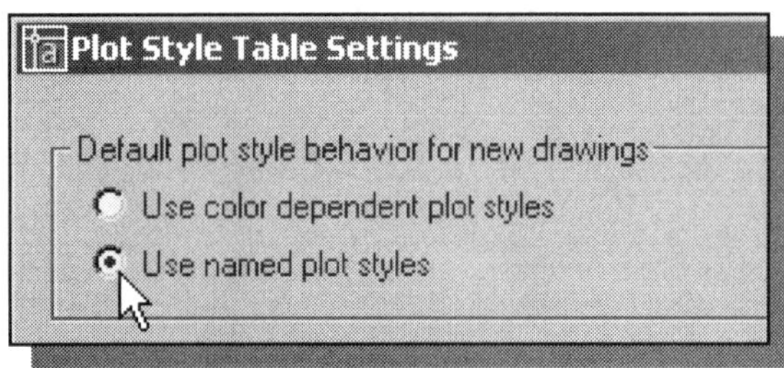

4. In the *Plot Style Table Settings* dialogue box, switch ***ON*** the ***Use named plot styles*** option as shown.

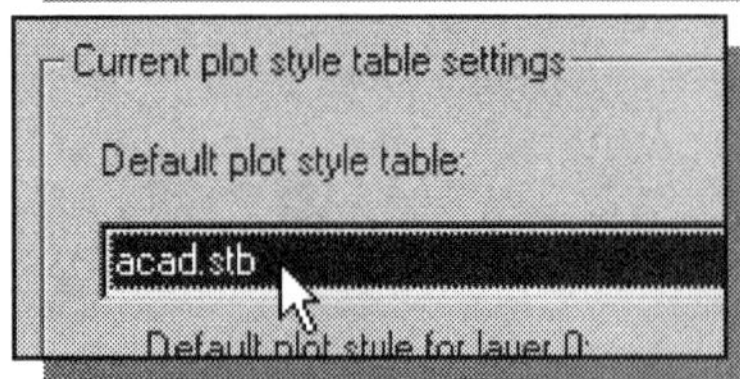

5. Choose the *acad.stb* as the default plot style table as shown.

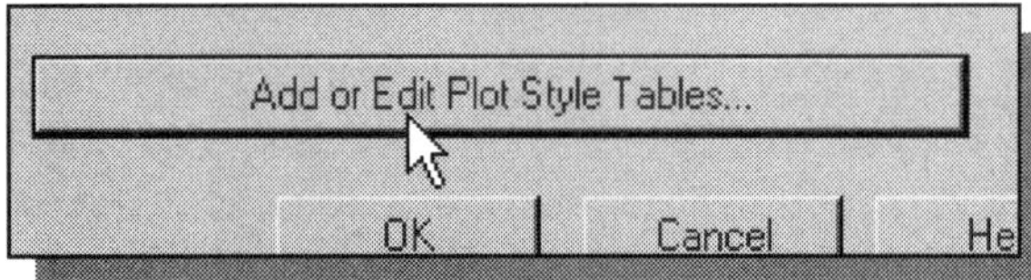

6. In the *Options* dialog box, click on the **Add or Edit Plot Style Tables** button.

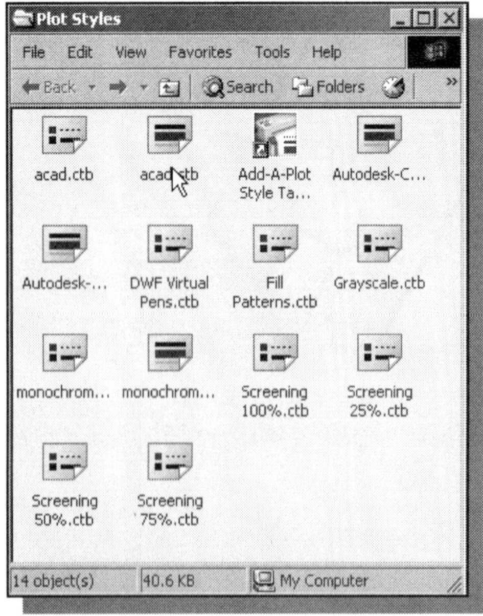

7. The *Plot Styles* folder appears on the screen.

8. Double-click the **acad.stb** icon with the left-mouse-button to open the plot style file.

9. In the *Plot Style Table Editor*, select the **Table View** tab.

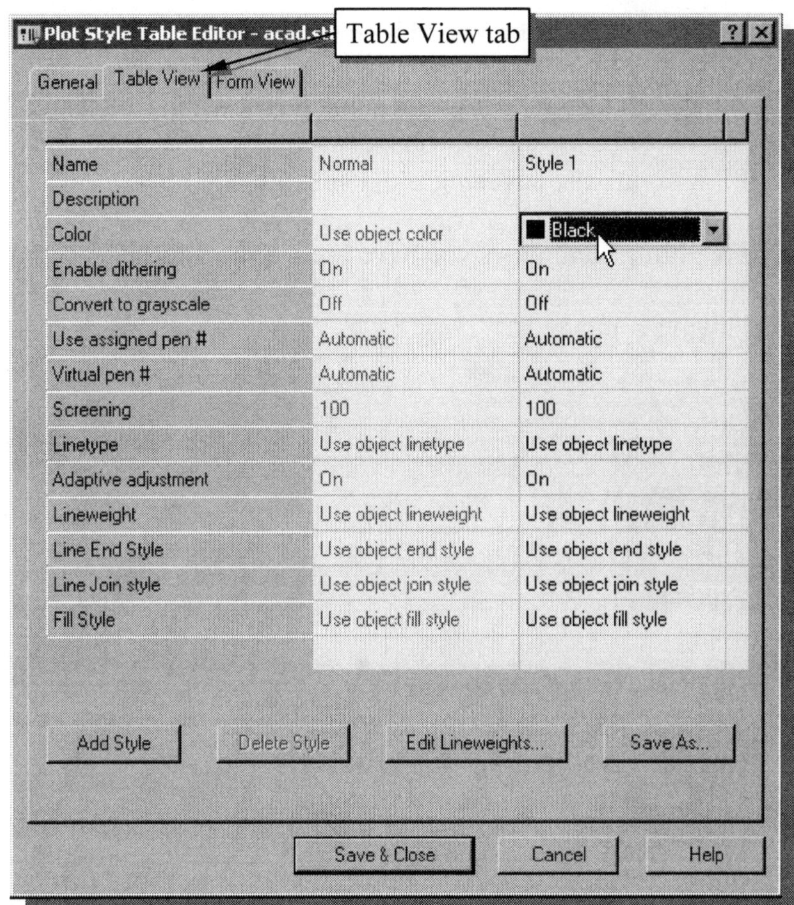

- The *Plot Style Table Editor* displays the plot styles that are in the current plot style table. The **Table View** and **Form View** tabs provide two methods to modify the existing plot style settings. Both tabs list all of the plot styles in the plot style table and their settings. In general, the **Table View** tab is more convenient if there is only a small number of plot styles. We can modify plot style color, screening, linetype, lineweight, and other settings. The first plot style in a named plot style table is *Normal* and represents an object's default properties (no plot style applied). We cannot modify or delete the *Normal* style.

10. Change the *Color* setting for *Style 1* to **Black**, so that all layers using this plot style will print using black.

11. Pick the **Save & Close** button to accept the settings and exit the *Plot Style Table Editor*.

➢ On your own, print out a copy of the *V-block* drawing using the modified plot style table.

Questions:

1. What is an auxiliary view and why would it be important?

2. When is a line viewed as a point? How can a line be shown in true length?

3. What is a GRIP? What are the advantages of using the GRIPS?

4. List three GRIPS editing commands you have used in the tutorial.

5. Identify the following commands:

(a)

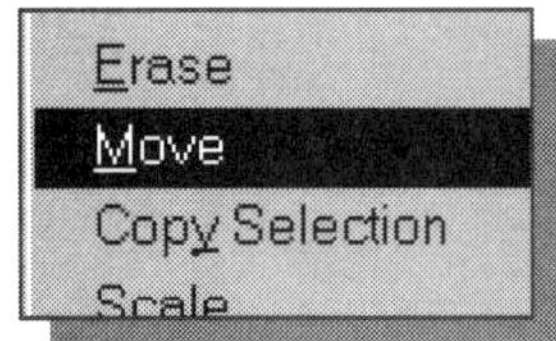

(b)

(c)

(d)

Exercises:

1. Dimensions are in inches.

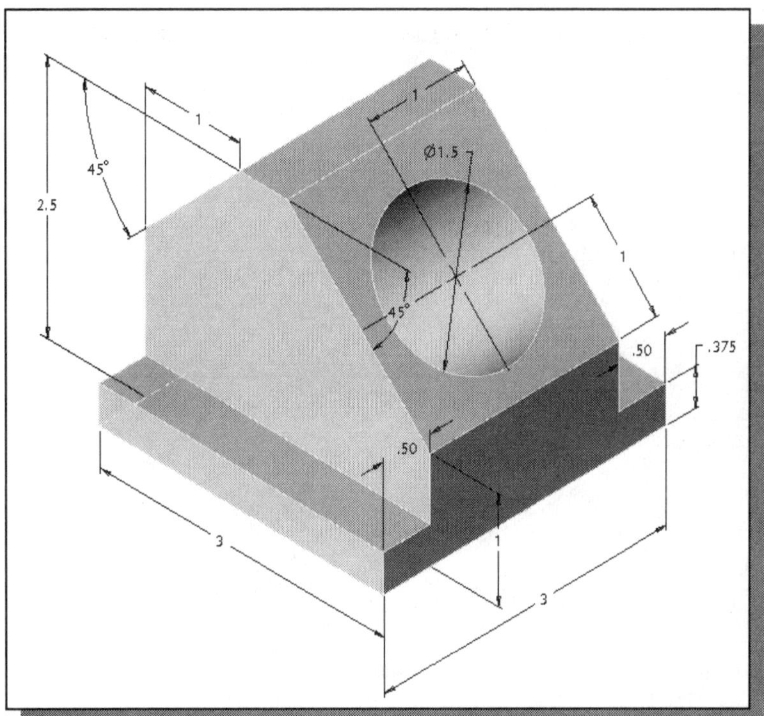

2. Dimensions are in inches.

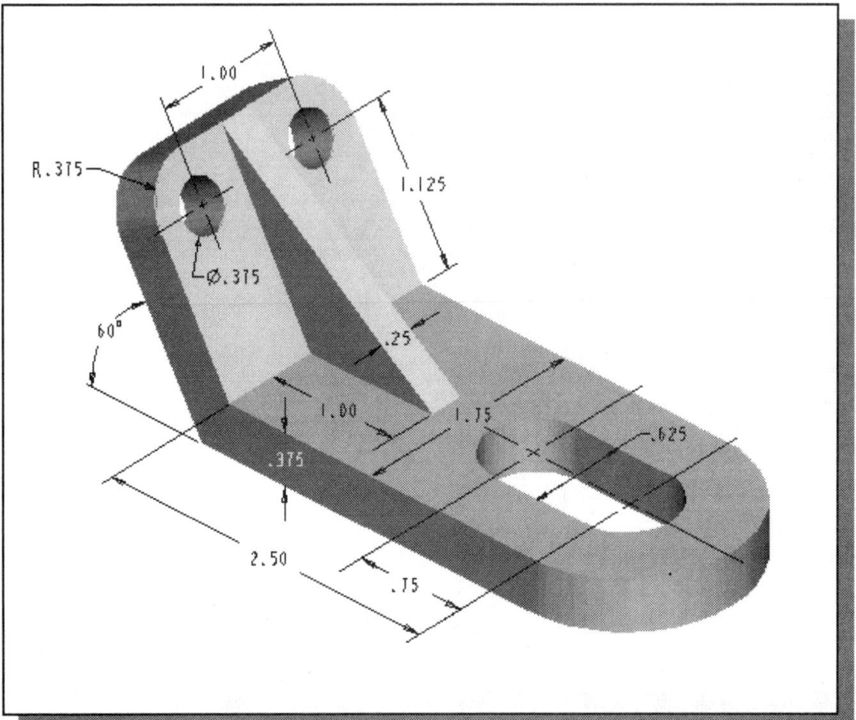

3. Dimensions are in Millimeters.

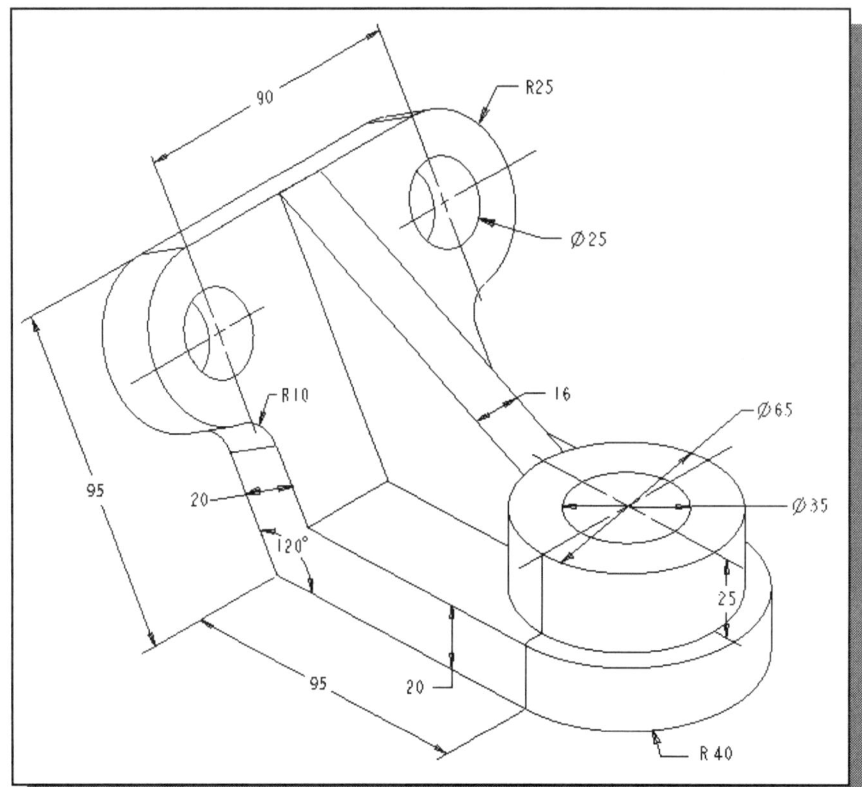

4. Dimensions are in inches.

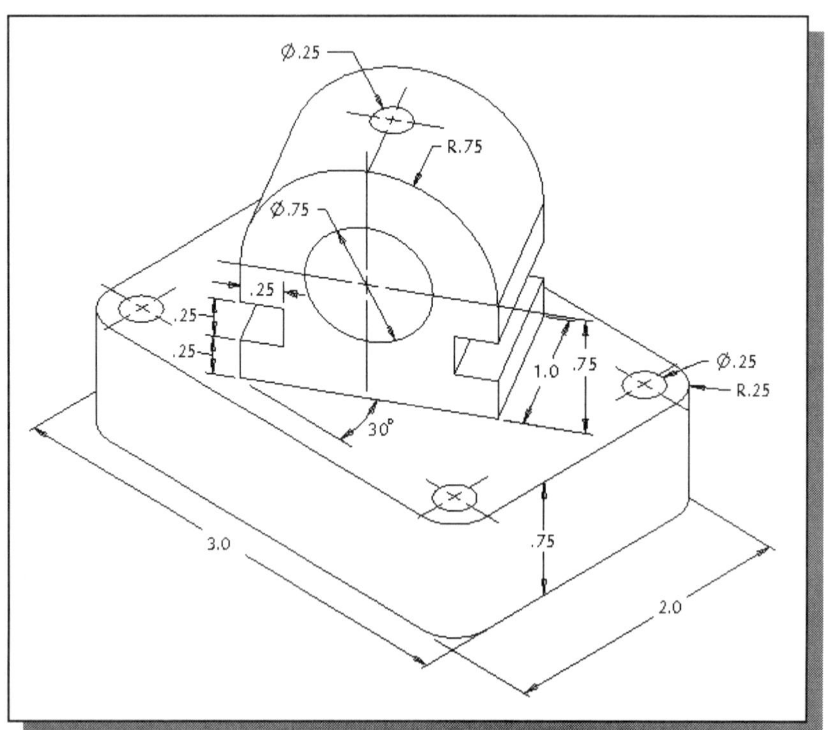

Lesson 9
Section Views

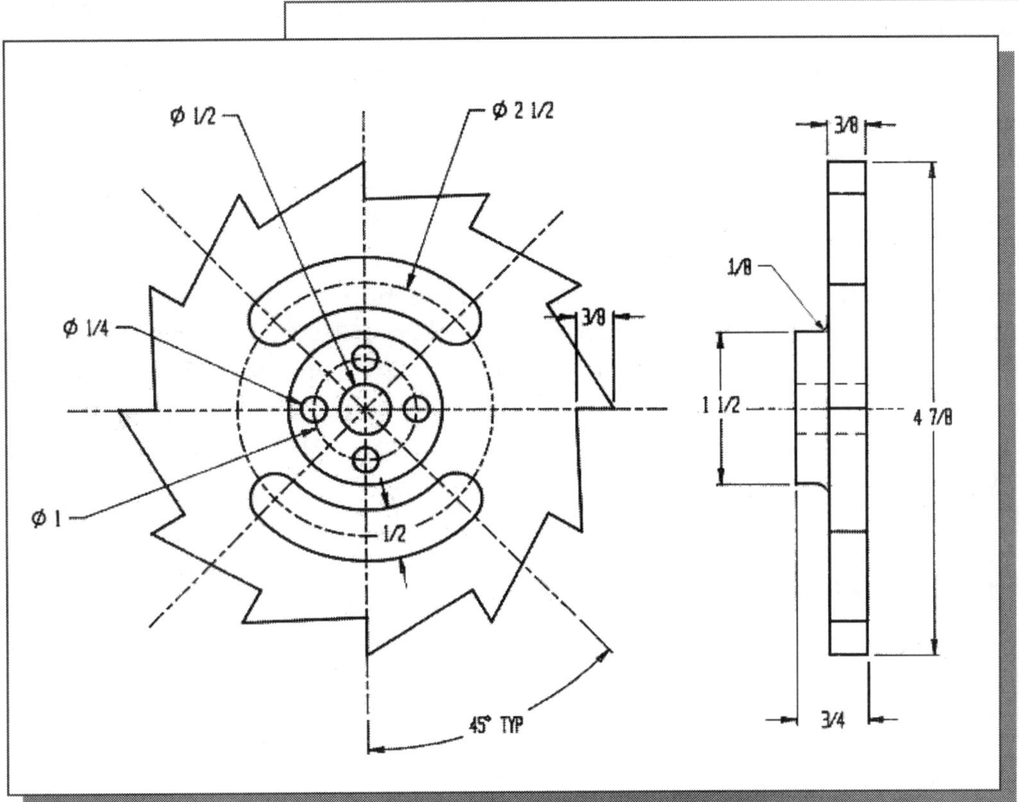

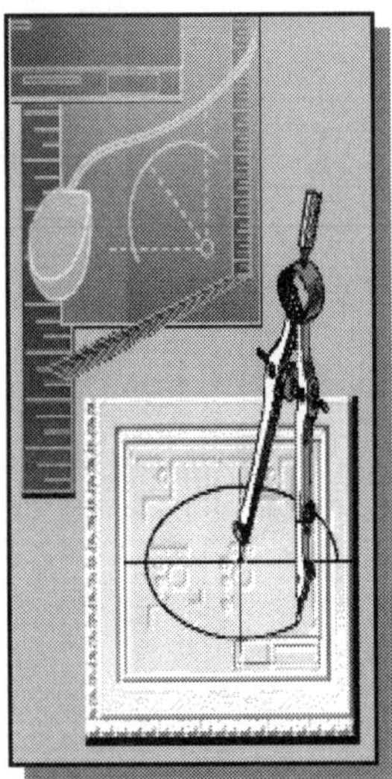

Learning Objectives

- Use CAD methods to create Section Views.
- Use the Object Snap Shortcut options.
- Change the Linetype Scale property.
- Stretch and move objects with GRIPS.
- Create cutting plane lines.
- Use the HATCH command.

Introduction

In the previous lessons, we have explored the basic CAD methods of creating orthographic views. By carefully selecting a limited number of views, the external features of most complicated designs can be fully described. However, we are frequently confronted with the necessity of showing the interiors of parts that cannot be shown clearly by means of hidden lines. We accomplish this by passing an imaginary cutting plane through the part and creating a cutaway view of the part. This type of view is known as a **section view**. In this lesson, we will demonstrate the procedure to construct a section view using **AutoCAD® 2005**.

In a section view, section lines, or cross-hatch lines, are added to indicate the surfaces that are cut by the imaginary cutting plane. The type of section line used to represent a surface varies according to the type of material. AutoCAD's **Hatch** command can be used to fill a pattern inside an area. We define a boundary that consists of an object or objects that completely enclose the area. **AutoCAD® 2005** comes with a solid fill and more than 50 industry-standard hatch patterns that we can use to differentiate the components of objects or represent object materials.

The *Bearing* Design

Starting Up AutoCAD 2000

1. Select the **AutoCAD 2005** option on the *Program* menu or select the **AutoCAD 2005** icon on the *Desktop*.

2. In the AutoCAD *Startup* dialog box, select the ***Template*** option.

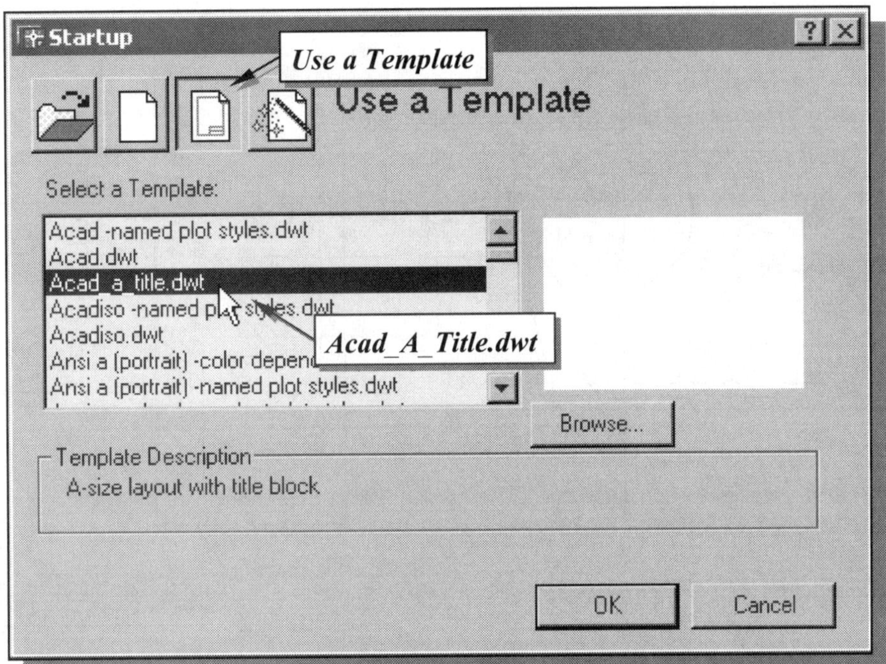

3. Select the ***Acad_A_Title*** template file from the list of template files. If the template file is not listed, click on the **Browse** button to locate and proceed to open a new drawing file.

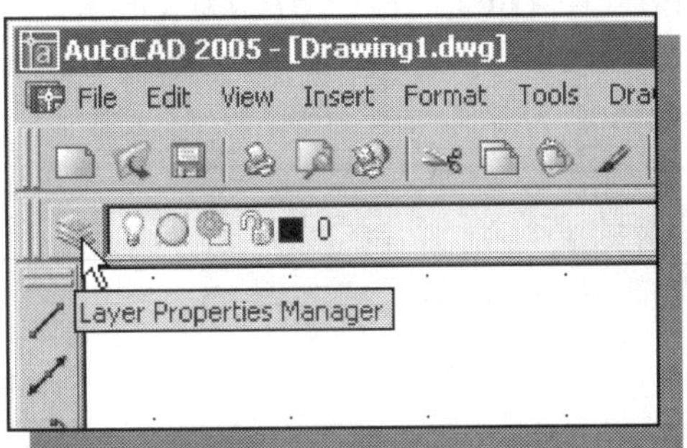

4. Pick ***Layer Properties Manager*** in the *Object Properties* toolbar.

5. Examine the layer property settings in the *Layer Properties Manager* dialog box.

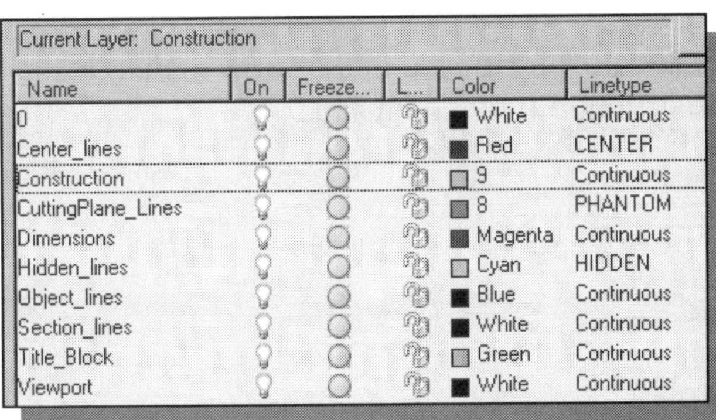

Current Layer: Construction

Name	On	Freeze...	L...	Color	Linetype
0				White	Continuous
Center_lines				Red	CENTER
Construction				9	Continuous
CuttingPlane_Lines				8	PHANTOM
Dimensions				Magenta	Continuous
Hidden_lines				Cyan	HIDDEN
Object_lines				Blue	Continuous
Section_lines				White	Continuous
Title_Block				Green	Continuous
Viewport				White	Continuous

6. On your own, set layer ***Construction*** as the *Current Layer*.

7. Click on the **OK** button to exit the *Layer Properties Manager* dialog box.

The *Bearing* Example

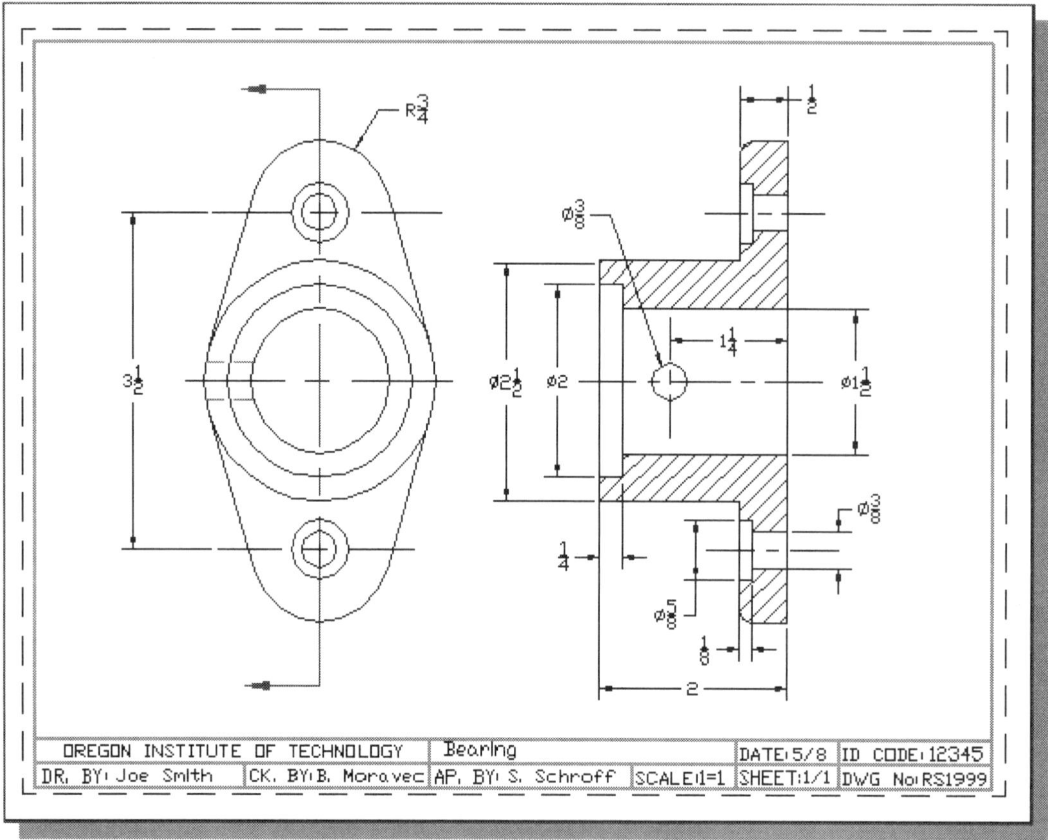

Setting up the principal views

1. In the *Status Bar* area, reset the options and turn ***ON*** the *OSNAP, OTRACK, LWT*, and *MODEL* options.

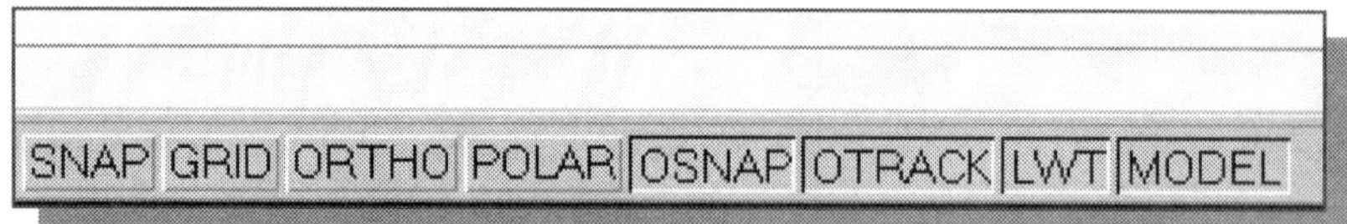

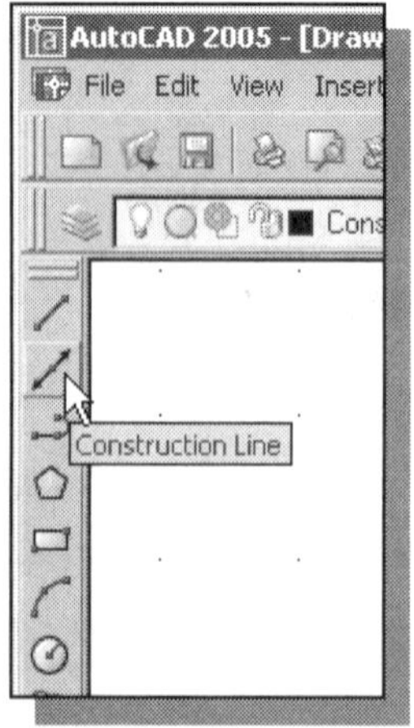

- We will first create construction lines for the front view.

2. Click the **Construction Line** icon in the *Draw* toolbar to activate the Construction Line command.

3. In the command prompt area, the message "*_xline Specify a point or [Hor/Ver/Ang/Bisect/Offset]:*" is displayed. On your own, create a vertical line and a horizontal line as shown in the figure below. These lines will be used as the references for the circular features of the design.

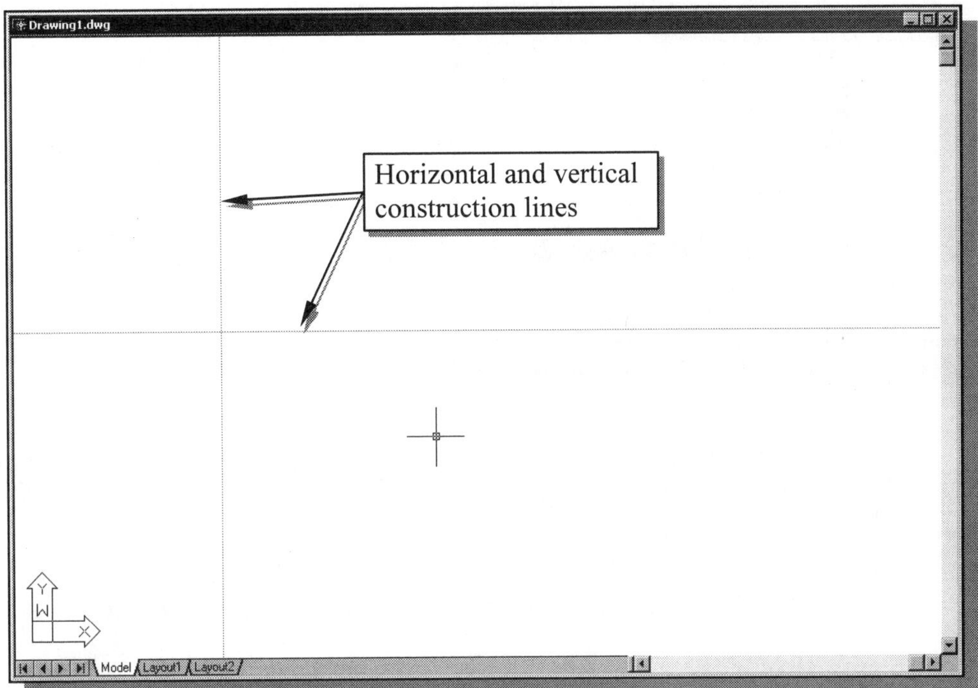

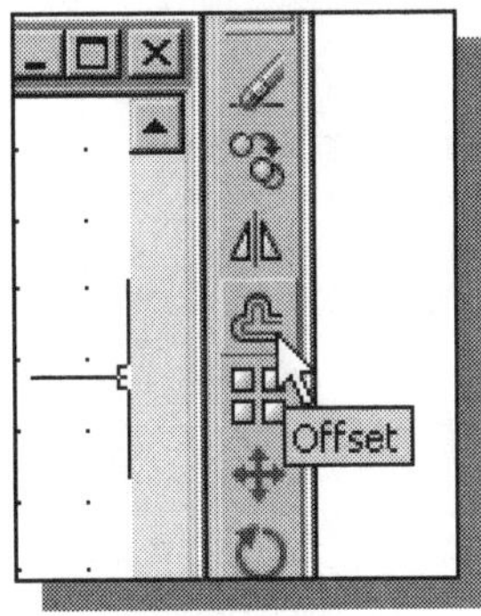

4. Click on the **Offset** icon in the *Modify* toolbar. In the command prompt area, the message "*Specify offset distance or [Through]:*" is displayed.

5. In the command prompt area, enter: ***1.75*** **[ENTER]**.

6. In the command prompt area, the message "*Select object to offset or <exit>:*" is displayed. Pick the **horizontal line** on the screen.

7. AutoCAD next expects us to identify the direction of the offset. Pick a location that is **above** the selected line.

8. We will also create a line that is below the original horizontal line at 1.75. Pick the original **horizontal line** on the screen.

9. Pick a location that is **below** the selected line.

10. Inside the graphics window, **right-mouse-click** to end the Offset command.

Creating object lines in the front-view

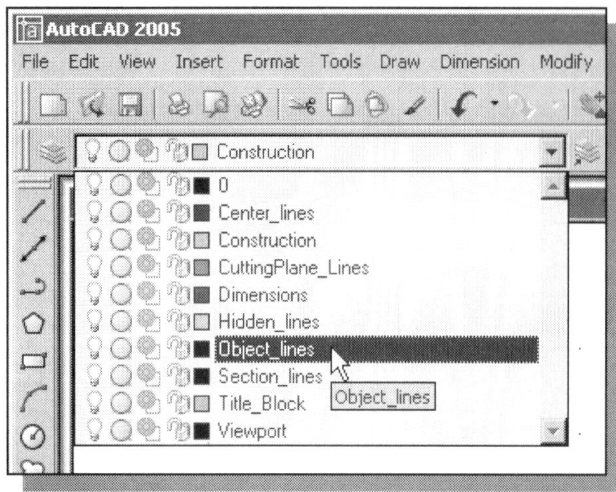

1. On the *Object Properties* toolbar, choose the ***Layer Control*** box with the left-mouse-button.

2. Move the cursor over the name of layer ***Object_Lines***; the tool tip "*Object_Lines*" appears.

3. **Left-mouse-click once** and layer *Object_Lines* is set as the *Current Layer*.

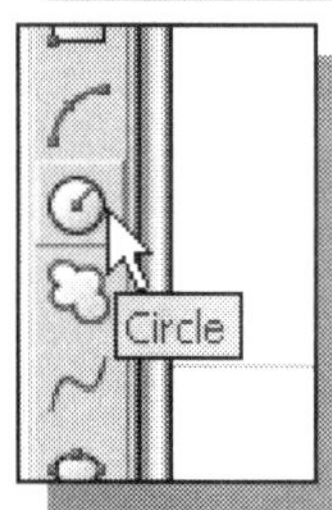

4. Click on the **Circle** icon in the *Draw* toolbar. In the command prompt area, the message "*Specify center point for circle or [3P/2P/Ttr (tan tan radius)]:*" is displayed.

5. Pick the center intersection point as the center of the circle.

6. In the command prompt area, the message "*Specify radius of circle or [Diameter]:*" is displayed. Enter: ***1.25*** **[ENTER]**.

7. Repeat the **Circle** command and create the two **diameter 1.5** circles as shown.

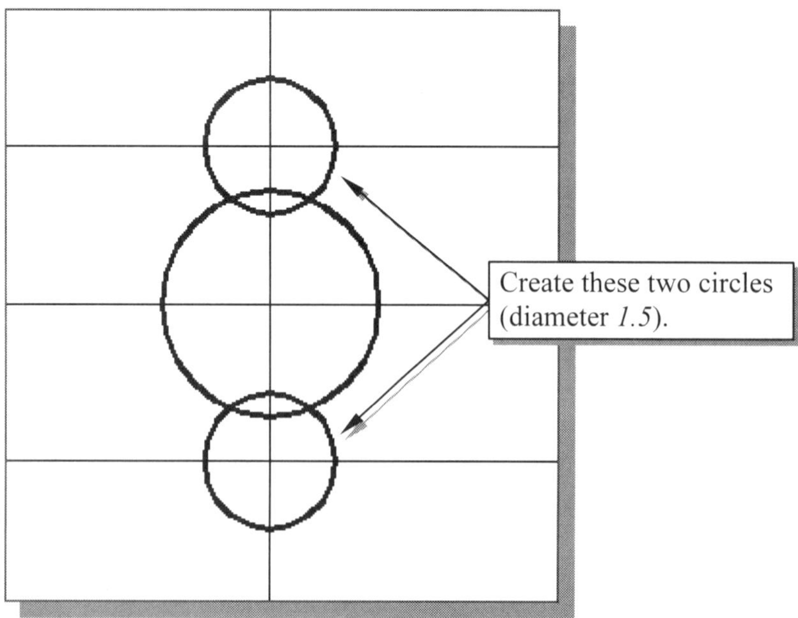

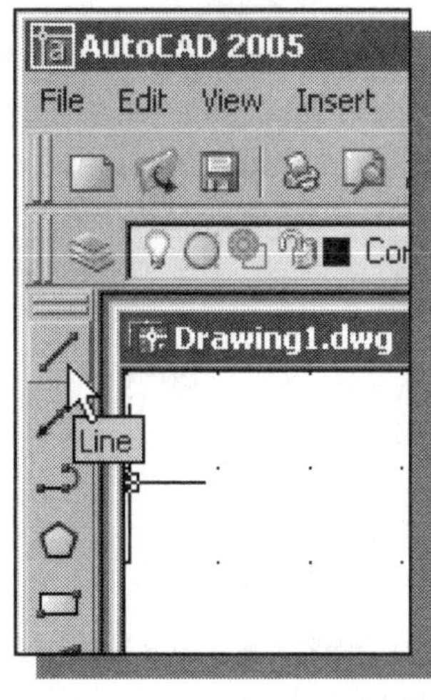

8. Select the **Line** command icon in the *Draw* toolbar. In the command prompt area, the message "*_line Specify first point:*" is displayed.

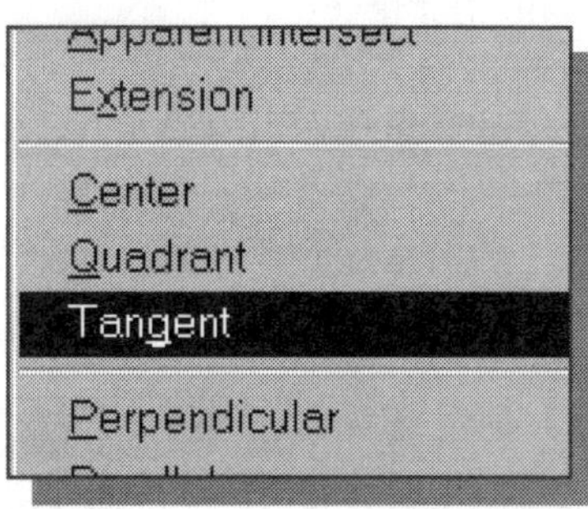

9. Inside the graphics window, hold down the **[SHIFT]** key and **right-mouse-click** once to bring up the *Object Snap* shortcut menu.

10. Select the **Tangent** option in popup window. Move the cursor near the circles and notice the *Tangent* marker appears at different locations.

- The Tangent option enables us to create tangent lines; **select objects by clicking near the expected tangency locations.**

11. Pick the top circle by clicking on the upper right section of the circle.

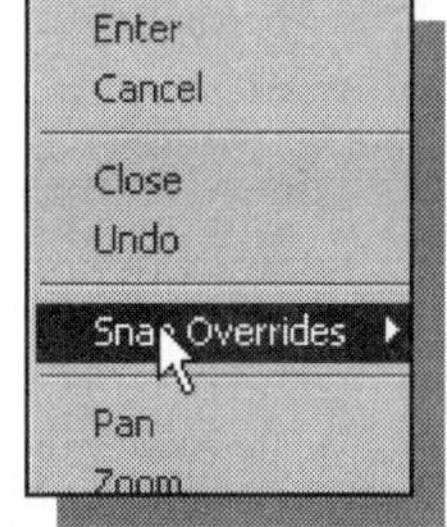

12. In the command prompt area, the message "*Specify the next point or [Undo]:*" is displayed. Inside the graphics window, **right-mouse-click** once and select **Snap Overrides**.

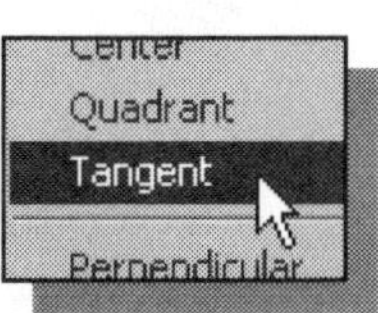

13. Select the **Tangent** option in the popup menu.

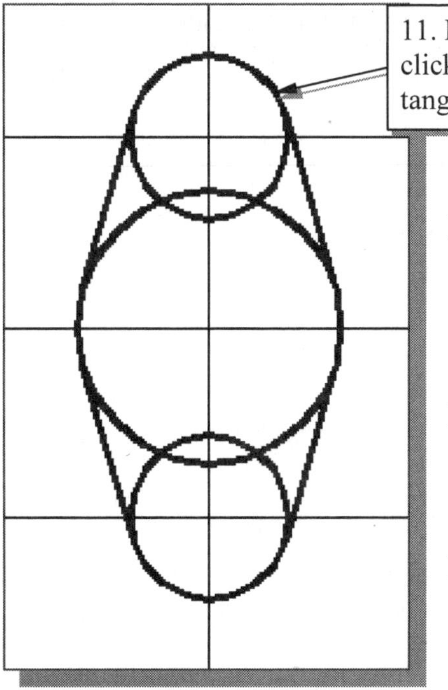

11. Pick the top circle by clicking near the expected tangency location.

14. Pick the center circle by clicking on the right side of the circle. A line tangent to the two circles appears on the screen.

15. Inside the graphics window, right-mouse-click and select **Enter** to end the Line command.

16. Repeat the **Line** command and create the four tangent lines as shown.

Editing the circles

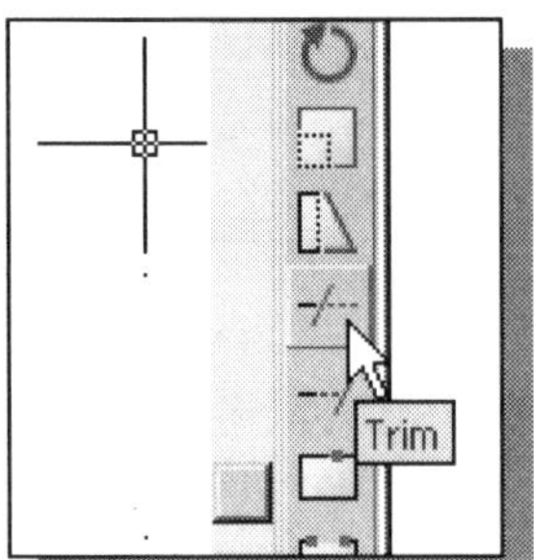

1. Select the **Trim** icon in the *Modify* toolbar. In the command prompt area, the message "*Select boundary edges... Select objects:*" is displayed.

2. Pick the four lines we just created as the *boundary edges*.

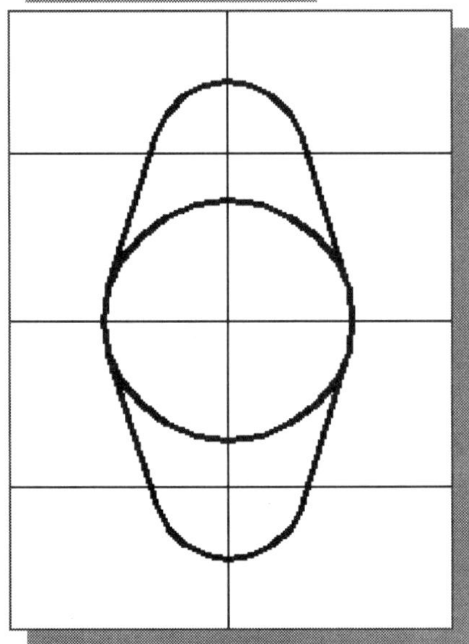

3. Inside the graphics window, **right-mouse-click** to proceed with the Trim command. The message "*Select object to trim or [Project/Edge/Undo]:*" is displayed in the command prompt area.

4. Trim the unwanted portions of the top and bottom circles and complete the outline of the front view as shown.

5. Inside the graphics window, right-mouse-click to activate the option menu and select **Enter** with the left-mouse-button to end the Trim command.

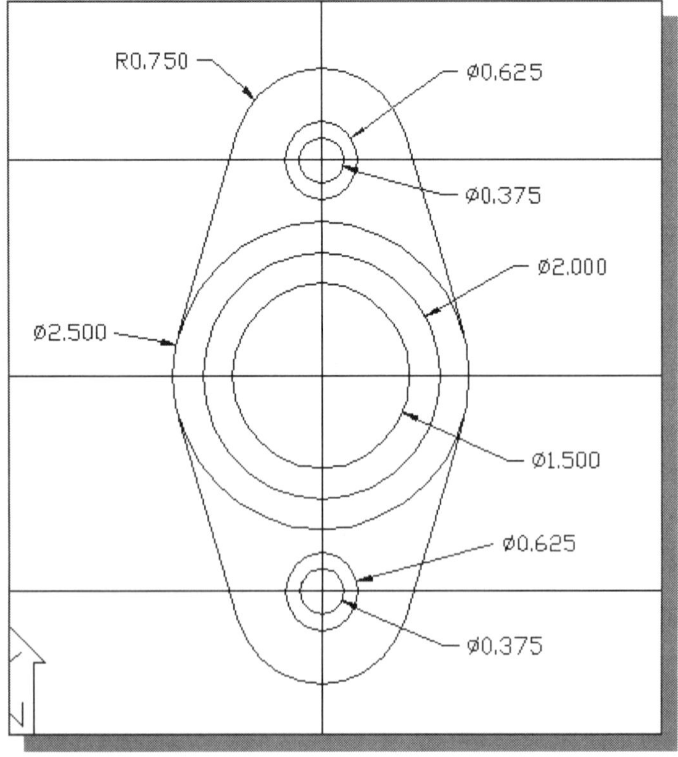

- On your own, create the additional circles as shown.

Setting up the side-view

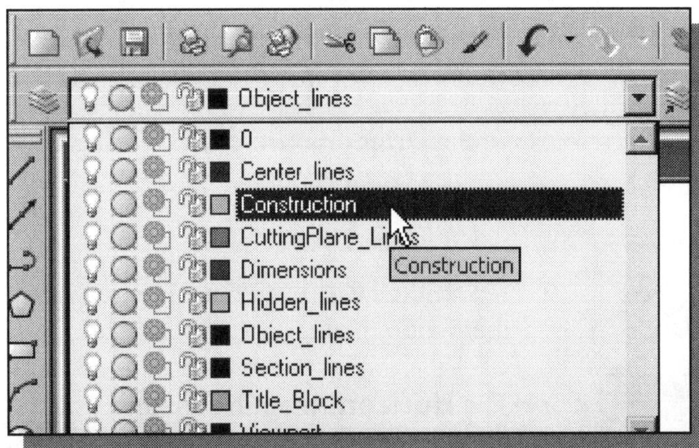

1. In the *Layer Control* box, set layer *Construction_Lines* as the *Current Layer*.

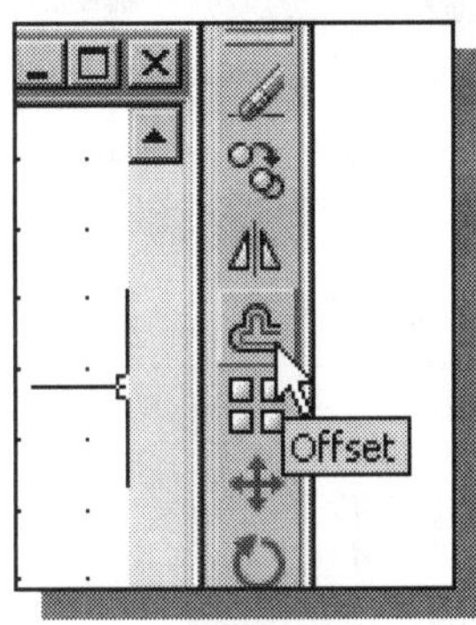

2. Select the **Offset** icon in the *Modify* toolbar. In the command prompt area, the message "*Specify offset distance or [Through]:*" is displayed.

3. In the command prompt area, enter: ***5.0*** **[ENTER]**.

4. In the command prompt area, the message "*Select object to offset or <exit>:*" is displayed. Pick the **vertical line** on the screen.

5. AutoCAD next expects us to identify the direction of the offset. Pick a location that is toward the right side of the selected line.

6. Inside the graphics window, right-mouse-click to end the Offset command.

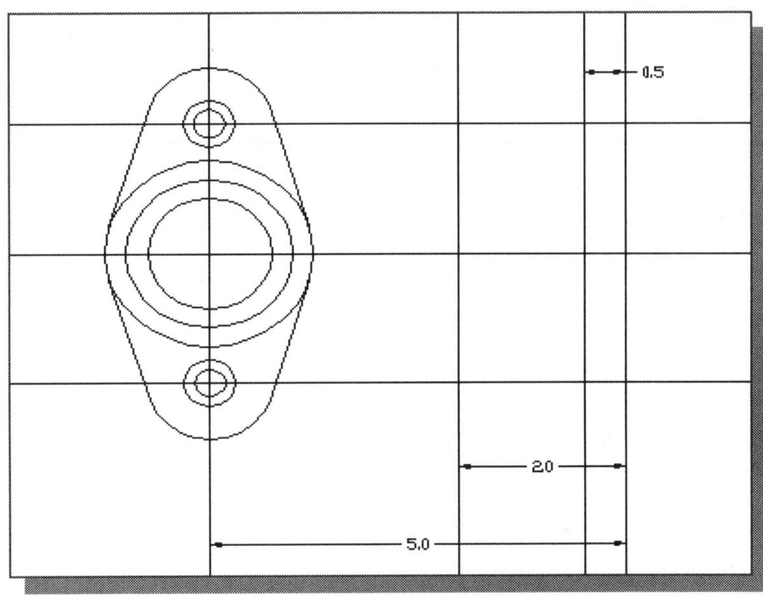

➢ On your own, repeat the Offset command and create two additional lines parallel to the line we just created as shown (distances of **0.5** and **2.0**).

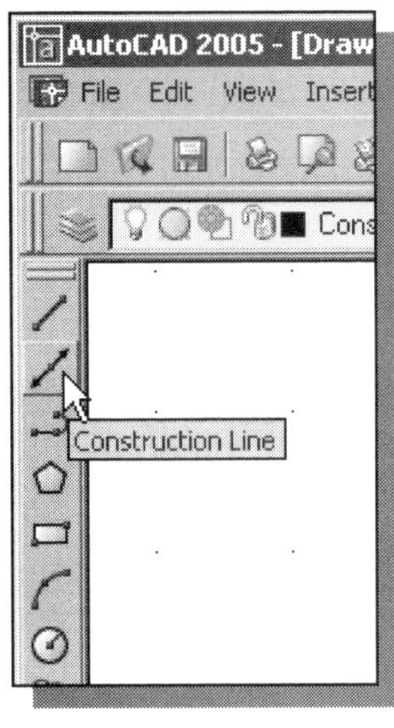

7. Select the **Construction Line** icon in the *Draw* toolbar. In the command prompt area, the message "*_xline Specify a point or [Hor/Ver/Ang/Bisect/Offset]:*" is displayed.

8. Inside the graphics window, right-mouse-click to bring up the popup menu.

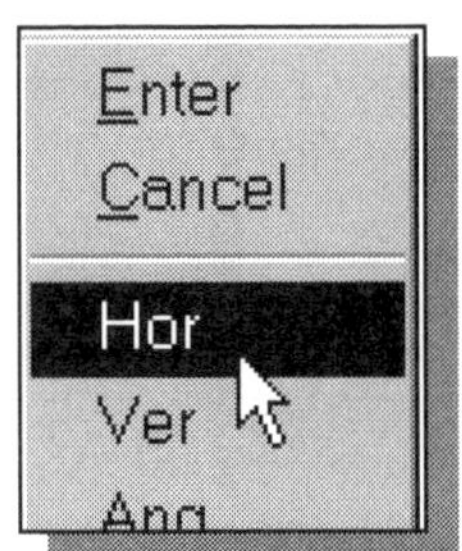

9. Select the **Hor** (horizontal) option in the popup menu.

➢ The **Horizontal** option enables us to create a horizontal line by specifying one point in the graphics window.

10. Create **projection lines** by clicking at the intersections between the vertical line and the circles (and arcs) in the front-view.

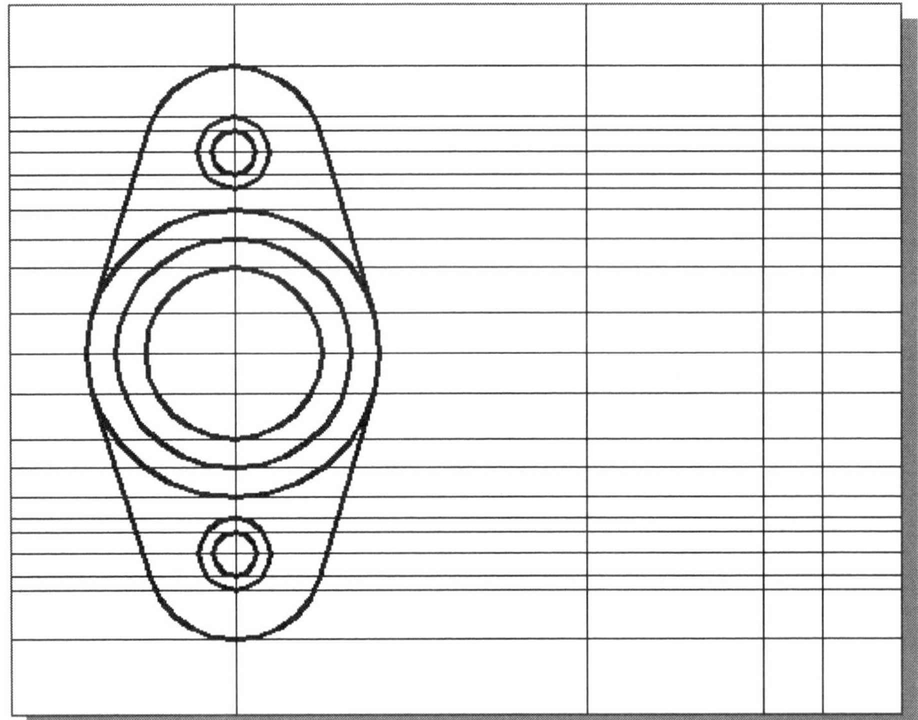

11. Also create two horizontal projection lines that pass through the two tangency-points on the ∅2.5 circle.

12. Inside the graphics window, right-mouse-click to end the Construction Line command.

➢ On your own, create object lines to show the outline of the side view.

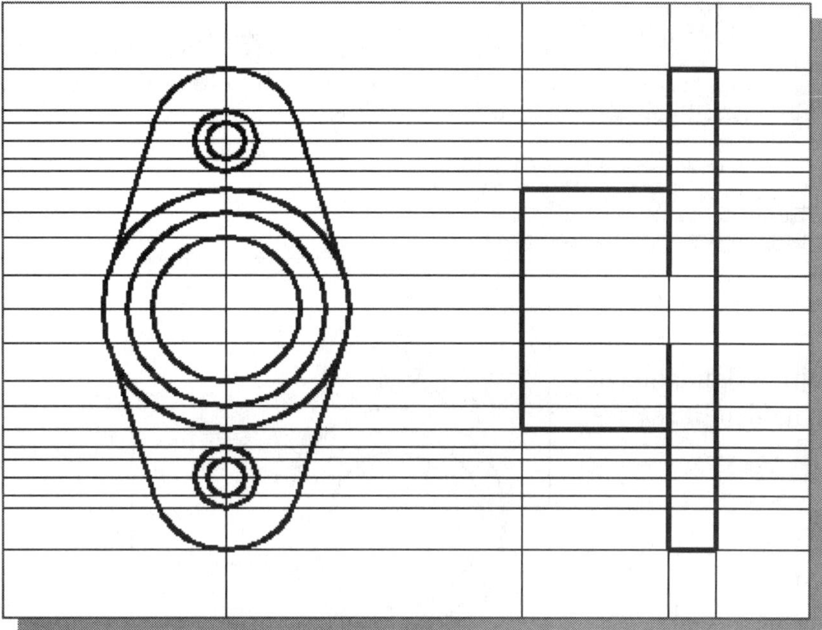

Adding hidden lines in the side-view

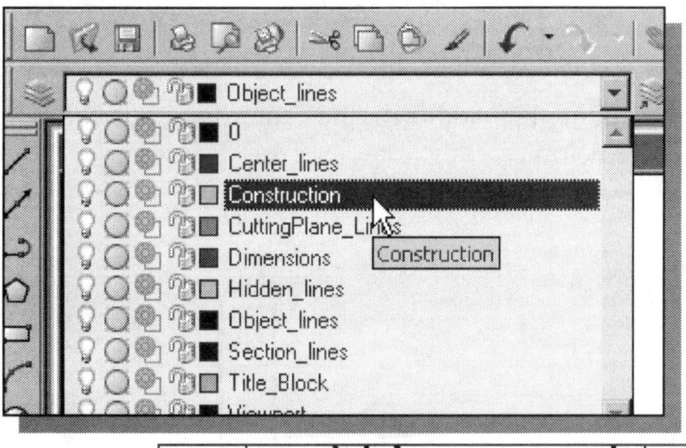

1. In the *Layer Control* box, set layer *Construction_Lines* as the *Current Layer*.

2. Use the **Offset** command and create the two additional vertical lines, for the counter-bore features, as shown.

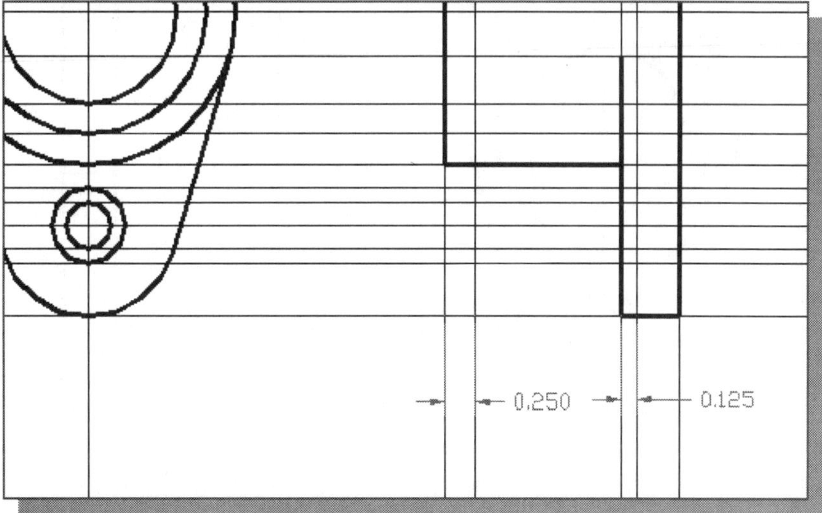

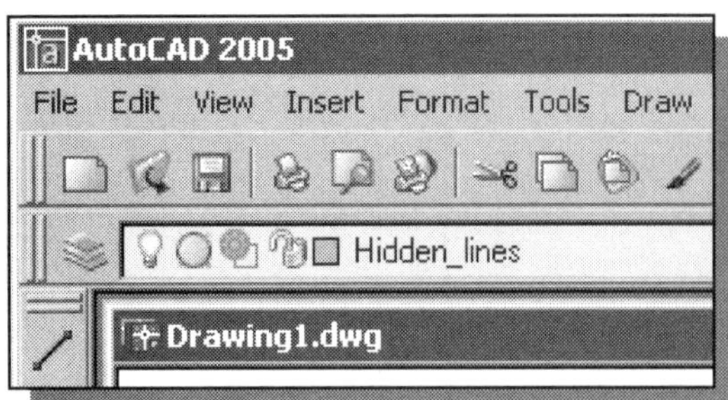

3. Set layer ***Hidden_Lines*** as the *Current Layer* in the *Layer Control* box.

4. Use the **Line** command and create the hidden lines as shown.

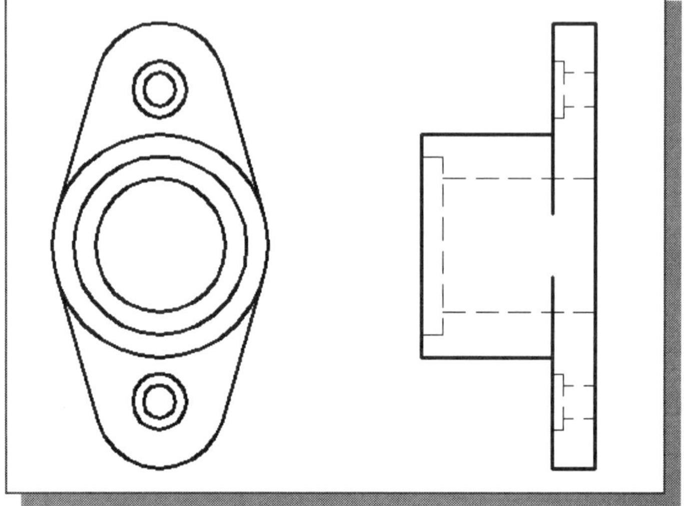

➢ On your own, complete the views by adding the side-drill, the centerlines, and the rounded corners as shown in the figure below.

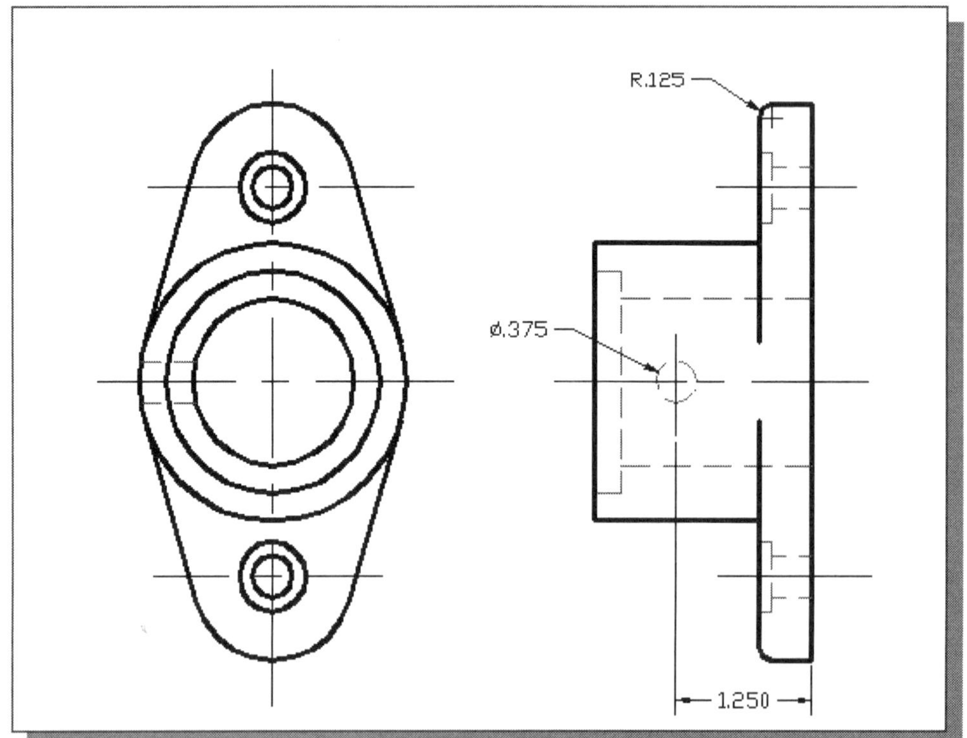

Changing the *Linetype Scale* property

❖ Looking at the side-drill feature and the centerlines we just created, not all of the lengths of the dash-dot linetypes appeared properly on the screen. The appearances of the dash-dot linetypes can be adjusted by modifying the ***Linetype Scale*** setting, which can be found under the *Object Property* option.

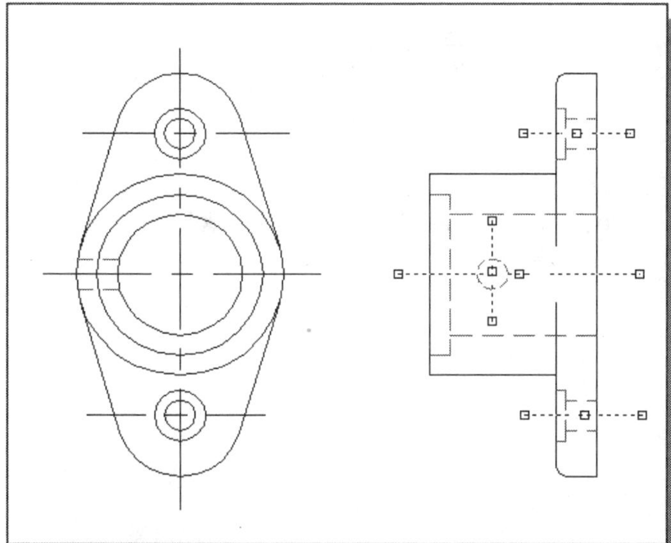

1. **Pre-select** the objects in the side view as shown (four lines and one circle).

2. In the *Standard* toolbar, select the **Properties** icon.

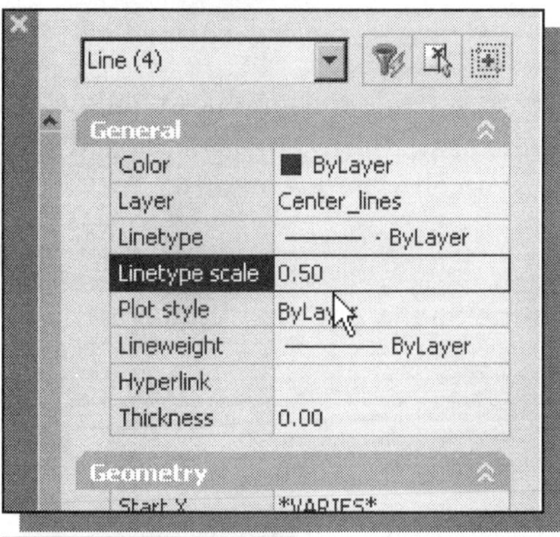

3. In the *Properties* dialog box, notice the default *Linetype scale* is 1.00.

4. Left-click on ***Linetype scale*** in the list and enter a new value: ***0.5*** **[ENTER]**.

5. Click on the **[X]** button to exit the *Properties* dialog box.

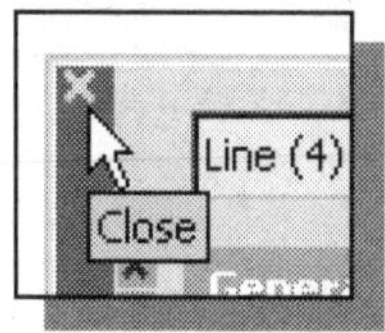

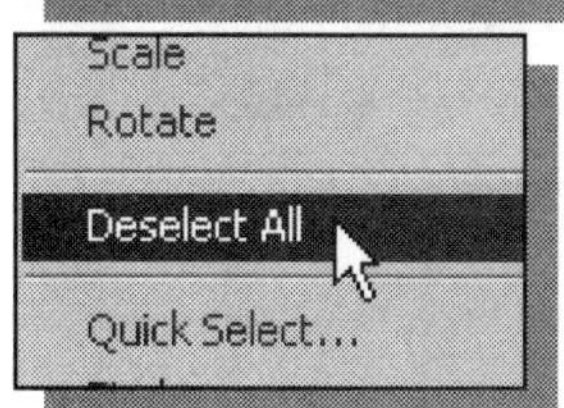

6. Inside the graphics window, **right-mouse-click** and select **Deselect All**.

➢ The appearances of the dash-dot linetypes of the selected objects are adjusted to half-size of the other objects. Keep in mind that the dash-dot linetypes may appear differently on paper, depending on the type of printer/plotter being used. You may want to do more adjustments after examining a printed/plotted copy of the drawing. It is also more common to adjust the *Linetype Scale* for all objects of the same linetype to maintain a consistent presentation of the drawing.

Stretching and moving objects with *GRIPS*

We can usually *stretch* an object by moving selected grips to new locations. Some grips will not stretch the object but will move the object. This is true of grips on text objects, blocks, midpoints of lines, centers of circles, centers of ellipses, and point objects.

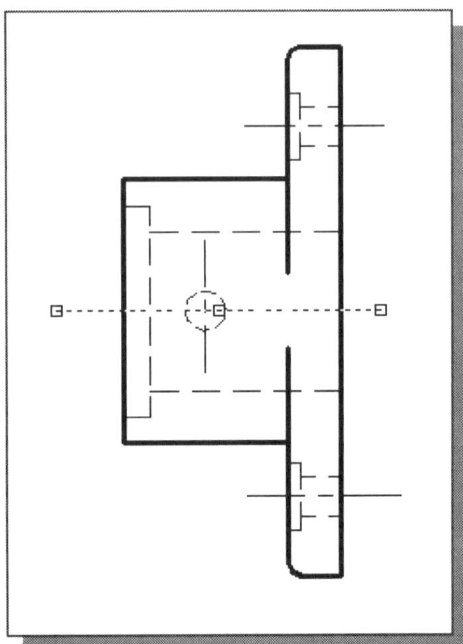

1. **Pre-select** the horizontal centerline that goes through the center of the part as shown.

2. Select the **right grip** by left-clicking once on the grip. Notice the grip is highlighted.

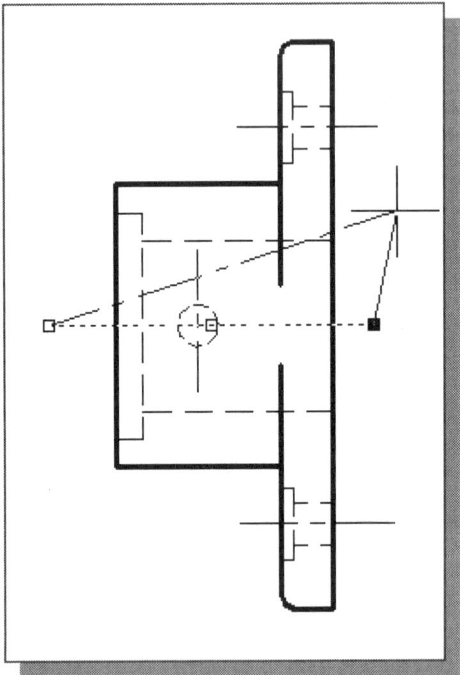

3. Move the cursor inside the graphics window and notice the center line is being stretched; the base point is attached to the cursor.

4. Pick a location on the screen to stretch the centerline.

5. Click on the **Undo** icon in the *Standard* toolbar area to undo the stretch we just did.

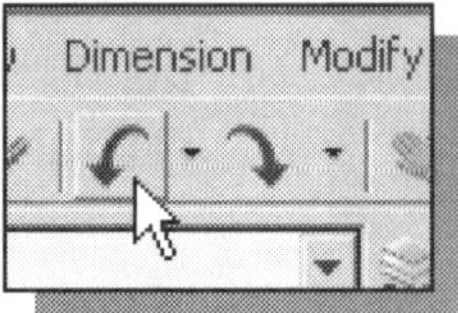

➢ On your own, experiment with moving the center grip of the centerline.

Drawing a cutting plane line

- Most section views require a cutting plane line to indicate the location on which the object is cut.

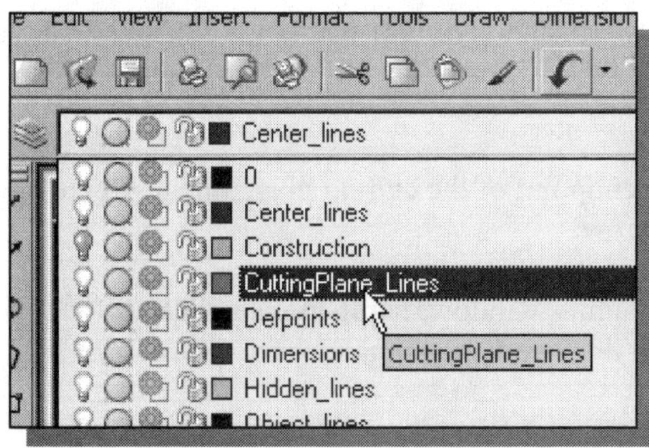

1. In the *Layer Control* box, turn ***OFF*** the *Construction_Lines* layer and set layer ***Cutting_Plane_Lines*** as the *Current Layer*.

2. Use the **Line** command and create the vertical cutting plane line aligned to the vertical centerline of the front view.

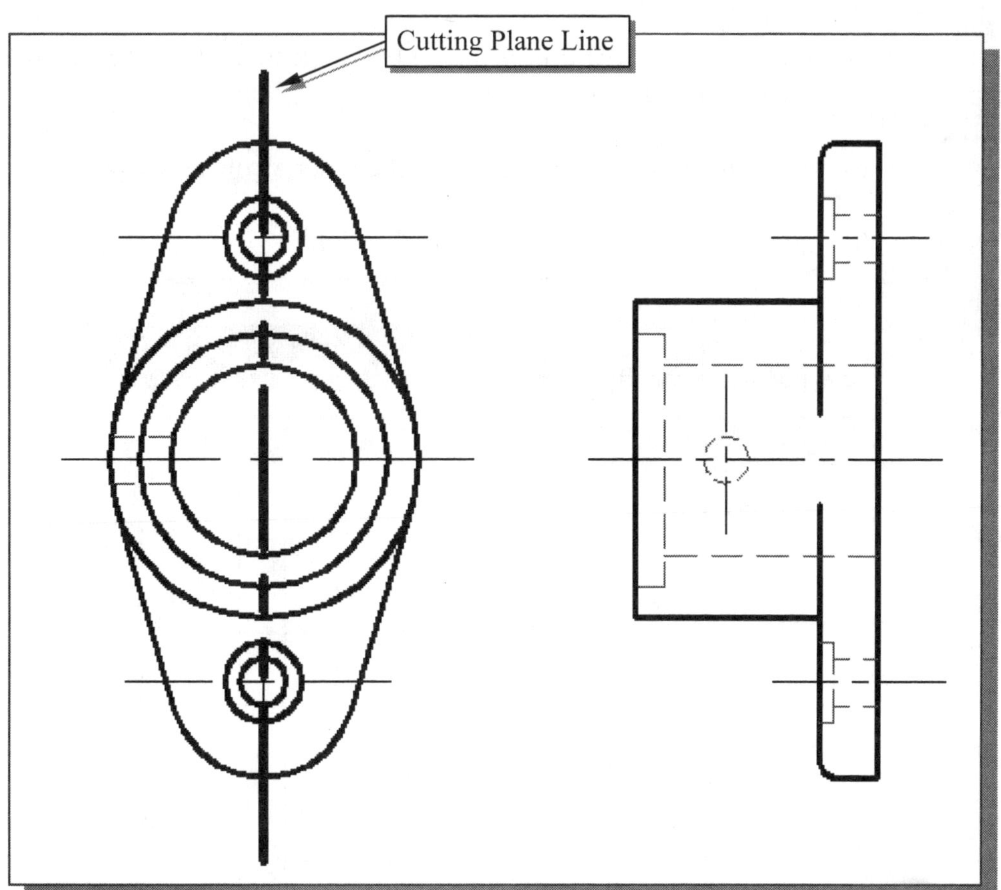

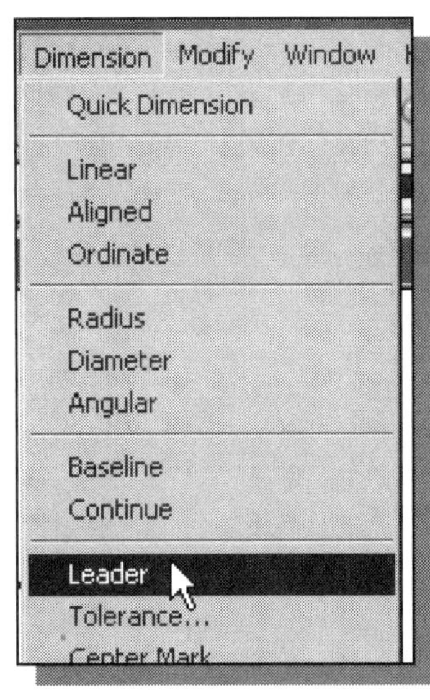

3. In the pull-down menus, select:

   [Dimension] → [Leader]

4. Move the cursor over the top endpoint of the cutting plane line to activate the *AutoTracking* option, and then select a point that is toward the left of the cutting plane line.

5. Pick the top endpoint of the cutting plane line to create a horizontal arrow.

6. Inside the graphics window, **right-mouse-click** to proceed with the **Leader** command.

7. In the command prompt area, the message "*Specify Text height <0.000>:*" is displayed. **Right-mouse-click** to accept the default **0.00** value.

8. In the command prompt area, the message "*Enter first line of annotation text <Mtext>:*" is displayed. **Right-mouse-click** to continue.

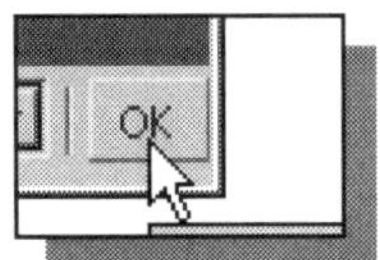

9. The *Multiline Text Editor* dialog box appears on the screen. Click on the **OK** button to close the dialog box.

10. Repeat the **Leader** command and create the other arrow as shown.

11. In the *Status Bar* area, turn ***OFF*** the *LWT* option.

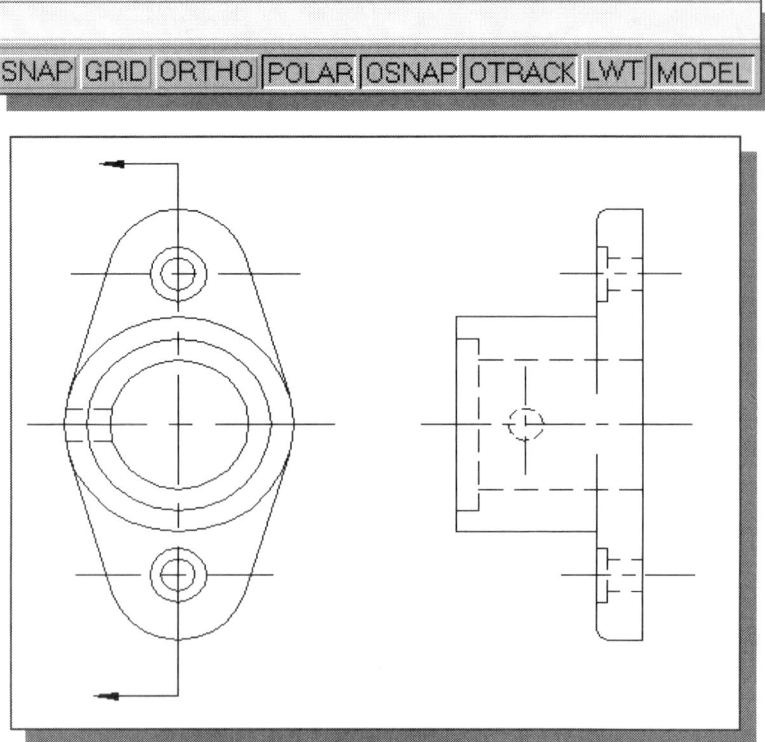

Converting the side-view into a section view

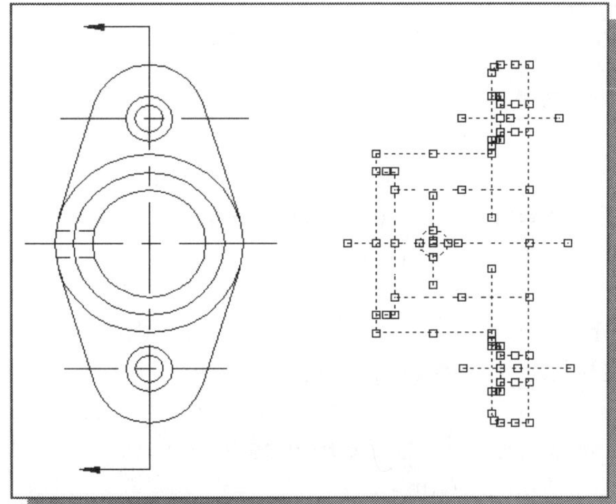

1. **Pre-select** all the objects in the side view by using a selection window.

2. Inside the graphics window, right-mouse-click to bring up the popup option menu and select the **Quick Select** option.

❖ The **Quick Select** option enables us to quickly select multiple objects by using various ***filter*** options.

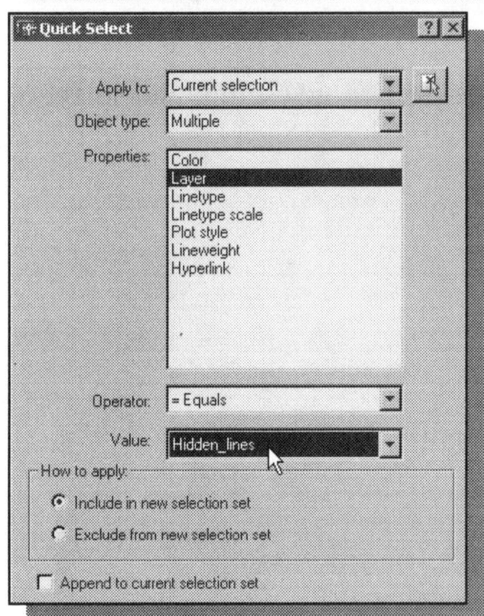

3. In the *Quick Select* dialog box, select **Layer** from the *Properties* list.

4. Set the *Value* box to **Hidden_Lines**.

5. In the *How to apply* section, set to the ***Include in new selection set*** option.

6. Click on the **OK** button to accept the settings.

❖ AutoCAD will now **filter out** objects that are not on layer *Hidden_lines*.

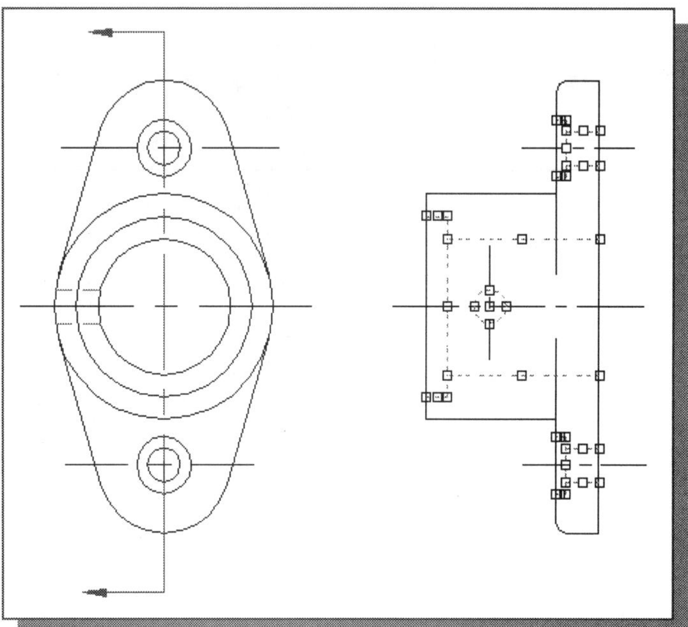

7. On the *Object Properties* toolbar, choose the *Layer Control* box with the left-mouse-button.

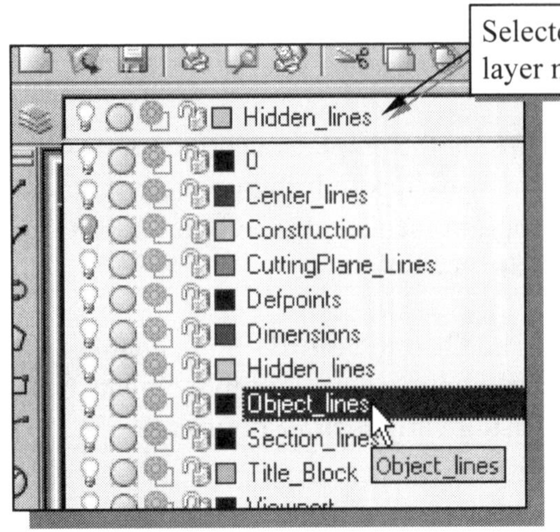

❖ Notice the layer name displayed in the *Layer Control* box is the selected object's assigned layer and layer properties.

8. In the *Layer Control* box, click on the ***Object_Lines*** layer name.

The selected objects are moved to the *Object_Lines* layer.

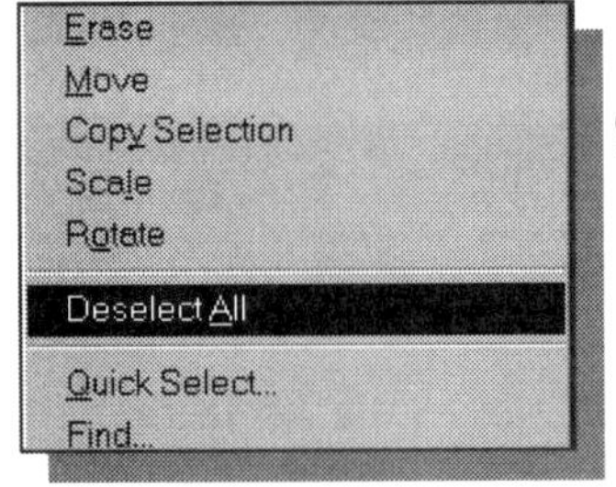

9. Inside the graphics window, **right-mouse-click** and select **Deselect All**.

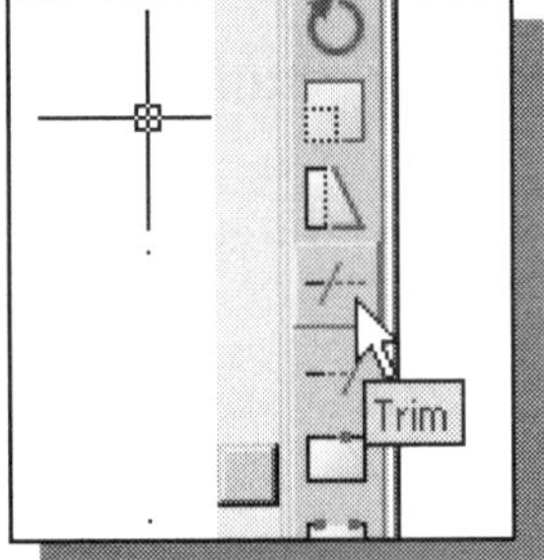

10. Use the **Trim** command and modify the side view as shown.

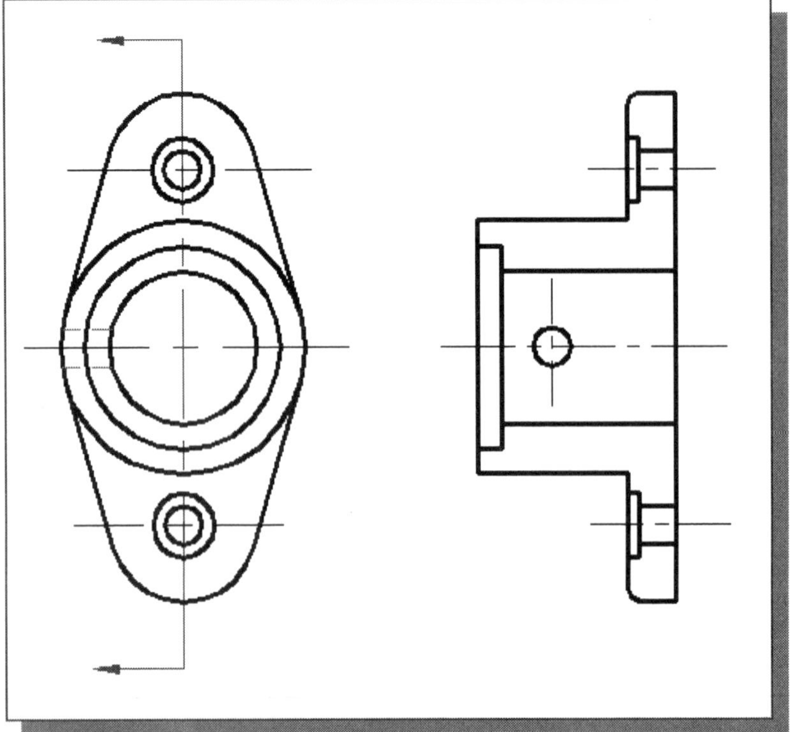

Adding section lines

1. In the *Layer Control* box, set layer ***Section_Lines*** as the *Current Layer*.

2. Select the **Hatch** icon in the *Draw* toolbar. The *Boundary Hatch* dialog box appears on the screen.

- We will use the *ANSI31* standard hatch pattern and create an associative hatch, which means the hatch is updated automatically if the boundaries are modified.

❖ We can define a boundary by ***Selecting Objects*** or ***Picking Points***. The ***Pick Points*** option is usually the easier and faster way to define boundaries. We specify locations inside the region to be crosshatched and AutoCAD will automatically derive the boundary definition from the location of the specified point.

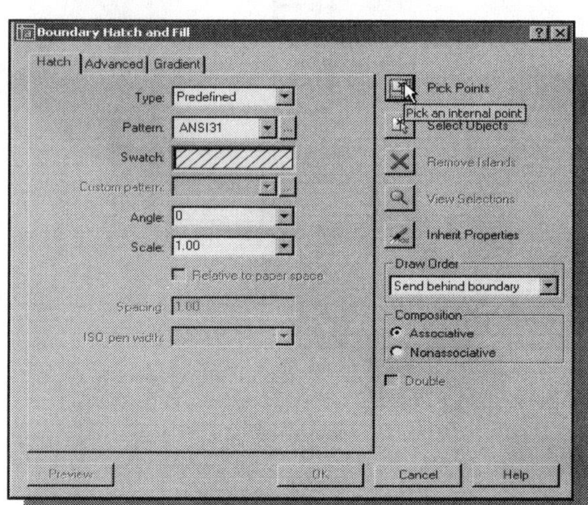

3. Click on the **Pick Points** icon.

4. In the command prompt area, the message "*Select internal point:*" is displayed.

5. **Left-click** inside the four regions as shown.

6. Inside the graphics window, right-mouse-click to bring up the popup menu and select **ENTER** to continue with the **Hatch** command.

7. Click on the **OK** button to close the *Boundary Hatch* dialog box.

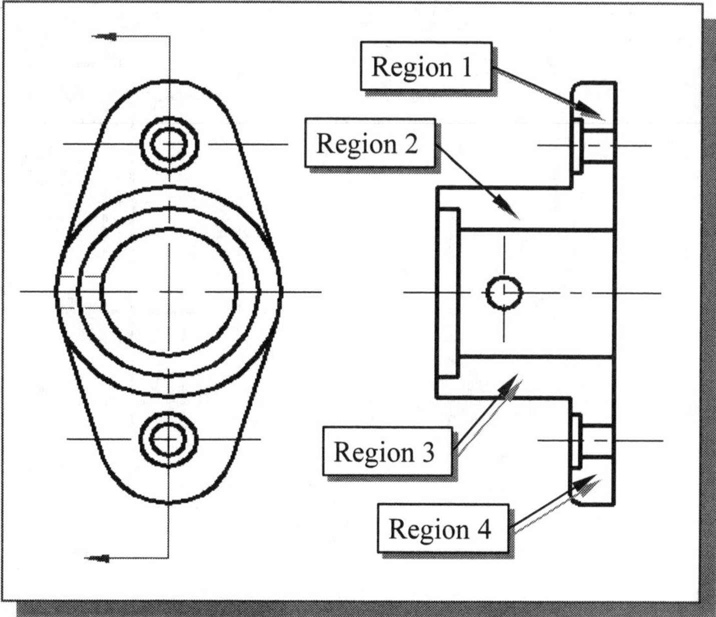

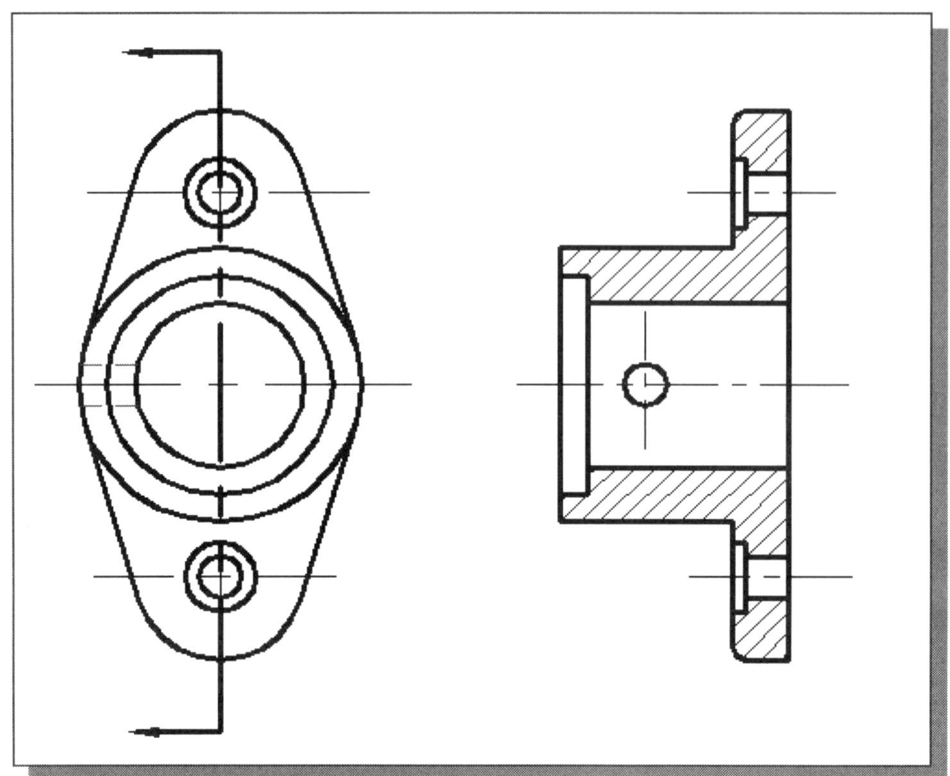

➢ Complete the drawing by adding the proper dimensions.

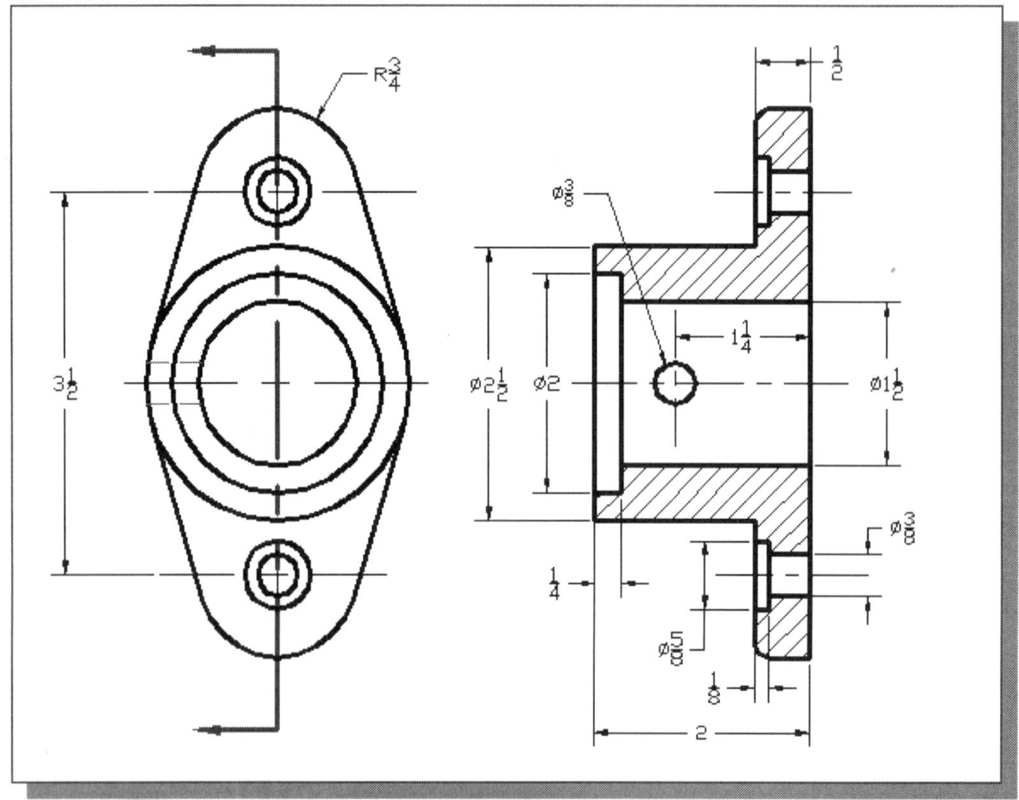

➢ On your own, create a drawing layout and print out the drawing.

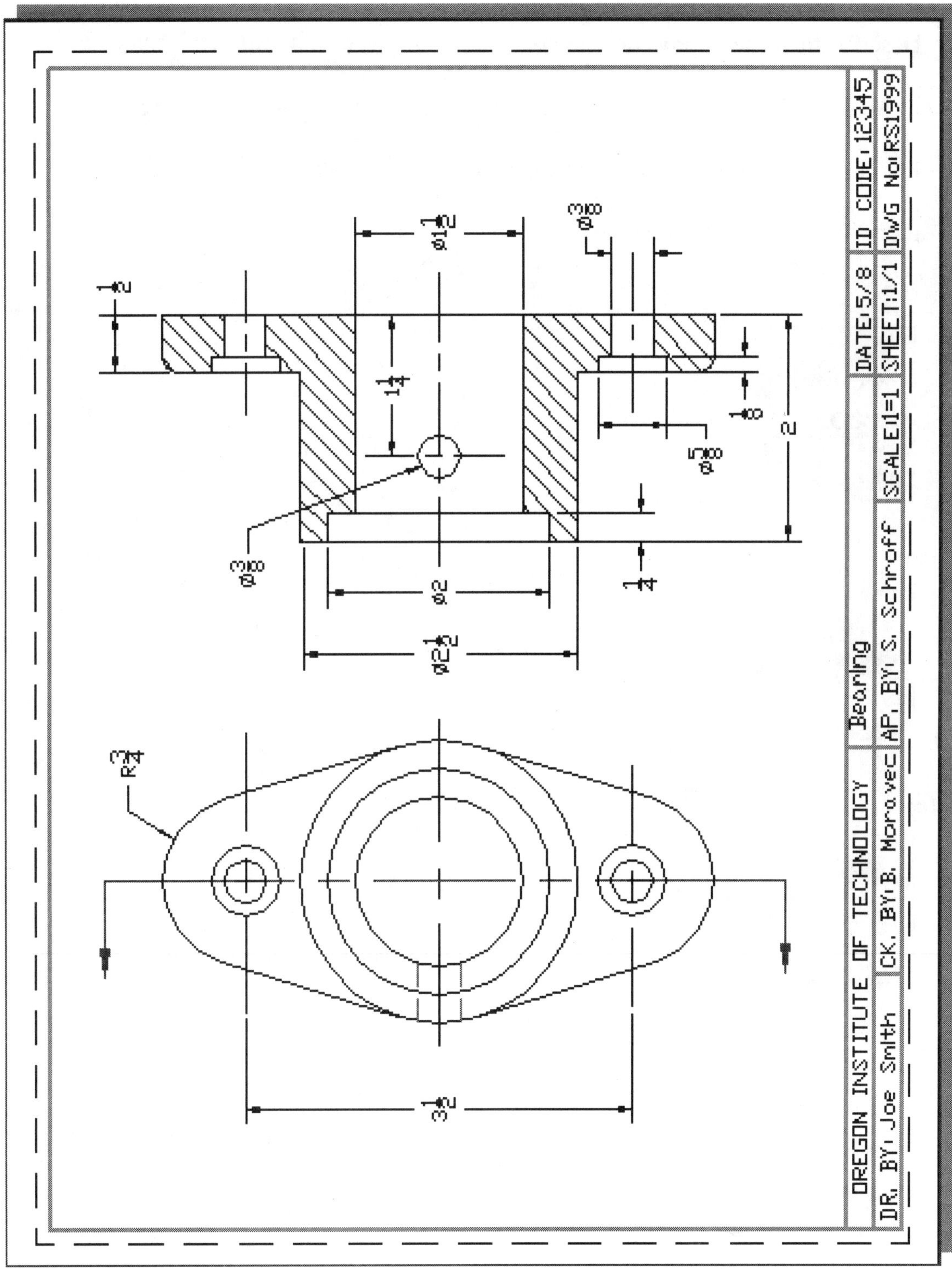

Questions:

1. When and why is a *section view* necessary?

2. Describe the general procedure to create a *section view* in **AutoCAD® 2005**.

3. In **AutoCAD® 2005**, can the angle and spacing of hatch patterns be altered?

4. Explain the concept of using a cutting plane line in a section view?

5. Identify the following commands:

(a)

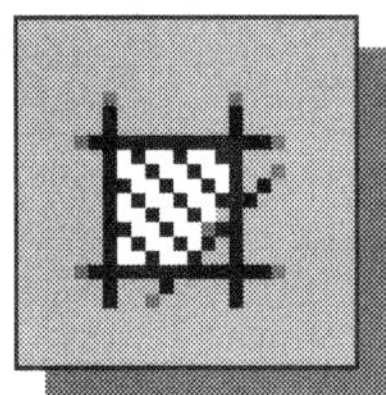

(b)

(c)

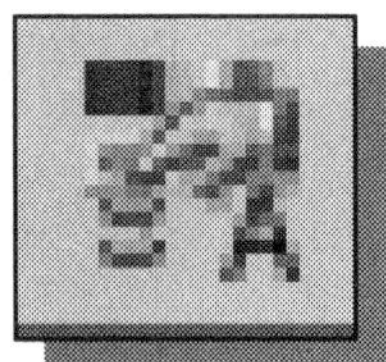

(d)

Exercises:

1.

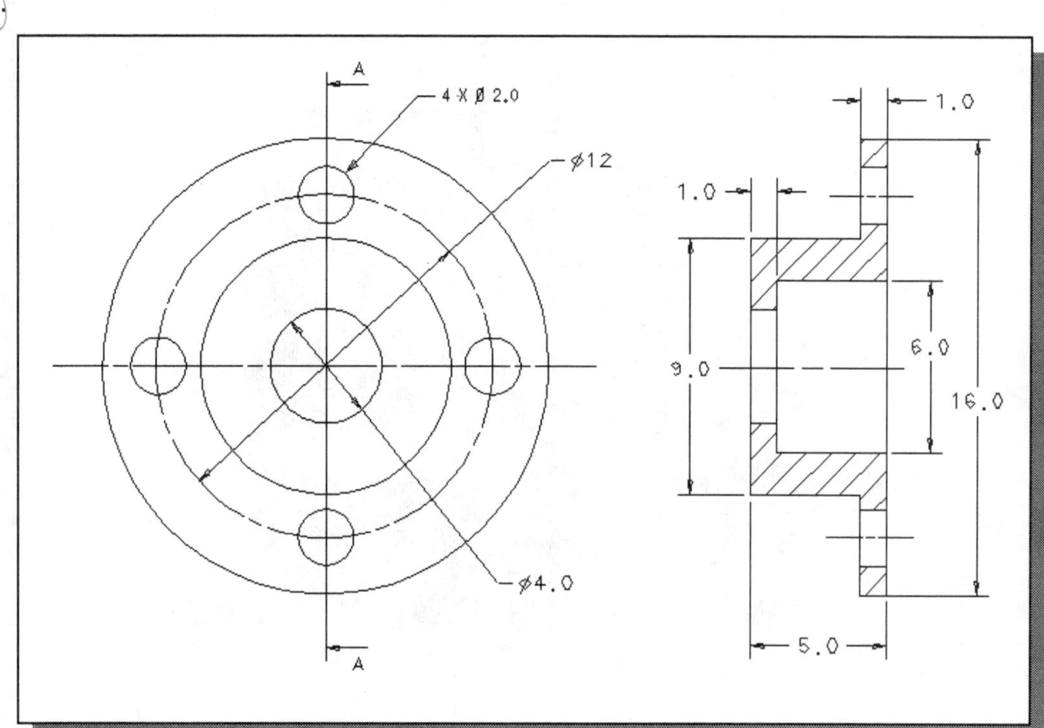

2.

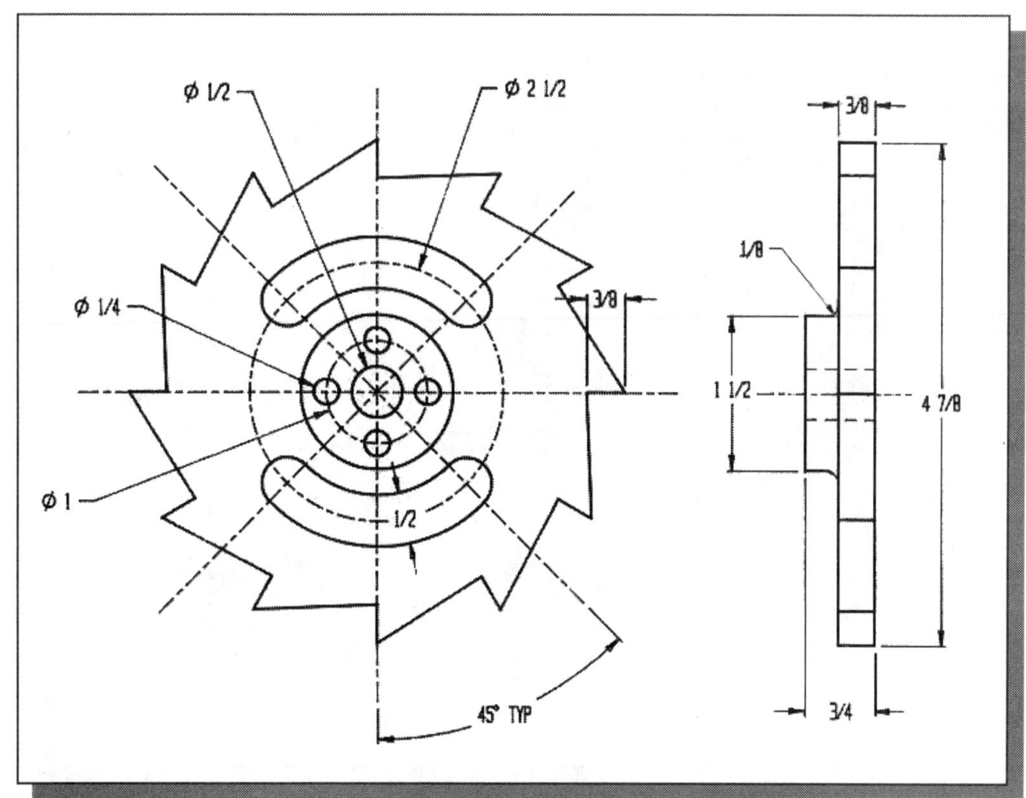

3.

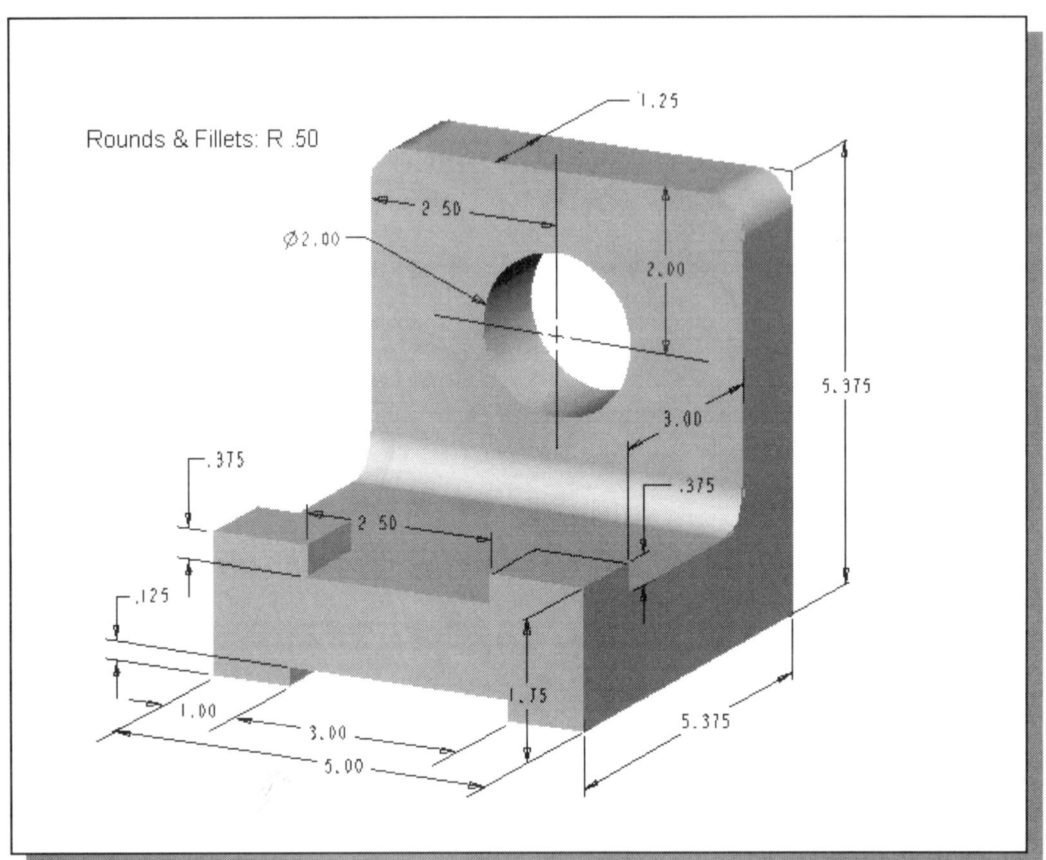

Rounds & Fillets: R .50
1.25
2.50
Ø2.00
2.00
5.375
3.00
.375
.375
2.50
.125
1.75
1.00
3.00
5.00
5.375

Ø1.00
2.00
KWY.375×.20
R.50
2.50
.50
R1.00

4.

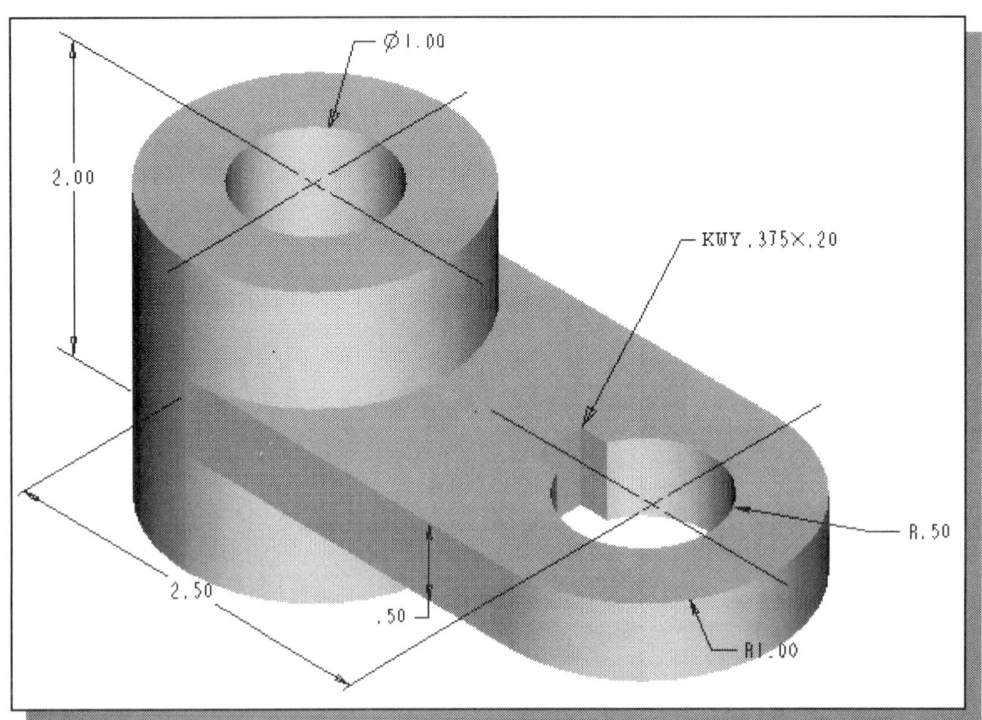

5.

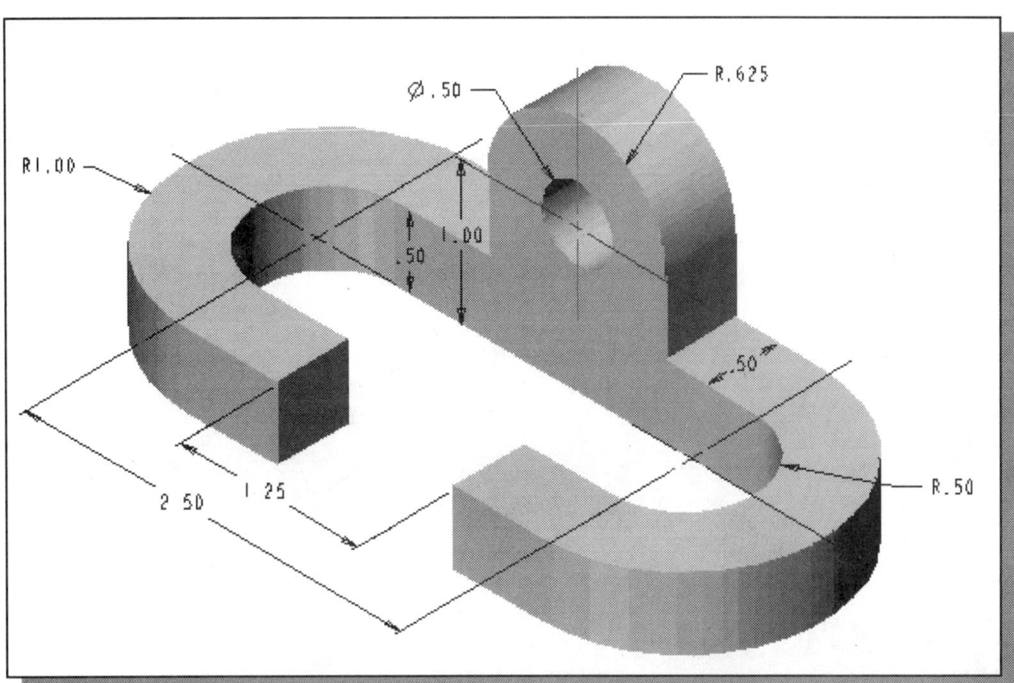

Ø.50
R.625
R1.00
1.00
.50
.50
R.50
2 50
1 25

.375 TYP.
2.00
R.50
1.25
Ø.50
2 50
1.00
Ø1.00
1.250
Ø.625
Rounds & Fillets: R.125

6.

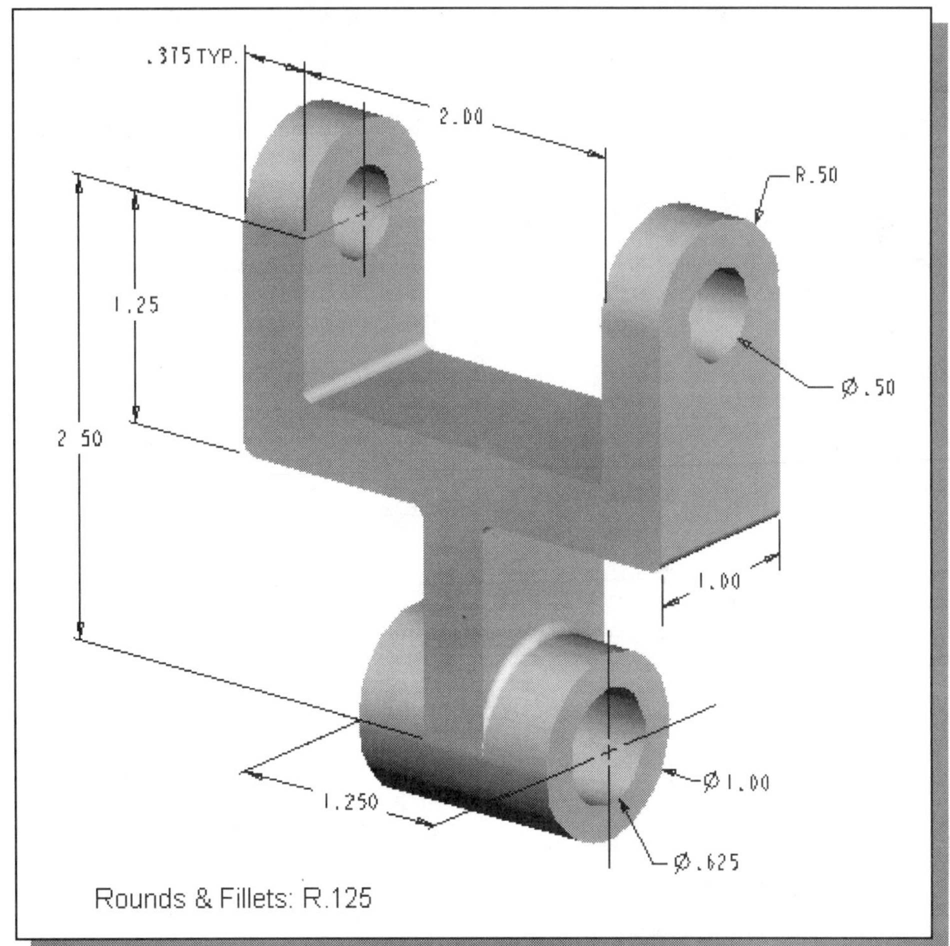

NOTES:

Lesson 10
Assembly Drawings and Blocks

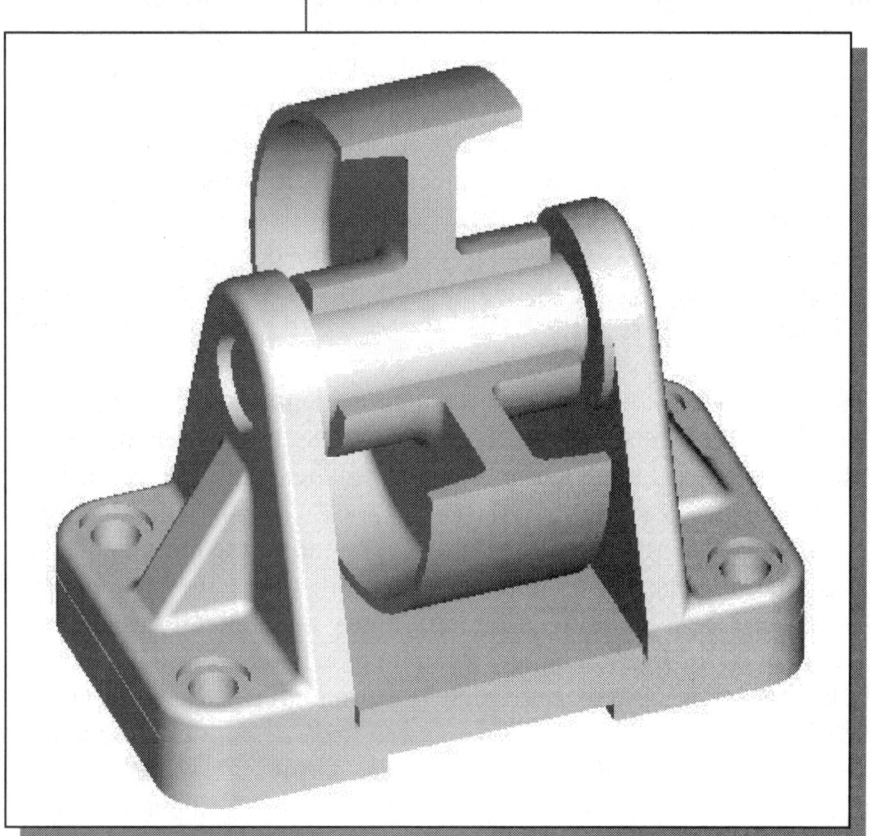

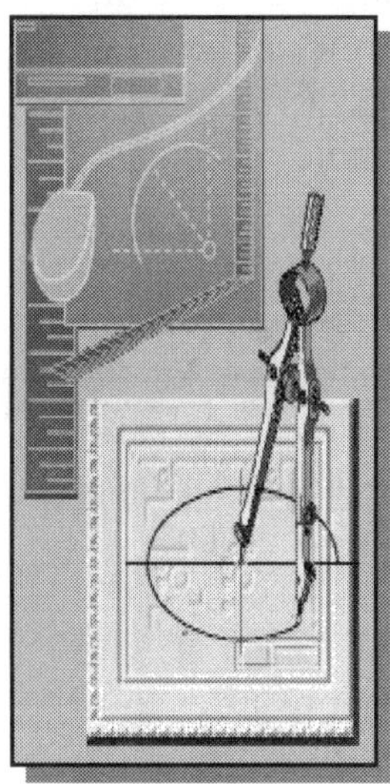

Learning Objectives

- Create an Assembly Drawing from Part files.
- Using AutoCAD with the Internet.
- Load Multiple Drawings into a single AutoCAD session.
- Define a Block.
- Create multiple copies using BLOCKS.
- Copy and paste with the Windows Clipboard.
- Use the MOVE and ROTATE commands.

Introduction

The term **assembly drawing** refers to the type of drawing in which the various parts of a design are shown in their relative positions in the finished product. Assembly drawings are used to represent the function of each part and the proper working relationships of the mating parts. Sectioning is used more extensively on assembly drawings than on detail drawings to show the relationship of various parts. Assembly drawings should not be overly detailed since precise information is provided on the detail drawings. In most cases dimensions are omitted on assembly drawings except for assembly dimensions such as important center distances, overall dimensions, and dimensions showing relationships between the parts. For the purpose of clarity, *subassembly drawings* are often made to give the information needed for the smaller units of a larger assembly. Several options are available in **AutoCAD® 2005** to assist us in creating assembly drawings.

In **AutoCAD® 2005**, a **block** is a collection of objects that is identified by a unique name and essentially behaves as if it is a single object. Using blocks can help us organize our design by associating the related objects into smaller units. We can insert, scale, and rotate multiple objects that belong to the same block with a single selection. We can insert the same block numerous times instead of re-creating the individual geometric objects each time. We can also import a block from a CAD file outside the current drawing. We can use blocks to build a standard library of frequently used symbols, components, or standard parts; the blocks can then be inserted into other drawings. Using blocks also helps us save disk space by storing all references to the same block as one block definition in the database. We can *explode* a block to separate its component objects, modify them, and redefine the block. **AutoCAD® 2005** updates all instances of that block based on the *block definition*. Blocks can also be nested, so that one block is a part of another block. Using blocks greatly reduces repetitious work.

In **AutoCAD® 2005**, we can load multiple drawings into a single AutoCAD session. This feature enables us to work with multiple drawings at the same time, and we can easily copy objects from one drawing to another by using the *Windows Clipboard*. Copying to and pasting from the *Clipboard* allow us to quickly assemble objects in different files and thus increase our productivity.

AutoCAD® 2005 also allows us to create a collaborative design environment, where files and resources can be shared through the Internet. We can open and save AutoCAD drawings to an Internet location, insert blocks by dragging drawings from a web site, and insert hyperlinks in drawings so that others can access related documents. To use the **AutoCAD® 2005** Internet features, *Microsoft Internet Explorer 6.0* (or a later version) and Internet or intranet connections are required.

In this lesson, we will demonstrate using the **AutoCAD® 2005** Internet features to access drawings through the Internet, as well as using blocks and the *Windows Clipboard* to create a subassembly drawing. We will use the bearing part that was created in the previous lesson.

The *Shaft Support* Subassembly

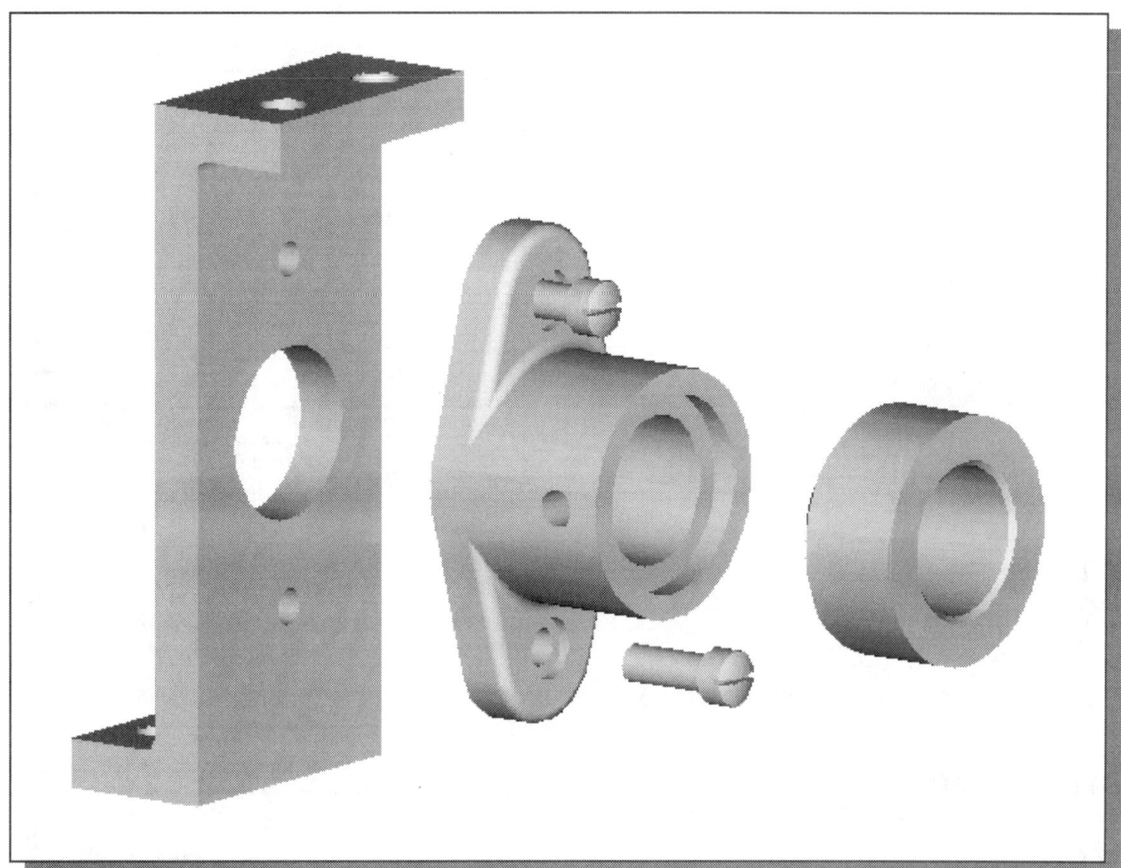

Additional parts

Besides the ***Bearing***, we will need three additional parts: (1) ***Cap-Screw***, (2) ***Collar*** and (3) ***Base-Plate***. Create the *Collar* and *Base-Plate* drawings as shown below, save the drawings as separate part files (*Collar*, *Base-Plate*). (Exit **AutoCAD® 2005** after you have created the files.)

(1) ***Cap-Screw***
(We will open this drawing through the Internet.)

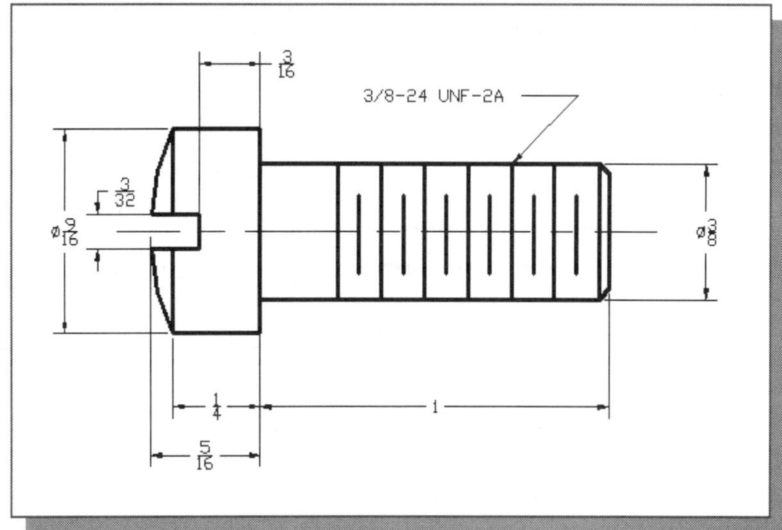

(2) ***Collar***

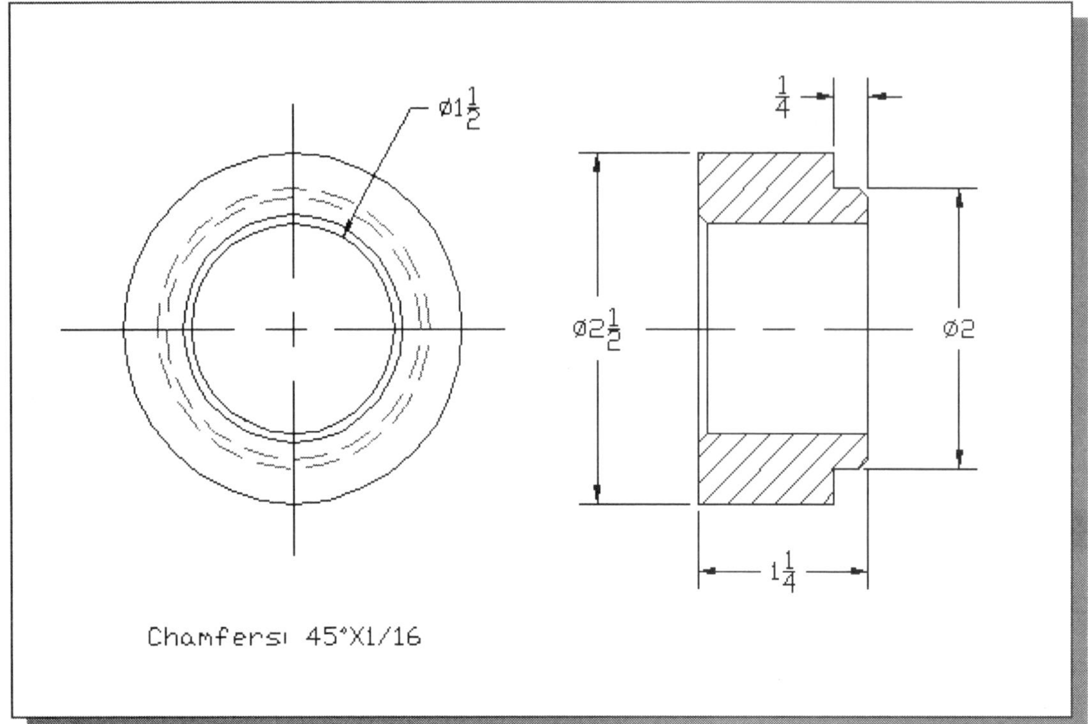

(3) ***Base-Plate***

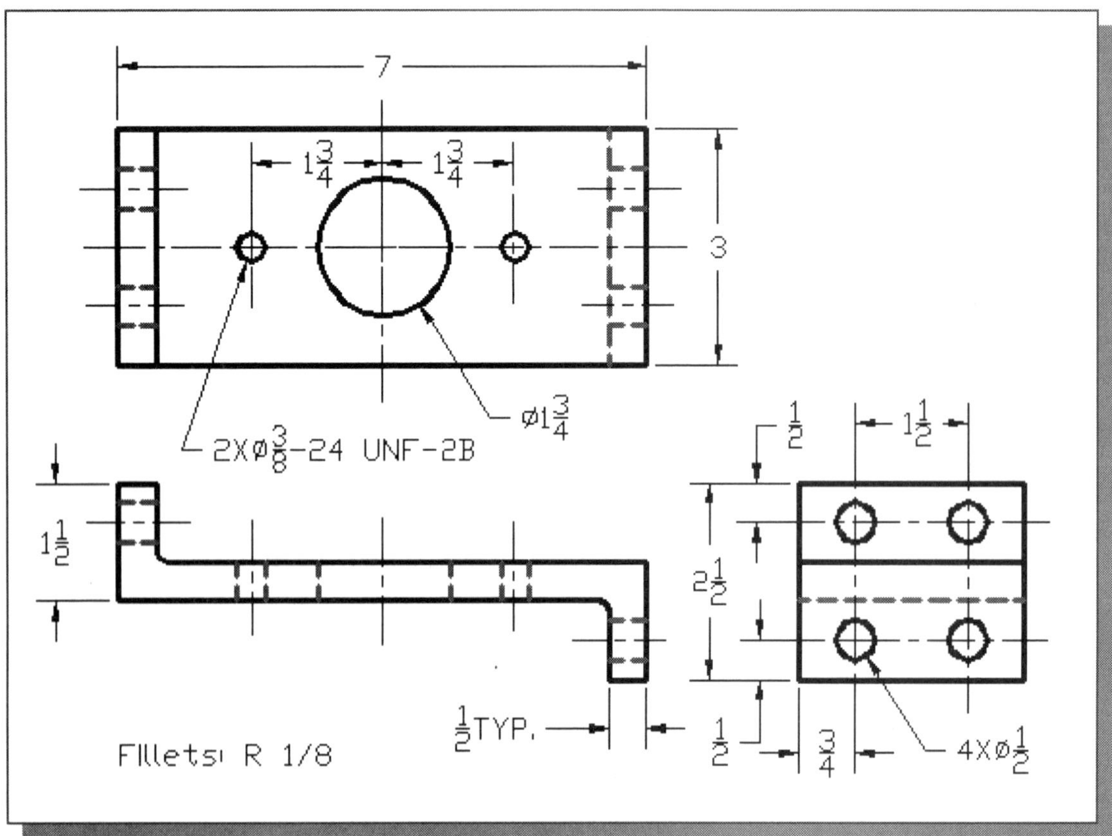

Starting Up AutoCAD 2005 and Loading Multiple Drawings

1. Select the **AutoCAD 2005** option on the *Program* menu or select the **AutoCAD 2005** icon on the *Desktop*.

2. In the AutoCAD *Startup* dialog box, select **Open a Drawing** with a single click of the left-mouse-button.

3. In the *File* list section, pick ***Bearing.dwg*** as the first drawing to be loaded. (If the file is not listed in the *File* list, use the **Browse** button to locate the file.)

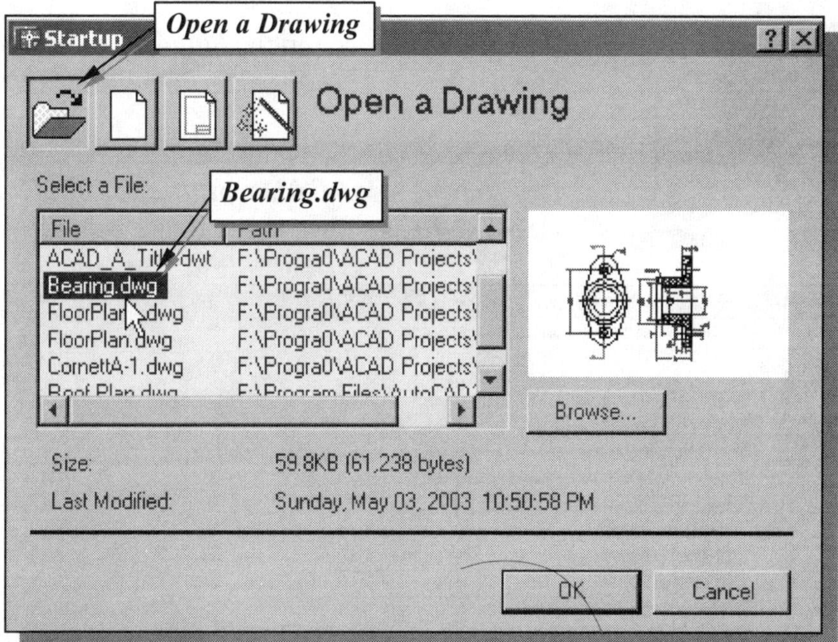

4. Click on the **OK** button to open the AutoCAD *Startup* dialog box.

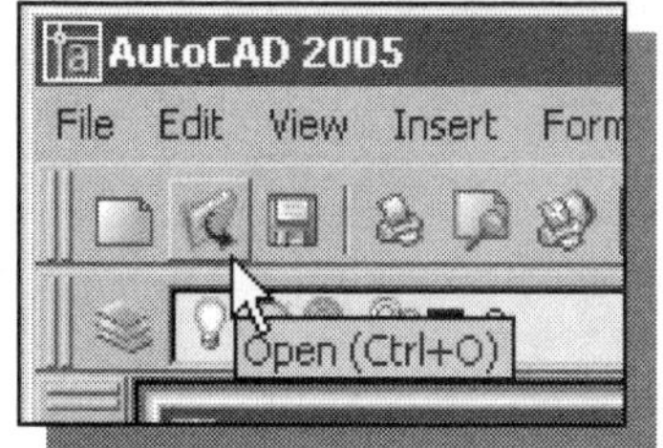

5. Select the **Open** icon in the *Standard* toolbar.

6. In the *Select File* dialog box, pick ***Base-Plate.dwg*** as the second drawing to be loaded.

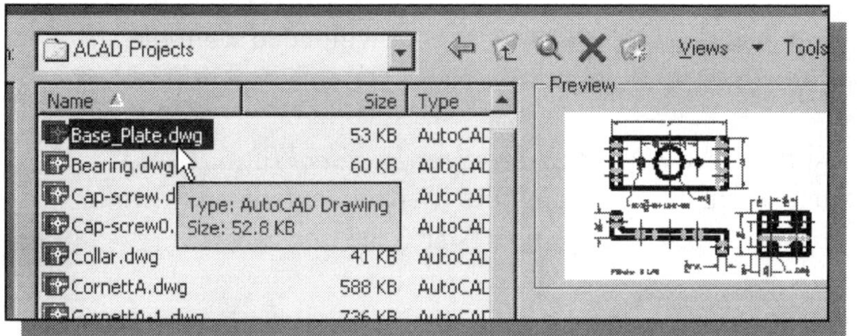

7. On your own, repeat the above steps and open the ***Collar.dwg*** file.

Using AutoCAD with the Internet

- **AutoCAD® 2005** allows us to share files and resources through the Internet. Drawings can be placed and opened to an Internet location, insert blocks by dragging drawings from a web site, and insert hyperlinks in drawings so that others can access related documents. Note that to use the **AutoCAD® 2005** Internet features, *Microsoft Internet Explorer 5.0* (or a later version) and Internet or Intranet connections are required.

  We will illustrate the procedure to open an AutoCAD file from the Internet by *Uniform Resource Locator* (URL).

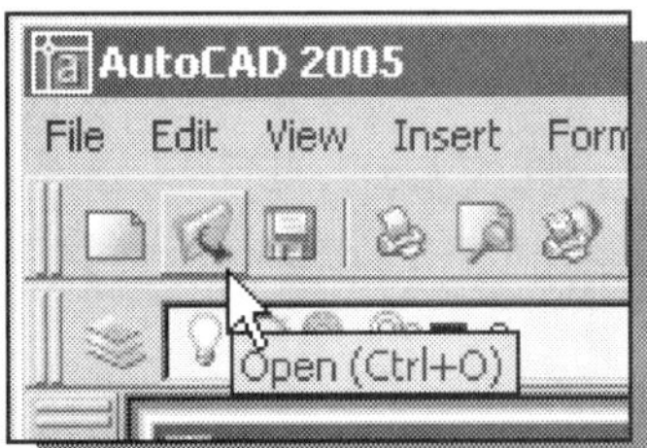

1. Click the **Open** icon in the *Standard* toolbar area as shown.

2. In the *Select File* dialog box, enter ***http://www.sdcACAD.com/acad2005/Cap-screw.dwg*** as shown in the figure below.

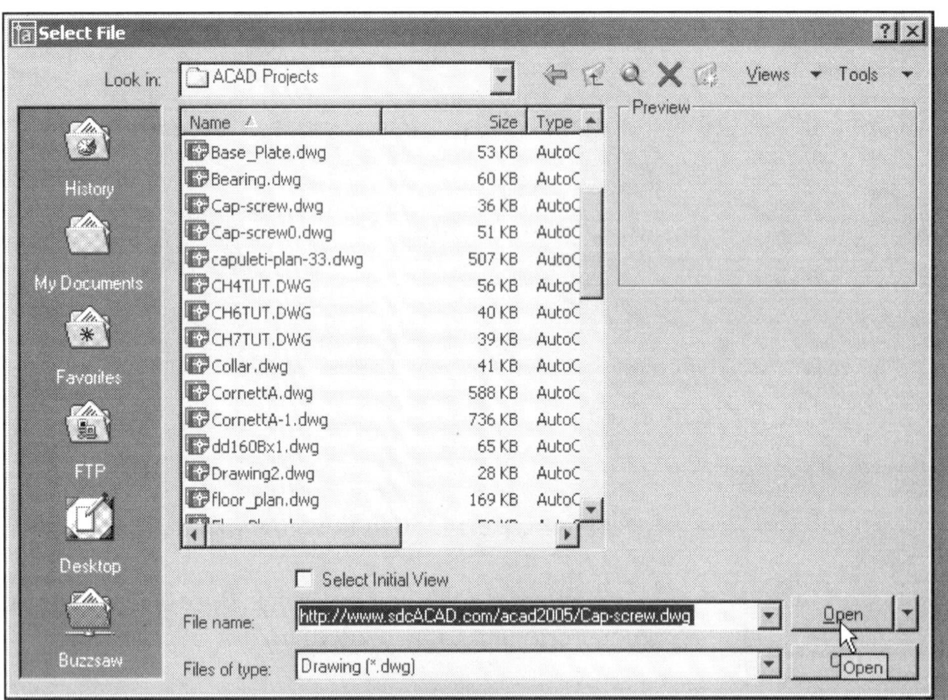

3. Click the **Open** icon and the *Cap-screw* file is downloaded from the www.sdcACAD.com web site to the local computer.

- The URL entered must be of the *Hypertext Transfer Protocol* (http://) and the complete filename must be entered including the filename extension (.dwg or .dwt). Also note that the directory and file names are case sensitive.

Rearrange the Displayed Windows

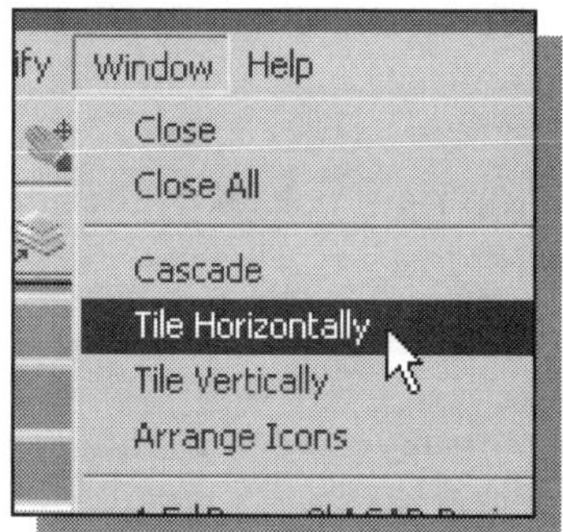

1. In the pull-down menus, select:

   [Window] → [Tile Horizontally]

➢ Note that the highlighted window and the graphics cursor indicate the **active window** in the current AutoCAD session. We can switch to any window by clicking inside the desired window.

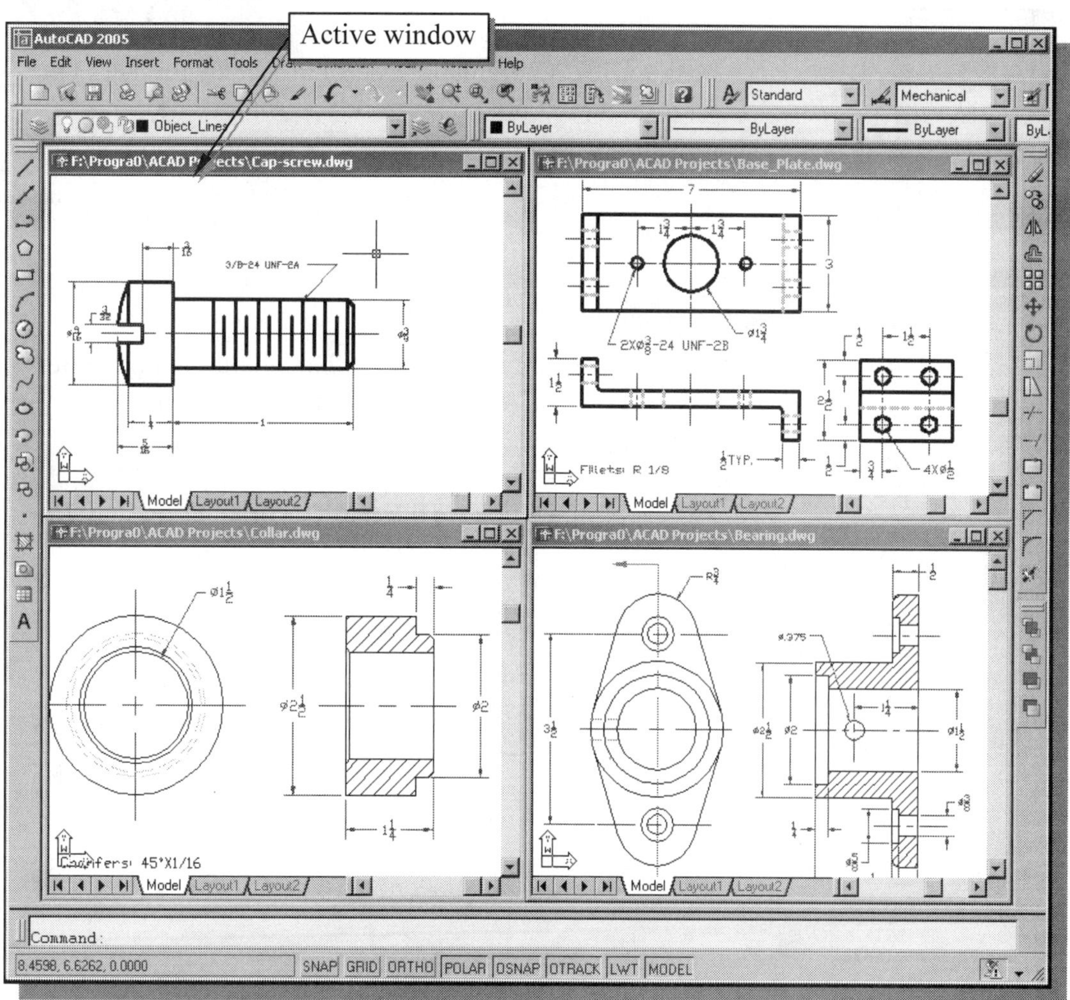

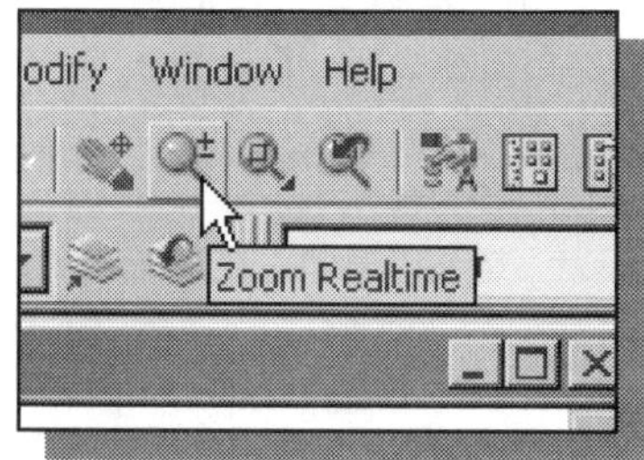

➢ On your own, adjust the display of each window by left-clicking inside each window and using the **Zoom Realtime** command.

Defining a *Block*

1. Set the ***Cap-Screw*** window as the *active window* by left-mouse-clicking inside the window.

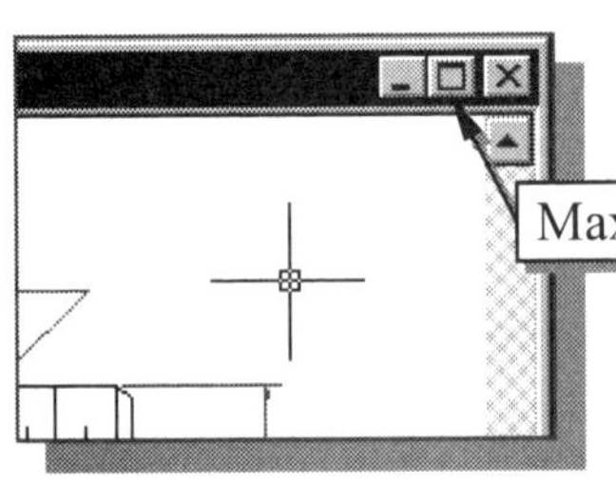

2. Click on the **Maximize** icon at the top right corner of the *Cap-Screw* window to enlarge the window.

3. In the *Layer Control* box, switch off all layers except the *Object_Lines* and *Center_Lines* layers.

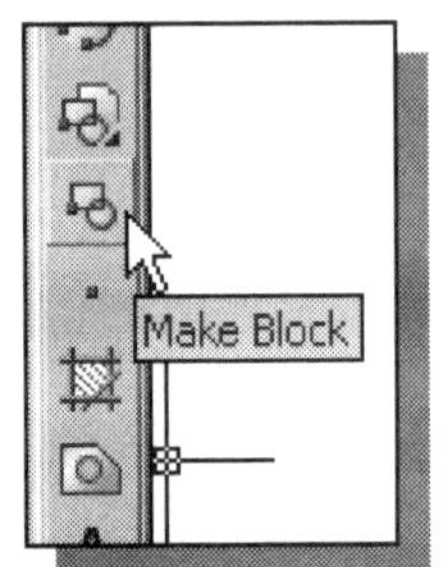

4. Pick the **Make Block** command icon in the *Draw* toolbar. The *Block Definition* dialog box appears on the screen.

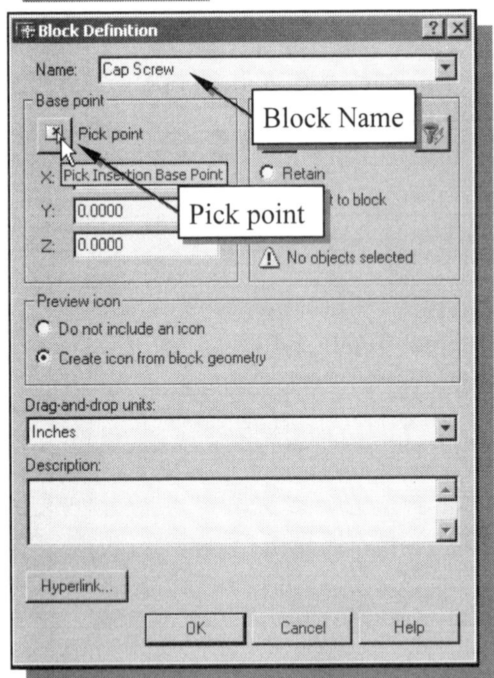

5. In the *Block Definition* dialog box, enter ***Cap Screw*** as the block *Name*.

6. Click on the **Pick point** button to define a reference point of the block.

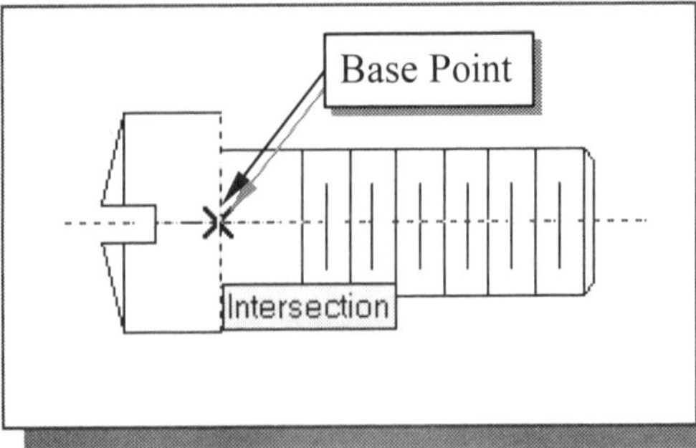

7. Pick the intersection of the centerline and the base of the *Cap-Screw* head as the base point.

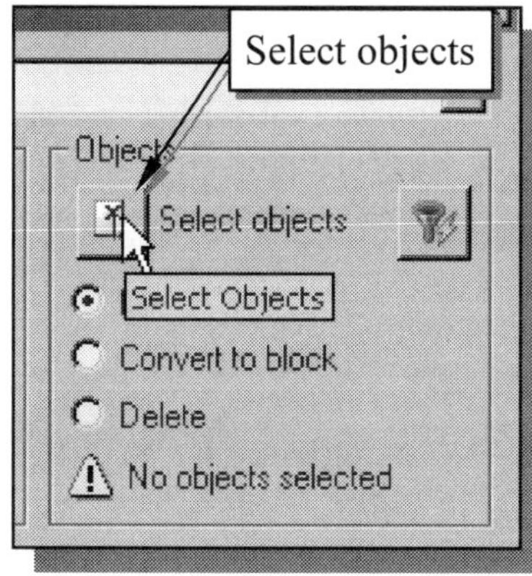

8. Click on the **Select Objects** icon to select the objects to be placed in the block.

9. Select all *object lines* and *centerlines* by using a selection window on the screen.

10. Inside the graphics window, **right-mouse-click** once to accept the selected objects.

- The selected objects will be included in the new block, and several options are available regarding the selected objects after the block is created. We can retain or delete the selected objects or convert them to a block instance.

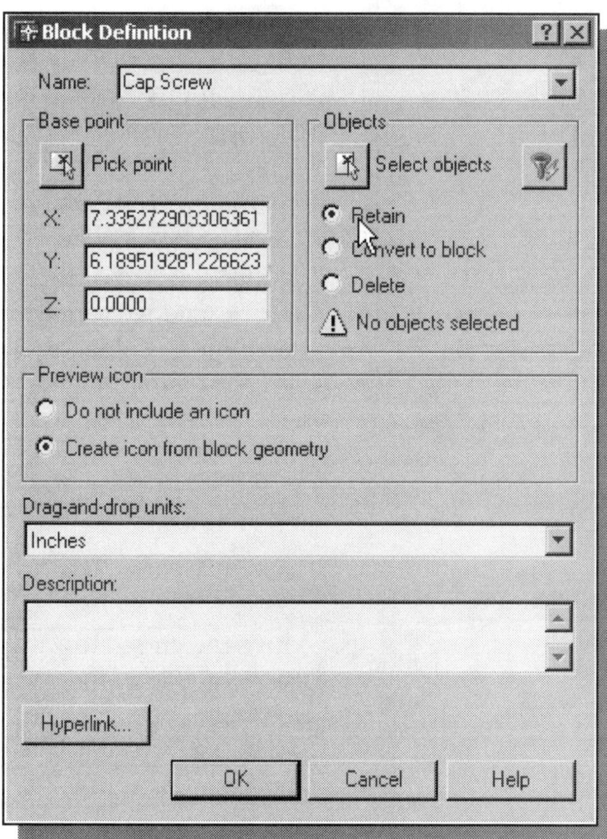

- ***Retain***: Keep the selected objects as regular objects in the drawing after creating the block.
- ***Convert to Block***: Convert the selected objects to a block instance in the drawing after creating the block.
- ***Delete***: Remove the selected objects from the drawing after creating the block.

11. Pick the ***Retain*** option to keep the objects as regular lines and arcs.

- Notice in the *Preview icon* section, the *Create icon from block geometry* option displays a small icon of the selected objects.

12. Click the **OK** button to accept the settings and proceed to create the new block.

Inserting a *Block*

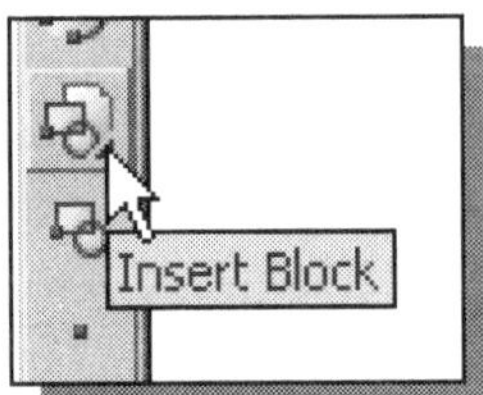

1. Pick the **Insert Block** command icon in the *Draw* toolbar. The *Block Definition* dialog box appears on the screen.

2. In the *Insert* dialog box, notice the block name ***Cap screw*** appears in the block *Name* box. (Note: In this example, we created only one block; AutoCAD allows us to define multiple blocks in the same drawing.)

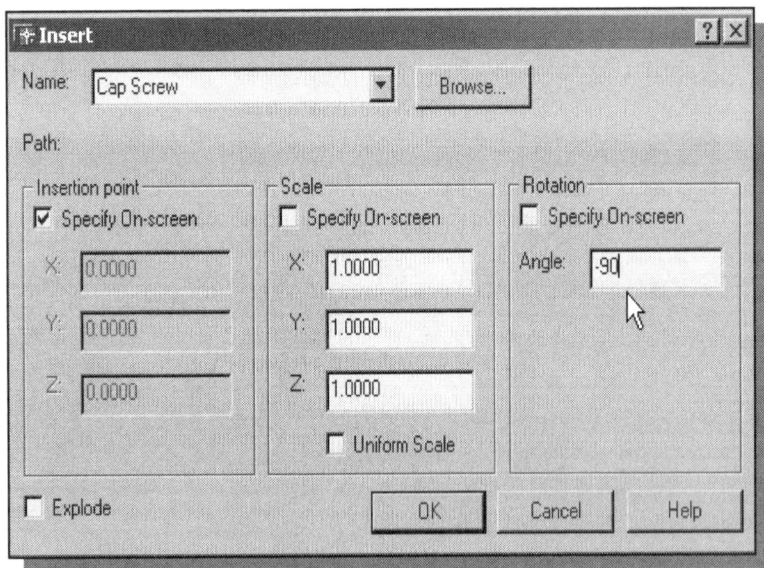

3. In the *Rotation* section, we will enter a ***-90*** angle to orient the *Cap-screw* in a vertical direction. Notice that other options are also available. The *Scale* option allows us to adjust the size of the block, and we can also position the block by entering coordinates.

4. Click on the **OK** button to accept the settings and proceed to insert the block into the drawing.

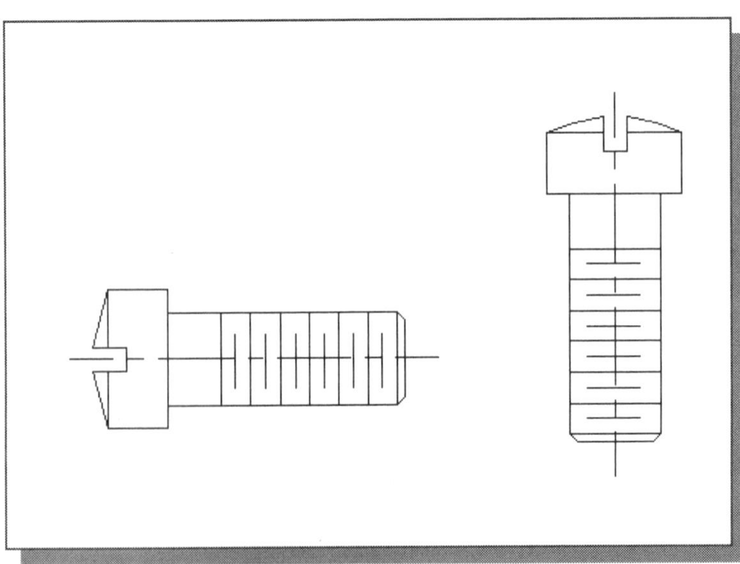

5. Move the cursor toward the right side of the original copy of the cap screw. Left-click to place a copy of the block.

➢ On your own, place additional copies of the block on the screen while experimenting with the *Block Scale* and *Rotation* options.

Starting the *Assembly drawing*

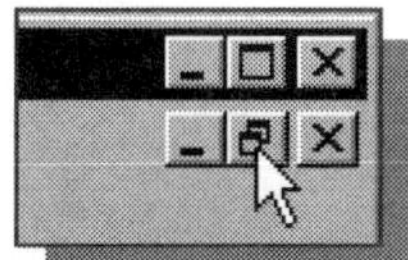

1. Switch back to the four tiled-windows display by left-clicking on the **Restore Down** icon near the upper right corner of the graphics window.

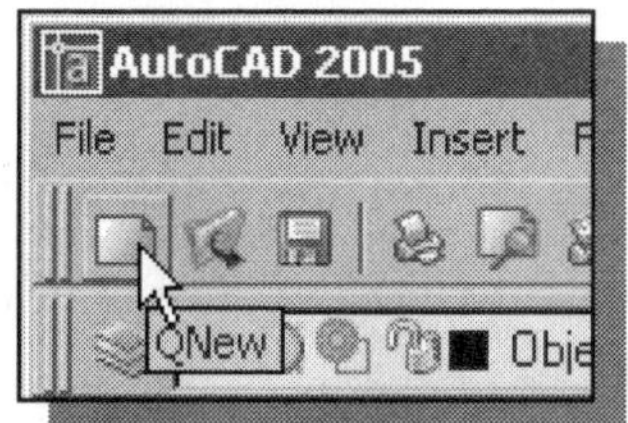

2. Select the **New** icon in the *Standard* toolbar area.

3. In the AutoCAD 2005 *Create New Drawing* dialog box, select the ***Use a Template*** option as shown in the figure.

4. Select the ***Acad_A_Title*** template file from the list of template files. If the file is saved in a separate folder, click on the **Browse** button to locate the file.

5. Click the **OK** button to open the selected template file.

6. On your own, resize the window as shown.

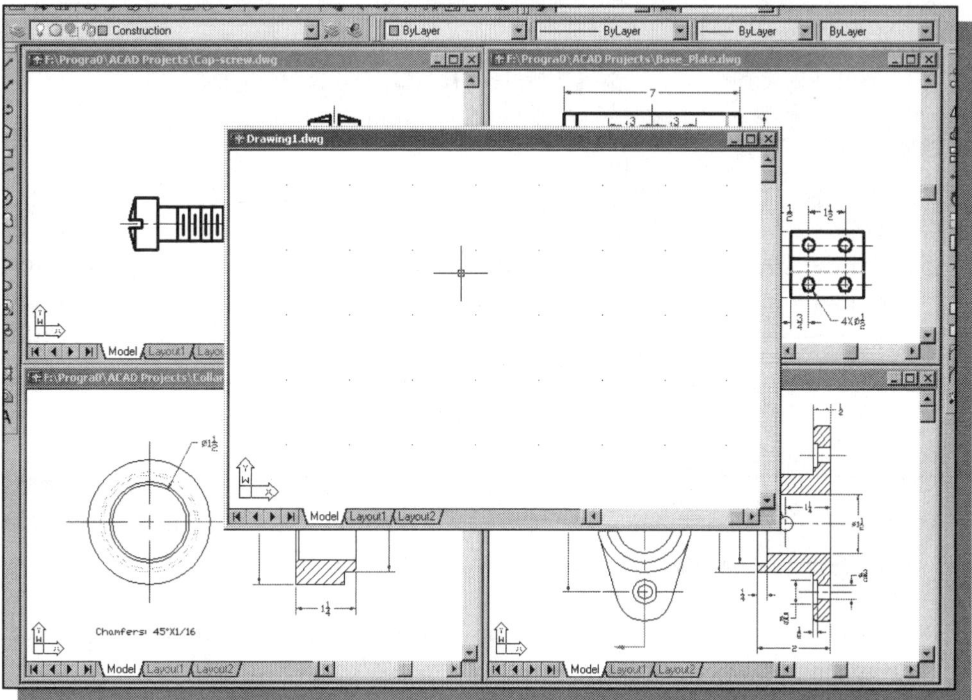

Copying and pasting with the *Windows Clipboard*

1. Set the ***Base-Plate*** window as the *current window* by left-mouse-clicking inside the window.

2. In the *Layer Control* box, switch off all layers except the *Object_Lines, Hidden_Lines*, and *Center_Lines* layers.

3. Select the **front view** of the *Base-Plate* by enclosing the front-view using a selection window.

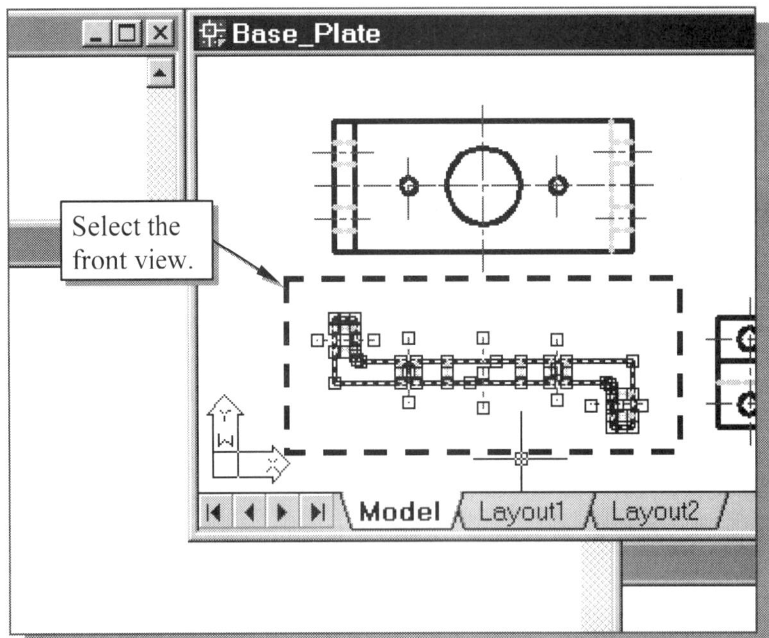

4. Select the **Copy to Clipboard** icon in the *Standard* toolbar area.

5. Set the ***Drawing1*** window as the *current window* by a left-mouse-click inside the window.

6. Select the **Paste from Clipboard** icon in the *Standard* toolbar area.

7. Position the front view of the *Base-Plate* near the bottom of the graphics window as shown in the next page.

❖ Note the selected items are copied into the new drawing and all of the layer settings are retained.

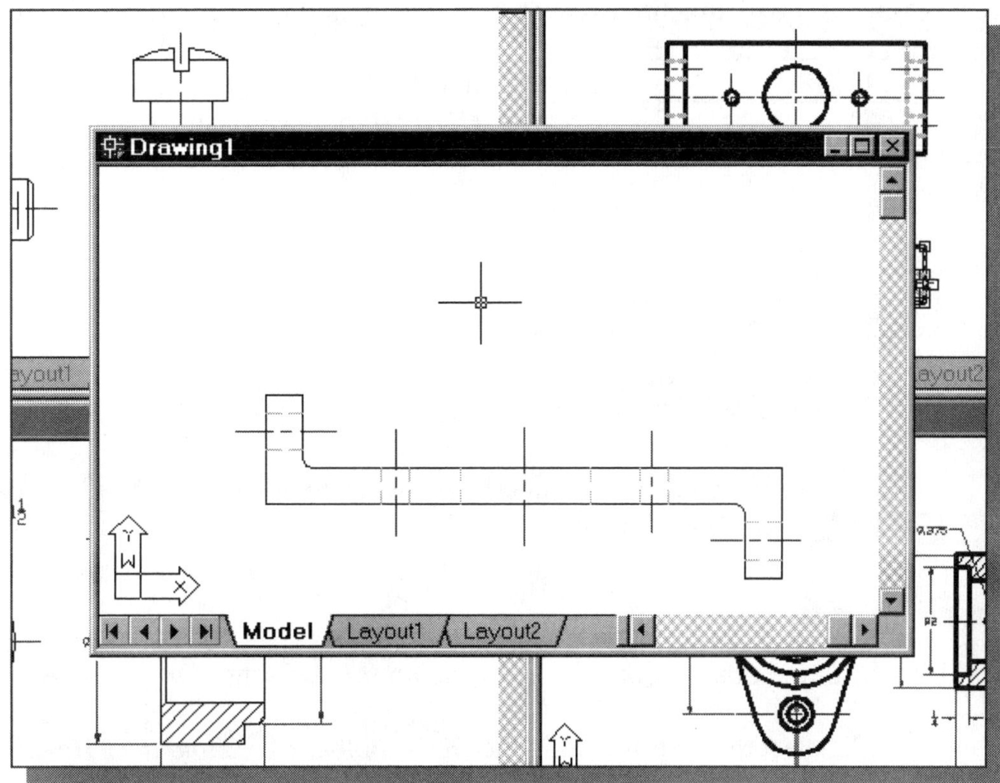

Converting the view into a section view

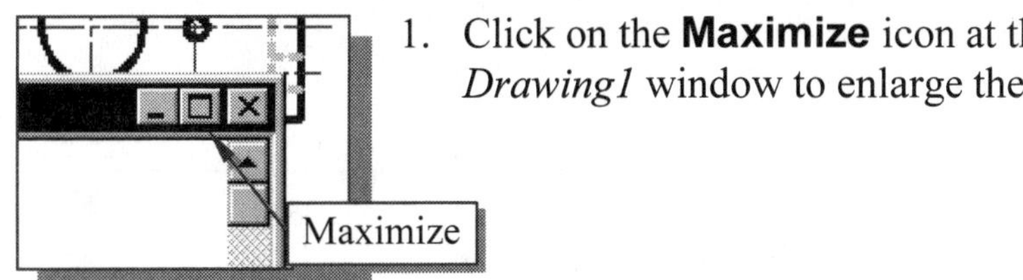

1. Click on the **Maximize** icon at the top right corner of the *Drawing1* window to enlarge the window.

2. **Pre-select** all the objects in the front view by using a selection window.

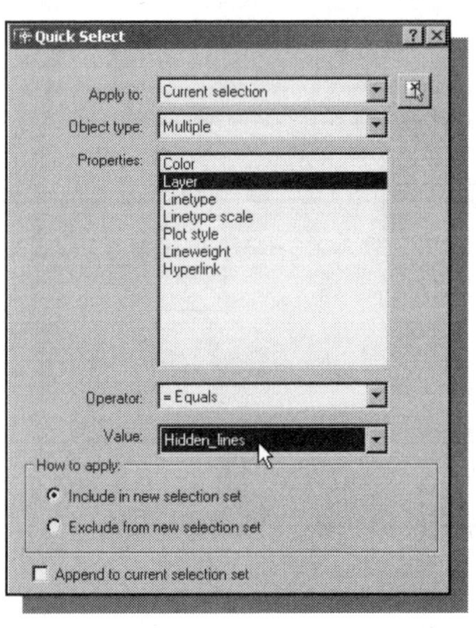

3. Inside the graphics window, right-mouse-click to bring up the popup option menu and select the **Quick Select** option.

4. In the *Quick Select* dialog box, select ***Layer*** from the *Properties* list.

5. Set the ***Value*** box to **Hidden_Lines**.

6. In the *How to apply* section, confirm the ***Include in new selection set*** option is selected.

7. Click on the **OK** button to accept the settings.

8. AutoCAD will now **filter out** objects that are not on layer *Hidden_Lines*.

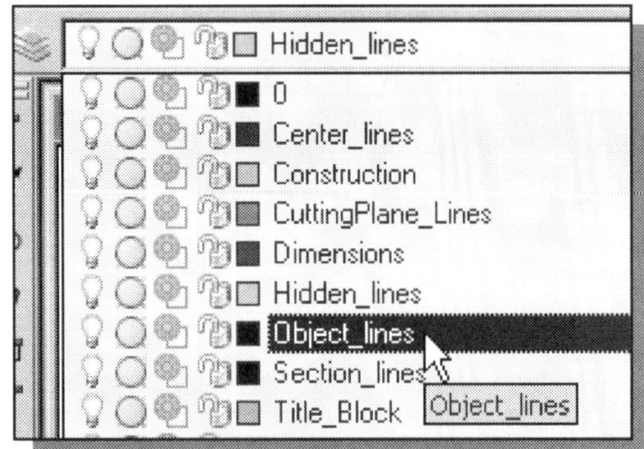

9. In the *Layer Control* box, click on the ***Object_Lines*** layer name to move the selected objects to the *Object_Lines* layer.

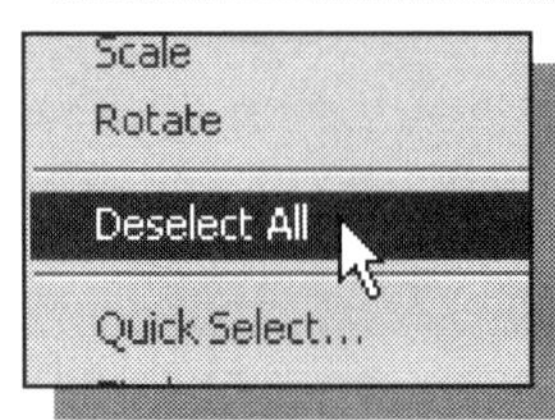

10. Inside the graphics window, **right-mouse-click** and select **Deselect All**.

11. In the *Layer Control* box, set layer ***Section_Lines*** as the *Current Layer*.

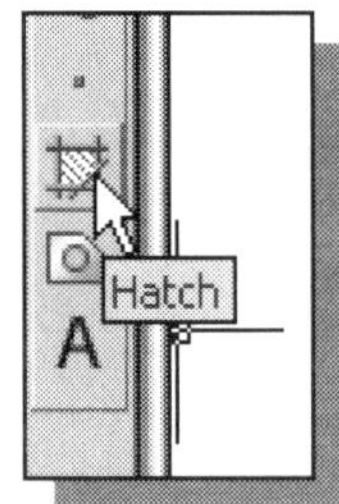

12. Select the **Hatch** icon in the *Draw* toolbar. The *Boundary Hatch* dialog box appears on the screen.

13. On your own, create the hatch-pattern as shown.

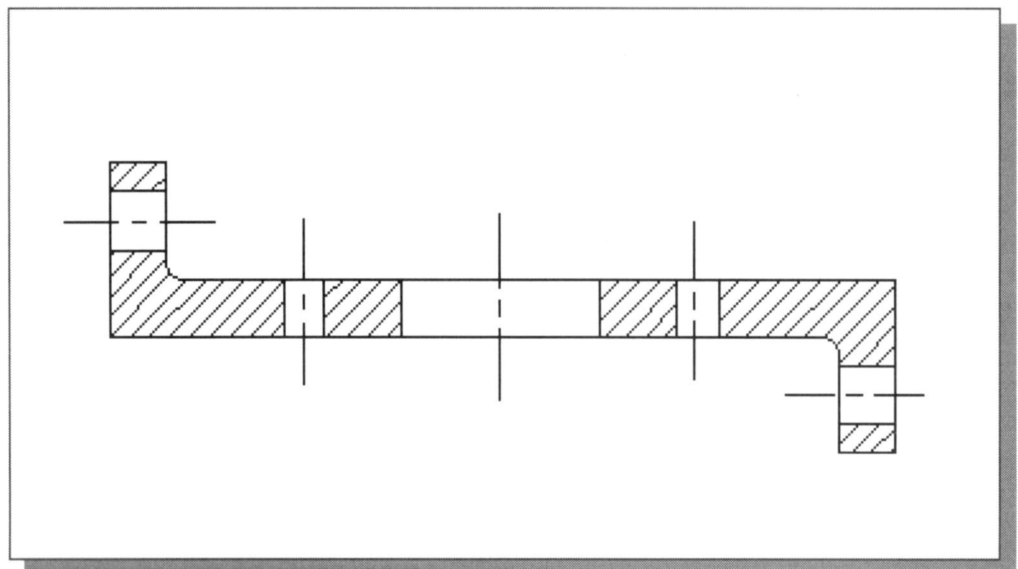

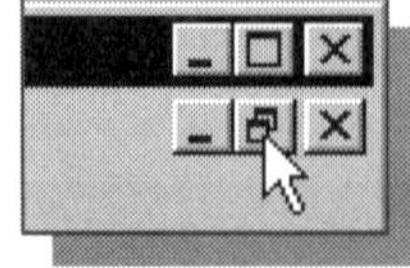

14. Switch back to the tiled-windows display by left-clicking on the Restore Down icon near the upper right corner of the graphics window.

Adding the *Bearing* to the assembly drawing

1. Set the ***Bearing*** window as the *current window* by a left-mouse-click inside the window.

2. In the *Layer Control* box, switch off all layers except the *Object_Lines, Hidden_Lines, Center_Lines*, and *Section_Lines* layers.

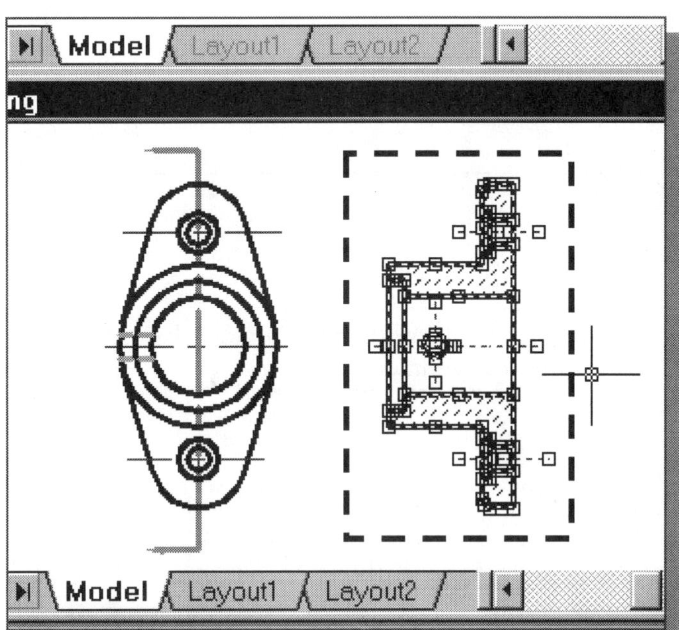

3. Select the **side view** of the *Bearing* by enclosing the side view using a selection window.

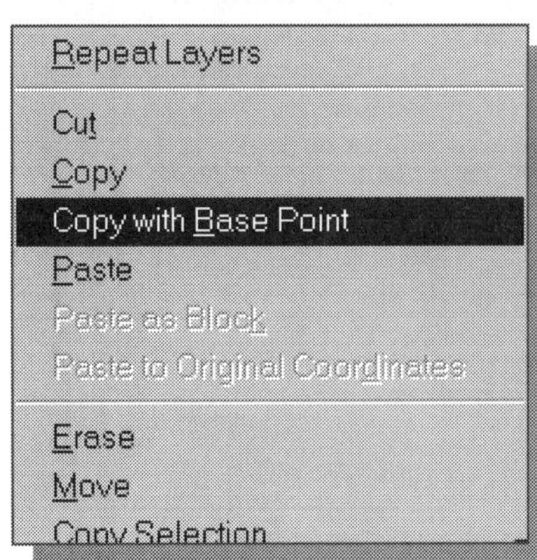

4. Inside the graphics window, **right-mouse-click** and select the **Copy with Base Point** option.

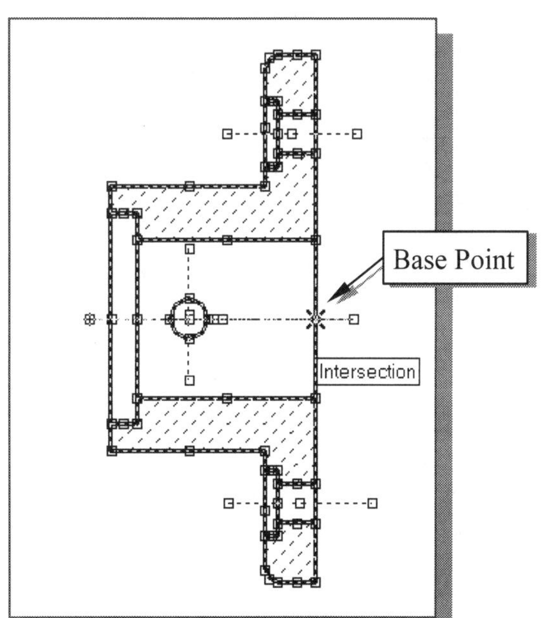

5. Pick the **center intersection** on the right vertical line of the side view as the base point.

6. Set the ***Drawing1*** window as the *current window* by left-mouse-clicking inside the window.

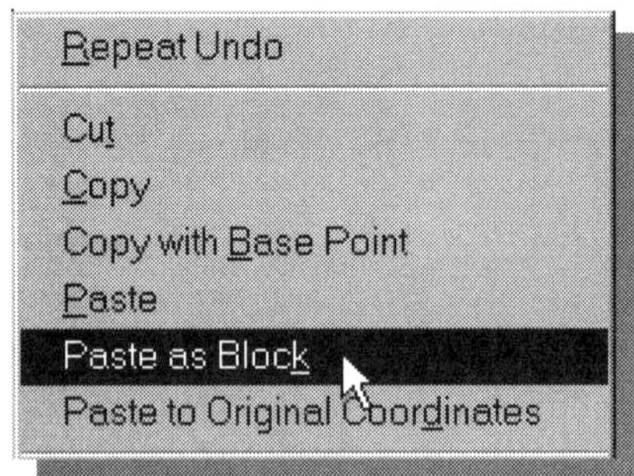

7. Inside the graphics window, right-mouse-click and select the **Paste as Block** option.

8. Align the side view of the *Bearing* to the top center-intersection of the *Base-Plate* as shown.

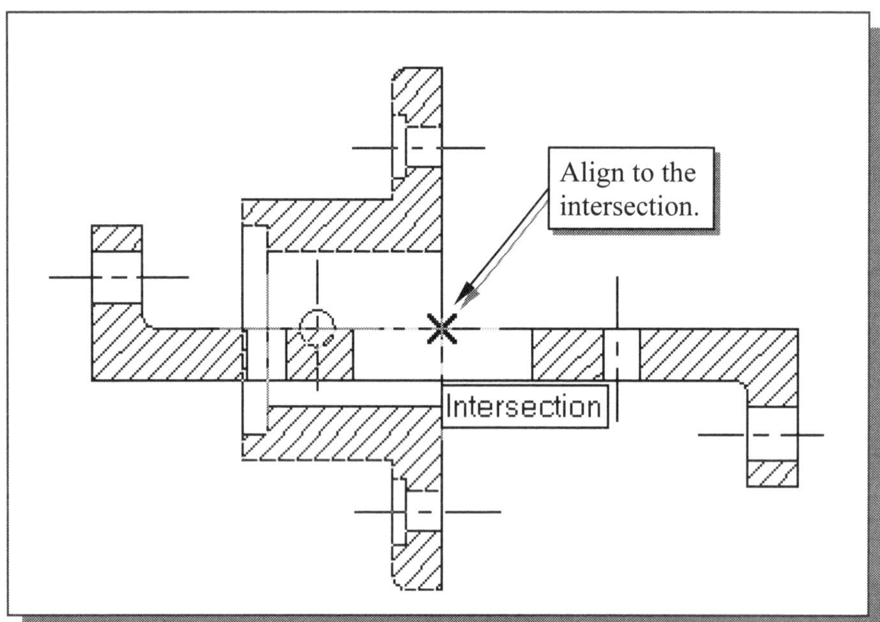

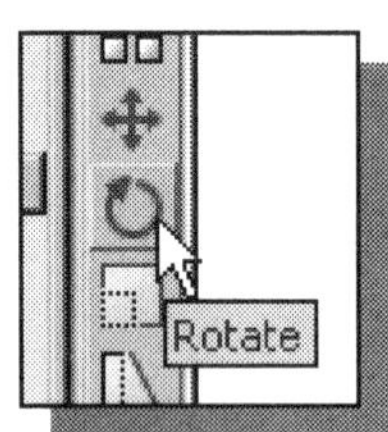

9. Click on the **Rotate** icon in the *Modify* toolbar.

10. Pick the side view of the *Bearing* we just placed into the assembly drawing. Notice the entire view is treated as a block object.

11. Inside the graphics window, **right-mouse-click** to accept the selection and proceed with the Rotate command.

12. Pick the base point as the rotation reference point.

13. Rotate and align the side view of the *Bearing* to the top of the *Base-Plate*.

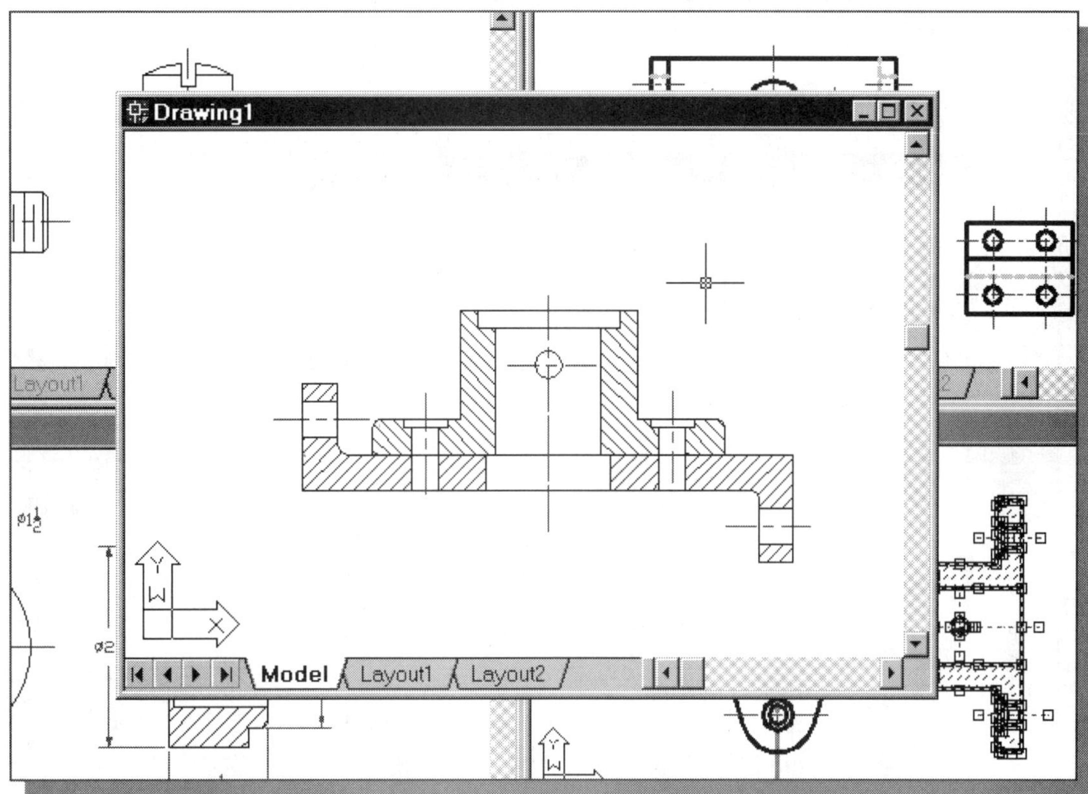

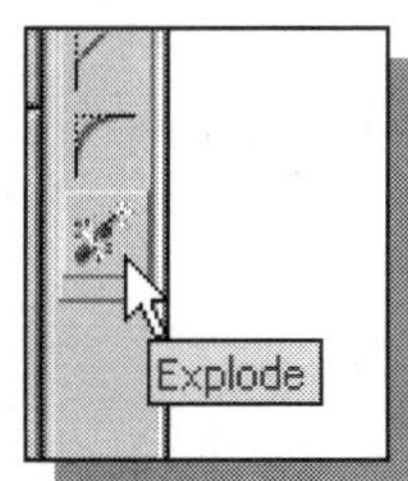

14. Select the **Explode** icon in the *Modify* toolbar.

15. Pick the *Bearing* to break the block into its component objects.

➢ On your own, copy and paste the collar to the top of the bearing.

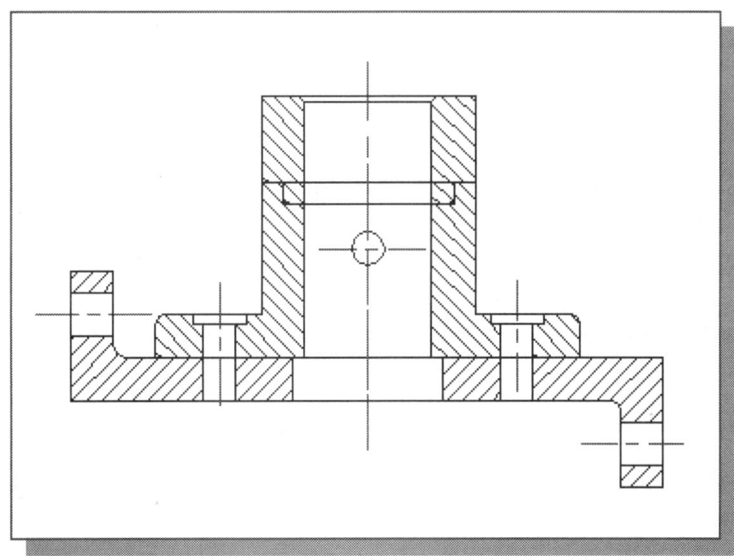

16. Use the **Explode, Trim**, and **Erase** commands and modify the assembly as shown.

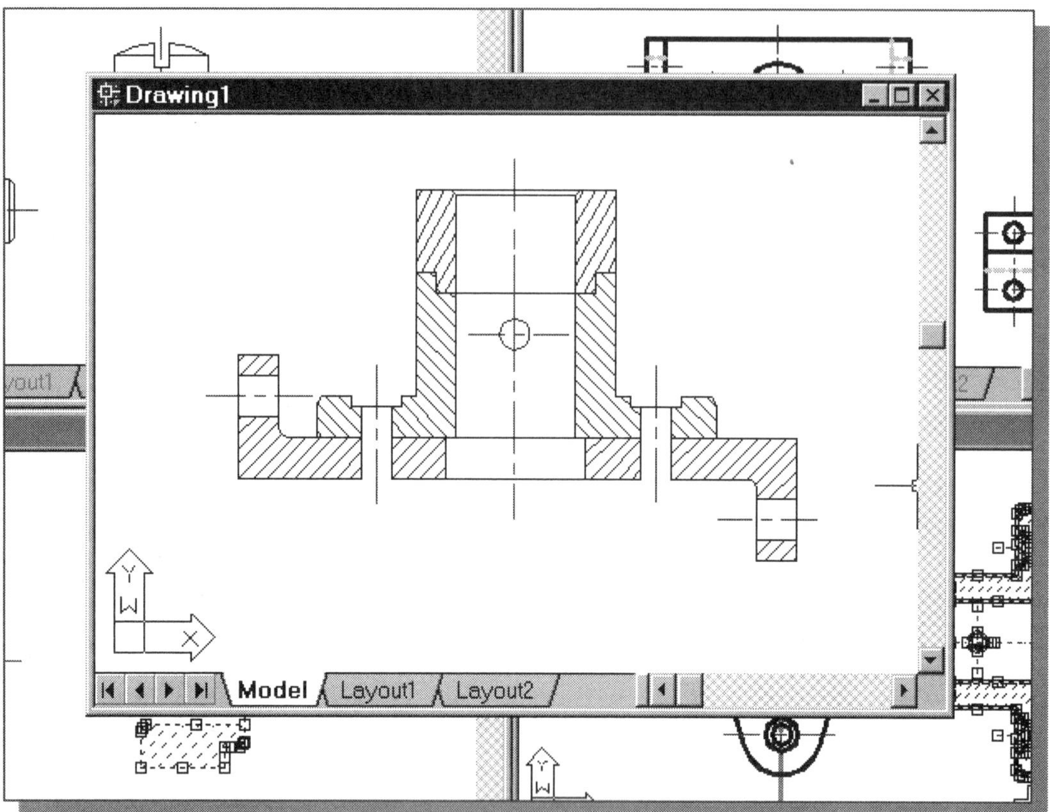

Adding the *Cap-Screws* to the assembly drawing

1. Set the ***Cap-Screw*** window as the *current window* by a left-mouse-click inside the window.

2. Pre-select the vertical *Cap-Screw*. Since all objects belong to a block we can quickly select the block.

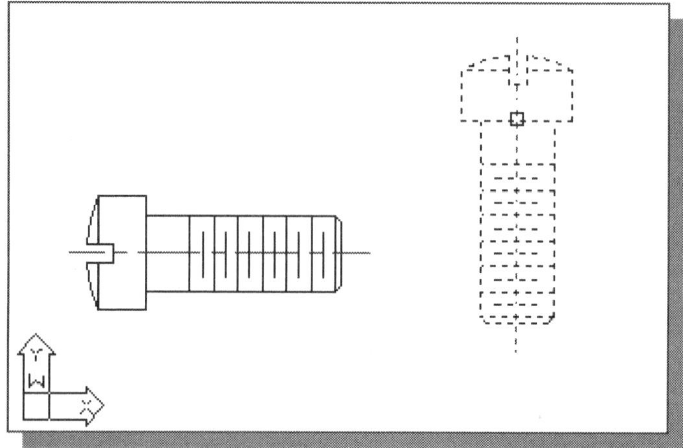

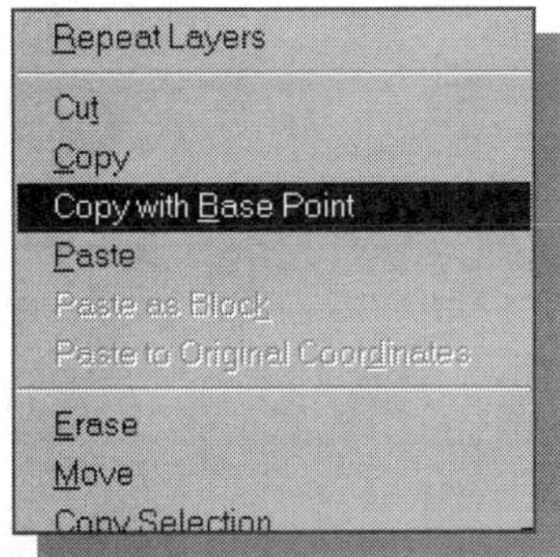

3. Inside the graphics window, **right-mouse-click** and select the **Copy with Base Point** option.

4. Pick the ***GRIP*** point as the copy base point.

5. Set the ***Drawing1*** window as the *current window* by left-mouse-clicking inside the window.

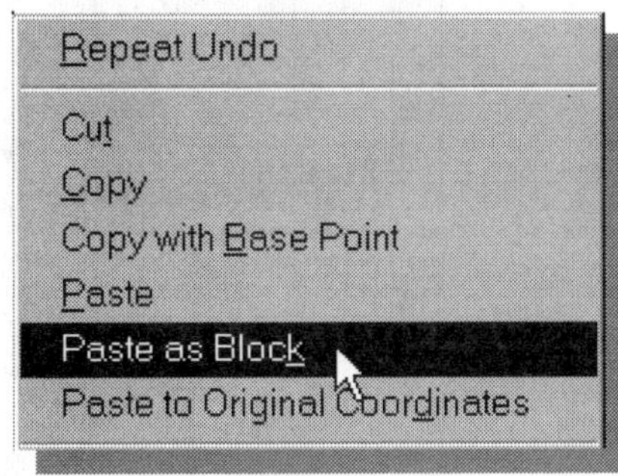

6. Inside the graphics window, **right-mouse-click** and select the **Paste** option.

7. Align the *Cap-Screw* as shown.

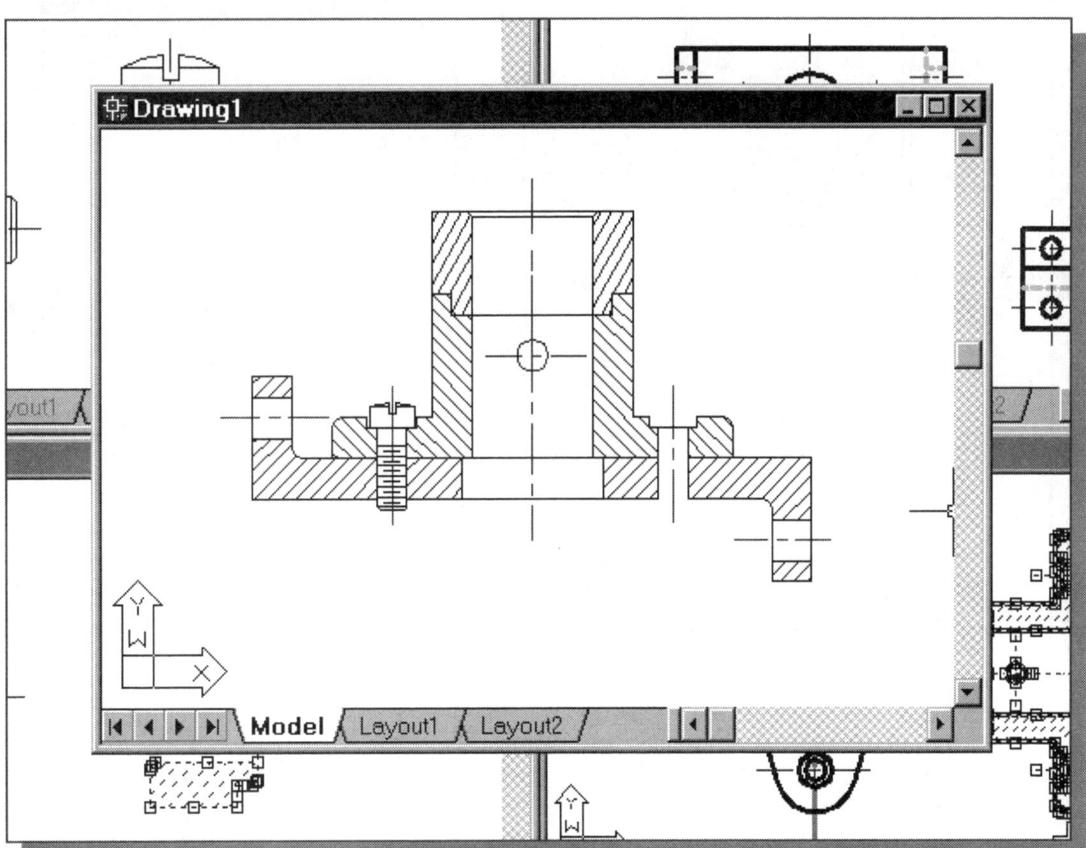

➢ On your own, repeat the steps and place another copy of the *Cap-Screw* in place.

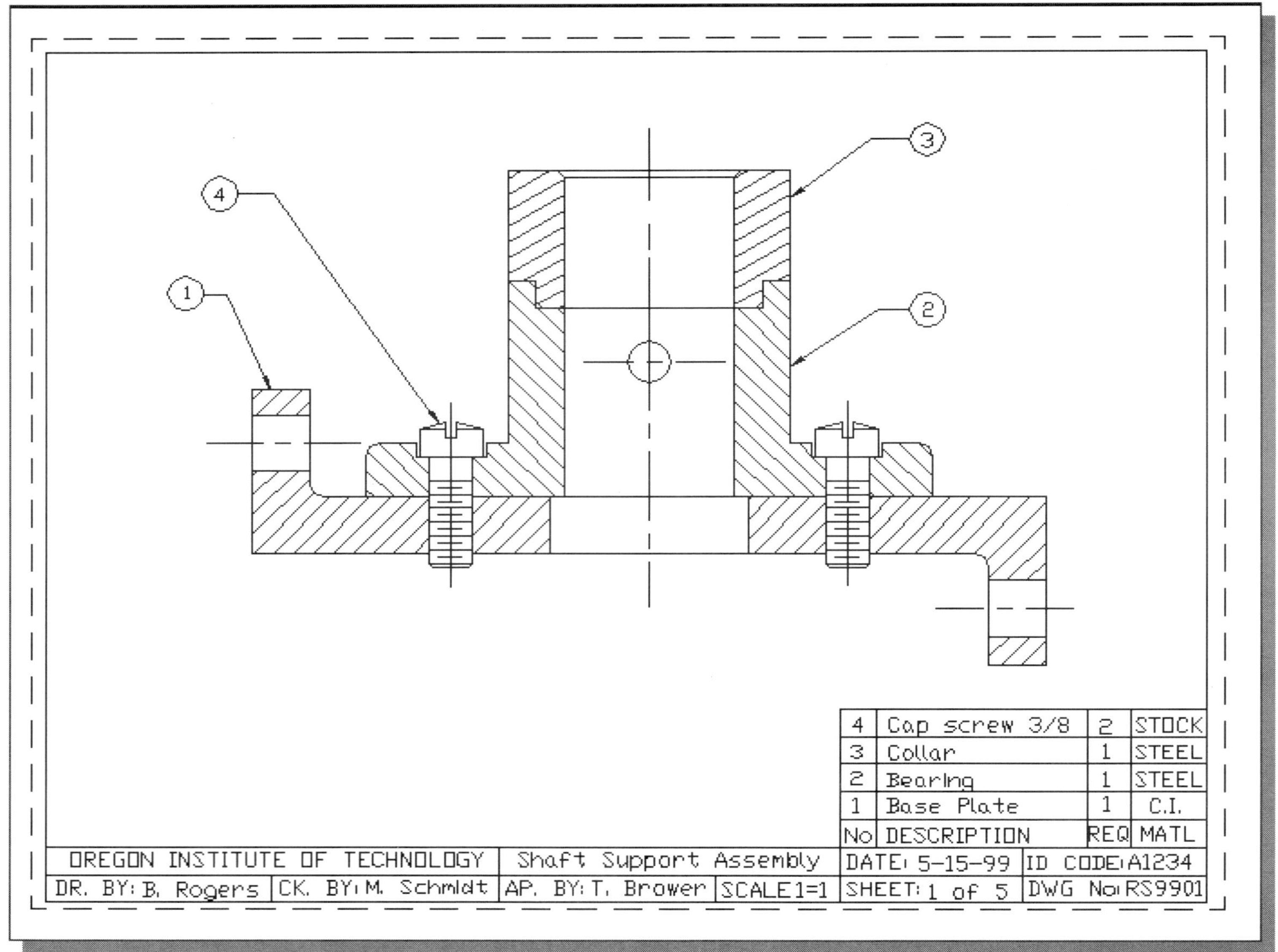

3
4
1
2
4 Cap screw 3/8 2 STOCK
3 Collar 1 STEEL
2 Bearing 1 STEEL
1 Base Plate 1 C.I.
No DESCRIPTION REQ MATL
OREGON INSTITUTE OF TECHNOLOGY
Shaft Support Assembly
DATE: 5-15-99
ID CODE: A1234
DR. BY: B. Rogers
CK. BY: M. Schmidt
AP. BY: T. Brower
SCALE 1=1
SHEET: 1 of 5
DWG No: RS9901

Questions:

1. What is an *assembly drawing*? What are the basic differences between an assembly drawing and a detail drawing?

2. What is a *block*? List some the advantages of using blocks in AutoCAD.

3. What are the differences between "*Copying and pasting with the Windows Clipboard*" and "*Copying with GRIPS* "?

4. Which command allows us to separate a block into its component objects?

5. Describe the differences between *PASTE* and *PASTE AS A BLOCK*.

6. Identify the following commands:

(a)

(b)

(c)

(d)

Exercise:

1. **Wheel Assembly** (Create a set of detail and assembly drawings. All Dimensions are in mm.)

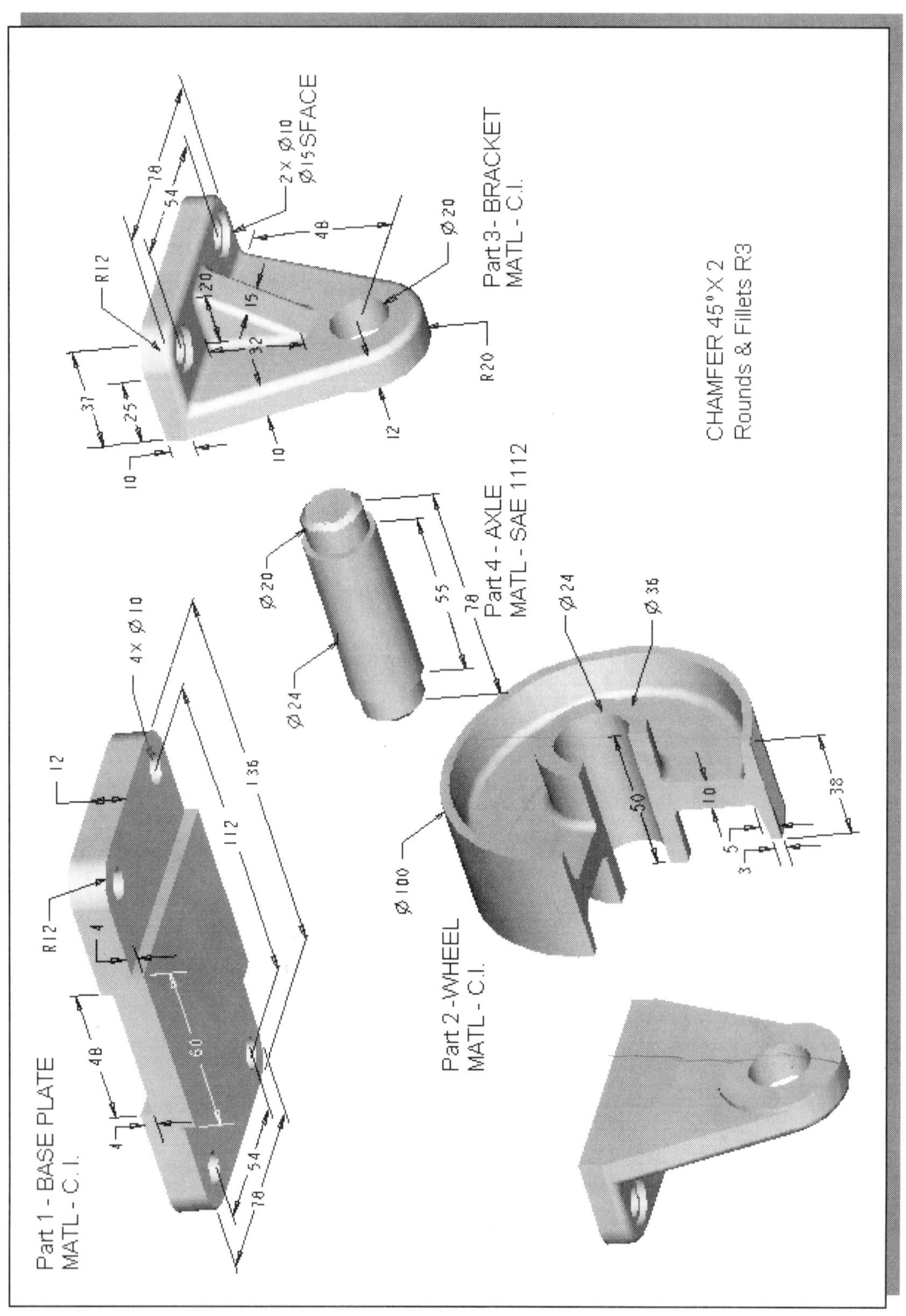

2. **Leveling Assembly** (Create a set of detail and assembly drawings. All Dimensions are in mm.)

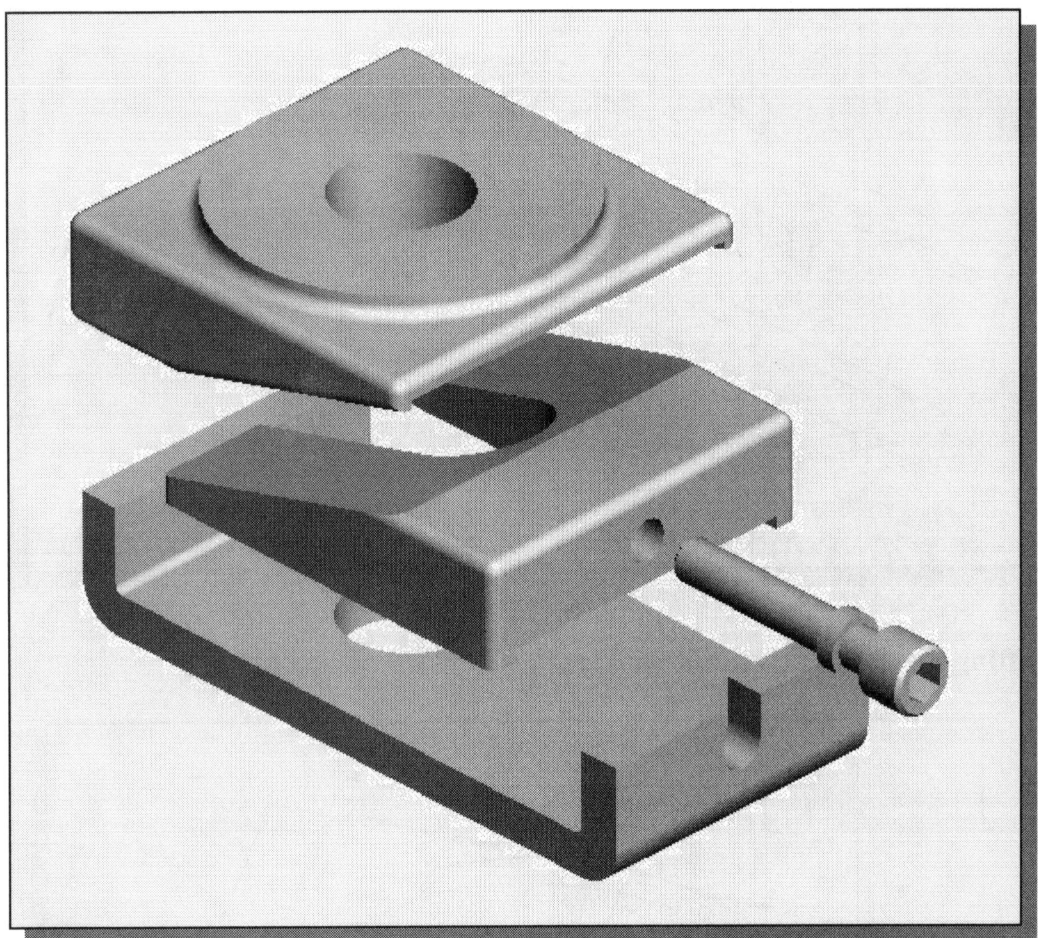

(a) Base Plate

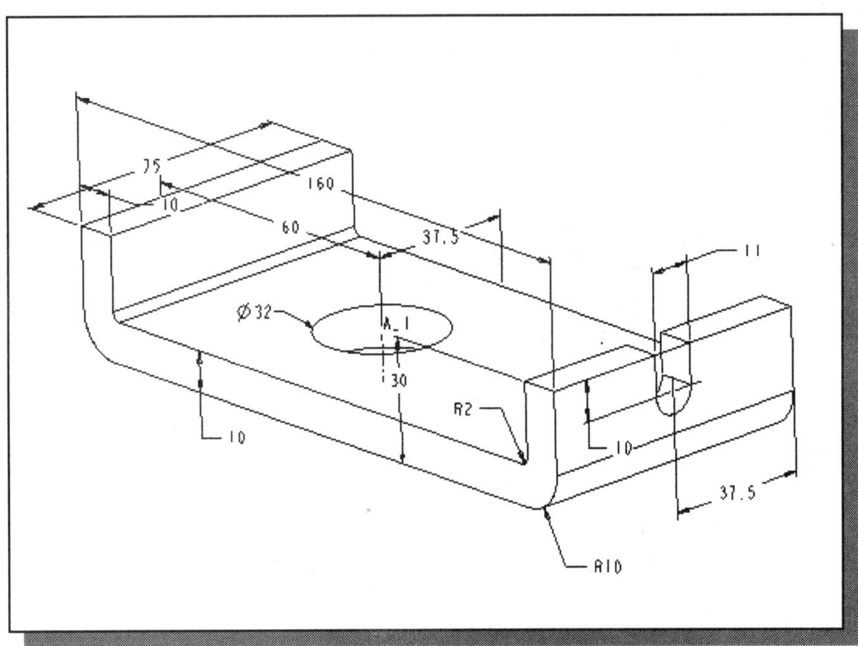

(b) **Sliding Block** (Rounds & Fillets: R3)

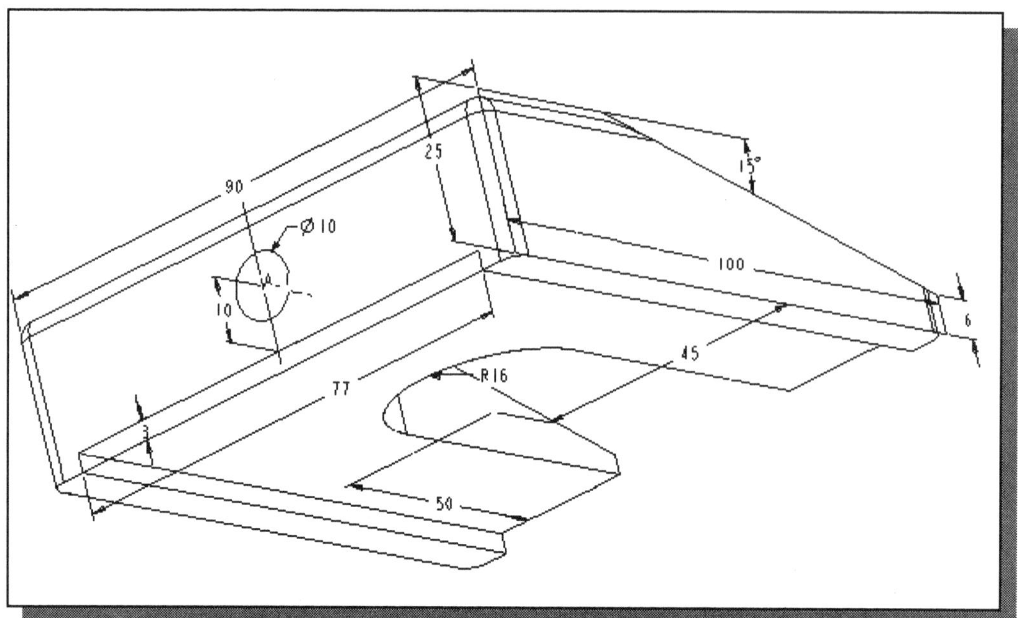

(c) **Lifting Block** (Rounds & Fillets: R3)

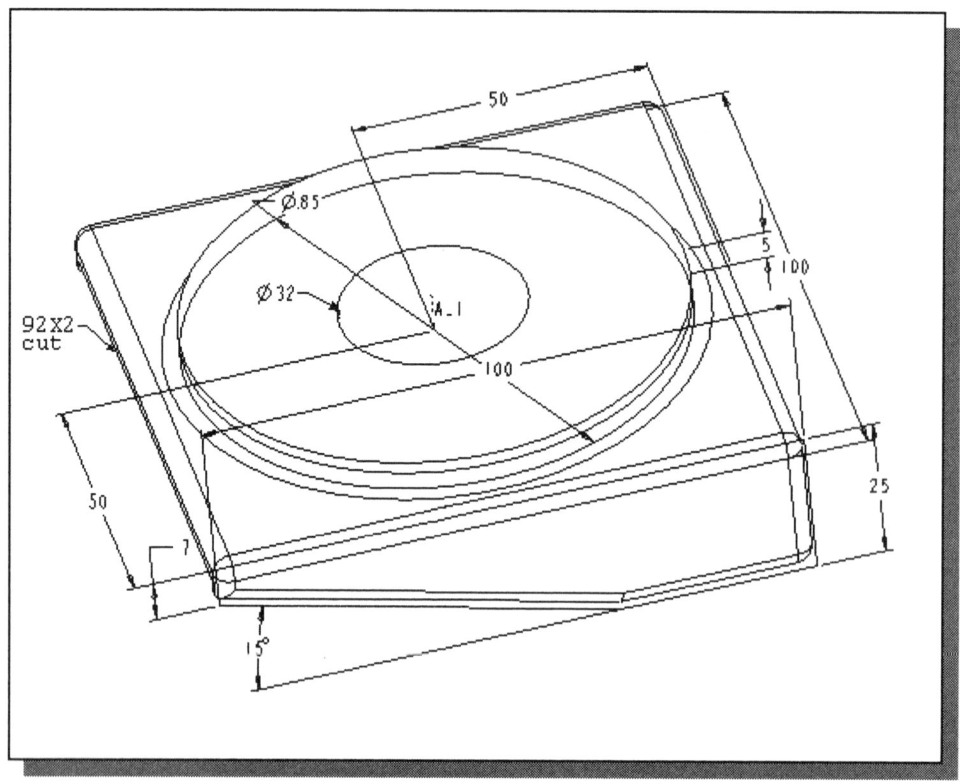

(d) **Adjusting Screw** (M10 X 1.5)

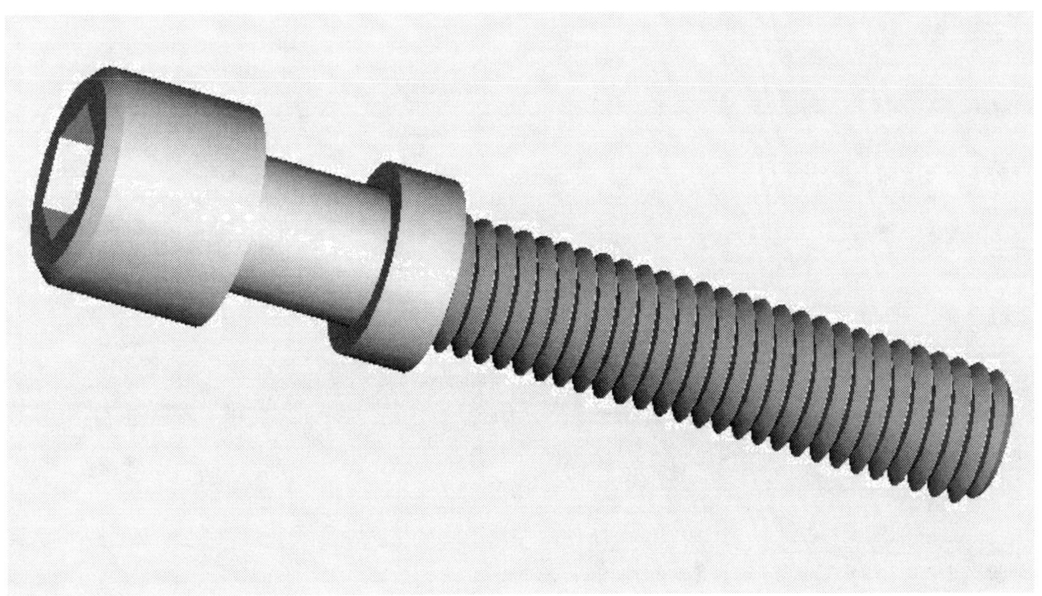

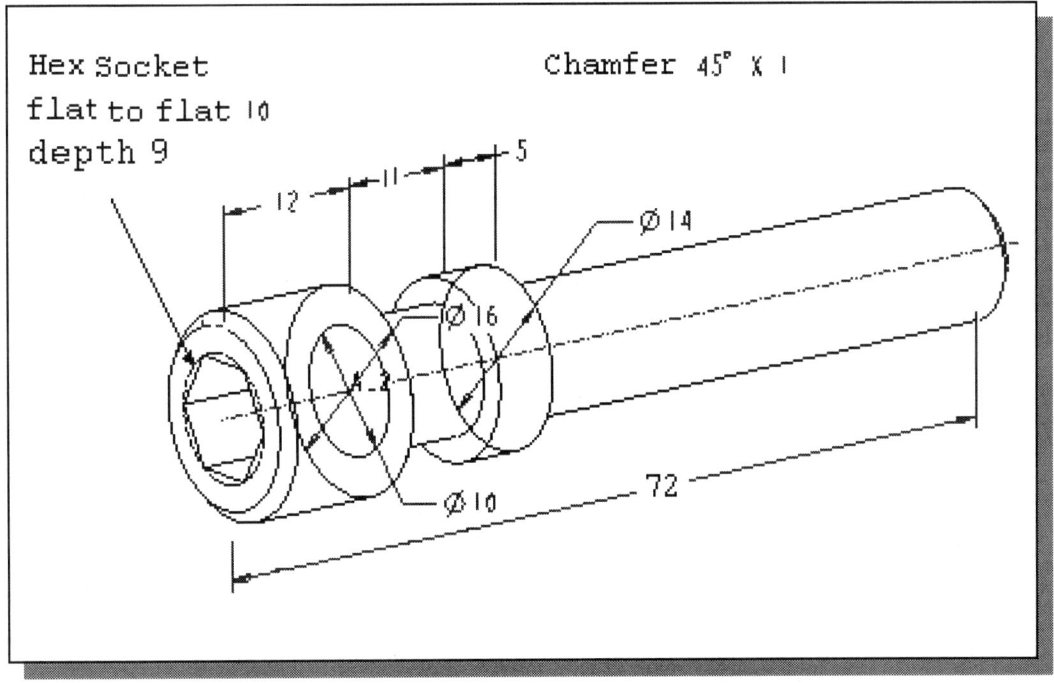

NOTES:

INDEX

G

H

I

L

M

N

O

P

Q

R

NOTES:

NOTES:

NOTES:

NOTES:

NOTES:

NOTES:

NOTES:

NOTES:

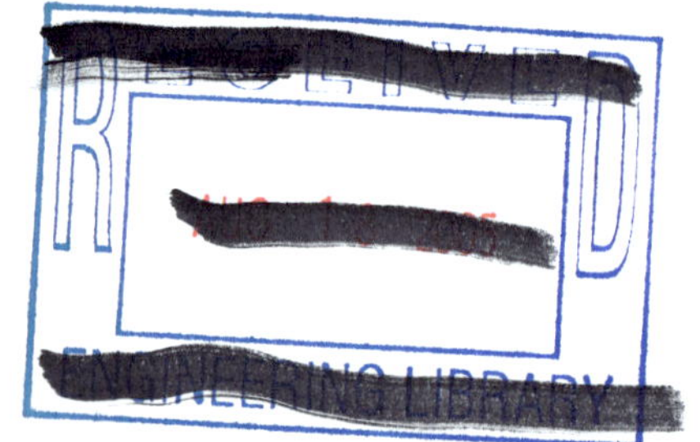